Foundations
of
Statistical
Natural
Language
Processing

Foundations
of
Statistical
Natural
Language
Processing

Christopher D. Manning

Hinrich Schütze

The MIT Press
Cambridge, Massachusetts
London, England

Second printing, 1999
© 1999 Massachusetts Institute of Technology
Second printing with corrections, 2000

Typeset in 10/13 Lucida Bright by the authors using LaTeX 2_ε.
Printed and bound in the United States of America.

Library of Congress Cataloging-in-Publication Information

Manning, Christopher D.
    Foundations of statistical natural language processing / Christopher D. Manning, Hinrich Schütze.
        p.   cm.
    Includes bibliographical references (p.   ) and index.
    ISBN 0-262-13360-1
        1. Computational linguistics—Statistical methods. I. Schütze, Hinrich. II. Title.
P98.5.S83M36 1999
410'.285—dc21   99-21137
                                                                      CIP

Brief Contents

Contents

IV Applications and Techniques   461

List of Tables

List of Figures

Table of Notations

$\cup$	Union of sets
$\cap$	Intersection of sets
$A - B$, $A \backslash B$	Set difference
$\overline{A}$	The complement of set A
$\varnothing$	The empty set
2^A, $\mathcal{P}(A)$	The power set of A
$|A|$	Cardinality of a set
$\sum$	Sum
$\prod$	Product
$p \Rightarrow q$	p implies q (logical inference)
$p \Leftrightarrow q$	p and q are logically equivalent
$\stackrel{\text{def}}{=}$	Defined to be equal to (only used if "=" is ambiguous)
$\mathbb{R}$	The set of real numbers
$\mathbb{N}$	The set of natural numbers
$n!$	The factorial of n
∞	Infinity
$|x|$	Absolute value of a number
$\ll$	Much smaller than
$\gg$	Much greater than
$f : A \to B$	A function f from values in A to B
$\max f$	The maximum value of f

$\min f$	The minimum value of f
$\arg\max f$	The argument for which f has its maximum value
$\arg\min f$	The argument for which f has its minimum value
$\lim_{x\to\infty} f(x)$	The limit of f as x tends to infinity
$f \propto g$	f is proportional to g
∂	Partial derivative
$\int$	Integral
$\log a$	The logarithm of a
$\exp(x), e^x$	The exponential function
$\lceil a \rceil$	The smallest integer i s.t. $i \geq a$
$\vec{x}$	A real-valued vector: $\vec{x} \in \mathbb{R}^n$
$|\vec{x}|$	Euclidean length of $\vec{x}$
$\vec{x} \cdot \vec{y}$	The dot product of $\vec{x}$ and $\vec{y}$
$\cos(\vec{x}, \vec{y})$	The cosine of the angle between $\vec{x}$ and $\vec{y}$
c_{ij}	Element in row i and column j of matrix C
C^{T}	Transpose of matrix C
$\hat{X}$	Estimate of X
$E(X)$	Expectation of X
$\mathrm{Var}(X)$	Variance of X
μ	Mean
σ	Standard deviation
$\bar{x}$	Sample mean
s^2	Sample variance
$P(A|B)$	The probability of A conditional on B
$X \sim \mathrm{p}(x)$	Random variable X is distributed according to p
$\mathrm{b}(r;\, n, p)$	The binomial distribution
$\binom{n}{r}$	Combination or binomial coefficient (the number of ways of choosing r objects from n)
$\mathrm{n}(x;\, \mu, \sigma)$	The normal distribution
$H(X)$	Entropy

$I(X; Y)$	Mutual information
$D(p \parallel q)$	Kullback-Leibler (KL) divergence
$C(\cdot)$	Count of the entity in parentheses
f_u	The relative frequency of u.
$w_{ij}, w_{(i)(j)}$	The words $w_i, w_{i+1}, \ldots, w_j$
$w_{i,j}$	The same as w_{ij}
$w_i, \ldots, w_j$	The same as w_{ij}
$O(n)$	Time complexity of an algorithm
*	Ungrammatical sentence or phrase or ill-formed word
?	Marginally grammatical sentence or marginally acceptable phrase

Note. Some chapters have separate notation tables for symbols that are used locally: table 6.2 (Statistical Inference), table 7.1 (Word Sense Disambiguation), table 9.1 (Markov Models), table 10.2 (Tagging), table 11.1 (Probabilistic Context-Free Grammars), and table 14.2 (Clustering).

Preface

THE NEED for a thorough textbook for Statistical Natural Language Processing hardly needs to be argued for in the age of on-line information, electronic communication and the World Wide Web. Increasingly, businesses, government agencies and individuals are confronted with large amounts of text that are critical for working and living, but not well enough understood to get the enormous value out of them that they potentially hide.

At the same time, the availability of large text corpora has changed the scientific approach to language in linguistics and cognitive science. Phenomena that were not detectable or seemed uninteresting in studying toy domains and individual sentences have moved into the center field of what is considered important to explain. Whereas as recently as the early 1990s quantitative methods were seen as so inadequate for linguistics that an important textbook for mathematical linguistics did not cover them in any way, they are now increasingly seen as crucial for linguistic theory.

In this book we have tried to achieve a balance between theory and practice, and between intuition and rigor. We attempt to ground approaches in theoretical ideas, both mathematical and linguistic, but simultaneously we try to not let the material get too dry, and try to show how theoretical ideas have been used to solve practical problems. To do this, we first present key concepts in probability theory, statistics, information theory, and linguistics in order to give students the foundations to understand the field and contribute to it. Then we describe the problems that are addressed in Statistical Natural Language Processing (NLP), like tagging and disambiguation, and a selection of important work so that students are grounded in the advances that have been made and, having understood the special problems that language poses, can move the field forward.

When we designed the basic structure of the book, we had to make a number of decisions about what to include and how to organize the material. A key criterion was to keep the book to a manageable size. (We didn't entirely succeed!) Thus the book is not a complete introduction to probability theory, information theory, statistics, and the many other areas of mathematics that are used in Statistical NLP. We have tried to cover those topics that seem most important in the field, but there will be many occasions when those teaching from the book will need to use supplementary materials for a more in-depth coverage of mathematical foundations that are of particular interest.

We also decided against attempting to present Statistical NLP as homogeneous in terms of the mathematical tools and theories that are used. It is true that a unified underlying mathematical theory would be desirable, but such a theory simply does not exist at this point. This has led to an eclectic mix in some places, but we believe that it is too early to mandate that a particular approach to NLP is right and should be given preference to others.

A perhaps surprising decision is that we do not cover speech recognition. Speech recognition began as a separate field to NLP, mainly growing out of electrical engineering departments, with separate conferences and journals, and many of its own concerns. However, in recent years there has been increasing convergence and overlap. It was research into speech recognition that inspired the revival of statistical methods within NLP, and many of the techniques that we present were developed first for speech and then spread over into NLP. In particular, work on language models within speech recognition greatly overlaps with the discussion of language models in this book. Moreover, one can argue that speech recognition is the area of language processing that currently is the most successful and the one that is most widely used in applications. Nevertheless, there are a number of practical reasons for excluding the area from this book: there are already several good textbooks for speech, it is not an area in which we have worked or are terribly expert, and this book seemed quite long enough without including speech as well. Additionally, while there is overlap, there is also considerable separation: a speech recognition textbook requires thorough coverage of issues in signal analysis and acoustic modeling which would not generally be of interest or accessible to someone from a computer science or NLP background, while in the reverse direction, most people studying speech would be uninterested in many of the NLP topics on which we focus.

Other related areas that have a somewhat fuzzy boundary with Statistical NLP are machine learning, text categorization, information retrieval, and cognitive science. For all of these areas, one can find examples of work that is not covered and which would fit very well into the book. It was simply a matter of space that we did not include important concepts, methods and problems like minimum description length, back-propagation, the Rocchio algorithm, and the psychological and cognitive-science literature on frequency effects on language processing.

The decisions that were most difficult for us to make are those that concern the boundary between statistical and non-statistical NLP. We believe that, when we started the book, there was a clear dividing line between the two, but this line has become much more fuzzy recently. An increasing number of non-statistical researchers use corpus evidence and incorporate quantitative methods. And it is now generally accepted in Statistical NLP that one needs to start with all the scientific knowledge that is available about a phenomenon when building a probabilistic or other model, rather than closing one's eyes and taking a clean-slate approach.

Many NLP researchers will therefore question the wisdom of writing a separate textbook for the statistical side. And the last thing we would want to do with this textbook is to promote the unfortunate view in some quarters that linguistic theory and symbolic computational work are not relevant to Statistical NLP. However, we believe that there is so much quite complex foundational material to cover that one simply cannot write a textbook of a manageable size that is a satisfactory and comprehensive introduction to all of NLP. Again, other good texts already exist, and we recommend using supplementary material if a more balanced coverage of statistical and non-statistical methods is desired.

STATISTICAL NATURAL LANGUAGE PROCESSING

A final remark is in order on the title we have chosen for this book. Calling the field *Statistical Natural Language Processing* might seem questionable to someone who takes their definition of a statistical method from a standard introduction to statistics. Statistical NLP as we define it comprises all quantitative approaches to automated language processing, including probabilistic modeling, information theory, and linear algebra.

While probability theory is the foundation for formal statistical reasoning, we take the basic meaning of the term 'statistics' as being broader, encompassing all quantitative approaches to data (a definition which one can quickly confirm in almost any dictionary). Although there is thus some potential for ambiguity, Statistical NLP has been the most widely used term to refer to non-symbolic and non-logical work on NLP over the past decade, and we have decided to keep with this term.

Acknowledgments. Over the course of the three years that we were working on this book, a number of colleagues and friends have made comments and suggestions on earlier drafts. We would like to express our gratitude to all of them, in particular, Einat Amitay, Chris Brew, Thorsten Brants, Andreas Eisele, Michael Ernst, Oren Etzioni, Marc Friedman, Éric Gaussier, Eli Hagen, Marti Hearst, Nitin Indurkhya, Michael Inman, Mark Johnson, Rosie Jones, Tom Kalt, Andy Kehler, Julian Kupiec, Michael Littman, Arman Maghbouleh, Amir Najmi, Kris Popat, Fred Popowich, Geoffrey Sampson, Hadar Shemtov, Scott Stoness, David Yarowsky, and Jakub Zavrel. We are particularly indebted to Bob Carpenter, Eugene Charniak, Raymond Mooney, and an anonymous reviewer for MIT Press, who suggested a large number of improvements, both in content and exposition, that we feel have greatly increased the overall quality and usability of the book. We hope that they will sense our gratitude when they notice ideas which we have taken from their comments without proper acknowledgement.

We would like to also thank: Francine Chen, Kris Halvorsen, and Xerox PARC for supporting the second author while writing this book, Jane Manning for her love and support of the first author, Robert Dale and Dikran Karagueuzian for advice on book design, and Amy Brand for her regular help and assistance as our editor.

Feedback. While we have tried hard to make the contents of this book understandable, comprehensive, and correct, there are doubtless many places where we could have done better. We welcome feedback to the authors via email to cmanning@acm.org or hinrich@hotmail.com.

In closing, we can only hope that the availability of a book which collects many of the methods used within Statistical NLP and presents them in an accessible fashion will create excitement in potential students, and help ensure continued rapid progress in the field.

Christopher Manning

Hinrich Schütze

February 1999

Road Map

IN GENERAL, this book is written to be suitable for a graduate-level semester-long course focusing on Statistical NLP. There is actually rather more material than one could hope to cover in a semester, but that richness gives ample room for the teacher to pick and choose. It is assumed that the student has prior programming experience, and has some familiarity with formal languages and symbolic parsing methods. It is also assumed that the student has a basic grounding in such mathematical concepts as set theory, logarithms, vectors and matrices, summations, and integration – we hope nothing more than an adequate high school education! The student may have already taken a course on symbolic NLP methods, but a lot of background is not assumed. In the directions of probability and statistics, and linguistics, we try to briefly summarize all the necessary background, since in our experience many people wanting to learn about Statistical NLP methods have no prior knowledge in these areas (perhaps this will change over time!). Nevertheless, study of supplementary material in these areas is probably necessary for a student to have an adequate foundation from which to build, and can only be of value to the prospective researcher.

What is the best way to read this book and teach from it? The book is organized into four parts: Preliminaries (part I), Words (part II), Grammar (part III), and Applications and Techniques (part IV).

Part I lays out the mathematical and linguistic foundation that the other parts build on. Concepts and techniques introduced here are referred to throughout the book.

Part II covers word-centered work in Statistical NLP. There is a natural progression from simple to complex linguistic phenomena in its four chapters on collocations, *n*-gram models, word sense disambiguation, and lexical acquisition, but each chapter can also be read on its own.

The four chapters in part III, Markov Models, tagging, probabilistic context free grammars, and probabilistic parsing, build on each other, and so they are best presented in sequence. However, the tagging chapter can be read separately with occasional references to the Markov Model chapter.

The topics of part IV are four applications and techniques: statistical alignment and machine translation, clustering, information retrieval, and text categorization. Again, these chapters can be treated separately according to interests and time available, with the few dependencies between them marked appropriately.

Although we have organized the book with a lot of background and foundational material in part I, we would not advise going through all of it carefully at the beginning of a course based on this book. What the authors have generally done is to review the really essential bits of part I in about the first 6 hours of a course. This comprises very basic probability (through section 2.1.8), information theory (through section 2.2.7), and essential practical knowledge – some of which is contained in chapter 4, and some of which is the particulars of what is available at one's own institution. We have generally left the contents of chapter 3 as a reading assignment for those without much background in linguistics. Some knowledge of linguistic concepts is needed in many chapters, but is particularly relevant to chapter 12, and the instructor may wish to review some syntactic concepts at this point. Other material from the early chapters is then introduced on a "need to know" basis during the course.

The choice of topics in part II was partly driven by a desire to be able to present accessible and interesting topics early in a course, in particular, ones which are also a good basis for student programming projects. We have found collocations (chapter 5), word sense disambiguation (chapter 7), and attachment ambiguities (section 8.3) particularly successful in this regard. Early introduction of attachment ambiguities is also effective in showing that there is a role for linguistic concepts and structures in Statistical NLP. Much of the material in chapter 6 is rather detailed reference material. People interested in applications like speech or optical character recognition may wish to cover all of it, but if *n*-gram language models are not a particular focus of interest, one may only want to read through section 6.2.3. This is enough to understand the concept of likelihood, maximum likelihood estimates, a couple of simple smoothing methods (usually necessary if students are to be building any probabilistic models on their own), and good methods for assessing the performance of systems.

In general, we have attempted to provide ample cross-references so that, if desired, an instructor can present most chapters independently with incorporation of prior material where appropriate. In particular, this is the case for the chapters on collocations, lexical acquisition, tagging, and information retrieval.

Exercises. There are exercises scattered through or at the end of every chapter. They vary enormously in difficulty and scope. We have tried to provide an elementary classification as follows:

- ⋆ Simple problems that range from text comprehension through to such things as mathematical manipulations, simple proofs, and thinking of examples of something.

- ⋆⋆ More substantial problems, many of which involve either programming or corpus investigations. Many would be suitable as an assignment to be done over two weeks.

- ⋆⋆⋆ Large, difficult, or open-ended problems. Many would be suitable as a term project.

WEBSITE

Website. Finally, we encourage students and teachers to take advantage of the material and the references on the companion *website*. It can be accessed directly at the URL http://www.sultry.arts.usyd.edu.au/fsnlp, or found through the MIT Press website http://mitpress.mit.edu, by searching for this book.

PART I

Preliminaries

"Statistical considerations are essential to an understanding of the operation and development of languages"

(Lyons 1968: 98)

"One's ability to produce and recognize grammatical utterances is not based on notions of statistical approximation and the like"

(Chomsky 1957: 16)

"You say: the point isn't the word, but its meaning, and you think of the meaning as a thing of the same kind as the word, though also different from the word. Here the word, there the meaning. The money, and the cow that you can buy with it. (But contrast: money, and its use.)"

(Wittgenstein 1968, Philosophical Investigations, §120)

"For a large class of cases—though not for all—in which we employ the word 'meaning' it can be defined thus: the meaning of a word is its use in the language."   *(Wittgenstein 1968, §43)*

"Now isn't it queer that I say that the word 'is' is used with two different meanings (as the copula and as the sign of equality), and should not care to say that its meaning is its use; its use, that is, as the copula and the sign of equality?"

(Wittgenstein 1968, §561)

1 *Introduction*

THE AIM of a linguistic science is to be able to characterize and explain the multitude of linguistic observations circling around us, in conversations, writing, and other media. Part of that has to do with the cognitive side of how humans acquire, produce, and understand language, part of it has to do with understanding the relationship between linguistic utterances and the world, and part of it has to do with understanding the linguistic structures by which language communicates. In order to

RULES approach the last problem, people have proposed that there are *rules* which are used to structure linguistic expressions. This basic approach has a long history that extends back at least 2000 years, but in this century the approach became increasingly formal and rigorous as linguists explored detailed grammars that attempted to describe what were well-formed versus ill-formed utterances of a language.

However, it has become apparent that there is a problem with this conception. Indeed it was noticed early on by Edward Sapir, who summed it up in his famous quote "All grammars leak" (Sapir 1921: 38). It is just not possible to provide an exact and complete characterization of well-formed utterances that cleanly divides them from all other sequences of words, which are regarded as ill-formed utterances. This is because people are always stretching and bending the 'rules' to meet their communicative needs. Nevertheless, it is certainly not the case that the rules are completely ill-founded. Syntactic rules for a language, such as that a basic English noun phrase consists of an optional determiner, some number of adjectives, and then a noun, do capture major patterns within the language. But somehow we need to make things looser, in accounting for the creativity of language use.

This book explores an approach that addresses this problem head on. Rather than starting off by dividing sentences into grammatical and ungrammatical ones, we instead ask, "What are the common patterns that occur in language use?" The major tool which we use to identify these patterns is counting things, otherwise known as statistics, and so the scientific foundation of the book is found in probability theory. Moreover, we are not merely going to approach this issue as a scientific question, but rather we wish to show how statistical models of language are built and successfully used for many natural language processing (NLP) tasks. While practical utility is something different from the validity of a theory, the usefulness of statistical models of language tends to confirm that there is something right about the basic approach.

Adopting a Statistical NLP approach requires mastering a fair number of theoretical tools, but before we delve into a lot of theory, this chapter spends a bit of time attempting to situate the approach to natural language processing that we pursue in this book within a broader context. One should first have some idea about *why* many people are adopting a statistical approach to natural language processing and of *how* one should go about this enterprise. So, in this first chapter, we examine some of the philosophical themes and leading ideas that motivate a statistical approach to linguistics and NLP, and then proceed to get our hands dirty by beginning an exploration of what one can learn by looking at statistics over texts.

1.1 Rationalist and Empiricist Approaches to Language

Some language researchers and many NLP practitioners are perfectly happy to just work on text without thinking much about the relationship between the mental representation of language and its manifestation in written form. Readers sympathetic with this approach may feel like skipping to the practical sections, but even practically-minded people have to confront the issue of what prior knowledge to try to build into their model, even if this prior knowledge might be clearly different from what might be plausibly hypothesized for the brain. This section briefly discusses the philosophical issues that underlie this question.

Between about 1960 and 1985, most of linguistics, psychology, artificial intelligence, and natural language processing was completely dominated by a *rationalist* approach. A rationalist approach is characterized

RATIONALIST

by the belief that a significant part of the knowledge in the human mind is not derived by the senses but is fixed in advance, presumably by genetic inheritance. Within linguistics, this rationalist position has come to dominate the field due to the widespread acceptance of arguments by Noam Chomsky for an innate language faculty. Within artificial intelligence, rationalist beliefs can be seen as supporting the attempt to create intelligent systems by handcoding into them a lot of starting knowledge and reasoning mechanisms, so as to duplicate what the human brain begins with.

POVERTY OF THE STIMULUS

Chomsky argues for this innate structure because of what he perceives as a problem of the *poverty of the stimulus* (e.g., Chomsky 1986: 7). He suggests that it is difficult to see how children can learn something as complex as a natural language from the limited input (of variable quality and interpretability) that they hear during their early years. The rationalist approach attempts to dodge this difficult problem by postulating that the key parts of language are innate – hardwired in the brain at birth as part of the human genetic inheritance.

EMPIRICIST

An *empiricist* approach also begins by postulating some cognitive abilities as present in the brain. The difference between the approaches is therefore not absolute but one of degree. One has to assume some initial structure in the brain which causes it to prefer certain ways of organizing and generalizing from sensory inputs to others, as no learning is possible from a completely blank slate, a *tabula rasa*. But the thrust of empiricist approaches is to assume that the mind does not begin with detailed sets of principles and procedures specific to the various components of language and other cognitive domains (for instance, theories of morphological structure, case marking, and the like). Rather, it is assumed that a baby's brain begins with general operations for association, pattern recognition, and generalization, and that these can be applied to the rich sensory input available to the child to learn the detailed structure of natural language. Empiricism was dominant in most of the fields mentioned above (at least the ones then existing!) between 1920 and 1960, and is now seeing a resurgence. An empiricist approach to NLP suggests that we can learn the complicated and extensive structure of language by specifying an appropriate general language model, and then inducing the values of parameters by applying statistical, pattern recognition, and machine learning methods to a large amount of language use.

Generally in Statistical NLP, people cannot actually work from observing a large amount of language use situated within its context in the world. So, instead, people simply use texts, and regard the textual context as a surrogate for situating language in a real world context. A body of texts is called a *corpus* – *corpus* is simply Latin for 'body,' and when you have several such collections of texts, you have *corpora*. Adopting such a corpus-based approach, people have pointed to the earlier advocacy of empiricist ideas by the British linguist J. R. Firth, who coined the slogan "You shall know a word by the company it keeps" (Firth 1957: 11). However an empiricist corpus-based approach is perhaps even more clearly seen in the work of American structuralists (the 'post-Bloomfieldians'), particularly Zellig Harris. For example, (Harris 1951) is an attempt to find discovery procedures by which a language's structure can be discovered automatically. While this work had no thoughts to computer implementation, and is perhaps somewhat computationally naive, we find here also the idea that a good grammatical description is one that provides a compact representation of a corpus of texts.

CORPUS
CORPORA

AMERICAN
STRUCTURALISTS

It is not appropriate to provide a detailed philosophical treatment of scientific approaches to language here, but let us note a few more differences between rationalist and empiricist approaches. Rationalists and empiricists are attempting to describe different things. Chomskyan (or *generative*) linguistics seeks to describe the language module of the human mind (the I-language) for which data such as texts (the E-language) provide only indirect evidence, which can be supplemented by native speaker intuitions. Empiricist approaches are interested in describing the E-language as it actually occurs. Chomsky (1965: 3–4) thus makes a crucial distinction between *linguistic competence*, which reflects the knowledge of language structure that is assumed to be in the mind of a native speaker, and *linguistic performance* in the world, which is affected by all sorts of things such as memory limitations and distracting noises in the environment. Generative linguistics has argued that one can isolate linguistic competence and describe it in isolation, while empiricist approaches generally reject this notion and want to describe actual use of language.

GENERATIVE
LINGUISTICS

LINGUISTIC
COMPETENCE

LINGUISTIC
PERFORMANCE

This difference underlies much of the recent revival of interest in empiricist techniques for computational work. During the second phase of work in artificial intelligence (roughly 1970–1989, say) people were concerned with the science of the mind, and the best way to address that was seen as building small systems that attempted to behave intelligently. This approach identified many key problems and approaches that are still with us today, but the work can be criticized on the grounds that it dealt only with very small (often pejoratively called 'toy') problems, and often did not provide any sort of objective evaluation of the general efficacy of the methods employed. Recently, people have placed greater emphasis on engineering practical solutions. Principally, they seek methods that can work on raw text as it exists in the real world, and objective comparative evaluations of how well different methods work. This new emphasis is sometimes reflected in naming the field 'Language Technology' or 'Language Engineering' instead of NLP. As we will discuss below, such goals have tended to favor Statistical NLP approaches, because they are better at automatic learning (*knowledge induction*), better at disambiguation, and also have a role in the science of linguistics.

INDUCTION

Finally, Chomskyan linguistics, while recognizing certain notions of competition between principles, depends on *categorical* principles, which sentences either do or do not satisfy. In general, the same was true of American structuralism. But the approach we will pursue in Statistical NLP draws from the work of Shannon, where the aim is to assign probabilities to linguistic events, so that we can say which sentences are 'usual' and 'unusual'. An upshot of this is that while Chomskyan linguists tend to concentrate on categorical judgements about very rare types of sentences, Statistical NLP practitioners are interested in good descriptions of the associations and preferences that occur in the totality of language use. Indeed, they often find that one can get good real world performance by concentrating on common types of sentences.

CATEGORICAL

1.2 Scientific Content

Many of the applications of the methods that we present in this book have a quite *applied* character. Indeed, much of the recent enthusiasm for statistical methods in natural language processing derives from people seeing the prospect of statistical methods providing practical solutions to real problems that have eluded solution using traditional NLP methods. But if statistical methods were just a practical engineering approach, an approximation to difficult problems of language that science has not yet been able to figure out, then their interest to us would be rather limited. Rather, we would like to emphasize right at the beginning that there are clear and compelling scientific reasons to be interested in the frequency with which linguistic forms are used, in other words, statistics, as one approaches the study of language.

1.2.1   Questions that linguistics should answer

What questions does the study of language concern itself with? As a start we would like to answer two basic questions:

- What kinds of things do people say?

- What do these things say/ask/request about the world?

From these two basic questions, attention quickly spreads to issues about how knowledge of language is acquired by humans, and how they actually go about generating and understanding sentences in real time. But let us just concentrate on these two basic questions for now. The first covers all aspects of the structure of language, while the second deals with semantics, pragmatics, and discourse – how to connect utterances with the world. The first question is the bread and butter of corpus linguistics, but the patterns of use of a word can act as a surrogate for deep understanding, and hence can let us also address the second question using corpus-based techniques. Nevertheless patterns in corpora more easily reveal the syntactic structure of a language, and so the majority of work in Statistical NLP has dealt with the first question of what kinds of things people say, and so let us begin with it here.

How does traditional (structuralist/generative) linguistics seek to answer this question? It abstracts away from any attempt to describe the kinds of things that people usually say, and instead seeks to describe a *competence grammar* that is said to underlie the language (and which generative approaches assume to be in the speaker's head). The extent to which such theories approach the question of what people say is merely to suggest that there is a set of sentences – grammatical sentences – which are licensed by the competence grammar, and then other strings of words are ungrammatical. This concept of *grammaticality* is meant to be judged purely on whether a sentence is structurally well-formed, and not according to whether it is the kind of thing that people would say or whether it is semantically anomalous. Chomsky gave *Colorless green ideas sleep furiously* as an example of a sentence that is grammatical, al-

COMPETENCE
GRAMMAR

GRAMMATICALITY

though semantically strange and not the kind of thing you would expect people to say. Syntactic grammaticality is a categorical binary choice.[1]

Now, initially, a distinction between grammatical and ungrammatical sentences does not seem so bad. We immediately notice when a non-native speaker says something really wrong – something ungrammatical – and we are able to correct such sentences to grammatical ones. In contrast, except when there are bad speech errors, a native speaker normally produces grammatical sentences. But there are at least two reasons why we should seek more. Firstly, while maintaining a binary split between grammatical and ungrammatical sentences may seem plausible in simple cases, it becomes increasingly far-fetched as we extend our investigation. Secondly, regardless of this, there are many reasons to be interested in the frequency with which different sentences and sentence types are used, and simply dividing sentences into grammatical and ungrammatical sentences gives no information about this. For instance, very often non-native speakers say or write things that are not in any way syntactically ungrammatical, but just somehow subtly odd. Here's an example from a student essay:

(1.1)   In addition to this, she insisted that women were regarded as a different existence from men unfairly.

CONVENTIONALITY

We might respond to this passage by saying that we can understand the message, but it would sound better expressed slightly differently. This is a statement about the *conventionality* of certain modes of expression. But a convention is simply a way in which people frequently express or do something, even though other ways are in principle possible.

The fact that sentences do not divide neatly into two sets – grammatical and ungrammatical ones – is well known to anyone who has been in linguistics for a while. For many of the complicated sentences of interest to theoretical linguistics, it is difficult for human beings to decide whether they are grammatical or not. For example, try your hand at judging the grammaticality of the following sentences drawn (not at random)

---

1. Some versions of Chomsky's 1980s theory, Government-Binding theory (GB), provide a minor degree of gradedness by suggesting that sentences that disobey some constraints are only sort of weird while ones that disobey other constraints are truly horrible, but the formal theory, in GB and elsewhere, provides little support for these notions. Linguists generally rely on an informal system of stars and question marks for initially grading sentences (where * (ungrammatical) > ?* > ?? > ? (questionable)), but these gradations are converted into a binary grammatical/ungrammatical distinction when people try to develop the principles of grammar.

from (van Riemsdijk and Williams 1986) – a textbook, not even a research paper – before peeking at the answers in the footnote.[2]

(1.2)   a. John I believe Sally said Bill believed Sue saw.

b. What did Sally whisper that she had secretly read?

c. John wants very much for himself to win.

d. (Those are) the books you should read before it becomes difficult to talk about.

e. (Those are) the books you should read before talking about becomes difficult.

f. Who did Jo think said John saw him?

g. That a serious discussion could arise here of this topic was quite unexpected.

h. The boys read Mary's stories about each other.

We find that most people disagree with more than one of van Riemsdijk and Williams's claims about which sentences are grammatical. This result raises real questions about what, if anything, generative linguistics is describing.

    This difficulty has led to many statements in the linguistics literature about judgements being difficult, or the facts quite obscure, as if somehow there is a categorical answer to whether each sentence is grammatical, but it is hard for human beings to work out what that answer is. Yet, despite these manifest difficulties, most of theoretical linguistics continues to work in a framework that defines such observations to be out of the realm of interest (relegating them to performance effects). We believe that this is unsustainable. On the other hand, it must be noticed that most simple sentences are either clearly acceptable or unacceptable and we would want our theory to be able to account for this observation. Perhaps the right approach is to notice the parallel with other cases of

CATEGORICAL PERCEPTION

categorical perception that have been described in the psychological literature. For instance, although the timing of voicing onset which differentiates a /p/ sound from a /b/ sound is a continuous variable (and its typical

---

2. Answers: a. OK, b. bad, c. OK, d. OK, e. bad, f. OK, g. OK, h. bad.

value varies between languages), human beings perceive the results categorically, and this is why a theory of phonology based on categorical phonemes is largely viable, despite all the movements and variations in phonological production occurring in a continuous space. Similarly for syntax, a categorical theory may suffice for certain purposes. Nevertheless, we would argue that the difficulties in giving grammaticality judgements to complex and convoluted sentences show the implausibility of extending a binary distinction between grammatical and ungrammatical strings to all areas of language use.

1.2.2 Non-categorical phenomena in language

But beyond the above difficulties in giving grammaticality judgements, if we peek into the corners of language, we see clear evidence of failures of categorical assumptions, and circumstances where considerations of frequency of use are essential to understanding language. This suggests that while a *categorical view of language* may be sufficient for many purposes, CATEGORICAL VIEW OF we must see it as an approximation that also has its limitations (just as LANGUAGE Newtonian physics is good for many purposes but has its limits).[3]

One source of data on non-categorical phenomena in language is to look at the history of language change (others are looking at sociolinguistic variation and competing hypotheses during language acquisition). Over time, the words and syntax of a language change. Words will change their meaning and their part of speech. For instance, English *while* used to be exclusively a noun meaning 'time,' a usage that survives mainly in a few fixed phrases such as *to take a while*, but changed to be mainly used as a complementizer introducing subordinate clauses (*While you were out, . . .*). It doesn't make sense to say that categorically until some day in 1742 *while* was only a noun and then it became a complementizer – even if this claim is only being made for certain speakers rather than the speech community as a whole. Rather, one would expect a gradual change. One hypothesis is that if the frequency of use of a word in various contexts gradually changes so that it departs from the typical profile of use of words in the category to which it formerly belonged, and rather its profile of use comes to more resemble words of another category, then

---

3. Readers not familiar with linguistics and NLP may have trouble understanding this section and may wish to skip it, but to return to it after reading chapter 3. The historical examples include various archaic spellings – the standardization of English spelling is a relatively modern phenomenon. Reading them aloud is often helpful for decoding them.

it will come to be reanalyzed as a word of that different category. During the period of change, one would expect to see evidence of noncategorical behavior.

Blending of parts of speech: *near*

At first blush it appears that the word *near* can be used either as an adjective as in (1.3a) or as a preposition (1.3b):

(1.3)   a. We will review that decision in the near future.

        b. He lives near the station.

Evidence for *near* as an adjective includes its position between a determiner and noun as in (1.3a) – a classic adjective position – and the fact that it can form an adverb by adding *-ly*: *We nearly lost.* Evidence for *near* as a preposition includes that it can head the locative phrase complements of verbs like *live* as in (1.3b) – a classic role for prepositions, and that such a phrase can be modified by *right*, which is normally restricted to modifying prepositional phrases: *He lives right near the station* (cf. *He swam right across the lake* vs. *??That's a right red car*). So far, though, this data is not that surprising: many words in English seem to have multiple parts of speech. For example, many words are both nouns and verbs, such as *play*: *They saw a play* vs. *They play lacrosse on Thursdays.* But the interesting thing is that *near* can simultaneously show adjective properties and preposition properties, and thus appears to behave as a category blend. This happens in sentences like:

(1.4)   a. He has never been nearer the center of the financial establishment.

        b. We live nearer the water than you thought.

Realization in the comparative form (*nearer*) is a hallmark of adjectives (and adverbs). Other categories do not form comparatives and superlatives.[4] On the other hand, grammatical theory tells us that adjectives and nouns do not take direct objects, hence we have to insert prepositions

---

4. The thoughtful reader might note that some prepositions do have related forms ending in *-er* which are perhaps related to comparatives (*upper, downer, inner, outer*), but we note that none of these prepositions have a superlative that is formed in analogy to regular adjectival superlatives, as *near* does (that is, *nearest*), and that none of these other forms in *-er* can be used in preposition-like uses. We cannot say: **John lives inner Sydney than Fred.*

after adjectives and say *unsure **of** his beliefs* or *convenient **for** people who work long hours*. In this sense *nearer* is behaving like a preposition by heading a locative phrase and taking a direct object. Thus in these sentences *nearer* is simultaneously showing properties of adjectives and prepositions that are not available to the other category. Hence it is exhibiting a blended status somewhere between these two parts of speech, which are normally taken as categorically distinct.

Language change: *kind of* and *sort of*

New uses for the word sequences *kind of* and *sort of* present a convincing example of how different frequencies of use in certain constructions can lead to what is apparently categorical change. In modern English, the expressions *sort of* and *kind of* have at least two distinct uses. In one, *sort* or *kind* functions as a noun with *of* as a following preposition introducing a prepositional phrase, as in sentences such as *What sort of animal made these tracks?* But there is another usage in which these expressions can best be thought of as degree modifiers, akin to *somewhat* or *slightly*:

(1.5) a. We are kind of hungry.

   b. He sort of understood what was going on.

We can tell that *kind/sort of* is not behaving as a normal noun preposition sequence here because it is appearing in contexts – such as between the subject noun phrase and the verb – where normally one cannot insert a noun-preposition sequence (for example, one cannot say **He variety of understood what was going on*).

   Historically, *kind* and *sort* were clearly nouns. Among other things, they could be preceded by a determiner and followed by a PP:

(1.6) a. A nette sent in to the see, and of alle kind of fishis gedrynge. [1382]

   b. I knowe that sorte of men ryght well. [1560]

Unambiguous degree modifier uses did not appear until the nineteenth century:

(1.7) a. I kind of love you, Sal—I vow. [1804]

   b. It sort o' stirs one up to hear about old times. [1833]

It does not appear that this new construction was borrowed from another language. Rather it appears to be a language internal development. How could this innovation have come about?

A plausible hypothesis is to notice that when we have *kind/sort of* preceding an adjective, then it is actually ambiguous between these two readings:

(1.8)   a. [NP a [kind] [PP of [NPdense rock]]]

        b. [NP a [AP [MOD kind of] dense] rock]

And what one finds is that between the sixteenth and the nineteenth century, there was a significant rise in the use of *kind/sort of* in this [Det {*sort/kind*} of AdjP N] frame:

(1.9)   a. Their finest and best, is a kind of course red cloth. [c. 1600]

        b. But in such questions as the present, a hundred contradictory views may preserve a kind of imperfect analogy. [1743]

(Note that *course* is here a variant spelling of *coarse*.) In this environment, *sort/kind of* fills a slot that could be occupied by a noun head followed by a preposition, but it also fills a slot that could be occupied by a degree modifier (with a different syntactic structure). As this usage became more common, *kind/sort of* was more commonly being used in a typical degree modifier slot; in other words, it grew to look syntactically more like a degree modifier. Moreover, the semantics of these particular nouns was such that they could easily be thought of as degree modifiers. This frequency change seems to have driven a change in syntactic category, and in time the use of *kind/sort of* was extended to other contexts such as modifying verb phrases.

The general point here is that while language change can be sudden (due to either external or internal factors), it is generally gradual. The details of gradual change can only be made sense of by examining frequencies of use and being sensitive to varying strengths of relationships, and this type of modeling requires statistical, as opposed to categorical, observations.

Although there have only been a few attempts to use Statistical NLP for explaining complex linguistic phenomena, what is exciting about the subject matter of this book from the point of view of theoretical linguistics is that this new way of looking at language may be able to account for things such as non-categorical phenomena and language change much better than anything existing today.

1.2.3   Language and cognition as probabilistic phenomena

A more radical argument for probability as part of a scientific understanding of language is that human cognition is probabilistic and that language must therefore be probabilistic too since it is an integral part of cognition. A frequent response to our previous examples of non-categorical phenomena in language is that they are marginal and rare. Most sentences are either clearly grammatical or clearly ungrammatical. And most of the time, words are used in only one part of speech, without blending. But if language and cognition as a whole are best explained probabilistically, then probability theory must be a central part of an explanatory theory of language.

The argument for a probabilistic approach to cognition is that we live in a world filled with uncertainty and incomplete information. To be able to interact successfully with the world, we need to be able to deal with this type of information. Suppose you want to determine whether it is safe to wade through a river. You see that the water is flowing slowly, so probably it won't drag you away. You are pretty certain that no piranhas or alligators live in this area. You integrate all this information in evaluating how safe it is to cross the river. Now, if someone tells you, "the water is only knee-deep if you walk towards that tall tree over there", then this linguistic information will be just one more source of information to incorporate. Processing the words, forming an idea of the overall meaning of the sentence, and weighing it in making a decision is no different in principle from looking at the current, forming an idea of the speed of the water, and taking this sensory information into account. So the gist of this argument is that the cognitive processes used for language are identical or at least very similar to those used for processing other forms of sensory input and other forms of knowledge. These cognitive processes are best formalized as probabilistic processes or at least by means of some quantitative framework that can handle uncertainty and incomplete information.

The facts of language often look quite different depending on whether or not one is sympathetic to an important role for quantitative methods in linguistics. A famous example is Chomsky's dictum that probabil-

GRAMMATICALITY   ity theory is inappropriate for formalizing the notion of *grammaticality*.

He argued that computing the probability of sentences from a corpus of utterances would assign the same low probability to all unattested sentences, grammatical and ungrammatical ones alike, and hence not account for linguistic productivity (Chomsky 1957: 16). This argument only makes sense if one has a bias against probabilistic representation of concepts in general. Consider the cognitive representation of the concept *tall*. Suppose you see a man who is seven feet tall and it is the first person you've ever seen of that height. You will easily recognize this person as a *tall* man, not as an uncategorizable man. Similarly, it will be easy for you to recognize a person of another unattested height, say four feet, as definitely not *tall*. In this book, we will look at probabilistic models that can easily learn and represent this type of regularity and make the right judgement for unattested examples. Indeed, a major part of Statistical NLP is deriving good probability estimates for unseen events. The premise that all unattested instances will be treated alike in a probabilistic framework does not hold.

We believe that much of the skepticism towards probabilistic models for language (and for cognition in general) stems from the fact that the well-known early probabilistic models (developed in the 1940s and 1950s) are extremely simplistic. Because these simplistic models clearly do not do justice to the complexity of human language, it is easy to view probabilistic models in general as inadequate. One of the insights we hope to promote in this book is that complex probabilistic models can be as explanatory as complex non-probabilistic models – but with the added advantage that they can explain phenomena that involve the type of uncertainty and incompleteness that is so pervasive in cognition in general and in language in particular.

These issues relate to the treatment of semantics in Statistical NLP. We mentioned earlier that most existing work in Statistical NLP has concentrated on the lower levels of grammatical processing, and people have sometimes expressed skepticism as to whether statistical approaches can ever deal with meaning. But the difficulty in answering this question is mainly in defining what 'meaning' is! It is often useful in practice if 'meaning' is viewed as symbolic expressions in some language, such as when translating English into a database query language like SQL. This sort of translation can certainly be done using a Statistical NLP system (we discuss the process of translation in chapter 13). But from a Statistical NLP perspective, it is more natural to think of meaning as residing in the distribution of contexts over which words and utterances are used.

USE THEORY OF
MEANING

Philosophically, this brings us close to the position adopted in the later writings of Wittgenstein (that is, Wittgenstein 1968), where the meaning of a word is defined by the circumstances of its use (a *use theory of meaning*) – see the quotations at the beginning of the chapter. Under this conception, much of Statistical NLP research directly tackles questions of meaning.

1.3 The Ambiguity of Language: Why NLP Is Difficult

An NLP system needs to determine something of the structure of text – normally at least enough that it can answer "Who did what to whom?" Conventional parsing systems try to answer this question only in terms of possible structures that could be deemed grammatical for some choice of words of a certain category. For example, given a reasonable grammar, a standard NLP system will say that sentence (1.10) has 3 syntactic analyses, often called *parses*:

(1.10)   Our company is training workers.

The three differing parses might be represented as in (1.11):

(1.11)   a.

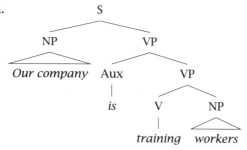

        b.

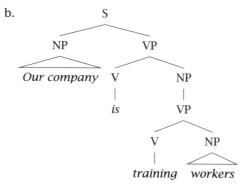

c.

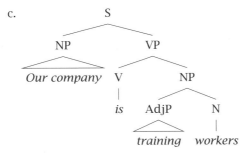

There is (a), the one humans perceive, where *is training* is the verb group, and two others with *is* as the main verb: in (b) the rest is a gerund (cf. *Our problem is training workers*), while in (c) *training* modifies *workers* (cf. *Those are training wheels*). The last two parses are semantically anomalous, but in most current systems semantic analysis is done only after syntactic analysis (if at all). This means that, as sentences get longer and grammars get more comprehensive, such ambiguities lead to a terrible multiplication of parses. For instance, Martin et al. (1987) report their system giving 455 parses for the sentence in (1.12):[5]

(1.12) List the sales of the products produced in 1973 with the products produced in 1972.

Therefore, a practical NLP system must be good at making disambiguation decisions of word sense, word category, syntactic structure, and semantic scope. But the goal of maximizing coverage while minimizing resultant ambiguity is fundamentally inconsistent with symbolic NLP systems, where extending the coverage of the grammar to obscure constructions simply increases the number of undesired parses for common sentences and vice versa. Furthermore, experience with AI approaches to parsing and disambiguation, which seek models with deep understanding, has shown that hand-coded syntactic constraints and preference rules are time consuming to build, do not scale up well, and are brittle in the face of the extensive use of metaphor in language (Lakoff 1987).

SELECTIONAL
RESTRICTIONS

For instance a traditional approach is to use *selectional restrictions*, and say, for example, that a verb like *swallow* requires an animate being as its subject and a physical object as its object. But such a restriction would disallow common and straightforward metaphorical extensions of the usage of *swallow* such as these:

---

5. See also Church and Patil (1982) for similar examples.

(1.13) a. I swallowed his story, hook, line, and sinker.

b. The supernova swallowed the planet.

Disambiguation strategies that rely on manual rule creation and hand-tuning produce a knowledge acquisition bottleneck, and still perform poorly when evaluated on naturally occurring text.

A Statistical NLP approach seeks to solve these problems by automatically learning lexical and structural preferences from corpora. Rather than parsing solely using syntactic categories, such as part of speech labels, we recognize that there is a lot of information in the relationships between words, that is, which words tend to group with each other. This collocational knowledge can be exploited as a window onto deeper semantic relationships. In particular, the use of statistical models offers a good solution to the ambiguity problem: statistical models are robust, generalize well, and behave gracefully in the presence of errors and new data. Thus Statistical NLP methods have led the way in providing successful disambiguation in large scale systems using naturally occurring text. Moreover, the parameters of Statistical NLP models can often be estimated automatically from text corpora, and this possibility of automatic learning not only reduces the human effort in producing NLP systems, but raises interesting scientific issues regarding human language acquisition.

1.4 Dirty Hands

1.4.1 Lexical resources

LEXICAL RESOURCES

So much for motivation. How does one actually proceed? Well, first of all, one needs to get one's hands on some *lexical resources*: machine-readable text, dictionaries, thesauri, and also tools for processing them. We will briefly introduce a few important ones here since we will be referring to them throughout the book. You can consult the website for more information on how to actually get your hands on them.

BROWN CORPUS

BALANCED CORPUS

The *Brown corpus* is probably the most widely known corpus. It is a tagged corpus of about a million words that was put together at Brown university in the 1960s and 1970s. It is a *balanced corpus*. That is, an attempt was made to make the corpus a representative sample of American English at the time. Genres covered are press reportage, fiction, scientific text, legal text, and many others. Unfortunately, one has to pay to obtain the Brown corpus, but it is relatively inexpensive for research

purposes. Many institutions with NLP research have a copy available, so
LANCASTER-OSLO-
BERGEN CORPUS   ask around. The *Lancaster-Oslo-Bergen (LOB) corpus* was built as a British
English replication of the Brown corpus.

SUSANNE CORPUS   The *Susanne corpus* is a 130,000 word subset of the Brown corpus,
which has the advantage of being freely available. It is also annotated
with information on the syntactic structure of sentences – the Brown corpus only disambiguates on a word-for-word basis. A larger corpus of
PENN TREEBANK   syntactically annotated (or parsed) sentences is the *Penn Treebank*. The
text is from the *Wall Street Journal*. It is more widely used, but not available for free.

CANADIAN HANSARDS   The *Canadian Hansards*, the proceedings of the Canadian parliament,
BILINGUAL CORPUS   are the best known example of a *bilingual corpus*, a corpus that contains
PARALLEL TEXTS   *parallel texts* in two or more languages that are translations of each other.
Such parallel texts are important for statistical machine translation and
other cross-lingual NLP work. The Hansards are another resource that
one has to pay for.

WORDNET   In addition to texts, we also need dictionaries. *WordNet* is an electronic
dictionary of English. Words are organized into a hierarchy. Each node
SYNSET   consists of a *synset* of words with identical (or close to identical) meanings. There are also some other relations between words that are defined,
such as meronymy or part-whole relations. WordNet is free and can be
downloaded from the internet.
▼ More details on corpora can be found in chapter 4.

1.4.2 Word counts

Once we have downloaded some text, there are a number of quite interesting issues in its low-level representation, classification, and processing. Indeed, so many that chapter 4 is devoted to these questions. But
for the moment, let us suppose that our text is being represented as a
list of words. For the investigation in this section, we will be using Mark
Twain's *Tom Sawyer*.

There are some obvious first questions to ask. What are the most common words in the text? The answer is shown in table 1.1. Notice how
this list is dominated by the little words of English which have important
FUNCTION WORDS   grammatical roles, and which are usually referred to as *function words*,
such as determiners, prepositions, and complementizers. The one really
exceptional word in the list is *Tom* whose frequency clearly reflects the
text that we chose. This is an important point. In general the results one

Word	Freq.	Use
the	3332	determiner (article)
and	2972	conjunction
a	1775	determiner
to	1725	preposition, verbal infinitive marker
of	1440	preposition
was	1161	auxiliary verb
it	1027	(personal/expletive) pronoun
in	906	preposition
that	877	complementizer, demonstrative
he	877	(personal) pronoun
I	783	(personal) pronoun
his	772	(possessive) pronoun
you	686	(personal) pronoun
Tom	679	proper noun
with	642	preposition

Table 1.1   Common words in *Tom Sawyer*.

gets depends on the corpus or sample used. People use large and varied samples to try to avoid anomalies like this, but in general the goal of using a truly 'representative' sample of all of English usage is something of a chimera, and the corpus will reflect the materials from which it was constructed. For example, if it includes material from linguistics research papers, then words like *ergativity, causativize,* and *lexicalist* may well occur, but otherwise they are unlikely to be in the corpus at all, no matter how large it is.

How many words are there in the text? This question can be interpreted in two ways. The question about the sheer length of the text is distin-
WORD TOKENS guished by asking how many *word tokens* there are. There are 71,370. So this is a very small corpus by any standards, just big enough to illustrate a few basic points. Although *Tom Sawyer* is a reasonable length novel, it is somewhat less than half a megabyte of online text, and for broad coverage statistical grammars we will often seek collections of text that are orders of magnitude larger. How many different words, or in
WORD TYPES other words, how many *word types* appear in the text? There are 8,018. This is actually quite a small number for a text its size, and presumably reflects the fact that *Tom Sawyer* is written in a colloquial style for chil-

Word Frequency	Frequency of Frequency
1	3993
2	1292
3	664
4	410
5	243
6	199
7	172
8	131
9	82
10	91
11–50	540
51–100	99
> 100	102

Table 1.2 Frequency of frequencies of word types in *Tom Sawyer*.

dren (for instance, a sample of newswire the same size contained slightly over 11,000 word types). In general in this way one can talk about *to-kens*, individual occurrences of something, and *types*, the different things present. One can also calculate the ratio of tokens to types, which is simply the average frequency with which each type is used. For *Tom Sawyer*, it is 8.9.[6]

TOKENS

TYPES

The above statistics tell us that words in the corpus occur 'on average' about 9 times each. But one of the greatest problems in Statistical NLP is that word types have a very uneven distribution. Table 1.2 shows how many word types occur with a certain frequency. Some words are very common, occurring over 700 times and therefore individually accounting for over 1% of the words in the novel (there are 12 such words in table 1.1). Overall, the most common 100 words account for slightly over half (50.9%) of the word tokens in the text. On the other extreme, note that almost half (49.8%) of the word types occur only once in the corpus. Such words are referred to as *hapax legomena*, Greek for 'read only once.' Even beyond these words, note that the vast majority of word types oc-

HAPAX LEGOMENA

---

6. This ratio is not a valid measure of something like 'text complexity' just by itself, since the value varies with the size of the text. For a valid comparison, one needs to normalize the lengths of the texts, such as by calculating the measure over windows of 1,000 words.

cur extremely infrequently: over 90% of the word types occur 10 times or less. Nevertheless, very rare words make up a considerable proportion of the text: 12% of the text is words that occur 3 times or less.

Such simple text counts as these can have a use in applications such as cryptography, or to give some sort of indication of style or authorship. But such primitive statistics on the distribution of words in a text are hardly terribly linguistically significant. So towards the end of the chapter we will begin to explore a research avenue that has slightly more linguistic interest. But these primitive text statistics already tell us the reason that Statistical NLP is difficult: it is hard to predict much about the behavior of words that you never or barely ever observed in your corpus. One might initially think that these problems would just go away when one uses a larger corpus, but this hope is not borne out: rather, lots of words that we do not see at all in *Tom Sawyer* will occur – once or twice – in a large corpus. The existence of this long tail of rare words is the basis for the most celebrated early result in corpus linguistics, Zipf's law, which we will discuss next.

1.4.3   Zipf's laws

In his book *Human Behavior and the Principle of Least Effort*, Zipf argues that he has found a unifying principle, the Principle of Least Effort, which underlies essentially the entire human condition (the book even includes some questionable remarks on human sexuality!). The Principle of Least Effort argues that people will act so as to minimize their probable average rate of work (i.e., not only to minimize the work that they would have to do immediately, but taking due consideration of future work that might result from doing work poorly in the short term). The evidence for this theory is certain empirical laws that Zipf uncovered, and his presentation of these laws begins where his own research began, in uncovering certain statistical distributions in language. We will not comment on his general theory here, but will mention some of his empirical language laws.

The famous law: Zipf's law

If we count up how often each word (type) of a language occurs in a large corpus, and then list the words in order of their frequency of occurrence, we can explore the relationship between the frequency of a word f and

RANK   its position in the list, known as its *rank r*. Zipf's law says that:

Word	Freq. (f)	Rank (r)	$f \cdot r$	Word	Freq. (f)	Rank (r)	$f \cdot r$
the	3332	1	3332	turned	51	200	10200
and	2972	2	5944	you'll	30	300	9000
a	1775	3	5235	name	21	400	8400
he	877	10	8770	comes	16	500	8000
but	410	20	8400	group	13	600	7800
be	294	30	8820	lead	11	700	7700
there	222	40	8880	friends	10	800	8000
one	172	50	8600	begin	9	900	8100
about	158	60	9480	family	8	1000	8000
more	138	70	9660	brushed	4	2000	8000
never	124	80	9920	sins	2	3000	6000
Oh	116	90	10440	Could	2	4000	8000
two	104	100	10400	Applausive	1	8000	8000

Table 1.3 Empirical evaluation of Zipf's law on *Tom Sawyer*.

(1.14) $f \propto \dfrac{1}{r}$

or, in other words:

(1.15)   There is a constant k such that $f \cdot r = k$

For example, this says that the 50th most common word should occur with three times the frequency of the 150th most common word. This relationship between frequency and rank appears first to have been noticed by Estoup (1916), but was widely publicized by Zipf and continues to bear his name. We will regard this result not actually as a law, but as a roughly accurate characterization of certain empirical facts.

Table 1.3 shows an empirical evaluation of Zipf's law on the basis of *Tom Sawyer*. Here, Zipf's law is shown to approximately hold, but we note that it is quite a bit off for the three highest frequency words, and further that the product $f \cdot r$ tends to bulge a little for words of rank around 100, a slight bulge which can also be noted in many of Zipf's own studies. Nevertheless, Zipf's law is useful as a rough description of the frequency distribution of words in human languages: there are a few very common words, a middling number of medium frequency words, and many low frequency words. Zipf saw in this a deep significance.

According to his theory both the speaker and the hearer are trying to minimize their effort. The speaker's effort is conserved by having a small vocabulary of common words and the hearer's effort is lessened by having a large vocabulary of individually rarer words (so that messages are less ambiguous). The maximally economical compromise between these competing needs is argued to be the kind of reciprocal relationship between frequency and rank that appears in the data supporting Zipf's law. However, for us, the main upshot of Zipf's law is the practical problem that for most words our data about their use will be exceedingly sparse. Only for a few words will we have lots of examples.

The validity and possibilities for the derivation of Zipf's law is studied extensively by Mandelbrot (1954). While studies of larger corpora sometimes show a closer match to Zipf's predictions than our examples here, Mandelbrot (1954: 12) also notes that "bien que la formule de Zipf donne l'allure générale des courbes, elle en représente très mal les détails [although Zipf's formula gives the general shape of the curves, it is very bad in reflecting the details]." Figure 1.1 shows a rank-frequency plot of the words in one corpus (the Brown corpus) on doubly logarithmic axes. Zipf's law predicts that this graph should be a straight line with slope -1. Mandelbrot noted that the line is often a bad fit, especially for low and high ranks. In our example, the line is too low for most low ranks and too high for ranks greater than 10,000.

To achieve a closer fit to the empirical distribution of words, Mandelbrot derives the following more general relationship between rank and frequency:

$$(1.16) \qquad f = P(r + \rho)^{-B} \quad \text{or} \quad \log f = \log P - B \log(r + \rho)$$

Here P, B and ρ are parameters of a text, that collectively measure the richness of the text's use of words. There is still a hyperbolic distribution between rank and frequency, as in the original equation (1.14). If this formula is graphed on doubly logarithmic axes, then for large values of r, it closely approximates a straight line descending with slope $-B$, just as Zipf's law. However, by appropriate setting of the other parameters, one can model a curve where the predicted frequency of the most frequent words is lower, while thereafter there is a bulge in the curve: just as we saw in the case of *Tom Sawyer*. The graph in figure 1.2 shows that Mandelbrot's formula is indeed a better fit than Zipf's law for our corpus. The slight bulge in the upper left corner and the larger slope

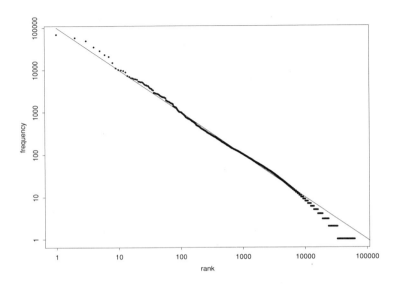

Figure 1.1 Zipf's law. The graph shows rank on the X-axis versus frequency on the Y-axis, using logarithmic scales. The points correspond to the ranks and frequencies of the words in one corpus (the Brown corpus). The line is the relationship between rank and frequency predicted by Zipf for $k = 100,000$, that is $f \times r = 100,000$.

of $B = 1.15$ model the lowest and highest ranks better than the line in figure 1.1 predicted by Zipf.

If we take $B = 1$ and $\rho = 0$ then Mandelbrot's formula simplifies to the one given by Zipf (see exercise 1.3). Based on data similar to the corpora we just looked at, Mandelbrot argues that Zipf's simpler formula just is not true in general: "lorsque Zipf essayait de représenter tout par cette loi, il essayait d'habiller tout le monde avec des vêtements d'une seule taille [when Zipf tried to represent everything by this (i.e., his) law, he tried to dress everyone with clothes of a single cut]". Nevertheless, Mandelbrot sees the importance of Zipf's work as stressing that there are often phenomena in the world that are not suitably modeled by Gaussian (normal) distributions, that is, 'bell curves,' but by hyperbolic distributions – a fact discovered earlier in the domain of economics by Pareto.

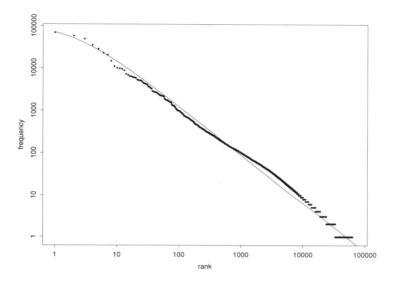

Figure 1.2   Mandelbrot's formula. The graph shows rank on the X-axis versus frequency on the Y-axis, using logarithmic scales. The points correspond to the ranks and frequencies of the words in one corpus (the Brown corpus). The line is the relationship between rank and frequency predicted by Mandelbrot's formula for $P = 10^{5.4}$, $B = 1.15$, $\rho = 100$.

Other laws

References to Zipf's law in the Statistical NLP literature invariably refer to the above law, but Zipf actually proposed a number of other empirical laws relating to language which were also taken to illustrate the Principle of Least Effort. At least two others are of some interest to the concerns of Statistical NLP. One is the suggestion that the number of meanings of a word is correlated with its frequency. Again, Zipf argues that conservation of speaker effort would prefer there to be only one word with all meanings while conservation of hearer effort would prefer each meaning to be expressed by a different word. Assuming that these forces are equally strong, Zipf argues that the number of meanings m of a word obeys the law:

(1.17) $m \propto \sqrt{f}$

or, given the previous law, that:

$$(1.18) \quad m \propto \frac{1}{\sqrt{r}}$$

Zipf finds empirical support for this result (in his study, words of frequency rank about 10,000 average about 2.1 meanings, words of rank about 5000 average about 3 meanings, and words of rank about 2000 average about 4.6 meanings).

A second result concerns the tendency of content words to clump. For a word one can measure the number of lines or pages between each occurrence of the word in a text, and then calculate the frequency F of different interval sizes I. For words of frequency at most 24 in a 260,000 word corpus, Zipf found that the number of intervals of a certain size was inversely related to the interval size ($F \propto I^{-P}$, where p varied between about 1 and 1.3 in Zipf's studies). In other words, most of the time content words occur near another occurrence of the same word.

▼ The topic of word senses is discussed in chapter 7, while the clumping of content words is discussed in section 15.3.

Other laws of Zipf's include that there is an inverse relationship between the frequency of words and their length, that the greater the frequency of a word or morpheme, the greater the number of different permutations (roughly, compounds and morphologically complex forms) it will be used in, and yet further laws covering historical change and the frequency of phonemes.

The significance of power laws

As a final remark on Zipf's law, we note that there is a debate on how surprising and interesting Zipf's law and 'power laws' in general are as a description of natural phenomena. It has been argued that randomly generated text exhibits Zipf's law (Li 1992). To show this, we construct a generator that randomly produces characters from the 26 letters of the alphabet and the blank (that is, each of these 27 symbols has an equal chance of being generated next). Simplifying slightly, the probability of a word of length n being generated is $\left(\frac{26}{27}\right)^n \frac{1}{27}$: the probability of generating a non-blank character n times and the blank after that. One can show that the words generated by such a generator obey a power law of the form Mandelbrot suggested. The key insights are (i) that there are 26 times more words of length $n + 1$ than length n, and (ii) that there is a constant ratio by which words of length n are more frequent than words of length $n + 1$. These two opposing trends combine into the regularity of Mandelbrot's law. See exercise 1.4.

There is in fact a broad class of probability distributions that obey power laws when the same procedure is applied to them that is used to compute the Zipf distribution: first counting events, then ranking them according to their frequency (Günter et al. 1996). Seen from this angle, Zipf's law seems less valuable as a characterization of language. But the basic insight remains: what makes frequency-based approaches to language hard is that almost all words are rare. Zipf's law is a good way to encapsulate this insight.

1.4.4 Collocations

COLLOCATION

Lexicographers and linguists (although rarely those of a generative bent) have long been interested in collocations. A *collocation* is any turn of phrase or accepted usage where somehow the whole is perceived to have an existence beyond the sum of the parts. Collocations include compounds (*disk drive*), phrasal verbs (*make up*), and other stock phrases (*bacon and eggs*). They often have a specialized meaning or are idiomatic, but they need not be. For example, at the time of writing, a favorite expression of bureaucrats in Australia is *international best practice*. Now there appears to be nothing idiomatic about this expression; it is simply two adjectives modifying a noun in a productive and semantically compositional way. But, nevertheless, the frequent use of this phrase as a fixed expression accompanied by certain connotations justifies regarding it as a collocation. Indeed, any expression that people repeat because they have heard others using it is a candidate for a collocation.

▼ Collocations are discussed in detail in chapter 5. We see later on that collocations are important in areas of Statistical NLP such as machine translation (chapter 13) and information retrieval (chapter 15). In machine translation, a word may be translated differently according to the collocation it occurs in. An information retrieval system may want to index only 'interesting' phrases, that is, those that are collocations.

Lexicographers are also interested in collocations both because they show frequent ways in which a word is used, and because they are multiword units which have an independent existence and probably should appear in a dictionary. They also have theoretical interest: to the extent that most of language use is people reusing phrases and constructions

Frequency	Word 1	Word 2
80871	of	the
58841	in	the
26430	to	the
21842	on	the
21839	for	the
18568	and	the
16121	that	the
15630	at	the
15494	to	be
13899	in	a
13689	of	a
13361	by	the
13183	with	the
12622	from	the
11428	New	York
10007	he	said
9775	as	a
9231	is	a
8753	has	been
8573	for	a

Table 1.4 Commonest bigram collocations in the *New York Times*.

that they have heard, this serves to de-emphasize the Chomskyan focus on the creativity of language use, and to give more strength to something like a Hallidayan approach that considers language to be inseparable from its pragmatic and social context.

Now collocations may be several words long (such as *international best practice*) or they may be discontinuous (such as *make [something] up*), but let us restrict ourselves to the simplest case and wonder how we can automatically identify contiguous two word collocations. It was mentioned above that collocations tend to be frequent usages. So the first idea to try might be simply to find the most common two word sequences in a text. That is fairly easily done, and, for a corpus of text from the *New York Times* (see page 153), the results are shown in table 1.4. Unfortunately, this method does not seem to succeed very well at capturing the collocations present in the text. It is not surprising that these pairs of words

BIGRAMS (normally referred to as *bigrams*) occur commonly. They simply represent common syntactic constructions involving individually extremely common words. One problem is that we are not normalizing for the frequency of the words that make up the collocation. Given that *the, of*, and *in* are extremely common words, and that the syntax of prepositional and noun phrases means that a determiner commonly follows a preposition, we should expect to commonly see *of the* and *in the*. But that does not make these word sequences collocations. An obvious next step is to somehow take into account the frequency of each of the words. We will look at methods that do this in chapter 5.

A modification that might be less obvious, but which is very effective, is to *filter* the collocations and remove those that have parts of speech (or syntactic categories) that are rarely associated with interesting collocations. There simply are no interesting collocations that have a preposition as the first word and an article as the second word. The two most frequent patterns for two word collocations are "adjective noun" and "noun noun" (the latter are called noun-noun compounds). Table 1.5 shows which bigrams are selected from the corpus if we only keep adjective-noun and noun-noun bigrams. Almost all of them seem to be phrases that we would want to list in a dictionary – with some exceptions like *last year* and *next year*.

Our excursion into 'collocation discovery' illustrates the back and forth in Statistical NLP between modeling and data analysis. Our initial model was that a collocation is simply a frequent bigram. We analyzed the results we got based on this model, identified problems and then came up with a refined model (collocation = frequent bigram with a particular part-of-speech pattern). This model needs further refinement because of bigrams like *next year* that are selected incorrectly. Still, we will leave our investigation of collocations for now, and continue it in chapter 5.

1.4.5 Concordances

As a final illustration of data exploration, suppose we are interested in the syntactic frames in which verbs appear. People have researched how to get a computer to find these frames automatically, but we can also just use the computer as a tool to find appropriate data. For such purposes, KEY WORD IN people often use a *Key Word In Context* (KWIC) concordancing program CONTEXT which produces displays of data such as the one in figure 1.3. In such a display, all occurrences of the word of interest are lined up beneath

Frequency	Word 1	Word 2	Part-of-speech pattern
11487	New	York	A N
7261	United	States	A N
5412	Los	Angeles	N N
3301	last	year	A N
3191	Saudi	Arabia	N N
2699	last	week	A N
2514	vice	president	A N
2378	Persian	Gulf	A N
2161	San	Francisco	N N
2106	President	Bush	N N
2001	Middle	East	A N
1942	Saddam	Hussein	N N
1867	Soviet	Union	A N
1850	White	House	A N
1633	United	Nations	A N
1337	York	City	N N
1328	oil	prices	N N
1210	next	year	A N
1074	chief	executive	A N
1073	real	estate	A N

Table 1.5 Frequent bigrams after filtering. The most frequent bigrams in the *New York Times* after applying a part-of-speech filter.

1	could find a target. The librarian	"showed	off" – running hither and thither w
2	elights in. The young lady teachers	"showed	off" – bending sweetly over pupils
3	ingly. The young gentlemen teachers	"showed	off" with small scoldings and other
4	seeming vexation). The little girls	"showed	off" in various ways, and the littl
5	n various ways, and the little boys	"showed	off" with such diligence that the a
6	t genuwyne?" Tom lifted his lip and	showed	the vacancy. "Well, all right," sai
7	is little finger for a pen. Then he	showed	Huckleberry how to make an H and an
8	ow's face was haggard, and his eyes	showed	the fear that was upon him. When he
9	not overlook the fact that Tom even	showed	a marked aversion to these inquests
10	own. Two or three glimmering lights	showed	where it lay, peacefully sleeping,
11	ird flash turned night into day and	showed	every little grass-blade, separate
12	that grew about their feet. And it	showed	three white, startled faces, too. A
13	he first thing his aunt said to him	showed	him that he had brought his sorrows
14	p from her lethargy of distress and	showed	good interest in the proceedings. S
15	ent a new burst of grief from Becky	showed	Tom that the thing in his mind had
16	shudder quiver all through him. He	showed	Huck the fragment of candle-wick pe

Figure 1.3 Key Word In Context (KWIC) display for the word *showed*.

$$\text{NP}_{agent} \text{ showed off } (\text{PP}[\textit{with/in}]_{manner})$$

$$\text{NP}_{agent} \text{ showed } (\text{NP}_{recipient}) \left(\left\{ \begin{array}{l} \text{NP}_{content} \\ \text{CP}[\textit{that}]_{content} \\ \text{VP}[\text{inf}]_{content} \\ \textit{how } \text{VP}[\text{inf}]_{content} \\ \text{CP}[\textit{where}]_{content} \end{array} \right\} \right)$$

$$\text{NP}_{agent} \text{ showed NP}[\textit{interest}] \text{ PP}[\textit{in}]_{content}$$

$$\text{NP}_{agent} \text{ showed NP}[\textit{aversion}] \text{ PP}[\textit{to}]_{content}$$

Figure 1.4 Syntactic frames for *showed* in *Tom Sawyer*.

one another, with surrounding context shown on both sides. Commonly, KWIC programs allow you to sort the matches by left or right context. However, if we are interested in syntactic frames, rather than particular words, such sorting is of limited use. The data shows occurrences of the word *showed* within the novel *Tom Sawyer*. There are 5 uses of *showed off* (actually all within one paragraph of the text), each in double quotes, perhaps because it was a neologism at the time, or perhaps because Twain considered the expression slang. All of these uses are intransitive, although some take prepositional phrase modifiers. Beyond these, there are four straightforward transitive verb uses with just a direct object (6, 8, 11, 12) – although there are interesting differences between them with 8 being nonagentive, and 12 illustrating a sense of 'cause to be visible.' There is one ditransitive use which adds the person being shown (16). Three examples make who was shown the object NP and express the content either as a *that*-clause (13, 15) or as a non-finite question-form complement clause (7). One other example has a finite question-form complement clause (10) but omits mention of the person who is shown. Finally two examples have an NP object followed by a prepositional phrase and are quite idiomatic constructions (9, 14): *show an aversion PP[to]* and *show an interest PP[in]*. But note that while quite idiomatic, they are not completely frozen forms, since in both cases the object noun is productively modified to make a more complex NP. We could systematize the patterns we have found as in figure 1.4.

Collecting information like this about patterns of occurrence of verbs can be useful not only for purposes such as dictionaries for learners of foreign languages, but for use in guiding statistical parsers. A substantial part of the work in Statistical NLP consists (or should consist!) of poring over large amounts of data, like concordance lines and lists of candidates for collocations. At the outset of a project this is done to understand the important phenomena, later to refine the initial modeling, and finally to evaluate what was achieved.

1.5   Further Reading

Chomsky (1965: 47ff, 1980: 234ff, 1986) discusses the distinction between rationalist and empiricist approaches to language, and presents arguments for the rationalist position. A recent detailed response to these arguments from an 'empiricist' is (Sampson 1997). For people from a generative (computational) linguistics background wondering what Statistical NLP can do for them, and how it relates to their traditional concerns, Abney (1996b) is a good place to start. The observation that there must be a preference for certain kinds of generalizations in order to bootstrap induction was pointed out in the machine learning literature by Mitchell
BIAS   (1980), who termed the preference *bias*. The work of Firth is highly influential within certain strands of the British corpus linguistics tradition, and is thoroughly covered in (Stubbs 1996). References from within the Statistical NLP community perhaps originate in work from AT&T, see for instance (Church and Mercer 1993: 1). The Hallidayan approach to language is presented in (Halliday 1994).

GRAMMATICALITY   Thorough discussions of *grammaticality* judgements in linguistics are found in (Schütze 1996) and (Cowart 1997). Cowart argues for making use of the judgements of a population of speakers, which is quite compatible with the approach of this book, and rather against the Chomskyan approach of exploring the grammar of a single speaker. A good entry point to the literature on categorical perception is (Harnad 1987).

Lauer (1995b: ch. 3) advocates an approach involving probability distributions over meanings. See the Further Reading of chapter 12 for references to other Statistical NLP work that involves mapping to semantic representations.

The discussion of *kind/sort of* is based on Tabor (1994), which should be consulted for the sources of the citations used. Tabor provides a connectionist model which shows how the syntactic change discussed can be caused by changing frequencies of use. A lot of interesting recent work
GRAMMATICALIZA-   on gradual syntactic change can be found in the literature on *grammati-*
TION   *calization* (Hopper and Traugott 1993).

Two proponents of an important role for probabilistic mechanisms in cognition are Anderson (1983, 1990) and Suppes (1984). See (Oaksford and Chater 1998) for a recent collection describing different cognitive architectures, including connectionism. The view that language is best explained as a cognitive phenomenon is the central tenet of cognitive linguistics (Lakoff 1987; Langacker 1987, 1991), but many cognitive linguists would not endorse probability theory as a formalization of cognitive linguistics. See also (Schütze 1997).

The novel *Tom Sawyer* is available in the public domain on the internet, currently from sources including the Virginia Electronic Text Center (see the website).

Zipf's work began with (Zipf 1929), his doctoral thesis. His two major books are (Zipf 1935) and (Zipf 1949). It is interesting to note that Zipf was reviewed harshly by linguists in his day (see, for instance, (Kent 1930) and (Prokosch 1933)). In part these criticisms correctly focussed on the grandiosity of Zipf's claims (Kent (1930: 88) writes: "problems of phonology and morphology are not to be solved *en masse* by one grand general formula"), but they also reflected, even then, a certain ambivalence to the application of statistical methods in linguistics. Nevertheless, prominent American structuralists, such as Martin Joos and Morris Swadesh, did become involved in data collection for statistical studies, with Joos (1936) emphasizing that the question of whether to use statistical methods in linguistics should be evaluated separately from Zipf's particular claims.

As well as (Mandelbrot 1954), Mandelbrot's investigation of Zipf's law is summarized in (Mandelbrot 1983) – see especially chapters 38, 40, and 42. Mandelbrot attributes the direction of his life's work (leading to his well known work on fractals and the Mandelbrot set) to reading a review of (Zipf 1949).

Concordances were first constructed by hand for important literary and religious works. Computer concordancing began in the late 1950s for the purposes of categorizing and indexing article titles and abstracts. Luhn (1960) developed the first computer concordancer and coined the term KWIC *KWIC*.

1.6 Exercises

Exercise 1.1 [★★ Requires some knowledge of linguistics]
Try to think of some other cases of noncategorical phenomena in language, perhaps related to language change. For starters, look at the following pairs of

sentences, and try to work out the problems they raise. (Could these problems be solved simply by assigning the words to two categories, or is there evidence of mixed categoriality?)

(1.19)   a. On the weekend the children had *fun*.

          b. That's the *funnest* thing we've done all holidays.

(1.20)   a. Do you get much *email* at work?

          b. This morning I had *emails* from five clients, all complaining.

Exercise 1.2   [★ ★   Probably best attempted after reading chapter 4]

Replicate some of the results of section 1.4 on some other piece of text. (Alternatively, you could use the same text that we did so that you can check your work easily. In this case, you should only expect results similar to ours, since the exact numbers depend on various details of what is treated as a word, how case distinctions are treated, etc.)

Exercise 1.3   [★]

Show that Mandelbrot's law simplifies to Zipf's law for $B = 1$ and $\rho = 0$.

Exercise 1.4   [★ ★]

Construct a table like table 1.3 for the random character generator described above on page 29 (which generates the letters *a* through *z* and blank with equal probability of $1/27$).

Exercise 1.5   [★ ★]

Think about ways of identifying collocations that might be better than the methods used in this chapter.

Exercise 1.6   [★ ★]

If you succeeded in the above exercise, try the method out and see how well it appears to perform.

Exercise 1.7   [★ ★]

Write a program to produce KWIC displays from a text file. Have the user be able to select the word of interest and the size of the surrounding context.

"In 1786, I found, that in Germany they were engaged in a species of political inquiry, to which they had given the name of Statistics; and though I apply a different idea to that word, for by Statistical is meant in Germany, an inquiry for the purpose of ascertaining the political strength of a country, or questions respecting matters of state; whereas, the idea I annex to the term, is an inquiry into the state of a country, for the purpose of ascertaining the quantum of happiness enjoyed by its inhabitants, and the means of its future improvement; yet, as I thought that a new word might attract more public attention, I resolved on adopting it."

(Sir J. Sinclair Statist. Acc. Scot. XX. App. p. xiii, 1798)

2 *Mathematical Foundations*

THIS CHAPTER presents some introductory material on probability and information theory, while the next chapter presents some essential knowledge of linguistics. A thorough knowledge of one or more of the fields of probability and statistics, information theory, and linguistics is desirable, and perhaps even necessary, for doing original research in the field of Statistical NLP. We cannot provide a thorough well-motivated introduction to each of these three fields within this book, but nevertheless, we attempt to summarize enough material to allow understanding of everything that follows in the book. We do however assume knowledge of parsing, either from a computer science or computational linguistics perspective. We also assume a reasonable knowledge of mathematical symbols and techniques, perhaps roughly to the level of a first year undergraduate course, including the basics of such topics as: set theory, functions and relations, summations, polynomials, calculus, vectors and matrices, and logarithms. Mathematical notations that we use are summarized in the Table of Notations.

If you are familiar with one of the areas covered in these two chapters, then you should probably just skim the corresponding section. If you're not familiar with a topic, we think it is probably best to try to read through each section, but you will probably need to reread sections when the techniques in them are put to use. These chapters don't say much about applications – they present the preparatory theory for what follows.

2.1 Elementary Probability Theory

This section sketches the essentials of probability theory necessary to understand the rest of this book.

2.1.1 Probability spaces

PROBABILITY THEORY

Probability theory deals with predicting how likely it is that something will happen. For example, if one tosses three coins, how likely is it that they will all come up heads? Although our eventual aim is to look at language, we begin with some examples with coins and dice, since their behavior is simpler and more straightforward.

The notion of the likelihood of something is formalized through the concept of an *experiment* (or *trial*) – the process by which an observation is made. In this technical sense, tossing three coins is an experiment. All that is crucial is that the experimental protocol is well defined. We assume a collection of *basic outcomes* (or *sample points*) for our experiment, the *sample space* Ω. Sample spaces may either be *discrete*, having at most a countably infinite number of basic outcomes, or *continuous*, having an uncountable number of basic outcomes (for example, measuring a person's height). For language applications and in this introduction, we will mainly deal with discrete sample spaces which only contain a finite number of basic outcomes. Let an *event A* be a subset of Ω. For example, in the coin experiment, the first coin being a head, and the second and third coming down tails is one basic outcome, while any result of one head and two tails is an example of an event. Note also that Ω represents the certain event, the space of all possible experimental outcomes, and $\varnothing$ represents the impossible event. We say that an experimental outcome must be an event. The foundations of probability theory depend on the set of events $\mathcal{F}$ forming a σ-field – a set with a maximal element Ω and arbitrary complements and unions. These requirements are trivially satisfied by making the set of events, the *event space*, the power set of the sample space (that is, the set of all subsets of the sample space, often written $2^{\mathcal{F}}$).

Probabilities are numbers between 0 and 1, where 0 indicates impossibility and 1 certainty. A *probability function* (also known as a *probability distribution*) distributes a probability mass of 1 throughout the sample space Ω. Formally, a discrete probability function is any function $P: \mathcal{F} \rightarrow [0, 1]$ such that:

EXPERIMENT
TRIAL

BASIC OUTCOMES
SAMPLE SPACE
DISCRETE
CONTINUOUS

EVENT

σ-FIELD

EVENT SPACE

PROBABILITY
FUNCTION
PROBABILITY
DISTRIBUTION

- $P(\Omega) = 1$

DISJOINT
- Countable additivity: For *disjoint* sets $A_j \in \mathcal{F}$ (i.e., $A_j \cap A_k = \varnothing$ for $j \neq k$)

(2.1)
$$P\left(\bigcup_{j=1}^{\infty} A_j\right) = \sum_{j=1}^{\infty} P(A_j)$$

We call $P(A)$ the probability of the event A. These axioms say that an event that encompasses, say, three distinct possibilities must have a probability that is the sum of the probabilities of each possibility, and that since an experiment must have some basic outcome as its result, the probability of that is 1. Using basic set theory, we can derive from these axioms a set of further properties of probability functions; see exercise 2.1.

PROBABILITY SPACE
A well-founded *probability space* consists of a sample space Ω, a σ-field of events $\mathcal{F}$, and a probability function P. In Statistical NLP applications, we always seek to properly define such a probability space for our models. Otherwise, the numbers we use are merely ad hoc scaling factors, and there is no mathematical theory to help us. In practice, though, corners often have been, and continue to be, cut.

Example 1:   A fair coin is tossed 3 times. What is the chance of 2 heads?

Solution: The experimental protocol is clear. The sample space is:

$$\Omega = \{HHH, HHT, HTH, HTT, THH, THT, TTH, TTT\}$$

Each of the basic outcomes in Ω is equally likely, and thus has probability $1/8$. A situation where each basic outcome is equally likely is called a UNIFORM DISTRIBUTION *uniform distribution*. In a finite sample space with equiprobable basic outcomes, $P(A) = \frac{|A|}{|\Omega|}$ (where $|A|$ is the number of elements in a set A). The event of interest is:

$$A = \{HHT, HTH, THH\}$$

So:

$$P(A) = \frac{|A|}{|\Omega|} = \frac{3}{8}$$

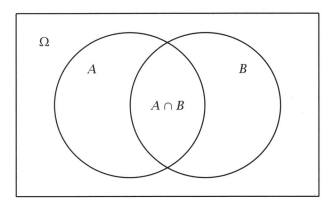

Figure 2.1 A diagram illustrating the calculation of conditional probability $P(A|B)$. Once we know that the outcome is in B, the probability of A becomes $P(A \cap B)/P(B)$.

2.1.2 Conditional probability and independence

CONDITIONAL
PROBABILITY

PRIOR PROBABILITY

POSTERIOR
PROBABILITY

Sometimes we have partial knowledge about the outcome of an experiment and that naturally influences what experimental outcomes are possible. We capture this knowledge through the notion of *conditional probability*. This is the updated probability of an event given some knowledge. The probability of an event before we consider our additional knowledge is called the *prior probability* of the event, while the new probability that results from using our additional knowledge is referred to as the *posterior probability* of the event. Returning to example 1 (the chance of getting 2 heads when tossing 3 coins), if the first coin has been tossed and is a head, then of the 4 remaining possible basic outcomes, 2 result in 2 heads, and so the probability of getting 2 heads now becomes $\frac{1}{2}$. The conditional probability of an event A given that an event B has occurred ($P(B) > 0$) is:

(2.2) $$P(A|B) = \frac{P(A \cap B)}{P(B)}$$

Even if $P(B) = 0$ we have that:

(2.3) $P(A \cap B) = P(B)P(A|B) = P(A)P(B|A)$ [The multiplication rule]

We can do the conditionalization either way because set intersection is symmetric ($A \cap B = B \cap A$). One can easily visualize this result by looking at the diagram in figure 2.1.

The generalization of this rule to multiple events is a central result that will be used throughout this book, the *chain rule*:

(2.4) $$P(A_1 \cap \ldots \cap A_n) = P(A_1)P(A_2|A_1)P(A_3|A_1 \cap A_2) \cdots P(A_n| \cap_{i=1}^{n-1} A_i)$$

▼ The chain rule is used in many places in Statistical NLP, such as working out the properties of Markov models in chapter 9.

INDEPENDENCE

Two events A, B are *independent* of each other if $P(A \cap B) = P(A)P(B)$. Unless $P(B) = 0$ this is equivalent to saying that $P(A) = P(A|B)$ (i.e., knowing that B is the case does not affect the probability of A). This equivalence follows trivially from the chain rule. Otherwise events are

DEPENDENCE
CONDITIONAL
INDEPENDENCE

dependent. We can also say that A and B are *conditionally independent* given C when $P(A \cap B|C) = P(A|C)P(B|C)$.

2.1.3 Bayes' theorem

BAYES' THEOREM

Bayes' theorem lets us swap the order of dependence between events. That is, it lets us calculate $P(B|A)$ in terms of $P(A|B)$. This is useful when the former quantity is difficult to determine. It is a central tool that we will use again and again, but it is a trivial consequence of the definition of conditional probability and the chain rule introduced in equations (2.2) and (2.3):

(2.5) $$P(B|A) = \frac{P(B \cap A)}{P(A)} = \frac{P(A|B)P(B)}{P(A)}$$

NORMALIZING
CONSTANT

The righthand side denominator $P(A)$ can be viewed as a *normalizing constant*, something that ensures that we have a probability function. If we are simply interested in which event out of some set is most likely given A, we can ignore it. Since the denominator is the same in all cases, we have that:

(2.6) $$\arg\max_B \frac{P(A|B)P(B)}{P(A)} = \arg\max_B P(A|B)P(B)$$

However, we can also evaluate the denominator by recalling that:

$$P(A \cap B) = P(A|B)P(B)$$
$$P(A \cap \overline{B}) = P(A|\overline{B})P(\overline{B})$$

So we have:

$$P(A) = P(A \cap B) + P(A \cap \overline{B}) \qquad \text{[additivity]}$$
$$= P(A|B)P(B) + P(A|\overline{B})P(\overline{B})$$

B and $\overline{B}$ serve to split the set A into two disjoint parts (one possibly empty), and so we can evaluate the conditional probability on each, and then sum, using additivity. More generally, if we have some group of sets PARTITION B_i that *partition* A, that is, if $A \subseteq \cup_i B_i$ and the B_i are disjoint, then:

$$(2.7) \quad P(A) = \sum_i P(A|B_i)P(B_i)$$

This gives us the following equivalent but more elaborated version of Bayes' theorem:

Bayes' theorem: If $A \subseteq \cup_{i=1}^n B_i$, $P(A) > 0$, and $B_i \cap B_j = \varnothing$ for $i \neq j$ then:

$$(2.8) \quad P(B_j|A) = \frac{P(A|B_j)P(B_j)}{P(A)} = \frac{P(A|B_j)P(B_j)}{\sum_{i=1}^n P(A|B_i)P(B_i)}$$

Example 2:   Suppose one is interested in a rare syntactic construction, perhaps parasitic gaps, which occurs on average once in 100,000 sentences. Joe Linguist has developed a complicated pattern matcher that attempts to identify sentences with parasitic gaps. It's pretty good, but it's not perfect: if a sentence has a parasitic gap, it will say so with probability 0.95, if it doesn't, it will wrongly say it does with probability 0.005. Suppose the test says that a sentence contains a parasitic gap. What is the probability that this is true?

Solution: Let G be the event of the sentence having a parasitic gap, and let T be the event of the test being positive. We want to determine:

$$
\begin{aligned}
P(G|T) &= \frac{P(T|G)P(G)}{P(T|G)P(G) + P(T|\overline{G})P(\overline{G})} \\[2mm]
&= \frac{0.95 \times 0.00001}{0.95 \times 0.00001 + 0.005 \times 0.99999} \approx 0.002
\end{aligned}
$$

Here we use having the construction or not as the partition in the denominator. Although Joe's test seems quite reliable, we find that using it won't help as much as one might have hoped. On average, only 1 in every 500 sentences that the test identifies will actually contain a parasitic gap. This poor result comes about because the prior probability of a sentence containing a parasitic gap is so low.

▼ Bayes' theorem is central to the noisy channel model described in section 2.2.4.

First die	Second die											
	1	2	3	4	5	6						
6	7	8	9	10	11	12						
5	6	7	8	9	10	11						
4	5	6	7	8	9	10						
3	4	5	6	7	8	9						
2	3	4	5	6	7	8						
1	2	3	4	5	6	7						
x		2	3	4	5	6	7	8	9	10	11	12
$p(X=x)$		$\frac{1}{36}$	$\frac{1}{18}$	$\frac{1}{12}$	$\frac{1}{9}$	$\frac{5}{36}$	$\frac{1}{6}$	$\frac{5}{36}$	$\frac{1}{9}$	$\frac{1}{12}$	$\frac{1}{18}$	$\frac{1}{36}$

Figure 2.2 A random variable X for the sum of two dice. Entries in the body of the table show the value of X given the underlying basic outcomes, while the bottom two rows show the pmf $p(x)$.

2.1.4 Random variables

RANDOM VARIABLE

A *random variable* is simply a function $X: \Omega \rightarrow \mathbb{R}^n$ (commonly with $n = 1$), where $\mathbb{R}$ is the set of real numbers. Rather than having to work with some irregular event space which differs with every problem we look at, a random variable allows us to talk about the probabilities of numerical values that are related to the event space. We think of an abstract *stochastic process* that generates numbers with a certain probability distribution. (The word *stochastic* simply means 'probabilistic' or 'randomly generated,' but is especially commonly used when referring to a sequence of results assumed to be generated by some underlying probability distribution.)

STOCHASTIC PROCESS

A discrete random variable is a function $X: \Omega \rightarrow S$ where S is a countable subset of $\mathbb{R}$. If $X: \Omega \rightarrow \{0, 1\}$, then X is called an *indicator random variable* or a *Bernoulli trial*.

INDICATOR RANDOM
VARIABLE
BERNOULLI TRIAL

Example 3: Suppose the events are those that result from tossing two dice. Then we could define a discrete random variable X that is the sum of their faces: $S = \{2, \ldots, 12\}$, as indicated in figure 2.2.

Because a random variable has a numeric range, we can often do mathematics more easily by working with the values of a random variable, rather than directly with events. In particular we can define the *probability mass function* (pmf) for a random variable X, which gives the proba-

PROBABILITY MASS
FUNCTION

bility that the random variable has different numeric values:

(2.9) **pmf** $p(x) = p(X = x) = P(A_x)$ where $A_x = \{\omega \in \Omega : X(\omega) = x\}$

We will write pmfs with a lowercase roman letter (even when they are variables). If a random variable X is distributed according to the pmf $p(x)$, then we will write $X \sim p(x)$.

Note that $p(x) > 0$ at only a countable number of points (to satisfy the stochastic constraint on probabilities), say $\{x_i : i \in \mathbb{N}\}$, while $p(x) = 0$ elsewhere. For a discrete random variable, we have that:

$$\sum_i p(x_i) = \sum_i P(A_{x_i}) = P(\Omega) = 1$$

Conversely, any function satisfying these constraints can be regarded as a mass function.

▼ Random variables are used throughout the introduction to information theory in section 2.2.

2.1.5 Expectation and variance

EXPECTATION The *expectation* is the *mean* or average of a random variable.
MEAN

If X is a random variable with a pmf $p(x)$ such that $\sum_x |x| \, p(x) < \infty$ then the expectation is:

(2.10) $$E(X) = \sum_x x \, p(x)$$

Example 4: If rolling one die and Y is the value on its face, then:

$$E(Y) = \sum_{y=1}^{6} y \, p(y) = \frac{1}{6} \sum_{y=1}^{6} y = \frac{21}{6} = 3\frac{1}{2}$$

This is the expected average found by totaling up a large number of throws of the die, and dividing by the number of throws.

If $Y \sim p(y)$ is a random variable, any function $g(Y)$ defines a new random variable. If $E(g(Y))$ is defined, then:

(2.11) $$E(g(Y)) = \sum_y g(y) \, p(y)$$

For instance, by letting g be a linear function $g(Y) = aY + b$, we see that $E(g(Y)) = aE(Y) + b$. We also have that $E(X + Y) = E(X) + E(Y)$ and if X and Y are independent, then $E(XY) = E(X)E(Y)$.

VARIANCE   The *variance* of a random variable is a measure of whether the values of the random variable tend to be consistent over trials or to vary a lot. One measures it by finding out how much on average the variable's values deviate from the variable's expectation:

$$(2.12) \quad \begin{aligned} \mathrm{Var}(X) &= E((X - E(X))^2) \\ &= E(X^2) - E^2(X) \end{aligned}$$

STANDARD DEVIATION   The commonly used *standard deviation* of a variable is the square root of the variance. When talking about a particular distribution or set of data, the mean is commonly denoted as μ, the variance as σ^2, and the standard deviation is hence written as σ.

Example 5:   What is the expectation and variance for the random variable introduced in example 3, the sum of the numbers on two dice?

Solution: For the expectation, we can use the result in example 4, and the formula for combining expectations in (or below) equation (2.11):

$$E(X) = E(Y + Y) = E(Y) + E(Y) = 3\frac{1}{2} + 3\frac{1}{2} = 7$$

The variance is given by:

$$\mathrm{Var}(X) = E((X - E(X))^2) = \sum_x \mathrm{p}(x)(x - E(X))^2 = 5\frac{5}{6}$$

Because the results for rolling two dice are concentrated around 7, the variance of this distribution is less than for an '11-sided die,' which returns a uniform distribution over the numbers 2–12. For such a uniformly distributed random variable U, we find that $\mathrm{Var}(U) = 10$.

▼ Calculating expectations is central to Information Theory, as we will see in section 2.2. Variances are used in section 5.2.

2.1.6   Notation

In these sections, we have distinguished between P as a probability function and p as the probability mass function of a random variable. However, the notations $P(\cdot)$ and $\mathrm{p}(\cdot)$ do not always refer to the same function. Any time that we are talking about a different probability space, then we are talking about a different function. Sometimes we will denote these

different functions with subscripts on the function to make it clear what
we are talking about, but in general people just write P and rely on context and the names of the variables that are arguments to the function to
disambiguate. It is important to realize that one equation is often referring to several different probability functions, all ambiguously referred
to as P.

2.1.7 Joint and conditional distributions

Often we define many random variables over a sample space giving us a
joint (or multivariate) probability distribution. The joint probability mass
function for two discrete random variables X, Y is:

$$p(x, y) = P(X = x, Y = y)$$

MARGINAL
DISTRIBUTION

Related to a joint pmf are *marginal pmfs*, which total up the probability
masses for the values of each variable separately:

$$p_X(x) = \sum_y p(x, y) \qquad p_Y(y) = \sum_x p(x, y)$$

In general the marginal mass functions do not determine the joint mass
function. But if X and Y are independent, then $p(x, y) = p_X(x)\, p_Y(y)$.
For example, for the probability of getting two sixes from rolling two
dice, since these events are independent, we can compute that:

$$p(Y = 6, Z = 6) = p(Y = 6)\, p(Z = 6) = \frac{1}{6} \times \frac{1}{6} = \frac{1}{36}$$

There are analogous results for joint distributions and probabilities for
the intersection of events. So we can define a conditional pmf in terms of
the joint distribution:

$$p_{X|Y}(x|y) = \frac{p(x, y)}{p_Y(y)} \quad \text{for } y \text{ such that } p_Y(y) > 0$$

and deduce a chain rule in terms of random variables, for instance:

$$p(w, x, y, z) = p(w)\, p(x|w)\, p(y|w, x)\, p(z|w, x, y)$$

2.1.8 Determining P

So far we have just been assuming a probability function P and giving it
the obvious definition for simple examples with coins and dice. But what

do we do when dealing with language? What do we say about the probability of a sentence like *The cow chewed its cud*? In general, for language events, unlike dice, *P* is unknown. This means we have to *estimate P*. We do this by looking at evidence about what *P* must be like based on a sample of data. The proportion of times a certain outcome occurs is called the *relative frequency* of the outcome. If $C(u)$ is the number of times an outcome *u* occurs in *N* trials then $\frac{C(u)}{N}$ is the relative frequency of *u*. The relative frequency is often denoted f_u. Empirically, if one performs a large number of trials, the relative frequency tends to stabilize around some number. That this number exists provides a basis for letting us calculate probability estimates.

Techniques for how this can be done are a major topic of this book, particularly covered in chapter 6. Common to most of these techniques is to estimate *P* by assuming that some phenomenon in language is acceptably modeled by one of the well-known families of distributions (such as the binomial or normal distribution), which have been widely studied in statistics. In particular a binomial distribution can sometimes be used as an acceptable model of linguistic events. We introduce a couple of families of distributions in the next subsection. This is referred to as a *parametric* approach and has a couple of advantages. It means we have an explicit probabilistic model of the process by which the data was generated, and determining a particular probability distribution within the family only requires the specification of a few parameters, since most of the nature of the curve is fixed in advance. Since only a few parameters need to be determined, the amount of training data required is not great, and one can calculate how much training data is sufficient to make good probability estimates.

But, some parts of language (such as the distributions of words in newspaper articles in a particular topic category) are irregular enough that this approach can run into problems. For example, if we assume our data is binomially distributed, but in fact the data looks nothing like a binomial distribution, then our probability estimates might be wildly wrong.

For such cases, one can use methods that make no assumptions about the underlying distribution of the data, or will work reasonably well for a wide variety of different distributions. This is referred to as a *nonparametric* or *distribution-free* approach. If we simply empirically estimate *P* by counting a large number of random events (giving us a discrete distribution, though we might produce a continuous distribution from

Margin terms:

ESTIMATION

RELATIVE FREQUENCY

PARAMETRIC

NON-PARAMETRIC
DISTRIBUTION-FREE

such data by interpolation, assuming only that the estimated probability density function should be a fairly smooth curve), then this is a non-parametric method. However, empirical counts often need to be modified or smoothed to deal with the deficiencies of our limited training data, a topic discussed in chapter 6. Such smoothing techniques usually assume a certain underlying distribution, and so we are then back in the world of parametric methods. The disadvantage of nonparametric methods is that we give our system less prior information about how the data are generated, so a great deal of training data is usually needed to compensate for this.

▼ Non-parametric methods are used in automatic classification when the underlying distribution of the data is unknown. One such method, nearest neighbor classification, is introduced in section 16.4 for text categorization.

2.1.9   Standard distributions

DISTRIBUTION
PARAMETERS

Certain probability mass functions crop up commonly in practice. In particular, one commonly finds the same basic form of a function, but just with different constants employed. Statisticians have long studied these families of functions. They refer to the family of functions as a *distribution* and to the numbers that define the different members of the family as *parameters*. Parameters are constants when one is talking about a particular pmf, but variables when one is looking at the family. When writing out the arguments of a distribution, it is usual to separate the random variable arguments from the parameters with a semicolon (;). In this section, we just briefly introduce the idea of distributions with one example each of a discrete distribution (the binomial distribution), and a continuous distribution (the normal distribution).

Discrete distributions: The binomial distribution

BINOMIAL
DISTRIBUTION

A *binomial distribution* results when one has a series of trials with only two outcomes (i.e., Bernoulli trials), each trial being independent from all the others. Repeatedly tossing a (possibly unfair) coin is the prototypical example of something with a binomial distribution. Now when looking at linguistic corpora, it is never the case that the next sentence is truly independent of the previous one, so use of a binomial distribution is always an approximation. Nevertheless, for many purposes, the dependency be-

tween words falls off fairly quickly and we can assume independence. In
any situation where one is counting whether something is present or ab-
sent, or has a certain property or not, and one is ignoring the possibility
of dependencies between one trial and the next, one is at least implicitly using a binomial distribution, so this distribution actually crops up
quite commonly in Statistical NLP applications. Examples include: looking through a corpus to find an estimate of the percent of sentences in
English that have the word *the* in them or finding out how commonly
a verb is used transitively by looking through a corpus for instances of a
certain verb and noting whether each use is transitive or not.

The family of binomial distributions gives the number r of successes
out of n trials given that the probability of success in any trial is p:

$$(2.13) \qquad \mathrm{b}(r;\, n, p) = \binom{n}{r} p^r (1 - p)^{n-r} \quad \text{where} \quad \binom{n}{r} = \frac{n!}{(n-r)!r!} \quad 0 \le r \le n$$

The term $\binom{n}{r}$ counts the number of different possibilities for choosing
r objects out of n, not considering the order in which they are chosen.
Examples of some binomial distributions are shown in figure 2.3. The binomial distribution has an expectation of np and a variance of $np(1 - p)$.

Example 6:   Let R have as value the number of heads in n tosses of a
(possibly weighted) coin, where the probability of a head is p.

Then we have the binomial distribution:

$$\mathrm{p}(R = r) = \mathrm{b}(r;\, n, p)$$

(The proof of this is by counting: each basic outcome with r heads and
$n - r$ tails has probability $h^r (1 - h)^{n-r}$, and there are $\binom{n}{r}$ of them.)

▼ The binomial distribution turns up in various places in the book, such
as when counting n-grams in chapter 6, and for hypothesis testing in
section 8.2.

▼ The generalization of a binomial trial to the case where each of the trials has more than two basic outcomes is called a multinomial experiment,
MULTINOMIAL   and is modeled by the *multinomial distribution*. A zeroth order n-gram
DISTRIBUTION   model of the type we discuss in chapter 6 is a straightforward example
of a multinomial distribution.

▼ Another discrete distribution that we discuss and use in this book is the
Poisson distribution (section 15.3.1). Section 5.3 discusses the Bernoulli
distribution, which is simply the special case of the binomial distribution
where there is only one trial. That is, we calculate $\mathrm{b}(r;\, 1, p)$.

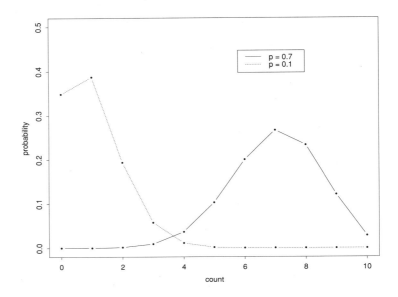

Figure 2.3 Two examples of binomial distributions: b(r; 10, 0.7) and b(r; 10, 0.1).

Continuous distributions: The normal distribution

So far we have looked only at discrete probability distributions and discrete random variables, but many things, such as measurements of heights and lengths, are best understood as having a continuous domain, over the real numbers $\mathbb{R}$. In this book, we do not outline the mathematics of continuous distributions. Suffice it to say that there are generally analogous results, except with points becoming intervals, and sums becoming integrals. However, we will occasionally have need to refer to continuous probability distributions, so we will give one example here: the normal distribution, which is central to all work in probability and statistics.

BELL CURVE

NORMAL
DISTRIBUTION

For many things in the world, such as the heights or IQs of people, one gets a distribution that is known in the media as a *bell curve*, but which is referred to in statistics as a *normal distribution*. Some normal distribution curves are shown in figure 2.4. The values of the graphed functions, probability density functions (pdf), do not directly give the probabilities of the points along the x-axis (indeed, the probability of a point is always 0 for a continuous distribution). Rather the probability

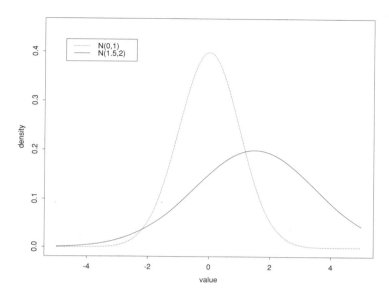

Figure 2.4 Example normal distribution curves: n(x; 0, 1) and n(x; 1.5, 2).

of a result within a certain interval on the x-axis is given by the area delimited by that region, the x-axis and the function curve.

The normal distribution has two parameters for the mean μ, and the standard deviation σ, and the curve is given by:

$$(2.14) \qquad \text{n}(x;\ \mu, \sigma) = \frac{1}{\sqrt{2\pi}\sigma} e^{-(x-\mu)^2/(2\sigma^2)}$$

STANDARD NORMAL DISTRIBUTION

The curve where $\mu = 0$ and $\sigma = 1$ is referred to as the *standard normal distribution*. A few figures for areas under this curve are given in the appendix.

GAUSSIANS

While it is much better to refer to such a curve as a 'normal distribution' than as a 'bell curve,' if you really want to fit into the Statistical NLP or pattern recognition communities, you should instead learn to refer to these functions as *Gaussians*, and to remark things like, 'Maybe we could model that using 3 Gaussians' at appropriate moments.[1]

___

1. Carl Friedrich Gauss was the first to use normal curves to model experimental data, using them to model the errors made by astronomers and surveyors in repeated measurements of the same quantity, but the normal curve was discovered by Abraham de Moivre.

In much of statistics, the discrete binomial distribution is approximated by the continuous normal distribution – one can see the basic similarity in the shapes of the curves by comparing figures 2.3 and 2.4. Such an approximation is acceptable when both basic outcomes have a reasonable probability of occurring or the amount of data is very large (roughly, when $np(1 - p) > 5$). But, in natural language, events like occurrences of the phrase *shade tree mechanics* are so rare, that even if you have a huge amount of text, there will be a significant difference between the appropriate binomial curve and the approximating normal curve, and so use of normal approximations can be unwise.

▼ Gaussians are often used in clustering, as discussed in chapter 14. In particular, here we have only discussed the one-dimensional or univariate normal distribution, while we present there the generalization to many dimensions (the multivariate normal distribution).

▼ Other continuous distributions discussed in this book are the hyperbolic distributions discussed in section 1.4.3, and the *t* distribution used for hypothesis testing in section 5.3.

2.1.10   Bayesian statistics

FREQUENTIST STATISTICS

BAYESIAN STATISTICS

So far, we have presented a brief introduction to orthodox *frequentist statistics*. Not everyone is agreed on the right philosophical foundations for statistics, and the main rival is a *Bayesian* approach to statistics. Actually, the Bayesians even argue among themselves, but we are not going to dwell on the philosophical issues here. We want to just briefly introduce the Bayesian approach because Bayesian methods are very useful in Statistical NLP, and we will come across them in later chapters.

Bayesian updating

MAXIMUM LIKELIHOOD ESTIMATE

PRIOR BELIEF

Suppose one takes a coin and tosses it 10 times, and gets 8 heads. Then from a frequentist point of view, the result is that this coin comes down heads 8 times out of 10. This is what is called the *maximum likelihood estimate*, as discussed further in section 6.2.1. However, if one has looked the coin over, and there doesn't seem anything wrong with it, one would be very reluctant to accept this estimate. Rather, one would tend to think that the coin would come down equally head and tails over the long run, and getting 8 heads out of 10 is just the kind of thing that happens sometimes given a small sample. In other words one has a *prior belief* that influences one's beliefs even in the face of apparent evidence against it. Bayesian statistics measure degrees of belief, and are calculated by starting with prior beliefs and updating them in the face of evidence, by use of Bayes' theorem.

For example, let μ_m be the model[2] that asserts $P(\text{head}) = m$. Let s be a particular sequence of observations yielding i heads and j tails. Then, for any m, $0 \le m \le 1$:

(2.15) $P(s|\mu_m) = m^i (1-m)^j$

From a frequentist point of view, we wish to find the MLE:

$$\arg\max_m P(s|\mu_m)$$

To do this, we can differentiate the above polynomial, and find its maximum, which fortunately gives the intuitive answer of $\frac{i}{i+j}$, or 0.8 for the case of 8 heads and 2 tails.

But now suppose that one wants to quantify one's belief that the coin is probably a regular, fair one. One can do that by assuming a prior probability distribution over how likely it is that different models μ_m are true. Since one would want most of the probability mass close to $\frac{1}{2}$, one might use something like a Gaussian distribution centered on $\frac{1}{2}$, but since polynomials are the only things we can remember how to differentiate, let us instead assume that one's prior belief is modeled by the distribution:

(2.16) $P(\mu_m) = 6m(1-m)$

This polynomial was chosen because its distribution is centered on $\frac{1}{2}$, and, conveniently, the area under the curve between 0 and 1 is 1.

When one sees an observation sequence s one wants to know one's new belief in the fairness of the coin. One can calculate this from (2.15) and (2.16) by Bayes' theorem:

(2.17) $\begin{aligned} P(\mu_m|s) &= \frac{P(s|\mu_m)P(\mu_m)}{P(s)} \\ &= \frac{m^i(1-m)^j \times 6m(1-m)}{P(s)} \end{aligned}$

---

2. By a model we mean whatever theoretical edifices we construct to explain something in the world. A probabilistic model might comprise the specification of a distribution and certain parameter values. Thus, we are introducing some notational sloppiness in equation (2.15), since previously we were conditioning on an event, that is, a subset of the event space, and now we are conditioning on a model, but we will allow ourselves that freedom.

$$= \frac{6m^{i+1}(1-m)^{j+1}}{P(s)}$$

Now $P(s)$ is the prior probability of s. Let us assume for the moment that it does not depend on μ_m, and therefore that we can ignore it while finding the m that maximizes this equation. If we then differentiate the numerator so as find its maximum, we can determine that for the case of 8 heads and 2 tails:

$$\arg\max_m P(\mu_m|s) = \frac{3}{4}$$

Because our prior was weak (the polynomial is a quite flat curve centered over $\frac{1}{2}$), we have moved a long way in the direction of believing that the coin is biased, but the important point is that we haven't moved all the way to 0.8. If we had assumed a stronger prior, we would have moved a smaller distance from $\frac{1}{2}$. (See exercise 2.8.)

But what do we make of the denominator $P(s)$? Well, since we have just seen s, one might conclude that this is 1, but that is not what it means. Rather, it is the *marginal probability* which is obtained by adding up all the $P(s|\mu_m)$ weighted by the probability of μ_m, as we saw earlier in equation (2.8). For the continuous case, we have the integral:

MARGINAL
PROBABILITY

(2.18) $$P(s) = \int_0^1 P(s|\mu_m)P(\mu_m)dm$$

$$= \int_0^1 6m^{i+1}(1-m)^{j+1}dm$$

This just happens to be an instance of the beta integral, another continuous distribution well-studied by statisticians, and so we can look up a book to find out that:

(2.19) $$P(s) = \frac{6(i+1)!(j+1)!}{(i+j+3)!}$$

NORMALIZATION
FACTOR

But the important point is that the denominator is just a *normalization factor*, which ensures that what we calculate for $P(\mu_m|s)$ in (2.17) is actually a probability function.

In the general case where data come in sequentially and we can reasonably assume independence between them, we start off with an a priori probability distribution, and when a new datum comes in, we can update our beliefs by calculating the maximum of the a posteriori distribution, what is sometimes referred to as the MAP probability. This then becomes the new prior, and the process repeats on each new datum. This process is referred to as *Bayesian updating*.

BAYESIAN UPDATING

Bayesian decision theory

But there is another thing that we can do with this new approach: use it to evaluate which model or family of models better explains some data. Suppose that we did not actually see the sequence of coin tosses but just heard the results shouted out over the fence. Now it may be the case, as we have assumed so far, that the results reported truly reflect the results of tossing a single, possibly weighted coin. This is the theory μ, which is a family of models, with a parameter representing the weighting of the coin. But an alternative theory is that at each step someone is tossing two fair coins, and calling out "tails" if *both* of them come down tails, and heads otherwise. Let us call this new theory ν. According to ν, if s is a particular observed sequence of i heads and j tails, then:

$$(2.20) \quad P(s|\nu) = \left(\frac{3}{4}\right)^i \left(\frac{1}{4}\right)^j$$

Note that one of these theories has a free parameter (the weighting of the coin m), while the other has no parameters. Let us assume that, a priori, both of these theories are equally likely, for instance:

$$(2.21) \quad P(\mu) = P(\nu) = \frac{1}{2}$$

We can now attempt to work out which theory is more likely given the data we have seen. We use Bayes' theorem again, and write down:

$$P(\mu|s) = \frac{P(s|\mu)P(\mu)}{P(s)} \qquad P(\nu|s) = \frac{P(s|\nu)P(\nu)}{P(s)}$$

The potentially confusing point here is that we have made a quick change in our notation. The quantity we are now describing as $P(s|\mu)$ is the quantity that we wrote as just $P(s)$ in (2.19) – since at that time we were assuming that theory μ_m was true and we were just trying to determine m, whereas what we are now writing as $P(s)$ is the prior probability of s, not knowing whether μ is true or not. With that gotten straight, LIKELIHOOD RATIO we can calculate the *likelihood ratio* between these two models. The $P(s)$ terms in the denominators cancel, and we can work out the rest using equations (2.19), (2.20), and (2.21):

$$(2.22) \quad \frac{P(\mu|s)}{P(\nu|s)} = \frac{P(s|\mu)P(\mu)}{P(s|\nu)P(\nu)}$$

$$= \frac{\frac{6(i+1)!(j+1)!}{(i+j+3)!}}{\left(\frac{3}{4}\right)^i \left(\frac{1}{4}\right)^j}$$

10 Results Reported			20 Results Reported		
Heads	Tails	Likelihood ratio	Heads	Tails	Likelihood ratio
0	10	4.03×10^4	0	20	1.30×10^{10}
1	9	2444.23	2	18	2.07×10^7
2	8	244.42	4	16	1.34×10^5
3	7	36.21	6	14	2307.06
4	6	7.54	8	12	87.89
5	5	2.16	10	10	6.89
6	4	0.84	12	8	1.09
7	3	0.45	14	6	0.35
8	2	0.36	16	4	0.25
9	1	0.37	18	2	0.48
10	0	0.68	20	0	3.74

Table 2.1 Likelihood ratios between two theories. The left three columns are for a sequence s of 10 pieces of data, and the right three columns for a sequence of 20 pieces of data.

If this ratio is greater than 1, we should prefer μ, and otherwise we should prefer ν (or commonly people take the log of this ratio and see if that value is greater than or less than zero).

We can calculate this ratio for different combinations of heads and tails. Table 2.1 shows likelihood values for sequences of 10 and 20 results. If there are few heads, then the likelihood ratio is greater than one, and the possibly weighted coin theory wins, since it is never strongly incompatible with any data (because of its free parameter). On the other hand, if the distribution is roughly what we'd expect according to the two fair coins theory (a lot more heads than tails) then the likelihood ratio is smaller than one, and the simpler two fair coins theory wins. As the quantity of data available becomes greater, the ratio of heads needs to be nearer $\frac{3}{4}$ in order for the two fair coins model to win. If these are the only two theories under consideration, and we choose the one that wins in such a likelihood ratio, then we have made what is called the *Bayes*

BAYES OPTIMAL
DECISION

optimal decision.

▼ If there are more theories, we can compare them all and decide on the most likely one in the same general manner. An example of this and more general discussion of Bayesian decision theory can be found in our discussion of word sense disambiguation in section 7.2.1.

2.1.11 Exercises

Exercise 2.1 [★]

This exercise indicates the kind of facility with set theory needed for this book, and summarizes a few useful results in probability theory. Use set theory and the axioms defining a probability function to show that:

a. $P(A \cup B) = P(A) + P(B) - P(A \cap B)$ [the addition rule]

b. $P(\varnothing) = 0$

c. $P(\overline{A}) = 1 - P(A)$

d. $A \subseteq B \Rightarrow P(A) \leq P(B)$

e. $P(B - A) = P(B) - P(A \cap B)$

Exercise 2.2 [★]

Assume the following sample space:

(2.23) $\Omega = \{\text{is-noun}, \text{has-plural-s}, \text{is-adjective}, \text{is-verb}\}$

and the function $f : 2^{\Omega} \rightarrow [0, 1]$ with the following values:

x	$f(x)$
{ is-noun }	0.45
{ has-plural-s }	0.2
{ is-adjective }	0.25
{ is-verb }	0.3

Can f be extended to all of 2^{Ω} such that it is a well-formed probability distribution? If not, how would you model these data probabilistically?

Exercise 2.3 [★]

Compute the probability of the event 'A period occurs after a three-letter word and this period indicates an abbreviation (not an end-of-sentence marker),' assuming the following probabilities.

(2.24) $P(\text{is-abbreviation}|\text{three-letter-word}) = 0.8$

(2.25) $P(\text{three-letter-word}) = 0.0003$

Exercise 2.4 [★]

Are X and Y as defined in the following table independently distributed?

x	0	0	1	1
y	0	1	0	1
$p(X = x, Y = y)$	0.32	0.08	0.48	0.12

Exercise 2.5   [★]

In example 5, we worked out the expectation of the sum of two dice in terms of the expectation of rolling one die. Show that one gets the same result if one calculates the expectation for two dice directly.

Exercise 2.6   [★★]

Consider the set of grades you have received for courses taken in the last two years. Convert them to an appropriate numerical scale. What is the appropriate distribution for modeling them?

Exercise 2.7   [★★]

Find a linguistic phenomenon that the binomial distribution is a good model for. What is your best estimate for the parameter p?

Exercise 2.8   [★★]

For $i = 8$ and $j = 2$, confirm that the maximum of equation (2.15) is at 0.8, and that the maximum of equation (2.17) is 0.75. Suppose our prior belief had instead been captured by the equation:

$$P(\mu_m) = 30m^2(1 - m)^2$$

What then would the MAP probability be after seeing a particular sequence of 8 heads and 2 tails? (Assume the theory μ_m and a prior belief that the coin is fair.)

2.2 Essential Information Theory

The field of information theory was developed in the 1940s by Claude Shannon, with the initial exposition reported in (Shannon 1948). Shannon was interested in the problem of maximizing the amount of information that you can transmit over an imperfect communication channel such as a noisy phone line (though actually many of his concerns stemmed from codebreaking in World War II). For any source of 'information' and any 'communication channel,' Shannon wanted to be able to determine theoretical maxima for (i) data compression – which turns out to be given by the Entropy H (or more fundamentally, by the Kolmogorov complexity K), and (ii) the transmission rate – which is given by the Channel Capacity C. Until Shannon, people had assumed that necessarily, if you send your message at a higher speed, then more errors must occur during the transmission. But Shannon showed that providing that you transmit the information in your message at a slower rate than the Channel Capacity, then you can make the probability of errors in the transmission of your message as small as you would like.

2.2.1 Entropy

ALPHABET

Let p(x) be the probability mass function of a random variable X, over a discrete set of symbols (or *alphabet*) X:

$$p(x) = P(X = x), \quad x \in X$$

For example, if we toss two coins and count the number of heads, we have a random variable: p(0) = 1/4, p(1) = 1/2, p(2) = 1/4.

ENTROPY
SELF-INFORMATION

The *entropy* (or *self-information*) is the average uncertainty of a single random variable:

(2.26)   **Entropy** $H(\mathrm{p}) = H(X) = -\sum_{x \in X} \mathrm{p}(x) \log_2 \mathrm{p}(x)$

Entropy measures the amount of information in a random variable. It is normally measured in bits (hence the log to the base 2), but using any other base yields only a linear scaling of results. For the rest of this book, an unadorned log should be read as log to the base 2. Also, for this definition to make sense, we define $0 \log 0 = 0$.

Example 7: Suppose you are reporting the result of rolling an 8-sided die. Then the entropy is:

$$H(X) = -\sum_{i=1}^{8} \mathrm{p}(i) \log \mathrm{p}(i) = -\sum_{i=1}^{8} \frac{1}{8} \log \frac{1}{8} = -\log \frac{1}{8} = \log 8 = 3 \text{ bits}$$

This result is what we would expect. Entropy, the amount of information in a random variable, can be thought of as the average length of the message needed to transmit an outcome of that variable. If we wish to send the result of rolling an eight-sided die, the most efficient way is to simply encode the result as a 3 digit binary message:

1	2	3	4	5	6	7	8
001	010	011	100	101	110	111	000

The transmission cost of each result is 3 bits, and there is no cleverer way of encoding the results with a lower average transmission cost. In general, an optimal code sends a message of probability p(i) in $\lceil -\log \mathrm{p}(i) \rceil$ bits.

The minus sign at the start of the formula for entropy can be moved inside the logarithm, where it becomes a reciprocal:

(2.27) $H(X) = \sum_{x \in X} \mathrm{p}(x) \log \dfrac{1}{\mathrm{p}(x)}$

People without any statistics background often think about a formula like this as a sum of the quantity $p(x) \log(1/p(x))$ for each x. While this is mathematically impeccable, it is the wrong way to think about such equations. Rather you should think of $\sum_{x \in X} p(x) \ldots$ as an idiom. It says to take a weighted average of the rest of the formula (which will be a function of x), where the weighting depends on the probability of each x. Technically, this idiom defines an *expectation*, as we saw earlier. Indeed,

$$(2.28) \quad H(X) = E\left(\log \frac{1}{p(X)}\right)$$

Example 8: Simplified Polynesian Simplified Polynesian[3] appears to be just a random sequence of letters, with the letter frequencies as shown:

p	t	k	a	i	u
1/8	1/4	1/8	1/4	1/8	1/8

Then the per-letter entropy is:

$$
\begin{aligned}
H(P) &= - \sum_{i \in \{p,t,k,a,i,u\}} P(i) \log P(i) \\
&= -[4 \times \frac{1}{8} \log \frac{1}{8} + 2 \times \frac{1}{4} \log \frac{1}{4}] \\
&= 2\frac{1}{2} \text{ bits}
\end{aligned}
$$

This is supported by the fact that we can design a code that on average takes $2\frac{1}{2}$ bits to transmit a letter:

p	t	k	a	i	u
100	00	101	01	110	111

Note that this code has been designed so that fewer bits are used to send more frequent letters, but still so that it can be unambiguously decoded – if a code starts with a 0 then it is of length two, and if it starts with a 1 it is of length 3. There is much work in information theory on the design of such codes, but we will not further discuss them here.

TWENTY QUESTIONS   One can also think of entropy in terms of the *Twenty Questions* game. If you can ask yes/no questions like 'Is it a *t* or an *a*?' or 'Is it a consonant?' then on average you will need to ask $2\frac{1}{2}$ questions to identify each letter with total certainty (assuming that you ask good questions!). In

---

3. Polynesian languages, such as Hawai'ian, are well known for their small alphabets.

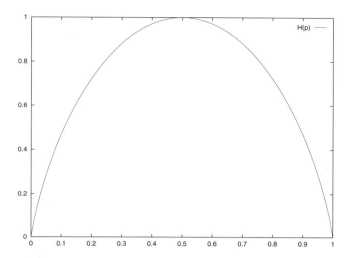

Figure 2.5   The entropy of a weighted coin. The horizontal axis shows the probability of a weighted coin to come up heads. The vertical axis shows the entropy of tossing the corresponding coin once.

other words, entropy can be interpreted as a measure of the size of the 'search space' consisting of the possible values of a random variable and its associated probabilities.

Note that: (i) $H(X) \geq 0$, (ii) $H(X) = 0$ only when the value of X is determinate, hence providing no new information, and that (iii) entropy increases with the message length. The information needed to transmit the results of tossing a possibly weighted coin depends on the probability p that it comes up heads, and on the number of tosses made. The entropy for a single toss is shown in figure 2.5. For multiple tosses, since each is independent, we would just multiply the number in the graph by the number of tosses.

2.2.2   Joint entropy and conditional entropy

The joint entropy of a pair of discrete random variables $X, Y \sim p(x, y)$ is the amount of information needed on average to specify both their values. It is defined as:

$$(2.29) \quad H(X, Y) = -\sum_{x \in X} \sum_{y \in Y} p(x, y) \log p(x, y)$$

The conditional entropy of a discrete random variable Y given another X, for $X, Y \sim p(x, y)$, expresses how much extra information you still need to supply on average to communicate Y given that the other party knows X:

$$(2.30) \quad H(Y|X) = \sum_{x \in X} p(x) H(Y|X = x)$$

$$= \sum_{x \in X} p(x) \left[- \sum_{y \in Y} p(y|x) \log p(y|x) \right]$$

$$= - \sum_{x \in X} \sum_{y \in Y} p(x, y) \log p(y|x)$$

There is also a Chain rule for entropy:

$$(2.31) \quad \begin{aligned} H(X, Y) &= H(X) + H(Y|X) \\ H(X_1, \dots, X_n) &= H(X_1) + H(X_2|X_1) + \dots + H(X_n|X_1, \dots, X_{n-1}) \end{aligned}$$

The products in the chain rules for probabilities here become sums because of the log:

$$\begin{aligned} H(X, Y) &= -E_{p(x,y)} (\log p(x, y)) \\ &= -E_{p(x,y)} (\log(p(x) \, p(y|x))) \\ &= -E_{p(x,y)} (\log p(x) + \log p(y|x)) \\ &= -E_{p(x)} (\log p(x)) - E_{p(x,y)} (\log p(y|x)) \\ &= H(X) + H(Y|X) \end{aligned}$$

Example 9: Simplified Polynesian revisited An important scientific idea is the distinction between a model and reality. Simplified Polynesian isn't a random variable, but we approximated it (or modeled it) as one. But now let's learn a bit more about the language. Further fieldwork has revealed that Simplified Polynesian has syllable structure. Indeed, it turns out that all words consist of sequences of CV (consonant-vowel) syllables. This suggests a better model in terms of two random variables C for the consonant of a syllable, and V for the vowel, whose joint distribution $P(C, V)$ and marginal distributions $P(C, \cdot)$ and $P(\cdot, V)$ are as follows:

(2.32)

	p	t	k	
a	$\frac{1}{16}$	$\frac{3}{8}$	$\frac{1}{16}$	$\frac{1}{2}$
i	$\frac{1}{16}$	$\frac{3}{16}$	0	$\frac{1}{4}$
u	0	$\frac{3}{16}$	$\frac{1}{16}$	$\frac{1}{4}$
	$\frac{1}{8}$	$\frac{3}{4}$	$\frac{1}{8}$	

Note that here the marginal probabilities are on a per-syllable basis, and are therefore double the probabilities of the letters on a per-letter basis, which would be:

(2.33)

p	t	k	a	i	u
1/16	3/8	1/16	1/4	1/8	1/8

We can work out the entropy of the joint distribution, in more than one way. Let us use the chain rule:[4]

$$H(C) = 2 \times \frac{1}{8} \times 3 + \frac{3}{4}(2 - \log 3)$$

$$= \frac{9}{4} - \frac{3}{4}\log 3 \text{ bits} \approx 1.061 \text{ bits}$$

$$H(V|C) = \sum_{c=p,t,k} p(C = c)H(V|C = c)$$

$$= \frac{1}{8}H\left(\frac{1}{2}, \frac{1}{2}, 0\right) + \frac{3}{4}H\left(\frac{1}{2}, \frac{1}{4}, \frac{1}{4}\right) + \frac{1}{8}H\left(\frac{1}{2}, 0, \frac{1}{2}\right)$$

$$= 2 \times \frac{1}{8} \times 1 + \frac{3}{4}\left[\frac{1}{2} \times 1 + 2 \times \frac{1}{4} \times 2\right]$$

$$= \frac{1}{4} + \frac{3}{4} \times \frac{3}{2}$$

$$= \frac{11}{8} \text{ bits} = 1.375 \text{ bits}$$

$$H(C, V) = H(C) + H(V|C)$$

$$= \frac{9}{4} - \frac{3}{4}\log 3 + \frac{11}{8}$$

$$= \frac{29}{8} - \frac{3}{4}\log 3 \approx 2.44 \text{ bits}$$

---

4. Within the calculation, we use an informal, but convenient, notation of expressing a finite-valued distribution as a sequence of probabilities, which we can calculate the entropy of.

Note that those 2.44 bits are now the entropy for a whole syllable (which was $2 \times 2\frac{1}{2} = 5$ for the original Simplified Polynesian example). Our better understanding of the language means that we are now much less uncertain, and hence less surprised by what we see on average than before.

Because the amount of information contained in a message depends on the length of the message, we normally want to talk in terms of the per-letter or per-word entropy. For a message of length n, the per-letter/word entropy, also known as the *entropy rate*, is:[5]

ENTROPY RATE

(2.34) $$H_{\text{rate}} = \frac{1}{n}H(X_{1n}) = -\frac{1}{n}\sum_{x_{1n}}p(x_{1n})\log p(x_{1n})$$

If we then assume that a language is a stochastic process consisting of a sequence of tokens $L = (X_i)$, for example a transcription of every word you utter in your life, or a corpus comprising everything that is sent down the newswire to your local paper, then we can define the entropy of a human language L as the entropy rate for that stochastic process:

(2.35) $$H_{\text{rate}}(L) = \lim_{n \to \infty}\frac{1}{n}H(X_1, X_2, \ldots, X_n)$$

We take the entropy rate of a language to be the limit of the entropy rate of a sample of the language as the sample gets longer and longer.

2.2.3 Mutual information

By the chain rule for entropy,

$$H(X, Y) = H(X) + H(Y|X) = H(Y) + H(X|Y)$$

Therefore,

$$H(X) - H(X|Y) = H(Y) - H(Y|X)$$

MUTUAL
INFORMATION

This difference is called the *mutual information* between X and Y. It is the reduction in uncertainty of one random variable due to knowing about another, or in other words, the amount of information one random variable contains about another. A diagram illustrating the definition of mutual information and its relationship to entropy is shown in figure 2.6 (adapted from Cover and Thomas (1991: 20)).

---

5. Commonly throughout this book we use two subscripts on something to indicate a subsequence. So, here, we use X_{ij} to represent the sequence of random variables $(X_i, \ldots, X_j)$ and similarly $x_{ij} = (x_i, \ldots, x_j)$. This notation is slightly unusual, but very convenient when sequences are a major part of the domain of discourse. So the reader should remember this convention and be on the lookout for it.

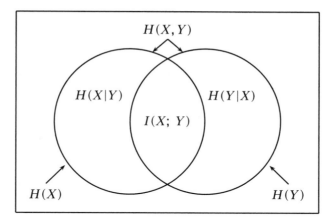

Figure 2.6   The relationship between mutual information I and entropy H.

Mutual information is a symmetric, non-negative measure of the common information in the two variables. People thus often think of mutual information as a measure of dependence between variables. However, it is actually better to think of it as a measure of independence because:

■ It is 0 only when two variables are independent, *but*

■ For two dependent variables, mutual information grows not only with the degree of dependence, but also according to the entropy of the variables.

Simple arithmetic gives us the following formulas for mutual information $I(X;\ Y)$:[6]

$$
\begin{aligned}
(2.36)\quad I(X;\ Y) \ &=\ H(X) - H(X|Y) \\
&=\ H(X) + H(Y) - H(X,Y) \\
&=\ \sum_x \mathrm{p}(x)\log\frac{1}{\mathrm{p}(x)} + \sum_y \mathrm{p}(y)\log\frac{1}{\mathrm{p}(y)} + \sum_{x,y}\mathrm{p}(x,y)\log\mathrm{p}(x,y) \\
&=\ \sum_{x,y}\mathrm{p}(x,y)\log\frac{\mathrm{p}(x,y)}{\mathrm{p}(x)\,\mathrm{p}(y)}
\end{aligned}
$$

Since $H(X|X) = 0$, note that:

$$H(X) = H(X) - H(X|X) = I(X;\ X)$$

---

6. Mutual information is conventionally written with a semi-colon separating the two arguments. We are unsure why.

This illustrates both why entropy is also called self-information, and how the mutual information between two totally dependent variables is not constant but depends on their entropy.

We can also derive conditional mutual information and a chain rule:

$$(2.37) \quad I(X; Y|Z) = I((X; Y)|Z) = H(X|Z) - H(X|Y, Z)$$

$$(2.38) \quad I(X_{1n}; Y) = I(X_1; Y) + \ldots + I(X_n; Y|X_1, \ldots, X_{n-1})$$
$$= \sum_{i=1}^{n} I(X_i; Y|X_1, \ldots, X_{i-1})$$

POINTWISE MUTUAL
INFORMATION

In this section we have defined the mutual information between two random variables. Sometimes people talk about the *pointwise mutual information* between two particular points in those distributions:

$$I(x, y) = \log \frac{p(x, y)}{p(x)\, p(y)}$$

This has sometimes been used as a measure of association between elements, but there are problems with using this measure, as we will discuss in section 5.4.

▼ Mutual information has been used many times in Statistical NLP, such as for clustering words (section 14.1.3). It also turns up in word sense disambiguation (section 7.2.2).

2.2.4 The noisy channel model

COMPRESSION

REDUNDANCY

Using information theory, Shannon modeled the goal of communicating down a telephone line – or in general across any channel – in the following way: The aim is to optimize in terms of throughput and accuracy the communication of messages in the presence of noise in the channel. It is assumed that the output of the channel depends probabilistically on the input. In general, there is a duality between *compression*, which is achieved by removing all redundancy, and transmission accuracy, which is achieved by adding controlled *redundancy* so that the input can be recovered even in the presence of noise. The goal is to encode the message in such a way that it occupies minimal space while still containing enough redundancy to be able to detect and correct errors. On receipt, the message is then decoded to give what was most likely the original message. This process is shown in figure 2.7.

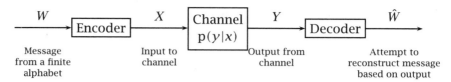

Figure 2.7 The noisy channel model.

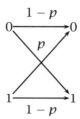

Figure 2.8 A binary symmetric channel. A 1 or a 0 in the input gets flipped on transmission with probability p.

CAPACITY

The central concept that characterizes a channel in information theory is its *capacity*. The channel capacity describes the rate at which one can transmit information through the channel with an arbitrarily low probability of being unable to recover the input from the output. For a memoryless channel, Shannon's second theorem states that the channel capacity can be determined in terms of mutual information as follows:

(2.39)
$$C = \max_{\mathrm{p}(X)} I(X; Y)$$

According to this definition, we reach a channel's capacity if we manage to design an input code X whose distribution maximizes the mutual information between the input and the output over all possible input distributions $\mathrm{p}(X)$.

As an example, consider the binary symmetric channel in figure 2.8. Each input symbol is either a 1 or a 0, and noise in the channel causes each symbol to be flipped in the output with probability p. We find that:

$$
\begin{aligned}
I(X; Y) &= H(Y) - H(Y|X) \\
&= H(Y) - H(\mathrm{p})
\end{aligned}
$$

Therefore,

$$\max_{\mathrm{p}(X)} I(X; Y) = 1 - H(\mathrm{p})$$

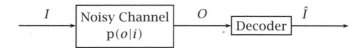

Figure 2.9   The noisy channel model in linguistics.

This last line follows because the mutual information is maximized by maximizing the entropy in the codes, which is done by making the input and hence the output distribution uniform, so their entropy is 1 bit. Since entropy is non-negative, $C \leq 1$. The channel capacity is 1 bit only if the entropy is zero, that is if $p = 0$ and the channel reliably transmits a 0 as 0 and a 1 as 1, or if $p = 1$ and it always flips bits. A completely noisy binary channel which transmits both 0s and 1s with equal probability as 0s and 1s (i.e., $p = \frac{1}{2}$) has capacity $C = 0$, since in this case there is no mutual information between X and Y. Such a channel is useless for communication.

It was one of the early triumphs of information theory that Shannon was able to show two important properties of channels. First, channel capacity is a well-defined notion. In other words, for each channel there is a smallest upper bound of $I(X; Y)$ over possible distributions $p(X)$. Second, in many practical applications it is easy to get close to the optimal channel capacity. We can design a code appropriate for the channel that will transmit information at a rate that is optimal or very close to optimal. The concept of capacity eliminates a good part of the guesswork that was involved in designing communications systems before Shannon. One can precisely evaluate how good a code is for a communication line and design systems with optimal or near-optimal performance.

The noisy channel model is important in Statistical NLP because a simplified version of it was at the heart of the renaissance of quantitative natural language processing in the 1970s. In the first large quantitative project after the early quantitative NLP work in the 1950s and 60s, researchers at IBM's T. J. Watson research center cast both speech recognition and machine translation as a noisy channel problem.

Doing linguistics via the noisy channel model, we do not get to control the encoding phase. We simply want to decode the output to give the most likely input, and so we work with the channel shown in figure 2.9. Many problems in NLP can be construed as an attempt to determine the most likely input given a certain output. We can determine

Application	Input	Output	p(i)	p($o\|i$)
Machine Translation	L_1 word sequences	L_2 word sequences	p(L_1) in a language model	translation model
Optical Character Recognition (OCR)	actual text	text with mistakes	prob of language text	model of OCR errors
Part Of Speech (POS) tagging	POS tag sequences	English words	prob of POS sequences	p($w\|t$)
Speech recognition	word sequences	speech signal	prob of word sequences	acoustic model

Table 2.2 Statistical NLP problems as decoding problems.

this as follows, by using Bayes' theorem, and then noting that the output probability is a constant:

$$(2.40) \qquad \hat{I} = \arg\max_i \mathrm{p}(i|o) = \arg\max_i \frac{\mathrm{p}(i)\,\mathrm{p}(o|i)}{\mathrm{p}(o)} = \arg\max_i \mathrm{p}(i)\,\mathrm{p}(o|i)$$

LANGUAGE MODEL

CHANNEL PROBABILITY

Here we have two probability distributions to consider: p(i) is the *language model*, the distribution of sequences of 'words' in the input language, and p($o|i$) is the *channel probability*.

As an example, suppose we want to translate a text from English to French. The noisy channel model for translation assumes that the true text is in French, but that, unfortunately, when it was transmitted to us, it went through a noisy communication channel and came out as English. So the word *cow* we see in the text was really *vache*, garbled by the noisy channel to *cow*. All we need to do in order to translate is to recover the

DECODE

original French – or to *decode* the English to get the French.[7]

The validity of the noisy channel model for translation is still giving rise to many a heated debate among NLP researchers, but there is no doubt that it is an elegant mathematical framework that has inspired a significant amount of important research. We will discuss the model in more detail in chapter 13. Other problems in Statistical NLP can also be seen as instantiations of the decoding problem. A selection is shown in table 2.2.

---

7. The French reader may be sympathetic with the view that English is really a form of garbled French that makes the language of *clarté* unnecessarily ambiguous!

2.2.5 Relative entropy or Kullback-Leibler divergence

RELATIVE ENTROPY

For two probability mass functions, p(x), q(x) their *relative entropy* is given by:

(2.41) $$D(p \parallel q) = \sum_{x \in X} p(x) \log \frac{p(x)}{q(x)}$$

where again we define $0 \log \frac{0}{q} = 0$ and otherwise $p \log \frac{p}{0} = \infty$. The relative entropy, also known as the *Kullback-Leibler divergence*, is a measure of how different two probability distributions (over the same event space) are. Expressed as an expectation, we have:

KULLBACK-LEIBLER
DIVERGENCE

(2.42) $$D(p \parallel q) = E_p \left(\log \frac{p(X)}{q(X)} \right)$$

Thus, the KL divergence between p and q is the average number of bits that are wasted by encoding events from a distribution p with a code based on a not-quite-right distribution q.

This quantity is always non-negative, and $D(p \parallel q) = 0$ iff p = q. For these reasons, some authors use the name 'KL distance,' but note that relative entropy is not a metric (in the sense in which the term is used in mathematics): it is not symmetric in p and q (see exercise 2.12), and it does not satisfy the *triangle inequality*.[8] Hence we will use the name 'KL divergence,' but nevertheless, informally, people often think about the relative entropy as the 'distance' between two probability distributions: it gives us a measure of how close two pmfs are.

TRIANGLE INEQUALITY

Mutual information is actually just a measure of how far a joint distribution is from independence:

(2.43) $$I(X; Y) = D(p(x, y) \parallel p(x) p(y))$$

We can also derive conditional relative entropy and a chain rule for relative entropy (Cover and Thomas 1991: 23):

(2.44) $$D(p(y|x) \parallel q(y|x)) = \sum_x p(x) \sum_y p(y|x) \log \frac{p(y|x)}{q(y|x)}$$

(2.45) $$D(p(x, y) \parallel q(x, y)) = D(p(x) \parallel q(x)) + D(p(y|x) \parallel q(y|x))$$

---

8. The triangle inequality is that for any three points x, y, z:

$$d(x, y) \leq d(x, z) + d(z, y)$$

▼ KL divergence is used for measuring selectional preferences in section 8.4.

2.2.6   The relation to language: Cross entropy

So far we have examined the notion of entropy, and seen roughly how it is a guide to determining efficient codes for sending messages, but how does this relate to understanding language? The secret to this is to return to the idea that entropy is a measure of our uncertainty. The more we know about something, the lower the entropy will be because we are less surprised by the outcome of a trial.

We can illustrate this with the examples used above. Consider again Simplified Polynesian from examples 8 and 9. This language has 6 letters. The simplest code is to use 3 bits for each letter of the language. This is equivalent to assuming that a good model of the language (where our 'model' is simply a probability distribution) is a uniform model. However, we noticed that not all the letters occurred equally often, and, noting these frequencies, produced a zeroth order model of the language. This had a lower entropy of 2.5 bits per letter (and we showed how this observation could be used to produce a more efficient code for transmitting the language). Thereafter, we noticed the syllable structure of the language, and developed an even better model that incorporated that syllable structure into it. The resulting model had an even lower entropy of 1.22 bits per letter. The essential point here is that if a model captures more of the structure of a language, then the entropy of the model should be lower. In other words, we can use entropy as a measure of the quality of our models.

Alternately, we can think of entropy as a matter of how surprised we will be. Suppose that we are trying to predict the next word in a Simplified Polynesian text. That is, we are examining $P(w|h)$, where w is the next word and h is the history of words seen so far. A measure of our *surprise* on seeing the next word can be derived in terms of the conditional probability assigned to w by our model m of the distribution of Simplified Polynesian words. Surprise can be measured by what we might term the *pointwise entropy* $H(w|h) = -\log_2 m(w|h)$. If the predictor is certain that word w follows a given history h and it is correct, then the information supplied to the predictor on seeing w is $-\log_2 1 = 0$. In other words, the predictor does not experience any surprise at all. On the other hand, if the model thinks that w cannot follow h, then $m(w|h) = 0$ and

SURPRISE

POINTWISE ENTROPY

so the information supplied to the predictor is infinite ($-\log_2 0 = \infty$). In this case our model is infinitely surprised, which is normally a very bad thing. Usually our models will predict a probability between these two extremes for each event and so the model will gain some information, or alternatively, be somewhat surprised, when it sees the next word, and the goal is to keep that level of surprise as low as possible. Summing over the surprise of the predictor at each word gives an expression for our total surprise:

$$
\begin{aligned}
H_{\text{total}} &= -\sum_{j=1}^{n} \log_2 m(w_j | w_1, w_2, \ldots, w_{j-1}) \\
&= -\log_2 m(w_1, w_2, \ldots, w_n)
\end{aligned}
$$

The second line above follows from the chain rule. Normally, we would want to normalize this measure by the length of the text so our notion of surprise is not dependent on the size of the text. This normalized measure gives the average surprise of the predictor per word.

So far this discussion has been rather informal, but we can formalize it through the notion of relative entropy. Suppose that we have some empirical phenomenon, in Statistical NLP usually utterances in a certain language. Assuming some mapping to numbers, we can represent it via a random variable X. Then we assume that there is some probability distribution over the utterances – for instance, you hear *Thank you* much more often than *On you*. So we take $X \sim p(x)$.

Now, unfortunately we do not know what $p(\cdot)$ is for empirical phenomena. But by looking at instances, for example by looking at a corpus of utterances, we can estimate roughly what p seems to be like. In other words, we can produce a model m of the real distribution, based on our best estimates. In making this model, what we want to do is to minimize $D(p \| m)$ – to have as accurate a probabilistic model as possible. Unfortunately, we normally cannot calculate this relative entropy – again, because we do not know what p is. However, there is a related quantity, the cross entropy, which we fortunately can get a handle on.

CROSS ENTROPY   The *cross entropy* between a random variable X with true probability distribution $p(x)$ and another pmf q (normally a model of p) is given by:

$$
\begin{aligned}
(2.46) \qquad H(X, q) &= H(X) + D(p \| q) \\
&= -\sum_{x} p(x) \log q(x)
\end{aligned}
$$

(2.47) $$= E_p\left(\log \frac{1}{q(x)}\right)$$

(Proof of this is left to the reader as exercise 2.13.)

Just as we defined the entropy of a language in section 2.2.2, we can define the cross entropy of a language $L = (X_i) \sim p(x)$ according to a model m by:

(2.48) $$H(L, m) = -\lim_{n \to \infty} \frac{1}{n} \sum_{x_{1n}} p(x_{1n}) \log m(x_{1n})$$

We do not seem to be making much progress, because it still seems that we cannot calculate this quantity without knowing p. But if we make certain assumptions that the language is 'nice,' then the cross entropy for the language can be calculated as:

(2.49) $$H(L, m) = -\lim_{n \to \infty} \frac{1}{n} \log m(x_{1n})$$

Using this second form, we can calculate the cross entropy based only on knowing our probability model and having a large body of utterances available. That is, we do not actually attempt to calculate the limit, but approximate it by calculating for a sufficiently large n:

(2.50) $$H(L, m) \approx -\frac{1}{n} \log m(x_{1n})$$

This measure is just the figure for our average surprise. Our goal will be to try to minimize this number. Because $H(X)$ is fixed (if unknown), this is equivalent to minimizing the relative entropy, which is a measure of how much our probability distribution departs from actual language use. The only additional requirement is that the text that we use to test the model must be an independent test set, and not part of the training corpus that we used to estimate the parameters of the model. Cross entropy is inversely related to the average probability a model assigns to words in test data. Lower model cross entropy normally leads to better performance in applications, but it need not do so if it is just a matter of improving the magnitude of probability estimates, but not their relative ordering. (See section 6.2.3 for more practical details on calculating the cross entropy of models.)

But what justifies going from equation (2.48) to equation (2.49)? The formula for language cross entropy has an expectation embedded within it:

(2.51) $$H(L, m) = \lim_{n \to \infty} \frac{1}{n} E\left(\log \frac{1}{m(X_{1n})}\right)$$

Recall that the expectation is a weighted average over all possible sequences. But in the above formula we are using a limit and looking at longer and longer sequences of language use. Intuitively, the idea is then that if we have seen a huge amount of the language, what we have seen is 'typical.' We no longer need to average over all samples of the language; the value for the entropy rate given by this particular sample will be roughly right.

The formal version of this is to say that if we assume that $L = (X_i)$ is a stationary ergodic process, then we can prove the above result. This is a consequence of the Shannon-McMillan-Breiman theorem, also known as the Asymptotic Equipartition Property:

Theorem: If H_{rate} is the entropy rate of a finite-valued stationary ergodic process (X_n), then:

$$-\frac{1}{n} \log \mathrm{p}(X_1, \dots, X_n) \to H, \quad \text{with probability 1}$$

We will not prove this theorem; see Cover and Thomas (1991: ch. 3, 15). An *ergodic* process is one that, roughly, cannot get into different substates that it will not escape from. An example of a non-ergodic process is one that in the beginning chooses one of two states: one in which it generates 0 forever, one in which it generates 1 forever. If a process is not ergodic, then even looking at one very long sequence will not necessarily tell us what its typical behavior is (for example, what is likely to happen when it gets restarted).

A *stationary* process is one that does not change over time. This is clearly wrong for language: new expressions regularly enter the language while others die out. And so, it is not exactly correct to use this result to allow the calculation of a value for cross entropy for language applications. Nevertheless, for a snapshot of text from a certain period (such as one year's newswire), we can assume that the language is near enough to unchanging, and so this is an acceptable approximation to truth. At any rate, this is the method regularly used.

ERGODIC

STATIONARY

2.2.7 The entropy of English

As noted above, English in general is not a stationary ergodic process. But we can nevertheless model it with various stochastic approximations. In particular, we can model English with what are known as *n-gram models*

n-GRAM MODELS

MARKOV CHAINS

MARKOV ASSUMPTION

or *Markov chains*. These models, which we discuss in detail in chapters 6 and 9, are ones where we assume a limited memory. We assume that the probability of the next word depends only on the previous k words in the input. This gives a kth order *Markov approximation*:

$$P(X_n = x_n | X_{n-1} = x_{n-1}, \ldots, X_1 = x_1) =$$
$$P(X_n = x_n | X_{n-1} = x_{n-1}, \ldots, X_{n-k} = x_{n-k})$$

If we are working on a character basis, for example, we are trying to guess what the next character in a text will be given the preceding k characters. Because of the redundancy of English, this is normally fairly easy. For instance, a generation of students have proved this by being able to make do with photocopies of articles that are missing the last character or two of every line.

By adding up counts of letters, letter digraphs (that is, sequences of two letters), and so on in English, one can produce upper bounds for the entropy of English.[9] We assume some such simplified model of English and compute its cross entropy against a text and this gives us an upper bound for the true entropy of English – since $D(p \parallel m) \geq 0$, $H(X, m) \geq H(X)$. Shannon did this, assuming that English consisted of just 27 symbols (the 26 letters of the alphabet and SPACE – he ignored case distinctions and punctuation). The estimates he derived were:

(2.52)

Model	Cross entropy (bits)	
zeroth order	4.76	(uniform model, so $\log 27$)
first order	4.03	
second order	2.8	
Shannon's experiment	1.3 (1.34)	(Cover and Thomas 1991: 140)

The first three lines show that as the order of the model increases, that is, as information about the frequencies of letters (first order) and digraphs (second order) is used, our model of English improves and the calculated cross entropy drops. Shannon wanted a tighter upper bound on the entropy of English, and derived one by human experiments – finding out how good at guessing the next letter in a text a human being was. This gave a much lower entropy bound for English. (A later experiment with

---

9. More strictly, one produces an estimate for the text on which the counts are based, and these counts are good for 'English' only to the extent that the text used is representative of English as a whole. Working at the character level, this is not too severe a problem, but it becomes quite important when working at the word level, as discussed in chapter 4.

more subjects on the same text that Shannon used produced the figure in parentheses, 1.34.)

Of course, the real entropy of English must be lower still: there are doubtless patterns in people's speech that humans do not pick up on (although maybe not that many!). But at present, the statistical language models that we can construct are much worse than human beings, and so the current goal is to produce models that are as good as English speakers at knowing which English utterances sound normal or common and which sound abnormal or marked.

▼ We return to *n*-gram models in chapter 6.

2.2.8   Perplexity

PERPLEXITY   In the speech recognition community, people tend to refer to *perplexity* rather than cross entropy. The relationship between the two is simple:

$$(2.53) \qquad \text{perplexity}(x_{1n}, \text{m}) \quad = \quad 2^{H(x_{1n}, \text{m})}$$

$$(2.54) \qquad\qquad\qquad\qquad\qquad = \quad \text{m}(x_{1n})^{-\frac{1}{n}}$$

We suspect that speech recognition people prefer to report the larger non-logarithmic numbers given by perplexity mainly because it is much easier to impress funding bodies by saying that "we've managed to reduce perplexity from 950 to only 540" than by saying that "we've reduced cross entropy from 9.9 to 9.1 bits." However, perplexity does also have an intuitive reading: a perplexity of k means that you are as surprised on average as you would have been if you had had to guess between k equiprobable choices at each step.

2.2.9   Exercises

Exercise 2.9   [★]

Take a (short) piece of text and compute the relative frequencies of the letters in the text. Assume these are the true probabilities. What is the entropy of this distribution?

Exercise 2.10   [★]

Take another piece of text and compute a second probability distribution over letters by the same method. What is the KL divergence between the two distributions? (You will need to 'smooth' the second distribution and replace any zero with a small quantity ϵ.)

Exercise 2.11 [⋆]

Cast the problem of word sense disambiguation as a noisy channel model, in analogy to the examples in table 2.2. Word sense disambiguation is the problem of determining which sense of an ambiguous word is used (e.g., 'industrial plant' vs. 'living plant' for *plant*) and will be covered in chapter 7.

Exercise 2.12 [⋆]

Show that the KL divergence is not symmetric by finding an example of two distributions p and q for which $D(p \parallel q) \neq D(q \parallel p)$.

Exercise 2.13 [⋆]

Prove the equality shown in the first two lines of (2.46).

Exercise 2.14 [⋆]

We arrived at the simplified way of computing cross entropy in equation (2.49) under the premise that the process we are dealing with is ergodic and stationary. List some characteristics of natural languages that show that these two properties are only approximately true of English.

Exercise 2.15 [⋆ ⋆]

Reproduce Shannon's experiment. Write a program that shows you a text one letter at a time. Run it on a text you have not seen. Can you confirm Shannon's estimate of the entropy of English?

Exercise 2.16 [⋆ ⋆]

Repeat the last exercise for one text that is 'easy' (e.g., a newsgroup posting) and one text that is 'hard' (e.g., a scientific article from a field you don't know well). Do you get different estimates? If the estimates are different, what difficulties does the experiment raise for interpreting the different estimates of the entropy of English?

2.3 Further Reading

Aho et al. (1986: ch. 4) cover parsing in computer science, and Allen (1995: ch. 3) covers parsing in computational linguistics. Most of the mathematics we use is covered in Part I of (Cormen et al. 1990), but not vector spaces and matrices, for which one should consult an introduction to linear algebra such as (Strang 1988).

Many books give good introductions to basic probability theory. A few good ones, listed in approximate order of increasing difficulty are (Moore and McCabe 1989; Freedman et al. 1998; Siegel and Castellan 1988; De-Groot 1975). Krenn and Samuelsson (1997) is particularly recommended as a much more thorough introduction to statistics aimed at a Statistical

NLP audience. Unfortunately most introduction to statistics textbooks follow a very fixed syllabus which is dominated by hypothesis testing as applied in experimental sciences such as biology and psychology. Often these concerns are rather distant from the issues of most relevance to Statistical NLP, and it can be helpful to also look at books covering quantitative methods for machine learning, such as (Mitchell 1997).

The coverage of information theory here barely scratches the surface of that field. Cover and Thomas (1991) provide a thorough introduction.

Brown et al. (1992b) present an estimate of 1.75 bits per character for the entropy of English based on predicting the next word, trained on an enormous corpus of English text.

3 *Linguistic Essentials*

THIS CHAPTER introduces basic linguistic concepts, which are necessary for making sense of discussions in the rest of the book. It may partly be a review of things you learned at school, but it will go into more depth for syntactic phenomena like attachment ambiguities and phrase structure that are important in NLP. Apart from syntax (sentence structure), we will cover some morphology (word formation) and semantics (meaning). The last section will give an overview of other areas of linguistics and pointers to further reading.

3.1 Parts of Speech and Morphology

SYNTACTIC
CATEGORIES
GRAMMATICAL
CATEGORIES
PARTS OF SPEECH
NOUN
VERB
ADJECTIVE
SUBSTITUTION TEST

Linguists group the words of a language into classes (sets) which show similar syntactic behavior, and often a typical semantic type. These word classes are otherwise called *syntactic* or *grammatical categories*, but more commonly still by the traditional name *parts of speech* (POS). Three important parts of speech are *noun*, *verb*, and *adjective*. *Nouns* typically refer to people, animals, concepts and things. The prototypical *verb* is used to express the action in a sentence. *Adjectives* describe properties of nouns. The most basic test for words belonging to the same class is the *substitution test*. Adjectives can be picked out as words that occur in the frame in (3.1):

$$(3.1) \quad \text{The} \left\{ \begin{array}{l} \text{sad} \\ \text{intelligent} \\ \text{green} \\ \text{fat} \\ \dots \end{array} \right\} \text{one is in the corner.}$$

In sentence (3.2), the noun *children* refers to a group of people (those of young age) and the noun *candy* to a particular type of food:

(3.2)   Children eat sweet candy.

The verb *eat* describes what children do with candy. The adjective *sweet* tells us about a property of candy, namely that it is sweet. Many words have multiple parts of speech: *candy* can also be a verb (as in *Too much boiling will candy the molasses*), and, at least in British English, *sweet* can be a noun, meaning roughly the same as *candy*. Word classes are normally divided into two. The *open* or *lexical categories* are ones like nouns, verbs and adjectives which have a large number of members, and to which new words are commonly added. The *closed* or *functional categories* are categories such as prepositions and determiners (containing words like *of, on, the, a*) which have only a few members, and the members of which normally have a clear grammatical use. Normally, the various parts of speech for a word are listed in an online *dictionary*, otherwise known as a *lexicon*.

OPEN WORD CLASS
LEXICAL CATEGORIES

CLOSED WORD CLASS
FUNCTIONAL
CATEGORIES

DICTIONARY
LEXICON

Traditional systems of parts of speech distinguish about 8 categories, but corpus linguists normally want to use more fine-grained classifications of word classes. There are well-established sets of abbreviations for naming these classes, usually referred to as POS *tags*. In this chapter, as we introduce syntactic categories, we will give the abbreviations used in the Brown corpus for the more important categories. For example, adjectives are tagged using the code JJ in the Brown corpus. Because of its pioneering role, the Brown corpus tags are particularly widely known.
▼ We briefly describe and compare several well-known tag sets in section 4.3.2.

TAGS

MORPHOLOGICAL
PROCESSES
PLURAL
SINGULAR

Word categories are systematically related by *morphological processes* such as the formation of the *plural* form (*dog-s*) from the *singular* form of the noun (*dog*). Morphology is important in NLP because language is productive: in any given text we will encounter words and word forms that we haven't seen before and that are not in our precompiled dictionary. Many of these new words are morphologically related to known words. So if we understand morphological processes, we can infer a lot about the syntactic and semantic properties of new words.

It is important to be able to handle morphology in English, but it's absolutely essential when it comes to highly inflecting languages like Finnish. In English, a regular verb has only 4 distinct forms, and irregular verbs have at most 8 forms. One can accomplish a fair amount without morphology, by just listing all word forms. In contrast, a Finnish verb has more than 10,000 forms! For a language like Finnish, it would be tedious and impractical to enumerate all verb forms as an enormous list.

INFLECTION
ROOT FORM
PREFIXES
SUFFIXES

The major types of morphological process are inflection, derivation, and compounding. *Inflections* are the systematic modifications of a *root form* by means of *prefixes* and *suffixes* to indicate grammatical distinctions like singular and plural. Inflection does not change word class or meaning significantly, but varies features such as tense, number, and plurality. All the inflectional forms of a word are often grouped as mani-

LEXEME

festations of a single *lexeme*.

DERIVATION

Derivation is less systematic. It usually results in a more radical change of syntactic category, and it often involves a change in meaning. An example is the derivation of the adverb *widely* from the adjective *wide* (by appending the suffix *-ly*). *Widely* in a phrase like *it is widely believed* means *among a large well-dispersed group of people*, a shift from the core meaning of *wide* (*extending over a vast area*). Adverb formation is also less systematic than plural inflection. Some adjectives like *old* or *difficult* don't have adverbs: **oldly* and **difficultly* are not words of English. Here are some other examples of derivations: the suffix *-en* transforms adjectives into verbs (*weak-en, soft-en*), the suffix *-able* transforms verbs into adjectives (*understand-able, accept-able*), and the suffix *-er* transforms verbs into nouns (*teach-er, lead-er*).

COMPOUNDING

Compounding refers to the merging of two or more words into a new word. English has many noun-noun compounds, nouns that are combinations of two other nouns. Examples are *tea kettle, disk drive*, or *college degree*. While these are (usually) written as separate words, they are pronounced as a single word, and denote a single semantic concept, which one would normally wish to list in the lexicon. There are also other compounds that involve parts of speech such as adjectives, verbs, and prepositions, such as *downmarket, (to) overtake*, and *mad cow disease*.

We will now introduce the major parts of speech of English.

3.1.1 Nouns and pronouns

Nouns typically refer to entities in the world like people, animals, and things. Examples are:

(3.3)   dog, tree, person, hat, speech, idea, philosophy

Type of inflection	Instances
number	singular, plural
gender	feminine, masculine, neuter
case	nominative, genitive, dative, accusative

Table 3.1 Common inflections of nouns.

English, which is morphologically impoverished compared to many other languages, has only one inflection of the noun, the plural form. It is usually formed by appending the suffix -*s*. Here are some nouns with their singular and plural forms.

(3.4)   dog : dogs   tree : trees   person : persons
         hat : hats   speech : speeches   woman : women
         idea : ideas philosophy : philosophies   child : children

The plural suffix has three pronunciations, /s/ as in *hats*, /z/, as in *boys*, and /əs/ as in *speeches*, the last case being represented by insertion of an *e* in the writing system. A few forms like *women* don't follow the regular pattern, and are termed *irregular*.

IRREGULAR

Number (singular and plural) is one common grammatical distinction that is marked on the noun. Two other types of inflection that are common for nouns across languages are gender and case as shown in table 3.1.

English does not have a system of gender inflections, but it does have different gender forms for the third person singular pronoun: *he* (masculine), *she* (feminine), and *it* (neuter). An example of gender inflection of nouns from Latin is the endings -*a* for feminine and -*us* for masculine. Examples: *fili-us* 'son, male child'; *fili-a* 'daughter, female child.' In some languages, grammatical gender is closely correlated with the sex of the person referred to as it is for these two Latin words (female → feminine, male → masculine, neither → neuter), but in other languages gender is a largely arbitrary grammatical category. An example linguists are fond of is the German word for girl, *Mädchen*, which is neuter.

In some languages, nouns appear in different forms when they have different functions (subject, object, etc.) in a sentence, and these forms

CASE

are called *cases*. For example, the Latin for 'son' is *filius* when the subject, but *filium* when the object of a verb. Many languages have a rich array of case inflections, with cases for locatives, instrumentals, etc. English has no real case inflections. The only case relationship that is systematically indicated is the genitive. The genitive describes the possessor. For example, the phrase *the woman's house* indicates that the woman owns the house. The genitive is usually written *'s*, but just as *'* after words that end in *s*, which includes most plural nouns such as in *the students' grievances*. Although *'s* initially looks like a case inflection, it is actually what is termed a *clitic*, also known as a *phrasal affix*, because it can appear not only attached to nouns, but after other words that modify a noun, as in *the person you met's house was broken into.*

CLITIC

PRONOUN   *Pronouns* are a separate small class of words that act like variables in that they refer to a person or thing that is somehow salient in the discourse context. For example, the pronoun *she* in sentence (3.5) refers to the most salient person (of feminine gender) in the context of use, which is Mary.

(3.5)   After *Mary* arrived in the village, *she* looked for a bed-and-breakfast.

As well as distinguishing the number of their antecedent, they also mark person (1st = speaker, 2nd = hearer, or 3rd = other discourse entities). They are the only words in English which appear in different forms when they are used as the subject and the object of a sentence. We call these forms the *nominative* or *subject case* and *accusative* or *object case* personal pronouns, respectively. Pronouns also have special forms, *possessive pronouns*, for when they are a possessor, as in *my car*, which we can view as genitive case forms. Somewhat oddly, English pronouns have another possessive form, often called the 'second' possessive personal pronoun, used when the object of the preposition *of* describes the possessor: *a friend of **mine***. Finally, there are *reflexive pronouns*, which are used similarly to ordinary (personal) pronouns except that they always refer to a nearby antecedent in the same sentence, normally the subject of the sentence. For example, *herself* in sentence (3.6a) must refer to Mary whereas *her* in sentence (3.6b) cannot refer to Mary (that is, Mary saw a woman other than herself in the mirror).

NOMINATIVE
SUBJECT CASE
ACCUSATIVE
OBJECT CASE
POSSESSIVE PRONOUNS

REFLEXIVE PRONOUNS

(3.6)   a. Mary saw herself in the mirror.

b. Mary saw her in the mirror.

ANAPHORS   Reflexive pronouns (and certain other expressions like *each other*) are often referred to as *anaphors*, and must refer to something very nearby in the text. Personal pronouns also refer to previously discussed people

	Nominative	Accusative	Possessive	2nd Possessive	Reflexive
Tag(s)	PPS (3SG)	PPO	PP$	PP$$	PPL
	PPSS (1SG,2SG,PL)				(PPLS for PL)
1SG	I	me	my	mine	myself
2SG	you	you	your	yours	yourself
3SG MASC	he	him	his	his	himself
3SG FEM	she	her	her	hers	herself
3SG NEUT	it	it	its	its	itself
1PL	we	us	our	ours	ourselves
2PL	you	you	your	yours	yourselves
3PL	they	them	their	theirs	themselves

Table 3.2 Pronoun forms in English. Second person forms do not distinguish number, except in the reflexive, while third person singular forms distinguish gender.

and things, but at a slightly greater distance. All the forms for pronouns, and their Brown tags are summarized in table 3.2.

Brown tags.   NN is the Brown tag for singular nouns (*candy, woman*). The Brown tag set also distinguishes two special types of nouns, *proper nouns* (or *proper names*), and *adverbial nouns*. Proper nouns are names like *Mary*, *Smith*, or *United States* that refer to particular persons or things. Proper nouns are usually capitalized. The tag for proper nouns is NNP.[1] Adverbial nouns (tag NR) are nouns like *home*, *west* and *tomorrow* that can be used without modifiers to give information about the circumstances of the event described, for example the time or the location. They have a function similar to *adverbs* (see below). The tags mentioned so far have the following plural equivalents: NNS (plural nouns), NNPS (plural proper nouns), and NRS (plural adverbial nouns). Many also have possessive or genitive extensions: NN$ (possessive singular nouns), NNS$ (possessive plural nouns), NNP$ (possessive singular proper nouns), NNPS$ (possessive plural proper nouns), and NR$ (possessive adverbial nouns). The tags for pronouns are shown in table 3.2.

PROPER NAMES
ADVERBIAL NOUNS

---

1. Actually, the Brown tag for proper nouns was NP, but we follow the Penn Treebank in substituting NNP, so that NP can maintain its conventional meaning within linguistics of a noun phrase (see below). We also follow the Penn Treebank in using a doubled N in the related tags mentioned subsequently.

3.1.2 Words that accompany nouns: Determiners and adjectives

DETERMINER

ARTICLE

Several other parts of speech most commonly appear accompanying nouns. *Determiners* describe the particular reference of a noun. A subtype of determiners is *articles*. The article *the* indicates that we're talking about someone or something that we already know about or can uniquely determine. We say *the tree* if we have already made reference to the tree or if the reference is clear from context such as when we are standing next to a tree and it is clear we are referring to it. The article *a* (or *an*) indicates that the person or thing we are talking about was not previously mentioned. If we say *a tree*, then we are indicating that we have not mentioned this tree before and its identity cannot be inferred from context. Other determiners include the *demonstratives*, such as *this* and *that*.

DEMONSTRATIVES

ADJECTIVE

Adjectives are used to describe properties of nouns. Here are some adjectives (in italics):

(3.7) a *red* rose, this *long* journey, many *intelligent* children, a very *trendy* magazine

ATTRIBUTIVE
ADNOMINAL
PREDICATIVE

Uses such as these modifying a noun are called *attributive* or *adnominal*. Adjectives also have a *predicative* use as a complement of *be*:

(3.8) The rose is *red*. The journey will be *long*.

AGREEMENT

Many languages mark distinctions of case, number, and gender on articles and adjectives as well as nouns, and we then say that the article or adjective *agrees* with the noun, that is, they have the same case, number, and gender. In English, the morphological modifications of adjectives are the derivational endings like *-ly* which we covered earlier, and the formation of *comparative* (*richer, trendier*), and *superlative* (*richest, trendiest*) forms. Only some, mainly shorter, adjectives form morphological comparatives and superlatives by suffixing *-er* and *-est*. For the rest, *periphrastic forms* are used (*more intelligent, most intelligent*). Periphrastic forms are formed with the auxiliary words, in this case *more* and *most*. The basic form of the adjective (*rich, trendy, intelligent*) is called the *positive* when contrasted with comparative and superlative. Comparative and superlative forms compare different degrees to which the property described by the adjective applies to nouns. The following example should be self-explanatory:

COMPARATIVE
SUPERLATIVE

PERIPHRASTIC FORMS

POSITIVE

(3.9) John is rich, Paul is richer, Mary is richest.

Brown tags. The Brown tag for adjectives (in the positive form) is JJ, for comparatives JJR, for superlatives JJT. There is a special tag, JJS, for the 'semantically' superlative adjectives *chief, main,* and *top.* Numbers are subclasses of adjectives. The cardinals, such as *one, two,* and *6,000,000,* have the tag CD. The ordinals, such as *first, second, tenth,* and *mid-twentieth* have the tag OD.

The Brown tag for articles is AT. Singular determiners, like *this, that,* have the tag DT; plural determiners (*these, those*) DTS; determiners that can be singular or plural (*some, any*) DTI, and 'double conjunction' determiners (*either, neither*) DTX.

QUANTIFIER *Quantifiers* are words that express ideas like 'all,' 'many,' 'some.' The determiners *some* and *any* can function as quantifiers. Other parts of speech that correspond to quantifiers have the tags ABN (pre-quantifier: *all, many*) and PN (nominal pronoun: *one, something, anything, somebody*). The tag for *there* when used to express existence at the beginning of a sentence is EX.

INTERROGATIVE A final group of words that occur with or instead of nouns are the *in-*
PRONOUNS *terrogative pronouns* and *determiners* which are used for questions and
INTERROGATIVE relative clauses. Their tags are WDT (*wh*-determiner: *what, which*), WP\$
DETERMINERS (possessive *wh*-pronoun: *whose*), WPO (objective *wh*-pronoun: *whom, which, that*), and WPS (nominative *wh*-pronoun: *who, which, that*).

3.1.3 Verbs

Verbs are used to describe actions (*She **threw** the stone*), activities (*She **walked** along the river*) and states (*I **have** $50*). A regular English verb has the following morphological forms:

BASE FORM ■ the root or *base form*: *walk*

■ the third singular present tense: *walks*

■ the gerund and present participle: *walking*

■ the past tense form and past/passive participle: *walked*

Most of these forms do duty in several functions. The base form is used
PRESENT TENSE for the *present tense.*

(3.10) I walk. You walk. We walk. You (guys) walk. They walk.

The third singular person has a different present tense form:

(3.11)   She walks. He walks. It walks.

INFINITIVE   The base form is also used for the *infinitive* with *to*:

(3.12)   She likes *to walk*. She has *to walk*. *To walk* is fun.

and after modals and in the bare infinitive:

(3.13)   She shouldn't *walk*. She helped me *walk*.

PROGRESSIVE   The *-ing* form is used for the *progressive* (indicating that an action is in progress):

(3.14)   She is walking. She was walking. She will be walking.

GERUND   and as the *gerund*, a derived form where the verb gains some or all of the properties of nouns:

(3.15)   This is the most vigorous *walking* I've done in a long time. *Walking* is fun.

The *-ed* form serves as past tense indicating an action that took place in the past:

(3.16)   She walked.

PRESENT PERFECT   It also functions as the past participle in the formation of *present perfect*:

(3.17)   She has walked.

PAST PERFECT   and *past perfect*:

(3.18)   She had walked.

IRREGULAR   A number of verbs are *irregular* and have different forms for past tense and past participle. Examples are *drive* and *take*:

(3.19)   a. She *drove* the car. She has never *driven* a car.

b. She *took* off on Monday. She had already *taken* off on Monday.

Just as nouns are commonly marked for features like number and case, verbs are also commonly marked for certain features. Table 3.3 summarizes grammatical features that are commonly indicated on verbs across languages. These features can be indicated either morphologically SYNTHETIC FORMS   (also called *synthetically*), as in the case of the English endings *-s*, *-ing*,

Feature Category	Instances
subject number	singular, plural
subject person	first (*I walk*), second (*you walk*), third (*she walks*)
tense	present tense, past tense, future tense
aspect	progressive, perfect
mood/modality	possibility, subjunctive, irrealis
participles	present participle (*walking*), past participle (*walked*)
voice	active, passive, middle

Table 3.3 Features commonly marked on verbs.

AUXILIARIES
VERB GROUP
ANALYTIC FORMS

and *-ed*), or by means of *auxiliaries*, words that accompany verbs in a *verb group* (also called *analytically*). English uses the auxiliaries *have*, *be*, and *will* (and others) to express aspect, mood, and some tense information. The present and past perfect are formed with *have* as we saw in sentences (3.17) and (3.18). The progressive is formed with *be* (3.14). Forms that are built using auxiliaries, as opposed to direct inflection as in the case of the English past tense, are referred to as *periphrastic forms*.

PERIPHRASTIC FORMS
MODAL AUXILIARIES

In English, there is a class of verbs with special properties: the *modal auxiliaries* or *modals*. Modals lack some of the forms of ordinary verbs (no infinitive, no progressive form), and always come first in the verb group. They express modalities like possibility (*may*, *can*) or obligation (*should*) as illustrated in the following examples:

(3.20)   a. With her abilities, she *can* do whatever she wants to.

b. He *may* or *may* not come to the meeting.

c. You *should* spend more time with your family.

In English, the formation of the future tense with the auxiliary *will* is in all ways parallel to that of other modalities:

(3.21)   She *will* come. She *will* not come.

Brown tags. The Brown tag set uses VB for the base form (*take*), VBZ for the third person singular (*takes*), VBD for the past tense (*took*), VBG for gerund and present participle (*taking*), and VBN for the past participle (*taken*). The tag for modal auxiliaries (*can, may, must, could, might, ...*) is MD. Since *be*, *have*, and *do* are important in forming tenses and moods, the Brown tag set has separate tags for all forms of these verbs. We omit them here, but they are listed in table 4.6.

3.1.4 Other parts of speech

Adverbs, prepositions, and particles

ADVERB

We have already encountered adverbs as an example of morphological derivation. *Adverbs* modify a verb in the same way that adjectives modify nouns. Adverbs specify place, time, manner or degree:

(3.22)   a. She *often* travels to Las Vegas.

       b. She *allegedly* committed perjury.

       c. She started her career off very *impressively*.

Some adverbs, such as *often*, are not derived from adjectives and lack the suffix *-ly*.

Some adverbs can also modify adjectives ((3.23a) and (3.23b)) and other adverbs (3.23c).

(3.23)   a. a *very* unlikely event

       b. a *shockingly* frank exchange

       c. She started her career off *very* impressively.

DEGREE ADVERBS

QUALIFIER

Certain adverbs like *very* are specialized to the role of modifying adjectives and adverbs and do not modify verbs. They are called *degree adverbs*. Their distribution is thus quite distinct from other adverbs, and they are sometimes regarded as a separate part of speech called *qualifiers*.

PREPOSITION

Prepositions are mainly small words that prototypically express spatial relationships:

(3.24)   *in* the glass, *on* the table, *over* their heads, *about* an interesting idea, *concerning* your recent invention

PARTICLE

PHRASAL VERBS

Most prepositions do double duty as particles. *Particles* are a subclass of prepositions that can enter into strong bonds with verbs in the formation of so-called *phrasal verbs*. We can best think of a phrasal verb as a separate lexical entry with syntactic and semantic properties different from the verb it was formed from. Here are some examples:

(3.25)   a. The plane *took off* at 8am.

b. Don't *give in* to him.

c. It is time to *take on* new responsibilities.

d. He was *put off* by so much rudeness.

Sometimes these constructions can occur with the preposition separated from the verb:

(3.26)   a. I didn't want to *take* that responsibility *on* right now.

b. He *put* me *off*.

These phrasal verbs have particular meanings that are quite specialized, and unpredictable from the verb and particle that make them up.

Sometimes we need to know the meaning of a sentence to be able to distinguish particles and prepositions: *up* is a preposition in (3.27a) and a particle in (3.27b). Note the meaning shift from the literal meaning of running on an incline in (3.27a) to the figurative meaning of building up a large bill in (3.27b).

(3.27)   a. She ran up a hill.

b. She ran up a bill.

Brown tags.   The tags for adverbs are RB (ordinary adverb: *simply*, *late*, *well*, *little*), RBR (comparative adverb: *later*, *better*, *less*), RBT (superlative adverb: *latest*, *best*, *least*), * (*not*), QL (qualifier: *very*, *too*, *extremely*), and QLP (post-qualifier: *enough*, *indeed*). Two tags stand for parts of speech that have both adverbial and interrogative functions: WQL (*wh*-qualifier: *how*) and WRB (*wh*-adverb: *how*, *when*, *where*).

The Brown tag for prepositions is IN, while particles have the tag RP.

Conjunctions and complementizers

COORDINATING
CONJUNCTION
COORDINATION

The remaining important word categories are coordinating and subordinating conjunctions. *Coordinating conjunctions* 'conjoin' or *coordinate* two words or phrases of (usually) the same category:

■ husband *and* wife [nouns]

- She bought *or* leased the car. [verbs]

- the green triangle *and* the blue square [noun phrases]

- She bought her car, *but* she also considered leasing it. [sentences]

CLAUSE
SUBORDINATING
CONJUNCTION

One function of coordinating conjunctions is to link two sentences (or *clauses*) as shown in the last example. This can also be done by *subordinating conjunctions*. In the examples below, the subordinating conjunction is shown in italics.

(3.28)   a. She said *that* he would be late.   [proposition]

b. She complained *because* he was late.   [reason]

c. I won't wait *if* he is late.   [condition]

d. She thanked him *although* he was late.   [concession]

e. She left *before* he arrived.   [temporal]

COMPLEMENTIZERS

Cases of subordinating conjunctions like *that* in (3.28a) or use of *for* which introduce arguments of the verb are often alternatively regarded as *complementizers*. The difference between coordination and subordination is that, as the terms suggest, coordination joins two sentences as equals whereas subordination attaches a secondary sentence to a primary sentence. The secondary sentence often expresses a proposition, a reason, a condition, a concession or a temporally related event.

Brown tags.   The tag for conjunctions is CC. The tag for subordinating conjunctions is CS.

3.2 Phrase Structure

WORD ORDER

PHRASES
SYNTAX

CONSTITUENT

Words do not occur in just any old order. Languages have constraints on *word order*. But it is also the case that the words in a sentence are not just strung together as a sequence of parts of speech, like beads on a necklace. Instead, words are organized into *phrases*, groupings of words that are clumped as a unit. *Syntax* is the study of the regularities and constraints of word order and phrase structure.

One fundamental idea is that certain groupings of words behave as *constituents*. Constituents can be detected by their being able to occur in various positions, and showing uniform syntactic possibilities for expansion. The examples in (3.29) and (3.30) show evidence from positioning and phrasal expansion for a constituent that groups nouns and their modifiers:

(3.29)   a. I put *the bagels* in the freezer.

           b. *The bagels*, I put in the freezer.

           c. I put in the fridge *the bagels* (that John had given me)

(3.30)
$$\left\{ \begin{array}{c} \text{She} \\ \text{the woman} \\ \text{the tall woman} \\ \text{the very tall woman} \\ \text{the tall woman with sad eyes} \\ \cdots \end{array} \right\} \text{saw} \left\{ \begin{array}{c} \text{him} \\ \text{the man} \\ \text{the short man} \\ \text{the very short man} \\ \text{the short man with red hair} \\ \cdots \end{array} \right\}.$$

PARADIGMATIC RELATIONSHIP

This is the notion of a *paradigmatic relationship* in Saussurean linguistics. All elements that can be replaced for each other in a certain syntactic position (like the noun phrase constituent above) are members of one *paradigm*. In contrast, two words bear a *syntagmatic relationship* if they can form a phrase (or *syntagma*) like *sewed clothes* or *sewed a dress*. An important class of syntagmatically related words are *collocations* (chapter 5).

PARADIGM
SYNTAGMATIC RELATIONSHIP
SYNTAGMA
COLLOCATIONS

    In this section we will briefly mention some of the major phrase types, and then introduce techniques linguists use to model phrase structure. The upshot will be to suggest that English sentences typically have an overall phrase structure that looks as follows:

(3.31)

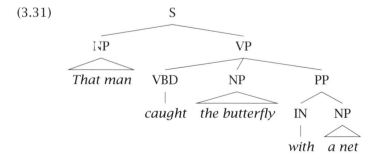

A whole sentence is given the category S. A sentence normally rewrites as a subject noun phrase and a verb phrase.

NOUN PHRASE

Noun phrases. A noun is usually embedded in a *noun phrase* (NP), a syntactic unit of the sentence in which information about the noun is gathered. The noun is the *head* of the noun phrase, the central constituent that determines the syntactic character of the phrase. Noun phrases are usually the *arguments* of verbs, the participants in the action, activity or state described by the verb. Noun phrases normally consist of an optional determiner, zero or more adjective phrases, a noun head, and then perhaps some post-modifiers, such as prepositional phrases or clausal modifiers, with the constituents appearing in that order. Clausal modifiers of nouns are referred to as *relative clauses*. Here is a large noun phrase that indicates many of these possibilities:

HEAD

RELATIVE CLAUSES

(3.32) The homeless old man in the park that I tried to help yesterday

PREPOSITIONAL PHRASES

Prepositional phrases. *Prepositional phrases* (PPs) are headed by a preposition and contain a noun phrase complement. They can appear within all the other major phrase types. They are particularly common in noun phrases and verb phrases where they usually express spatial and temporal locations and other attributes.

VERB PHRASE

Verb phrases. Analogous to the way nouns head noun phrases, the verb is the head of the *verb phrase* (VP). In general, the verb phrase organizes all elements of the sentence that depend syntactically on the verb (except that in most syntactic theories the verb phrase does not contain the subject noun phrase). Some examples of verb phrases appear in (3.33):

(3.33) a. *Getting to school on time* was a struggle.

b. He *was trying to keep his temper*.

c. That woman *quickly showed me the way to hide*.

ADJECTIVE PHRASES

Adjective phrases. Complex *adjective phrases* (APs) are less common, but encompass examples like the phrases shown in bold in these sentences: *She is **very sure of herself***; *He seemed a man who was **quite certain to succeed***.

3.2.1 Phrase structure grammars

A syntactic analysis of a sentence tells us how to determine the meaning of the sentence from the meaning of the words. For example, it will tell us who does what to whom in the event described in a sentence. Compare:

(3.34) Mary gave Peter a book.

(3.35) Peter gave Mary a book.

Sentences (3.34) and (3.35) use the same words, but have different meanings. In the first sentence, the book is transferred from Mary to Peter, in the second from Peter to Mary. It is the word order that allows us to infer who did what to whom.

FREE WORD ORDER Some languages like Latin or Russian permit many different ways of ordering the words in a sentence without a change in meaning, and instead use case markings to indicate who did what to whom. This type of language is called a *free word order* language, meaning that word order isn't used to indicate who the doer is – word order is then usually used mainly to indicate discourse structure. Other languages such as English are more restrictive in the extent to which words can move around in a sentence. In English, the basic word order is Subject – Verb – Object:

(3.36) *The children* (subject) *should* (auxiliary verb) eat *spinach* (object).

INTERROGATIVES
INVERTED
In general, this order is modified only to express particular 'mood' categories. In *interrogatives* (or questions), the subject and first auxiliary verb are *inverted*:

(3.37) *Should* (auxiliary verb) *the children* (subject) eat *spinach* (object)?

IMPERATIVES
If the statement would involve no auxiliary, a form of *do* appears in the initial position (*Did he cry?*). In *imperatives* (commands or requests), there is no subject (it is inferred to be the person who is addressed):

(3.38) Eat spinach!

DECLARATIVES Basic sentences are called *declaratives* when contrasted with interrogatives and imperatives.

REWRITE RULES The regularities of word order are often captured by means of *rewrite rules*. A rewrite rule has the form 'category → category*' and states that the symbol on the left side can be rewritten as the sequence of symbols on the right side. To produce a sentence of the language, we start with

START SYMBOL the *start symbol* 'S' (for sentence). Here is a simple set of rewrite rules:

(3.39)   S   →   NP VP   AT   →   *the*

NP   → $\begin{bmatrix} \text{AT NNS} \\ \text{AT NN} \\ \text{NP PP} \end{bmatrix}$ NNS   → $\begin{Bmatrix} children \\ students \\ mountains \end{Bmatrix}$

VP   → $\begin{bmatrix} \text{VP PP} \\ \text{VBD} \\ \text{VBD NP} \end{bmatrix}$ VBD   → $\begin{Bmatrix} slept \\ ate \\ saw \end{Bmatrix}$

P   →   IN NP   IN   → $\begin{Bmatrix} in \\ of \end{Bmatrix}$

NN   →   *cake*

LEXICON

CONTEXT-FREE
GRAMMARS

The rules on the righthand side rewrite one of the syntactic categories (or part of speech symbols) introduced in the previous sections into a word of the corresponding category. This part of the grammar is often separated off as the *lexicon*. The nature of these rules is that a certain syntactic category can be rewritten as one or more other syntactic categories or words. The possibilities for rewriting depend solely on the category, and not on any surrounding context, so such phrase structure grammars are commonly referred to as *context-free grammars*.

With these rules, we can derive sentences. Derivations (3.40) and (3.41) are two simple examples.

(3.40)   S
→ NP VP
→ AT NNS VBD
→ *The children slept*

(3.41)   S
→ NP VP
→ AT NNS VBD NP
→ AT NNS VBD AT NN
→ *The children ate the cake*

TERMINAL NODES
NONTERMINAL NODES
LOCAL TREE

The more intuitive way to represent phrase structure is as a tree. We refer to the leaf nodes of the tree as *terminal nodes* and to internal nodes as *nonterminal nodes*. In such a tree each nonterminal node and its immediate daughters, otherwise known as a *local tree* corresponds to the application of a rewrite rule. The order of daughters generates the word order of the sentence, and the tree has a single root node, which is the start symbol of the grammar. Trees (3.42) and (3.43) correspond to derivations (3.40) and (3.41). Each node in the tree shows something that we are hypothesising to be a *constituent*.

(3.42)

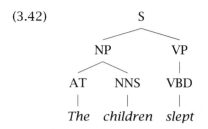

(3.43)

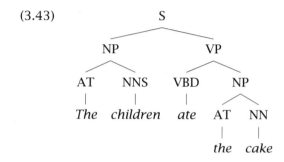

BRACKETING   A third and final way to show constituency is via a *(labeled) bracketing*. Sets of brackets delimit constituents and may be labeled to show the category of the nonterminal nodes. The labeled bracketing for (3.43) is (3.44):

(3.44)   [s [NP [AT *The*] [NNS *children*]] [VP[VBD *ate*] [NP [AT *the*] [NN *cake*]]]]

               A property of most formalizations of natural language syntax in terms
RECURSIVITY   of rewrite rules is *recursivity:* the fact that there are constellations in
               which rewrite rules can be applied an arbitrary number of times. In our
               example grammar, a PP contains an NP which can in turn contain an-
               other PP. Thus we can get recursive expansions as in the example in
               figure 3.1. Here, the sequence of prepositional phrases is generated by
               multiple application of the rewrite rule cycle "NP → NP PP; PP → IN NP."
               The derivation applies the cycle twice, but we could apply it three, four,
               or a hundred times.
                   Recursivity makes it possible for a single nonterminal symbol like VP or
               NP to be expanded to a large number of words. (For example, in figure 3.1
               the symbol VP is expanded to nine words: *ate the cake of the children in*

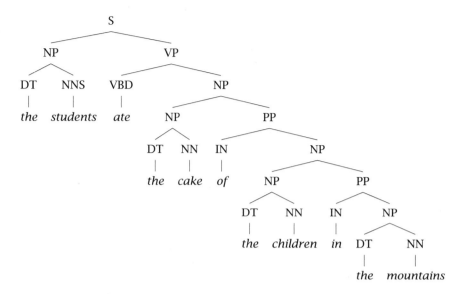

Figure 3.1 An example of recursive phrase structure expansion.

the mountains.) One consequence is that two words that were generated by a common rewrite rule and are syntactically linked can become separated by intervening words as the derivation of a sentence proceeds. These types of phenomena are called *non-local dependencies* because two words can be syntactically dependent even though they occur far apart in a sentence.

One example of a dependency that can be non-local is *subject-verb agreement*, the fact that the subject and verb of a sentence agree in number and person. We have *She walks, He walks, It walks* versus *I walk, You walk, We walk, They walk.* That is, the verb has the ending *-s* indicating third person singular if and only if the subject is in the third person singular. Subject and verb agree even if other words and phrases intervene as in the following example.

(3.45)   The **women** who found the wallet **were** given a reward.

If we looked only at immediate neighbors it would seem that we would have to say *the wallet was.* Only a complete syntactic analysis of the sentence reveals that *The women* is the subject and the form of *to be* has to be in the plural.

Another important case of non-local dependencies is the class known

LONG-DISTANCE
DEPENDENCIES
WH-EXTRACTION

as *long-distance dependencies,* such as *wh-extraction.*[2] The name is based on the theory that phrases such as *which book* in (3.46b) are moved (or extracted) from an underlying position (after the verb as in (3.46a)) to their "surface" position (the beginning of the sentence as in (3.46b)).

(3.46)   a. Should Peter buy *a book?*

b. *Which book* should Peter buy?

Without making any commitment to such a movement theory, it is clear that we have to recognize a long distance dependency between *buy* and *which book.* Otherwise we would not be able to tell that *book* is an argument of *buy.*

▼ Non-local phenomena are a challenge for some Statistical NLP approaches like *n*-grams that model local dependencies. An *n*-gram model would predict that the word after *wallet* in (3.45) is *was,* not *were.* These issues are further discussed at the beginning of chapter 11.

A final feature of many versions of phrase structure grammar is empty

EMPTY NODES

nodes. *Empty nodes* occur when a nonterminal may be rewritten as nothing. For example, noting that one can also say *Eat the cake!* without a subject NP, one might suggest adding a rule NP → ∅. An NP nonterminal is then allowed to be rewritten as nothing. This is often represented by putting a ∅ or an *e* under the node in the tree. Using this notation, the tree in (3.46b) could be given the structure in (3.47):

(3.47)

---

2. In the speech literature, the term 'long-distance dependencies' regularly refers to anything beyond the range of a trigram model. We have termed such effects 'non-local dependencies,' and have reserved the term 'long-distance dependencies' for its usual linguistic meaning of a dependency that appears to be able to cross any number of nodes in a phrase structure tree.

CONTEXT-FREE

The simple model of phrase structure that we have developed here adopts a *context-free* view of language. For example, once we have expanded 'VP' to 'VBD NP' and then to '*sewed* NP,' we can replace NP with whatever noun phrase we please. The context provided by the verb *sewed* is inaccessible when we decide how to expand NP. This inaccessibility of context is the key property of a context-free grammar. We could expand VP to a natural phrase like *sewed clothes*, but we can as easily choose a nonsensical expansion like *sewed wood blocks*.

▼ How to include necessary dependencies is a central topic in probabilistic parsing, which we discuss in chapter 12.

3.2.2   Dependency: Arguments and adjuncts

DEPENDENCY

Another important organizing notion is the concept of *dependents*. In a sentence like:

(3.48)   Sue watched the man at the next table.

Sue and *the man* are dependents of a watching event. We will say that they are the two arguments of the verb *watch*. The PP *at the next table* is a dependent of *man*. It modifies *man*.

SEMANTIC ROLES
AGENT
PATIENT

Most commonly, noun phrases are arguments of verbs. The arguments of verbs can be described at various levels. One can classify the arguments via *semantic roles*. The *agent* of an action is the person or thing that is doing something, the *patient* is the person or thing that is having something done to it, and other roles like *instrument* and *goal* describe yet other classes of semantic relationships. Alternatively, one can describe the syntactic possibilities for arguments in terms of grammatical relations. All English verbs take a *subject*, which is the noun phrase that appears before the verb. Many verbs take an *object* noun phrase, which normally appears immediately after the verb. Pronouns are in the subject case when they are subjects of a verb, and in the object case when they are objects of a verb. In our earlier example, here repeated as sentence (3.49), *children* is the subject of *eat* (the children are the agents of the action of eating), and *sweet candy* is the object of *eat* (the sweet candy is the thing being acted upon, the patient of the action):

SUBJECT
OBJECT

(3.49)   Children eat sweet candy.

Note that the morphological form of *candy* does not change. In English, pronouns are the only nouns that change their forms when used in the object case.

Some verbs take two object noun phrases after the verb, both in the object case:

(3.50)   She gave him the book.

INDIRECT OBJECT   In this sentence, *him* is the *indirect object* (describing the *recipient*, the
RECIPIENT   one who indirectly gets something) and *the book* is the *direct object* (de-
DIRECT OBJECT   scribing the patient). Other such verbs are verbs of sending and verbs of communication:

(3.51)   a. She *sent* her mother the book.

          b. She *emailed* him the letter.

Such verbs often allow an alternate expression of their arguments where the recipient appears in a prepositional phrase:

(3.52)   She sent the book to her mother.

Languages with case markings normally distinguish these NPs and express patients in the accusative case and recipients in the dative case.

There are systematic associations between semantic roles and grammatical functions, for example agents are usually subjects, but there are also some dissociations. In *Bill received a package from the mailman*, it is the mailman who appears to be the agent. The relationships between semantic roles and grammatical functions are also changed by voice alternations (the one feature in table 3.3 which we did not discuss earlier).
ACTIVE VOICE   Many language make a distinction between *active voice* and *passive voice*
PASSIVE VOICE   (or simply *active* and *passive*). Active corresponds to the default way of expressing the arguments of a verb: the agent is expressed as the subject, the patient as the object:

(3.53)   Children eat sweet candy.

In the passive, the patient becomes the subject, and the agent is demoted to an oblique role. In English this means that the order of the two arguments is reversed, and the agent is expressed by means of a prepositional *by*-phrase. The passive is formed with the auxiliary *be* and the past participle:

(3.54)   Candy is eaten by children.

In other languages, the passive alternation might just involve changes in case marking, and some morphology on the verb.

Subcategorization

As we have seen, different verbs differ in the number of entities (persons, animals, things) that they relate. One such difference is the contrast between *transitive* and *intransitive* verbs. Transitive verbs have a (direct) object, intransitive verbs don't:

TRANSITIVE
INTRANSITIVE

(3.55)   a. She brought a bottle of whiskey.

b. She walked (along the river).

In sentence (3.55a), *a bottle of whiskey* is the object of *brought*. We cannot use the verb *bring* without an object: we cannot say *She brought*. The verb *walk* is an example of an intransitive verb. There is no object in sentence (3.55). There is, however, a prepositional phrase expressing the location of the activity.

Syntacticians try to classify the dependents of verbs. The first distinction they make is between arguments and adjuncts. The subject, object, and direct object are arguments. In general, *arguments* express entities that are centrally involved in the activity of the verb. Most arguments are expressed as NPs, but they may be expressed as PPs, VPs, or as clauses:

ARGUMENTS

(3.56)   a. We deprived him *of food.*

b. John knows *that he is losing.*

Arguments are divided into the subject, and all non-subject arguments which are collectively referred to as *complements*.

COMPLEMENTS
ADJUNCTS

Adjuncts are phrases that have a less tight link to the verb. Adjuncts are always optional whereas many complements are obligatory (for example, the object of *bring* is obligatory). Adjuncts can also move around more easily than complements. Prototypical examples of adjuncts are phrases that tell us the time, place, or manner of the action or state that the verb describes as in the following examples:

(3.57)   a. She saw a Woody Allen movie *yesterday.*

b. She saw a Woody Allen movie *in Paris.*

c. She saw the Woody Allen movie *with great interest.*

d. She saw a Woody Allen movie *with a couple of friends.*

SUBORDINATE
CLAUSES   *Subordinate clauses* (sentences within a sentence) can also be either adjuncts or subcategorized arguments, and can express a variety of relationships to the verb. In the examples we saw earlier in (3.28), (a) involves an argument clause, while the rest are adjuncts.

Sometimes, it's difficult to distinguish adjuncts and complements. The prepositional phrase *on the table* is a complement in the first sentence (it is subcategorized for by *put* and cannot be omitted), an adjunct in the second (it is optional):

(3.58)   She put the book *on the table.*

(3.59)   He gave his presentation *on the stage.*

The traditional argument/adjunct distinction is really a reflection of the categorical basis of traditional linguistics. In many cases, such as the following, one seems to find an intermediate degree of selection:

(3.60)   a. I straightened the nail *with a hammer.*

b. He will retire *in Florida.*

It is not clear whether the PPs in italics should be regarded as being centrally involved in the event described by the verb or not. Within a Statistical NLP approach, it probably makes sense to talk instead about the degree of association between a verb and a dependent.

SUBCATEGORIZATION   We refer to the classification of verbs according to the types of complements they permit as *subcategorization.* We say that a verb *subcategorizes for* a particular complement. For example, *bring* subcategorizes for an object. Here is a list of subcategorized arguments with example sentences.

- **Subject.** *The children* eat candy.

- **Object.** The children eat *candy.*

- **Prepositional phrase.** She put the book *on the table.*

- **Predicative adjective.** We made the man *angry.*

- **Bare infinitive.** She helped me *walk.*

- **Infinitive with *to*.** She likes *to walk*.

- **Participial phrase.** She stopped *singing that tune* eventually.

- ***That*-clause.** She thinks *that it will rain tomorrow*. The *that* can usually be omitted: She thinks *it will rain tomorrow*.

- **Question-form clauses.** She is wondering *why it is raining in August*. She asked me *what book I was reading*.

While most of these complements are phrasal units that we have already seen, such as NPs and APs, the final entries are not, in that they are a unit bigger than an S. The clause *why it is raining in August* consists of a whole sentence *it is raining in August* plus an additional constituent out front. Such a "large clause" is referred to as an S′ (pronounced "S Bar") constituent. Relative clauses and main clause questions are also analyzed as S′ constituents.

Often verbs have several possible patterns of arguments. A particular set of arguments that a verb can appear with is referred to as a *subcategorization frame*. Here are some subcategorization frames that are common in English.

SUBCATEGORIZATION FRAME

- **Intransitive verb.** NP[subject]. *The woman walked.*

- **Transitive verb.** NP[subject], NP[object]. *John loves Mary.*

- **Ditransitive verb.** NP[subject], NP[direct object], NP[indirect object]. *Mary gave Peter flowers.*

- **Intransitive with PP.** NP[subject], PP. *I rent in Paddington.*

- **Transitive with PP.** NP[subject], NP[object], PP. *She put the book on the table.*

- **Sentential complement.** NP[subject], clause. *I know (that) she likes you.*

- **Transitive with sentential complement.** NP[subj], NP[obj], clause. *She told me that Gary is coming on Tuesday.*

Subcategorization frames capture *syntactic* regularities about complements. There are also *semantic* regularities which are called *selectional restrictions* or *selectional preferences*. For example, the verb *bark* prefers dogs as subjects. The verb *eat* prefers edible things as objects:

SELECTIONAL RESTRICTIONS SELECTIONAL PREFERENCES

(3.61)   *The Chihuahua* barked all night.

(3.62)   I eat *vegetables* every day.

Sentences that violate selectional preferences sound odd:

(3.63)   a. *The cat* barked all night.

b. I eat *philosophy* every day.

▼ Selectional preferences are further discussed in section 8.4.

3.2.3   X′ theory

Phrase structure rules as presented above do not predict any systematicity in the way that phrases in natural languages are made, nor any regularities for the appearance of different kinds of dependents in clauses.
However, modern syntax has stressed that there are a lot of such regu-
HEAD   larities. An important idea is that a word will be the *head* of a phrase.
The reason why we talk about noun phrases and prepositional phrases
is because they are a constituent consisting of a noun or preposition respectively, and all their dependents. The noun or preposition heads the
phrase.[3] Linguists have further argued that there is a broad systematicity
in the way dependents arrange themselves around a head in a phrase. A
head forms a small constituent with its complements. This constituent
can be modified by adjuncts to form a bigger constituent, and finally this
SPECIFIER   constituent can combine with a *specifier*, a subject or something like a
determiner to form a maximal phrase. An example of the general picture
is shown in (3.64):

(3.64)

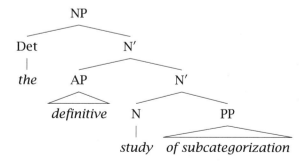

---

3. Recall, however, that verb phrases, as normally described, are slightly anomalous, since
they include all the complements of the verb, but not the subject.

The intermediate constituents are referred to as N′ nodes (pronounced "N bar nodes"). This is basically a two bar level theory (where we think of XP as X″), but is complicated by the fact that recursive *adjunction* of modifiers is allowed at the N′ level to express that a noun can have any number of adjectival phrase modifiers. Sometimes people use theories with more or fewer bar levels.

ADJUNCTION

The final step of the argument is that while there may be differences in word order, this general pattern of constituency is repeated across phrase types. This idea is referred to as X′ theory, where the X is taken to represent a variable across lexical categories.

3.2.4   Phrase structure ambiguity

GENERATION
PARSING

So far we have used rewrite rules to *generate* sentences. It is more common to use them in *parsing*, the process of reconstructing the derivation(s) or phrase structure tree(s) that give rise to a particular sequence of words. We call a phrase structure tree that is constructed from a sentence a *parse*. For example, the tree in (3.43) is a parse of sentence (3.41).

PARSE

In most cases, there are many different phrase structure trees that could all have given rise to a particular sequence of words. A parser based on a comprehensive grammar of English will usually find hundreds of parses for a sentence. This phenomenon is called phrase structure ambiguity or *syntactic ambiguity*. We saw an example of a syntactically ambiguous sentence in the introduction, example (1.10): *Our company is training workers.* One type of syntactic ambiguity that is particularly frequent is *attachment ambiguity*.

SYNTACTIC
AMBIGUITY

ATTACHMENT
AMBIGUITY

Attachment ambiguities occur with phrases that could have been generated by two different nodes. For example, according to the grammar in (3.39), there are two ways to generate the prepositional phrase *with a spoon* in sentence (3.65):

(3.65)   The children ate the cake with a spoon.

It can be generated as a child of a verb phrase, as in the parse tree shown in figure 3.2 (a), or as a child of one of the noun phrases, as in the parse tree shown in figure 3.2 (b).

Different attachments have different meanings. The 'high' attachment to the verb phrase makes a statement about the instrument that the children used while eating the cake. The 'low' attachment to the noun phrase tells us which cake was eaten (the cake with a spoon, and not, say, the

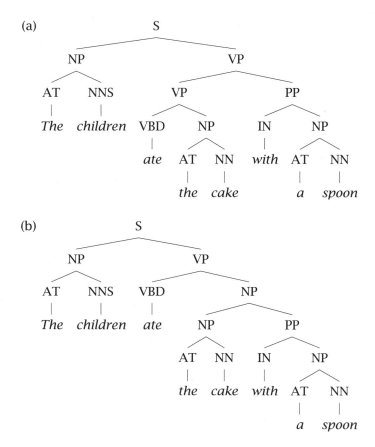

Figure 3.2 An example of a prepositional phrase attachment ambiguity.

cake with icing). So resolving attachment ambiguities can be important for finding the correct semantic interpretation.

A much-studied subclass of syntactic ambiguity is the phenomenon of *garden pathing*. A garden path sentence leads you along a path that suddenly turns out not to work. For example, there might turn out to be additional words in the sentence that do not seem to belong there:

GARDEN PATHS

(3.66)   The horse raced past the barn fell.

Sentence (3.66) from (Bever 1970) is probably the most famous example of a garden path sentence. By the time most people get to the word *barn*, they have constructed a parse that roughly corresponds to the meaning

'The horse ran past the barn.' But then there is an additional word *fell* that cannot be incrementally added to this parse. We have to backtrack to *raced* and construct a completely different parse, corresponding to the meaning *The horse fell after it had been raced past the barn.* Garden pathing is the phenomenon of first being tricked into adopting a spurious parse and then having to backtrack to try to construct the right parse.

Garden-path sentences are rarely a problem in spoken language. Semantic preferences, the generosity of speakers in following communicative maxims, and intonational patterns all usually prevent us from garden pathing (MacDonald et al. 1994; Tanenhaus and Trueswell 1995). We can see this in sentence (3.66) where an intonational break between *horse* and *raced* would tip the hearer off that *raced* introduces a reduced relative clause, not the verb of the main clause. However, garden-pathing can be a real problem when reading complex sentences of written English.

We have seen examples of sentences with more than one parse due to syntactic ambiguity. Most sentences are of this type. But it is also possible that a sentence will have no parse at all. The reason could be that a rule was used in the generation of the sentence that is not covered by the grammar. The other possibility is that the sentence is *ungrammatical* or not syntactically well-formed. Here is an example of an ungrammatical sentence.

UNGRAMMATICAL

(3.67)   *Slept children the.

It is important to distinguish ungrammaticality from semantic abnormality. Sentences like the following are odd, but they are jarring because their semantic interpretation is incoherent whereas (3.67) does not have an interpretation at all.

(3.68)   a. Colorless green ideas sleep furiously.

          b. The cat barked.

People often use a hash mark (#) to indicate semantic, pragmatic, or cultural oddness, as opposed to the marks we introduced earlier for syntactic illformedness.

3.3 Semantics and Pragmatics

Semantics is the study of the meaning of words, constructions, and utterances. We can divide semantics into two parts, the study of the meaning

LEXICAL SEMANTICS   of individual words (or *lexical semantics*) and the study of how meanings of individual words are combined into the meaning of sentences (or even larger units).

One way to approach lexical semantics is to study how word meanings are related to each other. We can organize words into a lexical hierarchy, as is the case, for example, in WordNet, which defines *hypernymy* and *hyponymy*. A hypernym or *hyperonym*[4] is a word with a more general sense, for example, *animal* is a hypernym of *cat*. A hyponym is a word with a more specialized meaning: *cat* is a hyponym of *animal*. (In general, if w^1 is a hypernym of w^2, then w^2 is a hyponym of w^1.) *Antonyms* are words with opposite meanings: *hot* and *cold* or *long* and *short*. The part-whole relationship is called *meronymy*. The word *tire* is a meronym of *car* and *leaf* is a meronym of *tree*. The whole corresponding to a part is called a *holonym*.

HYPERNYMY
HYPONYMY
HYPERONYM

ANTONYMS

MERONYMY

HOLONYM

SYNONYMS

HOMONYMS

Synonyms are words with the same meaning (or very similar meaning): *car* and *automobile* are synonyms. *Homonyms* are words that are written the same way, but are (historically or conceptually) really two different words with different meanings which seem unrelated. Examples are *suit* ('lawsuit' and 'set of garments') and *bank* ('river bank' and 'financial institution'). If a word's meanings (or *senses*) are related, we call it a *polyseme*. The word *branch* is polysemous because its senses ('natural subdivision of a plant' and 'a separate but dependent part of a central organization') are related. Lexical *ambiguity* can refer to both homonymy and polysemy. The subcase of homonymy where the two words are not only written the same way, but also have identical pronunciation, is called *homophony*. So the words *bass* for a species of fish and *bass* for a low-pitched sound are homonyms, but they are not homophones.

SENSES
POLYSEME

AMBIGUITY

HOMOPHONY

▼ Disambiguating word senses is the topic of chapter 7.

Once we have the meanings of individual words, we need to assemble them into the meaning of the whole sentence. That is a hard problem because natural language often does not obey the principle of *compositionality* by which the meaning of the whole can be strictly predicted from the meaning of the parts. The word *white* refers to very different colors in the following expressions:

COMPOSITIONALITY

(3.69)   white paper, white hair, white skin, white wine

White hair is grey, a white skin really has a rosy color, and white wine

---

4. The latter is prescriptively correct. The former is more commonly used.

is actually yellow (but yellow wine doesn't sound very appealing). The groupings *white hair*, *white skin*, and *white wine* are examples of *collocations*. The meaning of the whole is the sum of the meanings of the part plus some additional semantic component that cannot be predicted from the parts.

COLLOCATIONS

▼ Collocations are the topic of chapter 5.

If the relationship between the meaning of the words and the meaning of the phrase is completely opaque, we call the phrase an *idiom*. For example, the idiom *to kick the bucket* describes a process, dying, that has nothing to do with kicking and buckets. We may be able to explain the historical origin of the idiom, but in today's language it is completely non-compositional. Another example is the noun-noun compound *carriage return* for the character that marks the end of a line. Most younger speakers are not aware of its original meaning: returning the carriage of a typewriter to its position on the left margin of the page when starting a new line.

IDIOM

There are many other important problems in assembling the meanings of larger units, which we will not discuss in detail here. One example is the problem of *scope*. Quantifiers and operators have a scope which extends over one or more phrases or clauses. In the following sentence, we can either interpret the quantifier *everyone* as having scope over the negative *not* (meaning that not one person went to the movie), or we can interpret the negation as having scope over the quantifier (meaning that at least one person didn't go to the movie):

SCOPE

(3.70)   Everyone didn't go to the movie.

In order to derive a correct representation of the meaning of the sentence, we need to determine which interpretation is correct in context.

The next larger unit to consider after words and sentences is a *discourse*. Studies of discourse seek to elucidate the covert relationships between sentences in a text. In a narrative discourse, one can seek to describe whether a following sentence is an example, an elaboration, a restatement, etc. In a conversation one wants to model the relationship between turns and the kinds of speech acts involved (questions, statements, requests, acknowledgments, etc.). A central problem in *discourse analysis* is the resolution of *anaphoric relations*.

DISCOURSE ANALYSIS
ANAPHORIC
RELATIONS

(3.71)   a. Mary helped *Peter* get out of the cab. *He* thanked her.

b. Mary helped *the other passenger* out of the cab. *The man* had asked her to help him because of his foot injury.

Anaphoric relations hold between noun phrases that refer to the same person or thing. The noun phrases *Peter* and *He* in sentence (3.71a) and *the other passenger* and *The man* in sentence (3.71b) refer to the same person. The resolution of anaphoric relations is important for *information extraction*. In information extraction, we are scanning a text for a specific type of event such as natural disasters, terrorist attacks or corporate acquisitions. The task is to identify the participants in the event and other information typical of such an event (for example the purchase price in a corporate merger). To do this task well, the correct identification of anaphoric relations is crucial in order to keep track of the participants.

INFORMATION
EXTRACTION

(3.72)   Hurricane Hugo destroyed 20,000 Florida homes. At an estimated cost of one billion dollars, the disaster has been the most costly in the state's history.

If we identify *Hurricane Hugo* and *the disaster* as referring to the same entity in mini-discourse (3.72), we will be able to give *Hugo* as an answer to the question: *Which hurricanes caused more than a billion dollars worth of damage?*

PRAGMATICS   Discourse analysis is part of *pragmatics*, the study of how knowledge about the world and language conventions interact with literal meaning. Anaphoric relations are a pragmatic phenomenon since they are constrained by world knowledge. For example, for resolving the relations in discourse (3.72), it is necessary to know that hurricanes are disasters. Most areas of pragmatics have not received much attention in Statistical NLP, both because it is hard to model the complexity of world knowledge with statistical means and due to the lack of training data. Two areas that are beginning to receive more attention are the resolution of anaphoric relations and the modeling of speech acts in dialogues.

3.4   Other Areas

Linguistics is traditionally subdivided into phonetics, phonology, morphology, syntax, semantics, and pragmatics. Phonetics is the study of the physical sounds of language, phenomena like consonants, vowels and intonation. The subject of phonology is the structure of the sound systems in languages. Phonetics and phonology are important for speech recognition and speech synthesis, but since we do not cover speech, we will not cover them in this book. We will introduce the small number of phonetic and phonological concepts we need wherever we first refer to them.

SOCIOLINGUISTICS
HISTORICAL
LINGUISTICS

In addition to areas of study that deal with different levels of language, there are also subfields of linguistics that look at particular aspects of language. *Sociolinguistics* studies the interactions of social organization and language. The change of languages over time is the subject of *historical linguistics*. Linguistic typology looks at how languages make different use of the inventory of linguistic devices and how they can be classified into groups based on the way they use these devices. Language acquisition investigates how children learn language. Psycholinguistics focuses on issues of real-time production and perception of language and on the way language is represented in the brain. Many of these areas hold rich possibilities for making use of quantitative methods. Mathematical linguistics is usually used to refer to approaches using non-quantitative mathematical methods.

3.5 Further Reading

In-depth overview articles of a large number of the subfields of linguistics can be found in (Newmeyer 1988). In many of these areas, the influence of Statistical NLP can now be felt, be it in the widespread use of corpora, or in the adoption of quantitative methods from Statistical NLP.

De Saussure 1962 is a landmark work in structuralist linguistics. An excellent in-depth overview of the field of linguistics for non-linguists is provided by the Cambridge Encyclopedia of Language (Crystal 1987). See also (Pinker 1994) for a recent popular book. Marchand (1969) presents an extremely thorough study of the possibilities for word derivation in English. Quirk et al. (1985) provide a comprehensive grammar of English. Finally, a good work of reference for looking up syntactic (and many morphological and semantic) terms is (Trask 1993).

Good introductions to speech recognition and speech synthesis are: (Waibel and Lee 1990; Rabiner and Juang 1993; Jelinek 1997).

3.6   Exercises

Exercise 3.1   [⋆]

What are the parts of speech of the words in the following paragraph?

(3.73)   The lemon is an essential cooking ingredient. Its sharply fragrant juice and tangy rind is added to sweet and savory dishes in every cuisine. This enchanting book, written by cookbook author John Smith, offers a wonderful array of recipes celebrating this internationally popular, intensely flavored fruit.

Exercise 3.2   [⋆]

Think of five examples of noun-noun compounds.

Exercise 3.3   [⋆]

Identify subject, direct object and indirect object in the following sentence.

(3.74)   He baked her an apple pie.

Exercise 3.4   [⋆]

What is the difference in meaning between the following two sentences?

(3.75)   a. Mary defended her.

b. Mary defended herself.

Exercise 3.5   [⋆]

What is the standard word order in the English sentence (a) for declaratives, (b) for imperatives, (c) for interrogatives?

Exercise 3.6   [⋆]

What are the comparative and superlative forms for the following adjectives and adverbs?

(3.76)   good, well, effective, big, curious, bad

Exercise 3.7   [⋆]

Give base form, third singular present tense form, past tense, past participle, and present participle for the following verbs.

(3.77)   throw, do, laugh, change, carry, bring, dream

Exercise 3.8   [⋆]

Transform the following sentences into the passive voice.

(3.78)   a. Mary carried the suitcase up the stairs.

b. Mary gave John the suitcase.

Exercise 3.9   [★]

What is the difference between a preposition and a particle? What grammatical function does *in* have in the following sentences?

(3.79)   a. Mary lives in London.

         b. When did Mary move in?

         c. She puts in a lot of hours at work.

         d. She put the document in the wrong folder.

Exercise 3.10   [★]

Give three examples each of transitive verbs and intransitive verbs.

Exercise 3.11   [★]

What is the difference between a complement and an adjunct? Are the italicized phrases in the following sentences complements or adjuncts? What type of complements or adjuncts?

(3.80)   a. She goes to Church *on Sundays.*

         b. She went *to London.*

         c. Peter relies *on Mary* for help with his homework.

         d. The book is lying *on the table.*

         e. She watched him *with a telescope.*

Exercise 3.12   [★]

The italicized phrases in the following sentences are examples of attachment ambiguity. What are the two possible interpretations?

(3.81)   Mary saw the man *with the telescope.*

(3.82)   The company experienced growth in classified advertising *and preprinted inserts.*

Exercise 3.13   [★]

Are the following phrases compositional or non-compositional?

(3.83)   to beat around the bush, to eat an orange, to kick butt, to twist somebody's arm, help desk, computer program, desktop publishing, book publishing, the publishing industry

Exercise 3.14   [★]

Are phrasal verbs compositional or non-compositional?

Exercise 3.15   [★]

In the following sentence, either *a few actors* or *everybody* can take wide scope over the sentence. What is the difference in meaning?

(3.84)   A few actors are liked by everybody.

4 *Corpus-Based Work*

THIS CHAPTER begins with some brief advice on getting set up to do corpus-based work. The main requirements for Statistical NLP work are computers, corpora, and software. Many of the details of computers and corpora are subject to rapid change, and so it does not make sense to dwell on these. Moreover, in many cases, one will have to make do with the computers and corpora at one's local establishment, even if they are not in all respects ideal. Regarding software, this book does not attempt to teach programming skills as it goes, but assumes that a reader interested in implementing any of the algorithms described herein can already program in *some* programming language. Nevertheless, we provide in this section a few pointers to languages and tools that may be generally useful.

After that the chapter covers a number of interesting issues concerning the formats and problems one encounters when dealing with 'raw data' – plain text in some electronic form. A very important, if often neglected, issue is the low-level processing which is done to the text before the real work of the research project begins. As we will see, there are a number of difficult issues in determining what is a word and what is a sentence. In practice these decisions are generally made by imperfect heuristic methods, and it is thus important to remember that the inaccuracies of these methods affect all subsequent results.

Finally the chapter turns to marked up data, where some process – often a human being – has added explicit markup to the text to indicate something of the structure and semantics of the document. This is often helpful, but raises its own questions about the kind and content of the markup used. We introduce the rudiments of SGML markup (and thus also XML) and then turn to substantive issues such as the choice of tag sets used in corpora marked up for part of speech.

4.1   Getting Set Up

4.1.1   Computers

Text corpora are usually big. It takes quite a lot of computational resources to deal with large amounts of text. In the early days of computing, this was the major limitation on the use of corpora. For example in the earliest years of work on constructing the Brown corpus (the 1960s), just sorting all the words in the corpus to produce a word list would take 17 hours of (dedicated) processing time. This was because the computer (an IBM 7070) had the equivalent of only about 40 kilobytes of memory, and so the sort algorithm had to store the data being sorted on tape drives. Today one can sort this amount of data within minutes on even a modest computer.

As well as needing plenty of space to store corpora, Statistical NLP methods often consist of a step of collecting a large number of counts from corpora, which one would like to access speedily. This means that one wants a computer with lots of hard disk space, and lots of memory. In a rapidly changing world, it does not make much sense to be more precise than this about the hardware one needs. Fortunately, all the change is in a good direction, and often all that one will need is a decent personal computer with its RAM cheaply expanded (whereas even a few years ago, a substantial sum of money was needed to get a suitably fast computer with sufficient memory and hard disk space).

4.1.2   Corpora

A selection of some of the main organizations that distribute text corpora for linguistic purposes are shown in table 4.1. Most of these organizations charge moderate sums of money for corpora.[1] If your budget does not extend to this, there are now numerous sources of free text, ranging from email and web pages, to the many books and (maga)zines

---

1. Prices vary enormously, but are normally in the range of US$100–2000 per CD for academic and nonprofit organizations, and reflect the considerable cost of collecting and processing material.

Linguistic Data Consortium (LDC)	http://www.ldc.upenn.edu
European Language Resources Association (ELRA)	http://www.icp.grenet.fr/ELRA/
International Computer Archive of Modern English (ICAME)	http://nora.hd.uib.no/icame.html
Oxford Text Archive (OTA)	http://ota.ahds.ac.uk/
Child Language Data Exchange System (CHILDES)	http://childes.psy.cmu.edu/

Table 4.1   Major suppliers of electronic corpora with contact URLs.

that are available free on the web. Such free sources will not bring you linguistically-marked-up corpora, but often there are tools that can do the task of adding markup automatically reasonably well, and at any rate, working out how to deal with raw text brings its own challenges. Further resources for online text can be found on the website.

When working with a corpus, we have to be careful about the validity of estimates or other results of statistical analysis that we produce. A corpus is a special collection of textual material collected according to a certain set of criteria. For example, the Brown corpus was designed as a representative sample of written American English as used in 1961 (Francis and Kučera 1982: 5–6). Some of the criteria employed in its construction were to include particular texts in amounts proportional to actual publication and to exclude verse because "it presents special linguistic problems" (p. 5).

As a result, estimates obtained from the Brown corpus do not necessarily hold for British English or spoken American English. For example, the estimates of the entropy of English in section 2.2.7 depend heavily on the corpus that is used for estimation. One would expect the entropy of poetry to be higher than that of other written text since poetry can flout semantic expectations and even grammar. So the entropy of the Brown corpus will not help much in assessing the entropy of poetry. A more mundane example is text categorization (see chapter 16) where the performance of a system can deteriorate significantly over time because a sample drawn for training at one point can lose its representativeness after a year or two.

REPRESENTATIVE SAMPLE   The general issue is whether the corpus is a *representative sample* of the population of interest. A sample is representative if what we find for the sample also holds for the general population. We will not discuss methods for determining representativeness here since this issue is dealt with at length in the corpus linguistics literature. We also refer

BALANCED CORPUS   the reader to this literature for creating *balanced corpora*, which are put together so as to give each subtype of text a share of the corpus that is proportional to some predetermined criterion of importance. In Statistical NLP, one commonly receives as a corpus a certain amount of data from a certain domain of interest, without having any say in how it is constructed. In such cases, having more training text is normally more useful than any concerns of balance, and one should simply use all the text that is available.

In summary, there is no easy way of determining whether a corpus is representative, but it is an important issue to keep in mind when doing Statistical NLP work. The minimal questions we should attempt to answer when we select a corpus or report results are what type of text the corpus is representative of and whether the results obtained will transfer to the domain of interest.

▼ The effect of corpus variability on the accuracy of part-of-speech tagging is discussed in section 10.3.2.

4.1.3   Software

There are many programs available for looking at text corpora and analyzing the data that you see. In general, however, we assume that readers will be writing their own software, and so all the software that is really needed is a plain text editor, and a compiler or interpreter for a language of choice. However, certain other tools, such as ones for searching through text corpora can often be of use. We briefly describe some such tools later.

Text editors

You will want a plain text editor that shows fairly literally what is actually in the file. Fairly standard and cheap choices are Emacs for Unix (or Windows), TextPad for Windows, and BBEdit for Macintosh.

Regular expressions

In many places and in many programs, editors, etc., one wishes to find certain patterns in text, that are often more complex than a simple match against a sequence of characters. The most general widespread notation
REGULAR EXPRESSIONS   for such matches are *regular expressions* which can describe patterns

REGULAR LANGUAGE that are a *regular language*, the kind that can be recognized by a finite state machine. If you are not already familiar with regular expressions, you will want to become familiar with them. Regular expressions can be used in many plain text editors (Emacs, TextPad, Nisus, BBEdit, ...), with many tools (such as grep and sed), and as built-ins or libraries in many programming languages (such as Perl, C, ...). Introductions to regular expressions can be found in (Hopcroft and Ullman 1979; Sipser 1996; Friedl 1997).

Programming languages

Most Statistical NLP work is currently done in C/C++. The need to deal with large amounts of data collection and processing from large texts means that the efficiency gains of coding in a language like C/C++ are generally worth it. But for a lot of the ancillary processing of text, there are many other languages which may be more economical with human labor. Many people use Perl for general text preparation and reformatting. Its integration of regular expressions into the language syntax is particularly powerful. In general, interpreted languages are faster for these kinds of tasks than writing everything in C. Old timers might still use awk rather than Perl – even though what you can do with it is rather more limited. Another choice, better liked by programming purists is Python, but using regular expressions in Python just is not as easy as Perl. One of the authors still makes considerable use of Prolog. The built-in database facilities and easy handling of complicated data structures makes Prolog excel for some tasks, but again, it lacks the easy access to regular expressions available in Perl. There are other languages such as SNOBOL/SPITBOL or Icon developed for text computing, and which are liked by some in the humanities computing world, but their use does not seem to have permeated into the Statistical NLP community. In the last few years there has been increasing uptake of Java. While not as fast as C, Java has many other appealing features, such as being object-oriented, providing automatic memory management, and having many useful libraries.

Programming techniques

This section is not meant as a substitute for a general knowledge of computer algorithms, but we briefly mention a couple of useful tips.

Coding words.   Normally Statistical NLP systems deal with a large number of words, and programming languages like C(++) provide only quite limited facilities for dealing with words. A method that is commonly used in Statistical NLP and Information Retrieval is to map words to numbers on input (and only back to words when needed for output). This gives a lot of advantages because things like equality can be checked more easily and quickly on numbers. It also maps all tokens of a word to its type, which has a single number. There are various ways to do this. One good way is to maintain a large hash table (a hash function maps a set of objects into a specified range of integers, for example, $[0, \ldots, 127]$). A hash table allows one to see efficiently whether a word has been seen before, and if so return its number, or else add it and assign a new number. The numbers used might be indices into an array of words (especially effective if one limits the application to 65,000 or fewer words, so they can be stored as 16 bit numbers) or they might just be the address of the canonical form of the string as stored in the hashtable. This is especially convenient on output, as then no conversion back to a word has to be done: the string can just be printed.

There are other useful data structures such as various kinds of trees. See a book on algorithms such as (Cormen et al. 1990) or (Frakes and Baeza-Yates 1992).

Collecting count data.   For a lot of Statistical NLP work, there is a first step of collecting counts of various observations, as a basis for estimating probabilities. The seemingly obvious way to do that is to build a big data structure (arrays or whatever) in which one counts each event of interest. But this can often work badly in practice since this model requires a huge memory address space which is being roughly randomly accessed. Unless your computer has enough memory for all those tables, the program will end up swapping a lot and will run very slowly. Often a better approach is for the data collecting program to simply emit a token representing each observation, and then for a follow on program to sort and then count these tokens. Indeed, these latter steps can often be done by existing system utilities (such as sort and uniq on Unix systems). Among other places, such a strategy is very successfully used in the CMU-Cambridge Statistical Language Modeling toolkit which can be obtained from the web (see website).

4.2 Looking at Text

MARKUP

Text will usually come in either a raw format, or marked up in some way. *Markup* is a term that is used for putting codes of some sort into a computer file, that are not actually part of the text in the file, but explain something of the structure or formatting of that text. Nearly all computer systems for dealing with text use mark-up of some sort. Commercial word processing software uses markup, but hides it from the user by employing WYSIWYG (What You See Is What You Get) display. Normally, when dealing with corpora in Statistical NLP, we will want explicit markup that we can see. This is part of why the first tool in a corpus linguist's toolbox is a plain text editor.

There are a number of features of text in human languages that can make them difficult to process automatically, even at a low level. Here we discuss some of the basic problems that one should be aware of. The discussion is dominated by, but not exclusively concerned with, the most fundamental problems in *English* text.

4.2.1 Low-level formatting issues

Junk formatting/content

OCR

Depending on the source of the corpus, there may be various formatting and content that one cannot deal with, and is just junk that needs to be filtered out. This may include: document headers and separators, typesetter codes, tables and diagrams, garbled data in the computer file, etc. If the data comes from *OCR* (Optical Character Recognition), the OCR process may have introduced problems such as headers, footers and floating material (tables, figures, and footnotes) breaking up the paragraphs of the text. There will also usually be OCR errors where words have been misrecognized. If your program is meant to deal with only connected English text, then other kinds of content such as tables and pictures need to be regarded as junk. Often one needs a filter to remove junk content before any further processing begins.

Uppercase and lowercase

The original Brown corpus was all capitals (a * before a letter was used to indicate a capital letter in the original source text). All uppercase text is rarely seen these days, but even with modern texts, there are questions of how to treat capitalization. In particular, if we have two tokens that are identical except that one has certain letters in uppercase, should we treat them as the same? For many purposes we would like to treat *the*, *The*, and *THE* as the same, for example if we just want to do a study of the usage of definite articles, or noun phrase structure. This is easily done by converting all words to upper- or lowercase, but the problem is that at the same time we would normally like to keep the two types of *Brown* in *Richard Brown* and *brown paint* distinct. In many circumstances it is easy to distinguish *proper names* and hence to keep this distinction, but sometimes it is not. A simple heuristic is to change to lowercase letters capital letters at the start of a sentence (where English regularly capitalizes all words) and in things like headings and titles when there is a series of words that are all in capitals, while other words with capital letters are assumed to be names and their uppercase letters are preserved. This heuristic works quite well, but naturally, there are problems. The first problem is that one has to be able to correctly identify the ends of sentences, which is not always easy, as we discuss later. In certain genres (such as *Winnie the Pooh*), words may be capitalized just to stress that they are making a Very Important Point, without them indicating a proper name. At any rate, the heuristic will wrongly lowercase names that appear sentence initially or in all uppercase sequences. Often this source of error can be tolerated (because regular words are usually more common than proper names), but sometimes this would badly bias estimates. One can attempt to do better by keeping lists of proper names (perhaps with further information on whether they name a person, place, or company), but in general there is not an easy solution to the problem of accurate proper name detection.

PROPER NAMES

4.2.2   Tokenization: What is a word?

Normally, an early step of processing is to divide the input text into units called *tokens* where each is either a *word* or something else like a number or a punctuation mark. This process is referred to as *tokenization*. The treatment of punctuation varies. While normally people want to keep sentence boundaries (see section 4.2.4 below), often sentence-internal punctuation has just been stripped out. This is probably unwise. Recent work has emphasized the information contained in all punctuation. No matter how imperfect a representation, punctuation marks like commas and

TOKENS
WORD
TOKENIZATION

dashes give some clues about the macro structure of the text and what is likely to modify what.

The question of what counts as a word is a vexed one in linguistics, and often linguists end up suggesting that there are words at various levels, such as phonological words versus syntactic words, which need not all be the same. What is a humble computational linguist meant to do? GRAPHIC WORD Kučera and Francis (1967) suggested the practical notion of a *graphic word* which they define as "a string of contiguous alphanumeric characters with space on either side; may include hyphens and apostrophes, but no other punctuation marks." But, unfortunately, life is not that simple, even if one is just looking for a practical, workable definition. Kučera and Francis seem in practice to use intuition, since they regard as words numbers and monetary amounts like *$22.50* which do not strictly seem to obey the definition above. And things get considerably worse. Especially if using online material such as newsgroups and web pages for data, but even if sticking to newswires, one finds all sorts of oddities that should presumably be counted as words, such as references to *Micro$oft* or the web company *C|net*, or the various forms of smilies made out of punctuation marks, such as :-). Even putting aside such creatures, working out word tokens is a quite difficult affair. The main clue used in English is WHITESPACE the occurrence of *whitespace* – a space or tab or the beginning of a new line between words – but even this signal is not necessarily reliable. What are the main problems?

Periods

Words are not always surrounded by white space. Often punctuation marks attach to words, such as commas, semicolons, and periods (full stops). It at first seems easy to remove punctuation marks from word tokens, but this is problematic for the case of periods. While most periods are end of sentence punctuation marks, others mark an abbreviation such as in *etc.* or *Calif.* These abbreviation periods presumably should remain as part of the word, and in some cases keeping them might be important so that we can distinguish *Wash.*, an abbreviation for the state of Washington, from the capitalized form of the verb *wash*. Note especially that when an abbreviation like *etc.* appears at the end of the sentence, then only one period occurs, but it serves both functions of the period, simultaneously! An example occurred with *Calif.* earlier in this paragraph. HAPLOLOGY Within morphology, this phenomenon is referred to as *haplology*.

The issue of working out which punctuation marks do indicate the end of a sentence is discussed further in section 4.2.4.

Single apostrophes

It is a difficult question to know how to regard English contractions such as *I'll* or *isn't*. These count as one *graphic word* according to the definition above, but many people have a strong intuition that we really have two words here as these are contractions for *I will* and *is not*. Thus some processors (and some corpora, such as the Penn Treebank) split such contractions into two words, while others do not. Note the impact that not splitting them has. The traditional first syntax rule:

$$\text{S} \longrightarrow \text{NP} \quad \text{VP}$$

stops being obviously true of sentences involving contractions such as *I'm right*. On the other hand, if one does split, there are then funny words like *'s* and *n't* in your data.

Phrases such as *the dog's* and *the child's*, when not abbreviations for *the dog is* or *the dog has*, are commonly seen as containing *dog's* as the genitive or possessive case of *dog*. But as we mentioned in section 3.1.1, CLITIC this is not actually correct for English where *'s* is a *clitic* which can attach to other elements in a noun phrase, such as in *The house I rented yesterday's garden is really big*. Thus it is again unclear whether to regard *dog's* as one word or two, and again the Penn Treebank opts for the latter. Orthographic-word-final single quotations are an especially tricky case. Normally they represent the end of a quotation – and so should not be part of a word, but when following an *s*, they may represent an (unpronounced) indicator of a plural possessive, as in *the boys' toys* – and then should be treated as part of the word, if other possessives are being so treated. There is no easy way for a tokenizer to determine which function is intended in many such cases.

Hyphenation: Different forms representing the same word

Perhaps one of the most difficult areas is dealing with hyphens in the input. Do sequences of letters with a hyphen in between count as one word or two? Again, the intuitive answer seems to be sometimes one, sometimes two. This reflects the many sources of hyphens in texts.

One source is typographical. Words have traditionally been broken and hyphens inserted to improve justification of text. These line-breaking hyphens may be present in data if it comes from what was actually typeset. It would seem to be an easy problem to just look for hyphens at the end of a line, remove them and join the part words at the end of one line and the beginning of the next. But again, there is the problem of haplology. If there is a hyphen from some other source, then after that hyphen is regarded as a legitimate place to break the text, and only one hyphen appears not two. So it is not always correct to delete hyphens at the end of a line, and it is difficult in general to detect which hyphens were line-breaking hyphens and which were not.

Even if such line-breaking hyphens are not present (and they usually are not in truly electronic texts), difficult problems remain. Some things with hyphens are clearly best treated as a single word, such as *e-mail* or *co-operate* or *A-1-plus* (as in *A-1-plus commercial paper*, a financial rating). Other cases are much more arguable, although we usually want to regard them as a single word, for example, *non-lawyer, pro-Arab*, and *so-called.* The hyphens here might be termed lexical hyphens. They are commonly inserted before or after small word formatives, sometimes for the purpose of splitting up vowel sequences.

The third class of hyphens is ones inserted to help indicate the correct grouping of words. A common copy-editing practice is to hyphenate compound pre-modifiers, as in the example earlier in this sentence or in examples like these:

(4.1) a. the once-quiet study of superconductivity

b. a tough regime of business-conduct rules

c. the aluminum-export ban

d. a text-based medium

And hyphens occur in other places, where a phrase is seen as in some sense quotative or as expressing a quantity or rate:

(4.2) a. the idea of a child-as-required-yuppie-possession must be motivating them

b. a final "take-it-or-leave-it" offer

c. the 90-cent-an-hour raise

d. the 26-year-old

In these cases, we would probably want to treat the things joined by hyphens as separate words. In many corpora this type of hyphenation is very common, and it would greatly increase the size of the word vocabulary (mainly with items outside a dictionary) and obscure the syntactic structure of the text if such things were not split apart into separate words.[2]

A particular problem in this area is that the use of hyphens in many such cases is extremely inconsistent. Some texts and authorities use *cooperate*, while others use *co-operate*. As another example, in the Dow Jones newswire, one can find all of *database*, *data-base* and *data base* (the first and third are commonest, with the former appearing to dominate in software contexts, and the third in discussions of company assets, but without there being any clear semantic distinction in usage). Closer to home, look back at the beginning of this section. When we initially drafted this chapter, we (quite accidentally) used all of *markup*, *mark-up* and *mark(ed) up*. A careful copy editor would catch this and demand consistency, but a lot of the text we use has never been past a careful copy editor, and at any rate, we will commonly use texts from different sources which often adopt different conventions in just such matters. Note that this means that we will often have multiple forms, perhaps some treated as one word and others as two, for what is best thought of as a single LEXEME *lexeme* (a single dictionary entry with a single meaning).

Finally, while British typographic conventions put spaces between dashes and surrounding words, American typographic conventions normally have a long dash butting straight up against the words—like this. While sometimes this dash will be rendered as a special character or as multiple dashes in a computer file, the limitations of traditional computer character sets means that it can sometimes be rendered just as a hyphen, which just further compounds the difficulties noted above.

The same form representing multiple 'words'

In the main we have been collapsing distinctions and suggesting that one may wish to regard variant sequences of characters as really the

---

2. One possibility is to split things apart, but to add markup, as discussed later in this chapter, which records that the original was hyphenated. In this way no information is lost.

same word. It is important to also observe the opposite problem, where one might wish to treat the identical sequence of characters as different

words. This happens with *homographs*, where two lexemes have overlapping forms, such as *saw* as a noun for a tool, or as the past tense of the verb *see*. In such cases we might wish to assign occurrences of *saw* to two different lexemes.

▼ Methods of doing this automatically are discussed in chapter 7.

Word segmentation in other languages

Many languages do not put spaces in between words at all, and so the basic word division algorithm of breaking on whitespace is of no use at all. Such languages include major East-Asian languages/scripts, such as Chinese, Japanese, and Thai. Ancient Greek was also written by Ancient Greeks without word spaces. Spaces were introduced (together with ac-

cent marks, etc.) by those who came afterwards. In such languages, *word segmentation* is a much more major and challenging task.

While maintaining most word spaces, in German compound nouns are written as a single word, for example *Lebensversicherungsgesellschafts-angestellter* 'life insurance company employee.' In many ways this makes linguistic sense, as compounds *are* a single word, at least phonologically. But for processing purposes one may wish to divide such a compound, or at least to be aware of the internal structure of the word, and this becomes a limited word segmentation task. While not the rule, joining of compounds sometimes also happens in English, especially when they are common and have a specialized meaning. We noted above that one finds both *data base* and *database*. As another example, while *hard disk* is more common, one sometimes finds *harddisk* in the computer press.

Whitespace not indicating a word break

Until now, the problems we have dealt with have mainly involved splitting apart sequences of characters where the word divisions are not shown by whitespace. But the opposite problem of wanting to lump things together also occurs. Here, things are separated by whitespace but we may wish to regard them as a single word. One possible case is the reverse of the German compound problem. If one decides to treat *database* as one word, one may wish to treat it as one word even when it is written as *data base*. More common cases are things such as phone numbers, where we may wish to regard *9365 1873* as a single 'word,' or in the cases of multi-part names such as *New York* or *San Francisco*. An especially difficult case is when this problem interacts with hyphenation as in a phrase like this one:

(4.3)   the New York-New Haven railroad

Here the hyphen does not express grouping of just the immediately adjacent graphic words – treating *York-New* as a semantic unit would be a big mistake.

Other cases are of more linguistic interest. For many purposes, one would want to regard phrasal verbs (*make up, work out*) as a single lexeme (section 3.1.4), but this case is especially tricky since in many cases the particle is separable from the verb (*I couldn't* **work** *the answer* **out**), and so in general identification of possible phrasal verbs will have to be left to subsequent processing. One might also want to treat as a single lexeme certain other fixed phrases, such as *in spite of, in order to*, and *because of*, but typically a tokenizer will regard them as separate words. A partial implementation of this approach occurs in the LOB corpus where certain pairs of words such as *because of* are tagged with a single part of DITTO TAGS speech, here preposition, by means of using so-called *ditto tags*.

Variant coding of information of a certain semantic type

Many readers may have felt that the example of a phone number in the previous section was not very recognizable or convincing because *their* phone numbers are written as 812-4374, or whatever. However, even if one is not dealing with multilingual text, any application dealing with text from different countries or written according to different stylistic conventions has to be prepared to deal with typographical differences. In particular, some items such as phone numbers are clearly of one semantic sort, but can appear in many formats. A selection of formats for phone numbers with their countries, all culled from advertisements in one issue of the magazine *The Economist*, is shown in table 4.2. Phone numbers variously use spaces, periods, hyphens, brackets, and even slashes to group digits in various ways, often not consistently even within one country. Additionally, phone numbers may include international or national long distance codes, or attempt to show both (as in the first three UK entries in the table), or just show a local number, and there may or may not be explicit indication of this via other marks such as brackets and plus

Phone number	Country	Phone number	Country
0171 378 0647	UK	+45 43 48 60 60	Denmark
(44.171) 830 1007	UK	95-51-279648	Pakistan
+44 (0) 1225 753678	UK	+411/284 3797	Switzerland
01256 468551	UK	(94-1) 866854	Sri Lanka
(202) 522-2230	USA	+49 69 136-2 98 05	Germany
1-925-225-3000	USA	33 1 34 43 32 26	France
212. 995.5402	USA	++31-20-5200161	The Netherlands

Table 4.2 Different formats for telephone numbers appearing in an issue of *The Economist*.

signs. Trying to deal with myriad formats like this is a standard prob-

INFORMATION
EXTRACTION

lem in *information extraction*. It has most commonly been dealt with by building carefully handcrafted regular expressions to match formats, but given the brittleness of such an approach, there is considerable interest in automatic means for learning the formatting of semantic types.

▼ We do not cover information extraction extensively in this book, but there is a little further discussion in section 10.6.2.

Speech corpora

Our discussion has concentrated on written text, but the transcripts of speech corpora provide their own additional challenges. Speech corpora normally have more contractions, various sorts of more phonetic representations, show pronunciation variants, contain many sentence fragments, and include fillers like *er* and *um*. Example (4.4) – from the Switchboard corpus available from the LDC – shows a typical extract from a speech transcript:

(4.4)   Also I [cough] not convinced that the, at least the kind of people that I work with, I'm not convinced that that's really, uh, doing much for the progr-, for the, uh, drug problem.

4.2.3   Morphology

Another question is whether one wants to keep word forms like *sit*, *sits* and *sat* separate or to collapse them. The issues here are similar to those in the discussion of capitalization, but have traditionally been regarded as more linguistically interesting. At first, grouping such forms together and working in terms of lexemes feels as if it is the right thing to do. Do-

ing this is usually referred to in the literature as *stemming* in reference to a process that strips off affixes and leaves you with a stem. Alternatively,

the process may be referred to as *lemmatization* where one is attempting

to find the *lemma* or *lexeme* of which one is looking at an inflected form. These latter terms imply disambiguation at the level of lexemes, such as whether a use of *lying* represents the verb *lie-lay* 'to prostrate oneself' or *lie-lied* 'to fib.'

Extensive empirical research within the Information Retrieval (IR) community has shown that doing stemming does not help the performance of classic IR systems when performance is measured as an average over queries (Salton 1989; Hull 1996). There are always some queries for which stemming helps a lot. But there are others where performance goes down. This is a somewhat surprising result, especially from the viewpoint of linguistic intuition, and so it is important to understand why that is. There are three main reasons for this.

One is that while grouping the various forms of a stem seems a good thing to do, it often costs you a lot of information. For instance, while *operating* can be used in a periphrastic tense form as in *Bill is operating a tractor* (section 3.1.3), it is usually used in noun- and adjective-like uses such as *operating systems* or *operating costs*. It is not hard to see why a search for *operating systems* will perform better if it is done on inflected words than if one instead searches for all paragraphs that contain *operat-* and *system*. Or to consider another example, if someone enters *business* and the stemmer then causes retrieval of documents with *busy* in them, the results are unlikely to be beneficial.

Secondly, morphological analysis splits one token into several. However, often it is worthwhile to group closely related information into chunks, notwithstanding the blowout in the vocabulary that this causes. Indeed, in various Statistical NLP domains, people have been able to improve system performance by regarding frequent multiword units as a single distinctive token. Often inflected words are a useful and effective chunk size.

Thirdly, most information retrieval studies have been done on English – although recently there has been increasing multilingual work. English has very little morphology, and so the need for dealing intelligently with morphology is not acute. Many other languages have far richer systems of inflection and derivation, and then there is a pressing need for mor-

FULL-FORM LEXICON phological analysis. A *full-form lexicon* for such languages, one that separately lists all inflected forms of all words, would simply be too large. For instance, Bantu languages (spoken in central and southern Africa) display rich verbal morphology. Here is a form from KiHaya (Tanzania). Note the prefixes for subject and object agreement, and tense:

(4.5)   akabimúha
        a-ka-bi-mú-ha
        1SG-PAST-3PL-3SG-give
        'I gave them to him.'

For historical reasons, some Bantu language orthographies write many of these morphemes with whitespace in between them, but in the languages with 'conjunctive' orthographies, morphological analysis is badly needed. There is an extensive system of pronoun and tense markers appearing before the verb root, and quite a few other morphemes that can appear after the root, yielding a large system of combinatoric possibilities. Finnish is another language famous for millions of inflected forms for each verb.

One might be tempted to conclude from the paragraphs above that, in languages with rich morphology, one would gain by stripping inflectional morphology but not derivational morphology. But this hypothesis remains to be carefully tested in languages where there is sufficient inflectional morphology for the question to be interesting.

It is important to realize that this result from IR need not apply to any or all Statistical NLP applications. It need not even apply to all of IR. Morphological analysis might be much more useful in other applications. Stemming does not help in the non-interactive evaluation of IR systems, where a query is presented and processed without further input, and the results are evaluated in terms of the appropriateness of the set of documents returned. However, principled morphological analysis is valuable in IR in an interactive context, the context in which IR should really be evaluated. A computer does not care about weird stems like *busy* from *business*, but people do. They do not understand what is going on when *business* is stemmed to *busy* and a document with *busy* in it is returned.

It is also the case that nobody has systematically studied the possibility of letting people interactively influence the stemming. We believe that this could be very profitable, for cases like *saw* (where you want to stem for the sense 'see,' but not for the sense 'cutting implement'), or derivational cases where in some cases you want the stems (*arbitrary* from *arbitrariness*), but in some you do not (*busy* from *business*). But the suggestion that human input may be needed does show the difficulties of doing automatic stemming in a knowledge-poor environment of the sort that has often been assumed in Statistical NLP work (for both ideological and practical reasons).

▼ Stemming and IR in general are further discussed in chapter 15.

4.2.4 Sentences

What is a sentence?

The first answer to what is a sentence is "something ending with a '.', '?' or '!'." We have already mentioned the problem that only some periods mark the end of a sentence: others are used to show an abbreviation, or for both these functions at once. Nevertheless, this basic heuristic gets one a long way: in general about 90% of periods are sentence boundary indicators (Riley 1989). There are a few other pitfalls to be aware of. Sometimes other punctuation marks split up what one might want to regard as a sentence. Often what is on one or the other or even both sides of the punctuation marks colon, semicolon, and dash (':', ';', and '—') might best be thought of as a sentence by itself, as ':' in this example:

(4.6)   The scene is written with a combination of unbridled passion and sure-handed control: In the exchanges of the three characters and the rise and fall of emotions, Mr. Weller has captured the heartbreaking inexorability of separation.

Related to this is the fact that sometimes sentences do not nicely follow in sequence, but seem to nest in awkward ways. While normally nested things are not seen as sentences by themselves, but clauses, this classification can be strained for cases such as the quoting of direct speech, where we get subsentences:

(4.7)   "You remind me," she remarked, "of your mother."

A second problem with such indirect speech is that it is standard typesetting practice (particularly in North America) to place quotation marks after sentence final punctuation. Therefore, the end of the sentence is not after the period in the example above, but after the close quotation mark that follows the period.

The above remarks suggest that the essence of a heuristic sentence division algorithm is roughly as in figure 4.1. In practice most systems

- Place putative sentence boundaries after all occurrences of . ? ! (and maybe ; : —)

- Move the boundary after following quotation marks, if any.

- Disqualify a period boundary in the following circumstances:

  - If it is preceded by a known abbreviation of a sort that does not normally occur word finally, but is commonly followed by a capitalized proper name, such as *Prof.* or *vs.*

  - If it is preceded by a known abbreviation and not followed by an uppercase word. This will deal correctly with most usages of abbreviations like *etc.* or *Jr.* which can occur sentence medially or finally.

- Disqualify a boundary with a ? or ! if:

  - It is followed by a lowercase letter (or a known name).

- Regard other putative sentence boundaries as sentence boundaries.

Figure 4.1 Heuristic sentence boundary detection algorithm.

have used heuristic algorithms of this sort. With enough effort in their development, they can work very well, at least within the textual domain for which they were built. But any such solution suffers from the same problems of heuristic processes in other parts of the tokenization process. They require a lot of hand-coding and domain knowledge on the part of the person constructing the tokenizer, and tend to be brittle and domain-specific.

There has been increasing research recently on more principled methods of sentence boundary detection. Riley (1989) used statistical classification trees to determine sentence boundaries. The features for the classification trees include the case and length of the words preceding and following a period, and the a priori probability of different words to occur before and after a sentence boundary (the computation of which requires a large quantity of labeled training data). Palmer and Hearst (1994; 1997) avoid the need for acquiring such data by simply using the part of speech distribution of the preceding and following words, and using a neural network to predict sentence boundaries. This yields a robust, largely language independent boundary detection algorithm with high performance (about 98–99% correct). Reynar and Ratnaparkhi (1997) and Mikheev (1998) develop Maximum Entropy approaches to the problem, the latter achieving an accuracy rate of 99.25% on sentence boundary prediction.[3]

▼ Sentence boundary detection can be viewed as a classification problem. We discuss classification, and methods such as classification trees and maximum entropy models in chapter 16.

What are sentences like?

In linguistics classes, and when doing traditional computational linguistics exercises, sentences are generally short. This is at least in part because many of the parsing tools that have traditionally been used have a runtime exponential in the sentence length, and therefore become impractical for sentences over twelve or so words. It is therefore important to realize that typical sentences in many text genres are rather long. In newswire, the modal (most common) length is normally around 23 words. A chart of sentence lengths in a sample of newswire text is shown in table 4.3.

4.3   Marked-up Data

While much can be done from plain text corpora, by inducing the structure present in the text, people have often made use of corpora where some of the structure is shown, since it is then easier to learn more. This markup may be done by hand, automatically, or by a mixture of these two methods. Automatic means of learning structure are covered in the remainder of this book. Here we discuss the basics of markup. Some texts mark up just a little basic structure such as sentence and paragraph boundaries, while others mark up a lot, such as the full syntactic structure in corpora like the Penn Treebank and the Susanne corpus. However, the most common grammatical markup that one finds is a coding of words for part of speech, and so we devote particular attention to that.

---

3. *Accuracy* as a technical term is defined and discussed in section 8.1. However, the definition corresponds to one's intuitive understanding: it is the percent of the time that one is correctly classifying items.

Length	Number	Percent	Cum. %
1–5	1317	3.13	3.13
6–10	3215	7.64	10.77
11–15	5906	14.03	24.80
16–20	7206	17.12	41.92
21–25	7350	17.46	59.38
26–30	6281	14.92	74.30
31–35	4740	11.26	85.56
36–40	2826	6.71	92.26
41–45	1606	3.82	96.10
46–50	858	2.04	98.14
51–100	780	1.85	99.99
101+	6	0.01	100.00

Table 4.3 Sentence lengths in newswire text. Column "Percent" shows the percentage in each range, column "Cum. %" shows the cumulative percentage below a certain length.

4.3.1 Markup schemes

Various schemes have been used to mark up the structure of text. In the early days, these were developed on an ad hoc basis, as needs arose. One of the more important early examples was the COCOA format, which was used for including header information in texts (giving author, date, title, etc.). This information was enclosed within angle brackets with the first letter indicating the broad semantics of the field. Some other ad hoc systems of this sort are still in quite common use. The most common form of grammatical markup, which we discuss in great detail below, is indicating the part of speech of words by adding a part of speech tag to each word. These tags are commonly indicated by devices such as following each word by a slash or underline and then a short code naming the part of speech. The Penn Treebank uses a form of Lisp-like bracketing to mark up a tree structure over texts.

STANDARD
GENERALIZED MARKUP
LANGUAGE

However, currently by far the most common and supported form of markup is to use SGML (the *Standard Generalized Markup Language*). SGML is a general language that lets one define a grammar for texts, in particular for the type of markup they contain. The now-ubiquitous HTML is an instance of an SGML encoding. The Text Encoding Initiative (TEI) was a major attempt to define SGML encoding schemes suitable for marking up various kinds of humanities text resources ranging from poems and novels to linguistic resources like dictionaries. Another acronym to be

aware of is XML. XML defines a simplified subset of SGML that was particularly designed for web applications. However, the weight of commercial support behind XML and the fact that it avoids some of the rather arcane, and perhaps also archaic, complexities in the original SGML specification means that the XML subset is likely to be widely adopted for all other purposes as well.

This book does not delve deeply into SGML. We will give just the rudimentary knowledge needed to get going. SGML specifies that each doc-

ument type should have a *Document Type Definition* (DTD), which is a grammar for legal structures for the document. For example, it can state rules that a paragraph must consist of one or more sentences and nothing else. An SGML parser verifies that a document is in accordance with this DTD, but within Statistical NLP the DTD is normally ignored and people just process whatever text is found. An SGML document consists of one or more elements, which may be recursively nested. Elements normally begin with a begin tag and end with an end tag, and have document content in between. Tags are contained within angle brackets, and end tags begin with a forward slash character. As well as the tag name, the begin tag may contain additional attribute and value information. A couple of examples of SGML elements are shown below:

(4.8)   a. `<p><s>And then he left.</s>`
            `<s>He did not say another word.</s></p>`

       b. `<utt speak="Fred" date="10-Feb-1998">That is an ugly couch.</utt>`

The structure tagging shown in (4.8a), where the tag s is used for sentences and p for paragraphs, is particularly widespread. Example (4.8b) shows a tag with attributes and values. An element may also consist of just a single tag (without any matching end tag). In XML, such empty elements must be specially marked by ending the tag name with a forward slash character.

In general, when making use of SGML-encoded text in a casual way, one will wish to interpret some tags within angle brackets, and to simply ignore others. The other SGML syntax that one must be aware of is character and entity references. These begin with an ampersand and end with a semicolon. Character references are a way of specifying characters not available in the standard ASCII character set (minus the reserved SGML markup characters) via their numeric code. Entity references have symbolic names which were defined in the DTD (or are one of a few predefined entities). Entity references may expand to any text, but are commonly used just to encode a special character via a symbolic name. A few examples of character and entity references are shown in (4.9). They might be rendered in a browser or when printed as shown in (4.10).

(4.9) a. `&#x43; is the less than symbol`

   b. `r&eacute;sum&eacute;`

   c. `This chapter was written on &docdate;.`

(4.10) a. < is the less than symbol

   b. résumé

   c. This chapter was written on January 21, 1998.

There is much more to know about SGML, and some references appear in the Further Reading below, but this is generally enough for what the XML community normally terms the 'Desperate Perl Hacker' to get by.

4.3.2 Grammatical tagging

A common first step of analysis is to perform automatic grammatical tagging for categories roughly akin to conventional parts of speech, but often considerably more detailed (for instance, distinguishing comparative and superlative forms of adjectives, or singular from plural nouns). This section examines the nature of tag sets. What tag sets have been used? Why do people use different ones? Which one should you choose? ▼ How tagging is done automatically is the subject of chapter 10.

Tag sets

BROWN TAG SET

Historically, the most influential tag sets have been the one used for tagging the American Brown corpus (the *Brown tag set*) and the series of tag sets developed at the University of Lancaster, and used for tagging the Lancaster-Oslo-Bergen corpus and more recently the British National

Sentence	CLAWS c5	Brown	Penn Treebank	ICE
she	PNP	PPS	PRP	PRON(pers,sing)
was	VBD	BEDZ	VBD	AUX(pass,past)
told	VVN	VBN	VBN	V(ditr,edp)
that	CJT	CS	IN	CONJUNC(subord)
the	AT0	AT	DT	ART(def)
journey	NN1	NN	NN	N(com,sing)
might	VM0	MD	MD	AUX(modal,past)
kill	VVI	VB	VB	V(montr,infin)
her	PNP	PPO	PRP	PRON(poss,sing)
.	PUN	.	.	PUNC(per)

Figure 4.2   A sentence as tagged according to several different tag sets.

Tag set	Basic size	Total tags
Brown	87	179
Penn	45	
CLAWS1	132	
CLAWS2	166	
CLAWS c5	62	
London-Lund	197	

Table 4.4   Sizes of various tag sets.

Corpus (CLAWS1 through CLAWS5; CLAWS5 is also referred to as the *c5 tag set*). Recently, the *Penn Treebank tag set* has been the one most widely used in computational work. It is a simplified version of the Brown tag set. A brief summary of tag set sizes is shown in table 4.4. An example sentence shown tagged via several different tag sets is shown in figure 4.2. These tag sets are all for English. In general, tag sets incorporate morphological distinctions of a particular language, and so are not directly applicable to other languages (though often some of the design ideas can be transferred). Many tag sets for other languages have also been developed.

An attempt to align some tag sets, roughly organized by traditional parts of speech appears in tables 4.5 and 4.6, although we cannot guarantee that they are accurate in every detail. They are mostly alphabetical, but we have deviated from alphabetical order a little so as to group cat-

Category	Examples	Claws c5	Brown	Penn
Adjective	happy, bad	AJ0	JJ	JJ
Adjective, ordinal number	sixth, 72nd, last	ORD	OD	JJ
Adjective, comparative	happier, worse	AJC	JJR	JJR
Adjective, superlative	happiest, worst	AJS	JJT	JJS
Adjective, superlative, semantically	chief, top	AJ0	JJS	JJ
Adjective, cardinal number	3, fifteen	CRD	CD	CD
Adjective, cardinal number, one	one	PNI	CD	CD
Adverb	often, particularly	AV0	RB	RB
Adverb, negative	not, n't	XX0	*	RB
Adverb, comparative	faster	AV0	RBR	RBR
Adverb, superlative	fastest	AV0	RBT	RBS
Adverb, particle	up, off, out	AVP	RP	RP
Adverb, question	when, how, why	AVQ	WRB	WRB
Adverb, degree & question	how, however	AVQ	WQL	WRB
Adverb, degree	very, so, too	AV0	QL	RB
Adverb, degree, postposed	enough, indeed	AV0	QLP	RB
Adverb, nominal	here, there, now	AV0	RN	RB
Conjunction, coordination	and, or	CJC	CC	CC
Conjunction, subordinating	although, when	CJS	CS	IN
Conjunction, complementizer *that*	that	CJT	CS	IN
Determiner	this, each, another	DT0	DT	DT
Determiner, pronoun	any, some	DT0	DTI	DT
Determiner, pronoun, plural	these, those	DT0	DTS	DT
Determiner, prequalifier	quite	DT0	ABL	PDT
Determiner, prequantifier	all, half	DT0	ABN	PDT
Determiner, pronoun or double conj.	both	DT0	ABX	DT (CC)
Determiner, pronoun or double conj.	either, neither	DT0	DTX	DT (CC)
Determiner, article	the, a, an	AT0	AT	DT
Determiner, postdeterminer	many, same	DT0	AP	JJ
Determiner, possessive	their, your	DPS	PP$	PRP$
Determiner, possessive, second	mine, yours	DPS	PP$$	PRP
Determiner, question	which, whatever	DTQ	WDT	WDT
Determiner, possessive & question	whose	DTQ	WP$	WP$
Noun	aircraft, data	NN0	NN	NN
Noun, singular	woman, book	NN1	NN	NN
Noun, plural	women, books	NN2	NNS	NNS
Noun, proper, singular	London, Michael	NP0	NP	NNP
Noun, proper, plural	Australians, Methodists	NP0	NPS	NNPS
Noun, adverbial	tomorrow, home	NN0	NR	NN
Noun, adverbial, plural	Sundays, weekdays	NN2	NRS	NNS
Pronoun, nominal (indefinite)	none, everything, one	PNI	PN	NN
Pronoun, personal, subject	you, we	PNP	PPSS	PRP
Pronoun, personal, subject, 3SG	she, he, it	PNP	PPS	PRP
Pronoun, personal, object	you, them, me	PNP	PPO	PRP
Pronoun, reflexive	herself, myself	PNX	PPL	PRP
Pronoun, reflexive, plural	themselves, ourselves	PNX	PPLS	PRP
Pronoun, question, subject	who, whoever	PNQ	WPS	WP
Pronoun, question, object	who, whoever	PNQ	WPO	WP
Pronoun, existential there	there	EX0	EX	EX

Table 4.5 Comparison of different tag sets: adjective, adverb, conjunction, determiner, noun, and pronoun tags.

Category	Examples	Claws c5	Brown	Penn
Verb, base present form (not infinitive)	take, live	VVB	VB	VBP
Verb, infinitive	take, live	VVI	VB	VB
Verb, past tense	took, lived	VVD	VBD	VBD
Verb, present participle	taking, living	VVG	VBG	VBG
Verb, past/passive participle	taken, lived	VVN	VBN	VBN
Verb, present 3SG -*s* form	takes, lives	VVZ	VBZ	VBZ
Verb, auxiliary *do*, base	do	VDB	DO	VBP
Verb, auxiliary *do*, infinitive	do	VDB	DO	VB
Verb, auxiliary *do*, past	did	VDD	DOD	VBD
Verb, auxiliary *do*, present part.	doing	VDG	VBG	VBG
Verb, auxiliary *do*, past part.	done	VDN	VBN	VBN
Verb, auxiliary *do*, present 3SG	does	VDZ	DOZ	VBZ
Verb, auxiliary *have*, base	have	VHB	HV	VBP
Verb, auxiliary *have*, infinitive	have	VHI	HV	VB
Verb, auxiliary *have*, past	had	VHD	HVD	VBD
Verb, auxiliary *have*, present part.	having	VHG	HVG	VBG
Verb, auxiliary *have*, past part.	had	VHN	HVN	VBN
Verb, auxiliary *have*, present 3SG	has	VHZ	HVZ	VBZ
Verb, auxiliary *be*, infinitive	be	VBI	BE	VB
Verb, auxiliary *be*, past	were	VBD	BED	VBD
Verb, auxiliary *be*, past, 3SG	was	VBD	BEDZ	VBD
Verb, auxiliary *be*, present part.	being	VBG	BEG	VBG
Verb, auxiliary *be*, past part.	been	VBN	BEN	VBN
Verb, auxiliary *be*, present, 3SG	is, 's	VBZ	BEZ	VBZ
Verb, auxiliary *be*, present, 1SG	am, 'm	VBB	BEM	VBP
Verb, auxiliary *be*, present	are, 're	VBB	BER	VBP
Verb, modal	can, could, 'll	VM0	MD	MD
Infinitive marker	to	TO0	TO	TO
Preposition, to	to	PRP	IN	TO
Preposition	for, above	PRP	IN	IN
Preposition, of	of	PRF	IN	IN
Possessive	's, '	POS	$	POS
Interjection (or other isolate)	oh, yes, mmm	ITJ	UH	UH
Punctuation, sentence ender	. ! ?	PUN	.	.
Punctuation, semicolon	;	PUN	.	:
Punctuation, colon or ellipsis	: ...	PUN	:	:
Punctuation, comma	,	PUN	,	,
Punctuation, dash	–	PUN	–	–
Punctuation, dollar sign	$	PUN	not	$
Punctuation, left bracket	([{	PUL	(	(
Punctuation, right bracket	)] }	PUR	)	)
Punctuation, quotation mark, left	' "	PUQ	not	"
Punctuation, quotation mark, right	' "	PUQ	not	"
Foreign words (not in English lexicon)		UNC	(FW-)	FW
Symbol	[fj] *		not	SYM
Symbol, alphabetical	A, B, c, d	ZZ0		
Symbol, list item	A A. First			LS

Table 4.6 Comparison of different tag sets: Verb, preposition, punctuation and symbol tags. An entry of 'not' means an item was ignored in tagging, or was not separated off as a separate token.

egories that are sometimes collapsed. In this categorization, we use an elsewhere convention where the least marked category is used in all cases where a word cannot be placed within one of the more precise subclassifications. For instance, the plain Adjective category is used for adjectives that aren't comparatives, superlatives, numbers, etc. The complete Brown tag set was made larger by two decisions to augment the tag set. Normal tags could be followed by a hyphen and an attribute like TL (for a title word), or in the case of foreign words, the FW foreign word tag was followed by a hyphen and a part of speech assignment. Secondly, the Brown tag scheme makes use of 'combined tags' for graphic words that one might want to think of as multiple lexemes, such as *you'll*.[4] Normally such items were tagged with two tags joined with a plus sign, but for negation one just adds * to a tag. So *isn't* is tagged BEZ* and *she'll* is tagged PPS+MD. Additionally, possessive forms like *children's* are tagged with a tag ending in '$'. Normally, these tags are transparently derived from a base non-possessive tag, for instance, NNS$ in this case. These techniques of expanding the tag set are ignored in the comparison.

Even a cursory glance will show that the tag sets are very different. Part of this can be attributed to the overall size of the tag set. A larger tag set will obviously make more fine-grained distinctions. But this is not the only difference. The tag sets may choose to make distinctions in different areas. For example, the c5 tag set is larger overall than the Penn Treebank tag set, and it makes many more distinctions in some areas, but in other areas it has chosen to make many fewer. For instance, the Penn tag set distinguishes 9 punctuation tags, while c5 makes do with only 4. Presumably this indicates some difference of opinion on what is considered important. Tag sets also disagree more fundamentally in how to classify certain word classes. For example, while the Penn tag set simply regards subordinating conjunctions as prepositions (consonant with work in generative linguistics), the c5 tag set keeps them separate, and moreover implicitly groups them with other types of conjunctions. The notion of implicit grouping referred to here is that all the tag sets informally show relationships between certain sets of tags by having them begin with the same letter or pair of letters. This grouping is implicit in that although it is obvious to the human eye, they are formally just distinct symbolic

---

4. Compare the discussion above. This is also done in some other corpora, such as the London-Lund corpus, but the recent trend seems to have been towards dividing such graphic words into two for the purposes of tagging.

tags, and programs normally make no use of these families. However, in some other tag sets, such as the one for the International Corpus of English (Greenbaum 1993), an explicit system of high level tags with attributes for the expression of features has been adopted. There has also been some apparent development in people's ideas of what to encode. The early tag sets made very fine distinctions in a number of areas such as the treatment of certain sorts of qualifiers and determiners that were relevant to only a few words, albeit common ones. More recent tag sets have generally made fewer distinctions in such areas.

The design of a tag set

What features should guide the design of a tag set? Standardly, a tag set encodes both the target feature of classification, telling the user the useful information about the grammatical class of a word, and the predictive features, encoding features that will be useful in predicting the behavior of other words in the context. These two tasks should overlap, but they are not necessarily identical.

PART OF SPEECH   The notion of part of speech is actually complex, since parts of speech can be motivated on various grounds, such as semantic (commonly called notional) grounds, syntactic distributional grounds, or morphological grounds. Often these notions of part of speech are in conflict. For the purposes of prediction, one would want to use the definition of part of speech that best predicts the behavior of nearby words, and this is presumably strictly distributional tags. But in practice people have often used tags that reflect notional or morphological criteria. For example one of the uses of English present participles ending in *-ing* is as a gerund where they behave as a noun. But in the Brown corpus they are quite regularly tagged with the VBG tag, which is perhaps better reserved for verbal uses of participles. This happens even within clear noun compounds such as this one:

(4.11)   Fulton/NP-TL County/NN-TL Purchasing/VBG Department/NN

Ideally, we would want to give distinctive tags to words that have distinctive distributions, so that we can use that information to help processing elsewhere. This would suggest that some of the tags in, for example, the Penn Treebank tag set are too coarse to be good predictors. For instance, the complementizer *that* has a very distinct distribution from regular prepositions, and degree adverbs and the negative *not* have very different distributions from regular adverbs, but neither of these distinctions show up in the tag set. People have frequently made changes to add or remove distinctions according to their intuitions – for example, Charniak (1996) questions the decision of the Penn Treebank to tag auxiliaries with the same tags as other verbs, given that auxiliary verbs have a very distinctive distribution, and proceeds to retag them with an AUX tag. In general, the predictive value of making such changes in the set of distinctions in part of speech systems has not been very systematically evaluated. So long as the same tag set is used for prediction and classification, making such changes tends to be a two-edged sword: splitting tags to capture useful distinctions gives improved information for prediction, but makes the classification task harder.[5] For this reason, there is not necessarily a simple relationship between tag set size and the performance of automatic taggers.

4.4 Further Reading

The Brown corpus (the Brown University Standard Corpus of Present-Day American English) consists of just over a million words of written American English from 1961. It was compiled and documented by W. Nelson Francis and Henry Kučera (Francis and Kučera 1964; Kučera and Francis 1967; Francis and Kučera 1982). The details on early processing of the Brown corpus are from an email from Henry Kučera (posted to the corpora mailing list by Katsuhide Sonoda on 26 Sep 1996). The LOB (Lancaster-Oslo-Bergen) corpus was built as a British-English replication of the Brown Corpus during the 1970s (Johansson et al. 1978; Garside et al. 1987).

Identifying proper names is a major issue in Information Extraction. See (Cardie 1997) for an introduction.

A carefully designed and experimentally tested set of tokenization rules is the set used for the Susanne corpus (Sampson 1995: 52–59).

PUNCTUATION   Nunberg (1990) provides a linguistic perspective on the importance of *punctuation*. An introductory discussion of what counts as a word in linguistics can be found in (Crowley et al. 1995: 7–9). Lyons (1968: 194–206) provides a more thorough discussion. The examples in the section on hyphenation are mainly real examples from the Dow Jones newswire.

---

5. This is unless one category groups two very separate distributional clusters, in which case splitting the category can actually sometimes make classification easier.

Others are from e-mail messages to the corpora list by Robert Amsler and Mitch Marcus, 1996, and are used with thanks.

There are many existing systems for morphological analysis available, and some are listed on the website. An effective method of doing stemming in a knowledge-poor way can be found in Kay and Röscheisen (1993). Sproat (1992) contains a good discussion of the problems morphology presents for NLP and is the source of our German compound example.

The COCOA (COunt and COncordance on Atlas) format was used in corpora from ICAME and in related software such as LEXA (Hickey 1993).

SGML and XML are described in various books (Herwijnen 1994; McGrath 1997; St. Laurent 1998), and a lot of information, including some short readable introductions, is available on the web (see website).

The guidelines of the Text Encoding initiative (1994 P3 version) are published as McQueen and Burnard (1994), and include a very readable introduction to SGML in chapter 2. In general, though, rather than read the actual guidelines, one wants to look at tutorials such as Ide and Véronis (1995), or on the web, perhaps starting at the sites listed on the website. The full complexity of the TEI overwhelmed all but the most dedicated standard bearers. Recent developments include TEILite, which tries to pare the original standard down to a human-usable version, and the Corpus Encoding Standard, a TEI-conformant SGML instance especially designed for language engineering corpora.

Early work on CLAWS (Constituent-Likelihood Automatic Word-tagging System) and its tag set is described in (Garside et al. 1987). The more recent c5 tag set presented above is taken from (Garside 1995). The Brown tag set is described in (Francis and Kučera 1982) while the Penn tag set is described in (Marcus et al. 1993), and in more detail in (Santorini 1990).

This book is not an introduction to how corpora are used in linguistic studies (even though it contains a lot of methods and algorithms useful for such studies). However, recently there has been a flurry of new texts CORPUS LINGUISTICS on *corpus linguistics* (McEnery and Wilson 1996; Stubbs 1996; Biber et al. 1998; Kennedy 1998; Barnbrook 1996). These books also contain much more discussion of corpus design issues such as sampling and balance than we have provided here. For an article specifically addressing the problem of designing a representative corpus, see (Biber 1993).

More details about different tag sets are collected in Appendix B of (Garside et al. 1987) and in the web pages of the AMALGAM project (see website). The AMALGAM website also has a description of the tokenizing rules that they use, which can act as an example of a heuristic sentence divider and tokenizer. Grefenstette and Tapanainen (1994) provide another discussion of tokenization, showing the results of experiments employing simple knowledge-poor heuristics.

4.5 Exercises

Exercise 4.1 [⋆ ⋆]

As discussed in the text, it seems that for most purposes, we'd want to treat some hyphenated things as words (for instance, *co-worker, Asian-American*), but not others (for instance, *ain't-it-great-to-be-a-Texan, child-as-required-yuppie-possession*). Find hyphenated forms in a corpus and suggest some basis for which forms we would want to treat as words and which we would not. What are the reasons for your decision? (Different choices may be appropriate for different needs.) Suggest some methods to identify hyphenated sequences that should be broken up – e.g., ones that only appear as non-final elements of compound nouns:

> [N *[child-as-required-yuppie-possession] syndrome]*

Exercise 4.2 [⋆ ⋆   For linguists]

Take some linguistic problem that you are interested in (non-constituent coordination, ellipsis, idioms, heavy NP shift, pied-piping, verb class alternations, etc.). Could one hope to find useful data pertaining to this problem in a general corpus? Why or why not? If you think it might be possible, is there a reasonable way to search for examples of the phenomenon in either a raw corpus or one that shows syntactic structures? If the answer to both these questions is yes, then look for examples in a corpus and report on anything interesting that you find.

Exercise 4.3 [⋆ ⋆]

Develop a sentence boundary detection algorithm. Evaluate how successful it is. (In the construction of the *Wall Street Journal* section of the ACL-DCI CD-ROM (Church and Liberman 1991), a rather simplistic sentence boundary detection algorithm was used, and the results were not hand corrected, so many errors remain. If this corpus is available to you, you may want to compare your results with the sentence boundaries marked in the corpus. With luck, you should be able to write a system that performs considerably better!)

PART II

Words

*"When I say, for instance, 'I had a good breakfast this morning,'
it is clear that I am not in the throes of laborious thought, that
what I have to transmit is hardly more than a pleasurable
memory symbolically rendered in the grooves of habitual
expression. ... It is somewhat as though a dynamo capable of
generating enough power to run an elevator were operated
almost exclusively to feed an electric doorbell."*

(Sapir 1921: 14)

5 *Collocations*

A COLLOCATION is an expression consisting of two or more words that correspond to some conventional way of saying things. Or in the words of Firth (1957: 181): "Collocations of a given word are statements of the habitual or customary places of that word." Collocations include noun phrases like *strong tea* and *weapons of mass destruction*, phrasal verbs like *to make up*, and other stock phrases like *the rich and powerful*. Particularly interesting are the subtle and not-easily-explainable patterns of word usage that native speakers all know: why we say *a stiff breeze* but not *??a stiff wind* (while either *a strong breeze* or *a strong wind* is okay), or why we speak of *broad daylight* (but not *?bright daylight* or *??narrow darkness*).

COMPOSITIONALITY   Collocations are characterized by limited *compositionality*. We call a natural language expression compositional if the meaning of the expression can be predicted from the meaning of the parts. Collocations are not fully compositional in that there is usually an element of meaning added to the combination. In the case of *strong tea, strong* has acquired the meaning *rich in some active agent* which is closely related, but slightly different from the basic sense *having great physical strength*. Idioms are the most extreme examples of non-compositionality. Idioms like *to kick the bucket* or *to hear it through the grapevine* only have an indirect historical relationship to the meanings of the parts of the expression. We are not talking about buckets or grapevines literally when we use these idioms. Most collocations exhibit milder forms of non-compositionality, like the expression *international best practice* that we used as an example earlier in this book. It is very nearly a systematic composition of its parts, but still has an element of added meaning. It usually refers to administrative efficiency and would, for example, not be used to describe a cooking technique although that meaning would be compatible with its literal meaning.

There is considerable overlap between the concept of *collocation* and notions like *term, technical term,* and *terminological phrase.* As these names suggest, the latter three are commonly used when collocations are extracted from technical domains (in a process called *terminology extraction*). The reader should be warned, though, that the word *term* has a different meaning in information retrieval. There, it refers to both words and phrases. So it subsumes the more narrow meaning that we will use in this chapter.

Collocations are important for a number of applications: natural language generation (to make sure that the output sounds natural and mistakes like *powerful tea* or *to take a decision* are avoided), computational lexicography (to automatically identify the important collocations to be listed in a dictionary entry), parsing (so that preference can be given to parses with natural collocations), and corpus linguistic research (for instance, the study of social phenomena like the reinforcement of cultural stereotypes through language (Stubbs 1996)).

There is much interest in collocations partly because this is an area that has been neglected in structural linguistic traditions that follow Saussure and Chomsky. There is, however, a tradition in British linguistics, associated with the names of Firth, Halliday, and Sinclair, which pays close attention to phenomena like collocations. Structural linguistics concentrates on general abstractions about the properties of phrases and sentences. In contrast, Firth's *Contextual Theory of Meaning* emphasizes the importance of context: the context of the social setting (as opposed to the idealized speaker), the context of spoken and textual discourse (as opposed to the isolated sentence), and, important for collocations, the context of surrounding words (hence Firth's famous dictum that a word is characterized by the company it keeps). These contextual features easily get lost in the abstract treatment that is typical of structural linguistics.

CONTEXTUAL THEORY
OF MEANING

A good example of the type of problem that is seen as important in this contextual view of language is Halliday's example of strong vs. powerful tea (Halliday 1966: 150). It is a convention in English to talk about *strong tea*, not *powerful tea*, although any speaker of English would also understand the latter unconventional expression. Arguably, there are no interesting structural properties of English that can be gleaned from this contrast. However, the contrast may tell us something interesting about attitudes towards different types of substances in our culture (why do we use *powerful* for drugs like heroin, but not for cigarettes, tea and coffee?) and it is obviously important to teach this contrast to students who want to learn idiomatically correct English. Social implications of language use and language teaching are just the type of problem that British linguists following a Firthian approach are interested in.

In this chapter, we will introduce a number of approaches to finding collocations: selection of collocations by frequency, selection based on mean and variance of the distance between focal word and collocating word, hypothesis testing, and mutual information. We will then return to the question of what a collocation is and discuss in more depth different definitions that have been proposed and tests for deciding whether a phrase is a collocation or not. The chapter concludes with further readings and pointers to some of the literature that we were not able to include.

The reference corpus we will use in examples in this chapter consists of four months of the *New York Times* newswire: from August through November of 1990. This corpus has about 115 megabytes of text and roughly 14 million words. Each approach will be applied to this corpus to make comparison easier. For most of the chapter, the *New York Times* examples will only be drawn from fixed two-word phrases (or bigrams). It is important to keep in mind, however, that we chose this pool for convenience only. In general, both fixed and variable word combinations can be collocations. Indeed, the section on mean and variance looks at the more loosely connected type.

5.1 Frequency

Surely the simplest method for finding collocations in a text corpus is counting. If two words occur together a lot, then that is evidence that they have a special function that is not simply explained as the function that results from their combination.

Predictably, just selecting the most frequently occurring bigrams is not very interesting as is shown in table 5.1. The table shows the bigrams (sequences of two adjacent words) that are most frequent in the corpus and their frequency. Except for *New York*, all the bigrams are pairs of function words.

There is, however, a very simple heuristic that improves these results a lot (Justeson and Katz 1995b): pass the candidate phrases through a

$C(w^1\ w^2)$	w^1	w^2
80871	of	the
58841	in	the
26430	to	the
21842	on	the
21839	for	the
18568	and	the
16121	that	the
15630	at	the
15494	to	be
13899	in	a
13689	of	a
13361	by	the
13183	with	the
12622	from	the
11428	New	York
10007	he	said
9775	as	a
9231	is	a
8753	has	been
8573	for	a

Table 5.1 Finding Collocations: Raw Frequency. $C(\cdot)$ is the frequency of something in the corpus.

Tag Pattern	Example
A N	*linear function*
N N	*regression coefficients*
A A N	*Gaussian random variable*
A N N	*cumulative distribution function*
N A N	*mean squared error*
N N N	*class probability function*
N P N	*degrees of freedom*

Table 5.2 Part of speech tag patterns for collocation filtering. These patterns were used by Justeson and Katz to identify likely collocations among frequently occurring word sequences.

$C(w^1\ w^2)$	w^1	w^2	Tag Pattern
11487	New	York	A N
7261	United	States	A N
5412	Los	Angeles	N N
3301	last	year	A N
3191	Saudi	Arabia	N N
2699	last	week	A N
2514	vice	president	A N
2378	Persian	Gulf	A N
2161	San	Francisco	N N
2106	President	Bush	N N
2001	Middle	East	A N
1942	Saddam	Hussein	N N
1867	Soviet	Union	A N
1850	White	House	A N
1633	United	Nations	A N
1337	York	City	N N
1328	oil	prices	N N
1210	next	year	A N
1074	chief	executive	A N
1073	real	estate	A N

Table 5.3 Finding Collocations: Justeson and Katz' part-of-speech filter.

part-of-speech filter which only lets through those patterns that are likely to be 'phrases.'[1] Justeson and Katz (1995b: 17) suggest the patterns in table 5.2. Each is followed by an example from the text that they use as a test set. In these patterns A refers to an adjective, P to a preposition, and N to a noun.

Table 5.3 shows the most highly ranked phrases after applying the filter. The results are surprisingly good. There are only 3 bigrams that we would not regard as non-compositional phrases: *last year*, *last week*, and *first time*. *York City* is an artefact of the way we have implemented the Justeson and Katz filter. The full implementation would search for the longest sequence that fits one of the part-of-speech patterns and would thus find the longer phrase *New York City*, which contains *York City*.

The twenty highest ranking phrases containing *strong* and *powerful* all

1. Similar ideas can be found in (Ross and Tukey 1975) and (Kupiec et al. 1995).

w	$C(strong, w)$	w	$C(powerful, w)$
support	50	force	13
safety	22	computers	10
sales	21	position	8
opposition	19	men	8
showing	18	computer	8
sense	18	man	7
message	15	symbol	6
defense	14	military	6
gains	13	machines	6
evidence	13	country	6
criticism	13	weapons	5
possibility	11	post	5
feelings	11	people	5
demand	11	nation	5
challenges	11	forces	5
challenge	11	chip	5
case	11	Germany	5
supporter	10	senators	4
signal	9	neighbor	4
man	9	magnet	4

Table 5.4 The nouns w occurring most often in the patterns '*strong w*' and '*powerful w*.'

have the form A N (where A is either *strong* or *powerful*). We have listed them in table 5.4.

Again, given the simplicity of the method, these results are surprisingly accurate. For example, they give evidence that *strong challenge* and *powerful computers* are correct whereas *powerful challenge* and *strong computers* are not. However, we can also see the limits of a frequency-based method. The nouns *man* and *force* are used with both adjectives (*strong force* occurs further down the list with a frequency of 4). A more sophisticated analysis is necessary in such cases.

Neither *strong tea* nor *powerful tea* occurs in our *New York Times* corpus. However, searching the larger corpus of the World Wide Web we find 799 examples of *strong tea* and 17 examples of *powerful tea* (the latter mostly in the computational linguistics literature on collocations), which indicates that the correct phrase is *strong tea.*[2]

Justeson and Katz' method of collocation discovery is instructive in that it demonstrates an important point. A simple quantitative technique (the frequency filter in this case) combined with a small amount of linguistic knowledge (the importance of parts of speech) goes a long way. In the rest of this chapter, we will use a stop list that excludes words whose most frequent tag is not a verb, noun or adjective.

Exercise 5.1   [⋆]

Add part-of-speech patterns useful for collocation discovery to table 5.2, including patterns longer than two tags.

Exercise 5.2   [⋆]

Pick a document in which your name occurs (an email, a university transcript or a letter). Does Justeson and Katz's filter identify your name as a collocation?

Exercise 5.3   [⋆]

We used the World Wide Web as an auxiliary corpus above because neither *stong tea* nor *powerful tea* occurred in the *New York Times*. Modify Justeson and Katz's method so that it uses the World Wide Web as a resource of last resort.

5.2 Mean and Variance

Frequency-based search works well for fixed phrases. But many collocations consist of two words that stand in a more flexible relationship to one another. Consider the verb *knock* and one of its most frequent arguments, *door*. Here are some examples of knocking on or at a door from our corpus:

(5.1)   a. she knocked on his door

      b. they knocked at the door

      c. 100 women knocked on Donaldson's door

      d. a man knocked on the metal front door

The words that appear between *knocked* and *door* vary and the distance between the two words is not constant so a fixed phrase approach would not work here. But there is enough regularity in the patterns to allow us to determine that *knock* is the right verb to use in English for this situation, not *hit, beat* or *rap*.

---

2. This search was performed on AltaVista on March 28, 1998.

Sentence: *Stocks crash as rescue plan teeters*

Bigrams: *stocks crash*   *stocks as*   *stocks rescue*
                    crash as   *crash rescue*   *crash plan*
                                as rescue   *as plan*   *as teeters*
                                            rescue plan   *rescue teeters*
                                                        plan teeters

Figure 5.1   Using a three word collocational window to capture bigrams at a distance.

A short note is in order here on collocations that occur as a fixed phrase versus those that are more variable. To simplify matters we only look at fixed phrase collocations in most of this chapter, and usually at just bigrams. But it is easy to see how to extend techniques applicable to bigrams to bigrams at a distance. We define a collocational window (usually a window of 3 to 4 words on each side of a word), and we enter *every* word pair in there as a collocational bigram, as in figure 5.1. We then proceed to do our calculations as usual on this larger pool of bigrams.

However, the mean and variance based methods described in this section by definition look at the pattern of varying distance between two words. If that pattern of distances is relatively predictable, then we have evidence for a collocation like *knock ... door* that is not necessarily a fixed phrase. We will return to this point and a more in-depth discussion of what a collocation is towards the end of this chapter.

MEAN   One way of discovering the relationship between *knocked* and *door* is to
VARIANCE   compute the *mean* and *variance* of the offsets (signed distances) between the two words in the corpus. The mean is simply the average offset. For the examples in (5.1), we compute the mean offset between *knocked* and *door* as follows:

$$\frac{1}{4}(3 + 3 + 5 + 5) = 4.0$$

(This assumes a tokenization of *Donaldson's* as three words *Donaldson*, apostrophe, and *s*, which is what we actually did.) If there was an occurrence of *door* before *knocked*, then it would be entered as a negative number. For example, -3 for *the door that she knocked on*. We restrict our analysis to positions in a window of size 9 around the focal word *knocked*.

The variance measures how much the individual offsets deviate from the mean. We estimate it as follows.

(5.2)
$$s^2 = \frac{\sum_{i=1}^{n}(d_i - \bar{d})^2}{n - 1}$$

where n is the number of times the two words co-occur, d_i is the offset for co-occurrence i, and $\bar{d}$ is the sample mean of the offsets. If the offset is the same in all cases, then the variance is zero. If the offsets are randomly distributed (which will be the case for two words which occur together by chance, but not in a particular relationship), then the variance will be

SAMPLE DEVIATION high. As is customary, we use the *sample deviation* $s = \sqrt{s^2}$, the square root of the variance, to assess how variable the offset between two words is. The deviation for the four examples of *knocked / door* in the above case is 1.15:

$$s = \sqrt{\frac{1}{3}((3 - 4.0)^2 + (3 - 4.0)^2 + (5 - 4.0)^2 + (5 - 4.0)^2)} \approx 1.15$$

The mean and deviation characterize the distribution of distances between two words in a corpus. We can use this information to discover collocations by looking for pairs with low deviation. A low deviation means that the two words usually occur at about the same distance. Zero deviation means that the two words always occur at exactly the same distance.

We can also explain the information that variance gets at in terms of peaks in the distribution of one word with respect to another. Figure 5.2 shows the three cases we are interested in. The distribution of *strong* with respect to *opposition* has one clear peak at position -1 (corresponding to the phrase *strong opposition*). Therefore the variance of *strong* with respect to *opposition* is small ($s = 0.67$). The mean of -1.15 indicates that *strong* usually occurs at position -1 (disregarding the noise introduced by one occurrence at -4).

We have restricted positions under consideration to a window of size 9 centered around the word of interest. This is because collocations are essentially a local phenomenon. Note also that we always get a count of 0 at position 0 when we look at the relationship between two different words. This is because, for example, *strong* cannot appear in position 0 in contexts in which that position is already occupied by *opposition*.

Moving on to the second diagram in figure 5.2, the distribution of *strong* with respect to *support* is drawn out, with several negative positions having large counts. For example, the count of approximately 20

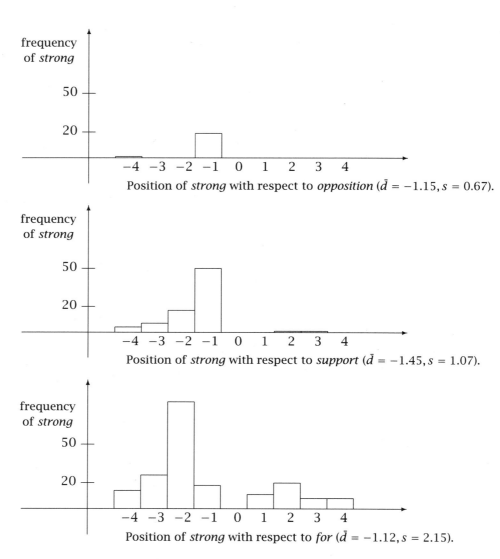

Figure 5.2   Histograms of the position of *strong* relative to three words.

s	$\bar{d}$	Count	Word 1	Word 2
0.43	0.97	11657	New	York
0.48	1.83	24	previous	games
0.15	2.98	46	minus	points
0.49	3.87	131	hundreds	dollars
4.03	0.44	36	editorial	Atlanta
4.03	0.00	78	ring	New
3.96	0.19	119	point	hundredth
3.96	0.29	106	subscribers	by
1.07	1.45	80	strong	support
1.13	2.57	7	powerful	organizations
1.01	2.00	112	Richard	Nixon
1.05	0.00	10	Garrison	said

Table 5.5 Finding collocations based on mean and variance. Sample deviation s and sample mean $\bar{d}$ of the distances between 12 word pairs.

at position -2 is due to uses like *strong leftist support* and *strong business support*. Because of this greater variability we get a higher s (1.07) and a mean that is between positions -1 and -2 (-1.45).

Finally, the occurrences of *strong* with respect to *for* are more evenly distributed. There is tendency for *strong* to occur before *for* (hence the negative mean of -1.12), but it can pretty much occur anywhere around *for*. The high deviation of $s = 2.15$ indicates this variability. This indicates that *for* and *strong* don't form interesting collocations.

The word pairs in table 5.5 indicate the types of collocations that can be found by this approach. If the mean is close to 1.0 and the deviation low, as is the case for *New York*, then we have the type of phrase that Justeson and Katz' frequency-based approach will also discover. If the mean is much greater than 1.0, then a low deviation indicates an interesting phrase. The pair *previous / games* (distance 2) corresponds to phrases like *in the previous 10 games* or *in the previous 15 games*; *minus / points* corresponds to phrases like *minus 2 percentage points*, *minus 3 percentage points* etc; *hundreds / dollars* corresponds to *hundreds of billions of dollars* and *hundreds of millions of dollars*.

High deviation indicates that the two words of the pair stand in no interesting relationship as demonstrated by the four high-variance examples in table 5.5. Note that means tend to be close to zero here as one would expect for a uniform distribution. More interesting are the cases in between, word pairs that have large counts for several distances in their collocational distribution. We already saw the example of *strong { business } support* in figure 5.2. The alternations captured in the other three medium-variance examples are *powerful { lobbying } organizations*, *Richard { M. } Nixon*, and *Garrison said / said Garrison* (remember that we tokenize *Richard M. Nixon* as four tokens: *Richard, M, ., Nixon*).

The method of variance-based collocation discovery that we have introduced in this section is due to Smadja. We have simplified things somewhat. In particular, Smadja (1993) uses an additional constraint that filters out 'flat' peaks in the position histogram, that is, peaks that are not surrounded by deep valleys (an example is at −2 for the combination *strong / for* in figure 5.2). Smadja (1993) shows that the method is quite successful at terminological extraction (with an estimated accuracy of 80%) and at determining appropriate phrases for natural language generation (Smadja and McKeown 1990).

Smadja's notion of collocation is less strict than many others'. The combination *knocked / door* is probably not a collocation we want to classify as terminology – although it may be very useful to identify for the purpose of text generation. Variance-based collocation discovery is the appropriate method if we want to find this type of word combination, combinations of words that are in a looser relationship than fixed phrases and that are variable with respect to intervening material and relative position.

5.3 Hypothesis Testing

One difficulty that we have glossed over so far is that high frequency and low variance can be accidental. If the two constituent words of a frequent bigram like *new companies* are frequently occurring words (as *new* and *companies* are), then we expect the two words to co-occur a lot just by chance, even if they do not form a collocation.

What we really want to know is whether two words occur together more often than chance. Assessing whether or not something is a chance event is one of the classical problems of statistics. It is usually couched in terms of hypothesis testing. We formulate a *null hypothesis* H_0 that there is no association between the words beyond chance occurrences, compute the probability p that the event would occur if H_0 were true, and then reject

NULL HYPOTHESIS

SIGNIFICANCE LEVEL H_0 if p is too low (typically if beneath a *significance level* of $p < 0.05$, 0.01, 0.005, or 0.001) and retain H_0 as possible otherwise.[3]

It is important to note that this is a mode of data analysis where we look at two things at the same time. As before, we are looking for particular patterns in the data. But we are also taking into account how much data we have seen. Even if there is a remarkable pattern, we will discount it if we haven't seen enough data to be certain that it couldn't be due to chance.

How can we apply the methodology of hypothesis testing to the problem of finding collocations? We first need to formulate a null hypothesis which states what should be true if two words do not form a collocation. For such a free combination of two words we will assume that each of the words w^1 and w^2 is generated completely independently of the other, and so their chance of coming together is simply given by:

$$P(w^1 w^2) = P(w^1)P(w^2)$$

The model implies that the probability of co-occurrence is just the product of the probabilities of the individual words. As we discuss at the end of this section, this is a rather simplistic model, and not empirically accurate, but for now we adopt independence as our null hypothesis.

5.3.1 The *t* test

Next we need a statistical test that tells us how probable or improbable it is that a certain constellation will occur. A test that has been widely used for collocation discovery is the *t* test. The *t* test looks at the mean and variance of a sample of measurements, where the null hypothesis is that the sample is drawn from a distribution with mean μ. The test looks at the difference between the observed and expected means, scaled by the variance of the data, and tells us how likely one is to get a sample of that mean and variance (or a more extreme mean and variance) assuming that the sample is drawn from a normal distribution with mean μ. To determine the probability of getting our sample (or a more extreme sample), we compute the *t* statistic:

(5.3) $$t = \frac{\bar{x} - \mu}{\sqrt{\frac{s^2}{N}}}$$

---

3. Significance at a level of 0.05 is the weakest evidence that is normally accepted in the experimental sciences. The large amounts of data commonly available for Statistical NLP tasks means that we can often expect to achieve greater levels of significance.

where $\bar{x}$ is the sample mean, s^2 is the sample variance, N is the sample size, and μ is the mean of the distribution. If the t statistic is large enough we can reject the null hypothesis. We can find out exactly how large it has to be by looking up the table of the t distribution we have compiled in the appendix (or by using the better tables in a statistical reference book, or by using appropriate computer software).

Here's an example of applying the t test. Our null hypothesis is that the mean height of a population of men is 158cm. We are given a sample of 200 men with $\bar{x} = 169$ and $s^2 = 2600$ and want to know whether this sample is from the general population (the null hypothesis) or whether it is from a different population of smaller men. This gives us the following t according to the above formula:

$$t = \frac{169 - 158}{\sqrt{\frac{2600}{200}}} \approx 3.05$$

If you look up the value of t that corresponds to a confidence level of $\alpha = 0.005$, you will find 2.576.[4] Since the t we got is larger than 2.576, we can reject the null hypothesis with 99.5% confidence. So we can say that the sample is not drawn from a population with mean 158cm, and our probability of error is less than 0.5%.

To see how to use the t test for finding collocations, let us compute the t value for *new companies*. What is the sample that we are measuring the mean and variance of? There is a standard way of extending the t test for use with proportions or counts. We think of the text corpus as a long sequence of N bigrams, and the samples are then indicator random variables that take on the value 1 when the bigram of interest occurs, and are 0 otherwise.

Using maximum likelihood estimates, we can compute the probabilities of *new* and *companies* as follows. In our corpus, *new* occurs 15,828 times, *companies* 4,675 times, and there are 14,307,668 tokens overall.

$$P(new) = \frac{15828}{14307668}$$

$$P(companies) = \frac{4675}{14307668}$$

---

4. A sample of 200 means 199 degress of freedom, which corresponds to about the same t as ∞ degrees of freedom. This is the row of the table where we looked up 2.576.

The null hypothesis is that occurrences of *new* and *companies* are independent.

$$H_0 : P(new\ companies) = P(new)P(companies)$$
$$= \frac{15828}{14307668} \times \frac{4675}{14307668} \approx 3.615 \times 10^{-7}$$

If the null hypothesis is true, then the process of randomly generating bigrams of words and assigning 1 to the outcome *new companies* and 0 to any other outcome is in effect a Bernoulli trial with $p = 3.615 \times 10^{-7}$ for the probability of *new company* turning up. The mean for this distribution is $\mu = 3.615 \times 10^{-7}$ and the variance is $\sigma^2 = p(1 - p)$ (see section 2.1.9), which is approximately p. The approximation $\sigma^2 = p(1 - p) \approx p$ holds since for most bigrams p is small.

It turns out that there are actually 8 occurrences of *new companies* among the 14,307,668 bigrams in our corpus. So, for the sample, we have that the sample mean is: $\bar{x} = \frac{8}{14307668} \approx 5.591 \times 10^{-7}$. Now we have everything we need to apply the t test:

$$t = \frac{\bar{x} - \mu}{\sqrt{\frac{s^2}{N}}} \approx \frac{5.591 10^{-7} - 3.615 10^{-7}}{\sqrt{\frac{5.591 10^{-7}}{14307668}}} \approx 0.999932$$

This t value of 0.999932 is not larger than 2.576, the critical value for $\alpha = 0.005$. So we cannot reject the null hypothesis that *new* and *companies* occur independently and do not form a collocation. That seems the right result here: the phrase *new companies* is completely compositional and there is no element of added meaning here that would justify elevating it to the status of collocation. (The t value is suspiciously close to 1.0, but that is a coincidence. See exercise 5.5.)

Table 5.6 shows t values for ten bigrams that occur exactly 20 times in the corpus. For the top five bigrams, we can reject the null hypothesis that the component words occur independently for $\alpha = 0.005$, so these are good candidates for collocations. The bottom five bigrams fail the test for significance, so we will not regard them as good candidates for collocations.

Note that a frequency-based method would not be able to rank the ten bigrams since they occur with exactly the same frequency. Looking at the counts in table 5.6, we can see that the t test takes into account the number of co-occurrences of the bigram ($C(w^1\ w^2)$) relative to the frequencies of the component words. If a high proportion of the occurrences of both words (*Ayatollah Ruhollah*, *videocassette recorder*) or at least a very high

t	$C(w^1)$	$C(w^2)$	$C(w^1 \, w^2)$	w^1	w^2
4.4721	42	20	20	Ayatollah	Ruhollah
4.4721	41	27	20	Bette	Midler
4.4720	30	117	20	Agatha	Christie
4.4720	77	59	20	videocassette	recorder
4.4720	24	320	20	unsalted	butter
2.3714	14907	9017	20	first	made
2.2446	13484	10570	20	over	many
1.3685	14734	13478	20	into	them
1.2176	14093	14776	20	like	people
0.8036	15019	15629	20	time	last

Table 5.6 Finding collocations: The *t* test applied to 10 bigrams that occur with frequency 20.

proportion of the occurrences of one of the words (*unsalted*) occurs in the bigram, then its *t* value is high. This criterion makes intuitive sense.

Unlike most of this chapter, the analysis in table 5.6 includes some stop words – without stop words, it is actually hard to find examples that fail significance. It turns out that most bigrams attested in a corpus occur significantly more often than chance. For 824 out of the 831 bigrams that occurred 20 times in our corpus the null hypothesis of independence can be rejected. But we would only classify a fraction as true collocations. The reason for this surprisingly high proportion of possibly dependent bigrams ($\frac{824}{831} \approx 0.99$) is that language – if compared with a random word generator – is very regular so that few completely unpredictable events happen. Indeed, this is the basis of our ability to perform tasks like word sense disambiguation and probabilistic parsing that we discuss in other chapters. The *t* test and other statistical tests are most useful as a method for *ranking* collocations. The level of significance itself is less useful. In fact, in most publications that we cite in this chapter, the level of significance is never looked at. All that is used is the scores and the resulting ranking.

5.3.2 Hypothesis testing of differences

The *t* test can also be used for a slightly different collocation discovery problem: to find words whose co-occurrence patterns best distinguish

t	$C(w)$	$C(strong\ w)$	$C(powerful\ w)$	Word
3.1622	933	0	10	computers
2.8284	2337	0	8	computer
2.4494	289	0	6	symbol
2.4494	588	0	6	machines
2.2360	2266	0	5	Germany
2.2360	3745	0	5	nation
2.2360	395	0	5	chip
2.1828	3418	4	13	force
2.0000	1403	0	4	friends
2.0000	267	0	4	neighbor
7.0710	3685	50	0	support
6.3257	3616	58	7	enough
4.6904	986	22	0	safety
4.5825	3741	21	0	sales
4.0249	1093	19	1	opposition
3.9000	802	18	1	showing
3.9000	1641	18	1	sense
3.7416	2501	14	0	defense
3.6055	851	13	0	gains
3.6055	832	13	0	criticism

Table 5.7 Words that occur significantly more often with *powerful* (the first ten words) and *strong* (the last ten words).

between two words. For example, in computational lexicography we may want to find the words that best differentiate the meanings of *strong* and *powerful*. This use of the *t* test was suggested by Church and Hanks (1989). Table 5.7 shows the ten words that occur most significantly more often with *powerful* than with *strong* (first ten words) and most significantly more often with *strong* than with *powerful* (second set of ten words).

The *t* scores are computed using the following extension of the *t* test to the comparison of the means of two normal populations:

$$(5.4) \qquad t = \frac{\bar{x}_1 - \bar{x}_2}{\sqrt{\frac{s_1^2}{n_1} + \frac{s_2^2}{n_2}}}$$

Here the null hypothesis is that the average difference is 0 ($\mu = 0$), so we have $\bar{x} - \mu = \bar{x} = \frac{1}{N} \sum (x_{1_i} - x_{2_i}) = \bar{x}_1 - \bar{x}_2$. In the denominator we add the variances of the two populations since the variance of the difference of two random variables is the sum of their individual variances.

Now we can explain table 5.7. The t values in the table were computed assuming a Bernoulli distribution (as we did for the basic version of the t test that we introduced first). If w is the collocate of interest (e.g., *computers* or *symbol*) and v^1 and v^2 are the words we are comparing (e.g., *powerful* and *strong*), then we have $\bar{x}_1 = s_1^2 = P(v^1 w)$, $\bar{x}_2 = s_2^2 = P(v^2 w)$. We again use the approximation $s^2 = p - p^2 \approx p$:

$$t \approx \frac{P(v^1 w) - P(v^2 w)}{\sqrt{\frac{P(v^1 w) + P(v^2 w)}{N}}}$$

We can simplify this as follows.

$$(5.5) \quad t \quad \approx \quad \frac{\frac{C(v^1 w)}{N} - \frac{C(v^2 w)}{N}}{\sqrt{\frac{C(v^1 w) + C(v^2 w)}{N^2}}}$$

$$= \quad \frac{C(v^1 w) - C(v^2 w)}{\sqrt{C(v^1 w) + C(v^2 w)}}$$

where $C(x)$ is the number of times x occurs in the corpus.

The application suggested by Church and Hanks (1989) for this form of the t test was lexicography. The data in table 5.7 are useful to a lexicographer who wants to write precise dictionary entries that bring out the difference between *strong* and *powerful*. Based on significant collocates, Church and Hanks analyze the difference as a matter of intrinsic vs. extrinsic quality. For example, *strong* support from a demographic group means that the group is very committed to the cause in question, but the group may not have any power. So *strong* describes an intrinsic quality. Conversely, a *powerful* supporter is somebody who actually has the power to move things. Many of the collocates we found in our corpus support Church and Hanks' analysis. But there is more complexity to the difference in meaning between the two words since what is extrinsic and intrinsic can depend on subtle matters like cultural attitudes. For example, we talk about *strong tea* on the one hand and *powerful drugs* on the other, a difference that tells us more about our attitude towards tea and drugs than about the semantics of the two adjectives (Church et al. 1991: 133).

	$w_1 = new$	$w_1 \neq new$
$w_2 = companies$	8	4667
	(*new companies*)	(e.g., *old companies*)
$w_2 \neq companies$	15820	14287181
	(e.g., *new machines*)	(e.g., *old machines*)

Table 5.8 A 2-by-2 table showing the dependence of occurrences of *new* and *companies*. There are 8 occurrences of *new companies* in the corpus, 4,667 bigrams where the second word is *companies*, but the first word is not *new*, 15,820 bigrams with the first word *new* and a second word different from *companies*, and 14,287,181 bigrams that contain neither word in the appropriate position.

5.3.3   Pearson's chi-square test

Use of the t test has been criticized because it assumes that probabilities are approximately normally distributed, which is not true in general (Church and Mercer 1993: 20). An alternative test for dependence which does not assume normally distributed probabilities is the χ^2 test (pronounced 'chi-square test'). In the simplest case, the χ^2 test is applied to 2-by-2 tables like table 5.8. The essence of the test is to compare the observed frequencies in the table with the frequencies expected for independence. If the difference between observed and expected frequencies is large, then we can reject the null hypothesis of independence.

Table 5.8 shows the distribution of *new* and *companies* in the reference corpus that we introduced earlier. Recall that $C(new) = 15,828$, $C(companies) = 4,675$, $C(new\ companies) = 8$, and that there are 14,307,668 tokens in the corpus. That means that the number of bigrams $w_i w_{i+1}$ with the first token not being *new* and the second token being *companies* is $4667 = 4675 - 8$. The two cells in the bottom row are computed in a similar way.

The χ^2 statistic sums the differences between observed and expected values in all squares of the table, scaled by the magnitude of the expected values, as follows:

$$(5.6) \quad X^2 = \sum_{i,j} \frac{(O_{ij} - E_{ij})^2}{E_{ij}}$$

where i ranges over rows of the table, j ranges over columns, O_{ij} is the observed value for cell (i, j) and E_{ij} is the expected value.

One can show that the quantity X^2 is asymptotically χ^2 distributed. In other words, if the numbers are large, then X^2 has a χ^2 distribution. We will return to the issue of how good this approximation is later.

The expected frequencies E_{ij} are computed from the marginal proba-bilities, that is, from the totals of the rows and columns converted into proportions. For example, the expected frequency for cell $(1, 1)$ (*new companies*) would be the marginal probability of *new* occurring as the first part of a bigram times the marginal probability of *companies* occur-ring as the second part of a bigram (multiplied by the number of bigrams in the corpus):

$$\frac{8 + 4667}{N} \times \frac{8 + 15820}{N} \times N \approx 5.2$$

That is, if *new* and *companies* occurred completely independently of each other we would expect 5.2 occurrences of *new companies* on average for a text of the size of our corpus.

The χ^2 test can be applied to tables of any size, but it has a simpler form for 2-by-2 tables: (see exercise 5.9)

(5.7) $$\chi^2 = \frac{N(O_{11}O_{22} - O_{12}O_{21})^2}{(O_{11} + O_{12})(O_{11} + O_{21})(O_{12} + O_{22})(O_{21} + O_{22})}$$

This formula gives the following χ^2 value for table 5.8:

$$\frac{14307668(8 \times 14287181 - 4667 \times 15820)^2}{(8 + 4667)(8 + 15820)(4667 + 14287181)(15820 + 14287181)} \approx 1.55$$

Looking up the χ^2 distribution in the appendix, we find that at a proba-bility level of $\alpha = 0.05$ the critical value is $\chi^2 = 3.841$ (the statistic has one degree of freedom for a 2-by-2 table). So we cannot reject the null hypothesis that *new* and *companies* occur independently of each other. Thus *new companies* is not a good candidate for a collocation.

This result is the same as we got with the t statistic. In general, for the problem of finding collocations, the differences between the t statistic and the χ^2 statistic do not seem to be large. For example, the 20 bigrams with the highest t scores in our corpus are also the 20 bigrams with the highest χ^2 scores.

However, the χ^2 test is also appropriate for large probabilities, for which the normality assumption of the t test fails. This is perhaps the reason that the χ^2 test has been applied to a wider range of problems in collocation discovery.

One of the early uses of the χ^2 test in Statistical NLP was the identifi-

	cow	¬ cow
vache	59	6
¬ vache	8	570934

Table 5.9 Correspondence of *vache* and *cow* in an aligned corpus. By applying the χ^2 test to this table one can determine whether *vache* and *cow* are translations of each other.

	corpus 1	corpus 2
word 1	60	9
word 2	500	76
word 3	124	20
	. . .	

Table 5.10 Testing for the independence of words in different corpora using χ^2. This test can be used as a metric for corpus similarity.

cation of translation pairs in aligned corpora (Church and Gale 1991b).[5] The data in table 5.9 (from a hypothetical aligned corpus) strongly suggest that *vache* is the French translation of English *cow*. Here, 59 is the number of aligned sentence pairs which have *cow* in the English sentence and *vache* in the French sentence etc. The χ^2 value is very high here: $\chi^2 = 456400$. So we can reject the null hypothesis that *cow* and *vache* occur independently of each other with high confidence. This pair is a good candidate for a translation pair.

An interesting application of χ^2 is as a metric for corpus similarity (Kilgarriff and Rose 1998). Here we compile an *n*-by-two table for a large *n*, for example $n = 500$. The two columns correspond to the two corpora. Each row corresponds to a particular word. This is schematically shown in table 5.10. If the ratio of the counts are about the same (as is the case in table 5.10, each word occurs roughly 6 times more often in corpus 1 than in corpus 2), then we cannot reject the null hypothesis that both corpora are drawn from the same underlying source. We can interpret this as a high degree of similarity. On the other hand, if the ratios vary wildly, then the X^2 score will be high and we have evidence for a high degree of dissimilarity.

---

5. They actually use a measure they call ϕ^2, which is X^2 multiplied by N. They do this since they are only interested in ranking translation pairs, so that assessment of significance is not important.

	H_1	H_2
$P(w^2\|w^1)$	$p = \frac{c_2}{N}$	$p_1 = \frac{c_{12}}{c_1}$
$P(w^2\|\neg w^1)$	$p = \frac{c_2}{N}$	$p_2 = \frac{c_2 - c_{12}}{N - c_1}$
c_{12} out of c_1 bigrams are w^1w^2	$b(c_{12}; c_1, p)$	$b(c_{12}; c_1, p_1)$
$c_2 - c_{12}$ out of $N - c_1$ bigrams are $\neg w^1w^2$	$b(c_2 - c_{12}; N - c_1, p)$	$b(c_2 - c_{12}; N - c_1, p_2)$

Table 5.11 How to compute Dunning's likelihood ratio test. For example, the likelihood of hypothesis H_2 is the product of the last two lines in the rightmost column.

Just as application of the t test is problematic because of the underlying normality assumption, so is application of χ^2 in cases where the numbers in the 2-by-2 table are small. Snedecor and Cochran (1989: 127) advise against using χ^2 if the total sample size is smaller than 20 or if it is between 20 and 40 and the expected value in any of the cells is 5 or less.

5.3.4 Likelihood ratios

LIKELIHOOD RATIO

Likelihood ratios are another approach to hypothesis testing. We will see below that they are more appropriate for sparse data than the χ^2 test. But they also have the advantage that the statistic we are computing, a *likelihood ratio*, is more interpretable than the X^2 statistic. It is simply a number that tells us how much more likely one hypothesis is than the other.

In applying the likelihood ratio test to collocation discovery, we examine the following two alternative explanations for the occurrence frequency of a bigram w^1w^2 (Dunning 1993):

- **Hypothesis 1.** $P(w^2|w^1) = p = P(w^2|\neg w^1)$

- **Hypothesis 2.** $P(w^2|w^1) = p_1 \neq p_2 = P(w^2|\neg w^1)$

Hypothesis 1 is a formalization of independence (the occurrence of w^2 is independent of the previous occurrence of w^1), Hypothesis 2 is a formalization of dependence which is good evidence for an interesting collocation.[6]

---

6. We assume that $p_1 \gg p_2$ if Hypothesis 2 is true. The case $p_1 \ll p_2$ is rare and we will ignore it here.

We use the usual maximum likelihood estimates for p, p_1 and p_2 and write c_1, c_2, and c_{12} for the number of occurrences of w^1, w^2 and w^1w^2 in the corpus:

(5.8) $$p = \frac{c_2}{N} \quad p_1 = \frac{c_{12}}{c_1} \quad p_2 = \frac{c_2 - c_{12}}{N - c_1}$$

Assuming a binomial distribution:

(5.9) $$b(k; n, x) = \binom{n}{k} x^k (1 - x)^{(n-k)}$$

the likelihood of getting the counts for w^1, w^2 and w^1w^2 that we actually observed is then $L(H_1) = b(c_{12}; c_1, p)b(c_2 - c_{12}; N - c_1, p)$ for Hypothesis 1 and $L(H_2) = b(c_{12}; c_1, p_1)b(c_2 - c_{12}; N - c_1, p_2)$ for Hypothesis 2. Table 5.11 summarizes this discussion. One obtains the likelihoods $L(H_1)$ and $L(H_2)$ just given by multiplying the last two lines, the likelihoods of the specified number of occurrences of w^1w^2 and $\neg w^1w^2$, respectively.

The log of the likelihood ratio λ is then as follows:

(5.10) $$\begin{aligned} \log \lambda &= \log \frac{L(H_1)}{L(H_2)} \\ &= \log \frac{b(c_{12}, c_1, p)b(c_2 - c_{12}, N - c_1, p)}{b(c_{12}, c_1, p_1)b(c_2 - c_{12}, N - c_1, p_2)} \\ &= \log L(c_{12}, c_1, p) + \log L(c_2 - c_{12}, N - c_1, p) \\ &\quad - \log L(c_{12}, c_1, p_1) - \log L(c_2 - c_{12}, N - c_1, p_2) \end{aligned}$$

where $L(k, n, x) = x^k (1 - x)^{n-k}$.

Table 5.12 shows the twenty bigrams of *powerful* which are highest ranked according to the likelihood ratio when the test is applied to the *New York Times* corpus (for which $N = 14,307,668$). We will explain below why we show the quantity $-2 \log \lambda$ instead of λ. We consider all occurring bigrams here, including rare ones that occur less than six times, since this test works well for rare bigrams. For example, *powerful cudgels*, which occurs 2 times, is identified as a possible collocation.

One advantage of likelihood ratios is that they have a clear intuitive interpretation. For example, the bigram *powerful computers* is $e^{0.5 \times 82.96} \approx 1.3 \times 10^{18}$ times more likely under the hypothesis that *computers* is more likely to follow *powerful* than its base rate of occurrence would suggest. This number is easier to interpret than the scores of the t test or the χ^2 test which we have to look up in a table.

$-2 \log \lambda$	$C(w^1)$	$C(w^2)$	$C(w^1 w^2)$	w^1	w^2
1291.42	12593	932	150	most	powerful
99.31	379	932	10	politically	powerful
82.96	932	934	10	powerful	computers
80.39	932	3424	13	powerful	force
57.27	932	291	6	powerful	symbol
51.66	932	40	4	powerful	lobbies
51.52	171	932	5	economically	powerful
51.05	932	43	4	powerful	magnet
50.83	4458	932	10	less	powerful
50.75	6252	932	11	very	powerful
49.36	932	2064	8	powerful	position
48.78	932	591	6	powerful	machines
47.42	932	2339	8	powerful	computer
43.23	932	16	3	powerful	magnets
43.10	932	396	5	powerful	chip
40.45	932	3694	8	powerful	men
36.36	932	47	3	powerful	486
36.15	932	268	4	powerful	neighbor
35.24	932	5245	8	powerful	political
34.15	932	3	2	powerful	cudgels

Table 5.12 Bigrams of *powerful* with the highest scores according to Dunning's likelihood ratio test.

But the likelihood ratio test also has the advantage that it can be more appropriate for sparse data than the χ^2 test. How do we use the likelihood ratio for hypothesis testing? If λ is a likelihood ratio of a particular form, then the quantity $-2 \log \lambda$ is asymptotically χ^2 distributed (Mood et al. 1974: 440). So we can use the values in table 5.12 to test the null hypothesis H_1 against the alternative hypothesis H_2. For example, we can look up the value of 34.15 for *powerful cudgels* in the table and reject H_1 for this bigram on a confidence level of $\alpha = 0.005$. (The critical value (for one degree of freedom) is 7.88. See the table of the χ^2 distribution in the appendix.)

The particular form of the likelihood ratio that is required here is that of a ratio between the maximum likelihood estimate over a subpart of the parameter space and the maximum likelihood estimate over the entire parameter space. For the likelihood ratio in (5.11), the entire space is the space of pairs (p_1, p_2) for the probability of w^2 occurring when w^1 preceded (p_1) and w^2 occurring when a different word preceded (p_2). We get the maximum likelihood for the data we observed if we assume the maximum likelihood estimates that we computed in (5.8). The subspace is the subset of cases for which $p_1 = p_2$. Again, the estimate in (5.8) gives us the maximum likelihood over the subspace given the data we observed. It can be shown that if λ is a ratio of two likelihoods of this type (one being the maximum likelihood over the subspace, the other over the entire space), then $-2 \log \lambda$ is asymptotically χ^2 distributed. 'Asymptotically' roughly means 'if the numbers are large enough'. Whether or not the numbers are large enough in a particular case is hard to determine, but Dunning has shown that for small counts the approximation to χ^2 is better for the likelihood ratio in (5.11) than, for example, for the X^2 statistic in (5.6). Therefore, the likelihood ratio test is in general more appropriate than Pearson's χ^2 test for collocation discovery.[7]

Relative frequency ratios. So far we have looked at evidence for collocations within one corpus. Ratios of *relative frequencies* between two or more different corpora can be used to discover collocations that are characteristic of a corpus when compared to other corpora (Damerau 1993). Although ratios of relative frequencies do not fit well into the hypothesis testing paradigm, we treat them here since they can be interpreted as likelihood ratios.

RELATIVE FREQUENCIES

Table 5.13 shows ten bigrams that occur exactly twice in our reference corpus (the 1990 *New York Times* corpus). The bigrams are ranked according to the ratio of their relative frequencies in our 1990 reference corpus versus their frequencies in a 1989 corpus (again drawn from the months August through November). For example, *Karim Obeid* occurs 68 times in the 1989 corpus. So the relative frequency ratio r is:

$$r = \frac{\frac{2}{14307668}}{\frac{68}{11731564}} \approx 0.024116$$

The bigrams in table 5.13 are mostly associated with news items that were more prevalent in 1989 than in 1990: The Muslim cleric Sheik Abdul

---

7. However, even $-2 \log \lambda$ is not approximated well by χ^2 if the expected values in the 2-by-2 contingency table are less than 1.0 (Read and Cressie 1988; Pedersen 1996).

Ratio	1990	1989	w^1	w^2
0.0241	2	68	Karim	Obeid
0.0372	2	44	East	Berliners
0.0372	2	44	Miss	Manners
0.0399	2	41	17	earthquake
0.0409	2	40	HUD	officials
0.0482	2	34	EAST	GERMANS
0.0496	2	33	Muslim	cleric
0.0496	2	33	John	Le
0.0512	2	32	Prague	Spring
0.0529	2	31	Among	individual

Table 5.13 Damerau's frequency ratio test. Ten bigrams that occurred twice in the 1990 *New York Times* corpus, ranked according to the (inverted) ratio of relative frequencies in 1989 and 1990.

Karim Obeid (who was abducted in 1989), the disintegration of communist Eastern Europe (*East Berliners*, *EAST GERMANS*, *Prague Spring*), the novel *The Russia House* by *John Le Carre*, a scandal in the Department of Housing and Urban Development (HUD), and the October 17 earthquake in the San Francisco Bay Area. But we also find artefacts like *Miss Manners* (whose column the *New York Times* newswire stopped carrying in 1990) and *Among individual*. The reporter Phillip H. Wiggins liked to use the latter phrase for his stock market reports (*Among individual Big Board issues . . .*), but he stopped writing for the *Times* in 1990.

The examples show that frequency ratios are mainly useful to find *subject-specific* collocations. The application proposed by Damerau is to compare a general text with a subject-specific text. Those words and phrases that on a relative basis occur most often in the subject-specific text are likely to be part of the vocabulary that is specific to the domain.

Exercise 5.4   [★ ★]

Identify the most significantly non-independent bigrams according to the *t* test in a corpus of your choice.

Exercise 5.5   [★]

It is a coincidence that the *t* value for *new companies* is close to 1.0. Show this by computing the *t* value of *new companies* for a corpus with the following counts. $C(new) = 30,000$, $C(companies) = 9,000$, $C(new\ companies) = 20$, and corpus size $N = 15,000,000$.

Exercise 5.6   [★]

We can improve on the method in section 5.2 by taking into account variance. In fact, Smadja does this and the algorithm described in (Smadja 1993) therefore bears some similarity to the *t* test.

Compute the *t* statistic in equation (5.3) for possible collocations by substituting mean and variance as computed in section 5.2 for $\bar{x}$ and s^2 and (a) assuming $\mu = 0$, and (b) assuming $\mu = \text{round}(\bar{x})$, that is, the closest integer. Note that we are not testing for bigrams here, but for collocations of word pairs that occur at any fixed small distance.

Exercise 5.7   [★★]

As we pointed out above, almost all bigrams occur significantly more often than chance if a stop list is used for prefiltering. Verify that there is a large proportion of bigrams that occur less often than chance if we do not filter out function words.

Exercise 5.8   [★★]

Apply the *t* test of differences to a corpus of your choice. Work with the following word pairs or with word pairs that are appropriate for your corpus: *man / woman, blue / green, lawyer / doctor.*

Exercise 5.9   [★]

Derive equation (5.7) from equation (5.6).

Exercise 5.10   [★★]

Find terms that distinguish best between the first and second part of a corpus of your choice.

Exercise 5.11   [★★]

Repeat the above exercise with random selection. Now you should find that fewer terms are significant. But some still are. Why? Shouldn't there be no differences between corpora drawn from the same source? Do this exercise for different significance levels.

Exercise 5.12   [★★]

Compute a measure of corpus similarity between two corpora of your choice.

Exercise 5.13   [★★]

Kilgarriff and Rose's corpus similarity measure can also be used for assessing corpus homogeneity. This is done by constructing a series of random divisions of the corpus into a pair of subcorpora. The test is then applied to each pair. If most of the tests indicated similarity, then it is a homogeneous corpus. Apply this test to a corpus of your choice.

$I(w^1, w^2)$	$C(w^1)$	$C(w^2)$	$C(w^1\ w^2)$	w^1	w^2
18.38	42	20	20	Ayatollah	Ruhollah
17.98	41	27	20	Bette	Midler
16.31	30	117	20	Agatha	Christie
15.94	77	59	20	videocassette	recorder
15.19	24	320	20	unsalted	butter
1.09	14907	9017	20	first	made
1.01	13484	10570	20	over	many
0.53	14734	13478	20	into	them
0.46	14093	14776	20	like	people
0.29	15019	15629	20	time	last

Table 5.14 Finding collocations: Ten bigrams that occur with frequency 20, ranked according to mutual information.

5.4   Mutual Information

POINTWISE MUTUAL
INFORMATION

An information-theoretically motivated measure for discovering interesting collocations is *pointwise mutual information* (Church et al. 1991; Church and Hanks 1989; Hindle 1990). Fano (1961: 27–28) originally defined mutual information between particular events x' and y', in our case the occurrence of particular words, as follows:

$$(5.11) \quad I(x', y') \quad = \quad \log_2 \frac{P(x'y')}{P(x')P(y')}$$

$$(5.12) \quad\qquad\qquad = \quad \log_2 \frac{P(x'|y')}{P(x')}$$

$$(5.13) \quad\qquad\qquad = \quad \log_2 \frac{P(y'|x')}{P(y')}$$

This type of mutual information, which we introduced in section 2.2.3, is roughly a measure of how much one word tells us about the other, a notion that we will make more precise shortly.

In information theory, mutual information is more often defined as holding between *random variables*, not *values of random variables* as we have defined it here (see the standard definition in section 2.2.3). We will see below that these two types of mutual information are quite different creatures.

When we apply this definition to the 10 collocations from table 5.6, we

	chambre	¬ *chambre*	MI	χ^2
house	31,950	12,004		
¬ *house*	4793	848,330	4.1	553610
	communes	¬ *communes*		
house	4974	38,980		
¬ *house*	441	852,682	4.2	88405

Table 5.15 Correspondence of *chambre* and *house* and *communes* and *house* in the aligned Hansard corpus. Mutual information gives a higher score to (*communes,house*), while the χ^2 test gives a higher score to the correct translation pair (*chambre,house*).

get the same ranking as with the *t* test (see table 5.14). As usual, we use maximum likelihood estimates to compute the probabilities, for example:

$$I(Ayatollah, Ruhollah) = \log_2 \frac{\frac{20}{14307668}}{\frac{42}{14307668} \times \frac{20}{14307668}} \approx 18.38$$

So what exactly is (pointwise) mutual information, $I(x', y')$, a measure of? Fano writes about definition (5.12):

> The amount of information provided by the occurrence of the event represented by [y'] about the occurrence of the event represented by [x'] is defined as [(5.12)].

For example, the mutual information measure tells us that the amount of information we have about the occurrence of *Ayatollah* at position i in the corpus increases by 18.38 bits if we are told that *Ruhollah* occurs at position $i + 1$. Or, since (5.12) and (5.13) are equivalent, it also tells us that the amount of information we have about the occurrence of *Ruhollah* at position $i + 1$ in the corpus increases by 18.38 bits if we are told that *Ayatollah* occurs at position i. We could also say that our uncertainty is reduced by 18.38 bits. In other words, we can be much more certain that *Ruhollah* will occur next if we are told that *Ayatollah* is the current word.

Unfortunately, this measure of 'increased information' is in many cases not a good measure of what an interesting correspondence between two events is, as has been pointed out by many authors. (We base our discussion here mainly on (Church and Gale 1991b) and (Maxwell 1992).) Consider the two examples in table 5.15 of counts of word correspondences between French and English sentences in the Hansard corpus, an aligned corpus of debates of the Canadian parliament (the table is similar to table 5.9). The reason that *house* frequently appears in translations of French sentences containing *chambre* and *communes* is that the most common use of *house* in the Hansard is the phrase *House of Commons* which corresponds to *Chambre de communes* in French. But it is easy to see that *communes* is a worse match for *house* than *chambre* since most occurrences of *house* occur without *communes* on the French side. As shown in the table, the χ^2 test is able to infer the correct correspondence whereas mutual information gives preference to the incorrect pair (*communes,house*).

We can explain the difference between the two measures easily if we look at definition (5.12) of mutual information and compare the quantities $I(chambre, house)$ and $I(communes, house)$:

$$\log \frac{P(house|chambre)}{P(house)} = \log \frac{\frac{31950}{31950+4793}}{P(house)} \approx \log \frac{0.87}{P(house)}$$

$$< \quad \log \frac{0.92}{P(house)} \approx \log \frac{\frac{4974}{4974+441}}{P(house)} = \log \frac{P(house|communes)}{P(house)}$$

The word *communes* in the French makes it more likely that *house* occurred in the English than *chambre* does. The higher mutual information value for *communes* reflects the fact that *communes* causes a larger decrease in uncertainty here. But as the example shows decrease in uncertainty does not correspond well to what we want to measure. In contrast, the χ^2 is a direct test of probabilistic dependence, which in this context we can interpret as the degree of association between two words and hence as a measure of their quality as translation pairs and collocations.

Table 5.16 shows a second problem with using mutual information for finding collocations. We show ten bigrams that occur exactly once in the first 1000 documents of the reference corpus and their mutual information score based on the 1000 documents. The right half of the table shows the mutual information score based on the entire reference corpus (about 23,000 documents).

The larger corpus of 23,000 documents makes some better estimates possible, which in turn leads to a slightly better ranking. The bigrams *marijuana growing* and *new converts* (arguably collocations) have moved up and *Reds survived* (definitely not a collocation) has moved down. However, what is striking is that even after going to a 10 times larger corpus 6 of the bigrams still only occur once and, as a consequence, have inaccurate maximum likelihood estimates and artificially inflated mutual

I_{1000}	w^1	w^2	w^1w^2	Bigram	I_{23000}	w^1	w^2	w^1w^2	Bigram
16.95	5	1	1	Schwartz eschews	14.46	106	6	1	Schwartz eschews
15.02	1	19	1	fewest visits	13.06	76	22	1	FIND GARDEN
13.78	5	9	1	FIND GARDEN	11.25	22	267	1	fewest visits
12.00	5	31	1	Indonesian pieces	8.97	43	663	1	Indonesian pieces
9.82	26	27	1	Reds survived	8.04	170	1917	6	marijuana growing
9.21	13	82	1	marijuana growing	5.73	15828	51	3	new converts
7.37	24	159	1	doubt whether	5.26	680	3846	7	doubt whether
6.68	687	9	1	new converts	4.76	739	713	1	Reds survived
6.00	661	15	1	like offensive	1.95	3549	6276	6	must think
3.81	159	283	1	must think	0.41	14093	762	1	like offensive

Table 5.16 Problems for Mutual Information from data sparseness. The table shows ten bigrams that occurred once in the first 1000 documents in the reference corpus ranked according to mutual information score in the first 1000 documents (left half of the table) and ranked according to mutual information score in the entire corpus (right half of the table). These examples illustrate that a large proportion of bigrams are not well characterized by corpus data (even for large corpora) and that mutual information is particularly sensitive to estimates that are inaccurate due to sparseness.

information scores. All 6 are not collocations and we would prefer a measure which ranks them accordingly.

None of the measures we have seen works very well for low-frequency events. But there is evidence that sparseness is a particularly difficult problem for mutual information. To see why, notice that mutual information is a log likelihood ratio of the probability of the bigram $P(w^1w^2)$ and the product of the probabilities of the individual words $P(w^1)P(w^2)$. Consider two extreme cases: perfect dependence of the occurrences of the two words (they only occur together) and perfect independence (the occurrence of one does not give us any information about the occurrence of the other). For perfect dependence we have:

$$I(x, y) = \log \frac{P(xy)}{P(x)P(y)} = \log \frac{P(x)}{P(x)P(y)} = \log \frac{1}{P(y)}$$

That is, among perfectly dependent bigrams, as they get rarer, their mutual information *increases*.

For perfect independence we have:

$$I(x, y) = \log \frac{P(xy)}{P(x)P(y)} = \log \frac{P(x)P(y)}{P(x)P(y)} = \log 1 = 0$$

Symbol	Definition	Current use	Fano
$I(x, y)$	$\log \frac{p(x,y)}{p(x)\,p(y)}$	pointwise mutual information	mutual information
$I(X; Y)$	$E \log \frac{p(X,Y)}{p(X)\,p(Y)}$	mutual information	average MI/expectation of MI

Table 5.17 Different definitions of *mutual information* in (Cover and Thomas 1991) and (Fano 1961).

We can say that mutual information is a good measure of independence. Values close to 0 indicate independence (independent of frequency). But it is a bad measure of dependence because for dependence the score depends on the frequency of the individual words. Other things being equal, bigrams composed of low-frequency words will receive a higher score than bigrams composed of high-frequency words. That is the opposite of what we would want a good measure to do since higher frequency means more evidence and we would prefer a higher rank for bigrams for whose interestingness we have more evidence. One solution that has been proposed for this is to use a cutoff and to only look at words with a frequency of at least 3. However, such a move does not solve the underlying problem, but only ameliorates its effects.

Since pointwise mutual information does not capture the intuitive notion of an interesting collocation very well, it is often not used when it is made available in practical applications (Fontenelle et al. 1994: 81) or it is redefined as $C(w^1 w^2) I(w^1, w^2)$ to compensate for the bias of the original definition in favor of low-frequency events (Fontenelle et al. 1994: 72, Hodges et al. 1996).

As we mentioned earlier, the definition of mutual information used here is common in corpus linguistic studies, but is less common in Information Theory. Mutual information in Information Theory refers to the EXPECTATION *expectation* of the quantity that we have used in this section:

$$I(X; Y) = E_{p(x,y)} \log \frac{p(X, Y)}{p(X)\,p(Y)}$$

The definition we have used in this chapter is an older one, termed pointwise mutual information (see section 2.2.3, Fano 1961: 28, and Gallager 1968). Table 5.17 summarizes the older and newer naming conventions. One quantity is the expectation of the other, so the two types of mutual information are quite different.

The example of mutual information demonstrates what should be self-evident: it is important to check what a mathematical concept is a formalization of. The notion of pointwise mutual information that we have used here ($\log \frac{p(w^1 w^2)}{p(w^1)\,p(w^2)}$) measures the reduction of uncertainty about the occurrence of one word when we are told about the occurrence of the other. As we have seen, such a measure is of limited utility for acquiring the types of linguistic properties we have looked at in this section.

Exercise 5.14 [⋆ ⋆]

Justeson and Katz's part-of-speech filter in section 5.1 can be applied to any of the other methods of collocation discovery in this chapter. Pick one and modify it to incorporate a part-of-speech filter. What advantages does the modified method have?

Exercise 5.15 [⋆ ⋆ ⋆]

Design and implement a collocation discovery tool for a translator's workbench. Pick either one method or a combination of methods that the translator can choose from.

Exercise 5.16 [⋆ ⋆ ⋆]

Design and implement a collocation discovery tool for a lexicographer's workbench. Pick either one method or a combination of methods that the lexicographer can choose from.

Exercise 5.17 [⋆ ⋆ ⋆]

Many news services tag references to companies in their news stories. For example, all references to the *General Electric Company* would be tagged with the same tag regardless of which variant of the name is used (e.g., *GE*, *General Electric*, or *General Electric Company*). Design and implement a collocation discovery tool for finding company names. How could one partially automate the process of identifying variants?

5.5 The Notion of Collocation

The notion of collocation may be confusing to readers without a background in linguistics. We will devote this section to discussing in more detail what a collocation is.

There are actually different definitions of the notion of collocation. Some authors in the computational and statistical literature define a collocation as two or more *consecutive* words with a special behavior, for example Choueka (1988):

> [A collocation is defined as] a sequence of two or more consecutive words, that has characteristics of a syntactic and semantic unit,

and whose exact and unambiguous meaning or connotation cannot be derived directly from the meaning or connotation of its components.

Most of the examples we have presented in this chapter also assumed adjacency of words. But in most linguistically oriented research, a phrase can be a collocation even if it is not consecutive (as in the example *knock ... door*). The following criteria are typical of linguistic treatments of collocations (see for example Benson (1989) and Brundage et al. (1992)), non-compositionality being the main one we have relied on here.

- **Non-compositionality.** The meaning of a collocation is not a straight-forward composition of the meanings of its parts. Either the meaning is completely different from the free combination (as in the case of idioms like *kick the bucket*) or there is a connotation or added element of meaning that cannot be predicted from the parts. For example, *white wine*, *white hair* and *white woman* all refer to slightly different colors, so we can regard them as collocations.

- **Non-substitutability.** We cannot substitute other words for for the components of a collocation even if, in context, they have the same meaning. For example, we can't say *yellow wine* instead of *white wine* even though *yellow* is as good a description of the color of white wine as *white* is (it is kind of a yellowish white).

- **Non-modifiability.** Many collocations cannot be freely modified with additional lexical material or through grammatical transformations. This is especially true for frozen expressions like idioms. For example, we can't modify *frog* in *to get a frog in one's throat* into *to get an ugly frog in one's throat* although usually nouns like *frog* can be modified by adjectives like *ugly*. Similarly, going from singular to plural can make an idiom ill-formed, for example in *people as poor as church mice.*

A nice way to test whether a combination is a collocation is to translate it into another language. If we cannot translate the combination word by word, then that is evidence that we are dealing with a collocation. For example, translating *make a decision* into French one word at a time we get *faire une décision* which is incorrect. In French we have to say *prendre une décision*. So that is evidence that *make a decision* is a collocation in English.

strength	power
to build up ~	to assume ~
to find ~	emergency ~
to save ~	discretionary ~
to sap somebody's ~	~ over [several provinces]
brute ~	supernatural ~
tensile ~	to turn off the ~
the ~ to [do X]	the ~ to [do X]
[our staff was] at full ~	the balance of ~
on the ~ of [your recommendation]	fire ~

Table 5.18   Collocations in the BBI Combinatory Dictionary of English for the words *strength* and *power*.

Some authors have generalized the notion of collocation even further and included cases of words that are strongly associated with each other, but do not necessarily occur in a common grammatical unit and with a particular order, cases like *doctor – nurse* or *plane – airport*. It is probably best to restrict collocations to the narrower sense of grammatically ASSOCIATION bound elements that occur in a particular order and use the terms *associ-* CO-OCCURRENCE *ation* and *co-occurrence* for the more general phenomenon of words that are likely to be used in the same context.

It is instructive to look at the types of collocations that a purely linguistic analysis of text will discover if plenty of time and person power is available so that the limitations of statistical analysis and computer technology need be of no concern. An example of such a purely linguistic analysis is the BBI Combinatory Dictionary of English (Benson et al. 1993). In table 5.18, we show some of the collocations (or combinations as the dictionary prefers to call them) of *strength* and *power* that the dictionary lists.[8] We can see immediately that a wider variety of grammatical patterns is considered here (in particular patterns involving prepositions and particles). Naturally, the quality of the collocations is also higher than computer-generated lists – as we would expect from a manually produced compilation.

We conclude our discussion of the concept of collocation by going through some subclasses of collocations that deserve special mention.

---

8. We cannot show collocations of *strong* and *powerful* because these adjectives are not listed as entries in the dictionary.

LIGHT VERBS   Verbs with little semantic content like *make, take* and *do* are called *light verbs* in collocations like *make a decision* or *do a favor*. There is hardly anything about the meaning of *make, take* or *do* that would explain why we have to say *make a decision* instead of *take a decision* and *do a favor* instead of *make a favor*, but for many computational purposes the correct light verb for combination with a particular noun must be determined and thus acquired from corpora if this information is not available in machine-readable dictionaries. Dras and Johnson (1996) examine one approach to this problem.

VERB PARTICLE   *Verb particle constructions* or *phrasal verbs* are an especially important
CONSTRUCTIONS   part of the lexicon of English. Many verbs in English like *to tell off* and
PHRASAL VERBS   *to go down* consist of a combination of a main verb and a particle. These verbs often correspond to a single lexeme in other languages (*réprimander, descendre* in French). This type of construction is a good example of a collocation with often non-adjacent words.

PROPER NAMES   *Proper nouns* (also called *proper names*) are usually included in the category of collocations in computational work although they are quite different from lexical collocations. They are most amenable to approaches that look for fixed phrases that reappear in exactly the same form throughout a text.

TERMINOLOGICAL   *Terminological expressions* or phrases refer to concepts and objects in
EXPRESSIONS   technical domains. Although they are often fairly compositional (e.g., *hydraulic oil filter*), it is still important to identify them to make sure that they are treated consistently throughout a technical text. For example, when translating a manual, we have to make sure that all instances of *hydraulic oil filter* are translated by the same term. If two different translations are used (even if they have the same meaning in some sense), the reader of the translated manual could get confused and think that two different entities are being described.

As a final example of the wide range of phenomena that the term collocation is applied to, let us point to the many different degrees of invariability that a collocation can show. At one extreme of the spectrum we have usage notes in dictionaries that describe subtle differences in usage between near-synonyms like *answer* and *reply* (*diplomatic answer* vs. *stinging reply*). This type of collocation is important for generating text that sounds natural, but getting a collocation wrong here is less likely to lead to a fatal error. The other extreme are completely frozen expressions like proper names and idioms. Here there is just one way of saying things and any deviation will completely change the meaning of what is said. Luckily, the less compositional and the more important a collocation, the easier it is to acquire it automatically.

5.6 Further Reading

See (Stubbs 1996) for an in-depth discussion of the British tradition of 'empiricist' linguistics.

The t test is covered in most general statistics books. Standard references are (Snedecor and Cochran 1989: 53) and (Moore and McCabe 1989: 541). Weinberg and Goldberg (1990: 306) and Ramsey and Schafer (1997) are more accessible for students with less mathematical background. These books also cover the χ^2 test, but not some of the other more specialized tests that we discuss here.

One of the first publications on the discovery of collocations was (Church and Hanks 1989), later expanded to (Church et al. 1991). The authors drew attention to an emerging type of corpus-based dictionary (Sinclair 1995) and developed a program of computational lexicography that combines corpus evidence, computational methods and human judgement to build more comprehensive dictionaries that better reflect actual language use.

There are a number of ways lexicographers can benefit from automated processing of corpus data. A lexicographer writes a dictionary entry after looking at a potentially large number of examples of a word. If the examples are automatically presorted according to collocations and other criteria (for example, the topic of the text), then this process can be made much more efficient. For example, phrasal verbs are sometimes neglected in dictionaries because they are not separate words. A corpus-based approach will make their importance evident to the lexicographer. In addition, a balanced corpus will reveal which of the uses are most frequent and hence most important for the likely user of a dictionary. Difference tests like the t test are useful for writing usage notes and for writing accurate definitions that reflect differences in usage between words. Some of these techniques are being used for the next generation of dictionaries (Fontenelle et al. 1994).

Eventually, a new form of dictionary could emerge from this work, a kind of dictionary-cum-corpus in which dictionary entry and corpus evidence support each other and are organized in a coherent whole. The COBUILD dictionary already has some of these characteristics (Sinclair

1995). Since space is less of an issue with electronic dictionaries plenty of corpus examples can be integrated into a dictionary entry for the interested user.

What we have said about the value of statistical corpus analysis for monolingual dictionaries applies equally to bilingual dictionaries, at least if an aligned corpus is available (Smadja et al. 1996).

Another important application of collocations is Information Retrieval (IR). Accuracy of retrieval can be improved if the similarity between a user query and a document is determined based on common collocations (or phrases) instead of common words (Fagan 1989; Evans et al. 1991; Strzalkowski 1995; Mitra et al. 1997). See Lewis and Jones (1996) and Krovetz (1991) for further discussion of the question of using collocation discovery and NLP in Information Retrieval and Nevill-Manning et al. (1997) for an alternative non-statistical approach to using phrases in IR. Steier and Belew (1993) present an interesting study of how the treatment of phrases (for example, for phrase weighting) should change as we move from a subdomain to a general domain. For example, *invasive procedure* is completely compositional and a less interesting collocation in the subdomain of medical articles, but becomes interesting and non-compositional when 'exported' to a general collection that is a mixture of many specialized domains.

Two other important applications of collocations, which we will just mention, are natural language generation (Smadja 1993) and cross-language information retrieval (Hull and Grefenstette 1998).

An important area that we haven't been able to cover is the discovery of proper nouns, which can be regarded as a kind of collocation. Proper nouns cannot be exhaustively covered in dictionaries since new people, places, and other entities come into existence and are named all the time. Proper nouns also present their own set of challenges: co-reference (How can we tell that IBM and International Business Machines refer to the same entity?), disambiguation (When does AMEX refer to the American Exchange, when to American Express?), and classification (Is this new entity that the text refers to the name of a person, a location or a company?). One of the earliest studies on this topic is (Coates-Stephens 1993). McDonald (1995) focuses on lexicosemantic patterns that can be used as cues for proper noun detection and classification. Mani and MacMillan (1995) and Paik et al. (1995) propose ways of classifying proper nouns according to type.

One frequently used measure for interestingness of collocations that

Z SCORE — we did not cover is the *z score*, a close relative of the *t* test. It is used in several software packages and workbenches for text analysis (Fontenelle et al. 1994; Hawthorne 1994). The *z* score should only be applied when the variance is known, which arguably is not the case in most Statistical NLP applications.

Fisher's exact test is another statistical test that can be used for judging how unexpected a set of observations is. In contrast to the *t* test and the χ^2 test, it is appropriate even for very small counts. However, it is hard to compute, and it is not clear whether the results obtained in practice are much different from, for example, the χ^2 test (Pedersen 1996).

Yet another approach to discovering collocations is to search for points in the word stream with either low or high uncertainty as to what the next (or previous) word will be. Points with high uncertainty are likely to be phrase boundaries, which in turn are candidates for points where a collocation may start or end, whereas points with low uncertainty are likely to be located within a collocation. See (Evans and Zhai 1996) and (Shimohata et al. 1997) for two approaches that use this type of information for finding phrases and collocations.

6 *Statistical Inference: n-gram Models over Sparse Data*

STATISTICAL NLP aims to do statistical inference for the field of natural language. *Statistical inference* in general consists of taking some data (generated in accordance with some unknown probability distribution) and then making some inferences about this distribution. For example, we might look at lots of instances of prepositional phrase attachments in a corpus, and use them to try to predict prepositional phrase attachments for English in general. The discussion in this chapter divides the problem into three areas (although they tend to overlap considerably): dividing the training data into equivalence classes, finding a good statistical estimator for each equivalence class, and combining multiple estimators.

As a running example of statistical estimation, we will examine the classic task of *language modeling*, where the problem is to predict the next word given the previous words. This task is fundamental to speech or optical character recognition, and is also used for spelling correction, handwriting recognition, and statistical machine translation. This sort of task is often referred to as a *Shannon game* following the presentation of the task of guessing the next letter in a text in (Shannon 1951). This problem has been well-studied, and indeed many estimation methods were first developed for this task. In general, though, the methods we develop are not specific to this task, and can be directly used for other tasks like word sense disambiguation or probabilistic parsing. The word prediction task just provides a clear easily-understood problem for which the techniques can be developed.

6.1   Bins: Forming Equivalence Classes

6.1.1   Reliability vs. discrimination

Normally, in order to do inference about one feature, we wish to find other features of the model that predict it. Here, we are assuming that past behavior is a good guide to what will happen in the future (that is, that the model is roughly stationary). This gives us a classification task: we try to predict the *target feature* on the basis of various *classificatory features*. When doing this, we effectively divide the data into equivalence classes that share values for certain of the classificatory features, and use this equivalence classing to help predict the value of the target feature on new pieces of data. This means that we are tacitly making *independence assumptions:* the data either does not depend on other features, or the dependence is sufficiently minor that we hope that we can neglect it without doing too much harm. The more classificatory features (of some relevance) that we identify, the more finely conditions that determine the unknown probability distribution of the target feature can potentially be teased apart. In other words, dividing the data into many *bins* gives us greater *discrimination*. Going against this is the problem that if we use a lot of bins then a particular bin may contain no or a very small number of training instances, and then we will not be able to do statistically *reliable* estimation of the target feature for that bin. Finding equivalence classes that are a good compromise between these two criteria is our first goal.

TARGET FEATURE
CLASSIFICATORY
FEATURES

INDEPENDENCE
ASSUMPTIONS

BINS

RELIABILITY

6.1.2   *n*-gram models

The task of predicting the next word can be stated as attempting to estimate the probability function P:

(6.1) $P(w_n | w_1, \ldots, w_{n-1})$

HISTORY

In such a stochastic problem, we use a classification of the previous words, the *history*, to predict the next word. On the basis of having looked at a lot of text, we know which words tend to follow other words.

For this task, we cannot possibly consider each textual history separately: most of the time we will be listening to a sentence that we have never heard before, and so there is no previous identical textual history on which to base our predictions, and even if we had heard the beginning of the sentence before, it might end differently this time. And so we

MARKOV ASSUMPTION

need a method of grouping histories that are similar in some way so as to give reasonable predictions as to which words we can expect to come next. One possible way to group them is by making a *Markov assumption* that only the prior local context – the last few words – affects the next word. If we construct a model where all histories that have the same last $n - 1$ words are placed in the same equivalence class, then we have an $(n - 1)^{\text{th}}$ order Markov model or an n-gram word model (the last word of the n-gram being given by the word we are predicting).

BIGRAM

TRIGRAM

FOUR-GRAM

DIGRAM

Before continuing with model-building, let us pause for a brief interlude on naming. The cases of n-gram models that people usually use are for $n = 2, 3, 4$, and these alternatives are usually referred to as a *bigram*, a *trigram*, and a *four-gram* model, respectively. Revealing this will surely be enough to cause any Classicists who are reading this book to stop, and to leave the field to uneducated engineering sorts: *gram* is a Greek root and so should be put together with Greek number prefixes. Shannon actually *did* use the term *digram*, but with the declining levels of education in recent decades, this usage has not survived. As non-prescriptive linguists, however, we think that the curious mixture of English, Greek, and Latin that our colleagues actually use is quite fun. So we will not try to stamp it out.[1]

Now in principle, we would like the n of our n-gram models to be fairly large, because there are sequences of words like:

(6.2)   Sue swallowed the large green ___.

PARAMETERS

where *swallowed* is presumably still quite strongly influencing which word will come next – *pill* or perhaps *frog* are likely continuations, but *tree*, *car* or *mountain* are presumably unlikely, even though they are in general fairly natural continuations after *the large green* ___. However, there is the problem that if we divide the data into too many bins, then there are a lot of parameters to estimate. For instance, if we conservatively assume that a speaker is staying within a vocabulary of 20,000 words, then we get the estimates for numbers of parameters shown in table 6.1.[2]

---

1. Rather than *four-gram*, some people do make an attempt at appearing educated by saying *quadgram*, but this is not really correct use of a Latin number prefix (which would give *quadrigram*, cf. *quadrilateral*), let alone correct use of a Greek number prefix, which would give us "a *tetragram* model."

2. Given a certain model space (here word n-gram models), the parameters are the numbers that we have to specify to determine a particular model within that model space.

Model	Parameters
1st order (bigram model):	$20,000 \times 19,999 = 400$ million
2nd order (trigram model):	$20,000^2 \times 19,999 = 8$ trillion
3th order (four-gram model):	$20,000^3 \times 19,999 = 1.6 \times 10^{17}$

Table 6.1 Growth in number of parameters for *n*-gram models.

So we quickly see that producing a five-gram model, of the sort that we thought would be useful above, may well not be practical, even if we have what we think is a very large corpus. For this reason, *n*-gram systems currently usually use bigrams or trigrams (and often make do with a smaller vocabulary).

One way of reducing the number of parameters is to reduce the value of *n*, but it is important to realize that *n*-grams are not the only way of forming equivalence classes of the history. Among other operations STEMMING of equivalencing, we could consider *stemming* (removing the inflectional endings from words) or grouping words into semantic classes (by use of a pre-existing thesaurus, or by some induced clustering). This is effectively reducing the vocabulary size over which we form *n*-grams. But we do not need to use *n*-grams at all. There are myriad other ways of forming equivalence classes of the history – it's just that they're all a bit more complicated than *n*-grams. The above example suggests that knowledge of the predicate in a clause is useful, so we can imagine a model that predicts the next word based on the previous word and the previous predicate (no matter how far back it is). But this model is harder to implement, because we first need a fairly accurate method of identifying the main predicate of a clause. Therefore we will just use *n*-gram models in this chapter, but other techniques are covered in chapters 12 and 14.

For anyone from a linguistics background, the idea that we would choose to use a model of language structure which predicts the next word simply by examining the previous two words – with no reference to the structure of the sentence – seems almost preposterous. But, actually, the

---

Since we are assuming nothing in particular about the probability distribution, the number of parameters to be estimated is the number of bins times one less than the number of values of the target feature (one is subtracted because the probability of the last target value is automatically given by the stochastic constraint that probabilities should sum to one).

lexical co-occurrence, semantic, and basic syntactic relationships that appear in this very local context are a good predictor of the next word, and such systems work surprisingly well. Indeed, it is difficult to beat a trigram model on the purely linear task of predicting the next word.

6.1.3 Building *n*-gram models

In the final part of some sections of this chapter, we will actually build some models and show the results. The reader should be able to recreate our results by using the tools and data on the accompanying website. The text that we will use is Jane Austen's novels, and is available from the website. This corpus has two advantages: (i) it is freely available through the work of Project Gutenberg, and (ii) it is not too large. The small size of the corpus is, of course, in many ways also a disadvantage. Because of the huge number of parameters of *n*-gram models, as discussed above, *n*-gram models work best when trained on enormous amounts of data. However, such training requires a lot of CPU time and diskspace, so a small corpus is much more appropriate for a textbook example. Even so, you will want to make sure that you start off with about 40Mb of free diskspace before attempting to recreate our examples.

As usual, the first step is to preprocess the corpus. The Project Gutenberg Austen texts are very clean plain ASCII files. But nevertheless, there are the usual problems of punctuation marks attaching to words and so on (see chapter 4) that mean that we must do more than simply split on whitespace. We decided that we could make do with some very simple search-and-replace patterns that removed all punctuation leaving whitespace separated words (see the website for details). We decided to use *Emma, Mansfield Park, Northanger Abbey, Pride and Prejudice,* and *Sense and Sensibility* as our corpus for building models, reserving *Persuasion* for testing, as discussed below. This gave us a (small) training corpus of $N = 617,091$ words of text, containing a vocabulary V of 14,585 word types.

By simply removing all punctuation as we did, our file is literally a long sequence of words. This isn't actually what people do most of the time. It is commonly felt that there are not very strong dependencies between sentences, while sentences tend to begin in characteristic ways. So people mark the sentences in the text – most commonly by surrounding them with the SGML tags <s> and </s>. The probability calculations at the start of a sentence are then dependent not on the last words of the preceding sentence but upon a 'beginning of sentence' context. We should additionally note that we didn't remove case distinctions, so capitalized words remain in the data, imperfectly indicating where new sentences begin.

6.2 Statistical Estimators

Given a certain number of pieces of training data that fall into a certain bin, the second goal is then finding out how to derive a good probability estimate for the target feature based on these data. For our running example of n-grams, we will be interested in $P(w_1 \cdots w_n)$ and the prediction task $P(w_n|w_1 \cdots w_{n-1})$. Since:

$$(6.3) \quad P(w_n|w_1 \cdots w_{n-1}) = \frac{P(w_1 \cdots w_n)}{P(w_1 \cdots w_{n-1})}$$

estimating good conditional probability distributions can be reduced to having good solutions to simply estimating the unknown probability distribution of n-grams.[3]

Let us assume that the training text consists of N words. If we append $n - 1$ dummy start symbols to the beginning of the text, we can then also say that the corpus consists of N n-grams, with a uniform amount of conditioning available for the next word in all cases. Let B be the number of bins (equivalence classes). This will be V^{n-1}, where V is the vocabulary size, for the task of working out the next word and V^n for the task of estimating the probability of different n-grams. Let $C(w_1 \cdots w_n)$ be the frequency of a certain n-gram in the training text, and let us say that there are N_r n-grams that appeared r times in the training text (i.e., $N_r = |\{w_1 \cdots w_n : C(w_1 \cdots w_n) = r\}|$). These frequencies of frequencies are very commonly used in the estimation methods which we cover below. This notation is summarized in table 6.2.

---

3. However, when smoothing, one has a choice of whether to smooth the n-gram probability estimates, or to smooth the conditional probability distributions directly. For many methods, these do not give equivalent results since in the latter case one is separately smoothing a large number of conditional probability distributions (which normally need to be themselves grouped into classes in some way).

N	Number of training instances
B	Number of bins training instances are divided into
w_{1n}	An n-gram $w_1 \cdots w_n$ in the training text
$C(w_1 \cdots w_n)$	Frequency of n-gram $w_1 \cdots w_n$ in training text
r	Frequency of an n-gram
$f(\cdot)$	Frequency estimate of a model
N_r	Number of bins that have r training instances in them
T_r	Total count of n-grams of frequency r in further data
h	'History' of preceding words

Table 6.2 Notation for the statistical estimation chapter.

6.2.1 Maximum Likelihood Estimation (MLE)

MLE estimates from relative frequencies

Regardless of how we form equivalence classes, we will end up with bins that contain a certain number of training instances. Let us assume a trigram model where we are using the two preceding words of context to predict the next word, and let us focus in on the bin for the case where the two preceding words were *comes across*. In a certain corpus, the authors found 10 training instances of the words *comes across*, and of those, 8 times they were followed by *as*, once by *more* and once by *a*. The question at this point is what probability estimates we should use for estimating the next word.

RELATIVE FREQUENCY   The obvious first answer (at least from a frequentist point of view) is to suggest using the *relative frequency* as a probability estimate:

$$
\begin{aligned}
P(as) &= 0.8 \\
P(more) &= 0.1 \\
P(a) &= 0.1 \\
P(x) &= 0.0 \quad \text{for } x \text{ not among the above 3 words}
\end{aligned}
$$

MAXIMUM LIKELIHOOD   This estimate is called the *maximum likelihood estimate* (MLE):
ESTIMATE

(6.4) $$P_{\text{MLE}}(w_1 \cdots w_n) = \frac{C(w_1 \cdots w_n)}{N}$$

(6.5) $$P_{\text{MLE}}(w_n | w_1 \cdots w_{n-1}) = \frac{C(w_1 \cdots w_n)}{C(w_1 \cdots w_{n-1})}$$

If one fixes the observed data, and then considers the space of all possible parameter assignments within a certain distribution (here a trigram model) given the data, then statisticians refer to this as a *likelihood function*. The maximum likelihood estimate is so called because it is the choice of parameter values which gives the highest probability to the training corpus.[4] The estimate that does that is the one shown above. It does not waste any probability mass on events that are not in the training corpus, but rather it makes the probability of observed events as high as it can subject to the normal stochastic constraints.

But the MLE is in general unsuitable for statistical inference in NLP. The problem is the sparseness of our data (even if we are using a large corpus). While a few words are common, the vast majority of words are very uncommon – and longer *n*-grams involving them are thus much rarer again. The MLE assigns a zero probability to unseen events, and since the probability of a long string is generally computed by multiplying the probabilities of subparts, these zeroes will propagate and give us bad (zero probability) estimates for the probability of sentences when we just happened not to see certain *n*-grams in the training text.[5] With respect to the example above, the MLE is not capturing the fact that there are other words which can follow *comes across*, for example *the* and *some*.

As an example of data sparseness, after training on 1.5 million words from the IBM Laser Patent Text corpus, Bahl et al. (1983) report that 23% of the trigram tokens found in further test data drawn from the same corpus were previously unseen. This corpus is small by modern standards, and so one might hope that by collecting much more data that the problem of data sparseness would simply go away. While this may initially seem hopeful (if we collect a hundred instances of *comes across*, we will probably find instances with it followed by *the* and *some*), in practice it is never a general solution to the problem. While there are a limited number of frequent events in language, there is a seemingly never end-

---

4. This is given that the occurrence of a certain *n*-gram is assumed to be a random variable with a binomial distribution (i.e., each *n*-gram is independent of the next). This is a quite untrue (though usable) assumption: firstly, each *n*-gram overlaps with and hence partly determines the next, and secondly, content words tend to clump (if you use a word once in a paper, you are likely to use it again), as we discuss in section 15.3.
5. Another way to state this is to observe that if our probability model assigns zero probability to any event that turns out to actually occur, then both the cross-entropy and the KL divergence with respect to (data from) the real probability distribution is infinite. In other words we have done a maximally bad job at producing a probability function that is close to the one we are trying to model.

RARE EVENTS ing tail to the probability distribution of rarer and rarer events, and we can never collect enough data to get to the end of the tail.[6] For instance *comes across* could be followed by any number, and we will never see every number. In general, we need to devise better estimators that allow for the possibility that we will see events that we didn't see in the training text.

All such methods effectively work by somewhat decreasing the probability of previously seen events, so that there is a little bit of probability mass left over for previously unseen events. Thus these methods are fre-

DISCOUNTING quently referred to as *discounting* methods. The process of discounting is

SMOOTHING often referred to as *smoothing*, presumably because a distribution without zeroes is smoother than one with zeroes. We will examine a number of smoothing methods in the following sections.

Using MLE estimates for *n*-gram models of Austen

Based on our Austen corpus, we made *n*-gram models for different values of *n*. It is quite straightforward to write one's own program to do this, by totalling up the frequencies of *n*-grams and $(n - 1)$-grams, and then dividing to get MLE probability estimates, but there is also software to do it on the website.

In practical systems, it is usual to not actually calculate *n*-grams for all words. Rather, the *n*-grams are calculated as usual only for the most common *k* words, and all other words are regarded as Out-Of-Vocabulary (OOV) items and mapped to a single token such as <UNK>. Commonly, this will be done for all words that have been encountered only once in the

HAPAX LEGOMENA training corpus (*hapax legomena*). A useful variant in some domains is to notice the obvious semantic and distributional similarity of rare numbers and to have two out-of-vocabulary tokens, one for numbers and one for everything else. Because of the Zipfian distribution of words, cutting out low frequency items will greatly reduce the parameter space (and the memory requirements of the system being built), while not appreciably affecting the model quality (hapax legomena often constitute half of the types, but only a fraction of the tokens).

We used the conditional probabilities calculated from our training corpus to work out the probabilities of each following word for part of a

---

6. Cf. Zipf's law – the observation that the relationship between a word's frequency and the rank order of its frequency is roughly a reciprocal curve – as discussed in section 1.4.3.

In person	*she*		*was*		*inferior*		*to*		*both*		*sisters*	
1-gram	$P(\cdot)$		$P(\cdot)$		$P(\cdot)$		$P(\cdot)$		$P(\cdot)$		$P(\cdot)$	
1	the	0.034	the	0.034	the	0.034	the	0.034	the	0.034	the	0.034
2	to	0.032	to	0.032	to	0.032	**to**	**0.032**	to	0.032	to	0.032
3	and	0.030	and	0.030	and	0.030			and	0.030	and	0.030
4	of	0.029	of	0.029	of	0.029			of	0.029	of	0.029
. . .												
8	was	0.015	**was**	**0.015**	was	0.015			was	0.015	was	0.015
. . .												
13	**she**	**0.011**			she	0.011			she	0.011	she	0.011
. . .												
254					both	0.0005			**both**	**0.0005**	both	0.0005
. . .												
435					sisters	0.0003					**sisters**	**0.0003**
. . .												
1701					**inferior**	**0.00005**						
2-gram	$P(\cdot\mid person)$		$P(\cdot\mid she)$		$P(\cdot\mid was)$		$P(\cdot\mid inferior)$		$P(\cdot\mid to)$		$P(\cdot\mid both)$	
1	and	0.099	had	0.141	not	0.065	to	0.212	be	0.111	of	0.066
2	who	0.099	**was**	**0.122**	a	0.052			the	0.057	to	0.041
3	to	0.076			the	0.033			her	0.048	in	0.038
4	in	0.045			to	0.031			have	0.027	and	0.025
. . .												
23	**she**	**0.009**							Mrs	0.006	she	0.009
. . .												
41									what	0.004	**sisters**	**0.006**
. . .												
293									**both**	**0.0004**		
. . .												
∞					**inferior**	**0**						
3-gram	$P(\cdot\mid In,person)$		$P(\cdot\mid person,she)$		$P(\cdot\mid she,was)$		$P(\cdot\mid was,inf.)$		$P(\cdot\mid inferior,to)$		$P(\cdot\mid to,both)$	
1	UNSEEN		did	0.5	not	0.057	UNSEEN		the	0.286	to	0.222
2			**was**	**0.5**	very	0.038			Maria	0.143	Chapter	0.111
3					in	0.030			cherries	0.143	Hour	0.111
4					to	0.026			her	0.143	Twice	0.111
. . .												
∞					**inferior**	**0**			**both**	**0**	**sisters**	**0**
4-gram	$P(\cdot\mid u,I,p)$		$P(\cdot\mid I,p,s)$		$P(\cdot\mid p,s,w)$		$P(\cdot\mid s,w,i)$		$P(\cdot\mid w,i,t)$		$P(\cdot\mid i,t,b)$	
1	UNSEEN		UNSEEN		in	1.0	UNSEEN		UNSEEN		UNSEEN	
. . .												
∞					**inferior**	**0**						

Table 6.3 Probabilities of each successive word for a clause from *Persuasion*. The probability distribution for the following word is calculated by Maximum Likelihood Estimate *n*-gram models for various values of *n*. The predicted likelihood rank of different words is shown in the first column. The actual next word is shown at the top of the table in italics, and in the table in bold.

sentence from our test corpus *Persuasion*. We will cover the issue of test corpora in more detail later, but it is vital for assessing a model that we try it on different data – otherwise it isn't a fair test of how well the model allows us to predict the patterns of language. Extracts from these probability distributions – including the actual next word shown in bold – are shown in table 6.3. The unigram distribution ignores context entirely, and simply uses the overall frequency of different words. But this is not entirely useless, since, as in this clause, most words in most sentences are common words. The bigram model uses the preceding word to help predict the next word. In general, this helps enormously, and gives us a much better model. In some cases the estimated probability of the word that actually comes next has gone up by about an order of magnitude (*was, to, sisters*). However, note that the bigram model is not guaranteed to increase the probability estimate. The estimate for *she* has actually gone down, because *she* is in general very common in Austen novels (being mainly books about women), but somewhat unexpected after the noun *person* – although quite possible when an adverbial phrase is being used, such as *In person* here. The failure to predict *inferior* after *was* shows problems of data sparseness already starting to crop up.

When the trigram model works, it can work brilliantly. For example, it gives us a probability estimate of 0.5 for *was* following *person she*. But in general it is not usable. Either the preceding bigram was never seen before, and then there is no probability distribution for the following word, or a few words have been seen following that bigram, but the data is so sparse that the resulting estimates are highly unreliable. For example, the bigram *to both* was seen 9 times in the training text, twice followed by *to*, and once each followed by 7 other words, a few of which are shown in the table. This is not the kind of density of data on which one can sensibly build a probabilistic model. The four-gram model is entirely useless. In general, four-gram models do not become usable until one is training on several tens of millions of words of data.

Examining the table suggests an obvious strategy: use higher order *n*-gram models when one has seen enough data for them to be of some use, but back off to lower order *n*-gram models when there isn't enough data. This is a widely used strategy, which we will discuss below in the section on combining estimates, but it isn't by itself a complete solution to the problem of *n*-gram estimates. For instance, we saw quite a lot of words following *was* in the training data – 9409 tokens of 1481 types – but *inferior* was not one of them. Similarly, although we had seen quite a lot of words in our training text overall, there are many words that did not appear, including perfectly ordinary words like *decides* or *wart*. So regardless of how we combine estimates, we still definitely need a way to give a non-zero probability estimate to words or *n*-grams that we happened not to see in our training text, and so we will work on that problem first.

6.2.2   Laplace's law, Lidstone's law and the Jeffreys-Perks law

Laplace's law

The manifest failure of maximum likelihood estimation forces us to examine better estimators. The oldest solution is to employ Laplace's law (1814; 1995). According to this law,

(6.6) $$P_{\text{Lap}}(w_1 \cdots w_n) = \frac{C(w_1 \cdots w_n) + 1}{N + B}$$

ADDING ONE   This process is often informally referred to as *adding one*, and has the effect of giving a little bit of the probability space to unseen events. But rather than simply being an unprincipled move, this is actually the Bayesian estimator that one derives if one assumes a uniform prior on events (i.e., that every *n*-gram was equally likely).

However, note that the estimates which Laplace's law gives are dependent on the size of the vocabulary. For sparse sets of data over large vocabularies, such as *n*-grams, Laplace's law actually gives far too much of the probability space to unseen events.

Consider some data discussed by Church and Gale (1991a) in the context of their discussion of various estimators for bigrams. Their corpus of 44 million words of Associated Press (AP) newswire yielded a vocabulary of 400,653 words (maintaining case distinctions, splitting on hyphens, etc.). Note that this vocabulary size means that there is a space of 1.6×10^{11} possible bigrams, and so *a priori* barely any of them will actually occur in the corpus. It also means that in the calculation of P_{Lap}, B is far larger than N, and Laplace's method is completely unsatisfactory in such circumstances. Church and Gale used half the corpus (22 million

EXPECTED FREQUENCY   words) as a training text. Table 6.4 shows the *expected frequency esti-*
ESTIMATES   *mates* of various methods that they discuss, and Laplace's law estimates that we have calculated. Probability estimates can be derived by dividing the frequency estimates by the number of *n*-grams, $N = 22$ million. For Laplace's law, the probability estimate for an *n*-gram seen *r* times is

$r = f_{MLE}$	$f_{empirical}$	f_{Lap}	f_{del}	f_{GT}	N_r	T_r
0	0.000027	0.000137	0.000037	0.000027	74 671 100 000	2 019 187
1	0.448	0.000274	0.396	0.446	2 018 046	903 206
2	1.25	0.000411	1.24	1.26	449 721	564 153
3	2.24	0.000548	2.23	2.24	188 933	424 015
4	3.23	0.000685	3.22	3.24	105 668	341 099
5	4.21	0.000822	4.22	4.22	68 379	287 776
6	5.23	0.000959	5.20	5.19	48 190	251 951
7	6.21	0.00109	6.21	6.21	35 709	221 693
8	7.21	0.00123	7.18	7.24	27 710	199 779
9	8.26	0.00137	8.18	8.25	22 280	183 971

Table 6.4 Estimated frequencies for the AP data from Church and Gale (1991a). The first five columns show the estimated frequency calculated for a bigram that actually appeared r times in the training data according to different estimators: r is the maximum likelihood estimate, $f_{empirical}$ uses validation on the test set, f_{Lap} is the 'add one' method, f_{del} is deleted interpolation (two-way cross validation, using the training data), and f_{GT} is the Good-Turing estimate. The last two columns give the frequencies of frequencies and how often bigrams of a certain frequency occurred in further text.

$(r+1)/(N+B)$, so the frequency estimate becomes $f_{Lap} = (r+1)N/(N+B)$. These estimated frequencies are often easier for humans to interpret than probabilities, as one can more easily see the effect of the discounting.

Although each previously unseen bigram has been given a very low probability, because there are so many of them, 46.5% of the probability space has actually been given to unseen bigrams.[7] This is far too much, and it is done at the cost of enormously reducing the probability estimates of more frequent events. How do we know it is far too much? The second column of the table shows an empirically determined estimate (which we discuss below) of how often unseen n-grams actually appeared in further text, and we see that the individual frequency of occurrence of previously unseen n-grams is much lower than Laplace's law predicts, while the frequency of occurrence of previously seen n-grams is much higher than predicted.[8] In particular, the empirical model finds that only 9.2% of the bigrams in further text were previously unseen.

---

7. This is calculated as $N_0 \times P_{Lap}(\cdot) = 74,671,100,000 \times 0.000137/22,000,000 = 0.465$.
8. It is a bit hard dealing with the astronomical numbers in the table. A smaller example which illustrates the same point appears in exercise 6.2.

Lidstone's law and the Jeffreys-Perks law

Because of this overestimation, a commonly adopted solution to the problem of multinomial estimation within statistical practice is Lidstone's law of succession, where we add not one, but some (normally smaller) positive value λ:

$$(6.7) \qquad P_{\text{Lid}}(w_1 \cdots w_n) = \frac{C(w_1 \cdots w_n) + \lambda}{N + B\lambda}$$

This method was developed by the actuaries Hardy and Lidstone, and Johnson showed that it can be viewed as a linear interpolation (see below) between the MLE estimate and a uniform prior. This may be seen by setting $\mu = N/(N + B\lambda)$:

$$(6.8) \qquad P_{\text{Lid}}(w_1 \cdots w_n) = \mu \frac{C(w_1 \cdots w_n)}{N} + (1 - \mu)\frac{1}{B}$$

The most widely used value for λ is $\frac{1}{2}$. This choice can be theoretically justified as being the expectation of the same quantity which is maximized by MLE and so it has its own names, the Jeffreys-Perks law, or *Expected Likelihood Estimation* (ELE) (Box and Tiao 1973: 34–36).

EXPECTED LIKELIHOOD ESTIMATION

In practice, this often helps. For example, we could avoid the objection above that two much of the probability space was being given to unseen events by choosing a small λ. But there are two remaining objections: (i) we need a good way to guess an appropriate value for λ in advance, and (ii) discounting using Lidstone's law always gives probability estimates linear in the MLE frequency and this is not a good match to the empirical distribution at low frequencies.

Applying these methods to Austen

Despite the problems inherent in these methods, we will nevertheless try applying them, in particular ELE, to our Austen corpus. Recall that up until now the only probability estimate we have been able to derive for the test corpus clause *she was inferior to both sisters* was the unigram estimate, which (multiplying through the bold probabilities in the top part of table 6.3) gives as its estimate for the probability of the clause 3.96×10^{-17}. For the other models, the probability estimate was either zero or undefined, because of the sparseness of the data.

Let us now calculate a probability estimate for this clause using a bigram model and ELE. Following the word *was*, which appeared 9409

Rank	Word	MLE	ELE
1	not	0.065	0.036
2	a	0.052	0.030
3	the	0.033	0.019
4	to	0.031	0.017
. . .			
=1482	inferior	0	0.00003

Table 6.5 Expected Likelihood Estimation estimates for the word following *was*.

times, *not* appeared 608 times in the training corpus, which overall contained 14589 word types. So our new estimate for $P(not|was)$ is $(608 + 0.5)/(9409 + 14589 \times 0.5) = 0.036$. The estimate for $P(not|was)$ has thus been discounted (by almost half!). If we do similar calculations for the other words, then we get the results shown in the last column of table 6.5. The ordering of most likely words is naturally unchanged, but the probability estimates of words that did appear in the training text are discounted, while non-occurring words, in particular the actual next word, *inferior*, are given a non-zero probability of occurrence. Continuing in this way to also estimate the other bigram probabilities, we find that this language model gives a probability estimate for the clause of 6.89×10^{-20}. Unfortunately, this probability estimate is actually *lower* than the MLE estimate based on unigram counts – reflecting how greatly all the MLE probability estimates for seen *n*-grams are discounted in the construction of the ELE model. This result substantiates the slogan used in the titles of (Gale and Church 1990a,b): poor estimates of context are worse than none. Note, however, that this does not mean that the model that we have constructed is entirely useless. Although the probability estimates it gives are extremely low, one can nevertheless use them to rank alternatives. For example, the model does correctly tell us that *she was inferior to both sisters* is a much more likely clause in English than *inferior to was both she sisters*, whereas the unigram estimate gives them both the same probability.

6.2.3   Held out estimation

How do we know that giving 46.5% of the probability space to unseen events is too much? One way that we can test this is empirically. We

HELD OUT ESTIMATOR

can take further text (assumed to be from the same source) and see how often bigrams that appeared r times in the training text tend to turn up in the further text. The realization of this idea is the *held out estimator* of Jelinek and Mercer (1985).

The held out estimator

For each n-gram, $w_1 \cdots w_n$, let:

$$C_1(w_1 \cdots w_n) = \text{frequency of } w_1 \cdots w_n \text{ in training data}$$
$$C_2(w_1 \cdots w_n) = \text{frequency of } w_1 \cdots w_n \text{ in held out data}$$

and recall that N_r is the number of bigrams with frequency r (in the training text). Now let:

$$(6.9) \qquad T_r = \sum_{\{w_1 \cdots w_n : C_1(w_1 \cdots w_n) = r\}} C_2(w_1 \cdots w_n)$$

That is, T_r is the total number of times that all n-grams that appeared r times in the training text appeared in the held out data. Then the average frequency of those n-grams is $\frac{T_r}{N_r}$ and so an estimate for the probability of one of these n-grams is:

$$(6.10) \qquad P_{\text{ho}}(w_1 \cdots w_n) = \frac{T_r}{N_r N} \qquad \text{where } C(w_1 \cdots w_n) = r$$

Pots of data for developing and testing models

TRAINING DATA

OVERTRAINING

TEST DATA

A cardinal sin in Statistical NLP is to test on your *training data*. But why is that? The idea of testing is to assess how well a particular model works. That can only be done if it is a 'fair test' on data that has not been seen before. In general, models induced from a sample of data have a tendency to be *overtrained*, that is, to expect future events to be like the events on which the model was trained, rather than allowing sufficiently for other possibilities. (For instance, stock market models sometimes suffer from this failing.) So it is essential to test on different data. A particular case of this is for the calculation of cross entropy (section 2.2.6). To calculate cross entropy, we take a large sample of text and calculate the per-word entropy of that text according to our model. This gives us a measure of the quality of our model, and an upper bound for the entropy of the language that the text was drawn from in general. But all that is only true if the *test data* is independent of the training data, and large enough to be indicative of the complexity of the language at hand. If we test on the training data, the cross entropy can easily be lower than the real entropy of the text. In the most blatant case we could build a model that has memorized the training text and always predicts the next word with probability 1. Even if we don't do that, we will find that MLE is an excellent language model if you are testing on training data, which is not the right result.

So when starting to work with some data, one should always separate it immediately into a training portion and a testing portion. The test data is normally only a small percentage (5–10%) of the total data, but has to be sufficient for the results to be reliable. You should always eyeball the training data – you want to use your human pattern-finding abilities to get hints on how to proceed. You shouldn't eyeball the test data – that's cheating, even if less directly than getting your program to memorize it.

HELD OUT DATA
VALIDATION DATA

Commonly, however, one wants to divide both the training and test data into two again, for different reasons. For many Statistical NLP methods, such as held out estimation of *n*-grams, one gathers counts from one lot of training data, and then one smooths these counts or estimates certain other parameters of the assumed model based on what turns up in further *held out* or *validation* data. The held out data needs to be independent of both the primary training data and the test data. Normally the stage using the held out data involves the estimation of many fewer parameters than are estimated from counts over the primary training data, and so it is appropriate for the held out data to be much smaller than the primary training data (commonly about 10% of the size). Nevertheless, it is important that there is sufficient data for any additional parameters of the model to be accurately estimated, or significant performance losses can occur (as Chen and Goodman (1996: 317) show).

DEVELOPMENT TEST
SET
FINAL TEST SET

A typical pattern in Statistical NLP research is to write an algorithm, train it, and test it, note some things that it does wrong, revise it and then to repeat the process (often many times!). But, if one does that a lot, not only does one tend to end up seeing aspects of the test set, but just repeatedly trying out different variant algorithms and looking at their performance can be viewed as subtly probing the contents of the test set. This means that testing a succession of variant models can again lead to overtraining. So the right approach is to have two test sets: a *development test set* on which successive variant methods are trialed and a *final test set* which is used to produce the final results that are published about the performance of the algorithm. One should expect performance on the final test set to be slightly lower than on the development test set (though sometimes one can be lucky).

The discussion so far leaves open exactly how to choose which parts of the data are to be used as testing data. Actually here opinion divides into two schools. One school favors selecting bits (sentences or even *n*-grams) randomly from throughout the data for the test set and using the rest of the material for training. The advantage of this method is that the testing data is as similar as possible (with respect to genre, register, writer, and vocabulary) to the training data. That is, one is training from as accurate a sample as possible of the type of language in the test data. The other possibility is to set aside large contiguous chunks as test data. The advantage of this is the opposite: in practice, one will end up using any NLP system on data that varies a little from the training data, as language use changes a little in topic and structure with the passage of time. Therefore, some people think it best to simulate that a little by choosing test data that perhaps isn't quite stationary with respect to the training data. At any rate, if using held out estimation of parameters, it is best to choose the same strategy for setting aside data for held out data as for test data, as this makes the held out data a better simulation of the test data. This choice is one of the many reasons why system results can be hard to compare: all else being equal, one should expect slightly worse performance results if using the second approach.

VARIANCE

While covering testing, let us mention one other issue. In early work, it was common to just run the system on the test data and present a single performance figure (for perplexity, percent correct or whatever). But this isn't a very good way of testing, as it gives no idea of the *variance* in the performance of the system. A much better way is to divide the test data into, say 20, smaller samples, and work out a test result on each of them. From those results, one can work out a mean performance figure, as before, but one can also calculate the variance that shows how much performance tends to vary. If using this method together with continuous chunks of training data, it is probably best to take the smaller testing samples from different regions of the data, since the testing lore tends to be full of stories about certain sections of data sets being "easy," and so it is better to have used a range of test data from different sections of the corpus.

If we proceed this way, then one system can score higher on average than another purely by accident, especially when within-system variance is high. So just comparing average scores is not enough for meaningful

	System 1	System 2
scores	71, 61, 55, 60, 68, 49,	42, 55, 75, 45, 54, 51
	42, 72, 76, 55, 64	55, 36, 58, 55, 67
total	609	526
n	11	11
mean $\bar{x}_i$	55.4	47.8
$s_i^2 = \sum (x_{ij} - \bar{x}_i)^2$	1,375.4	1,228.8
df	10	10

$$\text{Pooled } s^2 = \frac{1375.4 + 1228.8}{10 + 10} \approx 130.2$$

$$t = \frac{\bar{x}_1 - \bar{x}_2}{\sqrt{\frac{2s^2}{n}}} = \frac{55.4 - 47.8}{\sqrt{\frac{2 \cdot 130.2}{11}}} \approx 1.56$$

Table 6.6   Using the t test for comparing the performance of two systems. Since we calculate the mean for each data set, the denominator in the calculation of variance and the number of degrees of freedom is $(11 - 1) + (11 - 1) = 20$. The data do not provide clear support for the superiority of system 1. Despite the clear difference in mean scores, the sample variance is too high to draw any definitive conclusions.

system comparison. Instead, we need to apply a statistical test that takes into account both mean and variance. Only if the statistical test rejects the possibility of an accidental difference can we say with confidence that one system is better than the other.[9]

t TEST   An example of using the t test (which we introduced in section 5.3.1) for comparing the performance of two systems is shown in table 6.6 (adapted from (Snedecor and Cochran 1989: 92)). Note that we use a pooled estimate of the sample variance s^2 here under the assumption that the variance of the two systems is the same (which seems a reasonable assumption here: 609 and 526 are close enough). Looking up the t distribution in the appendix, we find that, for rejecting the hypothesis that the system 1 is better than system 2 at a probability level of $\alpha = 0.05$, the critical value is $t = 1.725$ (using a one-tailed test with 20 degrees of freedom). Since we have $t = 1.56 < 1.725$, the data fail the significance test. Although the averages are fairly distinct, we cannot conclude superiority of system 1 here because of the large variance of scores.

---

9. Systematic discussion of testing methodology for comparing statistical and machine learning algorithms can be found in (Dietterich 1998). A good case study, for the example of word sense disambiguation, is (Mooney 1996).

Using held out estimation on the test data

So long as the frequency of an n-gram $C(w_1 \cdots w_n)$ is the only thing that we are using to predict its future frequency in text, then we can use held out estimation performed on the test set to provide the correct answer of what the discounted estimates of probabilities should be in order to maximize the probability of the test set data. Doing this empirically measures how often n-grams that were seen r times in the training data actually do occur in the test text. The empirical estimates $f_{empirical}$ in table 6.4 were found by randomly dividing the 44 million bigrams in the whole AP corpus into equal-sized training and test sets, counting frequencies in the 22 million word training set and then doing held out estimation using the test set. Whereas other estimates are calculated only from the 22 million words of training data, this estimate can be regarded as an empirically determined gold standard, achieved by allowing access to the test data.

6.2.4   Cross-validation (deleted estimation)

The $f_{empirical}$ estimates discussed immediately above were constructed by looking at what actually happened in the test data. But the idea of held out estimation is that we can achieve the same effect by dividing the training data into two parts. We build initial estimates by doing counts on one part, and then we use the other pool of held out data to refine those estimates. The only cost of this approach is that our initial training data is now less, and so our probability estimates will be less reliable.

Rather than using some of the training data only for frequency counts and some only for smoothing probability estimates, more efficient schemes are possible where each part of the training data is used both as initial training data and as held out data. In general, such methods in CROSS-VALIDATION   statistics go under the name *cross-validation*.

Jelinek and Mercer (1985) use a form of two-way cross-validation that DELETED ESTIMATION   they call *deleted estimation*. Suppose we let N_r^a be the number of n-grams occurring r times in the ath part of the training data, and T_r^{ab} be the total occurrences of those bigrams from part a in the bth part. Now depending on which part is viewed as the basic training data, standard held out estimates would be either:

$$P_{ho}(w_1 \cdots w_n) = \frac{T_r^{01}}{N_r^0 N} \text{ or } \frac{T_r^{10}}{N_r^1 N} \qquad \text{where } C(w_1 \cdots w_n) = r$$

The more efficient deleted interpolation estimate does counts and smoothing on both halves and then does a weighted average of the two according to the proportion of words in N_r^0 versus N_r^1:

(6.11) $$P_{\text{del}}(w_1 \cdots w_n) = \frac{T_r^{01} + T_r^{10}}{N(N_r^0 + N_r^1)} \qquad \text{where } C(w_1 \cdots w_n) = r$$

On large training corpora, doing deleted estimation on the training data works better than doing held-out estimation using just the training data, and indeed table 6.4 shows that it produces results that are quite close to the empirical gold standard.[10] It is nevertheless still some way off for low frequency events. It overestimates the expected frequency of unseen objects, while underestimating the expected frequency of objects that were seen once in the training data. By dividing the text into two parts like this, one estimates the probability of an object by how many times it was seen in a sample of size $\frac{N}{2}$, assuming that the probability of a token seen r times in a sample of size $\frac{N}{2}$ is double that of a token seen r times in a sample of size N. However, it is generally true that as the size of the training corpus increases, the percentage of unseen n-grams that one encounters in held out data, and hence one's probability estimate for unseen n-grams, decreases (while never becoming negligible). It is for this reason that collecting counts on a smaller training corpus has the effect of overestimating the probability of unseen n-grams.

LEAVING-ONE-OUT

There are other ways of doing cross-validation. In particular Ney et al. (1997) explore a method that they call *Leaving-One-Out* where the primary training corpus is of size $N - 1$ tokens, while 1 token is used as held out data for a sort of simulated testing. This process is repeated N times so that each piece of data is left out in turn. The advantage of this training regime is that it explores the effect of how the model changes if any particular piece of data had not been observed, and Ney et al. show strong connections between the resulting formulas and the widely-used Good-Turing method to which we turn next.[11]

---

10. Remember that, although the empirical gold standard was derived by held out estimation, it was held out estimation based on looking at the test data! Chen and Goodman (1998) find in their study that for smaller training corpora, held out estimation outperforms deleted estimation.

11. However, Chen and Goodman (1996: 314) suggest that leaving one word out at a time is problematic, and that using larger deleted chunks in deleted interpolation is to be preferred.

6.2.5   Good-Turing estimation

The Good-Turing estimator

Good (1953) attributes to Turing a method for determining frequency or probability estimates of items, on the assumption that their distribution is binomial. This method is suitable for large numbers of observations of data drawn from a large vocabulary, and works well for n-grams, despite the fact that words and n-grams do not have a binomial distribution. The probability estimate in Good-Turing estimation is of the form $P_{GT} = r^*/N$ where r^* can be thought of as an adjusted frequency. The theorem underlying Good-Turing methods gives that for previously observed items:

$$(6.12) \qquad r^* = (r + 1)\frac{E(N_{r+1})}{E(N_r)}$$

where E denotes the expectation of a random variable (see (Church and Gale 1991a; Gale and Sampson 1995) for discussion of the derivation of this formula). The total probability mass reserved for unseen objects is then $E(N_1)/N$ (see exercise 6.5).

Using our empirical estimates, we can hope to substitute the observed N_r for $E(N_r)$. However, we cannot do this uniformly, since these empirical estimates will be very unreliable for high values of r. In particular, the most frequent n-gram would be estimated to have probability zero, since the number of n-grams with frequency one greater than it is zero! In practice, one of two solutions is employed. One is to use Good-Turing reestimation only for frequencies $r < k$ for some constant k (e.g., 10). Low frequency words are numerous, so substitution of the observed frequency of frequencies for the expectation is quite accurate, while the MLE estimates of high frequency words will also be quite accurate and so one doesn't need to discount them. The other is to fit some function S through the observed values of (r, N_r) and to use the smoothed values $S(r)$ for the expectation (this leads to a family of possibilities depending on exactly which method of curve fitting is employed – Good (1953) discusses several smoothing methods). The probability mass $\frac{N_1}{N}$ given to unseen items can either be divided among them uniformly, or by some more sophisticated method (see under Combining Estimators, below). So using this method with a uniform estimate for unseen events, we have:

Good-Turing Estimator: If $C(w_1 \cdots w_n) = r > 0$,

$$(6.13) \qquad P_{GT}(w_1 \cdots w_n) = \frac{r^*}{N} \quad \text{where } r^* = \frac{(r + 1)S(r + 1)}{S(r)}$$

If $C(w_1 \cdots w_n) = 0$,

(6.14) $\qquad P_{GT}(w_1 \cdots w_n) = \dfrac{1 - \sum_{r=1}^{\infty} N_r \frac{r^*}{N}}{N_0} \approx \dfrac{N_1}{N_0 N}$

Gale and Sampson (1995) present a simple and effective approach, Simple Good-Turing, which effectively combines these two approaches. As a smoothing curve they simply use a power curve $N_r = ar^b$ (with $b < -1$ to give the appropriate hyperbolic relationship), and estimate A and b by simple linear regression on the logarithmic form of this equation $\log N_r = a + b \log r$ (linear regression is covered in section 15.4.1, or in all introductory statistics books). However, they suggest that such a simple curve is probably only appropriate for high values of r. For low values of r, they use the measured N_r directly. Working up through frequencies, these direct estimates are used until for one of them there isn't a significant difference between r^* values calculated directly or via the smoothing function, and then smoothed estimates are used for all higher frequencies.[12] Simple Good-Turing can give exceedingly good estimators, as can be seen by comparing the Good-Turing column f_{GT} in table 6.4 with the empirical gold standard.

RENORMALIZATION Under any of these approaches, it is necessary to *renormalize* all the estimates to ensure that a proper probability distribution results. This can be done either by adjusting the amount of probability mass given to unseen items (as in equation (6.14)), or, perhaps better, by keeping the estimate of the probability mass for unseen items as $\frac{N_1}{N}$ and renormalizing all the estimates for previously seen items (as Gale and Sampson (1995) propose).

Frequencies of frequencies in Austen

COUNT-COUNTS To do Good-Turing, the first step is to calculate the frequencies of different frequencies (also known as *count-counts*). Table 6.7 shows extracts from the resulting list of frequencies of frequencies for bigrams and trigrams. (The numbers are reminiscent of the Zipfian distributions of

---

12. An estimate of r^* is deemed significantly different if the difference exceeds 1.65 times the standard deviation of the Good-Turing estimate, which is given by:

$$\sqrt{(r+1)^2 \frac{N_{r+1}}{N_r^2} \left(1 + \frac{N_{r+1}}{N_r}\right)}$$

	Bigrams				Trigrams			
r	N_r	r	N_r		r	N_r	r	N_r
1	138741	28	90		1	404211	28	35
2	25413	29	120		2	32514	29	32
3	10531	30	86		3	10056	30	25
4	5997	31	98		4	4780	31	18
5	3565	32	99		5	2491	32	19
6	2486		$\cdots$		6	1571		$\cdots$
7	1754	1264	1		7	1088	189	1
8	1342	1366	1		8	749	202	1
9	1106	1917	1		9	582	214	1
10	896	2233	1		10	432	366	1
	$\cdots$	2507	1			$\cdots$	378	1

Table 6.7 Extracts from the frequencies of frequencies distribution for bigrams and trigrams in the Austen corpus.

section 1.4.3 but different in the details of construction, and more exaggerated because they count sequences of words.) Table 6.8 then shows the reestimated counts r^* and corresponding probabilities for bigrams.

For the bigrams, the mass reserved for unseen bigrams, $N_1/N = 138741/617091 = 0.2248$. The space of bigrams is the vocabulary squared, and we saw 199,252 bigrams, so using uniform estimates, the probability estimate for each unseen bigram is: $0.2248/(14585^2 - 199252) = 1.058 \times 10^{-9}$. If we now wish to work out conditional probability estimates for a bigram model by using Good-Turing estimates for bigram probability estimates, and MLE estimates directly for unigrams, then we begin as follows:

$$P(she|person) = \frac{f_{GT}(person\ she)}{C(person)} = \frac{1.228}{223} = 0.0055$$

Continuing in this way gives the results in table 6.9, which can be compared with the bigram estimates in table 6.3. The estimates in general seem quite reasonable. Multiplying these numbers, we come up with a probability estimate for the clause of 1.278×10^{-17}. This is at least much higher than the ELE estimate, but still suffers from assuming a uniform distribution over unseen bigrams.

r	r^*	$P_{GT}(\cdot)$
0	0.0007	1.058×10^{-9}
1	0.3663	5.982×10^{-7}
2	1.228	2.004×10^{-6}
3	2.122	3.465×10^{-6}
4	3.058	4.993×10^{-6}
5	4.015	6.555×10^{-6}
6	4.984	8.138×10^{-6}
7	5.96	9.733×10^{-6}
8	6.942	1.134×10^{-5}
9	7.928	1.294×10^{-5}
10	8.916	1.456×10^{-5}
. . .		
28	26.84	4.383×10^{-5}
29	27.84	4.546×10^{-5}
30	28.84	4.709×10^{-5}
31	29.84	4.872×10^{-5}
32	30.84	5.035×10^{-5}
. . .		
1264	1263	0.002062
1366	1365	0.002228
1917	1916	0.003128
2233	2232	0.003644
2507	2506	0.004092

Table 6.8 Good-Turing estimates for bigrams: Adjusted frequencies and probabilities. Smoothed using the software on the website.

$P(she|person)$	0.0055
$P(was|she)$	0.1217
$P(inferior|was)$	6.9×10^{-8}
$P(to|inferior)$	0.1806
$P(both|to)$	0.0003956
$P(sisters|both)$	0.003874

Table 6.9 Good-Turing bigram frequency estimates for the clause from *Persuasion*.

6.2.6 Briefly noted

Ney and Essen (1993) and Ney et al. (1994) propose two discounting models: in the absolute discounting model, all non-zero MLE frequencies are discounted by a small constant amount δ and the frequency so gained is uniformly distributed over unseen events:

Absolute discounting: If $C(w_1 \cdots w_n) = r$,

$$(6.15) \quad P_{\text{abs}}(w_1 \cdots w_n) = \begin{cases} (r - \delta)/N & \text{if } r > 0 \\ \frac{(B - N_0)\delta}{N_0 N} & \text{otherwise} \end{cases}$$

(Recall that B is the number of bins.) In the linear discounting method, the non-zero MLE frequencies are scaled by a constant slightly less than one, and the remaining probability mass is again distributed across novel events:

Linear discounting: If $C(w_1 \cdots w_n) = r$,

$$(6.16) \quad P(w_1 \cdots w_n) = \begin{cases} (1 - \alpha)r/N & \text{if } r > 0 \\ \alpha/N_0 & \text{otherwise} \end{cases}$$

These estimates are equivalent to the frequent engineering move of making the probability of unseen events some small number ϵ instead of zero and then rescaling the other probabilities so that they still sum to one – the choice between them depending on whether the other probabilities are scaled by subtracting or multiplying by a constant. Looking again at the figures in table 6.4 indicates that absolute discounting seems like it could provide a good estimate. Examining the $f_{\text{empirical}}$ figures there, it seems that a discount of $\delta \approx 0.77$ would work well except for bigrams that have only been seen once previously (which would be underestimated). In general, we could use held out data to estimate a good value for δ. Extensions of the absolute discounting approach are very successful, as we discuss below. It is hard to justify linear discounting. In general, the higher the frequency of an item in the training text, the more accurate an unadjusted MLE estimate is, but the linear discounting method does not even approximate this observation.

A shortcoming of Lidstone's law is that it depends on the number of bins in the model. While some empty bins result from sparse data problems, many more may be principled gaps. Good-Turing estimation is one method where the estimates of previously seen items do not depend on the number of bins. Ristad (1995) explores the hypothesis that natural sequences use only a subset of the possible bins. He derives various forms for a *Natural Law of Succession*, including the following probability estimate for an *n*-gram with observed frequency $C(w_1 \cdots w_n) = r$:

NATURAL LAW OF
SUCCESSION

$$(6.17) \quad P_{\text{NLS}}(w_1 \cdots w_n) = \begin{cases} \frac{r+1}{N+B} & \text{if } N_0 = 0 \\ \frac{(r+1)(N+1+N_0-B)}{N^2+N+2(B-N_0)} & \text{if } N_0 > 0 \text{ and } r > 0 \\ \frac{(B-N_0)(B-N_0+1)}{N_0(N^2+N+2(B-N_0))} & \text{otherwise} \end{cases}$$

The central features of this law are: (i) it reduces to Laplace's law if something has been seen in every bin, (ii) the amount of probability mass assigned to unseen events decreases quadratically in the number N of trials, and (iii) the total probability mass assigned to unseen events is independent of the number of bins B, so there is no penalty for large vocabularies.

6.3   Combining Estimators

So far the methods we have considered have all made use of nothing but the raw frequency r of an *n*-gram and have tried to produce the best estimate of its probability in future text from that. But rather than giving the same estimate for all *n*-grams that never appeared or appeared only rarely, we could hope to produce better estimates by looking at the frequency of the $(n-1)$-grams found in the *n*-gram. If these $(n-1)$-grams are themselves rare, then we give a low estimate to the *n*-gram. If the $(n-1)$-grams are of moderate frequency, then we give a higher probability estimate for the *n*-gram.[13] Church and Gale (1991a) present a detailed study of this idea, showing how probability estimates for unseen bigrams can be estimated in terms of the probabilities of the unigrams that compose them. For unseen bigrams, they calculate the joint-if-independent probability $P(w_1)P(w_2)$, and then group the bigrams into bins based on this quantity. Good-Turing estimation is then performed on each bin to give corrected counts that are normalized to yield probabilities.

---

13. But if the $(n-1)$-grams are of very high frequency, then we may actually want to lower the estimate again, because the non-appearance of the *n*-gram is then presumably indicative of a principled gap.

But in this section we consider the more general problem of how to combine multiple probability estimates from various different models. If we have several models of how the history predicts what comes next, then we might wish to combine them in the hope of producing an even better model. The idea behind wanting to do this may either be smoothing, or simply combining different information sources.

For *n*-gram models, suitably combining various models of different orders is in general the secret to success. Simply combining MLE *n*-gram estimates of various orders (with some allowance for unseen words) using the simple linear interpolation technique presented below results in a quite good language model (Chen and Goodman 1996). One can do better, but not by simply using the methods presented above. Rather one needs to combine the methods presented above with the methods for combining estimators presented below.

6.3.1   Simple linear interpolation

One way of solving the sparseness in a trigram model is to mix that model with bigram and unigram models that suffer less from data sparseness. In any case where there are multiple probability estimates, we can make a linear combination of them, providing only that we weight the contribution of each so that the result is another probability function. Inside

LINEAR
INTERPOLATION
MIXTURE MODELS

Statistical NLP, this is usually called linear interpolation, but elsewhere the name *(finite) mixture models* is more common. When the functions being interpolated all use a subset of the conditioning information of the most discriminating function (as in the combination of trigram, bi-

DELETED
INTERPOLATION

gram and unigram models), this method is often referred to as *deleted interpolation*. For interpolating *n*-gram language models, such as deleted interpolation from a trigram model, the most basic way to do this is:

(6.18) $P_{li}(w_n|w_{n-2}, w_{n-1}) = \lambda_1 P_1(w_n) + \lambda_2 P_2(w_n|w_{n-1}) + \lambda_3 P_3(w_n|w_{n-1}, w_{n-2})$

where $0 \le \lambda_i \le 1$ and $\sum_i \lambda_i = 1$.

While the weights may be set by hand, in general one wants to find the combination of weights that works best. This can be done automatically by a simple application of the Expectation Maximization (EM) algorithm, as is discussed in section 9.2.1, or by other numerical algorithms. For instance, Chen and Goodman (1996) use Powell's algorithm, as presented in (Press et al. 1988). Chen and Goodman (1996) show that this simple model (with just slight complications to deal with previously unseen histories and to reserve some probability mass for out of vocabulary items) works quite well. They use it as the baseline model (see section 7.1.3) in their experiments.

6.3.2   Katz's backing-off

BACK-OFF MODELS

In *back-off models*, different models are consulted in order depending on their specificity. The most detailed model that is deemed to provide sufficiently reliable information about the current context is used. Again, back-off may be used to smooth or to combine information sources.

Back-off n-gram models were proposed by Katz (1987). The estimate for an n-gram is allowed to back off through progressively shorter histories:

$$(6.19)\quad P_{\text{bo}}(w_i | w_{i-n+1} \cdots w_{i-1}) = \begin{cases} (1 - d_{w_{i-n+1} \cdots w_{i-1}}) \frac{C(w_{i-n+1} \cdots w_i)}{C(w_{i-n+1} \cdots w_{i-1})} \\ \qquad\qquad \text{if } C(w_{i-n+1} \cdots w_i) > k \\ \alpha_{w_{i-n+1} \cdots w_{i-1}} P_{\text{bo}}(w_i | w_{i-n+2} \cdots w_{i-1}) \\ \qquad\qquad \text{otherwise} \end{cases}$$

If the n-gram of concern has appeared more than k times (k is normally set to 0 or 1), then an n-gram estimate is used, as in the first line. But the MLE estimate is discounted a certain amount (represented by the function d) so that some probability mass is reserved for unseen n-grams whose probability will be estimated by backing off. The MLE estimates need to be discounted in some manner, or else there would be no probability mass to distribute to the lower order models. One possibility for calculating the discount is the Good-Turing estimates discussed above, and this is what Katz actually used. If the n-gram did not appear or appeared k times or less in the training data, then we will use an estimate from a shorter n-gram. However, this back-off probability has to be multiplied by a normalizing factor α so that only the probability mass left over in the discounting process is distributed among n-grams that are estimated by backing off. Note that in the particular case where the $(n-1)$-gram in the immediately preceding history was unseen, the first line is inapplicable for any choice of w_i, and the back-off factor α takes on the value 1. If the second line is chosen, estimation is done recursively via an $(n-1)$-gram estimate. This recursion can continue down, so that one can start with a four-gram model and end up estimating the next word based on unigram frequencies.

While backing off in the absence of much data is generally reasonable, it can actually work badly in some circumstances. If we have seen the bigram $w_i w_j$ many times, and w_k is a common word, but we have never seen the trigram $w_i w_j w_k$, then at some point we should actually conclude that this is significant, and perhaps represents a 'grammatical zero,' rather than routinely backing off and estimating $P(w_k|h)$ via the bigram estimate $P(w_k|w_j)$. Rosenfeld and Huang (1992) suggest a more complex back-off model that attempts to correct for this.

Back-off models are sometimes criticized because their probability estimates can change suddenly on adding more data when the back-off algorithm selects a different order of n-gram model on which to base the estimate. Nevertheless, they are simple and in practice work well.

6.3.3 General linear interpolation

In simple linear interpolation, the weights were just a single number, but one can define a more general and powerful model where the weights are a function of the history. For k probability functions P_k the general form for a linear interpolation model is:

(6.20) $$P_{\text{li}}(w|h) = \sum_{i=1}^{k} \lambda_i(h) P_i(w|h)$$

where $\forall h$, $0 \le \lambda_i(h) \le 1$ and $\sum_i \lambda_i(h) = 1$.

Linear interpolation is commonly used because it is a very general way to combine models. Randomly adding in dubious models to a linear interpolation need not do harm providing one finds a good weighting of the models using the EM algorithm. But linear interpolation can make bad use of component models, especially if there is not a careful partitioning of the histories with different weights used for different sorts of histories. For instance, if the λ_i are just constants in an interpolation of n-gram models, the unigram estimate is always combined in with the same weight regardless of whether the trigram estimate is very good (because there is a lot of data) or very poor.

In general the weights are not set according to individual histories. Training a distinct $\lambda_{w_{(i-n+1)(i-1)}}$ for each $w_{(i-n+1)(i-1)}$ is not in general felicitous, because it would worsen the sparse data problem. Rather one wants to use some sort of equivalence classing of the histories. Bahl et al. (1983) suggest partitioning the λ into bins according to $C(w_{(i-n+1)(i-1)})$, and tying the parameters for all histories with the same frequency.

Chen and Goodman (1996) show that rather than this method of putting the λ parameters into bins, a better way is to group them according to the average number of counts per non-zero element:

(6.21)
$$\frac{C(w_{(i-n+1)(i-1)})}{|w_i : C(w_{(i-n+1)i}) > 0|}$$

That is, we take the average count over non-zero counts for n-grams $w_{i-n+1} \cdots w_{i-1} w^x$. We presume that the reason this works is that, because of the syntax of language, there are strong structural constraints on which words are possible or normal after certain other words. While it is central to most Statistical NLP language models that any word is allowed after any other – and this lets us deal with all possible disfluencies – nevertheless in many situations there are strong constraints on what can normally be expected due to the constraints of grammar. While some n-grams have just not been seen, others are 'grammatical zeroes,' to coin a phrase, because they do not fit with the grammatical rules of the language. For instance, in our Austen training corpus, both of the bigrams *great deal* and *of that* occur 178 times. But *of that* is followed in the corpus by 115 different words, giving an average count of 1.55, reflecting the fact that any adverb, adjective, or noun can felicitously follow within a noun phrase, and any capitalized word starting a new sentence is also a possibility. There are thus fairly few grammatical zeroes (mainly just verbs and prepositions). On the other hand, *great deal* is followed by only 36 words giving an average count of 4.94. While a new sentence start is again a possibility, grammatical possibilities are otherwise pretty much limited to conjunctions, prepositions, and the comparative form of adjectives. In particular, the preposition *of* follows 38% of the time. The higher average count reflects the far greater number of grammatical zeroes following this bigram, and so it is correct to give new unseen words a much lower estimate of occurrence in this context.

Finally, note that back-off models are actually a special case of the general linear interpolation model. In back-off models, the functions $\lambda_i(h)$ are chosen so that their value is 0 for a history h except for the coefficient of the model that would have been chosen using a back-off model, which has the value 1.

6.3.4   Briefly noted

Witten-Bell smoothing

Bell et al. (1990) and Witten and Bell (1991) introduce a number of smoothing algorithms for the goal of improving text compression. Their "Method C" is normally referred to as *Witten-Bell smoothing* and has been used for smoothing speech language models. The idea is to model the probability of a previously unseen event by estimating the probability of seeing such a new (previously unseen) event at each point as one proceeds through the training corpus. In particular, this probability is worked out relative to a certain history. So to calculate the probability of seeing a new word after, say, *sat in* one is calculating from the training data how often one saw a new word after *sat in*, which is just the count of the number of trigram types seen which begin with *sat in*. It is thus an instance of generalized linear interpolation:

$$(6.22) \quad P_{\text{WB}}(w_i | w_{(i-n+1)(i-1)}) = \lambda_{w_{(i-n+1)(i-1)}} P_{\text{MLE}}(w_i | w_{(i-n+1)(i-1)}) \\ + (1 - \lambda_{w_{(i-n+1)(i-1)}}) P_{\text{WB}}(w_i | w_{(i-n+2)(i-1)})$$

where the probability mass given to new *n*-grams is given by:

$$(6.23) \quad (1 - \lambda_{w_{(i-n+1)(i-1)}}) = \frac{|\{w_i : C(w_{i-n+1} \cdots w_i) > 0\}|}{|\{w_i : C(w_{i-n+1} \cdots w_i) > 0\}| + \sum_{w_i} C(w_{i-n+1} \cdots w_i)}$$

However, Chen and Goodman's (1998) results suggest that this method is not as good a smoothing technique for language models as others that we discuss in this section (performing particularly poorly when used on small training sets).

Linear Successive Abstraction

Samuelsson (1996) develops *Linear Successive Abstraction*, a method of determining the parameters of deleted interpolation style models without the need for their empirical determination on held out data. Samuelsson's results suggest similar performance within a part-of-speech tagger to that resulting from conventional deleted interpolation; we are unaware of any evaluation of this technique on word *n*-gram models.

Another simple but quite successful smoothing method examined by Chen and Goodman (1996) is the following. MacKay and Peto (1990) argue for a smoothed distribution of the form:

$$(6.24) \quad P_{\text{MP}}(w_i | w_{i-n+1} \cdots w_{i-1}) = \frac{C(w_{i-n+1} \cdots w_i) + \alpha P_{\text{MP}}(w_i | w_{i-n+2} \cdots w_{i-1})}{C(w_{i-n+1} \cdots w_{i-1}) + \alpha}$$

where α represents the number of counts added, in the spirit of Lidstone's law, but distributed according to the lower order distribution.

Model	Cross-entropy	Perplexity
Bigram	7.98 bits	252.3
Trigram	7.90 bits	239.1
Fourgram	7.95 bits	247.0

Table 6.10 Back-off language models with Good-Turing estimation tested on *Persuasion*.

Chen and Goodman (1996) suggest that the number of added counts should be proportional to the number of words seen exactly once, and suggest taking:

(6.25) $\alpha = \gamma (N_1 (w_{i-n+1} \cdots w_{i-1}) + \beta)$

where $N_1 (w_{i-n+1} \cdots w_{i-1}) = |\{w_i : C(w_{i-n+1} \cdots w_i) = 1\}|$, and then optimizing β and γ on held out data.

Kneser and Ney (1995) develop a back-off model based on an extension of absolute discounting which provides a new more accurate way of estimating the distribution to which one backs off. Chen and Goodman (1998) find that both this method and an extension of it that they propose provide excellent smoothing performance.

6.3.5   Language models for Austen

With the introduction of interpolation and back-off, we are at last at the point where we can build first-rate language models for our Austen corpus. Using the CMU-Cambridge Statistical Language Modeling Toolkit (see the website) we built back-off language models using Good-Turing estimates, following basically the approach of Katz (1987).[14] We then calculated the cross-entropy (and perplexity) of these language models on our test set, *Persuasion*. The results appear in table 6.10. The estimated probabilities for each following word, and the *n*-gram size used to estimate it for our sample clause is then shown in table 6.11. Our probability estimates are at last pleasingly *higher* than the unigram estimate with which we began!

While overall the trigram model outperforms the bigram model on the test data, note that on our example clause, the bigram model actually as-

---

14. The version of Good-Turing smoothing that the package implements only discounts low frequencies – words that occurred fewer than 7 times.

	$P(she\|h)$	$P(was\|h)$	$P(inferior\|h)$	$P(to\|h)$	$P(both\|h)$	$P(sisters\|h)$	Product
Unigram	0.011	0.015	0.00005	0.032	0.0005	0.0003	3.96×10^{-17}
Bigram	0.00529	0.1219	0.0000159	0.183	0.000449	0.00372	3.14×10^{-15}
n used	2	2	1	2	2	2	
Trigram	0.00529	0.0741	0.0000162	0.183	0.000384	0.00323	1.44×10^{-15}
n used	2	3	1	2	2	2	

Table 6.11 Probability estimates of the test clause according to various language models. The unigram estimate is our previous MLE unigram estimate. The other two estimates are back-off language models. The last column gives the overall probability estimate given to the clause by the model.

signs a higher probability. Overall, the fourgram model performs slightly worse than the trigram model. This is expected given the small amount of training data. Back-off models are in general not perfectly successful at simply ignoring inappropriately long contexts, and the models tend to deteriorate if too large *n*-grams are chosen for model building relative to the amount of data available.

6.4   Conclusions

A number of smoothing methods are available which often offer similar and good performance figures. Using Good-Turing estimation and linear interpolation or back-off to circumvent the problems of sparse data represent good current practice. Chen and Goodman (1996, 1998) present extensive evaluations of different smoothing algorithms. The conclusions of (Chen and Goodman 1998) are that a variant of Kneser-Ney back-off smoothing that they develop normally gives the best performance. It is outperformed by the Good-Turing smoothing method explored by Church and Gale (1991a) when training bigram models on more than 2 million words of text, and one might hypothesize that the same would be true of trigram models trained on a couple of orders of magnitude more text. But in all other circumstances, it seems to perform as well or better than other methods. While simple smoothing methods may be appropriate for exploratory studies, they are best avoided if one is hoping to produce systems with optimal performance. Active research continues on better ways of combining probability models and dealing with sparse data.

6.5 Further Reading

Important research studies on statistical estimation in the context of language modeling include (Katz 1987), (Jelinek 1990), (Church and Gale 1991a), (Ney and Essen 1993), and (Ristad 1995). Other discussions of estimation techniques can be found in (Jelinek 1997) and (Ney et al. 1997). Gale and Church (1994) provide detailed coverage of the problems with "adding one." An approachable account of Good-Turing estimation can be found in (Gale and Sampson 1995). The extensive empirical comparison of various smoothing methods in (Chen and Goodman 1996, 1998) are particularly recommended.

The notion of maximum likelihood across the values of a parameter was first defined in (Fisher 1922). See (Ney et al. 1997) for a proof that the relative frequency really is the maximum likelihood estimate.

Recently, there has been increasing use of maximum entropy methods for combining models. We defer coverage of maximum entropy models until chapter 16. See Lau et al. (1993) and Rosenfeld (1994, 1996) for applications to language models.

The early work cited in section 6.2.2 appears in: (Lidstone 1920), (Johnson 1932), and (Jeffreys 1948). See (Ristad 1995) for discussion. Good (1979: 395–396) covers Turing's initial development of the idea of Good-Turing smoothing. This article is reprinted with amplification in (Britton 1992).

6.6 Exercises

Exercise 6.1   [⋆ ⋆]

Explore figures for the percentage of unseen n-grams in test data (that differs from the training data). Explore varying some or all of: (i) the order of the model (i.e., n), (ii) the size of the training data, (iii) the genre of the training data, and (iv) how similar in genre, domain, and year the test data is to the training data.

Exercise 6.2   [⋆]

As a smaller example of the problems with Laplace's law, work out probability estimates using Laplace's law given that 100 samples have been seen from a potential vocabulary of 1000 items, and in that sample 9 items were seen 10 times, 2 items were seen 5 times and the remaining 989 items were unseen.

Exercise 6.3 [★]

Show that using ELE yields a probability function, in particular that

$$\sum_{w_1 \cdots w_n} P_{\text{ELE}}(w_1 \cdots w_n) = 1$$

Exercise 6.4 [★]

Using the word and bigram frequencies within the Austen test corpus given below, confirm the ELE estimate for the test clause *she was inferior to both sisters* given in section 6.2.2 (using the fact that the word before *she* in the corpus was *person*).

w	$C(w)$	$w_1 w_2$	$C(w_1 w_2)$
person	223	person she	2
she	6,917	she was	843
was	9,409	was inferior	0
inferior	33	inferior to	7
to	20,042	to both	9
both	317	both sisters	2

Exercise 6.5 [★]

Show that Good-Turing estimation is well-founded. I.e., you want to show:

$$\sum_{w_1 \cdots w_n} P_{\text{GT}}(w_1 \cdots w_n) = \frac{f_{\text{GT}}(w_1 \cdots w_n)}{N} = 1$$

Exercise 6.6 [★]

We calculated a Good-Turing probability estimate for *she was inferior to both sisters* using a bigram model with a uniform estimate of unseen bigrams. Make sure you can recreate these results, and then try doing the same thing using a trigram model. How well does it work?

Exercise 6.7 [★★]

Build language models for a corpus using the software pointed to on the website (or perhaps build your own). Experiment with what options give the best language model, as measured by cross-entropy.

Exercise 6.8 [★★]

Get two corpora drawn from different domains, and divide each into a training and a test set. Build language models based on the training data for each domain. Then calculate the cross-entropy figures for the test sets using both the language model trained on that domain, and the other language model. How much do the cross-entropy estimates differ?

Exercise 6.9 [⋆⋆]

Write a program that learns word n-gram models of some text (perhaps doing smoothing, but it is not really necessary for this exercise). Train separate models on articles from several Usenet newsgroups or other text from different genres and then generate some random text based on the models. How intelligible is the output for different values of n? Is the different character of the various newsgroups clearly preserved in the generated text?

Exercise 6.10 [⋆⋆]

Write a program that tries to identify the language in which a short segment of text is written, based on training itself on text written in known languages. For instance, each of the following lines is text in a different language:

> doen is ondubbelzinnig uit
> prétendre à un emploi
> uscirono fuori solo alcune
> look into any little problem

If you know a little about European languages, you can probably identify what language each sample is from. This is a classification task, in which you should usefully be able to use some of the language modeling techniques discussed in this chapter. (Hint: consider letter n-grams vs. word n-grams.) (This is a problem that has been investigated by others; see in particular (Dunning 1994). The website contains pointers to a number of existing language identification systems – including one that was originally done as a solution to this exercise!)

"The primary implication is that a task-independent set of word senses for a language is not a coherent concept. Word senses are simply undefined unless there is some underlying rationale for clustering, some context which classifies some distinctions as worth making and others as not worth making. For people, homonyms like 'pike' are a limiting case: in almost any situation where a person considers it worth their while attending to a sentence containing 'pike,' it is also worth their while making the fish/weapon distinction."

(Kilgarriff 1997: 19)

7 *Word Sense Disambiguation*

THIS CHAPTER gives an overview of work on word sense disambiguation within Statistical NLP. It introduces a few of the most important word sense disambiguation algorithms, and describes their resource requirements and performance.

SENSES
AMBIGUITY
What is the idea of word sense disambiguation? The problem to be solved is that many words have several meanings or *senses.* For such words given out of context, there is thus *ambiguity* about how they are to be interpreted. As a first example of ambiguity, consider the word *bank* and two of the senses that can be found in Webster's New Collegiate Dictionary (Woolf 1973):

■ the rising ground bordering a lake, river, or sea ...

■ an establishment for the custody, loan exchange, or issue of money, for the extension of credit, and for facilitating the transmission of funds

DISAMBIGUATION
The task of *disambiguation* is to determine which of the senses of an ambiguous word is invoked in a particular use of the word. This is done by looking at the context of the word's use.

This is how the problem has normally been construed in the word sense disambiguation literature. A word is assumed to have a finite number of discrete senses, often given by a dictionary, thesaurus, or other reference source, and the task of the program is to make a forced choice between these senses for the meaning of each usage of an ambiguous word, based on the context of use. However, it is important to realize at the outset that there are a number of reasons to be quite unhappy with such a statement of the task. The word *bank* is perhaps the most famous example of an ambiguous word, but it is really quite atypical. A more typical situation is that a word has various somewhat related senses, and it is unclear whether to and where to draw lines between them. For example, consider the word *title*. Some senses that we found in a dictionary were:

- Name/heading of a book, statute, work of art or music, etc.

- Material at the start of a film

- The right of legal ownership (of land)

- The document that is evidence of this right

- An appellation of respect attached to a person's name

SYNECDOCHE   - A written work [by *synecdoche*, i.e., putting a part for the whole]

One approach is simply to define the senses of a word as the meanings given to it in a particular dictionary. However, this is unsatisfactory from a scientific viewpoint because dictionaries often differ greatly in the number and kind of senses they list, not only because comprehensive dictionaries can be more complete, but fundamentally in the way word uses are gathered into senses. And often these groupings seem quite arbitrary. For example, the above list of senses distinguishes as two senses a right of legal title to property and a document that shows that right. However, this pattern of sense extension between a concept and something that shows the concept is pervasive and could have been, but was not, distinguished for other uses. For example the same ambiguity exists when talking about the title of a painting. For instance, one might remark in a gallery:

(7.1)   This work doesn't have a title.

That sentence could mean either that the work was not given a title by the author, or simply that the little placard giving the title, which usually appears by paintings in a gallery, is missing. It is also somewhat unclear why books, statutes and works of art or music are grouped together while films are separated out. The second definition could be seen as a special case of the first definition. It is quite common in many dictionaries for senses to be listed that are really special cases of another sense, if this sense is frequently and distinctively used in texts. These difficulties suggest that, for most words, the usages and hence the sense definitions are not to be thought of as like five kinds of cheese, among which one must choose, but more like a casserole which has some pieces of clearly distinct identifiable content, but a lot of stuff of uncertain and mixed origin in between.

Notwithstanding these philosophical objections, the problem of disambiguation is of clear importance in many applications of natural language processing. A system for automatic translation from English to German needs to translate *bank* as *Ufer* for the first sense given above ('ground bordering a lake or river'), and as *Bank* for the second sense ('financial institution'). An information retrieval system answering a query about 'financial banks' should return only documents that use *bank* in the second sense. Whenever a system's actions depend on the meaning of the text being processed, disambiguation is beneficial or even necessary.

There is another kind of ambiguity, where a word can be used as different parts of speech. For example, *butter* may be used as a noun, or as a verb, as in *You should butter your toast*. Determining the usage of a word TAGGING in terms of part of speech is referred to as *tagging*, and is discussed in chapter 10. How do these two notions relate? Using a word as a verb instead of as a noun is clearly a different usage, with a different meaning involved, and so this could be viewed as a word sense disambiguation problem. Conversely, differentiating word senses could be viewed as a tagging problem, but using semantic tags rather than part of speech tags. In practice, the two topics have been distinguished, partly because of differences between the nature of the problem, and partly because of the methods that have been used to approach them. In general, nearby structural cues are most useful for determining part of speech (e.g., is the preceding word a determiner?), but are almost useless for determining semantic sense within a part of speech. Conversely, quite distant content words are often very effective for determining a semantic sense, but are of little use for determining part of speech. Consequently, most part of speech tagging models simply use local context, while word sense disambiguation methods often try to use content words in a broader context.

The nature of ambiguity and disambiguation changes quite a bit depending on what material is available for training a word sense disambiguation system. After an initial section about methodology, this chapter has three main sections dealing with different types of training material. Section 7.2 describes *supervised disambiguation*, disambiguation based on a labeled training set. Section 7.3 describes *dictionary-based disambiguation*, disambiguation that is based on lexical resources such as dictionaries and thesauri. Section 7.4 deals with *unsupervised disam-*

biguation, the case in which only unlabeled text corpora are available for training. We conclude with an in-depth discussion of the notion of sense and pointers to further reading.

7.1   Methodological Preliminaries

Several important methodological issues come up in the context of word sense disambiguation. They are of general relevance to NLP, but have received special attention in this context. These are: supervised vs. unsupervised learning; the use of artificial evaluation data, known in the word sense disambiguation context as *pseudowords*; and the development of upper and lower bounds for the performance of algorithms, so that their success can be meaningfully interpreted.

7.1.1   Supervised and unsupervised learning

SUPERVISED LEARNING

UNSUPERVISED
LEARNING

CLUSTERING

CLASSIFICATION

A lot of algorithms are classified as to whether they involve supervised or unsupervised learning (Duda and Hart 1973: 45). The distinction is that with *supervised learning* we know the actual status (here, sense label) for each piece of data on which we train, whereas with *unsupervised learning* we do not know the classification of the data in the training sample. Unsupervised learning can thus often be viewed as a *clustering* task (see chapter 14), while supervised learning can usually be seen as a *classification* task (see chapter 16), or equivalently as a function-fitting task where one extrapolates the shape of a function based on some data points.

KNOWLEDGE SOURCES

However, in the Statistical NLP domain, things are often not this simple. Because the production of labeled training data is expensive, people will often want to be able to learn from unlabeled data, but will try to give their algorithms a head start by making use of various *knowledge sources*, such as dictionaries, or more richly structured data, such as aligned bilingual texts. In other methods, the system is seeded with labeled training data, but this data is augmented by further learning from unlabeled data. Rather than trying to force different methods on to a procrustean bed, it usually makes most sense to simply give a precise answer to the question: *What knowledge sources are needed for use of this method?* As we will see, sometimes there are alternative combinations of knowledge sources that can give similar information (e.g., using either aligned bilingual texts, or monolingual texts and a bilingual dictionary).

7.1.2 Pseudowords

In order to test the performance of disambiguation algorithms on a natural ambiguous word, a large number of occurrences has to be disambiguated by hand – a time-intensive and laborious task. In cases like this in which test data are hard to come by, it is often convenient to generate artificial evaluation data for the comparison and improvement of text processing algorithms. In the case of word sense disambiguation these

PSEUDOWORDS artificial data are called *pseudowords*.

Gale et al. (1992e) and Schütze (1992a) show how pseudowords, i.e., artificial ambiguous words, can be created by conflating two or more natural words. For example, to create the pseudoword *banana-door*, one replaces all occurrences of *banana* and *door* in a corpus by the artificial word *banana-door*. Pseudowords make it easy to create large-scale training and test sets for disambiguation while obviating the need for hand-labeling: we regard the text with pseudowords as the ambiguous source text, and the original as the text with the ambiguous words disambiguated.

7.1.3 Upper and lower bounds on performance

While it is important to measure the performance of one's algorithm, numerical evaluation by itself is meaningless without some discussion of how well the algorithm performs *relative to the difficulty of the task*. For example, whereas 90% accuracy is easy to achieve for part-of-speech tagging of English text, it is beyond the capacity of any existing machine translation system. The estimation of upper and lower bounds for the performance of an algorithm is a way to make sense of performance figures (Gale et al. 1992a). It is a good idea for many tasks in NLP, especially if there are no standardized evaluation sets for comparing systems.

UPPER BOUND The *upper bound* used is usually human performance. In the case of word sense disambiguation, if human judges disagree on the correct sense assignment for a particular context, then we cannot expect an automatic procedure to do better. Determining upper bounds is particularly interesting if the disambiguation algorithm uses a limited representation of contexts, for example just looking at the three words on each side of the ambiguous word. In such a situation, the reason for poor performance may just be that the contextual representations are not very informative so that even humans would not be able to disambiguate very well based on the same information. We can evaluate this by looking at human performance when based on the same limited contextual cues.[1]

An upper bound for word sense disambiguation was established by Gale et al. (1992a). Gale et al. performed tests with the following task: Subjects were given pairs of occurrences and had to decide whether they were instances of the same sense. The task resulted in upper bounds between 97% and 99%. However, most of the words in Gale et al.'s test set have few and clearly distinct senses. In contrast, there are many ambiguous words (in particular, high-frequency ones) that are similar to our example *title*, i.e., their senses are interrelated and overlapping. Interjudge agreement depends on the type of ambiguity: it is higher for words with clearly distinct senses (95% and higher) and lower for polysemous words with many related senses (perhaps as low as 65% to 70%).[2] The task is also easier when viewed as a yes/no decision task than as an arbitrary clustering task.

This means that we have to look at the properties of an individual ambiguous word to determine whether a disambiguation algorithm does a good job for it. For a word like *bank* we should aim for performance in the ninety percent range, whereas less stringent criteria should be applied to fuzzier cases like *title*, *side*, and *way*.

LOWER BOUND   The *lower bound* or *baseline* is the performance of the simplest possi-
BASELINE   ble algorithm, usually the assignment of all contexts to the most frequent sense. A baseline should always be given because raw performance numbers make it impossible to assess how hard disambiguation is for a particular word. An accuracy of 90% is an excellent result for an ambiguous word with two equiprobable senses. The same accuracy for a word with two senses in a 9 to 1 frequency ratio is trivial to achieve – by always selecting the most frequent sense.

▼ Upper and lower bounds are most relevant when we are dealing with a classification task and the evaluation measure is accuracy. Section 8.1 discusses other evaluation measures, in particular, precision and recall.

---

1. Although, for limited artificial contexts like this, it is of course possible that computers might be able to be more successful than human beings at extracting useful predictive information.
2. See (Jorgensen 1990). To be able to correctly compare the extent of inter-judge agreement across tasks, we need to correct for the expected chance agreement (which depends on the number of senses being distinguished). This is done by the kappa statistic (Siegel and Castellan 1988; Carletta 1996).

Symbol	Meaning
w	an ambiguous word
$s_1, \ldots, s_k, \ldots, s_K$	senses of the ambiguous word w
$c_1, \ldots, c_i, \ldots, c_I$	contexts of w in a corpus
$v_1, \ldots, v_j, \ldots, v_J$	words used as contextual features for disambiguation

Table 7.1 Notational conventions used in this chapter.

7.2   Supervised Disambiguation

In supervised disambiguation, a disambiguated corpus is available for training. There is a training set of exemplars where each occurrence of the ambiguous word w is annotated with a semantic label (usually its contextually appropriate sense s_k). This setting makes supervised disambiguation an instance of statistical classification, the topic of chapter 16. The task is to build a classifier which correctly classifies new cases based on their context of use c_i. This notation, which we will use throughout the remainder of the chapter, is shown in table 7.1.

We have selected two of the many supervised algorithms that have been applied to word sense disambiguation that exemplify two important theoretical approaches in statistical language processing: Bayesian classification (the algorithm proposed by Gale et al. (1992b)) and Information Theory (the algorithm proposed by Brown et al. (1991b)). They also demonstrate that very different sources of information can be employed successfully for disambiguation. The first approach treats the context of occurrence as a bag of words without structure, but it integrates information from many words in the context window. The second approach looks at only one informative feature in the context, which may be sensitive to text structure. But this feature is carefully selected from a large number of potential 'informants.'

7.2.1   Bayesian classification

The idea of the Bayes classifier which we will present for word senses is that it looks at the words around an ambiguous word in a large context window. Each content word contributes potentially useful information about which sense of the ambiguous word is likely to be used with it. The classifier does no feature selection. Instead it combines the evidence from all features. The specific formalization we describe is due to Gale et al. (1992b). The supervised training of the classifier assumes that we have a corpus where each use of ambiguous words is labeled with its correct sense.

BAYES CLASSIFIER   A *Bayes classifier* applies the *Bayes decision rule* when choosing a class,
BAYES DECISION RULE the rule that minimizes the probability of error (Duda and Hart 1973: 10–43):

(7.2)   **Bayes decision rule**
Decide s' if $P(s'|c) > P(s_k|c)$ for $s_k \neq s'$

The Bayes decision rule is optimal because it minimizes the probability of error. This is true because for each individual case it chooses the class (or sense) with the highest conditional probability and hence the smallest error rate. The error rate for a sequence of decisions (for example, disambiguating all instances of w in a multi-page text) will therefore also be as small as possible.

We usually do not know the value of $P(s_k|c)$, but we can compute it
BAYES' RULE   using *Bayes' rule* as in section 2.1.10:

$$P(s_k|c) = \frac{P(c|s_k)}{P(c)} P(s_k)$$

PRIOR PROBABILITY $P(s_k)$ is the *prior probability* of sense s_k, the probability that we have an instance of s_k if we do not know anything about the context. $P(s_k)$ is updated with the factor $\frac{P(c|s_k)}{P(c)}$ which incorporates the evidence which we
POSTERIOR   have about the context, and results in the *posterior probability* $P(s_k|c)$.
PROBABILITY   If all we want to do is choose the correct class, we can simplify the classification task by eliminating $P(c)$ (which is a constant for all senses and hence does not influence what the maximum is). We can also use logs of probabilities to make the computation simpler. Then, we want to assign w to the sense s' where:

(7.3)
$$
\begin{aligned}
s' &= \underset{s_k}{\arg\max}\, P(s_k|c) \\
&= \underset{s_k}{\arg\max}\, \frac{P(c|s_k)}{P(c)} P(s_k) \\
&= \underset{s_k}{\arg\max}\, P(c|s_k) P(s_k) \\
&= \underset{s_k}{\arg\max}\, [\log P(c|s_k) + \log P(s_k)]
\end{aligned}
$$

NAIVE BAYES

Gale et al.'s classifier is an instance of a particular kind of Bayes classifier, the *Naive Bayes* classifier. Naive Bayes is widely used in machine learning due to its efficiency and its ability to combine evidence from a large number of features (Mitchell 1997: ch. 6). It is applicable if the state of the world that we base our classification on is described as a series of attributes. In our case, we describe the context of w in terms of the words v_j that occur in the context.

NAIVE BAYES
ASSUMPTION

The *Naive Bayes assumption* is that the attributes used for description are all conditionally independent:

(7.4) **Naive Bayes assumption**
$$P(c|s_k) = P(\{v_j|v_j \text{ in } c\}|s_k) = \prod_{v_j \text{ in } c} P(v_j|s_k)$$

BAG OF WORDS

In our case, the Naive Bayes assumption has two consequences. The first is that all the structure and linear ordering of words within the context is ignored. This is often referred to as a *bag of words* model.[3] The other is that the presence of one word in the bag is independent of another. This is clearly not true. For example, *president* is more likely to occur in a context that contains *election* than in a context that contains *poet*. But, as in many other cases, the simplifying assumption makes it possible to adopt an elegant model that can be quite effective despite its shortcomings. Obviously, the Naive Bayes assumption is inappropriate if there are strong conditional dependencies between attributes. But there is a surprisingly large number of cases in which it does well, partly because the decisions made can still be optimal even if the probability estimates are inaccurate due to feature dependence (Domingos and Pazzani 1997).

With the Naive Bayes assumption, we get the following modified decision rule for classification:

(7.5) **Decision rule for Naive Bayes**
Decide s' if $s' = \arg\max_{s_k} [\log P(s_k) + \sum_{v_j \text{ in } c} \log P(v_j|s_k)]$

$P(v_j|s_k)$ and $P(s_k)$ are computed via Maximum-Likelihood estimation, perhaps with appropriate smoothing, from the labeled training corpus:

$$P(v_j|s_k) = \frac{C(v_j, s_k)}{C(s_k)}$$

---

3. A bag is like a set, but allows repeated elements (we use 'in' rather than '∈' in equation (7.4) because we are treating c as a bag).

1   **comment**: Training
2   **for** all senses s_k of w **do**
3   **for** all words v_j in the vocabulary **do**
4           $P(v_j|s_k) = \frac{C(v_j,s_k)}{C(v_j)}$
5   **end**
6   **end**
7   **for** all senses s_k of w **do**
8       $P(s_k) = \frac{C(s_k)}{C(w)}$
9   **end**
10 **comment**: Disambiguation
11 **for** all senses s_k of w **do**
12      $\text{score}(s_k) = \log P(s_k)$
13   **for** all words v_j in the context window c **do**
14          $\text{score}(s_k) = \text{score}(s_k) + \log P(v_j|s_k)$
15   **end**
16 **end**
17 choose $s' = \arg\max_{s_k} \text{score}(s_k)$

Figure 7.1   Bayesian disambiguation.

Sense	Clues for sense
medication	*prices, prescription, patent, increase, consumer, pharmaceutical*
illegal substance	*abuse, paraphernalia, illict, alcohol, cocaine, traffickers*

Table 7.2   Clues for two senses of *drug* used by a Bayesian classifier. Adapted from (Gale et al. 1992b: 419).

$$P(s_k) = \frac{C(s_k)}{C(w)}$$

where $C(v_j, s_k)$ is the number of occurrences of v_j in a context of sense s_k in the training corpus, $C(s_k)$ is the number of occurrences of s_k in the training corpus, and $C(w)$ is the total number of occurrences of the ambiguous word w. Figure 7.1 summarizes the algorithm.

Gale, Church and Yarowsky (1992b; 1992c) report that a disambiguation system based on this algorithm is correct for about 90% of occurrences for six ambiguous nouns in the Hansard corpus: *duty, drug, land, language, position,* and *sentence*.

Table 7.2 gives some examples of words that are good clues for two

Ambiguous word	Indicator	Examples: value → sense
prendre	object	*mesure* → *to take* *décision* → *to make*
vouloir	tense	present → *to want* conditional → *to like*
cent	word to the left	*per* → % number → *c.* [money]

Table 7.3 Highly informative indicators for three ambiguous French words.

senses of *drug* in the Hansard corpus. For example, *prices* is a good clue for the 'medication' sense. This means that $P(prices|\text{'medication'})$ is large and $P(prices|\text{'illicit substance'})$ is small and has the effect that a context of *drug* containing *prices* will have a higher score for 'medication' and a lower score for 'illegal substance' (as computed on line 14 in figure 7.1).

7.2.2 An information-theoretic approach

The Bayes classifier attempts to use information from all words in the context window to help in the disambiguation decision, at the cost of a somewhat unrealistic independence assumption. The information theoretic algorithm which we turn to now takes the opposite route. It tries to find a single contextual feature that reliably indicates which sense of the ambiguous word is being used. Some of Brown et al.'s (1991b) examples of indicators for French ambiguous words are listed in table 7.3. For the verb *prendre*, its object is a good indicator: *prendre une mesure* translates as *to **take** a measure*, *prendre une décision* as *to **make** a decision*. Similarly, the tense of the verb *vouloir* and the word immediately to the left of *cent* are good indicators for these two words as shown in table 7.3.

In order to make good use of an informant, its values need to be categorized as to which sense they indicate, e.g., *mesure* indicates *to take*, *décision* indicates *to make*. Brown et al. use the *Flip-Flop algorithm* for FLIP-FLOP ALGORITHM this purpose. Let $t_1, \ldots, t_m$ be the translations of the ambiguous word, and $x_1, \ldots, x_n$ the possible values of the indicator. Figure 7.2 shows the Flip-Flop algorithm for this case. The version of the algorithm described here only disambiguates between two senses. See Brown et al. (1991a) for an extension to more than two senses. Recall the definition of mutual

1 find random partition $P = \{P_1, P_2\}$ of $\{t_1, \ldots, t_m\}$
2 **while** (improving) **do**
3   find partition $Q = \{Q_1, Q_2\}$ of $\{x_1, \ldots, x_n\}$
4   that maximizes $I(P; Q)$
5   find partition $P = \{P_1, P_2\}$ of $\{t_1, \ldots, t_m\}$
7   that maximizes $I(P; Q)$
8 **end**

Figure 7.2 The Flip-Flop algorithm applied to finding indicators for disambiguation.

information from section 2.2.3:

$$I(X; Y) = \sum_{x \in X} \sum_{y \in Y} p(x, y) \log \frac{p(x, y)}{p(x)\, p(y)}$$

It can be shown that each iteration of the Flip-Flop algorithm increases the mutual information $I(P; Q)$ monotonically, so a natural stopping criterion is that $I(P; Q)$ does not increase any more or only insignificantly.

As an example, assume we want to translate *prendre* based on its object and that we have $\{t_1, \ldots, t_m\}$ = $\{take, make, rise, speak\}$ and $\{x_1, \ldots, x_n\}$ = $\{mesure, note, exemple, décision, parole\}$ (cf. (Brown et al. 1991b: 267)). The initial partition P of the senses might be P_1 = $\{take, rise\}$ and P_2 = $\{make, speak\}$. Which partition Q of the indicator values would give us maximum $I(P; Q)$? Obviously, the answer depends on the particular data we are working with. But let us assume that *prendre* is translated by *take* when occurring with the objects *mesure*, *note*, and *exemple* (corresponding to the phrases *take a measure*, *take notes*, and *take an example*), and translated by *make*, *speak*, and *rise* when occurring with *décision*, and *parole* (corresponding to the phrases *make a decision*, *make a speech* and *rise to speak*).

Then the partition that will maximize $I(P; Q)$ is Q_1 = $\{mesure, note, exemple\}$ and Q_2 = $\{décision, parole\}$ since this division of the indicator values gives us the most information for distinguishing the translations in P_1 from the translations in P_2. We only make an incorrect decision when *prendre la parole* is translated as *rise to speak*, but this cannot be avoided since *rise* and *speak* are in two different partition groups.

The next two steps of the algorithm then repartition P as P_1 = $\{take\}$ and P_2 = $\{make, rise, speak\}$ and Q as before. This partition is always correct for *take*. We would have to consider more than two 'senses' if we also wanted to distinguish between the other translations *make, rise* and *speak.*

A simple exhaustive search for the best partition of the French translations and the best possible indicator values would take exponential time. The Flip-Flop algorithm is an efficient linear-time algorithm for computing the best partition of values for a particular indicator, based on the splitting theorem (Breiman et al. 1984). We run the algorithm for all possible indicators and then choose the indicator with the highest mutual information. Brown et al. found that this was the accusative object for *prendre,* tense for *vouloir* and the preceding word for *cent* as shown in table 7.3.

Once an indicator and a particular partition of its values has been determined, disambiguation is simple:

1. For the occurrence of the ambiguous word, determine the value x_i of the indicator.

2. If x_i is in Q_1, assign the occurrence to sense 1, if x_i is in Q_2, assign the occurrence to sense 2.

Brown et al. (1991b) report a 20% improvement in the performance of a machine translation system (from 37 to 45 sentences correct out of 100) when the information-theoretic algorithm is incorporated into the system.

We call the algorithm *supervised* because it requires a labeled training set. However in Brown et al.'s (1991b) work, each occurrence of, say, French *cent* is 'labeled' not with its sense but by its corresponding English translation. These class labels are not the senses. For example, some of the labels of the French word *cent* are (English) *per* and the numbers 0, *one*, 2, and 8. The algorithm groups the labels into two classes, $Q_1 = \{per\}$ and $Q_2 = \{0, one, 2, 8\}$ which are then interpreted as the two senses of *cent,* corresponding to the English translations % (percent sign) and *cent* (with the variants *c.* and *sou*). There is thus a many-to-one mapping from labels to senses.

7.3 Dictionary-Based Disambiguation

If we have no information about the sense categorization of specific instances of a word, we can fall back on a general characterization of the senses. This section describes disambiguation methods that rely on the definition of senses in dictionaries and thesauri. Three different types of information have been used. Lesk (1986) exploits the sense definitions in the dictionary directly. Yarowsky (1992) shows how to apply the semantic categorization of words (derived from the categories in Roget's thesaurus) to the semantic categorization and disambiguation of contexts. In Dagan and Itai's method (1994), translations of the different senses are extracted from a bilingual dictionary and their distribution in a foreign language corpus is analyzed for disambiguation. Finally, we will see how a careful examination of the distributional properties of senses can lead to significant improvements in disambiguation. Commonly, ambiguous words are only used with one sense in any given discourse and with any given collocate (the *one sense per discourse* and *one sense per collocation* hypotheses).

7.3.1   Disambiguation based on sense definitions

Lesk (1986) starts from the simple idea that a word's dictionary definitions are likely to be good indicators for the senses they define.[4] Suppose that two of the definitions of *cone* are as follows:

1. a mass of ovule-bearing or pollen-bearing scales or bracts in trees of the pine family or in cycads that are arranged usually on a somewhat elongated axis,

2. something that resembles a cone in shape: as ... a crisp cone-shaped wafer for holding ice cream.

If either *tree* or *ice* occur in the same context as *cone*, then chances are that the occurrence belongs to the sense whose definition contains that word: sense 1 for *tree*, sense 2 for *ice*.

Let $D_1, \ldots, D_K$ be the dictionary definitions of the senses $s_1, \ldots, s_K$ of the ambiguous word w, represented as the bag of words occurring in the definition, and E_{v_j} the dictionary definition of a word v_j occurring in the context of use c of w, represented as the bag of words occurring in the definition of v_j. (If $s_{j_1}, \ldots, s_{j_L}$ are the senses of v_j, then $E_{v_j} = \bigcup_{j_i} D_{j_i}$. We simply ignore sense distinctions for the words v_j that occur in the context of w.) Then Lesk's algorithm can be described as shown in figure 7.3. For the overlap function, we can just count the number of common words in

---

4. Lesk credits Margaret Millar and Lawrence Urdang with the original proposal of the algorithm.

```
1  comment: Given: context c
2  for all senses s_k of w do
3      score(s_k) = overlap(D_k, ∪_{v_j in c} E_{v_j})
4  end
5  choose s' s.t. s' = arg max_{s_k} score(s_k)
```

Figure 7.3 Lesk's dictionary-based disambiguation algorithm. D_k is the set of words occurring in the dictionary definition of sense s_k. E_{v_j} is the set of words occurring in the dictionary definition of word v_j (that is, the union of all the sense definitions of v_j).

Sense		Definition
s_1	tree	a tree of the olive family
s_2	burned stuff	the solid residue left when combustible material is burned

Table 7.4   Two senses of *ash*.

Scores		Context
s_1	s_2	
0	1	This cigar burns slowly and creates a stiff *ash*.
1	0	The *ash* is one of the last trees to come into leaf.

Table 7.5 Disambiguation of *ash* with Lesk's algorithm. The score is the number of (stemmed) words that are shared by the sense definition and the context. The first sentence is disambiguated as 'burned stuff' because one word is shared with the definition of sense s_2, *burn*, and there are no common words for the other sense. In the second example, the word shared with the definition of s_1 ('tree') is *tree*.

the definition D_k of sense s_k and the union $\cup_{v_j \text{ in } c} E_{v_j}$ of the definitions of the words v_j in the context. Or we could use any of the similarity functions which we present in table 8.7.

One of Lesk's examples is the word *ash* with the senses in table 7.4. The two contexts in table 7.5 are correctly disambiguated when scored on the number of words common with the different sense definitions.

By itself, information of this sort derived from a dictionary is insufficient for high quality word sense disambiguation. Lesk reports accuracies between 50% and 70% when the algorithm is applied to a sample of ambiguous words. He suggests various optimizations that could improve performance. For example, one could run several iterations of the algorithm on a text. Instead of using the union of all words E_{v_j} occurring in the definition of v_j, one could only use the words in the definitions of the contextually appropriate senses as determined in the previous iteration of the algorithm. One would hope that the iterated algorithm eventually settles on the correct sense of each word in the text. Pook and Catlett (1988) suggest another improvement: to expand each word in the context with a list of synonyms from a thesaurus. Such an algorithm combines elements of dictionary-based and thesaurus-based disambiguation.

7.3.2   Thesaurus-based disambiguation

Thesaurus-based disambiguation exploits the semantic categorization provided by a thesaurus like Roget's (Roget 1946) or a dictionary with subject categories like Longman's (Procter 1978). The basic inference in thesaurus-based disambiguation is that the semantic categories of the words in a context determine the semantic category of the context as a whole, and that this category in turn determines which word senses are used.

The following simple thesaurus-based algorithm was proposed by Walker (1987: 254). The basic information used is that each word is assigned one or more subject codes in the dictionary. If the word is assigned several subject codes, then we assume that they correspond to the different senses of the word. Let $t(s_k)$ be the subject code of sense s_k of ambiguous word w occurring in context c. Then w can be disambiguated by counting the number of words for which the thesaurus lists $t(s_k)$ as a possible topic. We then choose the sense with the highest count as shown in figure 7.4.

Black (1988: 187) achieved only moderate success when applying Walker's algorithm to a sample of five ambiguous words: accuracies around 50%. However, the test words were difficult and highly ambiguous: *interest*, *point*, *power*, *state* and *terms*.

One problem with the algorithm is that a general categorization of words into topics is often inappropriate for a particular domain. For example, *mouse* may be listed as both a mammal and an electronic device in a thesaurus, but in a computer manual it will rarely be evidence for the thesaurus category 'mammal.' A general topic categorization may also have a problem of coverage. We will not find *Navratilova* in a thesaurus from the 1960s (and we may not find any proper nouns). Yet

1 **comment**: Given: context c
2 **for** all senses s_k of w **do**
3   score$(s_k) = \sum_{v_j \text{ in } c} \delta(t(s_k), v_j)$
4 **end**
5 choose s' s.t. $s' = \arg\max_{s_k} \text{score}(s_k)$

Figure 7.4   Thesaurus-based disambiguation. $t(s_k)$ is the subject code of sense s_k and $\delta(t(s_k), v_j) = 1$ iff $t(s_k)$ is one of the subject codes of v_j and 0 otherwise. The score is the number of words that are compatible with the subject code of sense s_k.

the occurrence of *Navratilova* is an excellent indicator of the category 'sports.'

The algorithm in figure 7.5 for the adaptation of a topic classification to a corpus was proposed by Yarowsky (1992). The algorithm adds words to a category t_i if they occur more often than chance in the contexts of t_i in the corpus. For example, *Navratilova* will occur more often in sports contexts than in other contexts, so it will be added to the sports category.

Yarowsky's algorithm in figure 7.5 uses the Bayes classifier introduced in section 7.2.1 for both adaptation and disambiguation. First we compute a score for each pair of a context c_i in the corpus and a thesaurus category t_l. For example, context (7.6) would get a high score for the thesaurus category 'sports,' assuming that the thesaurus lists *tennis* as a 'sports' word. In Yarowsky's experiments, a context is simply a 100-word window centered around the ambiguous word.

(7.6)   It is amazing that Navratilova, who turned 33 earlier this year, continues to play great tennis.

Making a Naive Bayes assumption, we can compute this score(c_i, t_l) as $\log P(t_l | c_i)$ where $P(t_l | c_i)$ is computed as follows.

(7.7) $$
\begin{aligned}
P(t_l | c_i) &= \frac{P(c_i | t_l)}{P(c_i)} P(t_l) \\
&= \frac{\prod_{v \text{ in } c_i} P(v | t_l)}{\prod_{v \text{ in } c_i} P(v)} P(t_l)
\end{aligned}
$$

We then use a threshold α in line 7 to determine which thesaurus categories are salient in a context. A fairly large value for this threshold should be chosen so that only contexts with good evidence for a category are assigned.

```
1  comment: Categorize contexts based on categorization of words
2  for all contexts c_i in the corpus do
3      for all thesaurus categories t_l do
4          score(c_i, t_l) = log P(c_i|t_l)/P(c_i) P(t_l)
5      end
6  end
7  t(c_i) = {t_l|score(c_i, t_l) > α}
8  comment: Categorize words based on categorization of contexts
9  for all words v_j in the vocabulary do
10     V_j = {c|v_j in c}
11 end
12 for all topics t_l do
13     T_l = {c|t_l ∈ t(c)}
14 end
15 for all words v_j, all topics t_l do
16     P(v_j|t_l) = |V_j ∩ T_l| / Σ_j |V_j ∩ T_l|
17 end
18 for all topics t_l do
19     P(t_l) = (Σ_j |V_j ∩ T_l|) / (Σ_l Σ_j |V_j ∩ T_l|)
20 end
21 comment: Disambiguation
22 for all senses s_k of w occurring in c do
23     score(s_k) = log P(t(s_k)) + Σ_{v_j in c} log P(v_j|t(s_k))
24 end
25 choose s' s.t. s' = arg max_{s_k} score(s_k)
```

Figure 7.5 Adaptive thesaurus-based disambiguation. Yarowsky's algorithms for adapting a semantic categorization of words and for thesaurus-based disambiguation. $P(v_j|t_l)$ on line 16 is estimated as the proportion of contexts of topic t_l that contain word v_j.

Now we can adjust the semantic categorization in the thesaurus to our corpus (represented as the set of contexts $\{c_i\}$). On line 16, we estimate $P(v_j|t_l)$ as the proportion of contexts of v_j that are in category t_l. If v_j is covered in the thesaurus, then this will adapt v_j's semantic categories to the corpus (for example, *stylus* may get a high score as a computer term even though the thesaurus only lists it in the category 'writing'). If v_j is not covered, then it will be added to the appropriate categories (the

Word	Sense	Roget category	Accuracy
bass	musical senses	MUSIC	99%
	fish	ANIMAL, INSECT	100%
star	space object	UNIVERSE	96%
	celebrity	ENTERTAINER	95%
	star shaped object	INSIGNIA	82%
interest	curiosity	REASONING	88%
	advantage	INJUSTICE	34%
	financial	DEBT	90%
	share	PROPERTY	38%

Table 7.6 Some results of thesaurus-based disambiguation. The table shows the senses of three ambiguous words, the Roget categories they correspond to, and the accuracy of the algorithm in figure 7.5. Adapted from (Yarowsky 1992).

case of *Navratilova*). The prior probability of t_l is simply computed as its relative frequency, adjusted for the fact that some contexts will have no semantic categories and others more than one (line 19).

The values $P(v_j|t_l)$ computed on line 16 are then used for disambiguation in analogy to the Bayesian algorithm we discussed earlier (see figure 7.1). Yarowsky (1992) recommends smoothing for some of the maximum likelihood estimates (see chapter 6).

Table 7.6 shows some results from (Yarowsky 1992). The method achieves high accuracy when thesaurus categories and senses align well with topics as in the case of *bass* and *star*. When a sense is spread out over several topics, the algorithm fails. Yarowsky calls these *topic-independent distinctions* between senses. For example, the sense 'advantage' of *interest* (as in *self-interest*) is not topic-specific. Self-interest can occur in music, entertainment, space exploration, finance, etc. Therefore, a topic-based classification does not do well on this sense.

TOPIC-INDEPENDENT DISTINCTIONS

7.3.3 Disambiguation based on translations in a second-language corpus

The third dictionary-based algorithm makes use of word correspondences in a bilingual dictionary (Dagan et al. 1991; Dagan and Itai 1994). We will refer to the language of application (the one for which we want

	Sense 1	Sense 2
Definition	legal share	attention, concern
Translation	*Beteiligung*	*Interesse*
English collocation	*acquire an interest*	*show interest*
Translation	*Beteiligung erwerben*	*Interesse zeigen*

Table 7.7 How to disambiguate *interest* using a second-language corpus.

to do disambiguation) as the *first language* and the target language in the bilingual dictionary as the *second language*. For example, if we want to disambiguate English based on a German corpus, then English is the first language, German is the second language, and we need an English-German dictionary (one with English headwords and German entries).

The basic idea of Dagan and Itai's algorithm is best explained with the example in table 7.7. English *interest* has two senses with two different translations in German. Sense 1 translates as *Beteiligung* (*legal share*, as in "a 50% interest in the company") and Sense 2 translates as *Interesse* (*attention, concern*, as in "her interest in mathematics"). (There are other senses of *interest* which we will ignore here.) In order to disambiguate an occurrence of *interest* in English, we identify the phrase it occurs in and search a German corpus for instances of the phrase. If the phrase occurs with only one of the translations of *interest* in German, then we assign the corresponding sense whenever *interest* is used in this phrase.

As an example, suppose *interest* is used in the phrase *showed interest*. The German translation of *show*, 'zeigen,' will only occur with *Interesse* since "legal shares" are usually not shown. We can conclude that *interest* in the phrase *to show interest* belongs to the sense *attention, concern*. On the other hand, the only frequently occurring translation of the phrase *acquired an interest* is *erwarb eine Beteiligung*, since *interest* in the sense 'attention, concern' is not usually acquired. This tells us that a use of *interest* as the object of *acquire* corresponds to the second sense, "legal share."

A simple implementation of this idea is shown in figure 7.6. For the above example the relation R is 'is-object-of' and the goal would be to disambiguate *interest* in $R(interest, show)$. To do this, we count the number of times that translations of the two senses of *interest* occur with translations of *show* in the second language corpus. The count of $R(Interesse, zeigen)$ would be higher than the count of $R(Beteiligung, zeigen)$, so we

1 **comment**: Given: a context c in which w occurs in relation $R(w, v)$
2 **for** all senses s_k of w **do**
3 $\text{score}(s_k) = |\{c \in S | \exists w' \in T(s_k), v' \in T(v) : R(w', v') \in c\}|$
4 **end**
5 choose $s' = \arg\max_{s_k} \text{score}(s_k)$

Figure 7.6   Disambiguation based on a second-language corpus. S is the second-language corpus, $T(s_k)$ is the set of possible translations of sense s_k, and $T(v)$ is the set of possible translations of v. The score of a sense is the number of times that one of its translations occurs with translations of v in the second-language corpus.

would choose the sense 'attention, concern,' corresponding to *Interesse*.

The algorithm used by Dagan and Itai is more complex: it disambiguates only if a decision can be made reliably. Consider the example of Hebrew *ro'sh* which has two possible English translations, *top* and *head*. Dagan and Itai found 10 examples of the relation *stand at head* and 5 examples of the relation *stand at top* in their English second-language corpus. This suggests that *stand at head* is more likely to translate the Hebrew phrase *'amad be-ro'sh* correctly. However, we can expect "stand at head" to be incorrect in a large proportion of the translations (approximately $\frac{5}{5+10} \approx 0.33$). In many cases, it is better to avoid a decision than to make an error with high probability. In a large system in which each component has a certain error rate, an accuracy of about 0.67 as in the above example is unacceptable. If a sentence passes through five components, each with an error rate of 0.33, then overall system accuracy could be as low as 14%: $(1 - 0.33)^5 \approx 0.14$. Dagan and Itai show how the probability of error can be estimated. They then make decisions only when the level of confidence is 90% or higher.

7.3.4   One sense per discourse, one sense per collocation

The dictionary-based algorithms we have looked at so far process each occurrence separately. But there are constraints between different occurrences that can be exploited for disambiguation. This section discusses work by Yarowsky (1995) which has focussed on two such constraints:

- **One sense per discourse.** The sense of a target word is highly consistent within any given document.

Discourse	Initial label	Context
d_1	living	the existence of *plant* and animal life
	living	classified as either *plant* or animal
	?	Although bacterial and *plant* cells are enclosed
d_2	living	contains a varied *plant* and animal life
	living	the most common *plant* life
	living	slight within Arctic *plant* species
	factory	are protected by *plant* parts remaining from

Table 7.8 Examples of the one sense per discourse constraint. The table shows contexts from two different documents, d_1 and d_2. One context in d_1 lacks sufficient local information for disambiguation ("?"). Local information is misleading for the last context in d_2. The one sense per discourse constraint can be used to counteract lacking or misleading information in such cases. It will correctly assign the unclassified and the misclassified contexts to 'living.' Adapted from (Yarowsky 1995).

- **One sense per collocation.** Nearby words provide strong and consistent clues to the sense of a target word, conditional on relative distance, order and syntactic relationship.

As an example for the first constraint consider the word *plant*. The constraint captures the intuition that if the first occurrence of *plant* is a use of the sense 'living being,' then later occurrences are likely to refer to living beings too. Table 7.8 shows two examples. This constraint is especially usable when the material to be disambiguated is a collection of small documents, or can be divided into short 'discourses' by the kind of method discussed in section 15.5. Then, this simple property of word senses can be used quite effectively as we will see below.

The second constraint makes explicit the basic assumption that most work on statistical disambiguation relies on: that word senses are strongly correlated with certain contextual features like other words in the same phrasal unit. Yarowsky's (1995) approach is similar to Brown et al.'s (1991b) information-theoretic method, which we introduced in section 7.2.2, in that he selects the strongest collocational feature for a particular context and disambiguates based only on this feature. Collocational features are ranked according to the following ratio:

$$(7.8) \qquad \frac{P(s_{k_1}|f)}{P(s_{k_2}|f)}$$

which basically is the ratio of the number of occurrences of sense s_{k_1} with collocation f divided by the number of occurrences of sense s_{k_2} with collocation f (again, smoothing is important if the collocation and/or senses occur infrequently, see Yarowsky (1994)).

Relying on only the strongest feature has the advantage that no integration of different sources of evidence is necessary. Many statistical methods, such as the Naive Bayes method used in section 7.2.1 or the dictionary-based methods presented earlier in this section, assume independence when evidence is combined. Since independence rarely holds, it is sometimes better to avoid the need for combining evidence altogether, and to rely on just one reliable piece of evidence. The more complex alternative is to accurately model the dependencies between sources of evidence (see chapter 16).

Figure 7.7 is a schematic description of an algorithm proposed by Yarowsky that combines both constraints. The algorithm iterates building two interdependent sets for each sense s_k. F_k contains characteristic collocations. E_k is the set of contexts of the ambiguous word w that are currently assigned to s_k.

On line 3, F_k is initialized from the dictionary definition of s_k or from another source (for example, a set of collocations entered manually by a lexicographer or a set of collocations from a small hand-labeled training set). E_k is initially empty.

The iteration begins by assigning all contexts with a characteristic collocation from F_k to E_k (line 11). For example, all contexts of *interest* in which *interest* is the object of the verb *show* would be assigned to $E_{\text{'attention, concern'}}$ if "is the object of *show*" is one of the collocations in $F_{\text{'attention, concern'}}$. The set of characteristic collocations is then recomputed by selecting those collocations that are most characteristic of the just updated E_k (line 14).

After this part of the algorithm has been completed, the constraint "one sense per discourse" is applied. All instances of the ambiguous word w are assigned to the majority sense in a document or discourse (line 20). Table 7.8 gave two examples of this process.

Yarowsky demonstrates that this algorithm is highly effective. Different versions achieve between 90.6% and 96.5% accuracy. The error rate is reduced by 27% when the discourse constraint (lines 18–21) is incorporated. This is a surprisingly good performance given that the algorithm does not need a labeled set of training examples.

```
 1  comment: Initialization
 2  for all senses s_k of w do
 3      F_k = the set of collocations in s_k's dictionary definition
 4  end
 5  for all senses s_k of w do
 6      E_k = ∅
 7  end
 8  comment: One sense per collocation
 9  while (at least one E_k changed in the last iteration) do
10      for all senses s_k of w do
11          E_k = {c_i | ∃ f_m : f_m ∈ c_i ∧ f_m ∈ F_k}
12      end
13      for all senses s_k of w do
14          F_k = {f_m | ∀ n ≠ k  P(s_k|f_m)/P(s_n|f_m) > α}
15      end
16  end
17  comment: One sense per discourse
18  for all documents d_m do
19      determine the majority sense s_k of w in d_m
20      assign all occurrences of w in d_m to s_k
21  end
```

Figure 7.7   Disambiguation based on "one sense per collocation" and "one sense per discourse."

7.4   Unsupervised Disambiguation

All that the methods discussed in the last section require for disambiguation are basic lexical resources, a small training set, or a few collocation seeds. Although this seems little to ask for, there are situations in which even such a small amount of information is not available. In particular, this is often the case when dealing with information from specialized domains, for which there may be no available lexical resources.[5] For example, information retrieval systems must be able to deal with text collections from any subject area. General dictionaries are less useful for domain-specific collections. A data base of chemical abstracts mostly

---

5. However, there are specialized dictionaries in some fields, such as for medical and scientific terms.

contains documents that belong to the category "chemistry" in a generic semantic classification. A generic thesaurus-based disambiguation algorithm would therefore be of little use. One cannot expect the user of an information retrieval system to define the senses of ambiguous words or to provide a training set for a new text collection. With the surge in on-line material in recent years, there is an increasing number of scenarios where outside sources of information are not available for disambiguation.

SENSE TAGGING

Strictly speaking, completely unsupervised disambiguation is not possible if we mean *sense tagging*: an algorithm that labels occurrences as belonging to one sense or another. Sense tagging requires that some characterization of the senses be provided. However, sense *discrimination* can be performed in a completely unsupervised fashion: one can cluster the contexts of an ambiguous word into a number of groups and discriminate between these groups without labeling them. Several such sense discrimination algorithms have been proposed. We will describe

CONTEXT-GROUP
DISCRIMINATION

one of them here, *context-group discrimination*, largely following Schütze (1998).[6] Note also the similarity to Brown et al.'s approach described in section 7.2.2. Brown et al. (1991b) cluster *translations* of an ambiguous word, which can be thought of as a type of prelabeling of the occurrences of the ambiguous word w. Here, we will look at a completely unsupervised algorithm that clusters unlabeled occurrences.

The probabilistic model is the same as that developed by Gale et al. (section 7.2.1). For an ambiguous word w with senses $s_1, \ldots, s_k, \ldots, s_K$, we estimate the conditional probability of each word v_j occurring in a context where w is being used in a particular sense s_k, that is, $P(v_j|s_k)$.

In contrast to Gale et al.'s Bayes classifier, parameter estimation in unsupervised disambiguation is not based on a labeled training set. Instead, we start with a random initialization of the parameters $P(v_j|s_k)$. The $P(v_j|s_k)$ are then reestimated by the EM algorithm (see section 14.2.2). After the random initialization, we compute for each context c_i of w the probability $P(c_i|s_k)$ that it was generated by sense s_k. We can use this preliminary categorization of the contexts as our training data and then reestimate the parameters $P(v_j|s_k)$ so as to maximize the likelihood of the data given the model. The algorithm is developed in figure 7.8.

The EM algorithm is guaranteed to increase the log likelihood of the

---

6. For consistency we reuse the probabilistic model introduced in section 7.2.1 and section 7.3.2, instead of Schütze's.

1. **Initialize** the parameters of the model μ randomly. The parameters are $P(v_j|s_k)$, $1 \le j \le J$, $1 \le k \le K$, and $P(s_k)$, $1 \le k \le K$.

   Compute the log of the likelihood of the corpus C given the model μ as the product of the probabilities $P(c_i)$ of the individual contexts c_i (where $P(c_i) = \sum_{k=1}^{K} P(c_i|s_k)P(s_k)$):

$$l(C|\mu) = \log \prod_{i=1}^{I} \sum_{k=1}^{K} P(c_i|s_k)P(s_k) = \sum_{i=1}^{I} \log \sum_{k=1}^{K} P(c_i|s_k)P(s_k)$$

2. While $l(C|\mu)$ is improving repeat:

   (a) **E-step.** For $1 \le k \le K$, $1 \le i \le I$ estimate h_{ik}, the posterior probability that s_k generated c_i, as follows:

$$h_{ik} = \frac{P(c_i|s_k)}{\sum_{k=1}^{K} P(c_i|s_k)}$$

   To compute $P(c_i|s_k)$, we make the by now familiar Naive Bayes assumption:

$$P(c_i|s_k) = \prod_{v_j \in c_i} P(v_j|s_k)$$

   (b) **M-step. Re-estimate** the parameters $P(v_j|s_k)$ and $P(s_k)$ by way of maximum likelihood estimation:

$$P(v_j|s_k) = \frac{\sum_{\{c_i:v_j \in c_i\}} h_{ik}}{Z_j}$$

   where $\sum_{\{c_i:v_j \in c_i\}}$ sums over all contexts in which v_j occurs and $Z_j = \sum_{k=1}^{K} \sum_{\{c_i:v_j \in c_i\}} h_{ik}$ is a normalizing constant.

   Recompute the probabilities of the senses as follows:

$$P(s_k) = \frac{\sum_{i=1}^{I} h_{ik}}{\sum_{k=1}^{K} \sum_{i=1}^{I} h_{ik}} = \frac{\sum_{i=1}^{I} h_{ik}}{I}$$

Figure 7.8 An EM algorithm for learning a word sense clustering. K is the number of desired senses; $c_1, \ldots, c_i, \ldots, c_I$ are the contexts of the ambiguous word in the corpus; and $v_1, \ldots, v_j, \ldots, v_J$ are the words being used as disambiguating features.

model given the data in each step. Therefore, the stopping criterion for the algorithm is to stop when the likelihood (computed in step 1) is no longer increasing significantly.

Once the parameters of the model have been estimated, we can disambiguate contexts of w by computing the probability of each of the senses based on the words v_j occurring in the context. Again, we make the Naive Bayes assumption and use the Bayes decision rule (7.5):

$$\text{Decide } s' \text{ if } s' = \arg\max_{s_k}[\log P(s_k) + \sum_{v_j \in c} \log P(v_j|s_k)]$$

The granularity of the sense classification of an ambiguous word can be chosen by running the algorithm for a range of values for K, the number of senses. The more senses there are, the more structure the model has, and therefore it will be able to explain the data better. As a result the best possible log likelihood of the model given the data will be higher with each new sense added. However, one can examine by how much the log likelihood increases with each new sense. If it increases strongly because the new sense explains an important part of the data, then this suggests that the new number of senses is justified. If the log likelihood increases only moderately, then the new sense only picks up random variation in the data and it is probably not justified.[7]

A simpler way to determine the number of senses is to make it dependent on how much training material is available. This approach is justified for an information retrieval application by Schütze and Pedersen (1995).

An advantage of unsupervised disambiguation is that it can be easily adapted to produce distinctions between usage types that are more fine-grained than would be found in a dictionary. Again, information retrieval is an application for which this is useful. The distinction between physical banks in the context of bank robberies and banks as abstract corporations in the context of corporate mergers can be highly relevant even if it is not reflected in dictionaries.

If the unsupervised algorithm is run for a large number of senses, say $K = 20$, then it will split dictionary senses into fine-grained contextual variants. For example, the sense 'lawsuit' of *suit* could be split into 'civil suit,' 'criminal suit,' etc. Usually, the induced clusters do not line up well with dictionary senses. Infrequent senses and senses that have few

---

7. One could choose the optimal number of senses automatically by testing on validation data, as discussed in chapter 6.

Word	Sense	Accuracy	
		μ	σ
suit	lawsuit	95	0
	the suit you wear	96	0
motion	physical movement	85	1
	proposal for action	88	13
train	line of railroad cars	79	19
	to teach	55	31

Table 7.9 Some results of unsupervised disambiguation. The table shows the mean μ and standard deviation σ for ten experiments with different initial conditions for the EM algorithm. Data are from (Schütze 1998: 110).

collocations are hard to isolate in unsupervised disambiguation. Senses like the use of *suit* in the sense 'to be appropriate for' as in *This suits me fine* are unlikely to be discovered. However, such hard to identify senses often carry less content than senses that are tied to a particular subject area. For an information retrieval system, it is probably more important to make the distinction between usage types like 'civil suit' vs. 'criminal suit' than to isolate the verbal sense 'to suit.'

Some results of unsupervised disambiguation are shown in table 7.9. We need to take into account the variability that is due to different initializations here (Step 1 in figure 7.8). The table shows both the average accuracy and the standard deviation over ten trials. For senses with a clear correspondence to a particular topic, the algorithm works well and variability is low. The word *suit* is an example. But the algorithm fails for words whose senses are topic-independent such as 'to teach' for *train* – this failure is not unlike other methods that work with topic information only. In addition to the low average performance, variability is also quite high for topic-independent senses. In general, performance is 5% to 10% lower than that of some of the dictionary-based algorithms as one would expect given that no lexical resources for training or defining senses are used.

7.5   What Is a Word Sense?

Now that we have looked at a wide range of different approaches to word sense disambiguation, let us revisit the question of what precisely a word sense is. It would seem natural to define senses as the mental representations of different meanings of a word. But given how little is known about the mental representation of meaning, it is hard to design experiments that determine how senses are represented by a subject. Some studies ask subjects to cluster contexts. The subject is given a pile of index cards, each with a sentence containing the ambiguous word, and instructions to sort the pile into coherent subgroups. While these experiments have provided many insights (for example, for research on the notion of semantic similarity, see Miller and Charles (1991)), it is not clear how well they model the use of words and senses in actual language comprehension and production. Determining linguistic similarity is not a task that people are confronted with in natural situations. Agreement between clusterings performed by different subjects is low (Jorgensen 1990).

Another problem with many psychological experiments on ambiguity is that they rely on introspection and whatever folk meaning a subject assumes for the word 'sense.' It is not clear that introspection is a valid methodology for getting at the true mental representations of senses since it fails to elucidate many other phenomena. For example, people tend to rationalize non-rational economic decisions (Kahneman et al. 1982).

The most frequently used methodology is to adopt the sense definitions in a dictionary and then to ask subjects to label instances in a corpus based on these definitions. There are different opinions on how well this technique works. Some researchers have reported high agreement between judges (Gale et al. 1992a) as we discussed above. High average agreement is likely if there are many ambiguous words with a skewed distribution, that is, one sense that is used in most of the occurrences. Sanderson and van Rijsbergen (1998) argue that such skewed distributions are typical of ambiguous words.

SKEWED DISTRIBUTION

However, randomly selecting ambiguous words as was done in (Gale et al. 1992a) introduces a bias which means that their figures may not reflect actual inter-judge agreement. Many ambiguous words with the highest disagreement rates are high-frequency words. So on a per-token basis inter-judge disagreement can be high even if it is lower on a per-type basis. In a recent experiment, Jean Véronis (p.c., 1998) found that there was not a single instance of the frequent French words *correct*, *historique*, *économie*, and *comprendre* with complete agreement among judges. The main reasons Véronis found for inter-judge disagreement were vague dictionary definitions and true ambiguity in the corpus.

Can we write dictionaries that are less vague? Fillmore and Atkins (1994) discuss such issues from a lexicographic perspective. Some authors argue that it is an inherent property of word meaning that several

CO-ACTIVATION

senses of a word can be used simultaneously or *co-activated* (Kilgarriff 1993; Schütze 1997; Kilgarriff 1997), which entails high rates of inter-judge disagreement. Of course, there are puns like (7.9) in which multiple senses are used in a way that seems so special that it would be acceptable for an NLP system to fail:

(7.9)   In AI, much of the I is in the beholder.

But Kilgarriff (1993) argues that such simultaneous uses of senses are quite frequent in ordinary language. An example is (7.10) where arguably two senses of *competition* are invoked: 'the act of competing' and 'the competitors.'

(7.10)   For better or for worse, this would bring competition to the licensed trade.

SYSTEMATIC
POLYSEMY

Many cases of 'coactivation' are cases of *systematic polysemy*, lexico-semantic rules that apply to a class of words and systematically change or extend their meaning. (See (Apresjan 1974), (Pustejovsky 1991), (Lakoff 1987), (Ostler and Atkins 1992), (Nunberg and Zaenen 1992), and (Copestake and Briscoe 1995) for theoretical work on systematic polysemy and (Buitelaar 1998) for a recent computational study.) The word *competition* is a case in point. A large number of English words have the same meaning alternation between 'the act of X' vs. 'the people doing X'. For example, *organization*, *administration*, and *formation* also exhibit it.

A different type of systematic ambiguity that cannot be neglected in practice is that almost all words can also be used as proper nouns, some of them frequently. Examples are *Brown*, *Bush*, and *Army*.

One response to low inter-judge agreement and the low performance of disambiguation algorithms for highly ambiguous words is to only consider coarse-grained distinctions, for example only those that manifest themselves across languages (Resnik and Yarowsky 1998). Systematic polysemy is likely to be similar in many languages, so we would not distinguish the two related senses of *competition* ('the act of competing' and 'the competitors') even if a monolingual dictionary lists them as different. This strategy is similar to ones used in other areas of NLP, such as parsing, where one defines an easier problem, shallow parsing, and does not attempt to solve the hardest problem, the resolution of attachment ambiguities.

Clustering approaches to word sense disambiguation (such as context-group disambiguation) adopt the same strategy. By definition, automatic clustering will only find groups of usages that can be successfully distinguished. This amounts to a restriction to a subpart of the problem that can be solved. Such solutions with a limited scope can be quite useful. Many translation ambiguities are coarse, so that a system restricted to coarse sense distinctions is sufficient. Context-group disambiguation has been successfully applied to information retrieval (Schütze and Pedersen 1995).

Such application-oriented notions of sense have the advantage that it is easy to evaluate them as long as the application that disambiguation is embedded in can be evaluated (for example, translation accuracy for machine translation, the measures of recall and precision – introduced in chapter 8 – for information retrieval). Direct evaluation of disambiguation accuracy and comparison of different algorithms is more difficult, but will be easier in the future with the development of standard evaluation sets. See Mooney (1996) for a comparative evaluation of a number of machine learning algorithms and Towell and Voorhees (1998) for the evaluation of a disambiguator for three highly ambiguous words (*hard*, *serve*, and *line*). A systematic evaluation of algorithms was undertaken

Senseval   as part of the *Senseval* project (unfortunately, after the writing of this chapter). See the website.

Another factor that influences what notion of sense is assumed, albeit implicitly, is the *type of information* that is used in disambiguation: co-occurrence (the bag-of-words model), relational information (subject, object, etc.), other grammatical information (such as part-of-speech), collocations (one sense per collocation) and discourse (one sense per discourse). For example, if only co-occurrence information is used, then only 'topical' sense distinctions are recognized, senses that are associated with different domains. The inadequacy of the bag-of-words model for many sense distinctions has been emphasized by Justeson and Katz (1995a). Leacock et al. (1998) look at the combination of topical and collocational information and achieve optimal results when both are used. Choueka and Lusignan (1985) show that humans do surprisingly well at sense discrimination if only a few words of adjacent context are shown – giving more context contributes little to human disambiguation performance. However, that does not necessarily mean that wider context is useless for the computer. Gale et al. (1992b) show that there is additional useful information in the context out to about 50 words on either side of the ambiguous word (using their algorithm), and that there is detectable information about sense distinctions out to a very large distance (thousands of words).

Different types of information may be appropriate to different degrees for different parts of speech. Verbs are best disambiguated by their arguments (subjects and objects), which implies the importance of local information. Many nouns have topically distinct word senses (like *suit* and *bank*) so that a wider context is more likely to be helpful.

Much research remains to be done on word sense disambiguation. In particular, it will become necessary to evaluate algorithms on a representative sample of ambiguous words, an effort few researchers have made so far. Only with more thorough evaluation will it be possible to fully understand the strengths and weaknesses of the disambiguation algorithms introduced in this chapter.

7.6 Further Reading

An excellent recent discussion of both statistical and non-statistical work on word sense disambiguation is (Ide and Véronis 1998). See also (Guthrie et al. 1996). An interesting variation of word sense disambiguation is *sentence boundary identification* (section 4.2.4). The problem is that periods in text can be used either to mark an abbreviation or to mark the end of a sentence. Palmer and Hearst (1997) show how the problem can be cast as the task of disambiguating two 'senses' of the period: ending an abbreviation vs. ending a sentence or both.

SENTENCE BOUNDARY
IDENTIFICATION

The common thread in this chapter has been the amount and type of lexical resources used by different approaches. In these remarks, we will first mention a few other methods that fit under the rubrics of supervised, dictionary-based, and unsupervised disambiguation, and then work that did not fit well into our organization of the chapter.

Two important supervised disambiguation methods are k nearest neighbors (kNN), also called memory-based learning (see page 295) and loglinear models. A nearest neighbor disambiguator is introduced in (Dagan et al. 1994, 1997b). The authors stress the benefits of kNN approaches for sparse data. See also (Ng and Lee 1996) and (Zavrel and Daelemans 1997). Decomposable models, a type of loglinear model, can be viewed as a generalization of Naive Bayes. Instead of treating all features as independent, features are grouped into mutually dependent subsets. Independence is then assumed only between features in different subsets, not for all pairs of features as is the case in the Naive Bayes classifier. Bruce and Wiebe (1994) apply decomposable models to disambiguation with good results.

Other disambiguation algorithms that rely on lexical resources are (Karov and Edelman 1998), (Guthrie et al. 1991), and (Dini et al. 1998). Karov and Edelman (1998) present a formalism that takes advantage of evidence both from a corpus and a dictionary, with good disambiguation results. Guthrie et al. (1991) use the subject field codes in (Procter 1978) in a way similar to the thesaurus classes in (Yarowsky 1992). Dini et al. (1998) apply transformation-based learning (see section 10.4.1) to tag ambiguous words with thesaurus categories.

Papers that use clustering include (Pereira et al. 1993; Zernik 1991b; Dolan 1994; Pedersen and Bruce 1997; Chen and Chang 1998). Pereira et al. (1993) cluster contexts of words in a way similar to Schütze (1998), but based on a different formalization of clustering. They do not directly describe a disambiguation algorithm based on the clustering result, but since in this type of unsupervised method assignment to clusters is equivalent to disambiguation, this would be a straightforward extension. See section 14.1.4 for the clustering algorithm they use. Chen and Chang (1998) and Dolan (1994) are concerned with constructing representations for senses by combining several subsenses into one 'supersense.' This type of clustering of subsenses is useful for constructing senses that are coarser than those a dictionary may provide and for relating sense definitions between two dictionaries.

An important issue that comes up in many different approaches to disambiguation is how to combine different types of evidence (McRoy 1992). See (Cottrell 1989; Hearst 1991; Alshawi and Carter 1994; Wilks and Stevenson 1998) for different proposals.

Although we only cover statistical approaches here, work on word sense disambiguation has a long tradition in Artificial Intelligence and Computational Linguistics. Two often-cited contributions are (Kelly and Stone 1975), a hand-constructed rule-based disambiguator, and (Hirst 1987), who exploits selectional restrictions for disambiguation. An excellent overview of non-statistical work on disambiguation can be found in the above-mentioned (Ide and Véronis 1998).

7.7   Exercises

Exercise 7.1   [⋆]

The lower bound of disambiguation accuracy depends on how much information is available. Describe a situation in which the lower bound could be lower than the performance that results from classifying all occurrences of a word as instances of its most frequent sense. (Hint: What knowledge is needed to calculate that lower bound?)

Exercise 7.2   [⋆ ⋆]

Supervised word sense disambiguation algorithms are quite easy to devise and train. Either implement one of the models discussed above, or design your own and implement it. How good is the performance? Training data are available from the Linguistic Data Consortium (the DSO corpus) and from the WordNet project (semcor). See the website for links to both.

Exercise 7.3   [⋆ ⋆]

Create an artificial training and test set using pseudowords. Evaluate one of the supervised algorithms on it.

Exercise 7.4   [⋆ ⋆]

Download a version of Roget's thesaurus from the web (see the website), and implement and evaluate a thesaurus-based algorithm.

Exercise 7.5   [⋆ ⋆]

The two supervised methods differ on two different dimensions: the number of features used (one vs. many) and the mathematical methodology (information theory vs. Bayesian classification). How would one design a Bayes classifier that uses only one feature and an information-theoretic method that uses many features?

Exercise 7.6   [⋆ ⋆]

In light of the discussion on closely related and 'co-activated' senses, discuss to what extent pseudowords model ambiguity well.

Exercise 7.7   [⋆ ⋆]

Lesk's algorithm counts how many words are shared between sense definition and context. This is not optimal since reliance on "non-descript" or stop words like *try* or *especially* can result in misclassifications. Try to come up with refinements of Lesk's algorithm that would weight words according to their expected value in discrimination.

Exercise 7.8   [⋆]

Two approaches use only one feature: information-theoretic disambiguation and Yarowsky's (1995) algorithm. Discuss differences and other similarities between the two approaches.

Exercise 7.9 [★]

Discuss the validity of the "one sense per discourse" constraint for different types of ambiguity (types of usages, homonyms etc.). Construct examples where the constraint is expected to do well and examples where it is expected to do poorly.

Exercise 7.10 [★ ★]

Evaluate the one sense per discourse constraint on a corpus. Find sections or articles with multiple uses of an ambiguous word, and work out how often they have different senses.

Exercise 7.11 [★]

The section on unsupervised disambiguation describes criteria for determining the number of senses of an ambiguous word. Can you think of other criteria? Assume (a) that a dictionary is available (but the word is not listed in it); (b) that a thesaurus is available (but the word is not listed in it).

Exercise 7.12 [★]

For a pair of languages that you are familiar with, find three cases of an ambiguous word in the first language for which the senses translate into different words and three cases of an ambiguous words for which at least two senses translate to the same word.

Exercise 7.13 [★]

Is it important to evaluate unsupervised disambiguation on a separate test set or does the unsupervised nature of the method make a distinction between training and test set unnecessary? (Hint: It can be important to have a separate test set. Why? See (Schütze 1998: 108).)

Exercise 7.14 [★]

Several of the senses of *title* discussed in the beginning of the chapter are related by systematic polysemy. Find other words with the same systematic polysemy.

Exercise 7.15 [★ ★]

Pick one of the disambiguation algorithms and apply it to sentence boundary identification.

"There is one, yt is called in the Malaca tongue Durion, and is so good that . . . it doth exceede in savour all others that euer they had seene, or tasted."

(Parke tr. Mendoza's Hist. China 393, 1588)

8 *Lexical Acquisition*

THE TOPIC of chapter 5 was the acquisition of *collocations*, phrases and other combinations of words that have a specialized meaning or some other special behavior important in NLP. In this chapter, we will cast our net more widely and look at the acquisition of more complex syntactic and semantic properties of words. The general goal of lexical acquisition is to develop algorithms and statistical techniques for filling the holes in existing machine-readable dictionaries by looking at the occurrence patterns of words in large text corpora. There are many lexical acquisition problems besides collocations: selectional preferences (for example, the verb *eat* usually takes food items as direct objects), subcategorization frames (for example, the recipient of *contribute* is expressed as a prepositional phrase with *to*), and semantic categorization (what is the semantic category of a new word that is not covered in our dictionary?). While we discuss simply the ability of computers to learn lexical information from online texts, rather than in any way attempting to model human language acquisition, to the extent that such methods are successful, they tend to undermine the classical Chomskyan arguments for an innate language faculty based on the perceived poverty of the stimulus.

Most properties of words that are of interest in NLP are not fully covered in machine-readable dictionaries. This is because of the productivity of natural language. We constantly invent new words and new uses of old words. Even if we could compile a dictionary that completely covered the language of today, it would inevitably become incomplete in a matter of months. This is the reason why lexical acquisition is so important in Statistical NLP.

A brief discussion of what we mean by *lexical* and the *lexicon* is in order. Trask (1993: 159) defines the lexicon as:

LEXICAL ENTRIES   That part of the grammar of a language which includes the *lexical entries* for all the words and/or morphemes in the language and which may also include various other information, depending on the particular theory of grammar.

The first part of the definition ("the lexical entries for all the words") suggests that we can think of the lexicon as a kind of expanded dictionary that is formatted so that a computer can read it (that is, machine-readable). The trouble is that traditional dictionaries are written for the needs of human users, not for the needs of computers. In particular, quantitative information is completely missing from traditional dictionaries since it is not very helpful for the human reader. So one important task of lexical acquisition for Statistical NLP is to augment traditional dictionaries with quantitative information.

The second part of the definition ("various other information, depending on the particular theory of grammar") draws attention to the fact that there is no sharp boundary between what is lexical information and what is non-lexical information. A general syntactic rule like S → NP VP is definitely non-lexical, but what about ambiguity in the attachment of prepositional phrases? In a sense, it is a syntactic problem, but it can be resolved by looking at the lexical properties of the verb and the noun that compete for the prepositional phrase as the following example shows:

(8.1)   a. The children ate the cake with their hands.

b. The children ate the cake with blue icing.

We can learn from a corpus that eating is something you can do with your hands and that cakes are objects that have icing as a part. After acquiring these lexical dependencies between *ate* and *hands* and *cake* and *icing*, we can correctly resolve the attachment ambiguities in example (8.1) such that *with their hands* attaches to *ate* and *with blue icing* attaches to *cake*.

In a sense, almost all of Statistical NLP involves estimating parameters tied to word properties, so a lot of statistical NLP work has an element of lexical acquisition to it. In fact, there are linguistic theories claiming that all linguistic knowledge is knowledge about words (Dependency Grammar (Mel'čuk 1988), Categorial Grammar (Wood 1993), Tree Adjoining Grammar (Schabes et al. 1988; Joshi 1993), 'Radical Lexicalism' (Karttunen 1986)) and all there is to know about a language is the lexicon, thus completely dispensing with grammar as an independent entity. In general, those properties that are most easily conceptualized on the level of the individual word are covered under the rubric 'lexical acquisition.' We have devoted separate chapters to the acquisition of collocations and word sense disambiguation simply because these are self-contained and warrant separate treatment as central problems in Statistical NLP. But they are as much examples of lexical acquisition as the problems covered in this chapter.

The four main areas covered in this chapter are verb subcategorization (the syntactic means by which verbs express their arguments), attachment ambiguity (as in example (8.1)), selectional preferences (the semantic characterization of a verb's arguments such as the fact that things that get eaten are usually food items), and semantic similarity between words. However, we first begin by introducing some evaluation measures which are commonly used to evaluate lexical acquisition methods and various other Statistical NLP systems, and conclude with a more in-depth discussion of the significance of lexical acquisition in Statistical NLP and some further readings.

8.1   Evaluation Measures

An important recent development in NLP has been the use of much more rigorous standards for the evaluation of NLP systems. It is generally agreed that the ultimate demonstration of success is showing improved performance at an application task, be that spelling correction, summarizing job advertisements, or whatever. Nevertheless, while developing systems, it is often convenient to assess components of the system on some artificial performance score (such as perplexity), improvements in which one can expect to be reflected in better performance for the whole system on an application task.

Evaluation in Information Retrieval (IR) makes frequent use of the notions of precision and recall, and their use has crossed over into work on evaluating Statistical NLP models, such as a number of the systems discussed in this chapter. For many problems, we have a set of targets (for example, targeted relevant documents, or sentences in which a word has a certain sense) contained within a larger collection. Our system then decides on a selected set (documents that it thinks are relevant, or sentences that it thinks contain a certain sense of a word, etc.). This situation is shown in figure 8.1. The selected and target groupings can be thought

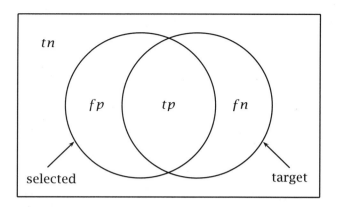

Figure 8.1 A diagram motivating the measures of precision and recall. The areas counted by the figures for true and false positives and true and false negatives are shown in terms of the target set and the selected set. Precision is $tp/|\text{selected}|$, the proportion of target (or correct) items in the selected (or retrieved) set. Recall is $tp/|\text{target}|$, the proportion of target items that were selected. In turn, $|\text{selected}| = tp + fp$, and $|\text{target}| = tp + fn$).

of as indicator random variables, and the joint distribution of the two variables can be expressed as a 2×2 contingency matrix:

(8.2)

	Actual	
System	target	¬ target
selected	tp	fp
¬selected	fn	tn

The numbers in each box show the frequency or count of the number of items in each region of the space. The cases accounted for by tp (*true positives*) and tn (*true negatives*) are the cases our system got right. The wrongly selected cases in fp are called *false positives*, *false acceptances* or *Type II errors*. The cases in fn that failed to be selected are called *false negatives*, *false rejections* or *Type I errors*.

TRUE POSITIVES

TRUE NEGATIVES

FALSE POSITIVES

TYPE II ERRORS

FALSE NEGATIVES

TYPE I ERRORS

PRECISION

Precision is defined as a measure of the proportion of selected items that the system got right:

(8.3) $\text{precision} = \dfrac{tp}{tp + fp}$

RECALL

Recall is defined as the proportion of the target items that the system selected:

(8.4) $\text{recall} = \dfrac{tp}{tp + fn}$

In applications like IR, one can generally trade off precision and re-call (one can select every document in the collection and get 100% recall but very low precision, etc.). This tradeoff can be plotted in a precision-recall curve, as we illustrate in section 15.1.2. Sometimes such a tradeoff doesn't make as much sense in NLP applications, but in any situation where there are some items that one is more sure of than others (such as in subcategorization frame learning in section 8.2), the same opportuni-ties for trading off precision vs. recall exist.

For this reason it can be convenient to combine precision and recall into
F MEASURE   a single measure of overall performance. One way to do this is the *F mea-*
E MEASURE   *sure*, a variant of the *E measure* introduced by van Rijsbergen (1979: 174), where $F = 1 - E$. The *F* measure is defined as follows:

(8.5) $F = \dfrac{1}{\alpha \frac{1}{P} + (1 - \alpha) \frac{1}{R}}$

where P is precision, R is recall and α is a factor which determines the weighting of precision and recall. A value of $\alpha = 0.5$ is often chosen for equal weighting of P and R. With this α value, the *F* measure simplifies to $2PR/(R + P)$.

A good question to ask is: "Wait a minute, in the table in (8.2), $tp + tn$ is the number of things I got right, and $fp + fn$ is the number of things I got wrong. Why don't we just report the percentage of things right or the percentage of things wrong?" One can do that, and these measures
ACCURACY   are known as *accuracy* and *error*. But it turns out that these often aren't
ERROR   good measures to use because in most of the kinds of problems we look at tn, the number of non-target, non-selected things, is huge, and dwarfs all the other numbers. In such contexts, use of precision and recall has three advantages:

- Accuracy figures are not very sensitive to the small, but interesting numbers $tp, fp,$ and fn, whereas precision and recall are. One can get extremely high accuracy results by simply selecting nothing.

- Other things being equal, the *F* measure prefers results with more true positives, whereas accuracy is sensitive only to the number of errors. This bias normally reflects our intuitions: We are interested in finding things, even at the cost of also returning some junk.

	tp	fp	fn	tn	Prec	Rec	F	Acc
(a)	25	0	125	99,850	1.000	0.167	0.286	0.9988
	50	100	100	99,750	0.333	0.333	0.333	0.9980
	75	150	75	99,700	0.333	0.500	0.400	0.9978
	125	225	25	99,625	0.357	0.833	0.500	0.9975
	150	275	0	99,575	0.353	1.000	0.522	0.9973
(b)	50	0	100	99,850	1.000	0.333	0.500	0.9990
	75	25	75	99,825	0.750	0.500	0.600	0.9990
	100	50	50	99,800	0.667	0.667	0.667	0.9990
	150	100	0	99,750	0.600	1.000	0.750	0.9990

Table 8.1 The F measure and accuracy are different objective functions. The table shows precision, recall, F measure (with $\alpha = 0.5$) and accuracy scores for certain selections of some number of items from out of a collection of 100,000 items of which 150 are genuine targets. The upper series (a) shows increasing F measure values, but decreasing accuracy. The lower series (b) shows identical accuracy scores, but again increasing F measure values. The bias of the F measure is towards maximizing the true positives, while accuracy is sensitive only to the number of classification errors.

- Using precision and recall, one can give a different cost to missing target items versus selecting junk.

Table 8.1 provides some examples which illustrate how accuracy and the F measure (with $\alpha = 0.5$) evaluate results differently.

FALLOUT   A less frequently used measure is *fallout*, the proportion of non-targeted items that were mistakenly selected.

(8.6) $$\text{fallout} = \frac{fp}{fp + tn}$$

Fallout is sometimes used as a measure of how hard it is to build a system that produces few false positives. If the number of non-targeted items is very large, then low precision due to large fp may be unavoidable because with a large background population of non-targeted items, it is unavoidable that some will be miscategorized.

ROC CURVE   In some fields of engineering recall-fallout trade-offs are more common than precision-recall trade-offs. One uses a so-called *ROC curve* (for *receiver operating characteristic*) to show how different levels of fallout (false positives as a proportion of all non-targeted events) influence recall

Frame	Functions	Verb	Example
NP NP	subject, object	greet	<u>She</u> greeted <u>me</u>.
NP S	subject, clause	hope	<u>She</u> hopes <u>he will attend</u>.
NP INF	subject, infinitive	hope	<u>She</u> hopes <u>to attend</u>.
NP NP S	subject, object, clause	tell	<u>She</u> told <u>me</u> <u>he will attend</u>.
NP NP INF	subject, object, infinitive	tell	<u>She</u> told <u>him</u> <u>to attend</u>.
NP NP NP	subject, (direct) object, indirect object	give	<u>She</u> gave <u>him</u> <u>the book</u>.

Table 8.2 Some subcategorization frames with example verbs and sentences. (adapted from (Brent 1993: 247)).

or sensitivity (true positives as a proportion of all targeted events). Think of a burglar alarm that has a knob for regulating its sensitivity. The ROC curve will tell you, for a certain rate of false positives, what the expected rate of true positives is. For example, for a false positives rate of being woken up once in a hundred nights with no burglars, one might achieve an expected rate of true positives of 95% (meaning 5% of burglaries will not be detected).

▼ Evaluation measures used in probabilistic parsing are discussed in section 12.1.8, and evaluation in IR is further discussed in section 15.1.2.

8.2 Verb Subcategorization

SUBCATEGORIZE FOR

SUBCATEGORIZATION
FRAME

Verbs *subcategorize for* different syntactic categories as we discussed in section 3.2.2. That is, they express their semantic arguments with different syntactic means. A particular set of syntactic categories that a verb can appear with is called a *subcategorization frame*. Examples of subcategorization frames are given in table 8.2. English verbs always subcategorize for a subject, so we sometimes omit subjects from subcategorization frames.

The phenomenon is called subcategorization because we can think of the verbs with a particular set of *semantic* arguments as one category. Each such category has several *subcategories* that express these semantic arguments using different *syntactic* means. For example, the class of verbs with semantic arguments *theme* and *recipient* has a subcategory that expresses these arguments with an object and a prepositional phrase (for example, *donate* in *He donated a large sum of money to the church*), and another subcategory that in addition permits a double-object construction (for example, *give* in *He gave the church a large sum of money*).

Knowing the possible subcategorization frames for verbs is important for parsing. The contrast in (8.7) shows why.

(8.7) a. She told the man where Peter grew up.

b. She found the place where Peter grew up.

If we know that *tell* has the subcategorization frame NP NP S (subject, object, clause), and that *find* lacks that frame, but has the subcategorization frame NP NP (subject, object), we can correctly attach the *where*-clause to *told* in the first sentence (as shown in (8.8a)) and to *place* in the second sentence (as shown in (8.8b)).

(8.8) a. She told [the man] [where Peter grew up].

b. She found [the place [where Peter grew up]].

Unfortunately, most dictionaries do not contain information on subcategorization frames. Even if we have access to one of the few dictionaries that do (e.g., Hornby 1974), the information on most verbs is incomplete. According to one account, up to 50% of parse failures can be due to missing subcategorization frames.[1] The most comprehensive source of subcategorization information for English is probably (Levin 1993). But even this excellent compilation does not cover all subcategorization frames and it does not have quantitative information such as the relative frequency of different subcategorization frames for a verb. And the need to cope with the productivity of language would make some form of acquisition from corpora necessary even if there were better sources available.

A simple and effective algorithm for learning some subcategorization frames was proposed by Brent (1993), implemented in a system called *Lerner*. Suppose we want to decide based on corpus evidence whether verb v takes frame f. Lerner makes this decision in two steps.

- **Cues.** Define a regular pattern of words and syntactic categories which indicates the presence of the frame with high certainty. Certainty is formalized as probability of error. For a particular cue c^j we define a probability of error ϵ_j that indicates how likely we are to make a mistake if we assign frame f to verb v based on cue c^j.

---

1. John Carroll, "Automatic acquisition of subcategorization frames and selectional preferences from corpora," talk given at the workshop "Practical Acquisition of Large-Scale Lexical Information" at CSLI, Stanford, on April 23, 1998.

- **Hypothesis testing.** The basic idea here is that we initially assume that the frame is *not* appropriate for the verb. This is our null hypothesis H_0. We reject this hypothesis if the cue c^j indicate with high probability that our H_0 is wrong.

Cues. Here is the regular pattern that Brent (1993: 247) uses as the cue for the subcategorization frame "NP NP" (transitive verbs):

(8.9)   Cue for frame "NP NP":
(OBJ | SUBJ_OBJ | CAP) (PUNC | CC)

where OBJ stands for personal pronouns that are necessarily accusative (or objective) like *me* and *him*, SUBJ_OBJ stands for personal pronouns that can be both subjects and objects like *you* and *it*, CAP is any capitalized word, PUNC is a punctuation mark, and CC is a subordinating conjunction like *if*, *before* or *as*.

This pattern is chosen because it is only likely to occur when a verb indeed takes the frame "NP NP." Suppose we have a sentence like (8.10) which matches the instantiation "CAP PUNC" of pattern (8.9).

(8.10)   [...] greet-V Peter-CAP ,-PUNC [...]

One can imagine a sentence like (8.11) where this pattern occurs and the verb does not allow the frame. (The matching pattern in (8.11) is *came*-V *Thursday*-CAP ,-PUNC.) But this case is very unlikely since a verb followed by a capitalized word that in turn is followed by a punctuation mark will almost always be one that takes objects and does not require any other syntactic arguments (except of course for the subject). So the probability of error is very low when we posit the frame 'NP NP' for a verb that occurs with cue (8.9).

(8.11)   I came Thursday, before the storm started.

Note that there is a tradeoff between how reliable a cue is and how often it occurs. The pattern "OBJ CC" is probably even less likely to be a misleading cue than "CAP PUNC." But if we narrowed (8.9) down to one reliable instantiation, we might have to sift through hundreds of occurrences of a verb to find the first occurrence with a cue, which would make the test applicable only to the most frequent verbs. This is a problem which we will return to later.

Hypothesis testing.   Once the cues for the frames of interest have been defined, we can analyze a corpus, and, for any verb-frame combination, count the number of times that a cue for the frame occurs with the verb. Suppose that verb v^i occurs a total of n times in the corpus and that there are $m \leq n$ occurrences with a cue for frame f^j. Then we can reject the null hypothesis H_0 that v^i does not permit f^j with the following probability of error:

$$(8.12) \qquad p_E = P(v^i(f^j) = 0 | C(v^i, c^j) \geq m) = \sum_{r=m}^{n} \binom{n}{r} \epsilon_j{}^r (1 - \epsilon_j)^{n-r}$$

where $v^i(f^j) = 0$ is shorthand for 'Verb v^i does not permit frame f^j,' $C(v^i, c^j)$ is the number of times that v^i occurs with cue c^j, and ϵ_j is the error rate for cue f^j, that is, the probability that we find cue c^j for a particular occurrence of the verb although the frame is not actually used.

Recall the basic idea of hypothesis testing (chapter 5, page 162): p_E is the probability of the observed data if the null hypothesis H_0 is correct. If p_E is small, then we reject H_0 because the fact that an unlikely event occurred indicates assuming H_0 was wrong. Our probability of error in this reasoning is p_E.

In equation (8.12), we assume a binomial distribution (section 2.1.9). Each occurrence of the verb is an independent coin flip for which the cue doesn't work with probability ϵ_j (that is, the cue occurs, but the frame doesn't), and for which it works correctly with probability $1 - \epsilon_j$ (either the cue occurs and correctly indicates the frame or the cue doesn't occur and thus doesn't mislead us).[2] It follows that an incorrect rejection of H_0 has probability p_E if we observe m or more cues for the frame. We will reject the null hypothesis if $p_E < \alpha$ for an appropriate level of significance α, for example, $\alpha = 0.02$. For $p_E \geq \alpha$, we will assume that verb v^i does not permit frame f^j.

An experimental evaluation shows that Lerner does well as far as precision is concerned. For most subcategorization frames, close to 100% of the verbs assigned to a particular frame are correctly assigned (Brent 1993: 255). However, Lerner does less well at recall. For the six frames covered by Brent (1993), recall ranges from 47% to 100%, but these numbers would probably be appreciably lower if a random sample of verb types had been selected instead of a random sample of verb tokens,

---

2. Lerner has a third component that we have omitted here: a way of determining ϵ_j for each frame. The interested reader should consult (Brent 1993).

a sampling method that results in a small proportion of low-frequency verbs.[3] Since low-frequency verbs are least likely to be comprehensively covered in existing dictionaries, they are arguably more important to get right than high-frequency verbs.

Manning (1993) addresses the problem of low recall by using a tagger and running the cue detection (that is, the regular expression matching for patterns like (8.9)) on the output of the tagger. It may seem worrying that we now have two error-prone systems, the tagger and the cue detector, which are combined, resulting in an even more error-prone system. However, in a framework of hypothesis testing, this is not necessarily problematic. The basic insight is that it doesn't really matter how reliable a cue is as an indicator for a subcategorization frame. Even an unreliable indicator can help us determine the subcategorization frame of a verb reliably if it occurs often enough and we do the appropriate hypothesis testing. For example, if cue c^j with error rate $\epsilon_j = 0.25$ occurs 11 out of 80 times, then we can still reject the null hypothesis that v^i does not permit c^j with $p_E \approx 0.011 < 0.02$ despite the low reliability of c^j.

Allowing low-reliability cues and additional cues based on tagger output increases the number of available cues significantly. As a result, a much larger proportion of verb occurrences have cues for a given frame. But more importantly, there are many subcategorization frames that have no high-reliability cues, for example, subcategorization for a preposition such as *on* in *he relies **on** relatives* or *with* in *she compared the results **with** earlier findings*. Since most prepositions occurring after verbs are not subcategorized for, there is simply no reliable cue for verbs subcategorizing for a preposition. Manning's method can learn a larger number of subcategorization frames, even those that have only low-reliability cues.

Table 8.3 shows a sample of Manning's results. We can see that precision is high: there are only three errors. Two of the errors are prepositional phrases (PPs): *to bridge between* and *to retire in*. It is often difficult to decide whether prepositional phrases are arguments (which are subcategorized for) or adjuncts (which aren't). One could argue that *retire* subcategorizes for the PP *in Malibu* in a sentence like *John retires in Malibu* since the verb and the PP-complement enter into a closer relationship than mere adverbial modification. (For example, one can infer that John ended up living in Malibu for a long time.) But the OALD does not list

---

3. Each occurrence of a verb in the Brown corpus had an equal chance of appearing in the sample which biases the sample against low-frequency verbs.

Verb	Correct	Incorrect	OALD
bridge	1	1	1
burden	2		2
depict	2		3
emanate	1		1
leak	1		5
occupy	1		3
remark	1	1	4
retire	2	1	5
shed	1		2
troop	0		3

Table 8.3 Some subcategorization frames learned by Manning's system. For each verb, the table shows the number of correct and incorrect subcategorization frames that were learned and the number of frames listed in the Oxford Advanced Learner's Dictionary (Hornby 1974). Adapted from (Manning 1993).

"NP *in*-PP" as a subcategorization frame, and this was what was used as the gold standard for evaluation.

The third error in the table is the incorrect assignment of the intransitive frame to *remark*. This is probably due to sentences like (8.13) which look like *remark* is used without any arguments (except the subject).

(8.13)   "And here we are 10 years later with the same problems," Mr. Smith remarked.

Recall in table 8.3 is relatively low. Recall here is the proportion of subcategorization frames listed in the OALD that were correctly identified. High precision and low recall are a consequence of the hypothesis testing framework adopted here. We only find subcategorization frames that are well attested. Conversely, this means that we do not find subcategorization frames that are rare. An example is the transitive use of *leak* as in *he leaked the news*, which was not found due to an insufficient number of occurrences in the corpus.

Table 8.3 is only a sample. Precision for the complete set of 40 verbs was 90%, recall was 43%. One way to improve these results would be to incorporate prior knowledge about a verb's subcategorization frame. While it is appealing to be able to learn just from raw data, without any help from a lexicographer's work, results will be much better if we take prior knowledge into account. The same pattern can be strong evidence for a new, unlisted subcategorization frame for one verb but evidence for a different frame with another verb. This is particularly true if we continue in the direction of more structured input to the subcategorization detector and use a parser instead of just a tagger. The simplest way of specifying prior knowledge would be to stipulate a higher prior for subcategorization frames listed in the dictionary.

As an example of how prior knowledge would improve accuracy, suppose we analyze a particular syntactic pattern (say, V NP S) and find two possible subcategorization frames f^1 (subject, object) and f^2 (subject, object, clause) with a slightly higher probability for f^1. This is our example (8.8). A parser could choose f^1 (subject, object) for a verb for which both frames have the same prior and f^2 (subject, object, clause) for a verb for which we have entered a bias against f^1 using some prior knowledge. For example, if we know that *email* is a verb of communication like *tell*, we may want to disfavor frames without clauses, and the parser would correctly choose frame f^2 (subject, object, clause) for *I emailed my boss where I had put the file with the slide presentation*. Such a system based on an incomplete subcategorization dictionary would make better use of a corpus than the systems described here and thus achieve better results.

Exercise 8.1   [$\star$]

A potential problem with the inclusion of low-reliability cues is that they 'water down' the effectiveness of high-reliability cues if we combine all cues in one regular expression pattern, resulting in lower recall. How can we modify the hypothesis test to address this problem? Hint: Consider a multinomial distribution.

Exercise 8.2   [$\star$]

Suppose a subcategorization frame for a verb is very rare. Discuss the difficulty of detecting such a frame with Brent and Manning's methods.

Exercise 8.3   [$\star$]

Could one sharpen the hypothesis test for a low-frequency subcategorization frame f^j by taking as the event space the set of occurrences of the verb that could potentially be instances of the subcategorization frame? Consider a verb that is mostly used transitively (with a direct object NP), but that has some occurrences that subcategorize only for a PP. The methods discussed above would count transitive uses as evidence against the possibility of any intransitive use. With an appropriately reduced event space, this would no longer be true. Discuss advantages and disadvantages of such an approach.

Exercise 8.4   [⋆]

A difficult problem in an approach using a fixed significance level ($\alpha = 0.02$ in Brent's work) and a categorical classification scheme (the verb takes a particular frame, yes/no) is to determine the threshold such that as many subcategorization classifications as possible are correct (high precision), but not too many frames are missed (high recall). Discuss how this problem might be alleviated in a probabilistic framework in which we determine $P(f^j|v^i)$ instead of making a binary decision.

Exercise 8.5   [⋆]

In an approach to subcategorization acquisition based on parsing and priors, how would you combine probabilistic parses and priors into a posterior estimate of the probability of subcategorization frames? Assume that the priors are given in the form $P(f^j|v^i)$, and that parsing a corpus gives you a number of estimates of the form $P(s_k|f^j)$ (the probability of sentence k given that verb v^i in the sentence occurs with frame f^j).

8.3 Attachment Ambiguity

A pervasive problem in parsing natural language is resolving attachment ambiguities. When we try to determine the syntactic structure of a sentence, a problem that we consider in general in chapter 12, there are often phrases that can be attached to two or more different nodes in the tree, and we have to decide which one is correct. PP attachment is the attachment ambiguity problem that has received the most attention in the Statistical NLP literature. We saw an example of it in chapter 3 example (3.65), here repeated as (8.14):

(8.14)   The children ate the cake with a spoon.

Depending on where we attach the prepositional phrase *with a spoon*, the sentence can either mean that the children were using a spoon to eat the cake (the PP is attached to *ate*), or that of the many cakes that they could have eaten the children ate the one that had a spoon attached (the PP is attached to *cake*). This latter reading is anomalous with this PP, but would be natural for the PP *with frosting*. See figure 3.2 in chapter 3 for the two different syntactic trees that correspond to the two attachments. This type of syntactic ambiguity occurs in every sentence in which a prepositional phrase follows an object noun phrase. The reason why the sentence in (1.12) had so many parses was because there were a lot of PPs (and participial relative clauses) which can attach at various places syntactically. In this section, we introduce a method for determining the attachment of *prepositional phrases* based on lexical information that is due to Hindle and Rooth (1993).

How are such ambiguities to be resolved? While one could imagine contextualizing a discourse where *with a spoon* was used as a differentiator of cakes, it was natural in the above example to see it as a tool for eating, and thus to choose the verb attachment. This seems to be true for many naturally occurring sentences:

(8.15)   a. Moscow sent more than 100,000 soldiers into Afghanistan ...

b. Sydney Water breached an agreement with NSW Health ...

In these examples, only one attachment results in a reasonable interpretation. In (8.15a), the PP *into Afghanistan* must attach to the verb phrase headed by *send*, while in (8.15b), the PP *with NSW Health* must attach to the NP headed by *agreement*. In cases like these, lexical preferences can be used to disambiguate. Indeed, it turns out that, in most cases, simple lexical statistics can determine which attachment is the correct one. These simple statistics are basically co-occurrence counts between the verb and the preposition on the one hand, and between the noun and the preposition on the other. In a corpus, we would find lots of cases where *into* is used with *send*, but only a few where *into* is used with *soldier*. So we can be reasonably certain that the PP headed by *into* in (8.15a) attaches to *send*, not to *soldiers*.

A simple model based on this information is to compute the following likelihood ratio λ (cf. section 5.3.4 on likelihood ratios).

(8.16) $$\lambda(v, n, p) \;=\; \log \frac{P(p|v)}{P(p|n)}$$

where $P(p|v)$ is the probability of seeing a PP with p after the verb v and $P(p|n)$ is the probability of seeing a PP with p after the noun n. We can then attach to the verb for $\lambda(v, n, p) > 0$ and to the noun for $\lambda(v, n, p) < 0$.

The trouble with this model is that it ignores the fact that other things being equal, there is a preference for attaching phrases "low" in the parse tree. For PP attachment, the lower node is the NP node. For example, the tree in figure 3.2 (b) attaches the PP *with the spoon* to the lower NP node, the tree in figure 3.2 (a) attaches it to the higher VP node. One can explain low attachments with a preference for local operations. When we process the PP, the NP is still fresh in our mind and so it is easier to attach the PP to it.

w	$C(w)$	$C(w, with)$
end	5156	607
venture	1442	155

Table 8.4 An example where the simple model for resolving PP attachment ambiguity fails.

The following example from the *New York Times* shows why it is important to take the preference for attaching low into account:

(8.17)   Chrysler confirmed that it would end its troubled venture with Maserati.

The preposition *with* occurs frequently after both *end* (e.g., *the show ended with a song*) and *venture* (e.g., *the venture with Maserati*). The data from the *New York Times* corpus in table 8.4,[4] when plugged into equation (8.16), predict attachment to the verb:

$$P(p|v) = \frac{607}{5156} \approx 0.118 > 0.107 \approx \frac{155}{1442} = P(p|n)$$

But that is the wrong decision here. The model is wrong because equation (8.16) ignores a bias for low attachment in cases where a preposition is equally compatible with the verb and the noun. We will now develop a probabilistic model for PP attachment that formalizes this bias.

8.3.1   Hindle and Rooth (1993)

In setting up the probabilistic model that is due to Hindle and Rooth (1993), we first define the event space. We are interested in sentences that are potentially ambiguous with respect to PP attachment. So we define the event space to consist of all clauses that have a transitive verb (a verb with an object noun phrase), an NP following the verb (the object noun phrase) and a PP following the NP.[5] Our goal is to resolve the PP attachment ambiguity in these cases.

In order to reduce the complexity of the model, we limit our attention to one preposition at a time (that is, we are not modeling possible interactions between PPs headed by different prepositions, see exercise 8.8),

---

4. We used the subset of texts from chapter 5.
5. Our terminology here is a little bit sloppy since the PP is actually part of the NP when it attaches to the noun, so, strictly speaking, it does not follow the NP. So what we mean here when we say "NP" is the base NP chunk without complements and adjuncts.

and, if there are two PPs with the same preposition in sequence, then we will only model the behavior of the first (see exercise 8.9).

To simplify the probabilistic model, we will not directly ask the question about whether a certain preposition is attached to a certain verb or noun. Rather, we will estimate how likely it is in general for a preposition to attach to a verb or noun. We will look at the following two questions, formalized by the sets of indicator random variables VA_p and NA_p:

VA_p: Is there a PP headed by p and following the verb v which attaches to v ($VA_p = 1$) or not ($VA_p = 0$)?

NA_p: Is there a PP headed by p and following the noun n which attaches to n ($NA_p = 1$) or not ($NA_p = 0$)?

Note that we are referring to any occurrence of the preposition p here rather than to a particular instance. So it is possible for both NA_p and VA_p to be 1 for some value of p. For instance, this is true for $p = on$ in the sentence:

(8.18)   He put the book [*on* World War II] [*on* the table].

For a clause containing the sequence "$v \ldots n \ldots \mathrm{PP}$," we wish to calculate the probability of the PP headed with preposition p attaching to the verb v and the noun n, conditioned on v and n:

$$
\begin{aligned}
(8.19) \quad P(VA_p, NA_p | v, n) &= P(VA_p | v, n) P(NA_p | v, n) \\
(8.20) \quad &= P(VA_p | v) P(NA_p | n)
\end{aligned}
$$

In (8.19), we assume conditional independence of the two attachments – that is, whether a PP occurs modifying n is independent of whether one occurs modifying v. In (8.20), we assume that whether the verb is modified by a PP does not depend on the noun and whether the noun is modified by a PP does not depend on the verb.

That we are treating attachment of a preposition to a verb and to a noun (i.e., VA_p and NA_p) as independent events seems counterintuitive at first since the problem as stated above posits a binary choice between noun and verb attachment. So, rather than being independent, attachment to the verb seems to imply non-attachment to the noun and vice versa. But we already saw in (8.18) that the definitions of VA_p and NA_p imply that both can be true. The advantage of the independence assumption is that it is easier to derive empirical estimates for the two variables separately rather than estimating their joint distribution. We will see below how we can estimate the relevant quantities from an unlabeled corpus.

Now suppose that we wish to determine the attachment of a PP that is immediately following an object noun. We can compute an estimate in terms of model (8.20) by computing the probability of $\text{NA}_p = 1$.

$$
\begin{aligned}
P(\text{Attach}(p) = n | v, n) &= P(\text{VA}_p = 0 \vee \text{VA}_p = 1 | v) \times P(\text{NA}_p = 1 | n) \\
&= 1.0 \times P(\text{NA}_p = 1 | n) \\
&= P(\text{NA}_p = 1 | n)
\end{aligned}
$$

So we do not need to consider whether $\text{VA}_p = 0$ or $\text{VA}_p = 1$, since while there could be other PPs in the sentence modifying the verb, they are immaterial to deciding the status of the PP immediately after the noun head.

In order to see that the case $\text{VA}_p = 1$ and $\text{NA}_p = 1$ does not make $\text{Attach}(p) = v$ true, let's look at what these two premises entail. First, there must be two prepositional phrases headed by a preposition of type p. This is because we assume that any given PP can only attach to one phrase, either the verb or the noun. Second, the first of these two PPs must attach to the noun, the second to the verb. If it were the other way round, then we would get crossing brackets. It follows that $\text{VA}_p = 1$ and $\text{NA}_p = 1$ implies that the first PP headed by p is attached to the noun, not to the verb. So $\text{Attach}(p) \neq v$ holds in this case.

In contrast, because there cannot be crossing lines in a phrase structure tree, in order for the first PP headed by the preposition p to attach to the verb, both $\text{VA}_p = 1$ and $\text{NA}_p = 0$ must hold. Substituting the appropriate values in model (8.20) we get:

$$
\begin{aligned}
P(\text{Attach}(p) = v | v, n) &= P(\text{VA}_p = 1, \text{NA}_p = 0 | v, n) \\
&= P(\text{VA}_p = 1 | v) P(\text{NA}_p = 0 | n)
\end{aligned}
$$

We can again assess $P(\text{Attach}(p) = v)$ and $P(\text{Attach}(p) = n)$ via a likelihood ratio λ.

$$
(8.21) \quad
\begin{aligned}
\lambda(v, n, p) &= \log_2 \frac{P(\text{Attach}(p) = v | v, n)}{P(\text{Attach}(p) = n | v, n)} \\
&= \log_2 \frac{P(\text{VA}_p = 1 | v) P(\text{NA}_p = 0 | v)}{P(\text{NA}_p = 1 | n)}
\end{aligned}
$$

We choose verb attachment for large positive values of λ and noun attachment for large negative values. We can also make decisions for values of

λ closer to zero (verb attachment for positive λ and noun attachment for negative λ), but there is a higher probability of error.

How do we estimate the probabilities $P(\text{VA}_p = 1|v)$ and $P(\text{NA}_p = 1|n)$ that we need for equation (8.22)? The simplest method is to rely on maximum likelihood estimates of the familiar form:

$$P(\text{VA}_p = 1|v) \;\;=\;\; \frac{C(v,p)}{C(v)}$$

$$P(\text{NA}_p = 1|n) \;\;=\;\; \frac{C(n,p)}{C(n)}$$

where $C(v)$ and $C(n)$ are the number of occurrences of v and n in the corpus, and $C(v,p)$ and $C(n,p)$ are the number of times that p attaches to v and p attaches to n. The remaining difficulty is to determine the attachment counts from an unlabeled corpus. In some sentences the attachment is obvious.

(8.22)   a. The road *to London* is long and winding.

b. She sent him *into the nursery* to gather up his toys.

The prepositional phrase in italics in (8.22a) must attach to the noun since there is no preceding verb, and the italicized PP in (8.22b) must attach to the verb since attachment to a pronoun like *him* is not possible. So we can bump up our counts for $C(road, to)$ and $C(send, into)$ by one based on these two sentences. But many sentences are ambiguous. That, after all, is the reason why we need an automatic procedure for the resolution of attachment ambiguity.

Hindle and Rooth (1993) propose a heuristic for determining $C(v,p)$ and $C(n,p)$ from unlabeled data that has essentially three steps.

1. Build an initial model by counting all unambiguous cases (examples like (8.22a) and (8.22b)).

2. Apply the initial model to all ambiguous cases and assign them to the appropriate count if λ exceeds a threshold (for example, $\lambda > 2.0$ for verb attachment and $\lambda < -2.0$ for noun attachment).

3. Divide the remaining ambiguous cases evenly between the counts (that is, increase both $C(v,p)$ and $C(n,p)$ by 0.5 for each ambiguous case).

Sentence (8.15a), here repeated as (8.23), may serve as an example of how the method is applied (Hindle and Rooth 1993: 109–110).

(8.23)   Moscow sent more than 100,000 soldiers into Afghanistan . . .

First we estimate the two probabilities we need for the likelihood ratio. The count data are from Hindle and Rooth's test corpus.

$$P(\text{VA}_{into} = 1 | send) \quad = \quad \frac{C(send, into)}{C(send)} = \frac{86}{1742.5} \approx 0.049$$

$$P(\text{NA}_{into} = 1 | soldiers) \quad = \quad \frac{C(soldiers, into)}{C(soldiers)} = \frac{1}{1478} \approx 0.0007$$

The fractional count is due to the step of the heuristic that divides the hardest ambiguous cases evenly between noun and verb. We also have:

(8.24) $P(\text{NA}_{into} = 0 | soldiers) = 1 - P(\text{NA}_{into} = 1 | soldiers) \approx 0.9993$

Plugging these numbers into formula (8.22), we get the following likelihood ratio.

$$\lambda(send, soldiers, into) \approx \log_2 \frac{0.049 \times 0.9993}{0.0007} \approx 6.13$$

So attachment to the verb is much more likely ($2^{6.13} \approx 70$ times more likely), which is the right prediction here. In general, the procedure is accurate in about 80% of cases if we always make a choice (Hindle and Rooth 1993: 115). We can trade higher precision for lower recall if we only make a decision for values of λ that exceed a certain threshold. For example, Hindle and Rooth (1993) found that precision was 91.7% and recall was 55.2% for $\lambda = 3.0$.

8.3.2   General remarks on PP attachment

Much of the early psycholinguistic literature on parsing emphasized the use of structural heuristics to resolve ambiguities, but they clearly don't help in cases like the PP attachments we have been looking at. For identical sequences of word classes, sometimes one parse structure is correct, and sometimes another. Rather, as suggested by Ford et al. (1982), lexical preferences seem very important here.

There are several major limitations to the model presented here. One is that it only considers the identity of the preposition and the noun and verb to which it might be attached. Sometimes other information is important (studies suggest human accuracy improves by around 5% when they see more than just a v, n, p triple). In particular, in sentences like those in (8.25), the identity of the noun that heads the NP inside the PP is clearly crucial:

The board approved [its acquisition] [by Royal Trustco Ltd.] [of Toronto] [for $27 a share] [at its monthly meeting].

Figure 8.2   Attachments in a complex sentence.

(8.25)   a. I examined the man with a stethoscope

b. I examined the man with a broken leg

Other information might also be important. For instance Hindle and Rooth (1993) note that a superlative adjective preceding the noun highly biased things towards an NP attachment (in their data). This conditioning was probably omitted by Hindle and Rooth because of the infrequent occurrence of superlative adjectives. However, a virtue of the likelihood ratio approach is that other factors can be incorporated in a principled manner (providing that they are assumed to be independent). Much other work has used various other features, in particular the identity of the head noun inside the PP (Resnik and Hearst 1993; Brill and Resnik 1994; Ratnaparkhi et al. 1994; Zavrel et al. 1997; Ratnaparkhi 1998). Franz (1996) is able to include lots of features within a loglinear model approach, but at the cost of reducing the most basic association strength parameters to categorical variables.

A second major limitation is that Hindle and Rooth (1993) consider only the most basic case of a PP immediately after an NP object which is modifying either the immediately preceding noun or verb. But there are many more possibilities for PP attachments than this. Gibson and Pearlmutter (1994) argue that psycholinguistic studies have been greatly biased by their overconcentration on this one particular case. A PP separated from an object noun by another PP may modify any of the noun inside the preceding PP, the object noun, or the preceding verb. Figure 8.2 shows a variety of the distant and complex attachment patterns that occur in texts. Additionally, in a complex sentence, a PP might not modify just the immediately preceding verb, but might modify a higher verb. See Franz (1997) for further discussion, and exercise 8.9.

Other attachment issues

Apart from prepositional phrases, attachment ambiguity also occurs with various kinds of adverbial and participial phrases and clauses, and in NOUN COMPOUNDS *noun compounds*. The issue of the scope of coordinations in parsing is also rather similar to an attachment decision, but we will not consider it further here.

A noun phrase consisting of a sequence of three or more nouns either has the left-branching structure [[N N] N] or the right-branching structure [N [N N]]. For example, *door bell manufacturer* is left-branching: *[[door bell] manufacturer]*. It's a manufacturer of door bells, not a manufacturer of bells that somehow has to do with doors. The phrase *woman aid worker* is an example of a right-branching NP: *[woman [aid worker]]*. The phrase refers to an aid worker who is female, not a worker working for or on *woman aid*. The left-branching case roughly corresponds to attachment of the PP to the verb ([V N P]), while the right-branching case corresponds to attachment to the noun ([V [N P]]).

We could directly apply the formalism we've developed for prepositional phrases to noun compounds. However, data sparseness tends to be a more serious problem for noun compounds than for prepositional phrases because prepositions are high-frequency words whereas most nouns are not. For this reason, one approach is to use some form of semantic generalization based on word classes in combination with attachment information. See Lauer (1995a) for one take on the problem (use of semantic classes for the PP attachment problem was explored by Resnik and Hearst (1993) with less apparent success). A different example of class-based generalization will be discussed in the next section.

As a final comment on attachment ambiguity, note that a large proportion of prepositional phrases exhibit 'indeterminacy' with respect to attachment (Hindle and Rooth 1993: 112). Consider the PP *with them* in (8.26):

(8.26)   We have not signed a settlement agreement *with them*.

When you sign an agreement with person X, then in most cases it is an agreement with X, but you also do the signing with X. It is rather unclear whether the PP should be attached to the verb or the noun or whether we should rather say that a PP like *with them* in sentence (8.26) should attach to *both* verb and noun. Lauer (1995a) found that a significant proportion of noun compounds also had this type of attachment indeterminacy. This is an example of a possibly important insight that came out of Statistical NLP work. Before Hindle and Rooth's study, computational linguists were not generally aware of how widespread attachment indeterminacy is (though see Church and Patil (1982) for a counterexample).

After becoming aware of this fact, we could just say that it doesn't matter how we attach in indeterminate cases. But the phenomenon might also motivate us to explore new ways of determining the contribution a prepositional phrase makes to the meaning of a sentence. The phenomenon of attachment indeterminacy suggests that it may not be a good idea to require that PP meaning always be mediated through a noun phrase or a verb phrase as current syntactic formalisms do.

Exercise 8.6 [★]

As is usually the case with maximum likelihood estimates, they suffer in accuracy if data are sparse. Modify the estimation procedure using one of the procedures suggested in chapter 6. Hindle and Rooth (1993) use an 'Add One' method in their experiments.

Exercise 8.7 [★]

Hindle and Rooth (1993) used a partially parsed corpus to determine $C(v, p)$, and $C(n, p)$. Discuss whether we could use an unparsed corpus and what additional problems we would have to grapple with.

Exercise 8.8 [★]

Consider sentences with two PPs headed by two different prepositions, for example, "He put the book on Churchill in his backpack." The model we developed could attach *on Churchill* to *put* when applied to the preposition *on* and *in his backpack* to *book* when applied to the preposition *in*. But that is an incorrect parse tree since it has crossing brackets. Develop a model that makes consistent decisions for sentences with two PPs headed by different prepositions.

Exercise 8.9 [★ ★]

Develop a model that resolves the attachment of the second PP in a sequence of the form: V ... N ... PP PP. There are three possible cases here: attachment to the verb, attachment to the noun and attachment to the noun in the first PP.

Exercise 8.10 [★]

Note the following difference between a) the acquisition methods for attachment ambiguity in this section and b) those for subcategorization frames in the last section and those for collocations in chapter 5. In the case of PP attachment, we are interested in what is *predictable*. We choose the pattern that best fits what we would predict to happen from the training corpus. (For example, a PP headed by *in* after *send*.) In the case of subcategorization and collocations, we are interested in what is *unpredictable*, that is, patterns that shouldn't occur if our model was right. Discuss this difference.

8.4   Selectional Preferences

Most verbs prefer arguments of a particular type. Such regularities are called *selectional preferences* or *selectional restrictions*. Examples are that the objects of the verb *eat* tend to be food items, the subjects of *think* tend to be people, and the subjects of *bark* tend to be dogs. These *semantic* constraints on arguments are analogous to the *syntactic* constraints we looked at earlier, subcategorization for objects, PPs, infinitives etc. We use the term *preferences* as opposed to *rules* because the preferences can be overridden in metaphors and other extended meanings. For example, *eat* takes non-food arguments in *eating one's words* or *fear eats the soul*.

The acquisition of selectional preferences is important in Statistical NLP for a number of reasons. If a word like *durian* is missing from our machine-readable dictionary, then we can infer part of its meaning from selectional restrictions. In the case of sentence (8.27), we can infer that a *durian* is a type of food.

(8.27)   Susan had never eaten a fresh durian before.

Another important use of selectional preferences is for ranking the possible parses of a sentence. We will give higher scores to parses where the verb has 'natural' arguments than to those with atypical arguments, a strategy that allows us to choose among parses that are equally good on syntactic criteria. Scoring the semantic wellformedness of a sentence based on selectional preferences is more amenable to automated language processing than trying to understand the meaning of a sentence more fully. This is because the semantic regularities captured in selectional preferences are often quite strong and, due to the tight syntactic link between a verb and its arguments, can be acquired more easily from corpora than other types of semantic information and world knowledge.

We will now introduce the model of selectional preferences proposed by Resnik (1993, 1996). In principle, the model can be applied to any class of words that imposes semantic constraints on a grammatically dependent phrase: verb↔subject, verb↔direct object, verb↔prepositional phrase, adjective↔noun, noun↔noun (in noun-noun compounds). But we will only consider the case 'verb↔direct object' here, that is, the case of verbs selecting a semantically restricted class of direct object noun phrases.

The model formalizes selectional preferences using two notions: selec-

SELECTIONAL
PREFERENCE
STRENGTH

tional preference strength and selectional association. *Selectional preference strength* measures how strongly the verb constrains its direct object. It is defined as the KL divergence between the prior distribution of direct objects (the distribution of direct objects for verbs in general) and the distribution of direct objects of the verb we are trying to characterize.

We make two assumptions to simplify the model. First, we only take the *head noun* of the direct object into account (for example, *apple* in *Susan ate the green apple*) since the head is the crucial part of the noun phrase that determines compatibility with the verb. Second, instead of dealing with individual nouns, we will instead look at *classes* of nouns. As usual, a class-based model facilitates generalization and parameter estimation. With these assumptions, we can define selectional preference strength $S(v)$ as follows:

(8.28) $$S(v) = D(P(C|v)\|P(C)) = \sum_c P(c|v) \log \frac{P(c|v)}{P(c)}$$

where $P(C)$ is the overall probability distribution of noun classes and $P(C|v)$ is the probability distribution of noun classes in the direct object position of v. We can take the noun classes from any lexical resource that groups nouns into classes. Resnik (1996) uses WordNet.

SELECTIONAL
ASSOCIATION

Based on selectional preference strength, we can define *selectional association* between a verb v and a class c as follows:

(8.29) $$A(v,c) = \frac{P(c|v) \log \frac{P(c|v)}{P(c)}}{S(v)}$$

That is, the association between a verb and a class is defined as the proportion that its summand $P(c|v) \log \frac{P(c|v)}{P(c)}$ contributes to the overall preference strength $S(v)$.

Finally, we need a rule for assigning association strength to nouns (as opposed to noun classes). If the noun n is in only one class c, then we simply define $A(v,n) \stackrel{\text{def}}{=} A(v,c)$. If the noun is a member of several classes, then we define its association strength as the highest association strength of any of its classes.

(8.30) $$A(v,n) = \max_{c \in \text{classes}(n)} A(v,c)$$

A noun like *chair* in (8.31) is in several classes because it is polysemous (or ambiguous).

(8.31) Susan interrupted the chair.

Noun class c	$P(c)$	$P(c\|eat)$	$P(c\|see)$	$P(c\|find)$
people	0.25	0.01	0.25	0.33
furniture	0.25	0.01	0.25	0.33
food	0.25	0.97	0.25	0.33
action	0.25	0.01	0.25	0.01
SPS $S(v)$		1.76	0.00	0.35

Table 8.5 Selectional Preference Strength (SPS). The argument distributions and selectional preference strengths of three verbs for a classification of nouns with four classes (based on hypothetical data).

In the case of *chair*, we have two candidate classes, 'furniture' and 'people' (the latter in the sense 'chairperson'). Equating $A(v, n)$ with the maximum $A(v, c)$ amounts to disambiguating the noun. In sentence (8.31) we will base the association strength $A(interrupt, chair)$ on the class 'people' since interrupting people is much more common than interrupting pieces of furniture, that is:

DISAMBIGUATION

$$A(interrupt, \text{people}) \gg A(interrupt, \text{furniture})$$

Hence:

$$
\begin{aligned}
A(interrupt, chair) &= \max_{c \in \text{classes}(chair)} A(interrupt, c) \\
&= A(interrupt, \text{people})
\end{aligned}
$$

So we can disambiguate *chair* as a by-product of determining the association of *interrupt* and *chair*.

The hypothetical data in table 8.5 (based on (Resnik 1996: 139)) may serve as a further illustration of the model. The table shows the prior distribution of object NPs over noun classes (assuming that there are only the four classes shown) and posterior distributions for three verbs. The verb *eat* overwhelmingly prefers food items as arguments; *see*'s distribution is not very different from the prior distribution since all physical objects can be seen; *find* has a uniform distribution over the first three classes, but 'disprefers' actions since actions are not really the type of entities that are found.

The selectional preference strengths of the three verbs are shown in the row 'SPS.' The numbers conform well with our intuition about the three verbs: *eat* is very specific with respect to the arguments it can take, *find* is less specific, and *see* has no selectional preferences (at least in our hypothetical data). Note that there is a clear interpretation of SPS as the amount of information we gain about the argument after learning about the verb. In the case of *eat*, SPS is 1.76, corresponding to almost 2 binary questions. That is just the number of binary questions we need to get from four classes (people, furniture, food, action) to one, namely the class 'food' that *eat* selects. (Binary logarithms were used to compute SPS and association strength.)

Computing the association strengths between verbs and noun classes, we find that the class 'food' is strongly preferred by *eat* (8.32) whereas the class 'action' is dispreferred by *find* (8.33). This example shows that the model formalizes selectional 'dispreferences' (negative numbers) as well as selectional preferences (positive numbers).

(8.32) $A(eat, \text{food}) \;=\; 1.08$

(8.33) $A(find, \text{action}) \;=\; -0.13$

The association strengths between *see* and all four noun classes are zero, corresponding to the intuition that *see* does not put strong constraints on its possible arguments.

The remaining problem is to estimate the probability that a direct object in noun class c occurs given a verb v, $P(c|v) = \frac{P(v,c)}{P(v)}$. The maximum likelihood estimate for $P(v)$ is $C(v)/\sum_{v'} C(v')$, the relative frequency of v with respect to all verbs. Resnik (1996) proposes the following estimate for $P(v,c)$:

(8.34) $$P(v,c) = \frac{1}{N} \sum_{n \in \text{words}(c)} \frac{1}{|\text{classes}(n)|} C(v,n)$$

where N is the total number of verb-object pairs in the corpus, $\text{words}(c)$ is the set of all nouns in class c, $\text{classes}(n)$ is the number of noun classes that contain n as a member and $C(v,n)$ is the number of verb-object pairs with v as the verb and n as the head of the object NP. This way of estimating $P(v,c)$ bypasses the problem of disambiguating nouns. If a noun that is a member of two classes c_1 and c_2 occurs with v, then we assign half of this occurrence to $P(v,c_1)$ and half to $P(v,c_2)$.

So far, we have only presented constructed examples. Table 8.6 shows some actual data from Resnik's experiments on the Brown corpus (Resnik 1996: 142). The verbs and nouns were taken from a psycholinguistic study (Holmes et al. 1989). The nouns in the left and right halves of the table are 'typical' and 'atypical' objects, respectively. For most verbs,

Verb v	Noun n	$A(v, n)$	Class	Noun n	$A(v, n)$	Class
answer	*request*	4.49	speech act	*tragedy*	3.88	communication
find	*label*	1.10	abstraction	*fever*	0.22	psych. feature
hear	*story*	1.89	communication	*issue*	1.89	communication
remember	*reply*	1.31	statement	*smoke*	0.20	article of commerce
repeat	*comment*	1.23	communication	*journal*	1.23	communication
read	*article*	6.80	writing	*fashion*	−0.20	activity
see	*friend*	5.79	entity	*method*	−0.01	method
write	*letter*	7.26	writing	*market*	0.00	commerce

Table 8.6 Association strength distinguishes a verb's plausible and implausible objects. The left half of the table shows typical objects, the right half shows atypical objects. In most cases, association strength $A(v, n)$ is a good predictor of object typicality.

association strength accurately predicts which object is typical. For example, it correctly predicts that *friend* is a more natural object for *see* than *method*. Most errors the model makes are due to the fact that it performs a form of disambiguation, by choosing the highest association strength among the possible classes of the noun (cf. the example of *chair* we discussed earlier). Even if a noun is an atypical object, if it has a rare interpretation as a plausible object, then it will be rated as typical. An example of this is *hear*. Both *story* and *issue* can be forms of communication, but this meaning is rarer for *issue*. Yet the model chooses the rare interpretation because it makes more sense for the verb *hear*.

Apart from the specific question of selectional preference, Resnik also investigates how well the model predicts whether or not a verb has the so-called *implicit object alternation* (or *unspecified object alternation*, see Levin (1993: 33)). An example is the alternation between sentences (8.35a) and (8.35b). The verb *eat* alternates between explicitly naming what was eaten (8.35a) and leaving the thing eaten implicit (8.35b).

IMPLICIT OBJECT
ALTERNATION

(8.35)   a. Mike ate the cake.

         b. Mike ate.

The explanation Resnik offers for this phenomenon is that the more constraints a verb puts on its object, the more likely it is to permit the implicit-object construction. The intuition is that for a verb like *eat* with a strong selectional preference, just knowing the verb gives us so much information about the direct object that we don't have to mention it. Resnik finds evidence that selectional preference strength is a good predictor of the permissibility of the implicit-object alternation for verbs.

We can now see why Resnik's model defines selectional preference strength (SPS) as the primary concept and derives association strength from it. SPS is seen as the more basic phenomenon which explains the occurrence of implicit objects as well as association strength.

An alternative is to define association strength directly as $P(c|v)$ – or as $P(n|v)$ if we don't want to go through an intermediate class representation. Approaches to computing $P(n|v)$ include distributional clustering (the work by Pereira et al. (1993) described in chapter 14) and methods for computing the similarity of nouns. If a measure of the similarity of nouns is available, then $P(n|v)$ can be computed from the distribution of nouns similar to n that are found in the argument slot of v. See the next section for more on this approach.

Exercise 8.11   [★]

As we pointed out above, we can use a model of selectional preferences for disambiguating nouns by computing the association strengths for different senses of the noun. This strategy assumes that we know what the senses of the noun are and which classes they are members of. How could one use selectional preferences to discover senses of nouns whose senses we don't know?

Exercise 8.12   [★]

Verbs can also be ambiguous as in the case of *fire* in these two sentences.

(8.36)   a. The president fired the chief financial officer.

          b. Mary fired her gun first.

How can the model be used to disambiguate verbs? Consider two scenarios, one in which we have a training set in which verb senses are labeled, one in which we don't.

Exercise 8.13   [★]

The model discussed in this section assigns the noun sense with the maximum association strength. This approach does not take prior probabilities into account. We may not want to choose an extremely rare sense of a noun even if it is the best fit as the object NP of a verb.

Example: The noun *shot* has the rare meaning 'marksman' as in *John was reputed to be a crack shot.* So, theoretically, we could choose this sense for *shot* in the sentence *John fired a shot*, corresponding to the meaning *John laid off a marksman.*

How could prior probabilities be used to avoid such incorrect inferences?

Exercise 8.14   [⋆ ⋆]

In the approach developed above, WordNet is treated as a flat set of noun classes, but it is actually a hierarchy. How could one make use of the information present in the hierarchy (for example, the fact, that the class 'dog' is a subclass of 'animal' which in turn is a subclass of 'entity')?

Exercise 8.15   [⋆ ⋆]

Verbs can be organized into a hierarchy too. How could one use hierarchical information about verbs for better parameter estimation?

Exercise 8.16   [⋆]

One assumption of the model is that it is the head noun that determines the compatibility of an object NP with the selectional preferences of the verb. However, as pointed out by Resnik (1996: 137), that is not always the case. Examples include negation (*you can't eat stones*), and certain adjectival modifiers (*he ate a chocolate firetruck*; *the tractor beam pulled the ship closer*); neither stones nor firetrucks are compatible with the selectional preferences of *eat*, but these sentences are still well-formed. Discuss this problem.

Exercise 8.17   [⋆]

Hindle and Rooth (1993) go through several iterations of estimating initial parameters of their model, disambiguating some ambiguous attachments and re-estimating parameters based on disambiguated instances. How could this approach be used to estimate the prior probabilities of noun classes in (8.34)? The goal would be to improve on the uniform distribution over possible classes assumed in the equation.

Exercise 8.18   [⋆]

Resnik's model expresses association strength as a proportion of selectional preference strength. This leads to interesting differences from an approach based on formalizing selectional preference as $P(n|v)$. Compare two noun-verb pairs with equal $P(n|v)$, that is, $P(n_1|v_1) = P(n_2|v_2)$. If the selectional preference strength of v_1 is much larger than that of v_2, then we get $A(v_1, c(n_1)) \ll A(v_2, c(n_2))$. So the two models make different predictions here. Discuss these differences.

8.5 Semantic Similarity

The holy grail of lexical acquisition is the acquisition of meaning. There are many tasks (like text understanding and information retrieval) for which Statistical NLP could make a big difference if we could automatically acquire meaning. Unfortunately, how to represent meaning in a way that can be operationally used by an automatic system is a largely unsolved problem. Most work on acquiring semantic properties of words

SEMANTIC SIMILARITY

has therefore focused on *semantic similarity*. Automatically acquiring a relative measure of how similar a new word is to known words (or how dissimilar) is much easier than determining what the meaning actually is.

GENERALIZATION

Despite its limitations, semantic similarity is still a useful measure to have. It is most often used for *generalization* under the assumption that semantically similar words behave similarly. An example would be the problem of selectional preferences that we discussed in the previous section. Suppose we want to find out how appropriate *durian* is as an argument of *eat* in sentence (8.37) (our previous example (8.27)):

(8.37)   Susan had never eaten a fresh durian before.

Suppose further that we don't have any information about *durian* except that it's semantically similar to *apple*, *banana*, and *mango*, all of which perfectly fit the selectional preferences of *eat*. Then we can generalize from the behavior of *apple*, *banana*, and *mango* to the semantically similar *durian* and hypothesize that *durian* is also a good argument of *eat*. This scheme can be implemented in various ways. We could base our treatment of *durian* only on the closest semantic neighbor (say, *mango*), or we could base it on a combination of evidence from a fixed number of nearest neighbors, a combination that can be weighted according to how semantically similar each neighbor is to *durian*.

CLASS-BASED
GENERALIZATION

Similarity-based generalization is a close relative of class-based generalization. In similarity-based generalization we only consider the closest neighbors in generalizing to the word of interest. In class-based generalization, we consider the whole class of elements that the word of interest is most likely to be a member of. (See exercise 8.20.)

Semantic similarity is also used for query expansion in information retrieval. A user who describes a request for information in her own words may not be aware of related terms which are used in the documents that the user would be most interested in. If a user describes a request for documents on Russian space misions using the word *astronaut*, then a query expansion system can suggest the term *cosmonaut* based on the semantic similarity between *astronaut* and *cosmonaut*.

k NEAREST NEIGHBORS
KNN

Another use of semantic similarity is for so-called *k nearest neighbors* (or *KNN*) classification, see section 16.4. We first need a training set of elements that are each assigned to a category. The elements might be words and the categories might be topic categories as they are used by newswire services ('financial,' 'agriculture,' 'politics' etc.). In KNN classification we assign a new element to the category that is most prevalent among its k nearest neighbors.

Before delving into the details of how to acquire measures of semantic similarity, let us remark that semantic similarity is not as intuitive and clear a notion as it may seem at first. For some, semantic similarity is an extension of synonymy and refers to cases of near-synonymy like the pair *dwelling/abode*. Often semantic similarity refers to the notion that two words are from the same *semantic domain* or *topic*. On this understanding of the term, words are similar if they refer to entities in the world that are likely to co-occur like *doctor, nurse, fever,* and *intravenous*, words that can refer to quite different entities or even be members of different syntactic categories.

SEMANTIC DOMAIN
TOPIC

One attempt to put the notion of semantic similarity on a more solid footing is provided by Miller and Charles (1991), who show that judgements of semantic similarity can be explained by the degree of *contextual interchangeability* or the degree to which one word can be substituted for another in context.

CONTEXTUAL
INTERCHANGEABILITY

Note that ambiguity presents a problem for all notions of semantic similarity. If a word is semantically similar to one sense of an ambiguous word, then it is rarely semantically similar to the other sense. For example, *litigation* is similar to the legal sense of *suit*, but not to the 'clothes' sense. When applied to ambiguous words, semantically similar usually means 'similar to the appropriate sense'.

8.5.1   Vector space measures

A large class of measures of semantic similarity are best conceptualized as measures of vector similarity. The two words whose semantic similarity we want to compute are represented as vectors in a multi-dimensional space. Figures 8.3, 8.4, and 8.5 give (constructed) examples of such multi-dimensional spaces (see also figure 15.5).

DOCUMENT SPACE

The matrix in figure 8.3 represents words as vectors in *document space*. Entry a_{ij} contains the number of times word j occurs in document i. Words are deemed similar to the extent that they occur in the same documents. In document space, *cosmonaut* and *astronaut* are dissimilar (no shared documents); *truck* and *car* are similar since they share a document: they co-occur in d_4.

WORD SPACE

The matrix in figure 8.4 represents words as vectors in *word space*. Entry b_{ij} contains the number of times word j co-occurs with word i.

	cosmonaut	astronaut	moon	car	truck
d_1	1	0	1	1	0
d_2	0	1	1	0	0
d_3	1	0	0	0	0
d_4	0	0	0	1	1
d_5	0	0	0	1	0
d_6	0	0	0	0	1

Figure 8.3 A document-by-word matrix A.

	cosmonaut	astronaut	moon	car	truck
cosmonaut	2	0	1	1	0
astronaut	0	1	1	0	0
moon	1	1	2	1	0
car	1	0	1	3	1
truck	0	0	0	1	2

Figure 8.4 A word-by-word matrix B.

	cosmonaut	astronaut	moon	car	truck
Soviet	1	0	0	1	1
American	0	1	0	1	1
spacewalking	1	1	0	0	0
red	0	0	0	1	1
full	0	0	1	0	0
old	0	0	0	1	1

Figure 8.5 A modifier-by-head matrix C. The nouns (or heads of noun phrases) in the top row are modified by the adjectives in the left column.

Co-occurrence can be defined with respect to documents, paragraphs or other units. Words are similar to the extent that they co-occur with the same words. Here, *cosmonaut* and *astronaut* are more similar than before since they both co-occur with *moon*.

We have defined co-occurrence in figure 8.4 with respect to the documents in figure 8.3. In other words, the following relationship holds:

TRANSPOSE $B = A^T A$. (Here $\cdot^T$ is the *transpose*, where we swap the rows and columns so that $X_{ij}^T = X_{ji}$.)

The matrix in figure 8.5 represents nouns (interpreted as heads of noun

MODIFIER SPACE   phrases) as vectors in *modifier space*. Entry c_{ij} contains the number of times that head j is modified by modifier i. Heads are similar to the extent that they are modified by the same modifiers. Again, *cosmonaut* and *astronaut* are similar. But, interestingly *moon* is dissimilar from *cosmonaut* and *astronaut* here, in contrast to the document space in figure 8.3 and the word space in figure 8.4. This contrast demonstrates that different spaces get at different types of semantic similarity. The type of undifferentiated co-occurrence information in document and word spaces

TOPICAL SIMILARITY   captures *topical similarity* (words pertaining to the same topic domain). Head-modifier information is more fine-grained. Although *astronaut* and *moon* are part of the same domain ('space exploration'), they are obviously entities with very different properties (a human being versus a celestial body). Different properties correspond to different modifiers, which explains why the two words come out as dissimilar on the head-modifier metric.[6]

The three matrices also have an interesting interpretation if we look at the similarity of *rows* instead of the similarity of *columns* (or, equivalently, look at the similarity of columns of the transposed matrices). Looking at the matrices this way, *A* defines similarity between documents. This is the standard way of defining similarity among documents and between documents and queries in information retrieval. Matrix *C* defines similarity between modifiers when transposed. For example, *red* and *old* are similar (they share *car* and *truck*), suggesting that they are used to modify the same types of nouns. Matrix *B* is *symmetric*, so looking at similarity of rows is no different from looking at similarity of columns.

So far we have appealed to an intuitive notion of vector similarity. Table 8.7 defines several measures that have been proposed to make this notion precise (adapted from (van Rijsbergen 1979: 39)). At first, we only

BINARY VECTORS   consider *binary vectors*, that is, vectors with entries that are either 0 or 1. The simplest way to describe a binary vector is as the set of dimensions on which it has non-zero values. So, for example, the vector for *cosmonaut* in figure 8.5 can be represented as the set {*Soviet, spacewalking*}. Having done this, we can calculate similarities using set operations, as in table 8.7.

---

6. See Grefenstette (1996) and Schütze and Pedersen (1997) for a discussion of the pros and cons of measuring word similarity based on associations versus head-modifier relationships.

Similarity measure	Definition
matching coefficient	$X \cap Y$
Dice coefficient	$\frac{2\|X \cap Y\|}{\|X\|+\|Y\|}$
Jaccard (or Tanimoto) coefficient	$\frac{\|X \cap Y\|}{\|X \cup Y\|}$
Overlap coefficient	$\frac{\|X \cap Y\|}{\min(\|X\|,\|Y\|)}$
cosine	$\frac{\|X \cap Y\|}{\sqrt{\|X\| \times \|Y\|}}$

Table 8.7 Similarity measures for binary vectors.

MATCHING COEFFICIENT

The first similarity measure, the *matching coefficient*, simply counts the number of dimensions on which both vectors are non-zero. In contrast to the other measures, it does not take into account the length of the vectors and the total number of non-zero entries in each.[7]

DICE COEFFICIENT

The *Dice coefficient* normalizes for length by dividing by the total number of non-zero entries. We multiply by 2 so that we get a measure that ranges from 0.0 to 1.0 with 1.0 indicating identical vectors.

JACCARD COEFFICIENT

The *Jaccard coefficient* penalizes a small number of shared entries (as a proportion of all non-zero entries) more than the Dice coefficient does. Both measures range from 0.0 (no overlap) to 1.0 (perfect overlap), but the Jaccard coefficient gives lower values to low-overlap cases. For example, two vectors with ten non-zero entries and one common entry get a Dice score of $2 \times 1/(10+10) = 0.1$ and a Jaccard score of $1/(10+10-1) \approx 0.05$. The Jaccard coefficient is frequently used in chemistry as a measure of similarity between chemical compounds (Willett and Winterman 1986).

OVERLAP COEFFICIENT

The *Overlap coefficient* has the flavor of a measure of inclusion. It has a value of 1.0 if every dimension with a non-zero value for the first vector is also non-zero for the second vector or vice versa (in other words if $X \subseteq Y$ or $Y \subseteq X$).

COSINE

The *cosine* is identical to the Dice coefficient for vectors with the same number of non-zero entries (see exercise 8.24), but it penalizes less in cases where the number of non-zero entries is very different. For example, if we compare one vector with one non-zero entry and another vector with 1000 non-zero entries and if there is one shared entry, then

---

7. This can be desirable to reflect our confidence in the similarity judgement. Hindle (1990) recommends a measure for noun similarity with this property.

we get a Dice coefficient of $2 \times 1/(1 + 1000) \approx 0.002$ and a cosine of $1/\sqrt{1000 \times 1} \approx 0.03$. This property of the cosine is important in Statistical NLP since we often compare words or objects that we have different amounts of data for, but we don't want to say they are dissimilar just because of that.

So far we have looked at binary vectors, but binary vectors only have one bit of information on each dimension. A more powerful representation for linguistic objects is the real-valued *vector space*. We will not give a systematic introduction to linear algebra here, but let us briefly review the basic concepts of vector spaces that we need in this book. A real-valued vector $\vec{x}$ of dimensionality n is a sequence of n real numbers, where x_i denotes the ith component of $\vec{x}$ (its value on dimension i). The components of a vector are properly written as a column:

VECTOR SPACE

(8.38) $$\vec{x} = \begin{pmatrix} x_1 \\ x_2 \\ \vdots \\ x_n \end{pmatrix}$$

However, we sometimes write vectors horizontally within paragraphs. We write $\mathbb{R}^n$ for the vector space of real-valued vectors with dimensionality n, so we have $\vec{x} \in \mathbb{R}^n$. In a Euclidean vector space, the *length of a vector* is defined as follows.

LENGTH OF A VECTOR

(8.39) $$|\vec{x}| = \sqrt{\sum_{i=1}^{n} x_i^2}$$

Finally, the dot product between two vectors is defined as $\vec{x} \cdot \vec{y} = \sum_{i=1}^{n} x_i y_i$.

The cosine, the last similarity measure we introduced for binary vectors, is also the most important one for real-valued vectors. The cosine measures the cosine of the angle between two vectors. It ranges from 1.0 $(\cos(0°) = 1.0)$ for vectors pointing in the same direction over 0.0 for orthogonal vectors $(\cos(90°) = 0.0)$ to -1.0 for vectors pointing in opposite directions $(\cos(180°) = -1.0)$.

For the general case of two n-dimensional vectors $\vec{x}$ and $\vec{y}$ in a real-valued space, the cosine measure can be calculated as follows:

(8.40) $$\cos(\vec{x}, \vec{y}) = \frac{\vec{x} \cdot \vec{y}}{|\vec{x}||\vec{y}|} = \frac{\sum_{i=1}^{n} x_i y_i}{\sqrt{\sum_{i=1}^{n} x_i^2}\sqrt{\sum_{i=1}^{n} y_i^2}}$$

This definition highlights another interpretation of the cosine, the interpretation as the *normalized correlation coefficient*. We compute how well

NORMALIZED CORRE-
LATION COEFFICIENT

the x_i and the y_i correlate and then divide by the (Euclidean) length of the two vectors to scale for the magnitude of the individual x_i and y_i.

NORMALIZATION   We call a vector *normalized* if it has unit length according to the Euclidean norm:

(8.41) $$|\vec{x}| = \sum_{i=1}^{n} x_i^2 = 1$$

For normalized vectors, the cosine is simply the dot product:

(8.42) $$\cos(\vec{x}, \vec{y}) = \vec{x} \cdot \vec{y}$$

EUCLIDEAN DISTANCE   The *Euclidean distance* between two vectors measures how far apart they are in the vector space:

(8.43) $$|\vec{x} - \vec{y}| = \sqrt{\sum_{i=1}^{n} (x_i - y_i)^2}$$

An interesting property of the cosine is that, if applied to normalized vectors, it will give the same ranking of similarities as Euclidean distance does. That is, if we only want to know which of two objects is closest to a third object, then cosine and Euclidean distance give the same answer for normalized vectors. The following derivation shows why ranking according to cosine and Euclidean distance comes out to be the same:

(8.44) $$
\begin{aligned}
(|\vec{x} - \vec{y}|)^2 &= \sum_{i=1}^{n} (x_i - y_i)^2 \\
&= \sum_{i=1}^{n} x_i^2 - 2 \sum_{i=1}^{n} x_i y_i + \sum_{i=1}^{n} y_i^2 \\
&= 1 - 2 \sum_{i=1}^{n} x_i y_i + 1 \\
&= 2(1 - \vec{x} \cdot \vec{y})
\end{aligned}
$$

Finally, the cosine has also been used as a similarity measure of probability distributions (Goldszmidt and Sahami 1998). Two distributions $\{p_i\}$ and $\{q_i\}$ are first transformed into $\{\sqrt{p_i}\}$ and $\{\sqrt{q_i}\}$. Taking the cosine of the two resulting vectors gives the measure $D = \sum_{i=1}^{n} \sqrt{p_i q_i}$, which can be interpreted as the sum over the geometric means of the $\{p_i\}$ and $\{q_i\}$.

Table 8.8 shows some cosine similarities computed for the *New York Times* corpus described in chapter 5. We compiled a 20,000-by-1,000 matrix similar to the word-by-word matrix in figure 8.4. As rows we selected

Focus word	Nearest neighbors							
garlic	*sauce*	.732	*pepper*	.728	*salt*	.726	*cup*	.726
fallen	*fell*	.932	*decline*	.931	*rise*	.930	*drop*	.929
engineered	*genetically*	.758	*drugs*	.688	*research*	.687	*drug*	.685
Alfred	*named*	.814	*Robert*	.809	*William*	.808	*W*	.808
simple	*something*	.964	*things*	.963	*You*	.963	*always*	.962

Table 8.8 The cosine as a measure of semantic similarity. For each of the five words in the left column, the table shows the words that were most similar according to the cosine measure when applied to a word-by-word co-occurrence matrix. For example, *sauce* is the word that is most similar to *garlic*. The cosine between the vectors of *sauce* and *garlic* is 0.732.

the 20,000 most frequent words, as columns the 1,000 most frequent words (after elimination of the 100 most frequent words in both cases). Instead of raw co-occurrence counts, we used the logarithmic weighting function $f(x) = 1 + \log(x)$ for non-zero counts (see section 15.2.2). A co-occurrence event was defined as two words occurring within 25 words of each other. The table shows cosine similarities between rows of the matrix.

For some word pairs, cosine in word space is a good measure of semantic similarity. The neighbors of *garlic* are generally close in meaning to garlic (with the possible exception of *cup*). The same is true for *fallen*. Note, however, that grammatical distinctions are not reflected because co-occurrence information is insensitive to word order and grammatical dependencies (the past participle *fallen* and the past tense *fell* are nearest neighbors of each other). The word *engineered* shows the corpus-dependency of the similarity measure. In the *New York Times*, the word is often used in the context of genetic engineering. A corpus of automobile magazine articles would give us a very different set of neighbors of *engineered*. Finally, the words *Alfred* and *simple* show us the limits of the chosen similarity measure. Some of the neighbors of *Alfred* are also names, but this is a case of part-of-speech similarity rather than semantic similarity. The neighbors of *simple* seem completely random. Since *simple* is frequently used and its occurrences are distributed throughout the corpus, co-occurrence information is not useful here to characterize the semantics of the word.

The examples we have given demonstrate the advantage of vector spaces as a representational medium: their simplicity. It is easy to visualize vectors in a two-dimensional or three-dimensional space. Equating similarity with the extent to which the vectors point in the same direction is equally intuitive. In addition, vector space measures are easy to compute. Intuitive simplicity and computational efficiency are probably the main reasons that vector space measures have been used for a long time in information retrieval, notably for word-by-document matrices (Lesk 1969; Salton 1971a; Qiu and Frei 1993). Work on using vector measures for word-by-word and modifier-by-head matrices is more recent (Grefenstette 1992b; Schütze 1992b). See (Grefenstette 1992a) and (Burgess and Lund 1997) for research demonstrating that vector-based similarity measures correspond to psychological notions of semantic similarity such as PRIMING the degree to which one word *primes* another.

8.5.2 Probabilistic measures

The problem with vector space based measures is that, except for the cosine, they operate on binary data (yes or no). The cosine is the only vector space measure that accommodates quantitative information, but it has its own problems. Computing the cosine assumes a Euclidean space. This is because the cosine is defined as the ratio of the lengths of two sides of a triangle. So we need a measure of length, the Euclidean metric. But a Euclidean space is not a well-motivated choice if the vectors we are dealing with are vectors of probabilities or counts – which is what most representations for computing semantic similarity are based on. To see this observe that the Euclidean distance between the probabilities 0.0 and 0.1 is the same as the distance between the probabilities 0.9 and 1.0. But in the first case we have the difference between impossibility and a chance of 1 in 10 whereas in the second there is only a small difference of about 10%. The Euclidean distance is appropriate for normally distributed quantities, not for counts and probabilities.

Matrices of counts like those in figures 8.3, 8.4, and 8.5 can be easily transformed into matrices of conditional probabilities by dividing each element in a row by the sum of all entries in the row (this amounts to using maximum likelihood estimates). For example, in the matrix in figure 8.5, the entry for (*American, astronaut*) would be transformed into $P(American|astronaut) = \frac{1}{2} = 0.5$. The question of semantic similarity can then be recast as a question about the similarity (or dissimilarity) of two probability distributions.

(Dis-)similarity measure	Definition
KL divergence	$D(p\|q) = \sum_i p_i \log \frac{p_i}{q_i}$
information radius (IRad)	$D(p\|\frac{p+q}{2}) + D(q\|\frac{p+q}{2})$
L_1 norm	$\sum_i |p_i - q_i|$

Table 8.9 Measures of (dis-)similarity between probability distributions.

Table 8.9 shows three measures of dissimilarity between probability
distributions investigated by Dagan et al. (1997b). We are already familiar
KL DIVERGENCE   with the KL divergence from section 2.2.5. It measures how well distribution q approximates distribution p; or, more precisely, how much information is lost if we assume distribution q when the true distribution is p.
The KL divergence has two problems for practical applications. First, we
get a value of ∞ if there is a 'dimension' with $q_i = 0$ and $p_i \neq 0$ (which will
happen often, especially if we use simple maximum likelihood estimates).
Secondly, KL divergence is asymmetric, that is, usually $D(p\|q) \neq D(q\|p)$.
The intuitive notion of semantic similarity and most other types of similarity we are interested in is symmetric, so the following should hold:
$\text{sim}(p, q) = \text{sim}(q, p)$.[8]

INFORMATION RADIUS   The second measure in table 8.9, *information radius* (or total divergence to the average as Dagan et al. (1997b) call it), overcomes both
these problems. It is symmetric ($\text{IRad}(p, q) = \text{IRad}(q, p)$) and there is
no problem with infinite values since $\frac{p_i+q_i}{2} \neq 0$ if either $p_i \neq 0$ or $q_i \neq 0$.
The intuitive interpretation of IRad is that it answers the question: How
much information is lost if we describe the two words (or random variables in the general case) that correspond to p and q with their average
distribution? IRad ranges from 0 for identical distributions to $2 \log 2$ for
maximally different distributions (see exercise 8.26). As usual we assume
$0 \log 0 = 0$.

L_1 NORM   A third measure considered by Dagan et al. (1997b) is the L_1 (or *Man-*
MANHATTAN NORM   *hattan) norm*. It also has the desirable properties of being symmetric and
well-defined for arbitrary p and q. We can interpret it as a measure of *the*
expected proportion of different events, that is, as the expected propor-

---

8. Note that in clustering, asymmetry can make sense since we are comparing two different entities, the individual word that we need to assign to a cluster and the representation
of the cluster. The question here is how well the cluster represents the word which is
different from similarity in the strict sense of the word. See (Pereira et al. 1993).

tion of events that are going to be different between the distributions p and q. This is because $\frac{1}{2}L_1(p,q) = 1 - \sum_i \min(p_i, q_i)$, and $\sum_i \min(p_i, q_i)$ is the expected proportion of trials with the same outcome.[9]

As an example consider the following conditional distributions computed from the data in figure 8.5.

$$p_1 = P(Soviet|cosmonaut) = 0.5$$
$$p_2 = 0$$
$$p_3 = P(spacewalking|cosmonaut) = 0.5$$
$$q_1 = 0$$
$$q_2 = P(American|astronaut) = 0.5$$
$$q_3 = P(spacewalking|astronaut) = 0.5$$

Here we have:

$$\frac{1}{2}L_1(p,q) = 1 - \sum_i \min(p_i, q_i) = 1 - 0.5 = 0.5$$

So if we looked at the sets of adjectives that occurred with a large number of uses of *cosmonaut* and *astronaut* in a corpus, then the overlap of the two sets would be expected to be 0.5, corresponding to the proportion of occurrences of *spacewalking* with each noun.

Dagan et al. (1997b) compared the three dissimilarity measures (KL, IRad, and L_1) on a task similar to the selectional preferences problem in section 8.4. Instead of looking at the fit of nouns as argument of verbs, they looked at the fit of verbs as predicates for nouns. For example, given a choice of the verbs *make* and *take* the similarity measures were used to determine that *make* is the right verb to use with *plans* (*make plans*) and *take* is the right verb to use with *actions* (*take actions*).

---

9. The following derivation shows that $\frac{1}{2}L_1(p,q) = 1 - \sum_i \min(p_i, q_i)$:

$$
\begin{aligned}
L_1(p,q) &= \sum_i |p_i - q_i| \\
&= \sum_i \left[\max(p_i, q_i) - \min(p_i, q_i)\right] \\
&= \sum_i \left[(p_i + q_i - \min(p_i, q_i)) - \min(p_i, q_i)\right] \\
&= \sum_i p_i + \sum_i q_i - 2\sum_i \min(p_i, q_i) \\
&= 2\left(1 - \sum_i \min(p_i, q_i)\right)
\end{aligned}
$$

Note that this also shows that $0 \le L_1(p,q) \le 2$ since $\sum_i \min(p,q) \ge 0$.

Here is how the similarity measure is used to compute the conditional probability $P(\text{verb}|\text{noun})$, which Dagan et al. (1997b) use as a measure of 'goodness of fit:'

$$(8.45) \quad P_{\text{SIM}}(v|n) = \sum_{n' \in S(n)} \frac{W(n, n')}{N(n)} P(v|n')$$

Here, v is the verb, n is the noun, $S(n)$ is the set of nouns closest to n according to the similarity measure,[10] $W(n, n')$ is a similarity measure derived from the dissimilarity measure and $N(n)$ is a normalizing factor: $N(n) = \sum_{n'} W(n, n')$.

This formulation makes it necessary to transform the dissimilarity measure (KL, IRad or L_1) into the similarity measure W. The following three transformations were used.

$$(8.46) \quad W_{\text{KL}}(p, q) = 10^{-\beta D(p\|q)}$$

$$(8.47) \quad W_{\text{IRad}}(p, q) = 10^{-\beta \text{IRad}(p\|q)}$$

$$(8.48) \quad W_{L_1}(p, q) = (2 - L_1(p, q))^{\beta}$$

The parameter β can be tuned for optimal performance.

Dagan et al. (1997b) show that IRad consistently performs better than KL and L_1. Consequently, they recommend IRad as the measure that is best to use in general.

This concludes our brief survey of measures of semantic similarity and dissimilarity. Vector space measures have the advantage of conceptual simplicity and of producing a similarity value that can be directly used for generalization. But they lack a clear interpretation of the computed measure. Probabilistic dissimilarity measures are on a more solid footing theoretically, but require an additional transformation to get to a measure of similarity that can be used for nearest neighbor generalization. Either approach is valuable in acquiring semantic properties of words from corpora by using similarity to transfer knowledge from known words to those that are not covered in the lexicon.

Exercise 8.19   [⋆]

Similarity-based generalization depends on the premise that similar things behave similarly. This premise is unobjectionable if the two uses of the word *similar* here refer to the same notion. But it is easy to fall into the trap of interpreting

---

10. For the experiments, $S(n)$ was chosen to be the entire set of nouns, but one can limit the words considered to those closest to the target word.

them differently. In that case, similarity-based generalization can give inaccurate results.

Find examples of such potentially dangerous cases, that is, examples where words that are similar with respect to one aspect behave very differently with respect to another aspect.

Exercise 8.20   [⋆]

Similarity-based and class-based generalization are more closely related than it may seem at first glance. Similarity-based generalization looks at the closest neighbors and weights the input from these neighbors according to their similarity. Class-based generalization looks at the most promising class and, in the simplest case, generalizes the novel word to the average of that class. But class-based generalization can be made to look like similarity-based generalization by integrating evidence from all classes and weighting it according to how well the element fits into each class. Similarity-based generalization looks like class-based generalization if we view each element as a class.

Discuss the relationship between the two types of generalization. What role do efficiency considerations play?

Exercise 8.21   [⋆]

Co-occurrence matrices like the one in figure 8.3 represent different types of information depending on how co-occurrence is defined. What types of words would you expect *fire* to be similar to for the following definitions of co-occurrence: co-occurrence within a document; co-occurrence within a sentence; co-occurrence with words at a maximum distance of three words to the right; co-occurrence with the word immediately adjacent to the right. (See Finch and Chater (1994) and Schütze (1995) for two studies that show how the latter type of immediate co-occurrence can be used to discover syntactic categories.)

Exercise 8.22   [⋆ ⋆]

The measures we have looked at compare simple objects like vectors and probability distributions. There have also been attempts to measure semantic similarity between more complex objects like trees (see (Sheridan and Smeaton 1992) for one example). How could one measure the (semantic?) similarity between trees? How might such an approach lead to a better measure of semantic similarity between words than 'flat' structures?

Exercise 8.23   [⋆]

Select two words heading columns in figure 8.3 and compute pairwise similarities using each of the measures in table 8.7 for each of the three matrices in figures 8.3 through 8.5.

Exercise 8.24   [⋆]

Show that dice and cosine coefficients are identical if the two vectors compared have the same number of non-zero entries.

Exercise 8.25   [⋆]

Semantic similarity can be context-dependent. For example, electrons and tennis balls are similar when we are talking about their form (both have a round shape) and dissimilar when we are talking about their sizes.

Discuss to what extent similarity is context-dependent and when this can hinder correct generalization.

Exercise 8.26   [⋆]

Show that divergence to the average (IRad) is bounded by $2 \log 2$.

Exercise 8.27   [⋆]

Select two words heading columns in figure 8.3 and compute the three measures of dissimilarity in table 8.9 for each of the matrices in figures 8.3 through 8.5. You will have to smooth the probabilities for KL divergence. Are the dissimilarity measures asymmetric for KL divergence?

Exercise 8.28   [⋆ ⋆]

Both the L_1 norm and the Euclidean norm are special cases of the Minkowski norm L_p:

$$(8.49) \qquad L_p(a, b) = \sqrt[p]{\sum_i |a_i - b_i|^p}$$

In this context, the Euclidean norm is also referred to as L_2. So the L_1 norm can be seen as a more appropriate version of the Euclidean norm for probability distributions.

Another norm that has been used for vectors is L_∞, that is L_p for $p \to \infty$ (Salton et al. 1983). What well-known function does L_∞ correspond to?

Exercise 8.29   [⋆]

Does a dissimilarity measure of 0 on one of the measures in table 8.9 imply that the other two measures are 0 too?

Exercise 8.30   [⋆]

If two probability distributions are maximally dissimilar according to one measure in table 8.9 (e.g., $\text{IRad}(p, q) = 2 \log 2$), does that imply that they are maximally dissimilar according to the other two?

8.6   The Role of Lexical Acquisition in Statistical NLP

Lexical acquisition plays a key role in Statistical NLP because available lexical resources are always lacking in some way. There are several reasons for this.

One reason is the cost of building lexical resources manually. For many types of lexical information, professional lexicographers will collect more accurate and comprehensive data than automatic procedures. But often manually constructed dictionaries are not available due to the cost of their construction. One estimate for the average time it takes to create a lexical entry from scratch is half an hour (Neff et al. 1993; obviously it depends on the complexity of the entry), so manual resource construction can be quite expensive.

There is one type of data that humans, including lexicographers, are notoriously bad at collecting: quantitative information. So the quantitative part of lexical acquisition almost always has to be done automatically, even if excellent manually constructed lexical resources are available for qualitative properties.

More generally, many lexical resources were designed for human consumption. The flip side of quantitative information being missing (which may be less important for people) is that the computer has no access to contextual information that is necessary to interpret lexical entries in conventional dictionaries. This is expressed aptly by Mercer (1993): "one cannot learn a new language by reading a bilingual dictionary." An example is the irregular plural *postmen* which is not listed as an exception in the lexical entry of *postman* in some dictionaries because it is obvious to a human reader that the plural of *postman* is formed in analogy to the plural of *man*. The best solution to problems like these is often the augmentation of a manual resource by automatic means.

PRODUCTIVITY

Despite the importance of these other considerations motivating automated lexical acquisition, the main reason for its importance is the inherent productivity of language. Natural language is in a constant state of flux, adapting to the changing world by creating names and words to refer to new things, new people and new concepts. Lexical resources have to be updated to keep pace with these changes. Some word classes are more likely to have coverage gaps than others. Most documents will mention proper nouns that we have not encountered before whereas there will hardly ever be newly created auxiliaries or prepositions. But the creativity of language is not limited to names. New nouns and verbs also occur at a high rate in many texts. Words that are covered in the dictionary may still need the application of lexical acquisition methods because they develop new senses or new syntactic usage patterns.

How can we quantify the amount of lexical information that has to be learned automatically, even if lexical resources are available? For a rough

Type of coverage problem	Example
proper noun	*Caramello, Château-Chalon*
foreign word	*perestroika*
code	*R101*
mathematical object	x_1
non-standard English	*havin'*
abbreviation	*NLP*
hyphenated word	*non-examination*
hyphen omitted	*bedclothes*
negated adjective	*unassailable*
adverbs	*ritualistically*
technical vocabulary	*normoglycaemia*
plural of mass noun	*estimations*
other cases	*deglutition, don'ts, affinitizes* (VBZ)

Table 8.10 Types of words occurring in the LOB corpus that were not covered by the OALD dictionary.

assessment, we can consult Zipf's law and other attempts to estimate the proportion of as yet unseen words and uses in text (see chapter 6 and, for example, (Baayen and Sproat 1996) and (Youmans 1991)).

LEXICAL COVERAGE   A more detailed analysis is provided in (Sampson 1989). Sampson tested the coverage of a dictionary with close to 70,000 entries (the OALD, Hornby 1974) for a 45,000 word subpart of the LOB corpus. (Numbers were not counted as words.) He found that about 3% of tokens were not listed in the dictionary. It is instructive to look at the different types of words that are the cause of coverage problems. Table 8.10 lists the major types found by Sampson and some examples.

More than half of the missing words were proper nouns. The other half is due to the other categories in the table. Some of the coverage problems would be expected not to occur in a larger dictionary (some frequent proper nouns and words like *unassailable*). But based on Sampson's findings, one would expect between one and two percent of tokens in a corpus to be missing from even a much larger dictionary. It is also important to note that this type of study only gets at character strings that are entirely missing from the dictionary. It is much harder to estimate at what rate known words are used with new senses or in novel syntactic constructions. Finally, the one to two percent of unknown words tend to

be among the most important in a document: the name of the person pro-
filed in an article or the abbreviation for a new scientific phenomenon. So
even if novel words constitute only a small percentage of the text, having
an operational representation for their properties is paramount.

It took a long time until the limitations of dictionaries and hand-crafted
knowledge bases for successful language processing became clear to NLP
researchers. A common strategy in early NLP research was to focus on a
small subdomain to attack what seemed to be the two most fundamental
problems: parsing and knowledge representation. As a result of this
focus on small subdomains, this early research "provided nothing for
general use on large-scale texts" and "work in computational linguistics
was largely inapplicable to anything but to sub-languages of very limited
semantic and syntactic scope" (Ide and Walker 1992).

Problems of lexical coverage started to take center stage in the late
eighties when interest shifted from subdomains to large corpora and robust systems, partly due to the influence of speech recognition research.
One of the earliest pieces of work on lexical acquisition from corpora was
done for the FORCE4 system developed by Walker and Amsler (1986) at
SRI International. Since then, lexical acquisition has become one of the
most active areas of Statistical NLP.

What does the future hold for lexical acquisition? One important trend
is to look harder for sources of prior knowledge that can constrain the
process of lexical acquisition. This is in contrast to earlier work that tried
to start 'from scratch' and favored deriving everything from the corpus.
Prior knowledge can be *discrete* as is the case when a lexical hierarchy like
WordNet is used or *probabilistic*, for example, when a prior distribution
over object noun classes is derived from a verb's dictionary entry and
this prior distribution is then refined based on corpora. Much of the hard
work of lexical acquisition will be in building interfaces that admit easy
specification of prior knowledge and easy correction of mistakes made in
automatic learning.

One important source of prior knowledge should be linguistic theory,
which has been surprisingly underutilized in Statistical NLP. In addition
to the attempts we have discussed here to constrain the acquisition process using linguistic insights, we refer the reader to Pustejovsky et al.
(1993), Boguraev and Pustejovsky (1995), and Boguraev (1993) for work
that takes linguistic theory as the foundation of acquisition. The last
two articles summarize the important work on computational lexicography done at Cambridge University (described in detail in (Boguraev and

Briscoe 1989)), which, although mostly non-statistical, contains important insights on how to combine theoretical linguistics and empirical acquisition from lexical resources.

Dictionaries are only one source of information that can be important in lexical acquisition in addition to text corpora. Other sources are encyclopedias, thesauri, gazeteers, collections of technical vocabulary and any other reference work or data base that is likely to contribute to a characterization of the syntactic and semantic properties of uncommon words and names.

The reader may have wondered why we have limited ourselves to textual sources. What about speech, images, video? Lexical acquisition has focused on text because words are less ambiguous descriptors of content than features that can be automatically extracted from audio and visual data. But we can hope that, as work on speech recognition and image understanding progresses, we will be able to ground the linguistic representation of words in the much richer context that non-textual media provide. It has been estimated that the average educated person reads on the order of one million words in a year, but hears ten times as many words spoken. If we succeed in emulating human acquisition of language by tapping into this rich source of information, then a breakthrough in the effectiveness of lexical acquisition can be expected.

8.7   Further Reading

There are several books and special issues of journals on lexical acquisition: (Zernik 1991a), (Ide and Walker 1992), (Church and Mercer 1993), and (Boguraev and Pustejovsky 1995). More recent work is covered in later issues of *Computational Linguistics*, *Natural Language Engineering*, and *Computers and the Humanities*. In what follows, we point the reader to some of the work on lexical acquisition we were not able to cover.

Other approaches to the resolution of attachment ambiguity include transformation-based learning (Brill and Resnik 1994) and loglinear models (Franz 1997). Collins and Brooks (1995) used a back-off model to address data sparseness issues. Attachment ambiguity in noun phrases also occurs in Romance languages. See (Bourigault 1993) for French and (Basili et al. 1997) for Italian.

An alternative to Resnik's information-theoretic approach to the acquisition of selectional preferences is work by Li and Abe (1995) that uses a

Minimum Description Length framework. In (Li and Abe 1996), this work is extended to take into account the dependency between two or more arguments of a verb. For example, *drive* can take *car* as a subject (*This car drives well*), but only if there is no object. This type of regularity can only be discovered we we look at all arguments of the verb simultaneously. See also (Velardi and Pazienza 1989) and (Webster and Marcus 1989) for early (non-probabilistic, but corpus-based) work on selectional preferences.

Once we have acquired information about the selectional preferences of a verb, we can exploit this knowledge to acquire subcategorization frames, the first problem we looked at in this chapter. Poznański and Sanfilippo (1995) and Aone and McKee (1995) take this approach. For example, a verb that takes an NP of type 'beneficiary' or 'recipient' is likely to subcategorize for a *to*-PP.

Apart from semantic similarity, the automatic enhancement of hierarchies has been another focus in the area of acquiring semantics. Hearst and Schütze (1995) and Hearst (1992) describe systems that insert new words into an existing semantic hierarchy and Coates-Stephens (1993) and Paik et al. (1995) do the same for proper nouns. Riloff and Shepherd (1997) and Roark and Charniak (1998) assign words to categories assuming a flat category structure (which can be regarded as a simplified semantic hierarchy).

Two other important types of semantic information that attempts have been made to acquire from corpora are antonyms (Justeson and Katz 1991) and metaphors (Martin 1991).

We suggested above that non-textual data are a worthwhile source of information to exploit. There are some research projects that investigate how lexical acquisition could take advantage of such data once the problem of how to automatically build a representation of the context of an utterance has been solved. Suppes et al. (1996) stress the importance of action-oriented matching between linguistic forms and their contextual meaning (as opposed to acquiring word meaning from passive perception). Siskind (1996) shows that even if the contextual representation is highly ambiguous (as one would expect in a realistic learning situation), lexical acquisition can proceed successfully.

As a last source of information for acquiring meaning, we mention work on exploiting morphology for this purpose. An example of a morphological regularity that implies a particular type of meaning is the progressive tense. In English, only non-stative verbs occur in the progressive tense. Oversimplifying somewhat, we can infer from the fact that we find *he is running* in a corpus, but not *he is knowing* that *know* is stative and *run* is non-stative. See (Dorr and Olsen 1997), (Light 1996) and (Viegas et al. 1996) for work along these lines. While none of these papers take a statistical approach, such morphological information could be a fertile ground for applying statistical methods.

We conclude these bibliographic remarks by pointing the reader to two important bodies of non-statistical work that warrant careful study by anybody interested in lexical acquisition. They are of great potential importance either because they suggest ways of combining statistical approaches with symbolic approaches (as in the regular-expression post-filtering of collocations in (Justeson and Katz 1995b)) or because the insights they offer can often be expressed in a statistical framework as well as in a non-statistical framework, making them a valuable source for future statistical work.

The first area is the work on building syntactic and semantic knowledge bases from machine-readable dictionaries described by Boguraev and Briscoe (1989) and Jensen et al. (1993). These two books are a good starting point for those who want to learn about the strengths and weaknesses of dictionaries for lexical acquisition. We have focused on corpus-based acquisition here because that has been the bias in Statistical NLP, but we believe that most future work will combine corpus-based and dictionary-based acquisition.

The second area is the application of regular expression matching to natural language processing. (See (Appelt et al. 1993), (Jacquemin 1994), (Voutilainen 1995), (Sproat et al. 1996), and (Jacquemin et al. 1997) for examples.) There are phenomena and processing steps in lexical acquisition that deal with purely symbolic information and that can be well modeled in terms of regular languages. (Tokenization of English is an example.) In such cases, the speed and simplicity of finite state automata cannot be matched by other methods (Roche and Schabes 1997; Levine et al. 1992).

PART III

Grammar

9 *Markov Models*

HIDDEN MARKOV MODELS (HMMs) have been the mainstay of the statistical modeling used in modern speech recognition systems. Despite their limitations, variants of HMMs are still the most widely used technique in that domain, and are generally regarded as the most successful. In this chapter we will develop the basic theory of HMMs, touch on their applications, and conclude with some pointers on extending the basic HMM model and engineering practical implementations.

HMM An *HMM* is nothing more than a probabilistic function of a Markov process. We have already seen an example of Markov processes in the *n*-gram MARKOV MODEL models of chapters 2 and 6. *Markov processes/chains/models* were first developed by Andrei A. Markov (a student of Chebyshev). Their first use was actually for a linguistic purpose – modeling the letter sequences in works of Russian literature (Markov 1913) – but Markov models were then developed as a general statistical tool. We will refer to vanilla Markov VISIBLE MARKOV models as *Visible Markov Models* (VMMs) when we want to be careful to MODELS distinguish them from HMMs.

We have placed this chapter at the beginning of the "grammar" part of the book because working on the order of words in sentences is a start at understanding their syntax. We will see that this is what a VMM does. HMMs operate at a higher level of abstraction by postulating additional "hidden" structure, and that allows us to look at the order of *categories* of words. After developing the theory of HMMs in this chapter, we look at the application of HMMs to part-of-speech tagging. The last two chapters in this part then deal with the probabilistic formalization of core notions of grammar like phrase structure.

9.1   Markov Models

Often we want to consider a sequence (perhaps through time) of random variables that *aren't* independent, but rather the value of each variable depends on previous elements in the sequence. For many such systems, it seems reasonable to assume that all we need to predict the future random variables is the value of the present random variable, and we don't need to know the values of all the past random variables in the sequence. For example, if the random variables measure the number of books in the university library, then, knowing how many books were in the library today might be an adequate predictor of how many books there will be tomorrow, and we don't really need to additionally know how many books the library had last week, let alone last year. That is, future elements of the sequence are conditionally independent of past elements, given the present element.

MARKOV ASSUMPTION
Suppose $X = (X_1, \ldots, X_T)$ is a sequence of random variables taking values in some finite set $S = \{s_1, \ldots, s_N\}$, the state space. Then the *Markov Properties* are:

Limited Horizon:

(9.1) $P(X_{t+1} = s_k | X_1, \ldots, X_t) = P(X_{t+1} = s_k | X_t)$

Time invariant (stationary):

(9.2) $= P(X_2 = s_k | X_1)$

X is then said to be a Markov chain, or to have the Markov property. One can describe a Markov chain by a stochastic transition matrix A:

(9.3) $a_{ij} = P(X_{t+1} = s_j | X_t = s_i)$

Here, $a_{ij} \geq 0, \forall i, j$ and $\sum_{j=1}^{N} a_{ij} = 1, \forall i$.

Additionally one needs to specify Π, the probabilities of different initial states for the Markov chain:

(9.4) $\pi_i = P(X_1 = s_i)$

Here, $\sum_{i=1}^{N} \pi_i = 1$. The need for this vector can be avoided by specifying that the Markov model always starts off in a certain extra initial state, s_0, and then using transitions from that state contained within the matrix A to specify the probabilities that used to be recorded in Π.

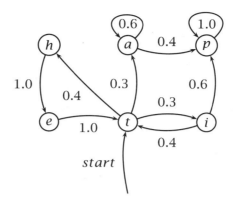

Figure 9.1 A Markov model.

From this general description, it should be clear that the word *n*-gram models we saw in chapter 6 are Markov models. Markov models can be used whenever one wants to model the probability of a linear sequence of events. For example, they have also been used in NLP for modeling valid phone sequences in speech recognition, and for sequences of speech acts in dialog systems.

Alternatively, one can represent a Markov chain by a state diagram as in figure 9.1. Here, the states are shown as circles around the state name, and the single start state is indicated with an incoming arrow. Possible transitions are shown by arrows connecting states, and these arcs are labeled with the probability of this transition being followed, given that you are in the state at the tail of the arrow. Transitions with zero probability are omitted from the diagram. Note that the probabilities of the outgoing arcs from each state sum to 1. From this representation, it should be clear that a Markov model can be thought of as a (nondeterministic) finite state automaton with probabilities attached to each arc. The Markov properties ensure that we have a finite state automaton. There are no long distance dependencies, and where one ends up next depends simply on what state one is in.

In a visible Markov model, we know what states the machine is passing through, so the state sequence or some deterministic function of it can be regarded as the output.

The probability of a sequence of states (that is, a sequence of random variables) $X_1, \ldots, X_T$ is easily calculated for a Markov chain. We find that we need merely calculate the product of the probabilities that occur on the arcs or in the stochastic matrix:

$$
\begin{aligned}
P(X_1, \ldots, X_T) &= P(X_1)P(X_2|X_1)P(X_3|X_1, X_2) \cdots P(X_T|X_1, \ldots, X_{T-1}) \\
&= P(X_1)P(X_2|X_1)P(X_3|X_2) \cdots P(X_T|X_{T-1}) \\
&= \pi_{X_1} \prod_{t=1}^{T-1} a_{X_t X_{t+1}}
\end{aligned}
$$

So, using the Markov model in figure 9.1, we have:

$$
\begin{aligned}
P(t, i, p) &= P(X_1 = t)P(X_2 = i|X_1 = t)P(X_3 = p|X_2 = i) \\
&= 1.0 \times 0.3 \times 0.6 \\
&= 0.18
\end{aligned}
$$

Note that what is important is whether we *can* encode a process as a Markov process, not whether we most naturally do. For example, recall the n-gram word models that we saw in chapter 6. One might think that, for $n \geq 3$, such a model is not a Markov model because it violates the Limited Horizon condition – we are looking a little into earlier history. But we can reformulate any n-gram model as a visible Markov model by simply encoding the appropriate amount of history into the state space (states are then $(n - 1)$-grams, for example (*was, walking, down*) would be a state in a fourgram model). In general, any fixed finite amount of history can always be encoded in this way by simply elaborating the state space as a crossproduct of multiple previous states. In such cases, we sometimes talk of an mth *order* Markov model, where m is the number of previous states that we are using to predict the next state. Note, thus, that an n-gram model is equivalent to an $(n - 1)^{\text{th}}$ order Markov model.

Exercise 9.1   [$\star$]

Build a Markov Model similar to figure 9.1 for one of the types of phone numbers in table 4.2.

9.2   Hidden Markov Models

In an HMM, you don't know the state sequence that the model passes through, but only some probabilistic function of it.

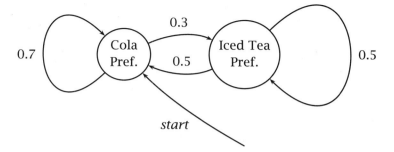

Figure 9.2   The crazy soft drink machine, showing the states of the machine and the state transition probabilities.

Example 1:   Suppose you have a crazy soft drink machine: it can be in two states, cola preferring (CP) and iced tea preferring (IP), but it switches between them randomly after each purchase, as shown in figure 9.2.

   Now, if, when you put in your coin, the machine always put out a cola if it was in the cola preferring state and an iced tea when it was in the iced tea preferring state, then we would have a visible Markov model. But instead, it only has a tendency to do this. So we need symbol *emission*

EMISSION
PROBABILITY
probabilities for the observations:

$$P(O_t = k | X_t = s_i, X_{t+1} = s_j) = b_{ijk}$$

For this machine, the output is actually independent of s_j, and so can be described by the following probability matrix:

(9.5)   Output probability given From state

	cola	iced tea (ice_t)	lemonade (lem)
CP	0.6	0.1	0.3
IP	0.1	0.7	0.2

   What is the probability of seeing the output sequence {lem, ice_t} if the machine always starts off in the cola preferring state?

Solution: We need to consider all paths that might be taken through the HMM, and then to sum over them. We know that the machine starts in state CP. There are then four possibilities depending on which of the two states the machine is in at the other two time instants. So the total probability is:

$$0.7 \times 0.3 \times 0.7 \times 0.1 + 0.7 \times 0.3 \times 0.3 \times 0.1 \quad +$$
$$0.3 \times 0.3 \times 0.5 \times 0.7 + 0.3 \times 0.3 \times 0.5 \times 0.7 \quad = \quad 0.084$$

Exercise 9.2   [⋆]
What is the probability of seeing the output sequence {col,lem} if the machine always starts off in the ice tea preferring state?

9.2.1   Why use HMMs?

HMMs are useful when one can think of underlying events probabilistically generating surface events. One widespread use of this is tagging – assigning parts of speech (or other classifiers) to the words in a text. We think of there being an underlying Markov chain of parts of speech from which the actual words of the text are generated. Such models are discussed in chapter 10.

When this general model is suitable, the further reason that HMMs are very useful is that they are one of a class of models for which there exist efficient methods of training through use of the Expectation Maximization (EM) algorithm. Given plenty of data that we assume to be generated by *some* HMM – where the model architecture is fixed but not the probabilities on the arcs – this algorithm allows us to automatically learn the model parameters that best account for the observed data.

Another simple illustration of how we can use HMMs is in generating parameters for linear interpolation of *n*-gram models. We discussed in chapter 6 that one way to estimate the probability of a sentence:

P(Sue drank her beer before the meal arrived)

was with an *n*-gram model, such as a trigram model, but that just using an *n*-gram model with fixed *n* tended to suffer because of data sparseness. Recall from section 6.3.1 that one idea of how to smooth *n*-gram LINEAR estimates was to use *linear interpolation* of *n*-gram estimates for various INTERPOLATION *n*, for example:

$$P_{\text{li}}(w_n | w_{n-1}, w_{n-2}) = \lambda_1 P_1(w_n) + \lambda_2 P_2(w_n | w_{n-1}) + \lambda_3 P_3(w_n | w_{n-1}, w_{n-2})$$

This way we would get some idea of how likely a particular word was, even if our coverage of trigrams is sparse. The question, then, is how to set the parameters λ_i. While we could make reasonable guesses as to

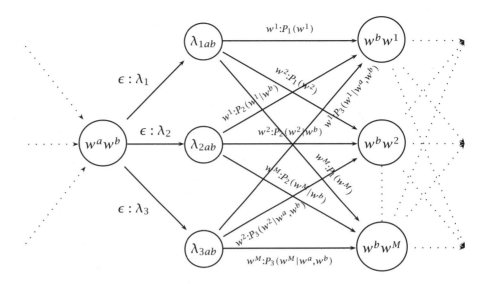

Figure 9.3 A section of an HMM for a linearly interpolated language model. The notation $o : p$ on arcs means that this transition is made with probability p, and that an o is output when this transition is made (with probability 1).

what parameter values to use (and we know that together they must obey the stochastic constraint $\sum_i \lambda_i = 1$), it seems that we should be able to find the optimal values automatically. And, indeed, we can (Jelinek 1990).

The key insight is that we can build an HMM with hidden states that represent the choice of whether to use the unigram, bigram, or trigram probabilities. The HMM training algorithm will determine the optimal weight to give to the arcs entering each of these hidden states, which in turn represents the amount of the probability mass that should be determined by each n-gram model via setting the parameters λ_i above.

Concretely, we build an HMM with four states for each word pair, one for the basic word pair, and three representing each choice of n-gram model for calculating the next transition. A fragment of the HMM is shown in figure 9.3. Note how this HMM assigns the same probabilities as the earlier equation: there are three ways for w^c to follow $w^a w^b$ and the total probability of seeing w^c next is then the sum of each of the n-gram probabilities that adorn the arcs multiplied by the corresponding parameter λ_i. The HMM training algorithm that we develop in this chapter can

Set of states	$S = \{s_1, \ldots s_N\}$
Output alphabet	$K = \{k_1, \ldots, k_M\} = \{1, \ldots, M\}$
Intial state probabilities	$\Pi = \{\pi_i\}, i \in S$
State transition probabilities	$A = \{a_{ij}\}, i, j \in S$
Symbol emission probabilities	$B = \{b_{ijk}\}, i, j \in S, k \in K$
State sequence	$X = (X_1, \ldots, X_{T+1}) \quad X_t : S \mapsto \{1, \ldots, N\}$
Output sequence	$O = (o_1, \ldots, o_T) \quad o_t \in K$

Table 9.1 Notation used in the HMM chapter.

then be applied to this network, and used to improve initial estimates for the parameters λ_{iab}. There are two things to note. This conversion works EPSILON TRANSITIONS by adding *epsilon transitions* – that is transitions that we wish to say do not produce an output symbol. Secondly, as presented, we now have separate parameters λ_{iab} for each word pair. But we would not want to adjust these parameters separately, as this would make our sparse data problem worse not better. Rather, for a fixed i, we wish to keep all (or at least classes of) the λ_{iab} parameters having the same value, which we do by using *tied states*. Discussion of both of these extensions to the basic HMM model will be deferred to section 9.4.

9.2.2 General form of an HMM

An HMM is specified by a five-tuple (S, K, Π, A, B), where S and K are the set of states and the output alphabet, and Π, A, and B are the probabilities for the initial state, state transitions, and symbol emissions, respectively. The notation that we use in this chapter is summarized in table 9.1. The random variables X_t map from state names to corresponding integers. In the version presented here, the symbol emitted at time t depends on both the state at time t and at time $t + 1$. This is sometimes called a ARC-EMISSION HMM *arc-emission HMM*, because we can think of the symbol as coming off the STATE-EMISSION HMM arc, as in figure 9.3. An alternative formulation is a *state-emission HMM*, where the symbol emitted at time t depends just on the state at time t. The HMM in example 1 is a state-emission HMM. But we can also regard it as a arc-emission HMM by simply setting up the b_{ijk} parameters so that $\forall k', k'', b_{ijk'} = b_{ijk''}$. This is discussed further in section 9.4.

Given a specification of an HMM, it is perfectly straightforward to simu-

```
1  t := 1;
2  Start in state s_i with probability π_i (i.e., X_1 = i)
3  forever do
4      Move from state s_i to state s_j with probability a_ij (i.e., X_{t+1} = j)
5      Emit observation symbol o_t = k with probability b_ijk
6      t := t + 1
7  end
```

Figure 9.4 A program for a Markov process.

late the running of a Markov process, and to produce an output sequence. One can do it with the program in figure 9.4. However, by itself, doing this is not terribly interesting. The interest in HMMs comes from *assuming* that some set of data was generated by a HMM, and then being able to calculate probabilities and probable underlying state sequences.

9.3   The Three Fundamental Questions for HMMs

There are three fundamental questions that we want to know about an HMM:

1. Given a model $\mu = (A, B, \Pi)$, how do we efficiently compute how likely a certain observation is, that is $P(O|\mu)$?

2. Given the observation sequence O and a model μ, how do we choose a state sequence $(X_1, \ldots, X_{T+1})$ that best explains the observations?

3. Given an observation sequence O, and a space of possible models found by varying the model parameters $\mu = (A, B, \pi)$, how do we find the model that best explains the observed data?

Normally, the problems we deal with are not like the soft drink machine. We don't know the parameters and have to estimate them from data. That's the third question. The first question can be used to decide between models which is best. The second question lets us guess what path was probably followed through the Markov chain, and this hidden path can be used for classification, for instance in applications to part of speech tagging, as we see in chapter 10.

9.3.1 Finding the probability of an observation

Given the observation sequence $O = (o_1, \ldots, o_T)$ and a model $\mu = (A, B, \Pi)$, we wish to know how to efficiently compute $P(O|\mu)$ – the probability of the observation given the model. This process is often referred to as *decoding*.

DECODING

For any state sequence $X = (X_1, \ldots, X_{T+1})$,

$$(9.6) \quad P(O|X, \mu) = \prod_{t=1}^{T} P(o_t | X_t, X_{t+1}, \mu)$$

$$= b_{X_1 X_2 o_1} b_{X_2 X_3 o_2} \cdots b_{X_T X_{T+1} o_T}$$

and,

$$(9.7) \quad P(X|\mu) = \pi_{X_1} a_{X_1 X_2} a_{X_2 X_3} \cdots a_{X_T X_{T+1}}$$

Now,

$$(9.8) \quad P(O, X|\mu) = P(O|X, \mu) P(X|\mu)$$

Therefore,

$$(9.9) \quad P(O|\mu) = \sum_{X} P(O|X, \mu) P(X|\mu)$$

$$= \sum_{X_1 \cdots X_{T+1}} \pi_{X_1} \prod_{t=1}^{T} a_{X_t X_{t+1}} b_{X_t X_{t+1} o_t}$$

This derivation is quite straightforward. It is what we did in example 1 to work out the probability of an observation sequence. We simply summed the probability of the observation occurring according to each possible state sequence. But, unfortunately, direct evaluation of the resulting expression is hopelessly inefficient. For the general case (where one can start in any state, and move to any other at each step), the calculation requires $(2T + 1) \cdot N^{T+1}$ multiplications.

Exercise 9.3   [⋆]

Confirm this claim.

DYNAMIC
PROGRAMMING
MEMOIZATION

The secret to avoiding this complexity is the general technique of *dynamic programming* or *memoization* by which we remember partial results rather than recomputing them. This general concept crops up in many other places in computational linguistics, such as chart parsing, and in computer science more generally (see (Cormen et al. 1990: ch. 16) for a general introduction). For algorithms such as HMMs, the dynamic programming problem is generally described in terms of *trellises* (also called *lattices*). Here, we make a square array of states versus time, and compute the probabilities of being at each state at each time in terms of the probabilities for being in each state at the preceding time instant. This is all best seen in pictures – see figures 9.5 and 9.6. A trellis can record the probability of all initial subpaths of the HMM that end in a certain state at a certain time. The probability of longer subpaths can then be worked out in terms of one shorter subpaths.

TRELLIS
LATTICE

The forward procedure

FORWARD PROCEDURE
The form of caching that is indicated in these diagrams is called the *forward procedure*. We describe it in terms of forward variables:

(9.10) $$\alpha_i(t) = P(o_1 o_2 \cdots o_{t-1}, X_t = i | \mu)$$

The forward variable $\alpha_i(t)$ is stored at (s_i, t) in the trellis and expresses the total probability of ending up in state s_i at time t (given that the observations $o_1 \cdots o_{t-1}$ were seen). It is calculated by summing probabilities for all incoming arcs at a trellis node. We calculate the forward variables in the trellis left to right using the following procedure:

1. Initialization

   $$\alpha_i(1) = \pi_i, \quad 1 \le i \le N$$

2. Induction

   $$\alpha_j(t+1) = \sum_{i=1}^{N} \alpha_i(t) a_{ij} b_{ijo_t}, \quad 1 \le t \le T, 1 \le j \le N$$

3. Total

   $$P(O|\mu) = \sum_{i=1}^{N} \alpha_i(T+1)$$

This is a much cheaper algorithm that requires only $2N^2 T$ multiplications.

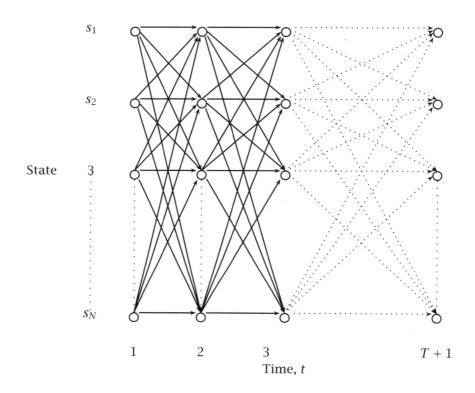

Figure 9.5 Trellis algorithms. The trellis is a square array of states versus times. A node at (s_i, t) can store information about state sequences which include $X_t = i$. The lines show the connections between nodes. Here we have a fully interconnected HMM where one can move from any state to any other at each step.

The backward procedure

It should be clear that we do not need to cache results working forward through time like this, but rather that we could also work backward. The BACKWARD PROCEDURE *backward procedure* computes backward variables which are the total probability of seeing the rest of the observation sequence given that we were in state s_i at time t. The real reason for introducing this less intuitive calculation, though, is because use of a combination of forward and backward probabilities is vital for solving the third problem of parameter

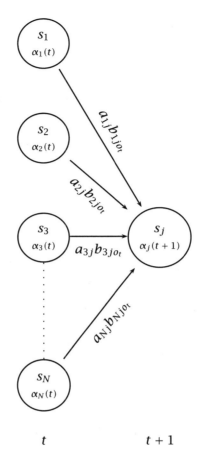

t $t+1$

Figure 9.6 Trellis algorithms: Closeup of the computation of forward probabilities at one node. The forward probability $\alpha_j(t+1)$ is calculated by summing the product of the probabilities on each incoming arc with the forward probability of the originating node.

reestimation.

Define backward variables

(9.11) $\beta_i(t) = P(o_t \cdots o_T | X_t = i, \mu)$

Then we can calculate backward variables working from right to left through the trellis as follows:

		Output		
		lem	ice_t	cola
Time (t):	1	2	3	4
$\alpha_{CP}(t)$	1.0	0.21	0.0462	0.021294
$\alpha_{IP}(t)$	0.0	0.09	0.0378	0.010206
$P(o_1 \cdots o_{t-1})$	1.0	0.3	0.084	0.0315
$\beta_{CP}(t)$	0.0315	0.045	0.6	1.0
$\beta_{IP}(t)$	0.029	0.245	0.1	1.0
$P(o_1 \cdots o_T)$	0.0315			
$\gamma_{CP}(t)$	1.0	0.3	0.88	0.676
$\gamma_{IP}(t)$	0.0	0.7	0.12	0.324
$\widehat{X_t}$	CP	IP	CP	CP
$\delta_{CP}(t)$	1.0	0.21	0.0315	0.01323
$\delta_{IP}(t)$	0.0	0.09	0.0315	0.00567
$\psi_{CP}(t)$		CP	IP	CP
$\psi_{IP}(t)$		CP	IP	CP
$\hat{X_t}$	CP	IP	CP	CP
$P(\hat{X})$	0.019404			

Table 9.2   Variable calculations for $O = $ (lem, ice_t, cola).

1. Initialization

$$\beta_i(T + 1) = 1, \quad 1 \leq i \leq N$$

2. Induction

$$\beta_i(t) = \sum_{j=1}^{N} a_{ij} b_{ijo_t} \beta_j(t + 1), \quad 1 \leq t \leq T, 1 \leq i \leq N$$

3. Total

$$P(O|\mu) = \sum_{i=1}^{N} \pi_i \beta_i(1)$$

Table 9.2 shows the calculation of forward and backward variables, and other variables that we will come to later, for the soft drink machine from example 1, given the observation sequence $O = $ (lem, ice_t, cola).

Combining them

More generally, in fact, we can use any combination of forward and backward caching to work out the probability of an observation sequence. Observe that:

$$
\begin{aligned}
P(O, X_t = i|\mu) &= P(o_1 \cdots o_T, X_t = i|\mu) \\
&= P(o_1 \cdots o_{t-1}, X_t = i, o_t \cdots o_T|\mu) \\
&= P(o_1 \cdots o_{t-1}, X_t = i|\mu) \\
&\qquad \times P(o_t \cdots o_T|o_1 \cdots o_{t-1}, X_t = i, \mu) \\
&= P(o_1 \cdots o_{t-1}, X_t = i|\mu)P(o_t \cdots o_T|X_t = i, \mu) \\
&= \alpha_i(t)\beta_i(t)
\end{aligned}
$$

Therefore:

$$
(9.12) \quad P(O|\mu) = \sum_{i=1}^{N} \alpha_i(t)\beta_i(t), \quad 1 \le t \le T+1
$$

The previous equations were special cases of this one.

9.3.2 Finding the best state sequence

The second problem was worded somewhat vaguely as "finding the state sequence that best explains the observations." That is because there is more than one way to think about doing this. One way to proceed would be to choose the states individually. That is, for each t, $1 \le t \le T+1$, we would find X_t that maximizes $P(X_t|O, \mu)$.

Let

$$
\begin{aligned}
(9.13) \quad \gamma_i(t) &= P(X_t = i|O, \mu) \\
&= \frac{P(X_t = i, O|\mu)}{P(O|\mu)} \\
&= \frac{\alpha_i(t)\beta_i(t)}{\sum_{j=1}^{N} \alpha_j(t)\beta_j(t)}
\end{aligned}
$$

The individually most likely state $\widehat{X_t}$ is:

$$
(9.14) \quad \widehat{X_t} = \arg\max_{1 \le i \le N} \gamma_i(t), \quad 1 \le t \le T+1
$$

This quantity maximizes the expected number of states that will be guessed correctly. However, it may yield a quite unlikely state *sequence*.

Therefore, this is not the method that is normally used, but rather the Viterbi algorithm, which efficiently computes the most likely state sequence.

Viterbi algorithm

Commonly we want to find the most likely complete path, that is:

$$\arg\max_X P(X|O, \mu)$$

To do this, it is sufficient to maximize for a fixed O:

$$\arg\max_X P(X, O|\mu)$$

VITERBI ALGORITHM   An efficient trellis algorithm for computing this path is the *Viterbi algorithm*. Define:

$$\delta_j(t) = \max_{X_1\cdots X_{t-1}} P(X_1 \cdots X_{t-1}, o_1 \cdots o_{t-1}, X_t = j|\mu)$$

This variable stores for each point in the trellis the probability of the most probable path that leads to that node. The corresponding variable $\psi_j(t)$ then records the node of the incoming arc that led to this most probable path. Using dynamic programming, we calculate the most probable path through the whole trellis as follows:

1. Initialization

   $$\delta_j(1) = \pi_j, \quad 1 \leq j \leq N$$

2. Induction

   $$\delta_j(t + 1) = \max_{1\leq i\leq N} \delta_i(t) a_{ij} b_{ijo_t}, \quad 1 \leq j \leq N$$

   Store backtrace

   $$\psi_j(t + 1) = \arg\max_{1\leq i\leq N} \delta_i(t) a_{ij} b_{ijo_t}, 1 \leq j \leq N$$

3. Termination and path readout (by backtracking). The most likely state sequence is worked out from the right backwards:

   $$
   \begin{aligned}
   \hat{X}_{T+1} &= \arg\max_{1\leq i\leq N} \delta_i(T + 1) \\
   \hat{X}_t &= \psi_{\hat{X}_{t+1}}(t + 1) \\
   P(\hat{X}) &= \max_{1\leq i\leq N} \delta_i(T + 1)
   \end{aligned}
   $$

In these calculations, one may get ties. We assume that in that case one path is chosen randomly. In practical applications, people commonly want to work out not only the best state sequence but the n-best sequences or a graph of likely paths. In order to do this people often store the $m < n$ best previous states at a node.

Table 9.2 above shows the computation of the most likely states and state sequence under both these interpretations – for this example, they prove to be identical.

9.3.3 The third problem: Parameter estimation

Given a certain observation sequence, we want to find the values of the model parameters $\mu = (A, B, \pi)$ which best explain what we observed. Using Maximum Likelihood Estimation, that means we want to find the values that maximize $P(O|\mu)$:

(9.15) $$\arg\max_{\mu} P(O_{\text{training}}|\mu)$$

FORWARD-BACKWARD ALGORITHM
EM ALGORITHM

There is no known analytic method to choose μ to maximize $P(O|\mu)$. But we can locally maximize it by an iterative hill-climbing algorithm. This algorithm is the *Baum-Welch* or *Forward-Backward algorithm*, which is a special case of the Expectation Maximization method which we will cover in greater generality in section 14.2.2. It works like this. We don't know what the model is, but we can work out the probability of the observation sequence using some (perhaps randomly chosen) model. Looking at that calculation, we can see which state transitions and symbol emissions were probably used the most. By increasing the probability of those, we can choose a revised model which gives a higher probability to the observation sequence. This maximization process is often referred to as *training* the model and is performed on *training data*.

TRAINING
TRAINING DATA

Define $p_t(i,j), 1 \leq t \leq T, 1 \leq i, j \leq N$ as shown below. This is the probability of traversing a certain arc at time t given observation sequence O; see figure 9.7.

(9.16) $$\begin{aligned} p_t(i,j) &= P(X_t = i, X_{t+1} = j|O, \mu) \\ &= \frac{P(X_t = i, X_{t+1} = j, O|\mu)}{P(O|\mu)} \end{aligned}$$

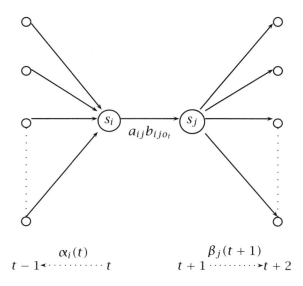

Figure 9.7 The probability of traversing an arc. Given an observation sequence and a model, we can work out the probability that the Markov process went from state s_i to s_j at time t.

$$= \frac{\alpha_i(t) a_{ij} b_{ijo_t} \beta_j(t+1)}{\sum_{m=1}^{N} \alpha_m(t) \beta_m(t)}$$

$$= \frac{\alpha_i(t) a_{ij} b_{ijo_t} \beta_j(t+1)}{\sum_{m=1}^{N} \sum_{n=1}^{N} \alpha_m(t) a_{mn} b_{mno_t} \beta_n(t+1)}$$

Note that $y_i(t) = \sum_{j=1}^{N} p_t(i, j)$.

Now, if we sum over the time index, this gives us expectations (counts):

$$\sum_{t=1}^{T} y_i(t) = \text{expected number of transitions from state } i \text{ in } O$$

$$\sum_{t=1}^{T} p_t(i, j) = \text{expected number of transitions from state } i \text{ to } j \text{ in } O$$

So we begin with some model μ (perhaps preselected, perhaps just chosen randomly). We then run O through the current model to estimate the expectations of each model parameter. We then change the model to maximize the values of the paths that are used a lot (while still respecting the stochastic constraints). We then repeat this process, hoping to converge on optimal values for the model parameters μ.

The reestimation formulas are as follows:

$$(9.17) \quad \hat{\pi}_i = \text{expected frequency in state } i \text{ at time } t = 1$$
$$= \gamma_i(1)$$

$$(9.18) \quad \hat{a}_{ij} = \frac{\text{expected number of transitions from state } i \text{ to } j}{\text{expected number of transitions from state } i}$$
$$= \frac{\sum_{t=1}^{T} p_t(i,j)}{\sum_{t=1}^{T} \gamma_i(t)}$$

$$(9.19) \quad \hat{b}_{ijk} = \frac{\text{expected number of transitions from } i \text{ to } j \text{ with } k \text{ observed}}{\text{expected number of transitions from } i \text{ to } j}$$
$$= \frac{\sum_{\{t:o_t=k,1\leq t\leq T\}} p_t(i,j)}{\sum_{t=1}^{T} p_t(i,j)}$$

Thus, from $\mu = (A, B, \Pi)$, we derive $\hat{\mu} = (\hat{A}, \hat{B}, \hat{\Pi})$. Further, as proved by Baum, we have that:

$$P(O|\hat{\mu}) \geq P(O|\mu)$$

This is a general property of the EM algorithm (see section 14.2.2). Therefore, iterating through a number of rounds of parameter reestimation will improve our model. Normally one continues reestimating the parameters until results are no longer improving significantly. This process of parameter reestimation does not guarantee that we will find the best model, however, because the reestimation process may get stuck in a *lo-cal maximum* (or even possibly just at a saddle point). In most problems of interest, the likelihood function is a complex nonlinear surface and there are many local maxima. Nevertheless, Baum-Welch reestimation is usually effective for HMMs.

LOCAL MAXIMUM

To end this section, let us consider reestimating the parameters of the crazy soft drink machine HMM using the Baum-Welch algorithm. If we let the initial model be the model that we have been using so far, then training on the observation sequence (lem, ice_t, cola) will yield the following values for $p_t(i,j)$:

(9.20)

		Time (and j)								
		1			**2**			**3**		
		CP	IP	γ_1	CP	IP	γ_2	CP	IP	γ_3
i	CP	0.3	0.7	1.0	0.28	0.02	0.3	0.616	0.264	0.88
	IP	0.0	0.0	0.0	0.6	0.1	0.7	0.06	0.06	0.12

and so the parameters will be reestimated as follows:

		Original			Reestimated		
Π	CP	1.0			1.0		
	IP	0.0			0.0		
		CP	IP		CP	IP	
A	CP	0.7	0.3		0.5486	0.4514	
	IP	0.5	0.5		0.8049	0.1951	
		cola	ice_t	lem	cola	ice_t	lem
B	CP	0.6	0.1	0.3	0.4037	0.1376	0.4587
	IP	0.1	0.7	0.2	0.1363	0.8537	0.0

Exercise 9.4   [⋆]

If one continued running the Baum-Welch algorithm on this HMM and this training sequence, what value would each parameter reach in the limit? Why?

The reason why the Baum-Welch algorithm is performing so strangely here
should be apparent: the training sequence is far too short to accurately represent the behavior of the crazy soft drink machine.

Exercise 9.5   [⋆]

Note that the parameter that is zero in Π stays zero. Is that a chance occurrence?
What would be the value of the parameter that becomes zero in B if we did another iteration of Baum-Welch reestimation? What generalization can one make
about Baum-Welch reestimation of zero parameters?

9.4   HMMs: Implementation, Properties, and Variants

9.4.1   Implementation

Beyond the theory discussed above, there are a number of practical issues in the implementation of HMMs. Care has to be taken to make the
implementation of HMM tagging efficient and accurate. The most obvious
issue is that the probabilities we are calculating consist of keeping on
multiplying together very small numbers. Such calculations will rapidly

underflow the range of floating point numbers on a computer (even if you store them as 'double'!).

The Viterbi algorithm only involves multiplications and choosing the largest element. Thus we can perform the entire Viterbi algorithm working with logarithms. This not only solves the problem with floating point underflow, but it also speeds up the computation, since additions are much quicker than multiplications. In practice, a speedy implementation of the Viterbi algorithm is particularly important because this is the runtime algorithm, whereas training can usually proceed slowly offline.

However, in the Forward-Backward algorithm as well, something still has to be done to prevent floating point underflow. The need to perform summations makes it difficult to use logs. A common solution is to employ auxiliary *scaling coefficients*, whose values grow with the time t so that the probabilities multiplied by the scaling coefficient remain within the floating point range of the computer. At the end of each iteration, when the parameter values are reestimated, these scaling factors cancel out. Detailed discussion of this and other implementation issues can be found in (Levinson et al. 1983), (Rabiner and Juang 1993: 365–368), (Cutting et al. 1991), and (Dermatas and Kokkinakis 1995). The main alternative is to just use logs anyway, despite the fact that one needs to sum. Effectively then one is calculating an appropriate scaling factor at the time of each addition:

SCALING COEFFICIENTS

(9.21)   **funct** *log_add* ≡
    if $(y - x > \log big)$
      then y
    elsif $(x - y > \log big)$
        then x
          else $\min(x, y) + \log(\exp(x - \min(x, y)) + \exp(y - \min(x, y)))$
    fi.

where *big* is a suitable large constant like 10^{30}. For an algorithm like this where one is doing a large number of numerical computations, one also has to be careful about round-off errors, but such concerns are well outside the scope of this chapter.

9.4.2 Variants

There are many variant forms of HMMs that can be made without fundamentally changing them, just as with finite state machines. One is to allow some arc transitions to occur without emitting any symbol, so-called *epsilon* or *null transitions* (Bahl et al. 1983). Another commonly used variant is to make the output distribution dependent just on a single state, rather than on the two states at both ends of an arc as you traverse an arc, as was effectively the case with the soft drink machine. Under this model one can view the output as a function of the state chosen, rather than of the arc traversed. The model where outputs are a function of the state has actually been used more often in Statistical NLP, because it corresponds naturally to a part of speech tagging model, as we see in chapter 10. Indeed, some people will probably consider us perverse for having presented the arc-emission model in this chapter. But we chose the arc-emission model because it is trivial to simulate the state-emission model using it, whereas doing the reverse is much more difficult. As suggested above, one does not need to think of the simpler model as having the outputs coming off the states, rather one can view the outputs as still coming off the arcs, but that the output distributions happen to be the same for all arcs that start at a certain node (or that end at a certain node, if one prefers).

This suggests a general strategy. A problem with HMM models is the large number of parameters that need to be estimated to define the model, and it may not be possible to estimate them all accurately if not much data is available. A straightforward strategy for dealing with this situation is to introduce assumptions that probability distributions on certain arcs or at certain states are the same as each other. This is referred to as *parameter tying*, and one thus gets *tied states* or *tied arcs*. Another possibility for reducing the number of parameters of the model is to decide that certain things are impossible (i.e., they have probability zero), and thus to introduce structural zeroes into the model. Making some things impossible adds a lot of structure to the model, and so can greatly improve the performance of the parameter reestimation algorithm, but is only appropriate in some circumstances.

9.4.3 Multiple input observations

We have presented the algorithms for a single input sequence. How does one train over multiple inputs? For the kind of HMM we have been assuming, where every state is connected to every other state (with a nonzero transition probability) – what is sometimes called an *ergodic model* – there is a simple solution: we simply concatenate all the observation sequences and train on them as one long input. The only real disadvantage to this is that we do not get sufficient data to be able to reestimate the initial probabilities π_i successfully. However, often people use HMM models that are not fully connected. For example, people sometimes use

FEED FORWARD MODEL

a *feed forward model* where there is an ordered set of states and one can only proceed at each time instant to the same or a higher numbered state. If the HMM is not fully connected – it contains structural zeroes – or if we do want to be able to reestimate the initial probabilities, then we need to extend the reestimation formulae to work with a sequence of inputs. Provided that we assume that the inputs are independent, this is straightforward. We will not present the formulas here, but we do present the analogous formulas for the PCFG case in section 11.3.4.

9.4.4 Initialization of parameter values

The reestimation process only guarantees that we will find a local maximum. If we would rather find the global maximum, one approach is to try to start the HMM in a region of the parameter space that is near the global maximum. One can do this by trying to roughly estimate good values for the parameters, rather than setting them randomly. In practice, good initial estimates for the output parameters $B = \{b_{ijk}\}$ turn out to be particularly important, while random initial estimates for the parameters A and Π are normally satisfactory.

9.5 Further Reading

The Viterbi algorithm was first described in (Viterbi 1967). The mathematical theory behind Hidden Markov Models was developed by Baum and his colleagues in the late sixties and early seventies (Baum et al. 1970), and advocated for use in speech recognition in lectures by Jack Ferguson from the Institute for Defense Analyses. It was applied to speech processing in the 1970s by Baker at CMU (Baker 1975), and by Jelinek and colleagues at IBM (Jelinek et al. 1975; Jelinek 1976), and then later found its way at IBM and elsewhere into use for other kinds of language modeling, such as part of speech tagging.

There are many good references on HMM algorithms (within the context of speech recognition), including (Levinson et al. 1983; Knill and Young 1997; Jelinek 1997). Particularly well-known are (Rabiner 1989; Rabiner and Juang 1993). They consider continuous HMMs (where the output is real valued) as well as the discrete HMMs we have considered here, contain information on applications of HMMs to speech recognition and may also be consulted for fairly comprehensive references on the development and the use of HMMs. Our presentation of HMMs is however most closely based on that of Paul (1990).

Within the chapter, we have assumed a fixed HMM architecture, and have just gone about learning optimal parameters for the HMM within that architecture. However, what size and shape of HMM should one choose for a new problem? Sometimes the nature of the problem determines the architecture, as in the applications of HMMs to tagging that we discuss in the next chapter. For circumstances when this is not the case, there has been some work on learning an appropriate HMM structure on the principle of trying to find the most compact HMM that can adequately describe the data (Stolcke and Omohundro 1993).

HMMs are widely used to analyze gene sequences in bioinformatics. See for instance (Baldi and Brunak 1998; Durbin et al. 1998). As linguists, we find it a little hard to take seriously problems over an alphabet of four symbols, but bioinformatics is a well-funded domain to which you can apply your new skills in Hidden Markov Modeling!

10 *Part-of-Speech Tagging*

THE ULTIMATE GOAL of research on Natural Language Processing is to parse and understand language. As we have seen in the preceding chapters, we are still far from achieving this goal. For this reason, much research in NLP has focussed on intermediate tasks that make sense of some of the structure inherent in language without requiring complete TAGGING understanding. One such task is part-of-speech tagging, or simply *tagging*. Tagging is the task of labeling (or tagging) each word in a sentence with its appropriate part of speech. We decide whether each word is a noun, verb, adjective, or whatever. Here is an example of a tagged sentence:

(10.1)   The-AT representative-NN put-VBD chairs-NNS on-IN the-AT table-NN.

The part-of-speech tags we use in this chapter are shown in table 10.1, and generally follow the Brown/Penn tag sets (see section 4.3.2). Note that another tagging is possible for the same sentence (with the rarer sense for *put* of an *option to sell*):

(10.2)   The-AT representative-JJ put-NN chairs-VBZ on-IN the-AT table-NN.

But this tagging gives rise to a semantically incoherent reading. The tagging is also syntactically unlikely since uses of *put* as a noun and uses of *chairs* as an intransitive verb are rare.

This example shows that tagging is a case of limited syntactic disambiguation. Many words have more than one syntactic category. In tagging, we try to determine which of these syntactic categories is the most likely for a particular use of a word in a sentence.

Tagging is a problem of limited scope: Instead of constructing a complete parse, we just fix the syntactic categories of the words in a sentence.

Tag	Part Of Speech
AT	article
BEZ	the word *is*
IN	preposition
JJ	adjective
JJR	comparative adjective
MD	modal
NN	singular or mass noun
NNP	singular proper noun
NNS	plural noun
PERIOD	. : ? !
PN	personal pronoun
RB	adverb
RBR	comparative adverb
TO	the word *to*
VB	verb, base form
VBD	verb, past tense
VBG	verb, present participle, gerund
VBN	verb, past participle
VBP	verb, non-3rd person singular present
VBZ	verb, 3rd singular present
WDT	*wh-* determiner (*what*, *which*)

Table 10.1   Some part-of-speech tags frequently used for tagging English.

For example, we are not concerned with finding the correct attachment of prepositional phrases. As a limited effort, tagging is much easier to solve than parsing, and accuracy is quite high. Between 96% and 97% of tokens are disambiguated correctly by the most successful approaches. However, it is important to realize that this impressive accuracy figure is not quite as good as it looks, because it is evaluated on a per-word basis. For instance, in many genres such as newspapers, the average sentence is over twenty words, and on such sentences, even with a tagging accuracy of 96% this means that there will be on average over one tagging error per sentence.

Even though it is limited, the information we get from tagging is still quite useful. Tagging can be used in information extraction, question answering, and shallow parsing. The insight that tagging is an intermediate layer of representation that is useful and more tractable than full parsing is due to the corpus linguistics work that was led by Francis and Kučera at Brown University in the 1960s and 70s (Francis and Kučera 1982).

The following sections deal with Markov Model taggers, Hidden Markov Model taggers and transformation-based tagging. At the end of the chapter, we discuss levels of accuracy for different approaches to tagging. But first we make some general comments on the types of information that are available for tagging.

10.1   The Information Sources in Tagging

How can one decide the correct part of speech for a word used in a context? There are essentially two sources of information. One way is to look at the tags of other words in the context of the word we are interested in. These words may also be ambiguous as to their part of speech, but the essential observation is that some part of speech sequences are common, such as AT JJ NN, while others are extremely unlikely or impossible, such as AT JJ VBP. Thus when choosing whether to give an NN or a VBP tag to the word *play* in the phrase *a new play*, we should obviously choose

SYNTAGMATIC the former. This type of *syntagmatic* structural information is the most obvious source of information for tagging, but, by itself, it is not very successful. For example, Greene and Rubin (1971), an early deterministic rule-based tagger that used such information about syntagmatic patterns correctly tagged only 77% of words. This made the tagging problem look quite hard. One reason that it looks hard is that many content words in English can have various parts of speech. For example, there is a very productive process in English which allows almost any noun to be turned into a verb, for example, *Next, you **flour** the pan*, or, *I want you to **web** our annual report*. This means that almost any noun should also be listed in a dictionary as a verb as well, and we lose a lot of constraining information needed for tagging.

These considerations suggest the second information source: just knowing the word involved gives a lot of information about the correct tag. Although *flour* can be used as a verb, an occurrence of *flour* is much more likely to be a noun. The utility of this information was conclusively demonstrated by Charniak et al. (1993), who showed that a 'dumb' tagger that simply assigns the most common tag to each word performs at the surprisingly high level of 90% correct.[1] This made tagging look quite easy – at least given favorable conditions, an issue to which we shall return. As a result of this, the performance of such a 'dumb' tagger has been used to give a baseline performance level in subsequent studies. And all modern taggers in some way make use of a combination of syntagmatic information (looking at information about tag sequences) and lexical information (predicting a tag based on the word concerned).

Lexical information is so useful because the distribution of a word's usages across different parts of speech is typically extremely uneven. Even for words with a number of parts of speech, they usually occur used as one particular part of speech. Indeed, this distribution is usually so marked that this one part of speech is often seen as basic, with others being derived from it. As a result, this has led to a certain tension over the way the term 'part of speech' has been used. In traditional grammars, one often sees a word in context being classified as something like 'a noun being used as an adjective,' which confuses what is seen as the 'basic' part of speech of the lexeme with the part of speech of the word as used in the current context. In this chapter, as in modern linguistics in general, we are concerned with determining the latter concept, but nevertheless, the distribution of a word across the parts of speech gives a great deal of additional information. Indeed, this uneven distribution is one reason why one might expect statistical approaches to tagging to be better than deterministic approaches: in a deterministic approach one can only say that a word can or cannot be a verb, and there is a temptation to leave out the verb possibility if it is very rare (since doing so will probably lift the level of overall performance), whereas within a statistical approach, we can say that a word has an extremely high *a priori* probability of being a noun, but there is a small chance that it might be being used as a verb, or even some other part of speech. Thus syntactic disambiguation can be argued to be one context in which a framework that allows quantitative information is more adequate for representing linguistic knowledge than a purely symbolic approach.

---

1. The general efficacy of this method was noted earlier by Atwell (1987).

10.2 Markov Model Taggers

10.2.1 The probabilistic model

In Markov Model tagging, we look at the sequence of tags in a text as a Markov chain. As discussed in chapter 9, a Markov chain has the following two properties:

- **Limited horizon.** $P(X_{i+1} = t^j | X_1, \ldots, X_i) = P(X_{i+1} = t^j | X_i)$

- **Time invariant (stationary).** $P(X_{i+1} = t^j | X_i) = P(X_2 = t^j | X_1)$

That is, we assume that a word's tag only depends on the previous tag (limited horizon) and that this dependency does not change over time (time invariance). For example, if a finite verb has a probability of 0.2 to occur after a pronoun at the beginning of a sentence, then this probability will not change as we tag the rest of the sentence (or new sentences). As with most probabilistic models, the two Markov properties only approximate reality. For example, the Limited Horizon property does not model long-distance relationships like *Wh*-extraction – this was in fact the core of Chomsky's famous argument against using Markov Models for natural language.

Exercise 10.1 [⋆]

What are other linguistic phenomena that are not modeled correctly by Markov chains? Which general property of language is common to these phenomena?

Exercise 10.2 [⋆]

Why is Time Invariance problematic for modeling language?

Following (Charniak et al. 1993), we will use the notation in table 10.2. We use subscripts to refer to words and tags in particular positions of the sentences and corpora we tag. We use superscripts to refer to word types in the lexicon of words and to refer to tag types in the tag set. In this compact notation, we can state the above Limited Horizon property as follows:

$$P(t_{i+1} | t_{1,i}) = P(t_{i+1} | t_i)$$

We use a *training set* of manually tagged text to learn the regularities of tag sequences. The maximum likelihood estimate of tag t^k following

w_i	the word at position i in the corpus
t_i	the tag of w_i
$w_{i,i+m}$	the words occurring at positions i through $i + m$ (alternative notations: $w_i \cdots w_{i+m}$, $w_i, \ldots, w_{i+m}$, $w_{i(i+m)}$)
$t_{i,i+m}$	the tags $t_i \cdots t_{i+m}$ for $w_i \cdots w_{i+m}$
w^l	the lth word in the lexicon
t^j	the jth tag in the tag set
$C(w^l)$	the number of occurrences of w^l in the training set
$C(t^j)$	the number of occurrences of t^j in the training set
$C(t^j, t^k)$	the number of occurrences of t^j followed by t^k
$C(w^l : t^j)$	the number of occurrences of w^l that are tagged as t^j
T	number of tags in tag set
W	number of words in the lexicon
n	sentence length

Table 10.2   Notational conventions for tagging.

t^j is estimated from the relative frequencies of different tags following a certain tag as follows:

$$P(t^k | t^j) = \frac{C(t^j, t^k)}{C(t^j)}$$

For instance, following on from the example of how to tag *a new play*, we would expect to find that $P(\text{NN}|\text{JJ}) \gg P(\text{VBP}|\text{JJ})$. Indeed, on the Brown corpus, $P(\text{NN}|\text{JJ}) \approx 0.45$ and $P(\text{VBP}|\text{JJ}) \approx 0.0005$.

With estimates of the probabilities $P(t_{i+1}|t_i)$, we can compute the probability of a particular tag sequence. In practice, the task is to find the most probable tag sequence for a sequence of words, or equivalently, the most probable state sequence for a sequence of words (since the states of the Markov Model here are tags). We incorporate words by having the Markov Model emit words each time it leaves a state. This is similar to the symbol emission probabilities b_{ijk} in HMMs from chapter 9:

$$P(O_n = k | X_n = s_i, X_{n+1} = s_j) = b_{ijk}$$

The difference is that we can directly observe the states (or tags) if we have a tagged corpus. Each tag corresponds to a different state. We can also directly estimate the probability of a word being emitted by a particular state (or tag) via Maximum Likelihood Estimation:

$$P(w^l|t^j) = \frac{C(w^l, t^j)}{C(t^j)}$$

Now we have everything in place to find the best tagging $t_{1,n}$ for a sentence $w_{1,n}$. Applying Bayes' rule, we can write:

$$
(10.3) \quad \underset{t_{1,n}}{\arg\max} \, P(t_{1,n}|w_{1,n}) = \underset{t_{1,n}}{\arg\max} \, \frac{P(w_{1,n}|t_{1,n})P(t_{1,n})}{P(w_{1,n})}
$$

$$
= \underset{t_{1,n}}{\arg\max} \, P(w_{1,n}|t_{1,n})P(t_{1,n})
$$

We now reduce this expression to parameters that can be estimated from the training corpus. In addition to the Limited Horizon assumption (10.5), we make two assumptions about words:

- words are independent of each other (10.4), and

- a word's identity only depends on its tag (10.5)

$$
(10.4) \quad P(w_{1,n}|t_{1,n})P(t_{1,n}) = \prod_{i=1}^{n} P(w_i|t_{1,n})
$$

$$
\times P(t_n|t_{1,n-1}) \times P(t_{n-1}|t_{1,n-2}) \times \cdots \times P(t_2|t_1)
$$

$$
(10.5) \quad = \prod_{i=1}^{n} P(w_i|t_i)
$$

$$
\times P(t_n|t_{n-1}) \times P(t_n - 1|t_{n-2}) \times \cdots \times P(t_2|t_1)
$$

$$
(10.6) \quad = \prod_{i=1}^{n} [P(w_i|t_i) \times P(t_i|t_{i-1})]
$$

(We define $P(t_1|t_0) = 1.0$ to simplify our notation.)

Exercise 10.3 [⋆]

These are simplifying assumptions. Give two examples each of phenomena where independence of words (10.4) and independence from previous and following tags (10.5) don't hold.

So the final equation for determining the optimal tags for a sentence is:

$$
(10.7) \quad \hat{t}_{1,n} = \underset{t_{1,n}}{\arg\max} \, P(t_{1,n}|w_{1,n}) = \prod_{i=1}^{n} P(w_i|t_i)P(t_i|t_{i-1})
$$

```
 1  for all tags t^j do
 2       for all tags t^k do
 3            P(t^k|t^j) := C(t^j,t^k) / C(t^j)
 4       end
 5  end
 6  for all tags t^j do
 7       for all words w^l do
 8            P(w^l|t^j) := C(w^l,t^j) / C(t^j)
 9       end
10  end
```

Figure 10.1 Algorithm for training a Visible Markov Model Tagger. In most implementations, a smoothing method is applied for estimating the $P(t^k|t^j)$ and $P(w^l|t^j)$.

			Second tag			
First tag	AT	BEZ	IN	NN	VB	PERIOD
AT	0	0	0	48636	0	19
BEZ	1973	0	426	187	0	38
IN	43322	0	1325	17314	0	185
NN	1067	3720	42470	11773	614	21392
VB	6072	42	4758	1476	129	1522
PERIOD	8016	75	4656	1329	954	0

Table 10.3 Idealized counts of some tag transitions in the Brown Corpus. For example, NN occurs 48636 times after AT.

The algorithm for training a Markov Model tagger is summarized in figure 10.1. The next section describes how to tag with a Markov Model tagger once it is trained.

Exercise 10.4   [⋆]
Given the data in table 10.3, compute maximum likelihood estimates as shown in figure 10.1 for $P(\text{AT}|\text{PERIOD})$, $P(\text{NN}|\text{AT})$, $P(\text{BEZ}|\text{NN})$, $P(\text{IN}|\text{BEZ})$, $P(\text{AT}|\text{IN})$, and $P(\text{PERIOD}|\text{NN})$. Assume that the total number of occurrences of tags can be obtained by summing over the numbers in a row (e.g., 1973+426+187 for BEZ).

Exercise 10.5   [⋆]
Given the data in table 10.4, compute maximum likelihood estimates as shown in figure 10.1 for $P(\text{bear}|t^k)$, $P(\text{is}|t^k)$, $P(\text{move}|t^k)$, $P(\text{president}|t^k)$, $P(\text{progress}|t^k)$, and $P(\text{the}|t^k)$. Take the total number of occurrences of tags from table 10.3.

	AT	BEZ	IN	NN	VB	PERIOD
bear	0	0	0	10	43	0
is	0	10065	0	0	0	0
move	0	0	0	36	133	0
on	0	0	5484	0	0	0
president	0	0	0	382	0	0
progress	0	0	0	108	4	0
the	69016	0	0	0	0	0
.	0	0	0	0	0	48809

Table 10.4 Idealized counts for the tags that some words occur with in the Brown Corpus. For example, 36 occurrences of *move* are with the tag NN.

Exercise 10.6 [★]

Compute the following two probabilities:

- $P(\text{AT NN BEZ IN AT NN} \mid \textit{The bear is on the move.})$
- $P(\text{AT NN BEZ IN AT VB} \mid \textit{The bear is on the move.})$

10.2.2 The Viterbi algorithm

We could evaluate equation (10.7) for all possible taggings $t_{1,n}$ of a sentence of length n, but that would make tagging exponential in the length of the input that is to be tagged. An efficient tagging algorithm is the Viterbi algorithm from chapter 9. To review, the Viterbi algorithm has three steps: (i) initialization, (ii) induction, and (iii) termination and path-readout. We compute two functions $\delta_i(j)$, which gives us the probability of being in state j (= tag j) at word i, and $\psi_{i+1}(j)$, which gives us the most likely state (or tag) at word i given that we are in state j at word $i + 1$. The reader may want to review the discussion of the Viterbi algorithm in section 9.3.2 before reading on. Throughout, we will refer to states as tags in this chapter because the states of the model correspond to tags. (But note that this is only true for a bigram tagger.)

The initialization step is to assign probability 1.0 to the tag PERIOD:

$$\delta_1(\text{PERIOD}) = 1.0$$

$$\delta_1(t) = 0.0 \ \text{ for } t \neq \text{PERIOD}$$

That is, we assume that sentences are delimited by periods and we prepend a period in front of the first sentence in our text for convenience.

1 **comment**: Given: a sentence of length n
2 **comment**: Initialization
3 $\delta_1(\text{PERIOD}) = 1.0$
4 $\delta_1(t) = 0.0$ for $t \neq \text{PERIOD}$
5 **comment**: Induction
6 **for** $i := 1$ **to** n **step** 1 **do**
7   **for** all tags t^j **do**
8 $\delta_{i+1}(t^j) := \max_{1 \leq k \leq T}[\delta_i(t^k) \times P(w_{i+1}|t^j) \times P(t^j|t^k)]$
9 $\psi_{i+1}(t^j) := \arg\max_{1 \leq k \leq T}[\delta_i(t^k) \times P(w_{i+1}|t^j) \times P(t^j|t^k)]$
10   **end**
11 **end**
12 **comment**: Termination and path-readout
13 $X_{n+1} = \arg\max_{1 \leq j \leq T} \delta_{n+1}(j)$
14 **for** $j := n$ **to** 1 **step** -1 **do**
15 $X_j = \psi_{j+1}(X_{j+1})$
16 **end**
17 $P(X_1, \ldots, X_n) = \max_{1 \leq j \leq T} \delta_{n+1}(t^j)$

Figure 10.2   Algorithm for tagging with a Visible Markov Model Tagger.

The induction step is based on equation (10.7), where $a_{jk} = P(t^k|t^j)$ and $b_{jkw^l} = P(w^l|t^j)$:

$$\delta_{i+1}(t^j) = \max_{1 \leq k \leq T}[\delta_i(t^k) \times P(w_{i+1}|t^j) \times P(t^j|t^k)], \quad 1 \leq j \leq T$$

$$\psi_{i+1}(t^j) = \arg\max_{1 \leq k \leq T}[\delta_i(t^k) \times P(w_{i+1}|t^j) \times P(t^j|t^k)], \quad 1 \leq j \leq T$$

Finally, termination and read-out steps are as follows, where $X_1, \ldots, X_n$ are the tags we choose for words $w_1, \ldots, w_n$:

$$X_n = \arg\max_{1 \leq j \leq T} \delta_n(t^j)$$

$$X_i = \psi_{i+1}(X_{i+1}), \quad 1 \leq i \leq n-1$$

$$P(X_1, \ldots, X_n) = \max_{1 \leq j \leq T} \delta_{n+1}(t^j)$$

Tagging with a Visible Markov Model tagger is summarized in figure 10.2.

Exercise 10.7   [$\star$]
Based on the probability estimates from the previous set of exercises, tag the following sentence using the Viterbi algorithm.

(10.8)   The bear is on the move.

Exercise 10.8

Some larger data sets of tag sequence probabilities and some suggested exercises are available on the website.

Terminological note: Markov Models vs. Hidden Markov Models. The reader may have noticed that for the purposes of tagging, the Markov Models in this chapter are treated as Hidden Markov Models. This is because we can observe the states of the Markov Model in training (the tags of the labeled corpus), but we only observe words in applying the Markov Model to the tagging task. We could say that the formalism used in Markov Model tagging is really a mixed formalism. We construct 'Visible' Markov Models in training, but treat them as Hidden Markov Models when we put them to use and tag new corpora.

10.2.3   Variations

Unknown words

We have shown how to estimate word generation probabilities for words that occur in the corpus. But many words in sentences we want to tag will not be in the training corpus. Some words will not even be in the dictionary. We discussed above that knowing the a priori distribution of the tags for a word (or at any rate the most common tag for a word) takes you a great deal of the way in solving the tagging problem. This means that unknown words are a major problem for taggers, and in practice, the differing accuracy of different taggers over different corpora is often mainly determined by the proportion of unknown words, and the smarts built into the tagger that allow it to try to guess the part of speech of unknown words.

  The simplest model for unknown words is to assume that they can be of any part of speech (or perhaps only any open class part of speech – that is nouns, verbs, etc., but not prepositions or articles). Unknown words are given a distribution over parts of speech corresponding to that of the lexicon as a whole. While this approach is serviceable in some cases, the loss of lexical information for these words greatly lowers the accuracy of the tagger, and so people have tried to exploit other features of the word and its context to improve the lexical probability estimates for unknown words. Often, we can use morphological and other cues to

Feature	Value	NNP	NN	NNS	VBG	VBZ
unknown word	yes	0.05	0.02	0.02	0.005	0.005
	no	0.95	0.98	0.98	0.995	0.995
capitalized	yes	0.95	0.10	0.10	0.005	0.005
	no	0.05	0.90	0.90	0.995	0.995
ending	-s	0.05	0.01	0.98	0.00	0.99
	-ing	0.01	0.01	0.00	1.00	0.00
	-tion	0.05	0.10	0.00	0.00	0.00
	other	0.89	0.88	0.02	0.00	0.01

Table 10.5 Table of probabilities for dealing with unknown words in tagging. For example, P(unknown word = yes|NNP) = 0.05 and P(ending = -*ing*|VBG) = 1.0.

make inferences about a word's possible parts of speech. For example, words ending in -*ed* are likely to be past tense forms or past participles. Weischedel et al. (1993) estimate word generation probabilities based on three types of information: how likely it is that a tag will generate an unknown word (this probability is zero for some tags, for example PN, personal pronouns); the likelihood of generation of uppercase/lowercase words; and the generation of hyphens and particular suffixes:

$$P(w^l|t^j) = \frac{1}{Z}P(\text{unknown word}|t^j)P(\text{capitalized}|t^j)P(\text{endings/hyph}|t^j)$$

where Z is a normalization constant. This model reduces the error rate for unknown words from more than 40% to less than 20%.

Charniak et al. (1993) propose an alternative model which depends both on roots and suffixes and can select from multiple morphological analyses (for example, *do-es* (a verb form) vs. *doe-s* (the plural of a noun)).

Most work on unknown words assumes independence between features. Independence is often a bad assumption. For example, capitalized words are more likely to be unknown, so the features 'unknown word' and 'capitalized' in Weischedel et al.'s model are not really independent. Franz (1996; 1997) develops a model for unknown words that takes dependence into account. He proposes a loglinear model that models *main* MAIN EFFECTS *effects* (the effects of a particular feature on its own) as well as *interac-* INTERACTIONS *tions* (such as the dependence between 'unknown word' and 'capitalized'). For an approach based on Bayesian inference see Samuelsson (1993).

Exercise 10.9 [⋆]

Given the (made-up) data in table 10.5 and Weischedel et al.'s model for unknown words, compute $P(fenestration|t^k)$, $P(fenestrates|t^k)$, $P(palladio|t^k)$, $P(palladios|t^k)$, $P(Palladio|t^k)$, $P(Palladios|t^k)$, and $P(guesstimating|t^k)$. Assume that NNP, NN, NNS, VBG, and VBZ are the only possible tags. Do the estimates seem intuitively correct? What additional features could be used for better results?

Exercise 10.10 [⋆⋆]

Compute better estimates of the probabilities in table 10.5 from the data on the web site.

Trigram taggers

The basic Markov Model tagger can be extended in several ways. In the model developed so far, we make predictions based on the preceding tag. BIGRAM TAGGER This is called a *bigram tagger* because the basic unit we consider is the preceding tag and the current tag. We can think of tagging as selecting the most probable bigram (modulo word probabilities).

We would expect more accurate predictions if more context is taken into account. For example, the tag RB (adverb) can precede both a verb in the past tense (VBD) and a past participle (VBN). So a word sequence like *clearly marked* is inherently ambiguous in a Markov Model with a 'memory' that reaches only one tag back. A *trigram tagger* has a two-TRIGRAM TAGGER tag memory and lets us disambiguate more cases. For example, *is clearly marked* and *he clearly marked* suggest VBN and VBD, respectively, because the trigram "BEZ RB VBN" is more frequent than the trigram "BEZ RB VBD" and because "PN RB VBD" is more frequent than "PN RB VBN." A trigram tagger was described in (Church 1988), which is probably the most cited publication on tagging and got many NLP researchers interested in the problem of part-of-speech tagging.

Interpolation and variable memory

Conditioning predictions on a longer history is not always a good idea. For example, there are usually no short-distance syntactic dependencies across commas. So knowing what part of speech occurred before a comma does not help in determining the correct part of speech after the comma. In fact, a trigram tagger may make worse predictions than a bigram tagger in such cases because of sparse data problems –

trigram transition probabilities are estimated based on rarer events, so the chances of getting a bad estimate are higher.

One way to address this problem is linear interpolation of unigram, bigram, and trigram probabilities:

$$P(t_i|t_{1,i-1}) = \lambda_1 P_1(t_i) + \lambda_2 P_2(t_i|t_{i-1}) + \lambda_3 P_3(t_i|t_{i-1,i-2})$$

This method of linear interpolation was covered in chapter 6 and how to estimate the parameters λ_i using an HMM was covered in chapter 9.

Some researchers have selectively augmented a low-order Markov model based on error analysis and prior linguistic knowledge. For example, Kupiec (1992b) observed that a first order HMM systematically mistagged the sequence "the bottom of" as "AT JJ IN." He then extended the order-one model with a special network for this construction so that the improbability of a preposition after a "AT JJ" sequence could be learned. This method amounts to manually selecting higher-order states for cases where an order-one memory is not sufficient.

A related method is the Variable Memory Markov Model (VMMM) (Schütze and Singer 1994). VMMMs have states of mixed "length" instead of the fixed-length states of bigram and trigram taggers. A VMMM tagger can go from a state that remembers the last two tags (corresponding to a trigram) to a state that remembers the last three tags (corresponding to a fourgram) and then to a state without memory (corresponding to a unigram). The number of symbols to remember for a particular sequence is determined in training based on an information-theoretic criterion. In contrast to linear interpolation, VMMMs condition the length of memory used for prediction on the current sequence instead of using a fixed weighted sum for all sequences. VMMMs are built top-down by splitting states. An alternative is to build this type of model bottom-up by way of MODEL MERGING *model merging* (Stolcke and Omohundro 1994a; Brants 1998).

The hierarchical non-emitting Markov model is an even more powerful model that was proposed by Ristad and Thomas (1997). By introducing non-emitting transitions (transitions between states that do not emit a word or, equivalently, emit the empty word ϵ), this model can store dependencies between states over arbitrarily long distances.

Smoothing

Linear interpolation is a way of smoothing estimates. We can use any of the other estimation methods discussed in chapter 6 for smoothing. For example, Charniak et al. (1993) use a method that is similar to Adding One (but note that, in general, it does not give a proper probability distribution ...):

$$P(t^j|t^{j+1}) = (1 - \epsilon)\frac{C(t^{j-1}, t^j)}{C(t^{j-1})} + \epsilon$$

Smoothing the word generation probabilities is more important than smoothing the transition probabilities since there are many rare words that will not occur in the training corpus. Here too, Adding One has been used (Church 1988). Church added 1 to the count of all parts of speech listed in the dictionary for a particular word, thus guaranteeing a non-zero probability for all parts of speech t^j that are listed as possible for w^l:

$$P(t^j|w^l) = \frac{C(t^j, w^l) + 1}{C(w^l) + K_l}$$

where K_l is the number of possible parts of speech of w^l.

Exercise 10.11 [⋆]
Recompute the probability estimates in exercises 10.4 and 10.5 with Adding One.

Reversibility

We have described a Markov Model that 'decodes' (or tags) from left to right. It turns out that decoding from right to left is equivalent. The following derivation shows why this is the case:

$$
\begin{aligned}
(10.9) \quad P(t_{1,n}) &= P(t_1)P(t_{1,2}|t_1)P(t_{2,3}|t_2)\ldots P(t_{n-1,n}|t_{n-1}) \\
&= \frac{P(t_1)P(t_{1,2})P(t_{2,3})\ldots P(t_{n-1,n})}{P(t_1)P(t_2)\ldots P(t_{n-1})} \\
&= P(t_n)P(t_{1,2}|t_2)P(t_{2,3}|t_3)\ldots P(t_{n-1,n}|t_n)
\end{aligned}
$$

Assuming that the probability of the initial and last states are the same (which is the case in tagging since both correspond to the tag PERIOD), 'forward' and 'backward' probability are the same. So it doesn't matter which direction we choose. The tagger described here moves from left to right. Church's tagger takes the opposite direction.

Maximum Likelihood: Sequence vs. tag by tag

As we pointed out in chapter 9, the Viterbi Algorithm finds the most likely sequence of states (or tags). That is, we maximize $P(t_{1,n}|w_{1,n})$. We could also maximize $P(t_i|w_{1,n})$ for all i which amounts to summing over different tag sequences.

As an example consider sentence (10.10):

(10.10)   Time flies like an arrow.

Let us assume that, according to the transition probabilities we've gathered from our training corpus, (10.11a) and (10.11b) are likely taggings (assume probability 0.01), (10.11c) is an unlikely tagging (assume probability 0.001), and that (10.11d) is impossible because transition probability $P(\text{VB}|\text{VBZ})$ is 0.0.

(10.11)   a. NN VBZ RB AT NN. $P(\cdot) = 0.01$

            b. NN NNS VB AT NN. $P(\cdot) = 0.01$

            c. NN NNS RB AT NN. $P(\cdot) = 0.001$

            d. NN VBZ VB AT NN. $P(\cdot) = 0$

For this example, we will obtain taggings (10.11a) and (10.11b) as the equally most likely sequences $P(t_{1,n}|w_{1,n})$. But we will obtain (10.11c) if we maximize $P(t_i|w_{1,n})$ for all i. This is because $P(X_2 = \text{NNS}|\textit{Time flies like an arrow}) = 0.011 = P(\text{b}) + P(\text{c}) > 0.01 = P(\text{a}) = P(X_2 = \text{VBZ}|\textit{Time flies like an arrow})$ and $P(X_3 = \text{RB}|\textit{Time flies like an arrow}) = 0.011 = P(\text{a}) + P(\text{c}) > 0.01 = P(\text{b}) = P(X_3 = \text{VB}|\textit{Time flies like an arrow})$.

Experiments conducted by Merialdo (1994: 164) suggest that there is no large difference in accuracy between maximizing the likelihood of individual tags and maximizing the likelihood of the sequence. Intuitively, it is fairly easy to see why this might be. With Viterbi, the tag transitions are more likely to be sensible, but if something goes wrong, we will sometimes get a sequence of several tags wrong; whereas with tag by tag, one error does not affect the tagging of other words, and so one is more likely to get occasional dispersed errors. In practice, since incoherent sequences (like "NN NNS RB AT NN" above) are not very useful, the Viterbi algorithm is the preferred method for tagging with Markov Models.

10.3   Hidden Markov Model Taggers

Markov Model taggers work well when we have a large tagged training set. Often this is not the case. We may want to tag a text from a specialized domain with word generation probabilities that are different from those in available training texts. Or we may want to tag text in a foreign language for which training corpora do not exist at all.

10.3.1 Applying HMMs to POS tagging

If we have no training data, we can use an HMM to learn the regularities of tag sequences. Recall that an HMM as introduced in chapter 9 consists of the following elements:

- a set of states

- an output alphabet

- initial state probabilities

- state transition probabilities

- symbol emission probabilities

As in the case of the Visible Markov Model, the states correspond to tags. The output alphabet consists either of the words in the dictionary or classes of words as we will see in a moment.

We could randomly initialize all parameters of the HMM, but this would leave the tagging problem too unconstrained. Usually dictionary information is used to constrain the model parameters. If the output alphabet consists of words, we set word generation (= symbol emission) probabilities to zero if the corresponding word-tag pair is not listed in the dictionary (e.g., JJ is not listed as a possible part of speech for *book*). Alternatively, we can group words into word equivalence classes so that all words that allow the same set of tags are in the same class. For example, we could group *bottom* and *top* into the class JJ-NN if both are listed with just two parts of speech, JJ and NN. The first method was proposed by Jelinek (1985), the second by Kupiec (1992b). We write $b_{j.l}$ for the probability that word (or word class) l is emitted by tag j. This means that as in the case of the Visible Markov Model the 'output' of a tag does not depend on which tag (= state) is next.

- **Jelinek's method.**

$$b_{j.l} = \frac{b_{j.l}^{\star} C(w^l)}{\sum_{w^m} b_{j.m}^{\star} C(w^m)}$$

where the sum is over all words w^m in the dictionary and

$$b^\star_{j.l} = \begin{cases} 0 & \text{if } t^j \text{ is not a part of speech allowed for } w^l \\ \frac{1}{T(w^l)} & \text{otherwise} \end{cases}$$

where $T(w^j)$ is the number of tags allowed for w^j.

Jelinek's method amounts to initializing the HMM with the maximum likelihood estimates for $P(w^k|t^i)$, assuming that words occur equally likely with each of their possible tags.

- **Kupiec's method.** First, group all words with the same possible parts of speech into 'metawords' u_L. Here L is a subset of the integers from 1 to T, where T is the number of different tags in the tag set:

$$u_L = \{w^l | j \in L \leftrightarrow t^j \text{is allowed for } w^l\} \quad \forall L \subseteq \{1, \ldots, T\}$$

For example, if NN $= t^5$ and JJ $= t^8$ then $u_{\{5,8\}}$ will contain all words for which the dictionary allows tags NN and JJ and no other tags.

We then treat these metawords u_L the same way we treated words in Jelinek's method:[2]

$$b_{j.L} = \frac{b^\star_{j.L} C(u_L)}{\sum_{u_{L'}} b^\star_{j.L'} C(u_{L'})}$$

where $C(u_{L'})$ is the number of occurrences of words from $u_{L'}$, the sum in the denominator is over all metawords $u_{L'}$, and

$$b^\star_{j.L} = \begin{cases} 0 & \text{if } j \notin L \\ \frac{1}{|L|} & \text{otherwise} \end{cases}$$

where $|L|$ is the number of indices in L.

The advantage of Kupiec's method is that we don't fine-tune a separate set of parameters for each word. By introducing equivalence classes, the total number of parameters is reduced substantially and this smaller set can be estimated more reliably. This advantage could turn into a disadvantage if there is enough training material to accurately estimate parameters word by word as Jelinek's method does. Some experiments

---

2. The actual initialization used by Kupiec is a variant of what we present here. We have tried to make the similarity between Jelinek's and Kupiec's methods more transparent.

D0	maximum likelihood estimates from a tagged training corpus
D1	correct ordering only of lexical probabilities
D2	lexical probabilities proportional to overall tag probabilities
D3	equal lexical probabilities for all tags admissible for a word
T0	maximum likelihood estimates from a tagged training corpus
T1	equal probabilities for all transitions

Table 10.6 Initialization of the parameters of an HMM. D0, D1, D2, and D3 are initializations of the lexicon, and T0 and T1 are initializations of tag transitions investigated by Elworthy.

conducted by Merialdo (1994) suggest that unsupervised estimation of a separate set of parameters for each word introduces error. This argument does not apply to frequent words, however. Kupiec therefore does not include the 100 most frequent words in equivalence classes, but treats them as separate one-word classes.

Training.   Once initialization is completed, the Hidden Markov Model is trained using the Forward-Backward algorithm as described in chapter 9.

Tagging.   As we remarked earlier, the difference between VMM tagging and HMM tagging is in how we *train* the model, not in how we *tag*. The formal object we end up with after training is a Hidden Markov model in both cases. For this reason, there is no difference when we apply the model in tagging. We use the Viterbi algorithm in exactly the same manner for Hidden Markov Model tagging as we do for Visible Markov Model tagging.

10.3.2   The effect of initialization on HMM training

The 'clean' (i.e., theoretically well-founded) way of stopping training with the Forward-Backward algorithm is the log likelihood criterion (stop when the log likelihood no longer improves). However, it has been shown that, for tagging, this criterion often results in overtraining. This issue was investigated in detail by Elworthy (1994). He trained HMMs from the different starting conditions in table 10.6. The combination of D0 and T0 corresponds to Visible Markov Model training as we described it at the beginning of this chapter. D1 orders the lexical probabilities correctly (for example, the fact that the tag VB is more likely for *make* than the tag NN), but the absolute values of the probabilities are randomized. D2 gives the same ordering of parts of speech to all words (for example, for the most frequent tag t^j, we would have $P(w|t^j)$ is greater than $P(w|t^k)$ for all other tags t^k). D3 preserves only information about which tags are possible for a word, the ordering is not necessarily correct. T1 initializes the transition probabilities to roughly equal numbers.[3]

CLASSICAL

EARLY MAXIMUM

INITIAL MAXIMUM

Elworthy (1994) finds three different patterns of training for different combinations of initial conditions. In the *classical* pattern, performance on the test set improves steadily with each training iteration. In this case the log likelihood criterion for stopping is appropriate. In the *early maximum* pattern, performance improves for a number of iterations (most often for two or three), but then decreases. In the *initial maximum* pattern, the very first iteration degrades performance.

The typical scenario for applying HMMs is that a dictionary is available, but no tagged corpus as training data (conditions D3 (maybe D2) and T1). For this scenario, training follows the early maximum pattern. That means that we have to be careful in practice not to overtrain. One way to achieve this is to test the tagger on a held-out validation set after each iteration and stop training when performance decreases.

Elworthy also confirms Merialdo's finding that the Forward-Backward algorithm degrades performance when a tagged training corpus (of even moderate size) is available. That is, if we initialize according to D0 and T0, then we get the initial maximum pattern. However, an interesting twist is that if training and test corpus are very different, then a few iterations do improve performance (the early maximum pattern). This is a case that occurs frequently in practice since we are often confronted with types of text for which we do not have similar tagged training text.

In summary, if there is a sufficiently large training text that is fairly similar to the intended text of application, then we should use Visible Markov Models. If there is no training text available or training and test text are very different, but we have at least some lexical information, then we should run the Forward-Backward algorithm for a few iterations. Only when we have no lexical information at all, should we train for a larger number of iterations, ten or more. But we cannot expect good perfor-

---

3. Exactly identical probabilities are generally bad as a starting condition for the EM algorithm since they often correspond to suboptimal local optima that can easily be avoided. We assume that D3 and T1 refer to approximately equal probabilities that are slightly perturbed to avoid ties.

mance in this case. This failure is not a defect in the forward-backward algorithm, but reflects the fact that the forward-backward algorithm is only maximizing the likelihood of the training data by adjusting the parameters of an HMM. The changes it is using to reduce the cross entropy may not be in accord with our true objective function – getting words assigned tags according to some predefined tag set. Therefore it is not capable of optimizing performance on that task.

Exercise 10.12   [⋆]

When introducing HMM tagging above, we said that random initialization of the model parameters (without dictionary information) is not a useful starting point for the EM algorithm. Why is this the case? What would happen if we just had the following eight parts of speech: preposition, verb, adverb, adjective, noun, article, conjunction, and auxiliary; and randomly initialized the HMM. Hint: The EM algorithm will concentrate on high-frequency events which have the highest impact on log likelihood (the quantity maximized).

How does this initialization differ from D3?

Exercise 10.13   [⋆]

The EM algorithm improves the log likelihood of the model given the data in each iteration. How is this compatible with Elworthy's and Merialdo's results that tagging accuracy often decreases with further training?

Exercise 10.14   [⋆]

The crucial bit of prior knowledge that is captured by both Jelinek's and Kupiec's methods of parameter initialization is which of the word generation probabilities should be zero and which should not. The implicit assumption here is that a generation probability set to zero initially will remain zero during training. Show that this is the case referring to the introduction of the Forward-Backward algorithm in chapter 9.

Exercise 10.15   [⋆ ⋆]

Get the Xerox tagger (see pointer on website) and tag texts from the web site.

10.4 Transformation-Based Learning of Tags

In our description of Markov models we have stressed at several points that the Markov assumptions are too crude for many properties of natural language syntax. The question arises why we do not adopt more sophisticated models. We could condition tags on preceding words (not just preceding tags) or we could use more context than trigram taggers by going to fourgram or even higher order taggers.

This approach is not feasible because of the large number of parameters we would need. Even with trigram taggers, we had to smooth and interpolate because maximum likelihood estimates were not robust enough. This problem would be exacerbated with models more complex than the Markov models introduced so far, especially if we wanted to condition transition probabilities on words.

We will now turn to transformation-based tagging. One of the strengths of this method is that it can exploit a wider range of lexical and syntactic regularities. In particular, tags can be conditioned on words and on more context. Transformation-based tagging encodes complex interdependencies between words and tags by selecting and sequencing transformations that transform an initial imperfect tagging into one with fewer errors. The training of a transformation-based tagger requires an order of magnitude fewer decisions than estimating the large number of parameters of a Markov model.

Transformation-based tagging has two key components:

- a specification of which 'error-correcting' transformations are admissible

- the learning algorithm

As input data, we need a tagged corpus and a dictionary. We first tag each word in the training corpus with its most frequent tag – that is what we need the dictionary for. The learning algorithm then constructs a ranked list of transformations that transforms the initial tagging into a tagging that is close to correct. This ranked list can be used to tag new text, by again initially choosing each word's most frequent tag, and then applying the transformations. We will now describe these components in more detail.

10.4.1   Transformations

A transformation consists of two parts, a triggering environment and a rewrite rule. Rewrite rules have the form $t^1 \rightarrow t^2$, meaning "replace tag t^1 by tag t^2." Brill (1995a) allows the triggering environments shown in table 10.7. Here the asterisk is the site of the potential rewriting and the boxes denote the locations where a trigger will be sought. For example, line 5 refers to the triggering environment "Tag t^j occurs in one of the three previous positions."

Schema	t_{i-3}	t_{i-2}	t_{i-1}	t_i	t_{i+1}	t_{i+1}	t_{i+3}
1			▭	*			
2				*	▭		
3		▭	▭	*			
4				*	▭	▭	
5	▭	▭	▭	*			
6				*	▭	▭	▭
7			▭	*	▭		
8		▭	▭	*	▭	▭	
9		▭		*	▭		

Table 10.7   Triggering environments in Brill's transformation-based tagger. Examples: Line 5 refers to the triggering environment "Tag t^j occurs in one of the three previous positions"; Line 9 refers to the triggering environment "Tag t^j occurs two positions earlier and tag t^k occurs in the following position."

Source tag	Target tag	Triggering environment
NN	VB	previous tag is TO
VBP	VB	one of the previous three tags is MD
JJR	RBR	next tag is JJ
VBP	VB	one of the previous two words is *n't*

Table 10.8   Examples of some transformations learned in transformation-based tagging.

Examples of the type of transformations that are learned given these triggering environments are shown in table 10.8. The first transformation specifies that nouns should be retagged as verbs after the tag TO. Later transformations with more specific triggers will switch some words back to NN (e.g., *school* in *go to school*). The second transformation in table 10.8 applies to verbs with identical base and past tense forms like *cut* and *put*. A preceding modal makes it unlikely that they are used in the past tense. An example for the third transformation is the retagging of *more* in *more valuable player*.

The first three transformations in table 10.8 are triggered by tags. The fourth one is triggered by a word. (In the Penn Treebank words like *don't* and *shouldn't* are split up into a modal and *n't*.) Similar to the second transformation, this one also changes a past tense form to a base form. A preceding *n't* makes a base form more likely than a past tense form.

```
1  C₀ := corpus with each word tagged with its most frequent tag
3  for k := 0 step 1 do
4      v := the transformation uᵢ that minimizes E(uᵢ(Cₖ))
6      if (E(Cₖ) − E(v(Cₖ))) < ϵ then break fi
7      Cₖ₊₁ := v(Cₖ)
8      τₖ₊₁ := v
9  end
10 Output sequence: τ₁, . . . , τₖ
```

Figure 10.3 The learning algorithm for transformation-based tagging. C_i refers to the tagging of the corpus in iteration i. E is the error rate.

Word-triggered environments can also be conditioned on the current word and on a combination of words and tags ("the current word is w^i and the following tag is t^j").

There is also a third type of transformation in addition to tag-triggered and word-triggered transformations. *Morphology-triggered transformations* offer an elegant way of integrating the handling of unknown words into the general tagging formalism. Initially, unknown words are tagged as proper nouns (NNP) if capitalized, as common nouns (NN) otherwise. Then morphology-triggered transformations like "Replace NN by NNS if the unknown word's suffix is -*s*" correct errors. These transformations are learned by the same learning algorithm as the tagging transformations proper. We will now describe this learning algorithm.

10.4.2   The learning algorithm

The learning algorithm of transformation-based tagging selects the best transformations and determines their order of application. It works as shown in figure 10.3.

Initially we tag each word with its most frequent tag. In each iteration of the loop, we choose the transformation that reduces the error rate most (line 4), where the error $E(C_k)$ is measured as the number of words that are mistagged in tagged corpus C_k. We stop when there is no transformation left that reduces the error rate by more than a prespecified threshold ϵ. This procedure is a greedy search for the optimal sequence of transformations.

We also have to make two decisions about how to apply the transformations, that is, how exactly to compute $\tau_i(C_k)$. First, we are going to stipulate that transformations are applied from left to right to the input. Secondly, we have to decide whether transformations should have an immediate or delayed effect. In the case of immediate effect, applications of the same transformation can influence each other. Brill implements delayed-effect transformations, which are simpler. This means that a transformation "A → B if the preceding tag is A" will transform AAAA to ABBB. AAAA would be transformed to ABAB if transformations took effect immediately.

An interesting twist on this tagging model is to use it for *unsupervised* learning as an alternative to HMM tagging. As with HMM tagging, the only information available in unsupervised tagging is which tags are allowable for each word. We can then take advantage of the fact that many words only have one tag and use that as the scoring function for selecting transformations. For example, we can infer that the tagging of *can* in *The can is open* as NN is correct if most unambiguous words in the environment "AT __ BEZ" are nouns with this tag. Brill (1995b) describes a system based on this idea that achieves tagging accuracies of up to 95.6%, a remarkable result for an unsupervised method. What is particularly interesting is that there is no overtraining – in sharp contrast to HMMs which are very prone to overtraining as we saw above. This is a point that we will return to presently.

10.4.3   Relation to other models

Decision trees

Transformation-based learning bears some similarity to decision trees (see section 16.1). We can view a decision tree as a mechanism that labels all leaves that are dominated by a node with the majority class label of that node. As we descend the tree we relabel the leaves of a child node if its label differs from that of the parent node. This way of looking at a decision tree shows the similarity to transformation-based learning where we also go through a series of relabelings, working on smaller and smaller subsets of the data.

In principle, transformation-based learning is strictly more powerful than decision trees as shown by Brill (1995a). That is, there exist classification tasks that can be solved using transformation-based learning that cannot be solved using decision trees. However, it is not clear that this 'extra power' of transformation-based learning is used in NLP applications.

The main practical difference between the two methods is that the training data are split at each node in a decision tree and that we apply a different sequence of 'transformations' for each node (the sequence corresponding to the decisions on the path from the root to that node). In transformation-based learning, each transformation in the learned transformation list is applied to all the data (leading to a rewriting when the triggering environment is met). As a result, we can directly minimize on the figure of merit that we are most interested in (number of tagging errors in the case of tagging) as opposed to indirect measures like entropy that are used for HMMs and decision trees. If we directly minimized tagging errors in decision tree learning, then it would be easy to achieve 100% accuracy for each leaf node. But performance on new data would be poor because each leaf node would be formed based on arbitrary properties of the training set that don't generalize. Transformation-based learning seems to be surprisingly immune to this form of overfitting (Ramshaw and Marcus 1994). This can be partially explained by the fact that we always learn on the whole data set.

One price we pay for this robustness is that the space of transformation sequences we have to search is huge. A naive implementation of transformation-based learning will therefore be quite inefficient. However, there are ways of searching the space more intelligently and efficiently (Brill 1995a).

Probabilistic models in general

In comparison to probabilistic models (including decision trees), transformation based learning does not make the battery of standard methods available that probability theory provides. For example, no extra work is necessary in a probabilistic model for a 'k-best' tagging – a tagging module that passes a number of tagging hypotheses with probabilities on to the next module downstream (such as the parser).

It is possible to extend transformation-based tagging to 'k-best' tagging by allowing rules of the form "add tag A to B if ..." so that some words will be tagged with multiple tags. However, the problem remains that we don't have an assessment of how likely each of the tags is. The first tag could be 100 times more likely than the next best one in one situation and all tags could be equally likely in another situation. This type of knowledge could be critical for constructing a parse.

An important characteristic of learning methods is the way prior knowledge can be encoded. Transformation-based tagging and probabilistic approaches have different strengths here. The specification of templates for the most appropriate triggering environments offers a powerful way of biasing the learner towards good generalizations in transformation-based learning. The templates in table 10.7 seem obvious. But they seem obvious only because of what we know about syntactic regularities. A large number of other templates that are obviously inappropriate are conceivable (e.g., "the previous even position in the sentence is a noun").

In contrast, the probabilistic Markov models make it easier to encode precisely what the prior likelihood for the different tags of a word are (for example, the most likely tag is ten times as likely or just one and a half times more likely). The only piece of knowledge we can give the learner in transformation-based tagging is which tag is most likely.

10.4.4 Automata

The reader may wonder why we describe transformation-based tagging in this textbook even though we said we would not cover rule-oriented approaches. While transformation-based tagging has a rule component, it also has a quantitative component. We are somewhat loosely using Statistical NLP in the sense of any corpus-based or quantitative method that uses counts from corpora, not just those that use the framework of probability theory. Transformation-based tagging clearly is a Statistical NLP method in this sense because transformations are selected based on a quantitative criterion.

However, the quantitative evaluation of transformations (by how much they improve the error rate) only occurs during training. Once learning is complete, transformation-based tagging is purely symbolic. That means that a transformation-based tagger can be converted into another symbolic object that is equivalent in terms of tagging performance, but has other advantageous properties like time efficiency.

This is the approach taken by Roche and Schabes (1995). They convert FINITE STATE TRANSDUCER a transformation-based tagger into an equivalent *finite state transducer*, a finite-state automaton that has a pair of symbols on each arc, one input symbol and one output symbol (in some cases several symbols can be output when an arc is traversed). A finite-state transducer passes over an input string and converts it into an output string by consuming the input symbols on the arcs it traverses and outputting the output symbols on the same arcs.

The construction algorithm proposed by Roche and Schabes has four steps. First, each transformation is converted into a finite-state trans-

ducer. Second, the transducer is converted into its *local extension*. Simply put, the local extension f_2 of a transducer f_1 is constructed such that running f_2 on an input string in one pass has the same effect as running f_1 on each position of the input string. This step takes care of cases like the following. Suppose we have a transducer that implements the transformation "replace A by B if one of the two preceding symbols is C." This transducer will have one arc with the input symbol A and the output symbol B. So for an input sequence like "CAA" we have to run it twice (at the second and third position) to correctly transduce "CAA" to "CBB." The local extension is constructed such that one pass will do this conversion.

In the third step, we compose all transducers into one single transducer whose effect is the same as running the individual transducers in sequence. This single transducer is generally non-deterministic. Whenever this transducer has to keep an event (like "C occurred at position i") in memory it will do this by launching two paths one assuming that a tag affected by a preceding C will occur later, one assuming that no such tag will occur. The appropriate path will be pursued further, the inappropriate path will be 'killed off' at the appropriate position in the string. This type of indeterminism is not efficient, so the fourth step is to convert the non-deterministic transducer into a deterministic one. This is not possible in general since non-deterministic transducers can keep events in memory for an arbitrary long sequence, which cannot be done by deterministic transducers. However, Roche and Schabes show that the transformations used in transformation-based tagging do not give rise to transducers with this property. We can therefore always transform a transformation-based tagger into a deterministic finite-state transducer.

The great advantage of a deterministic finite-state transducer is speed. A transformation-based tagger can take RKn elementary steps to tag a text where R is the number of transformations, K is the length of the triggering environment, and n is the length of the input text (Roche and Schabes 1995: 231). In contrast, finite-state transducers are linear in the length of the input text with a much smaller constant. Basically, we only hop from one state to the next as we read a word, look up its most likely tag (the initial state) and output the correct tag. This makes speeds of several tens of thousands of words per second possible. The speed of Markov model taggers can be an order of magnitude lower. This means that transducer-based tagging adds a very small overhead to operations like reading the input text from disk and its time demands are likely to be negligible compared to subsequent processing steps like parsing or message understanding.

There has also been work on transforming Hidden Markov models into finite state transducers (Kempe 1997). But, in this case, we cannot achieve complete equivalence since automata cannot perfectly mimic the floating point operations that need to be computed for the Viterbi algorithm.

10.4.5 Summary

The great advantage of transformation-based tagging is that it can condition tagging decisions on a richer set of events than the probabilistic models we looked at earlier. For example, information from the left and right can be used simultaneously and individual words (not just their tags) can influence the tagging of neighboring words. One reason transformation-based tagging can accommodate this richer set of triggering environments is probably that it primarily deals with binary information, which is less complex than probabilities.

It has also been claimed that transformations are easier to understand and modify than the transition and word generation probabilities in probabilistic tagging. However, it can be quite hard to foresee the effect of changing one transformation in a sequence, since complex interactions can occur when several dozen transformations are applied in sequence and each depends on the output of the previous one.

Work on the theoretical foundations of transformation-based tagging is still on-going. For example, the fact that transformation-based learning seems remarkably resistant to overfitting is so far an empirical result that is not well understood.

Even so, both learning and tagging are remarkably simple and intuitive in transformation-based tagging. Whether this simplicity is the principal criterion for choosing between a transformation-based or a probabilistic tagger, or whether the strength of probabilistic models in dealing with uncertainty and certain types of prior knowledge are more important considerations will depend on many factors such as what type of system the tagger is a component of and whether those working on this system are more comfortable with rule-based or probabilistic approaches.

Apart from tagging, transformation-based learning has also been applied to parsing (Brill 1993b), prepositional phrase attachment (Brill and Resnik 1994), and word sense disambiguation (Dini et al. 1998).

Exercise 10.16   [⋆]

Transformation-based learning is a form of greedy search. Is greedy search expected to find the optimal sequence of transformations? What would be alternatives?

Exercise 10.17   [⋆]

Most of the triggering environments in Brill (1995a) refer to preceding context. Why? Would you expect the same tendency for languages other than English?

Exercise 10.18   [⋆]

The set of possible triggering environments for words and tags is different in (Brill 1995a). For example, "one of the three preceding tags is X" is admissible as a triggering environment, but not "one of the three preceding words is X." What might be the reason for this difference? Consider the differences between the sizes of the search spaces for words and tags.

Exercise 10.19   [⋆]

Apart from choosing the most frequent tag as initialization, we can also assign all words to the same tag (say, NN) or use the output of another tagger which the transformation-based tagger can then improve. Discuss relative advantages of different initializations.

Exercise 10.20   [⋆⋆]

Get the Brill tagger (see pointer on website) and tag texts from the website.

10.5   Other Methods, Other Languages

10.5.1   Other approaches to tagging

Tagging has been one of the most active areas of research in NLP in the last ten years. We were only able to cover three of the most important approaches here. Many other probabilistic and quantitative methods have been applied to tagging, including all the methods we cover in chapter 16: neural networks (Benello et al. 1989), decision trees (Schmid 1994), memory-based learning (or k nearest neighbor approaches) (Daelemans et al. 1996), and maximum entropy models (Ratnaparkhi 1996).[4]

---

4. Ratnaparkhi's tagger, one of the highest performing statistical taggers, is publicly available. See the website.

There has also been work on how to construct a tagged corpus with a minimum of human effort (Brill et al. 1990). This problem poses itself when a language with as yet no tagged training corpus needs to be tackled or when in the case of already tagged languages we encounter text that is so different as to make existing tagged corpora useless.

Finally, some researchers have explored ways of constructing a tag set automatically in order to create syntactic categories that are appropriate for a language or a particular text sort (Schütze 1995; McMahon and Smith 1996).

10.5.2 Languages other than English

We have only covered part-of-speech tagging of English here. It turns out that English is a particularly suitable language for methods that try to infer a word's grammatical category from its position in a sequence of words. In many other languages, word order is much freer, and the surrounding words will contribute much less information about part of speech. However, in most such languages, the rich inflections of a word contribute more information about part of speech than happens in English. A full evaluation of taggers as useful preprocessors for high-level multilingual NLP tasks will only be possible after sufficient experimental results from a wide range of languages are available.

Despite these reservations, there exist now quite a number of tagging studies, at least for European languages. These studies suggest that the accuracy for other languages is comparable with that for English (Dermatas and Kokkinakis 1995; Kempe 1997), although it is hard to make such comparisons due to the incomparability of tag sets (tag sets are not universal, but all encode the particular functional categories of individual languages).

10.6 Tagging Accuracy and Uses of Taggers

10.6.1 Tagging accuracy

Accuracy numbers currently reported for tagging are most often in the range of 95% to 97%, when calculated over all words. Some authors give accuracy for ambiguous words only, in which case the accuracy figures are of course lower. However, performance depends considerably on factors such as the following.

- **The amount of training data available.** In general, the more the better.

- **The tag set.** Normally, the larger the tag set, the more potential ambiguity, and the harder the tagging task (but see the discussion in section 4.3.2). For example, some tag sets make a distinction between the preposition *to* and the infinitive marker *to*, and some don't. Using the latter tag set, one can't tag *to* wrongly.

- **The difference between training corpus and dictionary on the one hand and the corpus of application on the other.** If training and application text are drawn from the same source (for example, the same time period of a particular newspaper), then accuracy will be high. Normally the only results presented for taggers in research papers present results from this situation. If the application text is from a later time period, from a different source, or even from a different genre than the training text (e.g., scientific text vs. newspaper text), then performance can be poor.[5]

- **Unknown words.** A special case of the last point is coverage of the dictionary. The occurrence of many unknown words will greatly degrade performance. The percentage of words not in the dictionary can be very high when trying to tag material from some technical domain.

A change in any of these four conditions will impact tagging accuracy, sometimes dramatically. If the training set is small, the tag set large, the test corpus significantly different from the training corpus, or we are confronted with a larger than expected number of unknown words, then performance can be far below the performance range cited above. It is important to stress that these types of external conditions often have a stronger influence on performance than the choice of tagging method – especially when differences between methods reported are on the order of half a percent.

The influence of external factors also needs to be considered when we evaluate the surprisingly high performance of a 'dumb' tagger which always chooses a word's most frequent tag. Such a tagger can get an accuracy of about 90% in favorable conditions (Charniak et al. 1993). This high number is less surprising when we learn that the dictionary that was used in (Charniak et al. 1993) is based on the corpus of application, the

---

5. See Elworthy (1994) and Samuelsson and Voutilainen (1997) for experiments looking at performance for different degrees of similarity to the training set.

Brown corpus. Considerable manual effort went into the resources that make it now easy to determine what the most frequent tag for a word in the Brown corpus is. So it is not surprising that a tagger exploiting this dictionary information does well. The automatic tagger that was originally used to preprocess the Brown corpus only achieved 77% accuracy (Greene and Rubin 1971). In part this was due to its non-probabilistic nature, but in large part this was due to the fact that it could not rely on a large dictionary giving the frequency with which words are used in different parts of speech that was suitable for the corpus of application.

Even in cases where we have a good dictionary and the most-frequent-tag strategy works well, it is still important how well a tagger does in the range from 90% correct to 100% correct. For example, a tagger with 97% accuracy has a 63% chance of getting all tags in a 15-word sentence right, compared to 74% for a tagger with 98% accuracy. So even small improvements can make a significant difference in an application.

One of the best-performing tagging formalisms is non-quantitative: EngCG (*English Constraint Grammar*), developed at the University of Helsinki. Samuelsson and Voutilainen (1997) show that it performs better than Markov model taggers, especially if training and test corpora are not from the same source.[6] In EngCG, hand-written rules are compiled into finite-state automata (Karlsson et al. 1995; Voutilainen 1995). The basic idea is somewhat similar to transformation-based learning, except that a human being (instead of an algorithm) iteratively modifies a set of tagging rules so as to minimize the error rate. In each iteration, the current rule set is run on the corpus and an attempt is made to modify the rules so that the most serious errors are handled correctly. This methodology amounts to writing a small expert system for tagging. The claim has been made that for somebody who is familiar with the methodology, writing this type of tagger takes no more effort than building an HMM tagger (Chanod and Tapanainen 1995), though it could be argued that the methodology for HMM tagging is more easily accessible.

ENGLISH CONSTRAINT GRAMMAR

We conclude our remarks on tagging accuracy by giving examples of some of the most frequent errors. Table 10.9 shows some examples of common error types reported by Kupiec (1992b). The example phrases and fragments are all ambiguous, demonstrating that semantic context,

---

6. The accuracy figures for EngCG reported in the paper are better than 99% vs. better than 95% for a Markov Model tagger, but comparison is difficult since some ambiguities are not resolved by EngCG. EngCG returns a set of more than one tag in some cases.

Correct tag	Tagging error	Example
noun singular	adjective	*an executive order*
adjective	adverb	*more important issues*
preposition	particle	*He ran up a big . . .*
past tense	past participle	*loan needed to meet*
past participle	past tense	*loan needed to meet*

Table 10.9 Examples of frequent errors of probabilistic taggers.

or more syntactic context is necessary than a Markov model has access to. Syntactically, the word *executive* could be an adjective as well as a noun. The phrase *more important issues* could refer to a larger number of important issues or to issues that are more important. The word *up* is used as a preposition in *running up a hill*, as a particle in *running up a bill*. Finally, depending on the embedding, *needed* can be a past participle or a past tense form as the following two sentences from (Kupiec 1992b) show:

(10.12)   a. The loan needed to meet rising costs of health care.

            b. They cannot now handle the loan needed to meet rising costs of health care.

CONFUSION MATRIX   Table 10.10 shows a portion of a *confusion matrix* for the tagger described in (Franz 1995). Each row shows the percentage of the time words of a certain category were given different tags by the tagger. In a way the results are unsurprising. The errors occur in the cases where multiple class memberships are common. Particularly to be noted, however, is the low accuracy of tagging particles, which are all word types that can also act as prepositions. The distinction between particles and prepositions, while real, is quite subtle, and some people feel that it is not made very accurately even in hand-tagged corpora.[7]

10.6.2   Applications of tagging

The widespread interest in tagging is founded on the belief that many NLP applications will benefit from syntactically disambiguated text. Given this

---

7. Hence, as we shall see in chapter 12, it is often ignored in the evaluation of probabilistic parsers.

Correct	Tags assigned by the tagger							
Tags	DT	IN	JJ	NN	RB	RP	VB	VBG
DT	99.4	.3			.3			
IN	.4	97.5			1.5	.5		
JJ		.1	93.9	1.8	.9		.1	.4
NN			2.2	95.5			.2	.4
RB	.2	2.4	2.2	.6	93.2	1.2		
RP		24.7		1.1	12.6	61.5		
VB			.3	1.4			96.0	
VBG			2.5	4.4				93.0

Table 10.10 A portion of a confusion matrix for part of speech tagging. For each tag, a row of the table shows the percentage of the time that the tagger assigned tokens of that category to different tags. (Thus, in the full confusion matrix, the percentages in each row would add to 100%, but do not do so here, because only a portion of the table is shown.). Based on (Franz 1995).

ultimate motivation for part-of-speech tagging, it is surprising that there seem to be more papers on stand-alone tagging than on applying tagging to a task of immediate interest. We summarize here the most important applications for which taggers have been used.

PARTIAL PARSING   Most applications require an additional step of processing after tagging: *partial parsing*. Partial parsing can refer to various levels of detail of syntactic analysis. The simplest partial parsers are limited to finding the noun phrases of a sentence. More sophisticated approaches assign grammatical functions to noun phrases (subject, direct object, indirect object) and give partial information on attachments, for example, 'this noun phrase is attached to another (unspecified) phrase to the right'.

There is an elegant way of using Markov models for noun phrase recognition (see (Church 1988), but a better description can be found in (Abney 1996a)). We can take the output of the tagger and form a sequence of tag bigrams. For example, NN VBZ RB AT NN would be transformed into NN-VBZ VBZ-RB RB-AT AT-NN. This sequence of tag bigrams is then tagged with five symbols: noun-phrase-beginning, noun-phrase-end, noun-phrase-interior, noun-phrase-exterior (that is, this tag bigram is not part of a noun phrase), and between-noun-phrases (that is, at the position of this tag bigram there is a noun phrase immediately to the right and a noun phrase immediately to the left). The noun phrases are then all sequences of tags between a noun-phrase-beginning symbol (or a between-noun-phrases symbol) and a noun-phrase-end symbol (or a between-noun-phrases symbol), with noun-phrase-interior symbols in between.

The best known approaches to partial parsing are Fidditch, developed in the early eighties by Hindle (1994), and an approach called "parsing by chunks" developed by Abney (1991). These two systems do not use taggers because they predate the widespread availability of taggers. See also (Grefenstette 1994). Two approaches that are more ambitious than current partial parsers and attempt to bridge the gap between shallow and full parsing are the XTAG system (Doran et al. 1994) and chunk tagging (Brants and Skut 1998; Skut and Brants 1998).

In many systems that build a partial parser on top of a tagger, partial parsing is accomplished by way of regular expression matching over the output of the tagger. For example, a simple noun phrase may be defined as a sequence of article (AT), an arbitrary number of adjectives (JJ) and a singular noun (NN). This would correspond to the regular expression "AT JJ* NN." Since these systems focus on the final application, not on partial parsing we cover them in what follows not under the rubric "partial parsing," but grouped according to the application they are intended for. For an excellent overview of partial parsing (and tagging) see (Abney 1996a).

One important use of tagging in conjunction with partial parsing is for *lexical acquisition*. We refer the reader to chapter 8.

INFORMATION
EXTRACTION

Another important application is *information extraction* (which is also referred to as message understanding, data extraction, or text data mining). The goal in information extraction is to find values for the predefined slots of a template. For example, a template for weather reporting might have slots for the type of weather condition (tornado, snow storm), the location of the event (the San Francisco Bay Area), the time of the event (Sunday, January 11, 1998), and what the effect of the event was (power outage, traffic accidents, etc.). Tagging and partial parsing help identify the entities that serve as slot fillers and the relationships between them. A recent overview article on information extraction is (Cardie 1997). In a way one could think of information extraction as like tagging except that the tags are semantic categories, not grammatical parts of speech. However, in practice quite different techniques tend to be employed, because local sequences give less information about semantic categories than grammatical categories.

Tagging and partial parsing can also be applied to finding good indexing terms in information retrieval. The best unit for matching user queries and documents is often not the individual word. Phrases like *United States of America* and *secondary education* lose much of their meaning if they are broken up into words. Information retrieval performance can be improved if tagging and partial parsing are applied to noun phrase recognition and query-document matching is done on more meaningful units than individual terms (Fagan 1987; Smeaton 1992; Strzalkowski 1995). A related area of research is phrase normalization in which variants of terms are normalized and represented as the same basic unit (for example, *book publishing* and *publishing of books*). See (Jacquemin et al. 1997).

QUESTION ANSWERING   Finally, there has been work on so-called *question answering* systems which try to answer a user query that is formulated in the form of a question by returning an appropriate noun phrase such as a location, a person, or a date (Kupiec 1993b; Burke et al. 1997). For example, the question *Who killed President Kennedy?* might be answered with the noun phrase *Oswald* instead of returning a list of documents as most information retrieval systems do. Again, analyzing a query in order to determine what type of entity the user is looking for and how it is related to other noun phrases mentioned in the question requires tagging and partial parsing.

We conclude with a negative result: the best lexicalized probabilistic parsers are now good enough that they perform better starting with untagged text and doing the tagging themselves, rather than using a tagger as a preprocessor (Charniak 1997a). Therefore, the role of taggers appears to be as a fast lightweight component that gives sufficient information for many application tasks, rather than as a desirable preprocessing stage for all applications.

10.7 Further Reading

Early work on modeling natural language using Markov chains had been largely abandoned by the early sixties, partially due to Chomsky's criticism of the inadequacies of Markov models (Chomsky 1957: ch. 3). The lack of training data and computing resources to pursue an 'empirical' approach to natural language probably also played a role. Chomsky's criticism still applies: Markov chains cannot fully model natural language, in particular they cannot model many recursive structures (but cf. Ristad and Thomas (1997)). What has changed is that approaches that emphasize technical goals such as solving a particular task have become acceptable even if they are not founded on a theory that fully explains language as a cognitive phenomenon.

The earliest 'taggers' were simply programs that looked up the category of words in a dictionary. The first well-known program which attempted to assign tags based on syntagmatic contexts was the rule-based program presented in (Klein and Simmons 1963), though roughly the same idea is present in (Salton and Thorpe 1962). Klein and Simmons use the terms 'tags' and 'tagging,' though apparently interchangeably with 'codes' and 'coding.' The earliest probabilistic tagger known to us is (Stolz et al. 1965). This program initially assigned tags to some words (including all function words) via use of a lexicon, morphology rules, and other ad-hoc rules. The remaining open class words were then tagged using conditional probabilities calculated from tag sequences. Needless to say, this wasn't a well-founded probabilistic model.

Credit has to be given to two groups, one at Brown University, one at the University of Lancaster, who spent enormous resources to tag two large corpora, the Brown corpus and the Lancaster-Oslo-Bergen (LOB) corpus. Both groups recognized how invaluable a corpus annotated with tag information would be for further corpus research. Without these two tagged corpora, progress on part-of-speech tagging would have been hard if not impossible. The availability of a large quantity of tagged data is no doubt an important reason that tagging has been such an active area of research.

The Brown corpus was automatically pre-tagged with a rule-based tagger, TAGGIT (Greene and Rubin 1971). This tagger used lexical information only to limit the tags of words and only applied tagging rules when words in the surrounding context were unambiguously tagged. The output of the tagger was then manually corrected in an effort that took many years and supplied the training data for a lot of the quantitative work that was done later.

One of the first Markov Model taggers was created at the University of Lancaster as part of the LOB tagging effort (Garside et al. 1987; Marshall 1987). The heart of this tagger was the use of bigram tag sequence probabilities, with limited use of higher order context, but the differing probabilities of assigning a word to different parts of speech were handled by ad hoc discounting factors. The type of Markov Model tagger that tags based on both word probabilities and tag transition probabilities was introduced by Church (1988) and DeRose (1988).

During the beginning of the resurgence of quantitative methods in NLP, the level of knowledge of probability theory in the NLP community was so low that a frequent error in early papers is to compute the probability of the next tag in a Markov model as (10.14) instead of (10.13). At first sight, (10.14) can seem more intuitive. After all, we are looking at a word and want to determine its tag, so it is not far-fetched to assume the word as given and the tag as being conditioned on the word.

$$(10.13) \qquad \arg\max_{t_{1,n}} P(t_{1,n}|w_{1,n}) = \prod_{i=1}^{n} \left[P(w_i|t_i) \times P(t_i|t_{i-1}) \right]$$

$$(10.14) \qquad \arg\max_{t_{1,n}} P(t_{1,n}|w_{1,n}) = \prod_{i=1}^{n} \left[P(t_i|w_i) \times P(t_i|t_{i-1}) \right]$$

But, actually, equation (10.14) is not correct, and use of it results in lower performance (Charniak et al. 1993).

While the work of Church and DeRose was key in the resurgence of statistical methods in computational linguistics, work on hidden Markov model tagging had actually begun much earlier at the IBM research centers in New York state and Paris. Jelinek (1985) and Derouault and Merialdo (1986) are widely cited. Earlier references are Bahl and Mercer (1976) and Baker (1975), who attributes the work to Elaine Rich. Other early work in probabilistic tagging includes (Eeg-Olofsson 1985; Foster 1991).

DENOMINAL VERBS   A linguistic discussion of the conversion of nouns to verbs (*denominal verbs*) and its productivity can be found in Clark and Clark (1979). Huddleston (1984: ch. 3) contains a good discussion of the traditional definitions of parts of speech, their failings, and the notion of part of speech or word class as used in modern structuralist linguistics.

10.8   Exercises

Exercise 10.21   [⋆]

Usually, the text we want to tag is not segmented into sentences. An algorithm for identifying sentence boundaries is introduced in chapter 4, together with a general overview of the nitty-gritty of corpus processing.

Could we integrate sentence-boundary detection into the tagging methods introduced in this chapter? What would we have to change? How effective would you expect sentence-boundary detection by means of tagging to be?

Exercise 10.22   [★★]

Get the MULTEXT tagger (see the website) and tag some non-English text from the website.

11 Probabilistic Context Free Grammars

PEOPLE WRITE and say lots of different things, but the way people say things – even in drunken casual conversation – has some structure and regularity. The goal of syntax within linguistics is to try to isolate that structure. Until now, the only form of syntax we have allowed ourselves is methods for describing the ordering and arrangement of words, either directly in terms of the words, or in terms of word categories. In this chapter, we wish to escape the linear tyranny of these *n*-gram models and HMM tagging models, and to start to explore more complex notions of grammar.

Even in the most traditional forms of grammar, syntax is meant to show something more that just linear order. It shows how words group together and relate to each other as heads and dependents. The dominant method used for doing this within the last 50 or so years has been to place tree structures over sentences, as we saw in chapter 3. Language has a complex recursive structure, and such tree-based models – unlike Markov models – allow us to capture this. For instance Kupiec (1992b) notes that his HMM-based tagger has problems with constructions like:

(11.1)   The velocity of the seismic waves rises to . . .

because a singular verb (here, *rises*) is unexpected after a plural noun. Kupiec's solution is to augment the HMM model so it can recognize a rudimentary amount of NP structure, which in his model is encoded as a higher-order context extension glued on to his basic first order HMM. Leaving aside the technical details of the solution, the essential observation about verb agreement is that it is reflecting the hierarchical structure of the sentence, as shown in (11.2), and not the linear order of words.

(11.2)

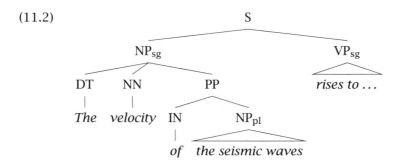

The verb agrees in number with the noun *velocity* which is the head of the preceding noun phrase, and not with the noun that linearly precedes it.

The simplest probabilistic model for recursive embedding is a *PCFG*, a *Probabilistic* (sometimes also called *Stochastic*) *Context Free Grammar* – which is simply a CFG with probabilities added to the rules, indicating how likely different rewritings are. We provide a detailed discussion of PCFGs in this chapter for a number of reasons: PCFGs are the simplest and most natural probabilistic model for tree structures, the mathematics behind them is well understood, the algorithms for them are a natural development of the algorithms employed with HMMs, and PCFGs provide a sufficiently general computational device that they can simulate various other forms of probabilistic conditioning (as we describe in section 12.1.9). Nevertheless, it is important to realize that PCFGs are only one of many ways of building probabilistic models of syntactic structure, and in the next chapter we study the domain of probabilistic parsing more generally.

A PCFG G consists of:

- A set of terminals, $\{w^k\}, k = 1, \ldots, V$

- A set of nonterminals, $\{N^i\}, i = 1, \ldots, n$

- A designated start symbol, N^1

- A set of rules, $\{N^i \rightarrow \zeta^j\}$, (where ζ^j is a sequence of terminals and nonterminals)

- A corresponding set of probabilities on rules such that:

(11.3) $\forall i \quad \sum_j P(N^i \rightarrow \zeta^j) = 1$

Notation	Meaning
G	Grammar (PCFG)
$\mathcal{L}$	Language (generated or accepted by a grammar)
t	Parse tree
$\{N^1, \ldots, N^n\}$	Nonterminal vocabulary (N^1 is start symbol)
$\{w^1, \ldots, w^V\}$	Terminal vocabulary
$w_1 \cdots w_m$	Sentence to be parsed
N_{pq}^j	Nonterminal N^j spans positions p through q in string
$\alpha_j(p, q)$	Outside probabilities (11.15)
$\beta_j(p, q)$	Inside probabilities (11.14)

Table 11.1 Notation for the PCFG chapter.

Note that when we write $P(N^i \to \zeta^j)$ in this chapter, we always mean $P(N^i \to \zeta^j | N^i)$. That is, we are giving the probability distribution of the daughters for a certain head. Such a grammar can be used either to parse or generate sentences of the language, and we will switch between these terminologies quite freely.

Before parsing sentences with a PCFG, we need to establish some notation. We will represent the sentence to be parsed as a sequence of words $w_1 \cdots w_m$, and use w_{ab} to denote the subsequence $w_a \cdots w_b$. We denote a single rewriting operation of the grammar by a single arrow $\to$. If as a result of one or more rewriting operations we are able to rewrite a nonterminal N^j as a sequence of words $w_a \cdots w_b$, then we will say DOMINATION that N^j *dominates* the words $w_a \cdots w_b$, and write either $N^j \stackrel{*}{\Rightarrow} w_a \cdots w_b$ or $\text{yield}(N^j) = w_a \cdots w_b$. This situation is illustrated in (11.4): a subtree with root nonterminal N^j dominating all and only the words from $w_a \cdots w_b$ in the string:

(11.4)

$$N^j$$

$$\overline{w_a \cdots w_b}$$

To say that a nonterminal N_j spans positions a through b in the string, but not to specify what words are actually contained in this subsequence, we will write N_{ab}^j. This notation is summarized in table 11.1.

The probability of a sentence (according to a grammar G) is given by:

(11.5) $\quad P(w_{1m}) \quad = \quad \sum_t P(w_{1m}, t) \quad$ where t is a parse tree of the sentence

S → NP VP	1.0	NP → NP PP	0.4
PP → P NP	1.0	NP → *astronomers*	0.1
VP → V NP	0.7	NP → *ears*	0.18
VP → VP PP	0.3	NP → *saw*	0.04
P → *with*	1.0	NP → *stars*	0.18
V → *saw*	1.0	NP → *telescopes*	0.1

Table 11.2 A simple Probabilistic Context Free Grammar (PCFG). The nonterminals are S, NP, PP, VP, P, V. We adopt the common convention whereby the start symbol N^1 is denoted by S. The terminals are the words in italics. The table shows the grammar rules and their probabilities. The slightly unusual NP rules have been chosen so that this grammar is in Chomsky Normal Form, for use as an example later in the section.

$$= \sum_{\{t:\text{yield}(t)=w_{1m}\}} P(t)$$

Moreover, it is easy to find the probability of a tree in a PCFG model. One just multiplies the probabilities of the rules that built its local subtrees.

Example 1:   Assuming the grammar in table 11.2, the sentence *astronomers saw stars with ears* has two parses with probabilities as shown in figure 11.1.

What are the assumptions of this model? The conditions that we need are:

- Place invariance. The probability of a subtree does not depend on where in the string the words it dominates are (this is like time invariance in HMMs):

(11.6) $\forall k \quad P(N^j_{k(k+c)} \to \zeta)$ is the same

- Context-free. The probability of a subtree does not depend on words not dominated by the subtree.

(11.7) $P(N^j_{kl} \to \zeta | \text{anything outside } k \text{ through } l) = P(N^j_{kl} \to \zeta)$

- Ancestor-free. The probability of a subtree does not depend on nodes in the derivation outside the subtree.

(11.8) $P(N^j_{kl} \to \zeta | \text{any ancestor nodes outside } N^j_{kl}) = P(N^j_{kl} \to \zeta)$

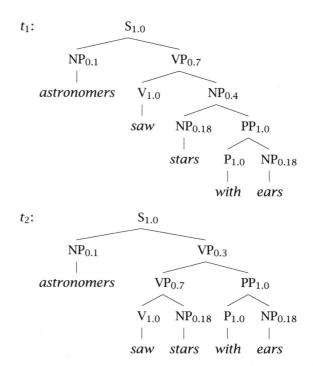

$$P(t_1) \; = \; 1.0 \times 0.1 \times 0.7 \times 1.0 \times 0.4 \times 0.18 \times 1.0 \times 1.0 \times 0.18$$
$$= \; 0.0009072$$
$$P(t_2) \; = \; 1.0 \times 0.1 \times 0.3 \times 0.7 \times 1.0 \times 0.18 \times 1.0 \times 1.0 \times 0.18$$
$$= \; 0.0006804$$
$$P(w_{15}) \; = \; P(t_1) + P(t_2) = 0.0015876$$

Figure 11.1 The two parse trees, their probabilities, and the sentence probability. This is for the sentence *astronomers saw stars with ears*, according to the grammar in table 11.2. Nonterminal nodes in the trees have been subscripted with the probability of the local tree that they head.

Using these conditions we can justify the calculation of the probability of a tree in terms of just multiplying probabilities attached to rules. But to show an example, we need to be able to distinguish tokens of a nonterminal. Therefore, let the upper left index in $^iN^j$ be an arbitrary identifying index for a particular token of a nonterminal. Then,

$$P\left(\begin{array}{c} ^1\text{S} \\ ^2\text{NP} \quad ^3\text{VP} \\ \textit{the} \ \ \textit{man} \ \ \textit{snores} \end{array}\right)$$

$$= \ P(^1\text{S}_{13} \rightarrow {}^2\text{NP}_{12}\,{}^3\text{VP}_{33}, {}^2\text{NP}_{12} \rightarrow \textit{the}_1\,\textit{man}_2, {}^3\text{VP}_{33} \rightarrow \textit{snores}_3)$$

$$= \ P(^1\text{S}_{13} \rightarrow {}^2\text{NP}_{12}\,{}^3\text{VP}_{33})P(^2\text{NP}_{12} \rightarrow \textit{the}_1\,\textit{man}_2 \mid {}^1\text{S}_{13} \rightarrow {}^2\text{NP}_{12}\,{}^3\text{VP}_{33})$$

$$\qquad P(^3\text{VP}_{33} \rightarrow \textit{snores}_3 \mid {}^1\text{S}_{13} \rightarrow {}^2\text{NP}_{12}\,{}^3\text{VP}_{33}, {}^2\text{NP}_{12} \rightarrow \textit{the}_1\,\textit{man}_2)$$

$$= \ P(^1\text{S}_{13} \rightarrow {}^2\text{NP}_{12}\,{}^3\text{VP}_{33})P(^2\text{NP}_{12} \rightarrow \textit{the}_1\,\textit{man}_2)P(^3\text{VP}_{33} \rightarrow \textit{snores}_3)$$

$$= \ P(\text{S} \rightarrow \text{NP VP})P(\text{NP} \rightarrow \textit{the man})P(\text{VP} \rightarrow \textit{snores})$$

where, after expanding the probability by the chain rule, we impose first the context-freeness assumption, and then the position-invariant assumption.

11.1 Some Features of PCFGs

Here we give some reasons to use a PCFG, and also some idea of their limitations:

- As grammars expand to give coverage of a large and diverse corpus of text, the grammars become increasingly ambiguous. There start to be many structurally different parses for most word sequences. A PCFG gives some idea of the plausibility of different parses.

- A PCFG does not give a very good idea of the plausibility of different parses, since its probability estimates are based purely on structural factors, and do not factor in lexical co-occurrence.

GRAMMAR INDUCTION

IDENTIFICATION IN
THE LIMIT

NEGATIVE EVIDENCE

- PCFGs are good for *grammar induction*. Gold (1967) showed that CFGs cannot be learned (in the sense of *identification in the limit* – that is, whether one can identify a grammar if one is allowed to see as much data produced by the grammar as one wants) without the use of *negative evidence* (the provision of ungrammatical examples). But PCFGs can be learned from positive data alone (Horning 1969). (However, doing grammar induction from scratch is still a difficult, largely unsolved problem, and hence much emphasis has been placed on learning from bracketed corpora, as we will see in chapter 12.)

- Robustness. Real text tends to have grammatical mistakes, disfluencies, and errors. This problem can be avoided to some extent with a PCFG by ruling out nothing in the grammar, but by just giving implausible sentences a low probability.

- PCFGs give a probabilistic language model for English (whereas a CFG does not).

- The predictive power of a PCFG as measured by entropy tends to be greater than that for a finite state grammar (i.e., an HMM) with the same number of parameters. (For such comparisons, we compute the number of parameters as follows. A V terminal, n nonterminal PCFG has $n^3 + nV$ parameters, while a K state M output HMM has $K^2 + MK$ parameters. While the exponent is higher in the PCFG case, the number of nonterminals used is normally quite small. See Lari and Young (1990) for a discussion of this with respect to certain artificial grammars.)

- In practice, a PCFG is a worse language model for English than an n-gram model (for $n > 1$). An n-gram model takes some local lexical context into account, while a PCFG uses none.

- PCFGs are not good models by themselves, but we could hope to combine the strengths of a PCFG and a trigram model. An early experiment that conditions the rules of a PCFG by word trigrams (and some additional context sensitive knowledge of the tree) is presented in Magerman and Marcus (1991) and Magerman and Weir (1992). Better solutions are discussed in chapter 12.

- PCFGs have certain biases, which may not be appropriate. All else being equal, in a PCFG, the probability of a smaller tree is greater than a larger tree. This is not totally wild – it is consonant with Frazier's (1978) Minimal Attachment heuristic – but it does not give a sensible model of actual sentences, which peak in frequency at some intermediate length. For instance, table 4.3 showed that the most frequent length for *Wall Street Journal* sentences is around 23 words. A PCFG gives too much of the probability mass to very short sentences. Similarly, all else being equal, nonterminals with a small number of expansions will be favored over nonterminals with many expansions in PCFG parsing, since the individual rewritings will have much higher probability (see exercise 12.3).

The one item here that deserves further comment is the claim that PCFGs define a language model. Initially, one might suspect that providing that the rules all obey equation (11.3), then $\sum_{\omega \in \mathcal{L}} P(\omega) = \sum_t P(t) = 1$. But actually this is only true if the *probability mass of rules* is accumulating in finite derivations. For instance, consider the grammar:

PROBABILITY MASS OF RULES

(11.9) $S \rightarrow rhubarb \quad P = \frac{1}{3}$

$S \rightarrow S\ S \qquad P = \frac{2}{3}$

This grammar will generate all strings *rhubarb ... rhubarb*. However, we find that the probability of those strings is:

(11.10) *rhubarb* $\qquad\qquad\qquad \frac{1}{3}$

rhubarb rhubarb $\qquad\qquad \frac{2}{3} \times \frac{1}{3} \times \frac{1}{3} = \frac{2}{27}$

rhubarb rhubarb rhubarb $\quad \left(\frac{2}{3}\right)^2 \times \left(\frac{1}{3}\right)^3 \times 2 = \frac{8}{243}$

...

The probability of the language is the sum of this infinite series $\frac{1}{3} + \frac{2}{27} + \frac{8}{243} + \ldots$, which turns out to be $\frac{1}{2}$. Thus half the probability mass has disappeared into infinite trees which do not generate strings of the language! Such a distribution is often termed *inconsistent* in the probability literature, but since this word has a rather different meaning in other fields related to NLP, we will term such a distribution *improper*. In practice, improper distributions are not much of a problem. Often, it doesn't really matter if probability distributions are improper, especially if we are mainly only comparing the magnitude of different probability estimates. Moreover, providing we estimate our PCFG parameters from parsed training corpora (see chapter 12), Chi and Geman (1998) show that one always gets a proper probability distribution.

INCONSISTENT

IMPROPER

11.2 Questions for PCFGs

Just as for HMMs, there are three basic questions we wish to answer:

- What is the probability of a sentence w_{1m} according to a grammar G: $P(w_{1m}|G)$?

- What is the most likely parse for a sentence: $\arg\max_t P(t|w_{1m}, G)$?

- How can we choose rule probabilities for the grammar G that maximize the probability of a sentence, $\arg\max_G P(w_{1m}|G)$?

CHOMSKY NORMAL FORM   In this chapter, we will only consider the case of *Chomsky Normal Form* grammars, which only have unary and binary rules of the form:

$$N^i \rightarrow N^j\ N^k$$
$$N^i \rightarrow w^j$$

The parameters of a PCFG in Chomsky Normal Form are:

(11.11) $P(N^j \rightarrow N^r\ N^s|G)$ If n nonterminals, an n^3 matrix of parameters
          $P(N^j \rightarrow w^k|G)$ If V terminals, nV parameters

For $j = 1, \ldots, n$,

(11.12) $$\sum_{r,s} P(N^j \rightarrow N^r\ N^s) + \sum_k P(N^j \rightarrow w^k) = 1$$

This constraint is seen to be satisfied for the grammar in table 11.2 (under the convention whereby all probabilities not shown are zero). Any CFG can be represented by a weakly equivalent CFG in Chomsky Normal Form.[1]

PROBABILISTIC REGULAR GRAMMARS   To see how we might efficiently compute probabilities for PCFGs, let us work from HMMs to *probabilistic regular grammars*, and then from there to PCFGs. Consider a probabilistic regular grammar (PRG), which has rules of the form:

$$N^i \rightarrow w^j\ N^k \quad \text{or} \quad N^i \rightarrow w^j \quad \text{and start state } N^1$$

This is similar to what we had for an HMM. The difference is that in an HMM there is a probability distribution over strings of a certain length:

$$\forall n \quad \sum_{w_{1n}} P(w_{1n}) = 1$$

---

1. Two grammars G_1 and G_2 are *weakly equivalent* if they both generate the same language $\mathcal{L}$ (with the same probabilities on sentences for stochastic equivalence). Two grammars are *strongly equivalent* if they additionally assign sentences the same tree structures (with the same probabilities, for the stochastic case).

Figure 11.2   A Probabilistic Regular Grammar (PRG).

whereas in a PCFG or a PRG, there is a probability distribution over the set of all strings that are in the language $\mathcal{L}$ generated by the grammar:

$$\sum_{\omega \in \mathcal{L}} P(\omega) = 1$$

To see the difference, consider:

P(John decided to bake a)

This would have a high probability in an HMM, since this is a quite likely beginning to a sentence, but a very low probability in a PRG or a PCFG, because it isn't a complete utterance.

We can think of a PRG as related to an HMM roughly as in figure 11.2. We add a start state and the transitions from it to the states of the HMM mirror the initial probabilities Π. To represent ending the string, we ad-SINK STATE   join to the HMM a finish state, often called a *sink state*, which one never leaves once one has entered it. From each HMM state one can continue in the basic HMM or shift to the sink state, which we interpret as the end of string in the PRG.

This gives the basic idea of how PRGs are related to HMMs. We can implement the PRG as an HMM where the states are nonterminals and the terminals are the output symbols, as follows:

States: NP $\longrightarrow$ N′ $\longrightarrow$ N′ $\longrightarrow$ N′ $\longrightarrow$ sink state
            | | | |
Outputs: *the*   *big*   *brown*   *box*

Recall how for an HMM we were able to efficiently do calculations in terms of forward and backward probabilities:

Forward probability $\alpha_i(t)$ = $P(w_{1(t-1)}, X_t = i)$
Backward probability $\beta_i(t)$ = $P(w_{tT} | X_t = i)$

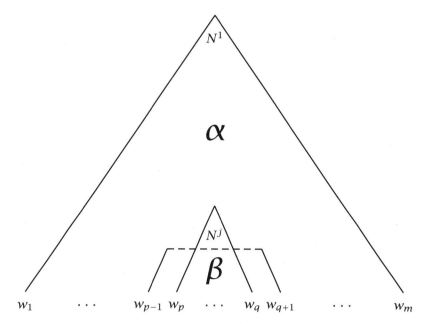

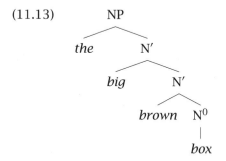

Figure 11.3   Inside and outside probabilities in PCFGs.

But now consider the PRG parse again, drawn as a tree:

(11.13)

In the tree, the forward probability corresponds to the probability of everything above and including a certain node, while the backward probability corresponds to the probability of everything below a certain node (given the node). This suggests an approach to dealing with the more general case of PCFGs. We introduce Inside and Outside probabilities, as indicated in figure 11.3, and defined as follows:

(11.14)   Outside probability $\alpha_j(p,q)$ = $P(w_{1(p-1)}, N_{pq}^j, w_{(q+1)m}|G)$

(11.15)   Inside probability $\beta_j(p,q)$ = $P(w_{pq}|N_{pq}^j, G)$

The inside probability $\beta_j(p,q)$ is the total probability of generating words $w_p \cdots w_q$ given that one is starting off with the nonterminal N^j. The outside probability $\alpha_j(p,q)$ is the total probability of beginning with the start symbol N^1 and generating the nonterminal N_{pq}^j and all the words outside $w_p \cdots w_q$.

11.3   The Probability of a String

11.3.1   Using inside probabilities

In general, we cannot efficiently calculate the probability of a string by simply summing the probabilities of all possible parse trees for the string, as there will be exponentially many of them. An efficient way to calcu-
INSIDE ALGORITHM   late the total probability of a string is by the *inside algorithm*, a dynamic programming algorithm based on the inside probabilities:

(11.16) $P(w_{1m}|G)$ $= P(N^1 \stackrel{*}{\Rightarrow} w_{1m}|G)$

(11.17) $= P(w_{1m}|N_{1m}^1, G)$ $= \beta_1(1,m)$

The inside probability of a substring is calculated by induction on the length of the string subsequence:

Base case: We want to find $\beta_j(k,k)$ (the probability of a rule $N^j \rightarrow w_k$):

$\beta_j(k,k)$ = $P(w_k|N_{kk}^j, G)$

                = $P(N^j \rightarrow w_k|G)$

Induction: We want to find $\beta_j(p,q)$, for $p < q$. As this is the inductive step using a Chomsky Normal Form grammar, the first rule must be of the form $N^j \rightarrow N^r \, N^s$, so we can proceed by induction, dividing the string in two in various places and summing the result:

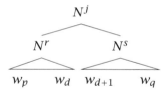

Then, $\forall j, 1 \leq p < q \leq m$,

$$
\begin{aligned}
\beta_j(p,q) &= P(w_{pq}|N_{pq}^j, G) \\
&= \sum_{r,s}\sum_{d=p}^{q-1} P(w_{pd}, N_{pd}^r, w_{(d+1)q}, N_{(d+1)q}^s|N_{pq}^j, G) \\
&= \sum_{r,s}\sum_{d=p}^{q-1} P(N_{pd}^r, N_{(d+1)q}^s|N_{pq}^j, G)P(w_{pd}|N_{pq}^j, N_{pd}^r, N_{(d+1)q}^s, G) \\
&\qquad \times P(w_{(d+1)q}|N_{pq}^j, N_{pd}^r, N_{(d+1)q}^s, w_{pd}, G) \\
&= \sum_{r,s}\sum_{d=p}^{q-1} P(N_{pd}^r, N_{(d+1)q}^s|N_{pq}^j, G)P(w_{pd}|N_{pd}^r, G) \\
&\qquad \times P(w_{(d+1)q}|N_{(d+1)q}^s, G) \\
&= \sum_{r,s}\sum_{d=p}^{q-1} P(N^j \to N^r N^s)\beta_r(p,d)\beta_s(d+1, q)
\end{aligned}
$$

Above, we first divided things up using the chain rule, then we made use of the context-free assumptions of PCFGs, and then rewrote the result using the definition of the inside probabilities. Using this recurrence relation, inside probabilities can be efficiently calculated bottom up.

Example 2: The above equation looks scary, but the calculation of inside probabilities is actually relatively straightforward. We're just trying to find all ways that a certain constituent can be built out of two smaller constituents by varying what the labels of the two smaller constituents are and which words each spans. In table 11.3, we show the computations of inside probabilities using the grammar of table 11.2 and the sentence explored in figure 11.1. The computations are shown using a *parse triangle* where each box records nodes that span from the row index to the column index.

PARSE TRIANGLE

▼ Further calculations using this example grammar and sentence are left to the reader in the Exercises.

	1	2	3	4	5
1	$\beta_{NP} = 0.1$		$\beta_S = 0.0126$		$\beta_S = 0.0015876$
2		$\beta_{NP} = 0.04$ $\beta_V = 1.0$	$\beta_{VP} = 0.126$		$\beta_{VP} = 0.015876$
3			$\beta_{NP} = 0.18$		$\beta_{NP} = 0.01296$
4				$\beta_P = 1.0$	$\beta_{PP} = 0.18$
5					$\beta_{NP} = 0.18$
	astronomers	*saw*	*stars*	*with*	*ears*

Table 11.3 Calculation of inside probabilities. Table cell (p,q) shows non-zero probabilities $\beta^i(p,q)$ calculated via the inside algorithm. The recursive computation of inside probabilities is done starting along the diagonal, and then moving in diagonal rows towards the top right corner. For the simple grammar of table 11.2, the only non-trivial case is cell $(2,5)$, which we calculate as:
$P(\text{VP} \rightarrow \text{V NP})\beta_V(2,2)\beta_{NP}(3,5) + P(\text{VP} \rightarrow \text{VP PP})\beta_{VP}(2,3)\beta_{PP}(4,5)$

11.3.2 Using outside probabilities

We can also calculate the probability of a string via the use of the outside probabilities. For any k, $1 \leq k \leq m$,

$$
(11.18) \qquad P(w_{1m}|G) = \sum_j P(w_{1(k-1)}, w_k, w_{(k+1)m}, N_{kk}^j|G)
$$

$$
= \sum_j P(w_{1(k-1)}, N_{kk}^j, w_{(k+1)m}|G)
$$

$$
\times P(w_k|w_{1(k-1)}, N_{kk}^j, w_{(k+1)n}, G)
$$

$$
(11.19) \qquad = \sum_j \alpha_j(k,k)P(N^j \rightarrow w_k)
$$

The outside probabilities are calculated top down. As we shall see, the inductive calculation of outside probabilities requires reference to inside probabilities, so we calculate outside probabilities second, using OUTSIDE ALGORITHM   the *outside algorithm*.

Base Case: The base case is the probability of the root of the tree being nonterminal N^i with nothing outside it:

$$
\alpha_1(1,m) = 1
$$

$$
\alpha_j(1,m) = 0 \quad \text{for } j \neq 1
$$

Inductive case: In terms of the previous step of the derivation, a node N_{pq}^j with which we are concerned might be on the left:

(11.20)

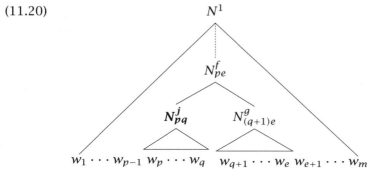

or right branch of the parent node:

(11.21)

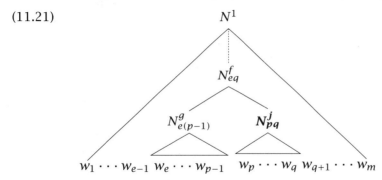

We sum over both possibilities, but restrict the first sum to $g \neq j$ so as not to double count in the case of rules of the form $X \to N^j N^j$:

$$
\begin{aligned}
\alpha_j(p,q) &= \Big[\sum_{f, g \neq j} \sum_{e=q+1}^{m} P(w_{1(p-1)}, w_{(q+1)m}, N_{pe}^f, N_{pq}^j, N_{(q+1)e}^g) \Big] \\
&\quad + \Big[\sum_{f,g} \sum_{e=1}^{p-1} P(w_{1(p-1)}, w_{(q+1)m}, N_{eq}^f, N_{e(p-1)}^g, N_{pq}^j) \Big] \\
&= \Big[\sum_{f, g \neq j} \sum_{e=q+1}^{m} P(w_{1(p-1)}, w_{(e+1)m}, N_{pe}^f) P(N_{pq}^j, N_{(q+1)e}^g | N_{pe}^f) \\
&\quad \times P(w_{(q+1)e} | N_{(q+1)e}^g) \Big] + \Big[\sum_{f,g} \sum_{e=1}^{p-1} P(w_{1(e-1)}, w_{(q+1)m}, N_{eq}^f) \\
&\quad \times P(N_{e(p-1)}^g, N_{pq}^j | N_{eq}^f) P(w_{e(p-1)} | N_{e(p-1)}^g) \Big]
\end{aligned}
$$

$$= \left[\sum_{f,g\neq j} \sum_{e=q+1}^{m} \alpha_f(p,e) P(N^f \to N^j \, N^g) \beta_g(q+1,e) \right]$$

$$+ \left[\sum_{f,g} \sum_{e=1}^{p-1} \alpha_f(e,q) P(N^f \to N^g \, N^j) \beta_g(e,p-1) \right]$$

As with an HMM, we can form a product of the inside and the outside probabilities:

$$\alpha_j(p,q)\beta_j(p,q) = P(w_{1(p-1)}, N^j_{pq}, w_{(q+1)m}|G) P(w_{pq}|N^j_{pq}, G)$$

$$= P(w_{1m}, N^j_{pq}|G)$$

But this time, the fact that we postulate a nonterminal node is important (whereas in the HMM case it is trivial that we are in *some* state at each point in time). Therefore, the probability of the sentence *and* that there is some constituent spanning from word p to q is given by:

(11.22) $$P(w_{1m}, N_{pq}|G) = \sum_j \alpha_j(p,q)\beta_j(p,q)$$

PRETERMINAL

However, we know that there will always be some nonterminal spanning the whole tree and each individual terminal (in a Chomsky Normal Form grammar). The nonterminal nodes whose only daughter is a single terminal node are referred to as *preterminal* nodes. Just in these cases this gives us the equations in (11.17) and (11.19) for the total probability of a string. Equation (11.17) is equivalent to $\alpha_1(1,m)\beta_1(1,m)$ and makes use of the root node, while equation (11.19) is equivalent to $\sum_j \alpha_j(k,k)\beta_j(k,k)$ and makes use of the fact that there must be some preterminal N^j above each word w_k.

11.3.3   Finding the most likely parse for a sentence

A Viterbi-style algorithm for finding the most likely parse for a sentence can be constructed by adapting the inside algorithm to find the element of the sum that is maximum, and to record which rule gave this maximum. This works as in the HMM case because of the independence assumptions of PCFGs. The result is an $O(m^3 n^3)$ PCFG parsing algorithm.

The secret to the Viterbi algorithm for HMMs is to define accumulators $\delta_j(t)$ which record the highest probability of a path through the trellis that leaves us at state j at time t. Recalling the link between HMMs and PCFGs through looking at PRGs, this time we wish to find the highest probability partial parse tree spanning a certain substring that is rooted with a certain nonterminal. We will retain the name δ and use accumulators:

$\delta_i(p, q)$ = the highest inside probability parse of a subtree N_{pq}^i

Using dynamic programming, we can then calculate the most probable parse for a sentence as follows. The initialization step assigns to each unary production at a leaf node its probability. For the inductive step, we again know that the first rule applying must be a binary rule, but this time we find the most probable one instead of summing over all such rules, and record that most probable one in the ψ variables, whose values are a list of three integers recording the form of the rule application which had the highest probability.

1. Initialization

$$\delta_i(p, p) = P(N^i \rightarrow w_p)$$

2. Induction

$$\delta_i(p, q) = \max_{\substack{1 \le j, k \le n \\ p \le r < q}} P(N^i \rightarrow N^j\ N^k)\delta_j(p, r)\delta_k(r+1, q)$$

Store backtrace

$$\psi_i(p, q) = \underset{(j, k, r)}{\arg\max}\, P(N^i \rightarrow N^j\ N^k)\delta_j(p, r)\delta_k(r+1, q)$$

3. Termination and path readout (by backtracking). Since our grammar has a start symbol N^1, then by construction, the probability of the most likely parse rooted in the start symbol is:[2]

(11.23) $$P(\hat{t}) = \delta_1(1, m)$$

We want to reconstruct this maximum probability tree $\hat{t}$. We do this by regarding $\hat{t}$ as a set of nodes $\{\hat{X}_x\}$ and showing how to construct this

---

2. We could alternatively find the highest probability node of any category that dominates the entire sentence as:

$$P(\hat{t}) = \max_{1 \le i \le n} \delta_i(1, m)$$

set. Since the grammar has a start symbol, the root node of the tree must be N_{1m}^1. We then show in general how to construct the left and right daughter nodes of a nonterminal node, and applying this process recursively will allow us to reconstruct the entire tree. If $X_x = N_{pq}^i$ is in the Viterbi parse, and $\psi_i(p,q) = (j,k,r)$, then:

$$
\begin{aligned}
\text{left}(\hat{X}_x) &= N_{pr}^j \\
\text{right}(\hat{X}_x) &= N_{(r+1)q}^k
\end{aligned}
$$

Note that where we have written 'arg max' above, it is possible for there not to be a unique maximum. We assume that in such cases the parser just chooses one maximal parse at random. It actually makes things considerably more complex to preserve all ties.

11.3.4 Training a PCFG

The idea of training a PCFG is grammar learning or grammar induction, but only in a certain limited sense. We assume that the structure of the grammar in terms of the number of terminals and nonterminals, and the name of the start symbol is given in advance. We also assume the set of rules is given in advance. Often one assumes that all possible rewriting rules exist, but one can alternatively assume some pre-given structure in the grammar, such as making some of the nonterminals dedicated preterminals that may only be rewritten as a terminal node. Training the grammar comprises simply a process that tries to find the optimal probabilities to assign to different grammar rules within this architecture.

INSIDE-OUTSIDE
ALGORITHM As in the case of HMMs, we construct an EM training algorithm, the *Inside-Outside algorithm*, which allows us to train the parameters of a PCFG on unannotated sentences of the language. The basic assumption is that a good grammar is one that makes the sentences in the training corpus likely to occur, and hence we seek the grammar that maximizes the likelihood of the training data. We will present training first on the basis of a single sentence, and then show how it is extended to the more realistic situation of a large training corpus of many sentences, by assuming independence between sentences.

To determine the probability of rules, what we would like to calculate is:

$$
\hat{P}(N^j \to \zeta) = \frac{C(N^j \to \zeta)}{\sum_\gamma C(N^j \to \gamma)}
$$

where $C(\cdot)$ is the count of the number of times that a particular rule is used. If parsed corpora are available, we can calculate these probabilities directly (as discussed in chapter 12). If, as is more common, a parsed training corpus is not available, then we have a hidden data problem: we wish to determine probability functions on rules, but can only directly see the probabilities of sentences. As we don't know the rule probabilities, we cannot compute relative frequencies, so we instead use an iterative algorithm to determine improving estimates. We begin with a certain grammar topology, which specifies how many terminals and nonterminals there are, and some initial probability estimates for rules (perhaps just randomly chosen). We use the probability of each parse of a training sentence according to this grammar as our confidence in it, and then sum the probabilities of each rule being used in each place to give an expectation of how often each rule was used. These expectations are then used to refine our probability estimates on rules, so that the likelihood of the training corpus given the grammar is increased.

Consider:

$$
\begin{aligned}
\alpha_j(p,q)\beta_j(p,q) &= P(N^1 \overset{*}{\Rightarrow} w_{1m}, N^j \overset{*}{\Rightarrow} w_{pq}|G) \\
&= P(N^1 \overset{*}{\Rightarrow} w_{1m}|G)P(N^j \overset{*}{\Rightarrow} w_{pq}|N^1 \overset{*}{\Rightarrow} w_{1m},G)
\end{aligned}
$$

We have already solved how to calculate $P(N^1 \overset{*}{\Rightarrow} w_{1m})$; let us call this probability π. Then:

$$
P(N^j \overset{*}{\Rightarrow} w_{pq}|N^1 \overset{*}{\Rightarrow} w_{1m}, G) = \frac{\alpha_j(p,q)\beta_j(p,q)}{\pi}
$$

and the estimate for how many times the nonterminal N^j is used in the derivation is:

(11.24) $$E(N^j \text{ is used in the derivation}) = \sum_{p=1}^{m}\sum_{q=p}^{m} \frac{\alpha_j(p,q)\beta_j(p,q)}{\pi}$$

In the case where we are not dealing with a preterminal, we substitute the inductive definition of β into the above probability and then $\forall r, s, p < q$:

$$
\begin{aligned}
&P(N^j \to N^r\, N^s \overset{*}{\Rightarrow} w_{pq}|N^1 \overset{*}{\Rightarrow} w_{1m}, G) \\
&= \frac{\sum_{d=p}^{q-1}\alpha_j(p,q)P(N^j \to N^r\, N^s)\beta_r(p,d)\beta_s(d+1,q)}{\pi}
\end{aligned}
$$

Therefore, the estimate for how many times this particular rule is used in the derivation can be found by summing over all ranges of words that the node could dominate:

(11.25) $E(N^j \rightarrow N^r\,N^s, N^j \text{ used})$

$$= \frac{\sum_{p=1}^{m-1}\sum_{q=p+1}^{m}\sum_{d=p}^{q-1}\alpha_j(p,q)P(N^j \rightarrow N^r\,N^s)\beta_r(p,d)\beta_s(d+1,q)}{\pi}$$

Now for the maximization step, we want:

$$P(N^j \rightarrow N^r\,N^s) = \frac{E(N^j \rightarrow N^r\,N^s, N^j \text{ used})}{E(N^j \text{ used})}$$

So, the reestimation formula is:

(11.26) $\hat{P}(N^j \rightarrow N^r\,N^s) = (11.25)/(11.24)$

$$= \frac{\sum_{p=1}^{m-1}\sum_{q=p+1}^{m}\sum_{d=p}^{q-1}\alpha_j(p,q)P(N^j \rightarrow N^r\,N^s)\beta_r(p,d)\beta_s(d+1,q)}{\sum_{p=1}^{m}\sum_{q=p}^{m}\alpha_j(p,q)\beta_j(p,q)}$$

Similarly for preterminals,

$$P(N^j \rightarrow w^k | N^1 \overset{*}{\Rightarrow} w_{1m}, G) = \frac{\sum_{h=1}^{m}\alpha_j(h,h)P(N^j \rightarrow w_h, w_h = w^k)}{\pi}$$

$$= \frac{\sum_{h=1}^{m}\alpha_j(h,h)P(w_h = w^k)\beta_j(h,h)}{\pi}$$

The $P(w_h = w^k)$ above is, of course, either 0 or 1, but we express things in the second form to show maximal similarity with the preceding case. Therefore,

(11.27) $\hat{P}(N^j \rightarrow w^k) = \dfrac{\sum_{h=1}^{m}\alpha_j(h,h)P(w_h = w^k)\beta_j(h,h)}{\sum_{p=1}^{m}\sum_{q=p}^{m}\alpha_j(p,q)\beta_j(p,q)}$

Unlike the case of HMMs, this time we cannot possibly avoid the problem of dealing with multiple training instances – one cannot use concatenation as in the HMM case. Let us assume that we have a set of training sentences $W = (W_1,\ldots,W_\omega)$, with $W_i = w_{i,1}\cdots w_{i,m_i}$. Let f_i, g_i, and h_i be the common subterms from before for use of a nonterminal at a branching node, at a preterminal node, and anywhere respectively, now calculated from sentence W_i:

(11.28) $f_i(p,q,j,r,s) = \dfrac{\sum_{d=p}^{q-1}\alpha_j(p,q)P(N^j \rightarrow N^r N^s)\beta_r(p,d)\beta_s(d+1,q)}{P(N^1 \overset{*}{\Rightarrow} W_i | G)}$

$g_i(h,j,k) = \dfrac{\alpha_j(h,h)P(w_h = w^k)\beta_j(h,h)}{P(N^1 \overset{*}{\Rightarrow} W_i | G)}$

$h_i(p,q,j) = \dfrac{\alpha_j(p,q)\beta_j(p,q)}{P(N^1 \overset{*}{\Rightarrow} W_i | G)}$

If we assume that the sentences in the training corpus are independent, then the likelihood of the training corpus is just the product of the probabilities of the sentences in it according to the grammar. Therefore, in the reestimation process, we can sum the contributions from multiple sentences to give the following reestimation formulas. Note that the denominators consider all expansions of the nonterminal, as terminals or nonterminals, to satisfy the stochastic constraint in equation (11.3) that a nonterminal's expansions sum to 1.

(11.29) $\quad \hat{P}(N^j \rightarrow N^r \, N^s) \quad = \quad \dfrac{\sum_{i=1}^{\omega} \sum_{p=1}^{m_i-1} \sum_{q=p+1}^{m_i} f_i(p,q,j,r,s)}{\sum_{i=1}^{\omega} \sum_{p=1}^{m_i} \sum_{q=p}^{m_i} h_i(p,q,j)}$

and

(11.30) $\quad \hat{P}(N^j \rightarrow w^k) = \dfrac{\sum_{i=1}^{\omega} \sum_{h=1}^{m_i} g_i(h,j,k)}{\sum_{i=1}^{\omega} \sum_{p=1}^{m_i} \sum_{q=p}^{m_i} h_i(p,q,j)}$

The Inside-Outside algorithm is to repeat this process of parameter reestimation until the change in the estimated probability of the training corpus is small. If G_i is the grammar (including rule probabilities) in the ith iteration of training, then we are guaranteed that the probability of the corpus according to the model will improve or at least get no worse:

$P(W|G_{i+1}) \geq P(W|G_i).$

11.4 Problems with the Inside-Outside Algorithm

However, the PCFG learning algorithm is not without problems:

1. Compared with linear models like HMMs, it is slow. For each sentence, each iteration of training is $O(m^3 n^3)$, where m is the length of the sentence, and n is the number of nonterminals in the grammar.

LOCAL MAXIMA 2. *Local maxima* are much more of a problem. Charniak (1993) reports that on each of 300 trials of PCFG induction (from randomly initialized parameters, using artificial data generated from a simple English-like PCFG) a different local maximum was found. Or in other words, the algorithm is very sensitive to the initialization of the parameters. This might perhaps be a good place to try another learning method. (For instance, the process of simulated annealing has been used with some success with neural nets to avoid problems of getting stuck in local maxima (Kirkpatrick et al. 1983; Ackley et al. 1985), but it is still perhaps too compute expensive for large-scale PCFGs.) Other partial solutions are restricting rules by initializing some parameters to zero or performing grammar minimization, or reallocating nonterminals away from "greedy" terminals. Such approaches are discussed in Lari and Young (1990).

3. Based on experiments on artificial languages, Lari and Young (1990) suggest that satisfactory grammar learning requires many more nonterminals than are theoretically needed to describe the language at hand. In their experiments one typically needed about $3n$ nonterminals to satisfactorily learn a grammar from a training text generated by a grammar with n nonterminals. This compounds the first problem.

4. While the algorithm is guaranteed to increase the probability of the training corpus, there is no guarantee that the nonterminals that the algorithm learns will have any satisfactory resemblance to the kinds of nonterminals normally motivated in linguistic analysis (NP, VP, etc.). Even if one initializes training with a grammar of the sort familiar to linguists, the training regime may completely change the meaning of nonterminal categories as it thinks best. As we have set things up, the only hard constraint is that N^1 must remain the start symbol. One option is to impose further constraints on the nature of the grammar. For instance, one could specialize the nonterminals so that they each only generate terminals *or* nonterminals. Using this form of grammar would actually also simplify the reestimation equations we presented above.

Thus, while grammar induction from unannotated corpora is possible in principle with PCFGs, in practice, it is extremely difficult. In different ways, many of the approaches of the next chapter address various of the limitations of using vanilla PCFGs.

11.5   Further Reading

A comprehensive discussion of topics like weak and strong equivalence, Chomsky Normal Form, and algorithms for changing arbitrary CFGs into various normal forms can be found in (Hopcroft and Ullman 1979). Standard techniques for parsing with CFGs in NLP can be found in most AI and NLP textbooks, such as (Allen 1995).

Probabilistic CFGs were first studied in the late 1960s and early 1970s, and initially there was an outpouring of work. Booth and Thomson (1973), following on from Booth (1969), define a PCFG as in this chapter (modulo notation). Among other results, they show that there are probability distributions on the strings of context free languages which cannot be generated by a PCFG, and derive necessary and sufficient conditions for a PCFG to define a proper probability distribution. Other work from this period includes: (Grenander 1967), (Suppes 1970), (Huang and Fu 1971), and several PhD theses (Horning 1969; Ellis 1969; Hutchins 1970). Tree structures in probability theory are normally referred to as *branching processes*, and are discussed in such work as (Harris 1963) and (Sankoff 1971).

BRANCHING
PROCESSES

During the 1970s, work on stochastic formal languages largely died out, and PCFGs were really only kept alive by the speech community, as an occasionally tried variant model. The Inside-Outside algorithm was introduced, and its convergence properties formally proved by Baker (1979). Our presentation essentially follows (Lari and Young 1990). This paper includes a proof of the algorithmic complexity of the Inside-Outside algorithm. Their work is further developed in (Lari and Young 1991).

For the extension of the algorithms presented here to arbitrary PCFGs, see (Charniak 1993) or (Kupiec 1991, 1992a).[3] Jelinek et al. (1990) and Jelinek et al. (1992a) provide a thorough introduction to PCFGs. In particular, these reports, and also Jelinek and Lafferty (1991) and Stolcke (1995), present incremental left-to-right versions of the Inside and Viterbi algorithms, which are very useful in contexts such as language models for speech recognition.

In the section on training a PCFG, we assumed a fixed grammar architecture. This naturally raises the question of how one should determine this architecture, and how one would learn it automatically. There has been a little work on automatically determining a suitable architecture using *Bayesian model merging*, a *Minimum Description Length* approach (Stolcke and Omohundro 1994b; Chen 1995), but at present this task is still normally carried out by using the intuitions of a linguist.

BAYESIAN MODEL
MERGING
MINIMUM
DESCRIPTION LENGTH

---

3. For anyone familiar with chart parsing, the extension is fairly straightforward: in a chart we always build maximally binary 'traversals' as we move the dot through rules. We can use this virtual grammar, with appropriate probabilities to parse arbitrary PCFGs (the rule that completes a constituent can have the same probability as the original rule, while all others have probability 1).

PCFGs have also been used in bioinformatics (e.g., Sakakibara et al. 1994), but not nearly as much as HMMs.

11.6   Exercises

Exercise 11.1   [⋆ ⋆]

Consider the probability of a (partial) syntactic parse tree giving part of the structure of a sentence:

$$P \left(\begin{array}{c} \text{NP} \\ \diagup \diagdown \\ \text{Det} \qquad \text{N}' \\ \diagup \diagdown \\ \text{Adj} \quad \text{N} \end{array} \right)$$

In general, as the (sub)tree gets large, we cannot accurately estimate the probability of such trees from any existing training corpus (a data sparseness problem).

As we saw, PCFGs approach this problem by estimating the probability of a tree like the one above from the joint probabilities of local subtrees:

$$P \left(\begin{array}{ccc} \text{NP} & & \text{N}' \\ \diagup \diagdown & , & \diagup \diagdown \\ \text{Det} \quad \text{N}' & \text{Adj} \quad \text{N} \end{array} \right)$$

However, how reasonable is it to assume independence between the probability distributions of these local subtrees (which is the assumption that licenses us to estimate the probability of a subtree as the product of the probability of each local tree it contains)?

Use a parsed corpus (e.g., the Penn Treebank) and find for some common subtrees whether the independence assumption seems justified or not. If it is not, see if you can find a method of combining the probabilities of local subtrees in such a way that it results in an empirically better estimate of the probability of a larger subtree.

Exercise 11.2   [⋆]

Using a parse triangle as in figure 11.3, calculate the outside probabilities for the sentence *astronomers saw stars with ears* according to the grammar in table 11.2. Start at the top righthand corner and work towards the diagonal.

Exercise 11.3   [⋆]

Using the inside and outside probabilities for the sentence *astronomers saw stars with ears* worked out in figure 11.3 and exercise 11.2, reestimate the probabilities of the grammar in table 11.2 by working through one iteration of the Inside-Outside algorithm. It is helpful to first link up the inside probabilities shown in figure 11.3 with the particular rules and subtrees used to obtain them.

What would the rule probabilities converge to with continued iterations of the Inside-Outside algorithm? Why?

Exercise 11.4 [★ ★ ★]

Recording possible spans of nodes in a parse triangle such as the one in figure 11.3 is the essence of the Cocke-Kasami-Younger (CKY) algorithm for parsing CFGs (Younger 1967; Hopcroft and Ullman 1979). Writing a CKY PCFG parser is quite straightforward, and a good exercise. One might then want to extend the parser from Chomsky Normal Form grammars to the more general case of context-free grammars. One way is to work out the general case oneself, or to consult the appropriate papers in the Further Reading. Another way is to write a grammar transformation that will take a CFG and convert it into a Chomsky Normal Form CFG by introducing specially-marked additional nodes where necessary, which can then be removed on output to display parse trees as given by the original grammar. This task is quite easy if one restricts the input CFG to one that does not contain any empty nodes (nonterminals that expand to give nothing).

Exercise 11.5 [★ ★ ★]

Rather than simply parsing a sequence of words, if interfacing a parser to a speech recognizer, one often wants to be able to parse a word lattice, of the sort shown in figure 12.1. Extend a PCFG parser so it works with word lattices. (Because the runtime of a PCFG parser is dependent on the number of words in the word lattice, a PCFG parser can be impractical when dealing with large speech lattices, but our CPUs keep getting faster every year!)

12 *Probabilistic Parsing*

CHUNKING

GRAMMAR INDUCTION

THE PRACTICE of parsing can be considered as a straightforward implementation of the idea of *chunking* – recognizing higher level units of structure that allow us to compress our description of a sentence. One way to capture the regularity of chunks over different sentences is to learn a grammar that explains the structure of the chunks one finds. This is the problem of *grammar induction*. There has been considerable work on grammar induction, because it is exploring the empiricist question of how to learn structure from unannotated textual input, but we will not cover it here. Suffice it to say that grammar induction techniques are reasonably well understood for finite state languages, but that induction is very difficult for context-free or more complex languages of the scale needed to handle a decent proportion of the complexity of human languages. It is not hard to induce *some* form of structure over a corpus of text. Any algorithm for making chunks – such as recognizing common subsequences – will produce some form of chunked representation of sentences, which we might interpret as a phrase structure tree. However, most often the representations one finds bear little resemblance to the kind of phrase structure that is normally proposed in linguistics and NLP.

Now, there is enough argument and disagreement within the field of syntax that one might find *someone* who has proposed syntactic structures similar to the ones that the grammar induction procedure which you have sweated over happens to produce. This can and has been taken as evidence for that model of syntactic structure. However, such an approach has more than a whiff of circularity to it. The structures found depend on the implicit inductive bias of the learning program. This suggests another tack. We need to get straight what structure we expect our

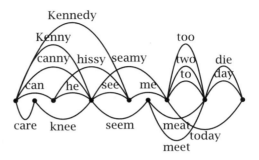

Figure 12.1   A word lattice (simplified).

PARSER
model to find *before* we start building it. This suggests that we should
begin by deciding what we want to do with parsed sentences. There are
various possible goals: using syntactic structure as a first step towards
semantic interpretation, detecting phrasal chunks for indexing in an IR
system, or trying to build a probabilistic parser that outperforms *n*-gram
models as a language model. For any of these tasks, the overall goal is
to produce a system that can place a provably useful structure over arbitrary sentences, that is, to build a *parser*. For this goal, there is no need
to insist that one begins with a *tabula rasa*. If one just wants to do a
good job at producing useful syntactic structure, one should use all the
prior information that one has. This is the approach that will be adopted
in this chapter.

The rest of this chapter is divided into two parts. The first introduces
some general concepts, ideas, and approaches of broad general relevance,
which turn up in various places in the statistical parsing literature (and a
couple which should turn up more often than they do). The second then
looks at some actual parsing systems that exploit some of these ideas,
and at how they perform in practice.

12.1   Some Concepts

12.1.1   Parsing for disambiguation

There are at least three distinct ways in which one can use probabilities
in a parser:

WORD LATTICE

■ **Probabilities for determining the sentence.** One possibility is to use a parser as a language model over a *word lattice* in order to determine what sequence of words running along a path through the lattice has highest probability. In applications such as speech recognizers, the actual input sentence is uncertain, and there are various hypotheses, which are normally represented by a word lattice as in figure 12.1.[1] The job of the parser here is to be a language model that tries to determine what someone probably said. A recent example of using a parser in this way is (Chelba and Jelinek 1998).

■ **Probabilities for speedier parsing.** A second goal is to use probabilities to order or prune the search space of a parser. The task here is to enable the parser to find the best parse more quickly while not harming the quality of the results being produced. A recent study of effective methods for achieving this goal is (Caraballo and Charniak 1998).

■ **Probabilities for choosing between parses.** The parser can be used to choose from among the many parses of the input sentence which ones are most likely.

In this section, and in this chapter, we will concentrate on the third use of probabilities over parse trees: using a statistical parser for disambiguation.

Capturing the tree structure of a particular sentence has been seen as key to the goal of disambiguation – the problem we discussed in chapter 1. For instance, to determine the meaning of the sentence in (12.1), we need to determine what are the meaningful units and how they relate. In particular we need to resolve ambiguities such as the ones represented in whether the correct parse for the sentence is (12.2a) or (12.2b), (12.2c) or (12.2d), or even (12.2e).

(12.1)   The post office will hold out discounts and service concessions as incentives.

---

1. Alternatively, they may be represented by an *n-best list*, but that has the unfortunate effect of multiplying out ambiguities in what are often disjoint areas of uncertainty in the signal.

(12.2)   a.

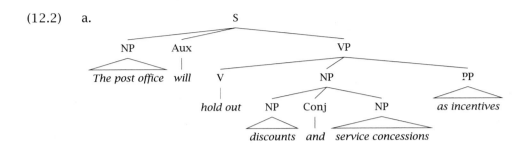

b.

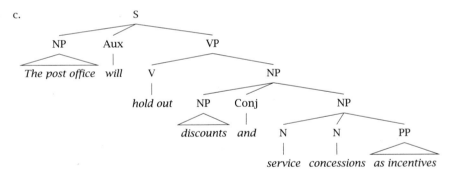

c.

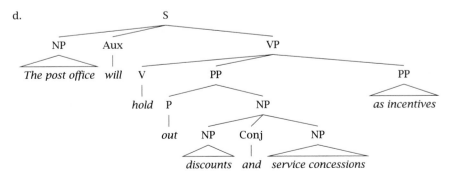

d.

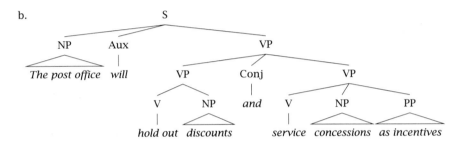

e.

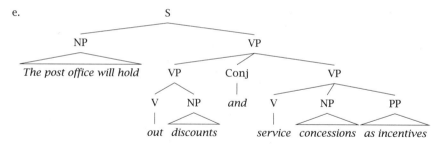

One might get the impression from computational linguistics books that such ambiguities are rare and artificial, because most books contain the same somewhat unnatural-sounding examples (ones about pens and boxes, or seeing men with telescopes). But that's just because simple short examples are practical to use. Such ambiguities are actually ubiquitous. To provide some freshness in our example (12.1), we adopted the following approach: we randomly chose a *Wall Street Journal* article, and used the first sentence as the basis for making our point. Finding ambiguities was not difficult.[2] If you are still not convinced about the severity of the disambiguation problem, then you should immediately do exercise 12.1 before continuing to read this chapter.

What is one to do about all these ambiguities? In classical categorical approaches, some ambiguities are seen as genuine syntactic ambiguities, and it is the job of the parser to return structures corresponding to all of these, but other weird things that one's parser spits out are seen as faults of the grammar, and the grammar writer will attempt to refine the grammar, in order to generate less crazy parses. For instance, the grammar writer might feel that (12.2d) should be ruled out, because *hold* needs an object noun phrase, and enforce that by a subcategorization frame placed on the verb *hold*. But actually that would be a mistake, because then the parser would not be able to handle a sentence such as: *The flood waters reached a height of 8 metres, but the sandbags held.*

In contrast, a statistically-minded linguist will not be much interested in how many parses his parser produces for a sentence. Normally there is still some categorical base to the grammar and so there is a fixed finite

2. We refrained from actually *using* the first sentence, since like so many sentences in newspapers, it was rather long. It would have been difficult to fit trees for a 38 word sentence on the page. But for reference, here it is: *Postmaster General Anthony Frank, in a speech to a mailers' convention today, is expected to set a goal of having computer-readable bar codes on all business mail by 1995, holding out discounts and service concessions as incentives.*

number of parses, but statistically-minded linguists can afford to be quite licentious about what they allow into their grammar, and so they usually are. What is important is the probability distribution over the parses generated by the grammar. We want to be able to separate out the few parses that are likely to be correct from the many that are syntactically possible, but extremely unlikely. In many cases, we are just interested in "the best parse," which is the one deemed to be most likely to be correct. Statistical parsers generally disambiguate and rate how likely different parses are as they parse, whereas in conventional parsers, the output trees would normally be sent to downstream models of semantics and world knowledge that would choose between the parses. A statistical parser usually disambiguates as it goes by using various extended notions of word and category collocation as a surrogate for semantic and world knowledge. This implements the idea that the ways in which a word tends to be used gives us at least some handle on its meaning.

12.1.2 Treebanks

We mentioned earlier that pure grammar induction approaches tend not to produce the parse trees that people want. A fairly obvious approach to this problem is to give a learning tool some examples of the kinds of parse trees that are wanted. A collection of such example parses is

TREEBANK   referred to as a *treebank*. Because of the usefulness of collections of correctly-parsed sentences for building statistical parsers, a number of people and groups have produced treebanks, but by far the most widely

PENN TREEBANK   used one, reflecting both its size and readily available status, is the *Penn Treebank*.

An example of a Penn Treebank tree is shown in figure 12.2. This example illustrates most of the major features of trees in the Penn treebank. Trees are represented in a straightforward (Lisp) notation via bracketing. The grouping of words into phrases is fairly flat (for example there is no disambiguation of compound nouns in phrases such as *Arizona real estate loans*), but the major types of phrases recognized in contemporary syntax are fairly faithfully represented. The treebank also makes some attempt to indicate grammatical and semantic functions (the **-SBJ** and **-LOC** tags in the figure, which are used to tag the subject and a locative, respectively), and makes use of empty nodes to indicate understood subjects and extraction gaps, as in the understood subject of the adverbial clause in the example, where the empty node is marked as *. In table 12.1,

```
( (S (NP-SBJ The move)
     (VP followed
         (NP (NP a round)
             (PP of
                 (NP (NP similar increases)
                     (PP by
                         (NP other lenders))
                     (PP against
                         (NP Arizona real estate loans)))))))
     ,
     (S-ADV (NP-SBJ *)
            (VP reflecting
                (NP (NP a continuing decline)
                    (PP-LOC in
                            (NP that market))))))
     .))
```

Figure 12.2   A Penn Treebank tree.

S	Simple clause (sentence)	CONJP	Multiword conjunction phrases
SBAR	S′ clause with complementizer	FRAG	Fragment
SBARQ	*Wh*-question S′ clause	INTJ	Interjection
SQ	Inverted *Yes/No* question S′ clause	LST	List marker
SINV	Declarative inverted S′ clause	NAC	Not A Constituent grouping
ADJP	Adjective Phrase	NX	Nominal constituent inside NP
ADVP	Adverbial Phrase	PRN	Parenthetical
NP	Noun Phrase	PRT	Particle
PP	Prepositional Phrase	RRC	Reduced Relative Clause
QP	Quantifier Phrase (inside NP)	UCP	Unlike Coordinated Phrase
VP	Verb Phrase	X	Unknown or uncertain
WHNP	*Wh-* Noun Phrase	WHADJP	*Wh-* Adjective Phrase
WHPP	*Wh-* Prepositional Phrase	WHADVP	*Wh-* Adverb Phrase

Table 12.1   Abbreviations for phrasal categories in the Penn Treebank. The common categories are gathered in the left column. The categorization includes a number of rare categories for various oddities.

we summarize the phrasal categories used in the Penn Treebank (which basically follow the categories discussed in chapter 3).

One oddity, to which we shall return, is that complex noun phrases are represented by an NP-over-NP structure. An example in figure 12.2 is the NP starting with *similar increases*. The lower NP node, often referred to as the 'baseNP' contain just the head noun and preceding material such as determiners and adjectives, and then a higher NP node (or sometimes two) contains the lower NP node and following arguments and modifiers. This structure is wrong by the standards of most contemporary syntactic theories which argue that NP postmodifiers belong with the head under some sort of N′ node, and lower than the determiner (section 3.2.3). On the other hand, this organization captures rather well the notion of CHUNKING *chunks* proposed by Abney (1991), where, impressionistically, the head noun and prehead modifiers seem to form one chunk, whereas phrasal postmodifiers are separate chunks. At any rate, some work on parsing has directly adopted this Penn Treebank structure and treats baseNPs as a unit in parsing.

Even when using a treebank, there is still an induction problem of extracting the grammatical knowledge that is implicit in the example parses. But for many methods, this induction is trivial. For example, to determine a PCFG from a treebank, we need do nothing more than count the frequencies of local trees, and then normalize these to give probabilities.

Many people have argued that it is better to have linguists constructing treebanks than grammars, because it is easier to work out the correct parse of individual actual sentences than to try to determine (often largely by intuition) what all possible manifestations of a certain rule or grammatical construct are. This is probably true in the sense that a linguist is unlikely to immediately think of all the possibilities for a construction off the top of his head, but at least an implicit grammar must be assumed in order to be able to treebank. In multiperson treebanking projects, there has normally been a need to make this grammar explicit. The treebanking manual for the Penn Treebank runs to over 300 pages.

12.1.3   Parsing models vs. language models

The idea of parsing is to be able to take a sentence s and to work out parse trees for it according to some grammar G. In probabilistic parsing, we would like to place a ranking on possible parses showing how likely each one is, or maybe to just return the most likely parse of a sentence. Thinking like this, the most natural thing to do is to define a probabilistic *parsing model*, which evaluates the probability of trees t for a sentence s by finding:

PARSING MODEL

(12.3) $P(t|s, G)$ where $\sum_t P(t|s, G) = 1$

Given a probabilistic parsing model, the job of a parser is to find the most probable parse of a sentence $\hat{t}$:

(12.4) $\hat{t} = \arg\max_t P(t|s, G)$

This is normally straightforward, but sometimes for practical reasons various sorts of heuristic or sampling parsers are used, methods which in most cases find the most probable parse, but sometimes don't.

One can directly estimate a parsing model, and people have done this, but they are a little odd in that one is using probabilities conditioned on a particular sentence. In general, we need to base our probability estimates on some more general class of data. The more usual approach is to start off by defining a language model, which assigns a probability to all trees generated by the grammar. Then we can examine the joint probability $P(t, s|G)$. Given that the sentence is determined by the tree (and recoverable from its leaf nodes), this is just $P(t|G)$, if yield$(t) = s$, and 0 otherwise. Under such a model, $P(t|G)$ is the probability of a particular parse of a particular sentence according to the grammar G. Below we suppress the conditioning of the probability according to the grammar, and just write $P(t)$ for this quantity.

LANGUAGE MODEL

In a language model, probabilities are for the entire language $\mathcal{L}$, so we have that:

(12.5) $\sum_{\{t:\ \text{yield}(t) \in \mathcal{L}\}} P(t) = 1$

We can find the overall probability of a sentence as:

(12.6) $P(s) = \sum_t P(s, t)$

$\qquad\qquad = \sum_{\{t:\ \text{yield}(t) = s\}} P(t)$

This means that it is straightforward to make a parsing model out of a language model. We simply divide the probability of a tree in the language model by the above quantity. The best parse is given by:

$$(12.7) \quad \hat{t} = \arg\max_t P(t|s) = \arg\max_t \frac{P(t,s)}{P(s)} = \arg\max_t P(t,s)$$

So a language model can always be used as a parsing model for the purpose of choosing between parses. But a language model can also be used for other purposes (for example, as a speech recognition language model, or for estimating the entropy of a language).

On the other hand, there is not a way to convert an arbitrary parsing model into a language model. Nevertheless, noticing some of the biases of PCFG parsing models that we discussed in chapter 11, a strand of work at IBM explored the idea that it might be better to build parsing models directly rather than defining them indirectly via a language model (Jelinek et al. 1994; Magerman 1995), and directly defined parsing models have also been used by others (Collins 1996). However, in this work, although the overall probabilities calculated are conditioned on a particular sentence, the atomic probabilities that the probability of a parse is decomposed into are not dependent on the individual sentence, but are still estimated from the whole training corpus. Moreover, when Collins (1997) refined his initial model (Collins 1996) so that parsing probabilities were defined via an explicit language model, this significantly increased the performance of his parser. So, while language models are not necessarily to be preferred to parsing models, they appear to provide a better foundation for modeling.

12.1.4   Weakening the independence assumptions of PCFGs

Context and independence assumptions

It is widely accepted in studies of language understanding that humans make wide use of the context of an utterance to disambiguate language as they listen. This use of context assumes many forms, for example the context where we are listening (to TV or in a bar), who we are listening to, and also the immediate prior context of the conversation. The prior discourse context will influence our interpretation of later sentences (this PRIMING is the effect known as *priming* in the psychological literature). People will find semantically intuitive readings for sentences in preference to weird ones. Furthermore, much recent work shows that these many sources of information are incorporated in real time while people parse sentences.[3] In our previous PCFG model, we were effectively making an independence assumption that none of these factors were relevant to the probability of a parse tree. But, in fact, all of these sources of evidence are relevant to and might be usable for disambiguating probabilistic parses. Even if we are not directly modeling the discourse context or its meaning, we can approximate these by using notions of collocation to help in more local semantic disambiguation, and the prior text as an indication of discourse context (for instance, we might detect the genre of the text, or its topic). To build a better statistical parser than a PCFG, we want to be able to incorporate at least some of these sources of information.

Lexicalization

There are two somewhat separable weaknesses that stem from the independence assumptions of PCFGs. The most often remarked on one is their lack of *lexicalization*. In a PCFG, the chance of a VP expanding as a verb followed by two noun phrases is independent of the choice of verb involved. This is ridiculous, as this possibility is much more likely with ditransitive verbs like *hand* or *tell*, than with other verbs. Table 12.2 uses data from the Penn Treebank to show how the probabilities of various common subcategorization frames differ depending on the verb that heads the VP.[4] This suggests that somehow we want to include more information about what the actual words in the sentence are when making decisions about the structure of the parse tree.

LEXICALIZATION

In other places as well, the need for lexicalization is obvious. A clear case is the issue of choosing phrasal attachment positions. As discussed at length in chapter 8, it is clear that the lexical content of phrases almost always provides enough information to decide the correct attachment site, whereas the syntactic category of the phrase normally provides very little information. One of the ways in which standard PCFGs are much

---

3. This last statement is not uncontroversial. Work in psycholinguistics that is influenced by a Chomskyan approach to language has long tried to argue that people construct syntactic parses first, and then choose between them in a disambiguation phase (e.g., Frazier 1978). But a variety of recent work (e.g., Tanenhaus and Trueswell 1995, Pearlmutter and MacDonald 1992) has argued against this and suggested that semantic and contextual information *does* get incorporated immediately during sentence understanding.
4. One can't help but suspect that some of the very low but non-zero entries might reveal errors in the treebank, but note that because functional tags are being ignored, an NP can appear after an intransitive verb if it is a temporal NP like *last week*.

	Verb			
Local tree	*come*	*take*	*think*	*want*
VP → V	9.5%	2.6%	4.6%	5.7%
VP → V NP	1.1%	32.1%	0.2%	13.9%
VP → V PP	34.5%	3.1%	7.1%	0.3%
VP → V SBAR	6.6%	0.3%	73.0%	0.2%
VP → V S	2.2%	1.3%	4.8%	70.8%
VP → V NP S	0.1%	5.7%	0.0%	0.3%
VP → V PRT NP	0.3%	5.8%	0.0%	0.0%
VP → V PRT PP	6.1%	1.5%	0.2%	0.0%

Table 12.2 Frequency of common subcategorization frames (local trees expanding VP) for selected verbs. The data show that the rule used to expand VP is highly dependent on the lexical identity of the verb. The counts ignore distinctions in verbal form tags. Phrase names are as in table 12.1, and tags are Penn Treebank tags (tables 4.5 and 4.6).

worse than *n*-gram models is that they totally fail to capture the lexical dependencies between words. We want to get this back, while maintaining a richer model than the purely linear word-level *n*-gram models. The most straightforward and common way to lexicalize a CFG is by having each phrasal node be marked by its head word, so that the tree in (12.8a) will be lexicalized as the tree in (12.8b).

(12.8)   a.   b.

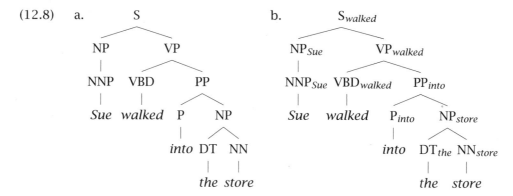

Central to this model of lexicalization is the idea that the strong lexical dependencies are between heads and their dependents, for example between a head noun and a modifying adjective, or between a verb and a noun phrase object, where the noun phrase object can in turn be approximated by its head noun. This is normally true and hence this is an effective strategy, but it is worth pointing out that there are some dependencies between pairs of non-heads. For example, for the object NP in (12.9):

(12.9)   I got [NP the easier problem [of the two] [to solve]].

both the posthead modifiers *of the two* and *to solve* are dependents of the prehead modifier *easier*. Their appearance is only weakly conditioned by the head of the NP *problem*. Here are two other examples of this sort, where the head is in bold, and the words involved in the nonhead dependency are in italics:

(12.10)   a. Her approach was *more quickly* **understood** *than mine.*

           b. He lives in what must be the *farthest* **suburb** *from the university.*

See also exercise 8.16.

Probabilities dependent on structural context

However, PCFGs are also deficient on purely structural grounds. Inherent to the idea of a PCFG is that probabilities are context-free: for instance, that the probability of a noun phrase expanding in a certain way is independent of where the NP is in the tree. Even if we in some way lexicalize PCFGs to remove the other deficiency, this assumption of structural context-freeness remains. But this grammatical assumption is actually quite wrong. For example, table 12.3 shows how the probabilities of expanding an NP node in the Penn Treebank differ wildly between subject position and object position. Pronouns, proper names and definite NPs appear more commonly in subject position while NPs containing posthead modifiers and bare nouns occur more commonly in object position. This reflects the fact that the subject normally expresses the sentence-internal topic. As another example, table 12.4 compares the expansions for the first and second object NPs of ditransitive verbs. The dispreference for pronouns to be second objects is well-known, and the preference for 'NP SBAR' expansions as second objects reflects the well-known tendency for heavy elements to appear at the end of the clause, but it would take a more thorough corpus study to understand some of the other effects. For instance, it is not immediately clear to us why bare plural

Expansion	% as Subj	% as Obj
NP → PRP	13.7%	2.1%
NP → NNP	3.5%	0.9%
NP → DT NN	5.6%	4.6%
NP → NN	1.4%	2.8%
NP → NP SBAR	0.5%	2.6%
NP → NP PP	5.6%	14.1%

Table 12.3 Selected common expansions of NP as Subject vs. Object, ordered by log odds ratio. The data show that the rule used to expand NP is highly dependent on its parent node(s), which corresponds to either a subject or an object.

Expansion	% as 1st Obj	% as 2nd Obj
NP → NNS	7.5%	0.2%
NP → PRP	13.4%	0.9%
NP → NP PP	12.2%	14.4%
NP → DT NN	10.4%	13.3%
NP → NNP	4.5%	5.9%
NP → NN	3.9%	9.2%
NP → JJ NN	1.1%	10.4%
NP → NP SBAR	0.3%	5.1%

Table 12.4 Selected common expansions of NP as first and second object inside VP. The data are another example of the importance of structural context for nonterminal expansions.

nouns are so infrequent in the second object position. But at any rate, the context-dependent nature of the distribution is again manifest.

The upshot of these observations is that we should be able to build a much better probabilistic parser than one based on a PCFG by better taking into account lexical and structural context. The challenge (as so often) is to find factors that give us a lot of extra discrimination while not defeating us with a multiplicity of parameters that lead to sparse data problems. The systems in the second half of this chapter present a number of approaches along these lines.

(a)   S
      NP VP
      N VP
      astronomers VP
      astronomers V NP
      astronomers saw NP
      astronomers saw N
      astronomers saw telescopes

(b)   S
      NP VP
      N VP
      astronomers VP
      astronomers V NP
      astronomers V N
      astronomers V *telescopes*
      astronomers saw telescopes

Figure 12.3 Two CFG derivations of the same tree.

12.1.5 Tree probabilities and derivational probabilities

In the PCFG framework, one can work out the probability of a tree by just multiplying the probabilities of each local subtree of the tree, where the probability of a local subtree is given by the rule that produced it. The tree can be thought of as a compact record of a branching process where one is making a choice at each node, conditioned solely on the label of the node. As we saw in chapter 3, within generative models of syntax,[5] one generates sentences from a grammar, classically by starting with a start symbol, and performing a derivation which is a sequence of top-down rewrites until one has a phrase marker all of whose leaf nodes are terminals (that is, words). For example, figure 12.3 (a) shows the derivation of a sentence using the grammar of table 11.2, where at each stage one non-terminal symbol gets rewritten according to the grammar. A straightforward way to make rewrite systems probabilistic is to define probability distributions over each choice point in the derivation. For instance, at the last step, we chose to rewrite the final N as *telescopes*, but could have chosen something else, in accord with the grammar. The linear steps of a derivational process map directly onto a standard stochastic process, where the states are productions of the grammar. Since the generative grammar can generate all sentences of the language, a derivational model is inherently a language model.

Thus a way to work out a probability for a parse tree is in terms of the probability of derivations of it. Now in general a given parse tree can have multiple derivations. For instance, the tree in (12.11) has not

_____

5. In the original sense of Chomsky (1957); in more recent work Chomsky has suggested that 'generative' means nothing more than 'formal' (Chomsky 1995: 162).

only the derivation in figure 12.3 (a), but also others, such as the one in figure 12.3 (b), where the second NP is rewritten before the V.

(12.11)

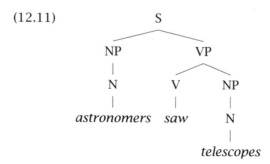

So, in general, to estimate the probability of a tree, we have to calculate:

(12.12) $P(t) = \displaystyle\sum_{\{d:\, d \text{ is a derivation of } t\}} P(d)$

However, in many cases, such as the PCFG case, this extra complication is unnecessary. It is fairly obvious to see (though rather more difficult to prove) that the choice of derivational order in the PCFG case makes no difference to the final probabilities.[6] Regardless of what probability distribution we assume over the choice of which node to rewrite next in a derivation, the final probability for a tree is otherwise the same. Thus we can simplify things by finding a way of choosing a unique derivation for each tree, which we will refer to as a *canonical derivation*. For instance, CANONICAL the leftmost derivation shown in figure 12.3 (a), where at each step we DERIVATION expand the leftmost non-terminal can be used as a canonical derivation. When this is possible, we can say:

(12.13) $P(t) = P(d)$ where *d* is the canonical derivation of *t*

Whether this simplification is possible depends on the nature of the probabilistic conditioning in the model. It is possible in the PCFG case because probabilities depend only on the parent node, and so it doesn't matter if other nodes have been rewritten yet or not. If more context is used, or there are alternative ways to generate the same pieces of structure, then the probability of a tree might well depend on the derivation. See sections 12.2.1 and 12.2.2.[7]

---

6. The proof depends on using the kind of derivation to tree mapping developed in (Hopcroft and Ullman 1979).
7. Even in such cases, one might choose to approximate tree probabilities by estimating

Let us write $\alpha_u \overset{r_i}{\rightarrow} \alpha_v$ for an individual rewriting step r_i rewriting the string α_u as α_v. To calculate the probability of a derivation, we use the chain rule, and assign a probability to each step in the derivation, conditioned by preceding steps. For a standard rewrite grammar, this looks like this:

(12.14) $$P(d) = P(S \overset{r_1}{\rightarrow} \alpha_1 \overset{r_2}{\rightarrow} \alpha_2 \overset{r_3}{\rightarrow} \ldots \overset{r_m}{\rightarrow} \alpha_m = s) = \prod_{i=1}^{m} P(r_i | r_1, \ldots r_{i-1})$$

We can think of the conditioning terms above, that is, the rewrite rules already applied, as the history of the parse, which we will refer to as h_i.

HISTORY-BASED GRAMMARS

So $h_i = (r_1, \ldots, r_{i-1})$. This is what led to the notion of *history-based grammars* (HBGs) explored initially at IBM. Since we can never model the entire history, normally what we have to do is form equivalence classes of the history via an equivalencing function π and estimate the above as:

(12.15) $$P(d) = \prod_{i=1}^{m} P(r_i | \pi(h_i))$$

This framework includes PCFGs as a special case. The equivalencing function for PCFGs simply returns the leftmost non-terminal remaining in the phrase marker. So, $\pi(h_i) = \pi(h_i')$ iff leftmost$_{NT}(\alpha_i) =$ leftmost$_{NT}(\alpha_i')$.

12.1.6 There's more than one way to do it

The way we augmented a CFG with probabilities in chapter 11 seems so natural that one might think that this is the only, or at least the only sensible, way to do it. The use of the term PCFG – probabilistic context-free grammar – tends to give credence to this view. Hence it is important to realize that this is untrue. Unlike the case of categorical context free languages, where so many different possibilities and parsing methods converge on strongly or weakly equivalent results, with probabilistic grammars, different ways of doing things normally lead to different probabilistic grammars. What is important from the probabilistic viewpoint is what the probabilities of different things are conditioned on (or looking from the other direction, what independence assumptions are made). While probabilistic grammars are sometimes equivalent – for example

---

them according to the probabilities of a canonical derivation, but this could be expected to have a detrimental effect on performance.

an HMM working from left-to-right gives the same results as one working from right-to-left, if the conditioning fundamentally changes, then
there will be a different probabilistic grammar, even if it has the same
categorical base. As an example of this, we will consider here another
way of building a probabilistic grammar with a CFG basis, Probabilistic
Left-Corner Grammars (PLCGs).

Probabilistic left-corner grammars

TOP-DOWN PARSING

If we think in parsing terms, a PCFG corresponds to a probabilistic version
of *top-down parsing*. This is because at each stage we are trying to predict
the child nodes given knowledge only of the parent node. Other parsing
methods suggest different models of probabilistic conditioning. Usually,
such conditioning is a *mixture of top-down and bottom-up information*.
One such possibility is suggested by a left-corner parsing strategy.

LEFT CORNER PARSER

Left corner parsers (Rosenkrantz and Lewis 1970; Demers 1977) work
by a combination of bottom-up and top-down processing. One begins
with a goal category (the root of what is currently being constructed),
and then looks at the left corner of the string (i.e., one shifts the next
terminal). If the left corner is the same category as the goal category,
then one can stop. Otherwise, one projects a possible local tree from
the left corner, by looking for a rule in the grammar which has the left
corner category as the first thing on its right hand side. The remaining
children of this projected local tree then become goal categories and one
recursively does left corner parsing of each. When this local tree is fin-
ished, one again recursively does left-corner parsing with the subtree as
the left corner, and the same goal category as we started with. To make
this description more precise, pseudocode for a simple left corner recognizer is shown in figure 12.4.[8] This particular parser assumes that lexical
material is introduced on the right-hand side of a rule, e.g., as N → *house*,
and that the top of the stack is to the left when written horizontally.
The parser works in terms of a stack of found and sought constituents,
the latter being represented on the stack as categories with a bar over
them. We use α to represent a single terminal or non-terminal (or the
empty string, if we wish to accommodate empty categories in the grammar), and y to stand for a (possibly empty) sequence of terminals and

---

8. The presentation here borrows from an unpublished manuscript of Mark Johnson and
Ed Stabler, 1993.

1 **comment**: Initialization
2 Place the predicted start symbol $\overline{S}$ on top of the stack
3 **comment**: Parser
4 **while** (an action is possible) **do** one of the following
5   **actions**
6   [Shift] Put the next input symbol on top of the stack
7   [Attach] If $\alpha\overline{\alpha}$ is on top of the stack, remove both
8   [Project] If α is on top of the stack and $A \rightarrow \alpha\ y$, replace α by $\overline{y}A$
9   **endactions**
10 **end**
11 **comment**: Termination
12 **if** empty(input) $\wedge$ empty(stack)
13   **then**
14   **exit** success
15   **else**
16   **exit** failure
17 **fi**

Figure 12.4 An LC stack parser.

SHIFTING
PROJECTING
ATTACHING

non-terminals. The parser has three operations, *shifting*, *projecting*, and *attaching*. We will put probability distributions over these operations. When to shift is deterministic: If the thing on top of the stack is a sought category $\overline{C}$, then one must shift, and one can never successfully shift at other times. But there will be a probability distribution over what is shifted. At other times we must decide whether to attach or project. The only interesting choice here is deciding whether to attach in cases where the left corner category and the goal category are the same. Otherwise we must project. Finally we need probabilities for projecting a certain local tree given the left corner (lc) and the goal category (gc). Under this model, we might have probabilities for this last operation like this:

$$P(\text{SBAR} \rightarrow \text{IN S}|lc = \text{IN}, gc = \text{S}) = 0.25$$
$$P(\text{PP} \rightarrow \text{IN NP}|lc = \text{IN}, gc = \text{S}) = 0.55$$

To produce a language model that reflects the operation of a left corner parser, we can regard each step of the parsing operation as a step in a derivation. In other words, we can generate trees using left corner probabilities. Then, just as in the last section, we can express the probability of a parse tree in terms of the probabilities of left corner derivations of that parse tree. Under left corner generation, each parse tree has a unique derivation and so we have:

$$P_{lc}(t) = P_{lc}(d) \quad \text{where } d \text{ is the LC derivation of } t$$

And the left corner probability of a sentence can then be calculated in the usual way:

$$P_{lc}(s) = \sum_{\{t:\ \text{yield}(t)=s\}} P_{lc}(t)$$

The probability of a derivation can be expressed as a product in terms of the probabilities of each of the individual operations in the derivation. Suppose that $(C_1, \ldots, C_m)$ is the sequence of operations in the LC parse derivation d of t. Then, by the chain rule, we have:

$$P(t) = P(d) = \prod_{i=1}^{m} P(C_i | C_1, \ldots, C_{i-1})$$

In practice, we cannot condition the probability of each parse decision on the entire history. The simplest left-corner model, which is all that we will develop here, assumes that the probability of each parse decision is largely independent of the parse history, and just depends on the state of the parser. In particular, we will assume that it depends simply on the left corner and top goal categories of the parse stack.

Each elementary operation of a left corner parser is either a shift, an attach or a left corner projection. Under the independence assumptions mentioned above, the probability of a shift will simply be the probability of a certain left corner child (lc) being shifted given the current goal category (gc), which we will model by P_{shift}. When to shift is deterministic. If a goal (i.e., barred) category is on top of the stack (and hence there is no left corner category), then one must shift. Otherwise one cannot. If one is not shifting, one must choose to attach or project, which we model by P_{att}. Attaching only has a non-zero probability if the left corner and the goal category are the same, but we define it for all pairs. If we do not attach, we project a constituent based on the left corner with probability P_{proj}. Thus the probability of each elementary operation C_i can be expressed in terms of probability distributions P_{shift}, P_{att}, and P_{proj} as follows:

(12.16) $P(C_i = \text{shift } lc) \quad = \quad \begin{cases} P_{shift}(lc|gc) & \text{if top is } gc \\ 0 & \text{otherwise} \end{cases}$

$$(12.17) \qquad P(C_i = \text{attach}) \quad = \quad \begin{cases} P_{att}(lc, gc) & \text{if top is not } gc \\ 0 & \text{otherwise} \end{cases}$$

$$(12.18) \qquad P(C_i = \text{proj } A \dot{\to} \gamma) \quad = \quad \begin{cases} (1 - P_{att}(lc, gc))P_{proj}(A \to \gamma | lc, gc) \\ \qquad\qquad\qquad \text{if top is not } gc \\ 0 \qquad\qquad\qquad \text{otherwise} \end{cases}$$

Where these operations obey the following constraints:

$$(12.19) \qquad\qquad \sum_{lc} P_{shift}(lc | gc) \quad = \quad 1$$

$$(12.20) \qquad\qquad \text{If } lc \neq gc, P_{att}(lc, gc) \quad = \quad 0$$

$$(12.21) \qquad \sum_{\{A \to \gamma: \gamma = lc \ \ldots\}} P_{proj}(A \to \gamma | lc, gc) \quad = \quad 1$$

From the above we note that the probabilities of the choice of different shifts and projections sum to one, and hence, since other probabilities are complements of each other, the probabilities of the actions available for each elementary operation sum to one. There are also no dead ends in a derivation, because unless A is a possible left corner constituent of gc, $P_{proj}(A \to \gamma | lc, gc) = 0$. Thus we have shown that these probabilities define a language model.[9] That is, $\sum_s P_{lc}(s | G) = 1$.

Manning and Carpenter (1997) present some initial exploration of this form of PLCGs. While the independence assumptions used above are still quite drastic, one nevertheless gets a slightly richer probabilistic model than a PCFG, because elementary left-corner parsing actions are conditioned by the goal category, rather than simply being the probability of a local tree. For instance, the probability of a certain expansion of NP can be different in subject position and object position, because the goal category is different. So the distributional differences shown in table 12.3 can be captured.[10] Manning and Carpenter (1997) show how, because of this, a PLCG significantly outperforms a basic PCFG.

Other ways of doing it

Left-corner parsing is a particularly interesting case: left-corner parsers work incrementally from left-to-right, combine top-down and bottom-up prediction, and hold pride of place in the family of Generalized Left Corner Parsing models discussed in exercise 12.6. Nevertheless it is not the

---

9. Subject to showing that the probability mass accumulates in finite trees, the issue discussed in chapter 11.
10. However, one might note that those in table 12.4 will not be captured.

only other possibility for making probabilistic parsers based on CFG parsing algorithms, and indeed other approaches were investigated earlier.

Working with bottom-up shift-reduce parsers is another obvious possibility. In particular, a thread of work has looked at making probabilistic versions of the Generalized LR parsing approach of Tomita (1991).
Briscoe and Carroll (1993) did the initial work in this area, but their
model is probabilistically improper in that the LR parse tables guide a
unification-based parser, and unification failures cause parse failures that
are not captured by the probability distributions. A solidly probabilistic
LR parser is described in (Inui et al. 1997).

12.1.7 Phrase structure grammars and dependency grammars

The dominant tradition within modern linguistics and NLP has been to
use phrase structure trees to describe the structure of sentences. But an
alternative, and much older, tradition is to describe linguistic structure in
terms of dependencies between words. Such a framework is referred to as

DEPENDENCY
GRAMMAR

a *dependency grammar*. In a dependency grammar, one word is the head
of a sentence, and all other words are either a dependent of that word,
or else dependent on some other word which connects to the headword
through a sequence of dependencies. Dependencies are usually shown as
curved arrows, as for example in (12.22).

(12.22)   The old man ate the rice slowly

Thinking in terms of dependencies is useful in Statistical NLP, but one
also wants to understand the relationship between phrase structure and
dependency models. In his work on disambiguating compound noun
structures (see page 286), Lauer (1995a; 1995b) argues that a dependency
model is better than an adjacency model. Suppose we want to disambiguate a compound noun such as *phrase structure model*. Previous work
had considered the two possible tree structures for this compound noun,
as shown in (12.23) and had tried to choose between them according to
whether corpus evidence showed a tighter collocational bond between
phrase↔structure or between *structure↔model*.

(12.23)   a.   b.

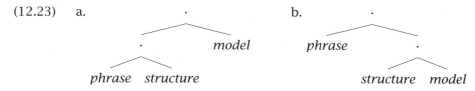

Lauer argues that instead one should examine the ambiguity in terms of dependency structures, as in (12.24), and there it is clear that the difference between them is whether *phrase* is a dependent of *structure* or whether it is a dependent of *model*. He tests this model against the adjacency model and shows that the dependency model outperforms the adjacency model.

(12.24)   a. phrase structure model   b. phrase structure model

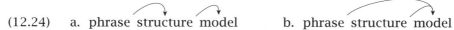

Now Lauer is right to point out that the earlier work had been flawed, and could maintain that it is easier to see what is going on in a dependency model. But this result does not show a fundamental advantage of dependency grammars over phrase structure grammars. The problem with the adjacency model was that in the trees, repeated annotated as (12.25), the model was only considering the nodes N^y and N^v, and ignoring the nodes N^x and N^u.

(12.25)   a. N^x b. N^u

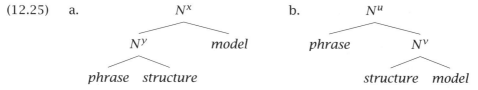

If one corrects the adjacency model so that one also considers the nodes N^x and N^u, and does the obvious lexicalization of the phrase structure tree, so that N^y is annotated with *structure* and N^v with *model* (since English noun compounds are right-headed), then one can easily see that the two models become equivalent. Under a lexicalized PCFG type model, we find that $P(N^x) = P(N^v)$, and so the way to decide between the possibilities is by comparing $P(N^y)$ vs. $P(N^u)$. But this is exactly equivalent to comparing the bond between *phrase* → *structure* and *phrase* → *model*.

There are in fact isomorphisms between various kinds of dependency grammars and corresponding types of phrase structure grammars. A dependency grammar using undirected arcs is equivalent to a phrase structure grammar where every rule introduces at least one terminal node. For

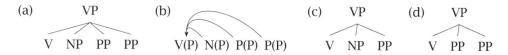

Figure 12.5 Decomposing a local tree into dependencies.

HEAD the more usual case of directed arcs, the equivalence is with 1-bar level X′ grammars. That is, for each terminal t in the grammar, there is a nonterminal $\bar{t}$, and the only rules in the grammar are of the form $\bar{t} \rightarrow \alpha\, t\, \beta$ where α and β are (possibly empty) sequences of non-terminals (cf. section 3.2.3). Another common option in dependency grammars is for the dependencies to be labeled. This in turn is equivalent to not only labeling one child of each local subtree as the *head* (as was implicitly achieved by the X-bar scheme), but labeling every child node with a relationship. Providing the probabilistic conditioning is the same, these results carry over to the probabilistic versions of both kinds of grammars.[11]

Nevertheless, dependency grammars have their uses in probabilistic parsing, and, indeed, have become increasingly popular. There appear to be two key advantages. We argued before that lexical information is key to resolving most parsing ambiguities. Because dependency grammars work directly in terms of dependencies between words, disambiguation decisions are being made directly in terms of these word dependencies. There is no need to build a large superstructure (that is, a phrase structure tree) over a sentence, and there is no need to make disambiguation decisions high up in that structure, well away from the words of the sentence. In particular, there is no need to worry about questions of how to lexicalize a phrase structure tree, because there simply is no structure that is divorced from the words of the sentence. Indeed, a dependency grammarian would argue that much of the superstructure of a phrase structure tree is otiose: it is not really needed for constructing an understanding of sentences.

The second advantage of thinking in terms of dependencies is that dependencies give one a way of decomposing phrase structure rules, and estimates of their probabilities. A problem with inducing parsers from the Penn Treebank is that, because the trees are very flat, there are lots

---

11. Note that there is thus no way to represent within dependency grammars the two or even three level X′ schemata that have been widely used in modern phrase structure approaches.

of rare kinds of flat trees with many children. And in unseen data, one will encounter yet other such trees that one has never seen before. This is problematic for a PCFG which tries to estimate the probability of a local subtree all at once. Note then how a dependency grammar decomposes this, by estimating the probability of each head-dependent relationship separately. If we have never seen the local tree in figure 12.5 (a) before, then in a PCFG model we would at best back off to some default 'unseen tree' probability. But if we decompose the tree into dependencies, as in (b), then providing we had seen other trees like (c) and (d) before, then we would expect to be able to give quite a reasonable estimate for the probability of the tree in (a). This seems much more promising than simply backing off to an 'unseen tree' probability, but note that we are making a further important independence assumption. For example, here we might be presuming that the probability of a PP attaching to a VP (that is, a preposition depending on a verb in dependency grammar terms) is independent of how many NPs there are in the VP (that is, how many noun dependents the verb has). It turns out that assuming complete independence of dependencies does not work very well, and we also need some system to account for the relative ordering of dependencies. To solve these problems, practical systems adopt various methods of allowing some conditioning between dependencies (as described below).

12.1.8   Evaluation

An important question is how to evaluate the success of a statistical parser. If we are developing a language model (not just a parsing model), then one possibility is to measure the cross entropy of the model with respect to held out data. This would be impeccable if our goal had merely been to find some form of structure in the data that allowed us to predict the data better. But we suggested earlier that we wanted to build probabilistic parsers that found particular parse trees that we had in mind, and so, while perhaps of some use as an evaluation metric, ending up doing evaluation by means of measuring cross entropy is rather inconsistent with our stated objective. Cross entropy or perplexity measures only the probabilistic weak equivalence of models, and not the tree structure that we regard as important for other tasks. In particular, probabilistically weakly equivalent grammars have the same cross entropy, but if they are not strongly equivalent, we may greatly prefer one or the other for our task.

Why are we interested in particular parse trees for sentences? People are rarely interested in syntactic analysis for its own sake. Presumably our ultimate goal is to build a system for information extraction, question answering, translation, or whatever. In principle a better way to evaluate parsers is to embed them in such a larger system and to investigate the differences that the various parsers make in such a task-based evaluation. These are the kind of differences that someone outside the parsing community might actually care about.

However, often a desire for simplicity and modularization means that it would be convenient to have measures on which a parser can be simply and easily evaluated, and which one might expect to lead to better performance on tasks. If we have good reason to believe that a certain style of parse tree is useful for further tasks, then it seems that what we could do is compare the parses found by the program with the results of hand-parsing of sentences, which we regard as a gold standard. But how should we evaluate our parsing attempts, or in other words, what is the

OBJECTIVE CRITERION

objective criterion that we are trying to maximize? The strictest criterion is to award the parser 1 point if it gets the parse tree completely right,

TREE ACCURACY
EXACT MATCH

and 0 points if it makes any kind of mistake. This is the *tree accuracy* or *exact match* criterion. It is the toughest standard, but in many ways it is a sensible one to use. In part this is because most standard parsing methods, such as the Viterbi algorithm for PCFGs try to maximize this quantity. So, since it is generally sensible for one's objective criterion to match what one's parser is maximizing, in a way using this criterion makes sense. However, clearly, in this line of reasoning, we are putting the cart before the horse. But for many potential tasks, partly right parses are not much use, and so it is a reasonable objective criterion. For example, things will not work very well in a database query system if one gets the scope of operators wrong, and it does not help much that the system got part of the parse tree right.

On the other hand, parser designers, like students, appreciate getting part-credit for mostly right parses, and for some purposes partially right parses can be useful. At any rate, the measures that have most commonly

PARSEVAL MEASURES

been used for parser evaluation are the *PARSEVAL measures*, which originate in an attempt to compare the performance of non-statistical parsers. These measures evaluate the component pieces of a parse. An example of a parsed tree, a gold standard tree, and the results on the PARSEVAL measures as they have usually been applied in Statistical NLP work is

PRECISION

shown in figure 12.6. Three basic measures are proposed: *precision* is

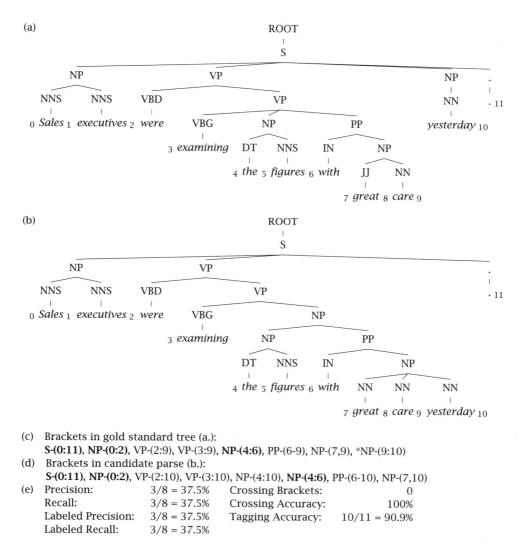

(c)   Brackets in gold standard tree (a.):
      S-(0:11), **NP-(0:2)**, VP-(2:9), VP-(3:9), **NP-(4:6)**, PP-(6-9), NP-(7,9), *NP-(9:10)
(d)   Brackets in candidate parse (b.):
      S-(0:11), **NP-(0:2)**, VP-(2:10), VP-(3:10), NP-(4:10), **NP-(4:6)**, PP-(6-10), NP-(7,10)
(e)   Precision: 3/8 = 37.5%   Crossing Brackets: 0
      Recall: 3/8 = 37.5%   Crossing Accuracy: 100%
      Labeled Precision: 3/8 = 37.5%   Tagging Accuracy: 10/11 = 90.9%
      Labeled Recall: 3/8 = 37.5%

Figure 12.6   An example of the PARSEVAL measures. The PARSEVAL measures
are easily calculated by extracting the ranges which are spanned by non-terminal
nodes, as indicated in (c) and (d) and then calculating the intersection, either
including or not including labels while doing so. The matching brackets are
shown in bold. The ROOT node is ignored in all calculations, and the preterminal
nodes are used only for the tagging accuracy calculation. The starred unary
node would be excluded in calculations according to the original standard, but
is included here.

B_1 (   )
B_2 (   )
B_3 (   )
B_4 (   )
         w_1 w_2 w_3 w_4 w_5 w_6 w_7 w_8

Figure 12.7 The idea of crossing brackets. Bracket B_1 crosses both brackets B_2 and B_4. All the other brackets are consistent. The guiding intuition is that crossing brackets cannot be combined into a single tree structure.

RECALL   how many brackets in the parse match those in the correct tree, *recall* measures how many of the brackets in the correct tree are in the parse,

CROSSING BRACKETS and *crossing brackets* gives the average of how many constituents in one tree cross over constituent boundaries in the other tree. A picture to help understand crossing brackets is in figure 12.7. Errors of this sort have often been seen as particularly dire. Rather than giving crossing brackets per tree (independent of tree size) an alternative is to report the non-crossing accuracy, the measure of the percentage of brackets that are not crossing brackets. The original PARSEVAL measures (because they were designed for implementations of various incompatible syntactic theories) ignored node labels, unary branching nodes, and performed various other (ad hoc) tree normalizations. However, if a parser is trying to duplicate parses being performed by hand, then it is reasonable to include node labels, and this is normally done, giving measures of labeled precision and recall. It is also reasonable to include unary nodes, except that the unary ROOT and preterminal nodes are not included.[12]

The PARSEVAL measures are not very discriminating. As we will see

---

12. The Penn Treebank gives all trees an unlabeled top node, here called ROOT. This is useful so that one can have rules rewriting the ROOT as the actual top node of the sentence, whether S or NP or whatever. (A surprising number of 'sentences' in newswire text are actually just noun phrases.) Including this node, and the preterminal nodes would inflate the precision and recall figures, as they are unary nodes which one could not get wrong. Including preterminal labels in the labeled measures is more defensible, but would mean that one's ability to do part of speech tagging is rolled into the performance of the parser, whereas some people feel it is best reported separately. Chains of unary nodes present some problems for these measures: the measures fail to capture the dominance ordering of the nodes, and, if multiple nodes have the same category, care must be taken in the calculation of recall. Finally we note that most evaluations of Statistical NLP parsers on the Penn Treebank have used their own ad-hoc normalizations, principally discounting sentence-internal punctuation and the distinction between the categories ADVP and PRT.

below, Charniak (1996) shows that according to these measures, one can do surprisingly well on parsing the Penn Treebank by inducing a vanilla PCFG which ignores all lexical content. This somewhat surprising result seems to reflect that in many respects the PARSEVAL measures are quite easy ones to do well on, particularly for the kind of tree structures assumed by the Penn Treebank. Firstly, it is important to note that they are measuring success at the level of individual decisions – and normally what makes NLP hard is that you have to make many consecutive decisions correctly to succeed. The overall success rate is then the nth power of the individual decision success rate – a number that easily becomes small.

But beyond this, there are a number of features particular to the structure of the Penn Treebank that make these measures particularly easy. Success on crossing brackets is helped by the fact that Penn Treebank trees are quite flat. To the extent that sentences have very few brackets in them, the number of crossing brackets is likely to be small. Identifying troublesome brackets that would lower precision and recall measures is also avoided. For example, recall that there is no disambiguation of compound noun structures within the Penn Treebank, which gives a completely flat structure to a noun compound (and any other prehead modifiers) as shown below (note that the first example also illustrates the rather questionable Penn Treebank practice of tagging hyphenated non-final portions of noun compounds as adjectives!).

(12.26)   [NP a/DT stock-index/JJ arbitrage/NN sell/NN program/NN]
           [NP a/DT joint/JJ venture/NN advertising/NN agency/NN]

Another case where peculiarities of the Penn Treebank help is the non-standard adjunction structures given to post noun-head modifiers, of the general form (NP (NP the man) (PP in (NP the moon))). As we discussed in section 8.3, a frequent parsing ambiguity is whether PPs attach to a preceding NP or VP – or even to a higher preceding node – and this is a situation where lexical or contextual information is more important than structural factors. Note now that the use of the above adjunction structure reduces the penalty for making this decision wrongly. For the different tree brackettings for Penn Treebank style structures and the type of N′ structure more commonly assumed in linguistics, as shown in figure 12.8, the errors assessed for different attachments are as shown in table 12.5. The forgivingness of the Penn Treebank scheme is manifest.

Penn VP attach   (VP saw (NP the man) (PP with (NP a telescope)))
Penn NP attach   (VP saw (NP (NP the man) (PP with (NP a telescope))))
Another VP attach   (VP saw (NP the (N′ man)) (PP with (NP a (N′ telescope)))))
Another NP attach   (VP saw (NP the (N′ man (PP with (NP a (N′ telescope))))))

Figure 12.8   Penn trees versus other trees.

| | Error | Errors assessed | | |
		Prec.	Rec.	CBs
Penn	VP instead of NP	0	1	0
	NP instead of VP	1	0	0
Another	VP instead of NP	2	2	1
	NP instead of VP	2	2	1

Table 12.5   Precision and recall evaluation results for PP attachment errors for different styles of phrase structure.

One can get the attachment wrong and not have any crossing brackets, and the errors in precision and recall are minimal.[13]

On the other hand, there is at least one respect in which the PARSEVAL measures seem too harsh. If there is a constituent that attaches very high (in a complex right-branching sentence), but the parser by mistake attaches it very low, then *every* node in the right-branching complex will be wrong, seriously damaging both precision and recall, whereas arguably only a single mistake was made by the parser. This is what happened to give the very bad results in figure 12.6. While there are two attachment errors in the candidate parse, the one that causes enormous damage in the results is attaching *yesterday* low rather than high (the parser which generated this example didn't know about temporal nouns, to its great detriment).

This all suggests that these measures are imperfect, and one might wonder whether something else should be introduced to replace them. One idea would be to look at dependencies, and to measure how many of the dependencies in the sentence are right or wrong. However, the difficulty in doing this is that dependency information is not shown in

---

13. This comparison assumes that one is including unary brackets. The general contrast remains even if one does not do so, but the badness of the non-Penn case is slightly reduced.

the Penn Treebank. While one can fairly successfully induce dependency relationships from the phrase structure trees given, there is no real gold standard available.

Returning to the idea of evaluating a parser with respect to a task, the correct approach is to examine whether success on the PARSEVAL measures is indicative of success on real tasks. Many small parsing mistakes might not affect tasks of semantic interpretation. This is suggested by results of (Bonnema 1996; Bonnema et al. 1997). For instance, in one experiment, the percentage of correct semantic interpretations was 88%, even though the tree accuracy of the parser was only 62%. The correlation between the PARSEVAL measures and task-based performance is briefly investigated by Hermjakob and Mooney (1997) with respect to their task of English to German translation. In general they find a quite good correlation between the PARSEVAL measures and generating acceptable translations. Labeled precision has by far the best correlation with a semantically adequate translation (0.78), whereas the correlation with the weaker measure of crossing brackets is much more modest (0.54). Whether there are other evaluation criteria that correlate better with success on final tasks, and whether different criteria better predict performance on different kinds of final tasks remain open questions. However, at the moment, people generally feel that these measures are adequate for the purpose of comparing parsers.

12.1.9 Equivalent models

When comparing two probabilistic grammars, it is easy to think that they are different because they are using different surface trappings, but what is essential is to work out what information is being used to condition the prediction of what. Providing the answers to that question are the same, then the probabilistic models are equivalent.

In particular, often there are three different ways of thinking about things: in terms of remembering more of the derivational history, looking at a bigger context in a phrase structure tree, or by enriching the vocabulary of the tree in deterministic ways.

Let us take a simple example. Johnson (1998) demonstrates the utility of using the grandparent node (G) as additional contextual information when rewriting a parent non-terminal (P) in a PCFG. For instance, consider the tree in (12.27).

(12.27)

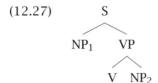

When expanding the NP non-terminals in (12.27), for NP_1, we would be using $P(NP \to \alpha | P = NP, G = S)$, while for NP_2 we would use $P(NP \to \alpha | P = NP, G = VP)$. This model can also capture the differences in the probability distributions for subject and object NPs shown in table 12.3 (while again failing to capture the distributional differences shown in table 12.4). Including information about the grandparent is surprisingly effective. Johnson shows that this simple model actually outperforms the probabilistic left-corner model presented earlier, and that in general it appears to be the most valuable simple enrichment of a PCFG model, short of lexicalization, and the concomitant need to handle sparse data that that introduces.

But the point that we wish to make here is that one can think of this model in three different ways: as using more of the derivational history, as using more of the parse tree context, or as enriching the category labels. The first way to think of it is in derivational terms, as in a history-based grammar. There we would be saying that we are doing a finer equivalence classing of derivational histories. For two derivational histories to be equivalent, not only would they have to have the same leftmost non-terminal remaining in the phrase marker, but both of these would have to have resulted from rewriting the same category. That is:

$$\pi(h) = \pi(h') \text{ iff } \begin{cases} \text{leftmost}_{NT}(\alpha_m) = \text{leftmost}_{NT}(\alpha'_m) = N^x \text{ \&} \\ \exists N^y : N^y \to \ldots N^x \ldots \in h \wedge N^y \to \ldots N^x \ldots \in h' \end{cases}$$

If two non-terminals were in different equivalence classes, they would be able to (and usually would) have different probabilities for rewriting.

But, instead of doing this, we could think of this new model simply in terms of the probability of tree structures, but suggest that rather than working out the probability of a local subtree just by looking at the nodes that comprise the subtree, we could also look at more surrounding context. One can get into trouble if one tries to look at the surrounding context in all directions at once, because then one can no longer produce a well-founded probabilistic model or parsing method – there has to be a certain directionality in the use of context. But if one is thinking of the tree being built top-down, then one can certainly include as much context from higher up in the tree as one wishes. Building equivalence classes of sequences of derivational steps is equivalent to building equivalence classes of partial trees. Just including the identity of the grandparent node is a particularly simple example of enriching context in this way.

Or thirdly, one can do what Johnson actually did and just use a generic PCFG parser, but enrich the vocabulary of the tree labels to encode this extra contextual information. Johnson simply relabeled every non-terminal with a composite label that recorded both the node's original label and its parent's label (for instance, NP_1 in (12.27) was relabeled as NP-S). Two nodes in the new trees had the same label if and only if both they and their parents had the same label in the original trees. Johnson could then use a standard PCFG parser over these new trees to simulate the effect of using extra contextual information in the original trees. All three of these methods produce equivalent probabilistic models. But the third method seems a particularly good one to remember, since it is frequently easier to write a quick program to produce transformed trees than to write a new probabilistic parser.

12.1.10   Building parsers: Search methods

TABLEAU

VITERBI ALGORITHM

For certain classes of probabilistic grammars, there are efficient algorithms that can find the highest probability parse in polynomial time. The way such algorithms work is by maintaining some form of *tableau* that stores steps in a parse derivation as they are calculated in a bottom-up fashion. The tableau is organized in such a way that if two subderivations are placed into one cell of the tableau, we know that both of them will be able to be extended in the same ways into larger subderivations and complete derivations. In such derivations, the lower probability one of the two will always lead to lower probability complete derivations, and so it may be discarded. Such algorithms are in general known as *Viterbi algorithms*, and we have seen a couple of examples in earlier chapters.

When using more complex statistical grammar formalisms, such algorithms may not be available. This can be for two reasons. There may not be (known) tabular parsing methods for these formalisms. But secondly, the above discussion assumed that by caching derivation probabilities one could efficiently find parse probabilities. Viterbi algorithms are a means of finding the highest probability derivation of a tree. They only allow us to find the highest probability parse for a tree if we can define a unique canonical derivation for each parse tree (as discussed earlier).

If there is not a one-to-one relationship between derivations and parses, then an efficient polynomial time algorithm for finding the highest probability tree may not exist. We will see an example below in section 12.2.1.

For such models, "the decoding problem" of finding the best parse becomes exponential. We nevertheless need some efficient way of moving through a large search space. If we think of a parsing problem as a search problem in this way, we can use any of the general search methods that have been developed within AI. But we will start with the original and best-known algorithm for doing this within the Statistical NLP community, the stack decoding algorithm.

The stack decoding algorithm

The stack decoding algorithm was initially developed by Jelinek (1969) for the purpose of decoding information transmissions across noisy channels. However, it is a method for exploring any tree-structured search space, such as commonly occurs in Statistical NLP algorithms. For example, a derivational parsing model gives a tree-structured search space, since we start with various choices for the first step of the derivation, and each of those will lead to a (normally different) range of choices for the second step of the derivation. It is an example of what in AI is known UNIFORM-COST as a *uniform-cost search* algorithm: one where one always expands the SEARCH least-cost leaf node first.

The stack decoding algorithm can be described via a priority queue object, an ordered list of items with operations of pushing an item and popping the highest-ranked item. Priority queues can be efficiently implemented using a heap data structure.[14] One starts with a priority queue that contains one item – the initial state of the parser. Then one goes into a loop where at each step one takes the highest probability item off the top of the priority queue, and extends it by advancing it from an n step derivation to an $n + 1$ step derivation (in general there will be multiple ways of doing this). These longer derivations are placed back on the priority queue ordered by probability. This process repeats until there is a complete derivation on top of the priority queue. If one assumes an infinite priority queue, then this algorithm is guaranteed to find the highest probability parse, because a higher probability partial derivation will always be extended before a lower probability one. That is, it is *complete*

---

14. This is described in many books on algorithms, such as (Cormen et al. 1990).

(guaranteed to find a solution if there is one) and *optimal* (guaranteed to find the best solution when there are several). If, as is common, a limited priority queue size is assumed, then one is not guaranteed to find the best parse, but the method is an effective heuristic for usually finding the best parse. The term *beam search* is used to describe systems which only keep and extend the best partial results. A *beam* may either be fixed size, or keep all results whose goodness is within a factor α of the goodness of the best item in the beam.

BEAM SEARCH

In the simplest version of the method, as described above, when one takes the highest probability item off the heap, one finds all the possible ways to extend it from an n step derivation to an $n+1$ step derivation, by seeing which next parsing steps are appropriate, and pushing the resulting $n+1$ step derivations back onto the heap. But Jelinek (1969) describes an optimization (which he attributes to John Cocke), where instead of doing that, one only applies the highest probability next step, and therefore pushes only the highest probability $n+1$ step derivation onto the stack, together with continuation information which can serve to point to the state at step n and the other extensions that were possible. Thereafter, if this state is popped from the stack, one not only determines and pushes on the highest probability $n+2$ step derivation, but one retrieves the continuation, applies the second highest probability rule, and pushes on the second highest probability $n+1$ step derivation (perhaps with its own continuation). This method of working with continuations is in practice very effective at reducing the beam size needed for effective parsing using the stack decoding algorithm.

A* search

Uniform-cost search can be rather inefficient, because it will expand all partial derivations (in a breadth-first-like manner) a certain distance, rather than directly considering whether they are likely to lead to a high probability complete derivation. There exist also *best-first search* algorithms which do the opposite, and judge which derivation to expand based on how near to a complete solution it is. But really what we want to do is find a method that combines both of these and so tries to expand the derivation that looks like it will lead to the highest probability parse, based on both the derivational steps already taken and the work still left to do. Working out the probability of the steps already taken is easy. The tricky part is working out the probability of the work still to do. It turns

BEST-FIRST SEARCH

out, though, that the right thing to do is to choose an optimistic estimate, meaning that the probability estimate for the steps still to be taken is always equal to or higher than the actual cost will turn out to be. If we can do that, it can be shown that the resulting search algorithm is still complete and optimal. Search methods that work in this way are called *A* search* algorithms. A* search algorithms are much more efficient because they direct the parser towards the partial derivations that look nearest to leading to a complete derivation. Indeed, A* search is *optimally efficient* meaning that no other optimal algorithm can be guaranteed to explore less of the search space.

A* SEARCH

OPTIMALLY EFFICIENT

Other methods

We have merely scratched the surface of the literature on search methods. More information can be found in most AI textbooks, for example (Russell and Norvig 1995: ch. 3–4).

We might end this subsection by noting that in cases where the Viterbi algorithm is inapplicable, one also usually gives up 'efficient' training: one cannot use the EM algorithm any more either. But one can do other things. One approach which has been explored at IBM is growing a decision tree to maximize the likelihood of a treebank (see section 12.2.2).

12.1.11   Use of the geometric mean

Any standard probabilistic approach ends up multiplying a large number of probabilities. This sequence of multiplications is justified by the chain rule, but most usually, large assumptions of conditional independence are made to make the models usable. Since these independence assumptions are often quite unjustifiable, large errors may accumulate. In particular, failing to model dependencies tends to mean that the estimated probability of a tree becomes far too low. Two other problems are sparse data where probability estimates for infrequent unseen constructs may also be far too low, and defective models like PCFGs that are wrongly biased to give short sentences higher probabilities than long sentences. As a result of this, sentences with bigger trees, or longer derivational histories tend to be penalized in existing statistical parsers. To handle this, it has sometimes been suggested (Magerman and Marcus 1991; Carroll 1994) that one should rather calculate the geometric mean (or equivalently the average log probability) of the various derivational steps. Such a move takes one out of the world of probabilistic approaches (however crude the assumptions) and into the world of *ad hoc* scoring functions for parsers. This approach can sometimes prove quite effective in practice, but it is treating the symptoms not the cause of the problem. For the goal of speeding up chart parsing, Caraballo and Charniak (1998) show that using the geometric mean of the probability of the rules making up a constituent works much better than simply using the probability of the constituent for rating which edges to focus on extending – this is both because the PCFG model is strongly biased to give higher probabilities to smaller trees, and because this measure ignores the probability of the rest of the tree. But they go on to show that one can do much better still by developing better probabilistic metrics of goodness.

12.2 Some Approaches

In the remainder of this chapter, we examine ways that some of the ideas presented above have been combined into statistical parsers. The presentations are quite brief, but give an overview of some of the methods that are being used and the current state of the art.

12.2.1 Non-lexicalized treebank grammars

A basic division in probabilistic parsers is between lexicalized parsers which deal with words, and those that operate over word categories. We will first describe non-lexicalized parsers. For a non-lexicalized parser, the input 'sentence' to parse is really just a list of word category tags, the preterminals of a normal parse tree. This obviously gives one much less information to go on than a sentence with real words, and in the second half we will discuss higher-performing lexicalized parsers. However, apart from general theoretical interest, the nice thing about non-lexicalized parsers is that the small terminal alphabet makes them easy to build. One doesn't have to worry too much about either computational efficiency or issues of smoothing sparse data.

PCFG estimation from a treebank: Charniak (1996)

Charniak (1996) addresses the important empirical question of how well a parser can do if it ignores lexical information. He takes the Penn Treebank, uses the part of speech and phrasal categories it uses (ignoring functional tags), induces a maximum likelihood PCFG from the trees by using the relative frequency of local trees as the estimates for rules in the obvious way, makes no attempt to do any smoothing or collapsing of rules, and sets out to try to parse unseen sentences.[15]

The result was that this grammar performed surprisingly well. Its performance in terms of precision, recall, and crossing brackets is not far below that of the best lexicalized parsers (see table 12.6). It is interesting to consider why this is. This result is surprising because such a parser will always choose the same resolution of an attachment ambiguity when confronted with the same structural context – and hence must often be wrong (cf. section 8.3). We feel that part of the answer is that these scoring measures are undiscerning on Penn Treebank trees, as we discussed in section 12.1.8. But it perhaps also suggests that while interesting parsing decisions, such as classic attachment ambiguities, clearly require semantic or lexical information, perhaps the majority of parsing decisions are mundane, and can be handled quite well by an unlexicalized PCFG. The precision, recall, and crossing brackets measures record average performance, and one can fare quite well on average with just a PCFG.

The other interesting point is that this result was achieved without any smoothing of the induced grammar, despite the fact that the Penn Treebank is well-known for its flat many-branching constituents, many of which are individually rare. As Charniak shows, the grammar induced from the Penn Treebank ends up placing almost no categorical constraints on what part of speech can occur next in a sentence, so one can parse any sentence. While it is certainly true that some rare local trees appear in the test set that were unseen during training, it is unlikely that they would ever occur in the highest probability parse, even if smoothing were done. Thus, under these circumstances, just using maximum likelihood estimates does no harm.

Partially unsupervised learning: Pereira and Schabes (1992)

We have discussed how the parameter estimation space for realistic-sized PCFGs is so big that the EM algorithm unaided tends to be of fairly little use, because it always gets stuck in a local maximum. One way to try to

---

15. We simplify slightly. Charniak did do a couple of things: recoding auxiliary verbs via an AUX tag, and incorporating a 'right-branching correction,' so as to get the parser to prefer right branching structures.

encourage the probabilities into a good region of the parameter space is proposed by Pereira and Schabes (1992) and Schabes et al. (1993). They begin with a Chomsky normal form grammar with 15 non-terminals over an alphabet of 45 part of speech tags as terminals, and train it not on raw sentences but on treebank sentences, where they ignore the non-terminal labels, but use the treebank bracketing. They employ a variant of the Inside-Outside algorithm constrained so as to only consider parses that do not cross Penn-Treebank nodes. Their parser always parses into binary constituents, but it can learn from any style of bracketing, which the parser regards as a partial bracketing of the sentence. We will not present here their modified versions of the Inside-Outside algorithm equations, but the basic idea is to reduce to zero the contribution to the reestimation equations of any proposed constituent which is not consistent with the treebank bracketing. Since bracketing decreases the number of rule split points to be considered, a bracketed training corpus also speeds up the Inside-Outside algorithm.

On a small test corpus, Pereira and Schabes (1992) show the efficacy of the basic method. Interestingly, both the grammars trained on unbracketed and bracketed training material converge on a very similar cross-entropy, but they differ hugely on how well their bracketings correspond to the desired bracketings present in the treebank. When the input was unbracketed, only 37% of the brackets the parser put on test sentences were correct, but when it had been trained on bracketed sentences, 90% of the brackets placed on test sentences were correct. Moreover, while EM training on the unbracketed data was successful in decreasing the cross-entropy, it was ineffective at improving the bracketing accuracy of the parser over the accuracy of the model resulting from random initialization of the parameters. This result underlines the discussion at the beginning of the chapter: current learning methods are effective at finding models with low entropy, but they are insufficient to learn syntactic structure from raw text. Only by chance will the inferred grammar agree with the usual judgements of sentence structure. At the present time, it is an open question whether the normally assumed hierarchical structure of language is underdetermined by the raw data, or whether the evidence for it is simply too subtle to be discovered by current induction techniques.

Schabes et al. (1993) test the same method on a larger corpus including longer sentences with similar results. They make use of one additional interesting idea, which is to impose a uniform right branching binary structure on all flat *n*-ary branching local trees of the Penn Treebank in the training data so as to maximize the speed-up to the Inside-Outside algorithm that comes from bracketing being present.

Parsing directly from trees: Data-Oriented Parsing

An interesting alternative to the grammar-based models that we have considered so far is to work out statistics directly on pieces of trees in a treebank, where the treebank is assumed to represent the body of parses that one has previously explored. Rather than deriving a grammar from the treebank, we let the parsing process use whichever fragments of trees appear to be useful. This has the apparent advantage that idiom chunks like *to take advantage of* will be used where they are present, whereas such chunks are not straightforwardly captured in PCFG-style models. Such an approach has been explored within the Data-Oriented Parsing (DOP) framework of Rens Bod and Remko Scha (Sima'an et al. 1994; Bod 1995, 1996, 1998). In this section, we will look at the DOP1 model.

Suppose we have a corpus of two sentences, as in (12.28):

(12.28)

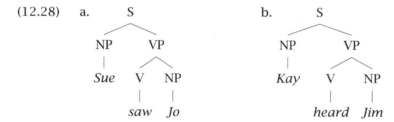

Then, to parse a new sentence like *Sue heard Jim*, we could do it by putting together tree fragments that we have already seen. For example we can compose these two tree fragments:

(12.29)

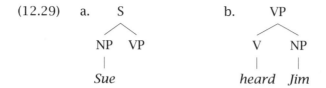

We can work out the probability of each tree fragment in the corpus, given that one is expanding a certain node, and, assuming independence, we can multiply these probabilities together (for instance, there are 8

fragments with VP as the parent node – fragments must include either all or none of the children of a node – among which (12.29b) occurs once, so its probability is 1/8). But that is only one derivation of this parse tree. In general there are many. Here is another one from our corpus, this time involving the composition of three tree fragments:

(12.30)

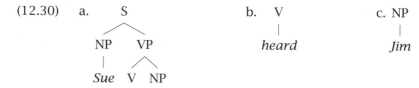

Since there are multiple fundamentally distinct derivations of a single tree in this DOP model, here we have an example of a grammar where the highest probability parse cannot be found efficiently by a Viterbi algo-rithm (Sima'an 1996) – see exercise 12.8. Parsing has therefore been done using *Monte Carlo simulation* methods. This is a technique whereby the probability of an event is estimated by taking random samples. One ran-domly produces a large number of derivations and uses these to estimate the most probable parse. With a large enough sample, these estimates can be made as accurate as desired, but the parsing process becomes slow.

MONTE CARLO
SIMULATION

The DOP approach is in some ways similar to the memory-based learn-ing (MBL) approach (Zavrel and Daelemans 1997) in doing prediction di-rectly from a corpus, but differs in that whereas the MBL approach pre-dicts based on a few similar exemplars, the DOP model uses statistics over the entire corpus.

The DOP model provides a different way of thinking, but it is important to realize that it is not *that* different to what we have been doing with PCFGs. After all, rather than writing grammar rules like S → NP VP and VP → V NP, we could instead write tree fragments:

(12.31)

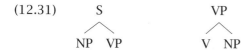

And the probabilities that we estimate for grammar rules from a tree-bank are exactly the same as would be assigned based on their relative frequency in the treebank on the DOP model.

The difference between PCFGs and what we have here is that rather than only having local trees of depth 1, we can have bigger tree frag-

PROBABILISTIC TREE
SUBSTITUTION
GRAMMAR

ments. The model can be formalized as a *Probabilistic Tree Substitution Grammar* (PTSG), which has five components just like the definition of a PCFG in chapter 11. However, rather than a set of rules, we have a set of tree fragments of arbitrary depth whose top and interior nodes are nonterminals and whose leaf nodes are terminals or nonterminals, and the probability function assigns probabilities to these fragments. PTSGs are thus a generalization of PCFGs, and are stochastically more powerful, because one can give particular probabilities to fragments – or just whole parses – which cannot be generated as a multiplication of rule probabilities in a PCFG. Bod (1995) shows that by starting with a PCFG model of depth 1 fragments and then progressively allowing in larger fragments parsing accuracy does increase significantly (this mirrors the result of Johnson (1998) on the utility of context from higher nodes in the tree). So the DOP model provides another way to build probabilistic models that use more conditioning context.

12.2.2   Lexicalized models using derivational histories

History-based grammars (HBGs)

Probabilistic methods based on the history of the derivation, and including a rich supply of lexical and other information, were first explored in large scale experiments at IBM, and are reported in (Black et al. 1993). This work exploited a one-to-one correspondence between leftmost derivations and parse trees, to avoid summing over possible derivations. The general idea was that all prior parse decisions could influence following parse decisions in the derivation, however, in the 1993 model, the only conditioning features considered were those on a path from the node currently being expanded to the root of the derivation, along with what number child of the parent a node is (from left to right).[16] Black et al. (1993) used decision trees to decide which features in the derivational history were important in determining the expansion of the current node. We will cover decision trees in section 16.1, but they can be thought of just as a tool that divides up the history into highly predictive equivalence classes.

---

16. Simply using a feature of being the nth child of the parent seems linguistically somewhat unpromising, since who knows what material may be in the other children, but this gives some handle on the varying distribution shown in table 12.4.

Unlike most other work, this work used a custom treebank, produced by the University of Lancaster. In the 1993 experiments, they restricted themselves to sentences completely covered by the most frequent 3000 words in the corpus (which effectively avoids many sparse data issues). Black et al. began with an existing hand-built broad-coverage feature-based unification grammar. This was converted into a PCFG by making equivalence classes out of certain labels (by ignoring or grouping certain features and feature-value pairs). This PCFG was then reestimated using a version of the Inside-Outside algorithm that prevents bracket crossing, as in the work of Pereira and Schabes (1992) discussed above.

Black et al. lexicalize their grammar so that phrasal nodes inherit two words, a lexical head H_1, and a secondary head H_2. The lexical head is the familiar syntactic head of the phrase, while the secondary head is another word that is deemed useful (for instance, in a prepositional phrase, the lexical head is the preposition, while the secondary head is the head of the complement noun phrase). Further, they define a set of about 50 each of syntactic and semantic categories, $\{Syn_p\}$ and $\{Sem_p\}$, to be used to classify non-terminal nodes. In the HBG parser, these two features, the two lexical heads, and the rule R to be applied at a node are predicted based on the same features of the parent node, and the index I expressing what number child of the parent node is being expanded. That is, we wish to calculate:

$$P(Syn, Sem, R, H_1, H_2 | Syn_p, Sem_p, R_p, I_{pc}, H_{1p}, H_{2p})$$

This joint probability is decomposed via the chain rule and each of the features is estimated individually using decision trees.

The idea guiding the IBM work was that rather than having a linguist tinker with a grammar to improve parsing preferences, the linguist should instead just produce a parser that is capable of parsing all sentences. One then gets a statistical parser to learn from the information in a treebank so that it can predict the correct parse by conditioning parsing steps on the derivation history. The HBG parser was tested on sentences of 7–17 words, by comparing its performance to the existing unification-based parser. The unification-based parser chose the correct parse for sentences about 60% of the time, while the HBG parser found the correct parse about 75% of the time, so the statistical parser was successful in producing a 37% reduction in error over the best disambiguation rules that the IBM linguist had produced by hand.

SPATTER

The HBG work was based on a language model, but work at IBM then started experimenting with building a parsing model directly. The early work reported in Jelinek et al. (1994) was developed as the SPATTER model in Magerman (1994, 1995), which we briefly review here.

SPATTER also works by determining probabilities over derivations, but it works in a bottom-up fashion, by starting with the words and building structure over them. Decision tree models are again used to pick out features of the derivational history that are predictive for a certain parsing decision. SPATTER began the trend of decomposing local phrase structure trees into individual parsing decisions, but rather than using a variant of dependency grammar, as in most other work, it used a somewhat odd technique of predicting which way the branch above a node pointed.

In SPATTER, a parse tree is encoded in terms of *words*, part of speech *tags*, non-terminal *labels*, and *extensions*, which encode the tree shape. Tagging was done as part of the parsing process. Since the grammar is fully lexicalized, the word and tag of the head child is always carried up to non-terminal nodes. If we start with some words and want to predict the subtree they form, things look something like this:

(12.32)

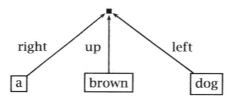

A node predicts an extension which expresses the type of the line above it connecting it to the parent node. There are five extensions: for subtrees with two or more branches, **right** is assigned to the leftmost child, **left** is assigned to the rightmost child, and **up** is assigned to any children in between, while **unary** is assigned to an 'only child' and **root** is assigned to the root node of the tree. (Note that right and left are thus switched!)

These features, including the POS tags of the words, are predicted by decision-tree models. For one node, features are predicted in terms of features of surrounding and lower nodes, where these features have already been determined. The models use the following questions (where X is one of the four features mentioned above):

- What is the X at the {current node/node {1/2} to the {left/right}}?

- What is the X at the current node's {first/second} {left/right}-most child?

- How many children does the node have?

- What is the span of the node in words?

- [For tags:] What are the two previous POS tags?

The parser was allowed to explore different derivation sequences, so it could start working where the best predictive information was available (although in practice possible derivational orders were greatly constrained). The probability of a parse was found by summing over derivations.

Some features of SPATTER, such as the extensions feature, were rather weird, and overall the result was a large and complex system that required a great deal of computer power to train and run (the decision tree training and smoothing algorithms were particularly computationally intensive). But there was no doubting its success. SPATTER showed that one could automatically induce from treebank data a successful statistical parser which clearly outperformed any existing hand-crafted parser in its ability to handle naturally occurring text.

12.2.3   Dependency-based models

Collins (1996)

More recently Collins (1996; 1997) has produced probabilistic parsing models from treebank data that are simpler, more intuitive, and more quickly computable than those explored in the preceding subsection, but which perform as well or better.

Collins (1996) introduces a lexicalized generally Dependency Grammar-like framework, except that baseNP units in the Penn Treebank are treated as chunks (using chunks in parsing in this way is reminiscent of the approach of Abney (1991)). The original model was again a parsing model. A sentence was represented as a bag of its baseNPs and other words (B) with dependencies (D) between them:

(12.33)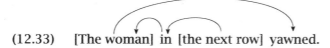
[The woman] in [the next row] yawned.

Then:

$$P(t|s) = P(B, D|s) = P(B|s) \times P(D|s, B)$$

Tagging was an independent process, and was performed by the maximum entropy tagger of Ratnaparkhi (1996). The probability estimate for baseNPs uses the idea of Church (1988) for identifying NPs (see section 10.6.2). Each gap G_i between words is classified as either the start or end of an NP, between two NPs or none of the above. Then the probability of a baseNP β of length m starting at w_u is given in terms of the predicted gap features as:

$$P(\beta|s) = \prod_{i=u+1}^{u+m} \hat{P}(G_i|w_{i-1}, t_{i-1}, w_i, t_i, c_i)$$

where c_i represents whether there is a 'comma' between the words or not. Deleted interpolation is used to smooth this probability.

For the dependency model, Collins replaced each baseNP with its head word and removed punctuation to give a reduced sentence. But punctuation is used to guide parsing. Part of what is clever about Collins' approach is that he works directly with the phrase structures of the Penn Treebank, but derives a notation for dependencies automatically from them. Dependencies are named based on the head and two child constituents. So if one has a subtree as in (12.34), the dependency between the PP and verb is labeled VBD_VP_PP.

(12.34)

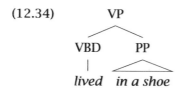

In other words, the dependency names are derived from purely categorial labels, but end up capturing much of the functional information that one would like to use in a parser. Nevertheless, the system does still have a few limitations – for instance, these dependency labels do not capture the difference between the two objects of a ditransitive verb.

Each dependency is assumed to be independent – a somewhat unrealistic assumption. Then, each word w_m apart from the main predicate of the sentence will be dependent on some head h_{w_m} via a dependency relationship $R_{w_m,h_{w_m}}$. Thus D can be written as a set of dependencies $\{d(w_i, h_{w_i}, R_{w_i,h_{w_i}})\}$, and we have that:

$$P(D|S,B) = \prod_{j=1}^{n} P(d(w_j, h_{w_j}, R_{w_j,h_{w_j}}))$$

Collins calculates the probability that two word-tag pairs $\langle w_i, t_i \rangle$ and $\langle w_j, t_j \rangle$ appear in the same reduced sentence with relationship R within the Penn treebank in the obvious way. He counts up how common one relationship is compared to the space of all relationships:

$$\hat{F}(R|\langle w_i, t_i \rangle, \langle w_j, t_j \rangle) = \frac{C(R, \langle w_i, t_i \rangle, \langle w_j, t_j \rangle)}{C(\langle w_i, t_i \rangle, \langle w_j, t_j \rangle)}$$

And then he normalizes this quantity to give a probability.

This model was then complicated by adding conditioning based on the 'distance' over which the dependency stretched, where distance was evaluated by an ad hoc function that included not only the distance, but direction, whether there was an intervening verb, and how many intervening commas there were.

The parser used a beam search with various pruning heuristics for efficiency. The whole system can be trained in 15 minutes, and runs quickly, performing well even when a quite small beam is used. Collins' parser slightly outperforms SPATTER, but the main advance seems to be in building a much simpler and faster system that performs basically as well. Collins also evaluates his system both using and not using lexical information and suggests that lexical information gives about a 10% improvement on labeled precision and recall. The odd thing about this result is that the unlexicalized version ends up performing rather worse than Charniak's PCFG parser. One might hypothesize that while splitting up local subtrees into independent dependencies is useful for avoiding data sparseness when dealing with a lexicalized model, it nevertheless means that one doesn't capture some (statistical) dependencies which are being profitably used in the basic PCFG model.

A lexicalized dependency-based language model

Collins (1997) redevelops the work of Collins (1996) as a generative language model (whereas the original had been a probabilistically deficient parsing model). He builds a sequence of progressively more complex models, at each stage getting somewhat improved performance. The general approach of the language model is to start with a parent node and a head and then to model the successive generation of dependents on both the left and right side of the head. In the first model, the probability of each dependent is basically independent of other dependents (it depends on the parent and head nodes' category, the head lexical item, and a final composite feature that is a function of distance, intervening words, and punctuation). Dependents continue to be generated until a special pseudo-nonterminal STOP is generated.

Collins then tries to build more complex models that do capture some of the (statistical) dependencies between different dependents of a head. What is of particular interest is that the models start bringing in a lot of traditional linguistics. The second model makes use of the argument/adjunct distinction and models the subcategorization frames of heads. A subcategorization frame is predicted for each head, and the generation of dependents is additionally conditioned on the bag of subcategorized arguments predicted that have not yet been generated. A problem caused by trying to model subcategorization is that various subcategorized arguments may not be overtly present in their normal place, due to processes like the implicit object alternation (section 8.4) or *Wh*-movement. In the final model Collins attempts to incorporate *Wh*-movement into the probabilistic model, through the use of traces and coindexed fillers (which are present in the Penn treebank). While the second model performs considerably better than the first, this final complication is not shown to give significantly better performance).

12.2.4 Discussion

Some overall parsing performance figures for some roughly comparable systems are shown in table 12.6.[17] At the time of writing, Collins' results are the best for a broad coverage statistical parser. It remains an open research problem to see whether one can weld useful elements of the IBM work (such as using held out data to estimate model parameters, the use

---

17. All these systems were trained on the Penn Treebank, and tested on an unseen test set of sentences of 2–40 words, also from the Penn Treebank. However, various details of the treatment of punctuation, choosing to ignore certain non-terminal distinctions, etc., nevertheless mean that the results are usually not *exactly* comparable. The results for SPATTER are the results Collins (1996) gives for running SPATTER on the same test set as his own parsers, and differ slightly from the results reported in (Magerman 1995).

	Sentences of $\leq$ 40 words			
	% LR	% LP	CB	% 0 CBs
Charniak (1996) PCFG	80.4	78.8	n/a	n/a
Magerman (1995) SPATTER	84.6	84.9	1.26	56.6
Collins (1996) best	85.8	86.3	1.14	59.9
Charniak (1997a) best	87.5	87.4	1.00	62.1
Collins (1997) best	88.1	88.6	0.91	66.5

Table 12.6 Comparison of some statistical parsing systems. LR = labeled recall, LP = labeled precision, CB = crossing brackets, n/a means that a result is not given (Charniak (1996) gives a result of 87.7% for non-crossing accuracy).

of decision trees, and more sophisticated deleted estimation techniques) with the key ideas of Collins' work to produce even better parsers. Additionally, we note that there are several other systems with almost as good performance, which use quite different parsing techniques, and so there still seems plenty of room for further investigation of other techniques. For instance, Charniak (1997a) uses probability estimates for conventional grammar rules (suitably lexicalized). The rule by which to expand a node is predicted based on the the node's category, its parent's category, and its lexical head. The head of each child is then predicted based on the child's category and the parent node's category and lexical head. Charniak provides a particularly insightful analysis of the differences in the conditioning used in several recent state-of-the-art statistical parsers and of what are probably the main determinants of better and worse performance.

Just as in tagging, the availability of rich lexical resources (principally, the Penn treebank) and the use of statistical techniques brought new levels of parsing performance. However, we note that recent incremental progress, while significant, has been reasonably modest. As Charniak (1997a: 601) points out:

This seems to suggest that if our goal is to get, say, 95% average labeled precision and recall, further incremental improvements on this basic scheme may not get us there.

Qualitative breakthroughs may well require semantically richer lexical resources and probabilistic models.

12.3   Further Reading

A variety of work on grammar induction can be found in the biennial proceedings of the International Colloquium on Grammar Inference (Carrasco and Oncina 1994; Miclet and de la Higuera 1996; Honavar and Slutzki 1998).

The current generation of work on probabilistic parsing of unrestricted text emerged within the DARPA Speech and Natural Language community. Commonly cited early papers include (Chitrao and Grishman 1990) and (Magerman and Marcus 1991). In particular, Magerman and Marcus make early reference to the varying structural properties of NPs in different positions.

Another thread of early work on statistical parsing occurred at the University of Lancaster. Atwell (1987) and Garside and Leech (1987) describe a constituent boundary finder that is similar to the NP finding of (Church 1988). A PCFG trained on a small treebank is then used to choose between possible constituents. Some discussion of the possibilities of using simulated annealing also appears. They suggest that their system could find an "acceptable" parse about 50% of the time.

Another important arena of work on statistical parsing is work within the pattern recognition community, an area pioneered by King-Sun Fu. See in particular (Fu 1974).

An approachable introduction to statistical parsing including part-of-speech tagging appears in (Charniak 1997b). The design of the Penn Treebank is discussed in (Marcus et al. 1993) and (Marcus et al. 1994). It is available from the Linguistic Data Consortium.

PARSEVAL MEASURES   The original *PARSEVAL measures* can be found in (Black et al. 1991) or (Harrison et al. 1991). A study of various parsing evaluation metrics, their relationships, and appropriate parsing algorithms for different objective functions can be found in (Goodman 1996).

DEPENDENCY GRAMMAR   The ideas of *dependency grammar* stretch back into the work of medieval Arab grammarians, but received a clear formal statement in the work of Tesnière (1959). Perhaps the earliest work on probabilistic dependency grammars was the Probabilistic Link Grammar model of Lafferty et al. (1992). Except for one particular quirky property where a word can be bi-linked in both directions, link grammar can be thought of as a notational variant of dependency grammar. Other work on dependency-based statistical parsers includes Carroll and Charniak (1992).

We have discussed only a few papers from the current flurry of work on statistical parsing. Systems with very similar performance to (Collins 1997), but very different grammar models, are presented by Charniak (1997a) and Ratnaparkhi (1997a). See also (Eisner 1996) for another recent approach to dependency-based statistical parsers, quite similar to (Collins 1997).

Most of the work here represents probabilistic parsing with a context-free base. There has been some work on probabilistic versions of more powerful grammatical frameworks. Probabilistic TAGs (*Tree-Adjoining Grammars*) are discussed by Resnik (1992) and Schabes (1992). Early work on probabilistic versions of unification grammars like Head-driven Phrase Structure Grammar (Pollard and Sag 1994) and Lexical-Functional Grammar (Kaplan and Bresnan 1982), such as (Brew 1995), used improper distributions, because the dependencies within the unification grammar were not properly accounted for. A firmer footing for such work is provided in the work of Abney (1997). See also (Smith and Cleary 1997). Bod et al. (1996) and Bod and Kaplan (1998) explore a DOP approach to LFG.

TREE-ADJOINING
GRAMMARS

Transformation-based learning has also been applied to parsing and grammar induction (Brill 1993a,c; Brill and Resnik 1994). See chapter 10 for a general introduction to the transformation-based learning approach.

TRANSFORMATION-
BASED
LEARNING

Hermjakob and Mooney (1997) apply a non-probabilistic parser based on machine learning techniques (decision lists) to the problem of treebank parsing, and achieve quite good results. The main take-home message for future Statistical NLP research in their work is the value they get from features for semantic classes, whereas most existing Statistical NLP work has tended to overemphasize syntactic features (for the obvious reason that they are what is most easily obtained from the currently available treebanks).

Chelba and Jelinek (1998) provide the first clear demonstration of a probabilistic parser outperforming a trigram model as a language model for *speech recognition*. They use a lexicalized binarized grammar (essentially equivalent to a dependency grammar) and predict words based on the two previous heads not yet contained in a bigger constituent.

SPEECH RECOGNITION

Most of the exposition in this chapter has treated parsing as an end in itself. Partly because parsers do not perform well enough yet, parsing has rarely been applied to higher-level tasks like speech recognition and language understanding. However, there is growing interest in *semantic parsing*, an approach that attempts to build a meaning representation of a sentence from its syntactic parse in a process that integrates syntactic and semantic processing. See (Ng and Zelle 1997) for a recent overview

SEMANTIC PARSING

article. A system that is statistically trained to process sentences all the way from words to discourse representations for an airline reservation application is described by Miller et al. (1996).

12.4   Exercises

Exercise 12.1   [★]

The second sentence in the *Wall Street Journal* article referred to at the start of the chapter is:

(12.35)   The agency sees widespread use of the codes as a way of handling the rapidly growing mail volume and controlling labor costs.

Find at least five well-formed syntactic structures for this sentence. If you cannot do this exercise, you should proceed to exercise 12.2.

Exercise 12.2   [★ ★]

Write a context-free grammar parser, which takes a grammar of rewrite rules, and uses it to find all the parses of a sentence. Use this parser and the grammar in (12.36) to parse the sentence in exercise 12.1. (The format of this grammar is verbose and ugly because it does not use the abbreviatory conventions, such as optionality, commonly used for phrase structure grammars. On the other hand, it is particularly easy to write a parser that handles grammars in this form.) How many parses do you get? (The answer you should get is 83.)

(12.36)   a. S → NP VP

b. VP → { VBZ NP | VBZ NP PP | VBZ NP PP PP }

c. VPG → VBG NP

d. NP → { NP CC NP | DT NBAR | NBAR }

e. NBAR → { AP NBAR | NBAR PP | VPG | N | N N }

f. PP → P NP

g. AP → { A | RB A }

h. N → { *agency, use, codes, way, mail, volume, labor, costs*}

i. DT → { *the, a* }

j. V → *sees*

k. A → { *widespread, growing* }

l. P → { *of, as* }

m. VBG → { *handling, controlling* }

n. RB → *rapidly*

o. CC → *and*

While writing the parser, leave provision for attaching probabilities to rules, so that you will be able to use the parser for experiments of the sort discussed later in the chapter.

Exercise 12.3 [★]

In chapter 11, we suggested that PCFGs have a bad bias towards using nonterminals with few expansions. Suppose that one has as a training corpus the treebank given below, where '$n\times$' indicates how many times a certain tree appears in the training corpus. What PCFG would one get from the treebank (using MLE as discussed in the text)? What is the most likely parse of the string '*a a*' using that grammar. Is this a reasonable result? Was the problem of bias stated correctly in chapter 11? Discuss.

$$
\left\{
\begin{array}{ccccc}
\text{S} & \text{S} & \text{S} & \text{S} & \text{S} \\
\wedge & \wedge & \wedge & \wedge & \wedge \\
10 \times \text{B B,} & 95 \times \text{A A,} & 325 \times \text{A A,} & 8 \times \text{A A,} & 428 \times \text{A A} \\
|\;\; | & |\;\; | & |\;\; | & |\;\; | & |\;\; | \\
a\; a & a\; a & f\; g & f\; a & g\; f
\end{array}
\right\}
$$

Exercise 12.4 [★★]

Can one combine a leftmost derivation of a CFG with an n-gram model to produce a probabilistically sound language model that uses phrase structure? If so, what kinds of independence assumptions does one have to make? (If the approach you work out seems interesting, you could try implementing it!)

Exercise 12.5 [★]

While a PLCG can have different probabilities for a certain expansion of NP in subject position and object position, we noted in a footnote that a PLCG could not capture the different distributions of NPs as first and second objects of a verb that were shown in table 12.4. Explain why this is so.

Exercise 12.6 [★★★]

As shown by Demers (1977), left-corner parsers, top-down parsers and bottom-up parsers can all be fit within a large family of Generalized Left-Corner Parsers whose behavior depends on how much of the input they have looked at before undertaking various actions. This suggests other possible probabilistic models implementing other points in this space. Are there other particularly useful points in this space? What are appropriate probabilistic models for them?

Exercise 12.7 [★★]

In section 12.2.1 we pointed out that a non-lexicalized parser will always choose the same attachment in the same structural configuration. However, thinking about the issue of PP attachment discussed in section 8.3, that does not quite mean that it must always choose noun attachments or always choose verb attachments for PPs. Why not? Investigate in a corpus whether there is any utility in being able to distinguish the cases that a PCFG can distinguish.

Exercise 12.8   [★]

The aim of this exercise is to appreciate why one cannot build a Viterbi algorithm for DOP parsing. For PCFG parsing, if we have built the two constituents/partial derivations shown in (12.37a) and (12.37b), and $P(N^i)$ in (12.37a) > $P(N^i)$ in (12.37b), then we can discard (12.37b) because any bigger tree built using (12.37b) will have a lower probability than a tree which is otherwise identical but substitutes (12.37a). But we cannot do this in the DOP model. Why not? Hint: Suppose that the tree fragment (12.37c) is in the corpus.

(12.37)   a. N^i b. N^i c. N^h

         N^j c d a N^k N^i N^g

        a b b c d a N^k

Exercise 12.9   [★★★]

Build, train, and test your own statistical parser using the Penn treebank. Your results are more likely to be useful to others if you chose some clear hypothesis to explore.

PART IV

Applications and Techniques

"Also knowing nothing official about, but having guessed and inferred considerable about, the powerful new mechanized methods in cryptography—methods which I believe succeed even when one does not know what language has been coded—one naturally wonders if the problem of translation could conceivably be treated as a problem in cryptography. When I look at an article in Russian, I say: 'This is really written in English, but it has been coded in some strange symbols. I will now proceed to decode.'"

(Weaver 1955: 18, quoting a letter he wrote in 1947)

"The best way of finding out the difficulties of doing something is to try to do it, so at this point I moved to the Artificial Intelligence Laboratory at MIT . . .

"The first great revelation was that the problems are difficult. Of course, these days this fact is a commonplace. But in the 1960s almost no one realized that machine vision was difficult. The field had to go through the same experience as the machine translation field did in its fiascoes of the 1950s before it was at last realized that here were some problems that had to be taken seriously."

(Marr 1982: 15)

13 *Statistical Alignment and Machine Translation*

MACHINE TRANSLATION, the automatic translation of text or speech from one language to another, is one the most important applications of NLP. The dream of building machines that let people from different cultures talk to each other easily is one of the most appealing ideas we as NLP researchers can use to justify our profession (and to get money from funding agencies).

Unfortunately, machine translation (MT) is a hard problem. It is true that nowadays you can buy inexpensive packages that call themselves translation programs. They produce low-quality translations which are sufficient for a translator who can post-edit the output or for people who know enough about a foreign language to be able to decipher the original with the help of a buggy translation. The goal of many NLP researchers is instead to produce close to error-free output that reads fluently in the target language. Existing systems are far from this goal for all but the most restricted domains (like weather reports, Isabelle 1987).

Why is machine translation hard? The best way to answer this question is to look at different approaches to MT that have been pursued. Some important approaches are schematically presented in figure 13.1.

WORD FOR WORD
The simplest approach is to translate *word for word* (the bottom arrow in figure 13.1). One obvious problem with this is that there is no one-to-one correspondence between words in different languages. Lexical ambiguity is one reason. One of the examples we discussed in chapter 7 is the English word *suit* which has different translations in French, depending on whether it means 'lawsuit' or 'set of garments.' One needs to look at context larger than the individual word to choose the correct French translation for ambiguous words like *suit*.

Another challenge for the word-for-word approach is that languages

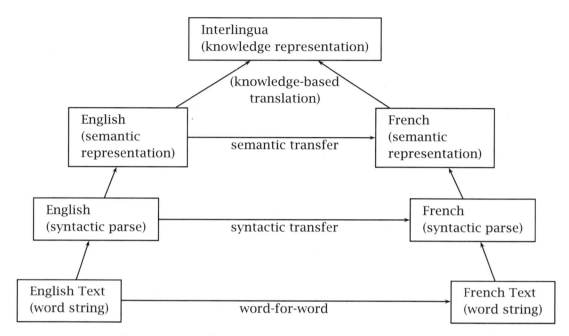

Figure 13.1   Different strategies for Machine Translation. Examples are for the case of translation from English (the source) to French (the target). Word-based methods translate the source word by word. Transfer methods build a structured representation of the source (syntactic or semantic), transform it into a structured representation of the target and generate a target string from this representation. Semantic methods use a richer semantic representation than parse trees with, for example, quantifier scope disambiguated. Interlingua methods translate via a language-independent knowledge representation. Adapted from (Knight 1997: figure 1).

SYNTACTIC TRANSFER
APPROACH

have different word orders. A naive word-for-word translation will usually get the word order in the target language wrong. This problem is addressed by the *syntactic transfer approach.*. We first parse the source text, then transform the parse tree of the source text into a syntactic tree in the target language (using appropriate rules), and then generate the translation from this syntactic tree. Note that we are again faced with ambiguity, syntactic ambiguity here, since we are assuming that we can correctly disambiguate the source text.

The syntactic transfer approach solves problems of word order, but of-

465

ten a syntactically correct translation has inappropriate semantics. For example, German *Ich esse gern* 'I like to eat' is a verb-adverb construction that translates literally as *I eat readily* (or *willingly, with pleasure, gladly*). There is no verb-adverb construction in English that can be used to express the meaning of *I like to eat.* So a syntax-based approach cannot work here.

SEMANTIC TRANSFER APPROACHIn *semantic transfer approaches*, we represent the meaning of the source sentence (presumably derived via an intermediate step of parsing as indicated by the arrows in figure 13.1), and then generate the translation from the meaning. This will fix cases of syntactic mismatch, but even this is not general enough to work for all cases. The reason is that even if the literal meaning of a translation is correct, it can still be unnatural to the point of being unintelligible. A classic example is the way that English and Spanish express direction and manner of motion (Talmy 1985). In Spanish, the direction is expressed using the verb and the manner is expressed with a separate phrase:

(13.1)   La botella entró a la cueva flotando.

With some effort, English speakers may be able to understand the literal translation 'the bottle entered the cave floating.' But if there are too many such literal translations in a text, then it becomes cumbersome to read. The correct English translation expresses the manner of motion using the verb and the direction using a preposition:

(13.2)   The bottle floated into the cave.

INTERLINGUA   An approach that does not rely on literal translations is translation via an *interlingua*. An interlingua is a knowledge representation formalism that is independent of the way particular languages express meaning. An interlingua has the added advantage that it efficiently addresses the problem of translating for a large number of languages, as is, for example, necessary in the European Community. Instead of building $O(n^2)$ translation systems, for all possible pairs of languages, one only has to build $O(n)$ systems to translate between each language and the interlingua. Despite these advantages, there are significant practical problems with interlingua approaches due to the difficulty of designing efficient and comprehensive knowledge representation formalisms and due to the large amount of ambiguity that has to be resolved to translate from a natural language to a knowledge representation language.

Where do statistical methods come into play in this? In theory, each of the arrows in figure 13.1 can be implemented based on a probabilistic model. For example, we can implement the arrow from the box "English Text (word string)" to the box "English Text (syntactic parse)" as a probabilistic parser (see chapters 11 and 12). Some components not shown in the figure could also be implemented statistically, for example, a word sense disambiguator. Such probabilistic implementation of selected modules is in fact the main use of statistical methods in machine translation at this point. Most systems are a mix of probabilistic and non-probabilistic components. However, there are a few completely statistical translation systems and we will describe one such system in section 13.3.

So why do we need a separate chapter on machine translation then, if a large part of the probabilistic work done for MT, such as probabilistic parsing and word sense disambiguation, is already covered in other chapters? Apart from a few specific MT problems (like probabilistic transfer, see the Further Reading), there is one task that mainly comes up in the MT context, the task of *text alignment*. Text alignment is not part of the translation process per se. Instead, text alignment is mostly used to create lexical resources such as bilingual dictionaries and parallel grammars, which then improve the quality of machine translation.

Surprisingly, there has been more work on text alignment in Statistical NLP than on machine translation proper, partly due the above-mentioned fact that many other components of MT systems like parsers and disambiguators are not MT-specific. For this reason, the bulk of this chapter will be about text alignment. We will then briefly discuss word alignment, the step necessary after text alignment for deriving a bilingual dictionary from a parallel text. The last two sections describe the best known attempt to construct a completely statistical MT system and conclude with some suggestions for further reading.

13.1   Text Alignment

PARALLEL TEXTS
BITEXTS

HANSARDS

A variety of work has applied Statistical NLP methods to multilingual texts. Most of this work has involved the use of *parallel texts* or *bitexts* – where the same content is available in several languages, due to document translation. The parallel texts most often used have been parliamentary proceedings (*Hansards*) or other official documents of countries with multiple official languages, such as Canada, Switzerland and Hong

Kong. One reason for using such texts is that they are easy to obtain
in quantity, but we suspect that the nature of these texts has also been
helpful to Statistical NLP researchers: the demands of accuracy lead the
translators of this sort of material to to use very consistent, literal translations. Other sources have been used (such as articles from newspapers
and magazines published in several languages), and yet other sources
are easily available (religious and literary works are often freely available in many languages), but these not only do not provide such a large
supply of text from a consistent period and genre, but they also tend to
involve much less literal translation, and hence good results are harder
to come by.

ALIGNMENT
Given that parallel texts are available online, a first task is to perform
gross large scale *alignment*, noting which paragraphs or sentences in one
language correspond to which paragraphs or sentences in another language. This problem has been well-studied and a number of quite successful methods have been proposed. Once this has been achieved, a
second problem is to learn which words tend to be translated by which
other words, which one could view as the problem of acquiring a bilingual dictionary from text. In this section we deal with the text alignment
problem, while the next section deals with word alignment and induction
of bilingual dictionaries from aligned text.

13.1.1   Aligning sentences and paragraphs

Text alignment is an almost obligatory first step for making use of multilingual text corpora. Text alignment can be used not only for the two
tasks considered in the following sections (bilingual lexicography and machine translation), but it is also a first step in using multilingual corpora
as knowledge sources in other domains, such as for word sense disambiguation, or multilingual information retrieval. Text alignment can also
be a useful practical tool for assisting translators. In many situations,
such as when dealing with product manuals, documents are regularly
revised and then each time translated into various languages. One can
reduce the burden on human translators by first aligning the old and revised document to detect changes, then aligning the old document with
its translation, and finally splicing in changed sections in the new document into the translation of the old document, so that a translator only
has to translate the changed sections.

The reason that text alignment is not trivial is that translators do not always translate one sentence in the input into one sentence in the output, although, naturally, this is the most common situation. Indeed, it is important at the outset of this chapter to realize the extent to which human translators change and rearrange material so the output text will flow well in the target language, even when they are translating material from quite technical domains. As an example, consider the extract from English and French versions of a document shown in figure 13.2. Although the material in both languages comprises two sentences, note that their content and organization in the two languages differs greatly. Not only is there a great deal of reordering (denoted imperfectly by bracketed groupings and arrows), but large pieces of material can just disappear: for example, the final English words *achieved above-average growth rates.* In the reordered French version, this content is just implied from the fact that we are talking about how in general sales of soft drinks were higher, *in particular, cola drinks.*

In the sentence alignment problem one seeks to say that some group of sentences in one language corresponds in content to some group of sentences in the other language, where either group can be empty so as to allow insertions and deletions. Such a grouping is referred to as a BEAD sentence alignment or *bead.* There is a question of how much content has to overlap between sentences in the two languages before the sentences are said to be in an alignment. In work which gives a specific criterion, normally an overlapping word or two is not taken as sufficient, but if a clause overlaps, then the sentences are said to be part of the alignment, no matter how much they otherwise differ. The commonest case of one sentence being translated as one sentence is referred to as a 1:1 sentence alignment. Studies suggest around 90% of alignments are usually of this sort. But sometimes translators break up or join sentences, yielding 1:2 or 2:1, and even 1:3 or 3:1 sentence alignments.

Using this framework, each sentence can occur in only one bead. Thus although in figure 13.2 the whole of the first French sentence is translated in the first English sentence, we cannot make this a 1:1 alignment, since much of the second French sentence also occurs in the first English sentence. Thus this is an example of a 2:2 alignment. If we are aligning at the sentence level, whenever translators move part of one sentence into another, we can only describe this by saying that some group of sentences in the source are parallel with some group of sentences in the translation. An additional problem is that in real texts there are a surprising number of cases of *crossing dependencies*, where the order of

CROSSING
DEPENDENCIES

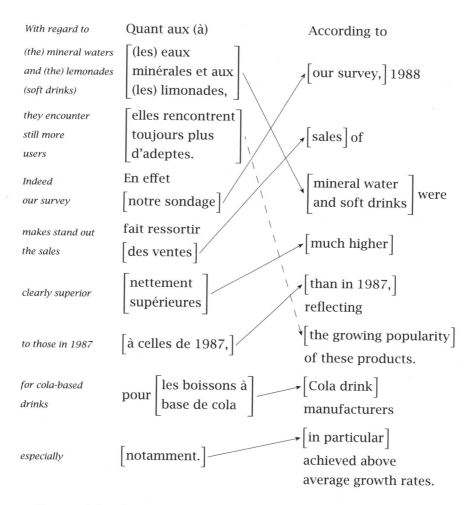

Figure 13.2 Alignment and correspondence. The middle and right columns show the French and English versions with arrows connecting parts that can be viewed as translations of each other. The italicized text in the left column is a fairly literal translation of the French text.

Paper	Languages	Corpus	Basis
Brown et al. (1991c)	English, French	Canadian Hansard	# of words
Gale and Church (1993)	English, French, German	Union Bank of Switzerland reports	# of characters
Wu (1994)	English, Cantonese	Hong Kong Hansard	# of characters
Church (1993)	various	various (incl. Hansard)	4-gram signals
Fung and McKeown (1994)	English, Cantonese	Hong Kong Hansard	lexical signals
Kay and Röscheisen (1993)	English, French, German	Scientific American	lexical (not probabilistic)
Chen (1993)	English, French	Canadian Hansard EEC proceedings	lexical
Haruno and Yamazaki (1996)	English, Japanese	newspaper, magazines	lexical (incl. dictionary)

Table 13.1 Sentence alignment papers. The table lists different techniques for text alignment, including the languages and corpora that were used as a testbed and (in column "Basis") the type of information that the alignment is based on.

sentences are changed in the translation (Dan Melamed, p.c., 1998). The algorithms we present here are not able to handle such cases accurately. Following the statistical string matching literature we can distinguish between *alignment* problems and *correspondence* problems, by adding the restriction that alignment problems do not allow crossing dependencies. If this restriction is added, then any rearrangement in the order of sentences must also be described as a many to many alignment. Given these restrictions, we find cases of 2:2, 2:3, 3:2, and, in theory at least, even more exotic alignment configurations. Finally, either deliberately or by mistake, sentences may be deleted or added during translation, yielding 1:0 and 0:1 alignments.

ALIGNMENT
CORRESPONDENCE

A considerable number of papers have examined aligning sentences in parallel texts between various languages. A selection of papers is shown in table 13.1. In general the methods can be classified along several dimensions. On the one hand there are methods that are simply length-based versus those methods that use lexical (or character string) content. Secondly, there is a contrast between methods that just give an average alignment in terms of what position in one text roughly corresponds with a certain position in the other text and those that align sentences to form sentence beads. We outline and compare the salient features of some of these methods here. In this discussion let us refer to the parallel texts in the two languages as S and T where each is a succession of sentences, so $S = (s_1, \ldots, s_I)$ and $T = (t_1, \ldots, t_J)$. If there are more than two languages, we reduce the problem to the two language case by doing pairwise alignments. Many of the methods we consider use dynamic programming methods to find the best alignment between the texts, so the reader may wish to review an introduction of dynamic programming such as Cormen et al. (1990: ch. 16).

13.1.2 Length-based methods

Much of the earliest work on sentence alignment used models that just compared the lengths of units of text in the parallel corpora. While it seems strange to ignore the richer information available in the text, it turns out that such an approach can be quite effective, and its efficiency allows rapid alignment of large quantities of text. The rationale of length-based methods is that short sentences will be translated as short sentences and long sentences as long sentences. Length usually is defined as the number of words or the number of characters.

Gale and Church (1993)

Statistical approaches to alignment attempt to find the alignment A with highest probability given the two parallel texts S and T:

(13.3) $\arg\max\limits_{A} P(A|S, T) = \arg\max\limits_{A} P(A, S, T)$

To estimate the probabilities involved here, most methods decompose the aligned texts into a sequence of aligned beads $(B_1, \ldots, B_K)$, and suggest that the probability of a bead is independent of the probability of other beads, depending only on the sentences in the bead. Then:

(13.4) $P(A, S, T) \approx \prod\limits_{k=1}^{K} P(B_k)$

The question then is how to estimate the probability of a certain type of alignment bead (such as 1:1, or 2:1) given the sentences in that bead.

The method of Gale and Church (1991; 1993) depends simply on the length of source and translation sentences measured in characters. The hypothesis is that longer sentences in one language should correspond to longer sentences in the other language. This seems uncontroversial, and turns out to be sufficient information to do alignment, at least with similar languages and literal translations.

The Union Bank of Switzerland (UBS) corpus used for their experiments provided parallel documents in English, French, and German. The texts in the corpus could be trivially aligned at a paragraph level, because paragraph structure was clearly marked in the corpus, and any confusions at this level were checked and eliminated by hand. For the experiments presented, this first step was important, since Gale and Church (1993) report that leaving it out and simply running the algorithm on whole documents tripled the number of errors. However, they suggest that the need for prior paragraph alignment can be avoided by applying the algorithm they discuss twice: firstly to align paragraphs within the document, and then again to align sentences within paragraphs. Shemtov (1993) develops this idea, producing a variant dynamic programming algorithm that is especially suited to dealing with deletions and insertions at the level of paragraphs instead of just at the sentence level.

Gale and Church's (1993) algorithm uses sentence length to evaluate how likely an alignment of some number of sentences in L_1 is with some number of sentences in L_2. Possible alignments in the study were limited to {1:1, 1:0, 0:1, 2:1, 1:2, 2:2}. This made it possible to easily find the most probable text alignment by using a dynamic programming algorithm, which tries to find the minimum possible distance between the two texts, or in other words, the best possible alignment. Let $D(i, j)$ be the lowest cost alignment between sentences $s_1, \ldots, s_i$ and $t_1, \ldots, t_j$. Then one can recursively define and calculate $D(i, j)$ by using the obvious base cases that $D(0, 0) = 0$, etc., and then defining:

$$D(i, j) = \min \begin{cases} D(i, j - 1) + \text{cost}(0\text{:}1 \text{ align } \varnothing, t_j) \\ D(i - 1, j) + \text{cost}(1\text{:}0 \text{ align } s_i, \varnothing) \\ D(i - 1, j - 1) + \text{cost}(1\text{:}1 \text{ align } s_i, t_j) \\ D(i - 1, j - 2) + \text{cost}(1\text{:}2 \text{ align } s_i, t_{j-1}, t_j) \\ D(i - 2, j - 1) + \text{cost}(2\text{:}1 \text{ align } s_{i-1}, s_i, t_j) \\ D(i - 2, j - 2) + \text{cost}(2\text{:}2 \text{ align } s_{i-1}, s_i, t_{j-1}, t_j) \end{cases}$$

For instance, one can start to calculate the cost of aligning two texts as indicated in figure 13.3. Dynamic programming allows one to efficiently consider all possible alignments and find the minimum cost alignment $D(I, J)$. While the dynamic programming algorithm is quadratic,

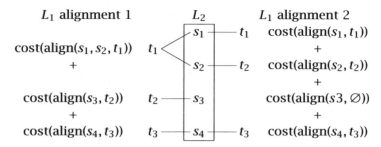

Figure 13.3   Calculating the cost of alignments. The costs of two different alignments are computed, one in the left column (which aligns t_1 with s_1 and s_2 and aligns t_2 with s_3) and one in the right column (which aligns s_3 with the empty sentence).

since it is only run between paragraph anchors, in practice things proceed quickly.

This leaves determining the cost of each type of alignment. This is done based on the length in characters of the sentences of each language in the bead, l_1 and l_2. One assumes that each character in one language gives rise to a random number of characters in the other language. These random variables are assumed to be independent and identically distributed, and the randomness can then be modeled by a normal distribution with mean μ and variance s^2. These parameters are estimated from data about the corpus. For μ, the authors compare the length of the respective texts. German/English = 1.1, and French/English = 1.06, so they are content to model μ as 1. The squares of the differences of the lengths of paragraphs are used to estimate s^2.

The cost above is then determined in terms of a distance measure between a list of sentences in one language and a list in the other. The distance measure δ compares the difference in the sum of the lengths of the sentences in the two lists to the mean and variance of the whole corpus: $\delta = (l_2 - l_1\mu)/\sqrt{l_1 s^2}$. The cost is of the form:

$$\text{cost}(l_1, l_2) = -\log P(\alpha \text{ align}|\delta(l_1, l_2, \mu, s^2))$$

where α align is one of the allowed match types (1:1, 2:1, etc.). The negative log is used just so one can regard this cost as a 'distance' measure: the highest probability alignment will correspond to the shortest 'distance' and one can just add 'distances.' The above probability is calculated using Bayes' law in terms of $P(\alpha \text{ align})P(\delta|\alpha \text{ align})$, and therefore the first term will cause the program to give a higher a priori probability to 1:1 matches, which are the most common.

So, in essence, we are trying to align beads so that the length of the sentences from the two languages in each bead are as similar as possible. The method performs well (at least on related languages like English, French and German). The basic method has a 4% error rate, and by using a method of detecting dubious alignments Gale and Church are able to produce a best 80% of the corpus on which the error rate is only 0.7%. The method works best on 1:1 alignments, for which there is only a 2% error rate. Error rates are high for the more difficult alignments; in particular the program never gets a 1:0 or 0:1 alignment correct.

Brown et al. (1991c)

The basic approach of Brown et al. (1991c) is similar to Gale and Church, but works by comparing sentence lengths in words rather than characters. Gale and Church (1993) argue that this is not as good because of the greater variance in number of words than number of characters between translations. Among the salient differences between the papers is a difference in goal: Brown et al. did not want to align whole articles, but just produce an aligned subset of the corpus suitable for further research. Thus for higher level section alignment, they used lexical anchors and simply rejected sections that did not align adequately. Using this method on the Canadian Hansard transcripts, they found that sometimes sections appeared in different places in the two languages, and this 'bad' text could simply be ignored. Other differences in the model used need not overly concern us, but we note that they used the EM algorithm to automatically set the various parameters of the model (see section 13.3). They report very good results, at least on 1:1 alignments, but note that sometimes small passages were misaligned because the algorithm ignores the identity of words (just looking at sentence lengths).

Wu (1994)

Wu (1994) begins by applying the method of Gale and Church (1993) to a corpus of parallel English and Cantonese text from the Hong Kong Hansard. He reports that some of the statistical assumptions underlying Gale and Church's model are not as clearly met when dealing with these unrelated languages, but nevertheless, outside of certain header passages, Wu reports results not much worse than those reported by Gale and Church. To improve accuracy, Wu explores using lexical cues, which heads this work in the direction of the lexical methods that we cover in section 13.1.4. Incidentally, it is interesting to note that Wu's 500 sentence test suite includes one each of a 3:1, 1:3 and 3:3 alignments – alignments considered too exotic to be generable by most of the methods we discuss, including Wu's.

13.1.3 Offset alignment by signal processing techniques

What ties these methods together is that they do not attempt to align beads of sentences but rather just to align position offsets in the two parallel texts so as to show roughly what offset in one text aligns with what offset in the other.

Church (1993)

Church (1993) argues that while the above length-based methods work well on clean texts, such as the Canadian Hansard, they tend to break down in real world situations when one is dealing with noisy optical character recognition (OCR) output, or files that contain unknown markup conventions. OCR programs can lose paragraph breaks and punctuation characters, and floating material (headers, footnotes, tables, etc.) can confuse the linear order of text to be aligned. In such texts, finding even paragraph and sentence boundaries can be difficult. Electronic texts should avoid most of these problems, but may contain unknown markup conventions that need to be treated as noise. Church's approach COGNATES is to induce an alignment by using cognates. *Cognates* are words that are similar across languages either due to borrowing or common inheritance from a linguistic ancestor, for instance, French *supérieur* and English *superior*. However, rather than considering cognate words (as in Simard et al. (1992)) or finding lexical correspondences (as in the methods to which we will turn next), the procedure works by finding cognates at the level of character sequences. The method is dependent on there being an ample supply of identical character sequences between the source and target languages, but Church suggests that this happens not only in languages with many cognates but in almost any language using the Roman alphabet, since there are usually many proper names and numbers present. He suggests that the method can even work with non-Roman

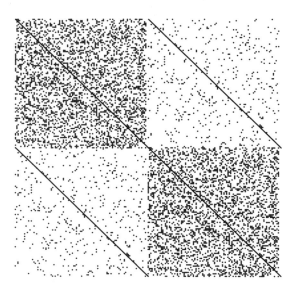

Figure 13.4 A sample dot plot. The source and the translated text are concatenated. Each coordinate (x, y) is marked with a dot iff there is a correspondence between position x and position y. The source text has more random correspondences with itself than with the translated text, which explains the darker shade of the upper left and, by analogy, the darker shade of the lower right. The diagonals are black because there is perfect correspondence of each text with itself (the diagonals in the upper left and the lower right), and because of the correspondences between the source text and its translation (diagonals in lower left and upper right).

writing systems, providing they are liberally sprinkled with names and numbers (or computer keywords!).

DOT-PLOT   The method used is to construct a *dot-plot*. The source and translated texts are concatenated and then a square graph is made with this text on both axes. A dot is placed at (x, y) whenever there is a match between positions x and y in this concatenated text. In Church (1993) the unit that is matched is character 4-grams. Various signal processing techniques are then used to compress the resulting plot. Dot plots have a characteristic look, roughly as shown in figure 13.4. There is a straight diagonal line, since each position (x, x) has a dot. There are then two darker rectangles in the upper left and lower right. (Since the source is more similar to itself, and the translation to itself than each to the other.) But the important information for text alignment is found in the other two, lighter colored quadrants. Either of these matches between the text of the two languages, and hence represents what is sometimes called a *bitext map*. In these quadrants, there are two other, fainter, roughly straight, diagonal lines. These lines result from the propensity of cognates to appear in the two languages, so that often the same character sequences appear in the source and the translation of a sentence. A heuristic search is then used to find the best path along the diagonal, and this provides an alignment in terms of offsets in the two texts. The details of the algorithm need not concern us, but in practice various methods are used so as not to calculate the entire dotplot, and *n*-grams are weighted by inverse frequency so as to give more importance to when rare *n*-grams match (with common *n*-grams simply being ignored). Note that there is no attempt here to align whole sentences as beads, and hence one cannot provide performance figures corresponding to those for most other methods we discuss. Perhaps because of this, the paper offers no quantitative evaluation of performance, although it suggests that error rates are "often very small." Moreover, while this method may often work well in practice, it can never be a fully general solution to the problem of aligning parallel texts, since it will fail completely when no or extremely few identical character sequences appear between the text and the translation. This problem can occur when different character sets are used, as with eastern European or Asian languages (although even in such case there are often numbers and foreign language names that occur on both sides).

BITEXT MAP

Fung and McKeown (1994)

Following earlier work in Fung and Church (1994), Fung and McKeown (1994) seek an algorithm that will work: (i) without having found sentence boundaries (as we noted above, punctuation is often lost in OCR), (ii) in only roughly parallel texts where some sections may have no corresponding section in the translation or vice versa, and (iii) with unrelated language pairs. In particular, they wish to apply this technique to a parallel corpus of English and Cantonese (Chinese). The technique is to infer a small bilingual dictionary that will give points of alignment. For each word, a *signal* is produced, as an *arrival vector* of integer numbers giv-

ARRIVAL VECTOR

ing the number of words between each occurrence of the word at hand.[1]
For instance, if a word appears at word offsets (1, 263, 267, 519) then
the arrival vector will be (262, 4, 252). These vectors are then compared
for English and Cantonese words. If the frequency or position of occurrence of an English and a Cantonese word differ too greatly it is assumed
that they cannot match, otherwise a measure of similarity between the
signals is calculated using Dynamic Time Warping – a standard dynamic
programming algorithm used in speech recognition for aligning signals
of potentially different lengths (Rabiner and Juang 1993: sec. 4.7). For all
such pairs of an English word and a Cantonese word, a few dozen pairs
with very similar signals are retained to give a small bilingual dictionary
with which to anchor the text alignment. In a manner similar to Church's
dot plots, each occurrence of this pair of words becomes a dot in a graph
of the English text versus the Cantonese text, and again one expects to
see a stronger signal in a line along the diagonal (producing a figure similar to figure 13.4). This best match between the texts is again found by
a dynamic programming algorithm and gives a rough correspondence in
offsets between the two texts. This second phase is thus much like the
previous method, but this method has the advantages that it is genuinely
language independent, and that it is sensitive to lexical content.

13.1.4   Lexical methods of sentence alignment

The previous methods attacked the lack of robustness of the length-
based methods in the face of noisy and imperfect input, but they do
this by abandoning the goal of aligning sentences, and just aligning text
offsets. In this section we review a number of methods which still align
beads of sentences like the first methods, but are more robust because
they use lexical information to guide the alignment process.

Kay and Röscheisen (1993)

The early proposals of Brown et al. (1991c) and Gale and Church (1993)
make little or no use of the actual lexical content of the sentences. However, it seems that lexical information could give a lot of confirmation of
alignments, and be vital in certain cases where a string of similar length

---

1. Since Chinese is not written divided into words, being able to do this depends on an
earlier text segmentation phase.

sentences appears in two languages (as often happens in reports when there are things like lists). Kay and Röscheisen (1993) thus use a partial alignment of lexical items to induce the sentence alignment. The use of lexical cues also means the method does not require a prior higher level paragraph alignment.

The method involves a process of convergence where a partial alignment at the word level induces a maximum likelihood alignment at the sentence level, which is used in turn to refine the word level alignment and so on. Word alignment is based on the assumption that two words should correspond if their distributions are the same. The steps are basically as follows:

- Assume the first and last sentences of the texts align. These are the initial anchors.

- Then until most sentences are aligned:

ENVELOPE

1. Form an *envelope* of possible alignments from the cartesian product of the list of sentences in the source language and the target language. Alignments are excluded if they cross anchors or their respective distances from an anchor differ too greatly. The difference is allowed to increase as distance from an anchor increases, giving a pillow shape of possible alignments, as in figure 13.5.

2. Choose pairs of words that tend to co-occur in these potential partial alignments. Choose words whose distributions are similar in the sense that most of the sentences in which one appears are alignable with sentences in which the other appears, and which are sufficiently common that alignments are not likely to be due to chance.

3. Find pairs of source and target sentences which contain many possible lexical correspondences. The most reliable of these pairs are used to induce a set of partial alignments which will be part of the final result. We commit to these alignments, and add them to our list of anchors, and then repeat the steps above.

ANNEALING SCHEDULE

The accuracy of the approach depends on the *annealing schedule.* If you accept many pairs as reliable in each iteration, you need fewer iterations but the results might suffer. Typically, about 5 iterations are needed for satisfactory results. This method does not assume any limitations on the types of possible alignments, and is very robust, in that

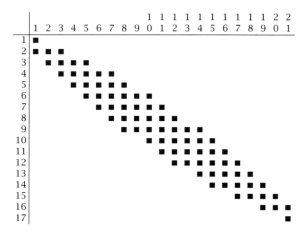

Figure 13.5   The pillow-shaped envelope that is searched. Sentences in the L_1 text are shown on the vertical axis (1–17), sentences in the L_2 text are shown on the horizontal axis (1–21). There is already an anchor between the beginning of both texts, and between sentences (17, 21). A '■' indicates that the two corresponding sentences are in the set of alignments that are considered in the current iteration of the algorithm. Based on (Kay and Röscheisen 1993: figure 3).

'bad' sentences just will not have any match in the final alignment. Results are again good. On Scientific American articles, Kay and Röscheisen (1993) achieved 96% coverage after four passes, and attributed the remainder to 1:0 and 0:1 matches. On 1000 Hansard sentences and using 5 passes, there were 7 errors, 5 of which they attribute not to the main algorithm but to the naive sentence boundary detection algorithm that they employed. On the other hand, the method is computationally intensive. If one begins with a large text with only the endpoints for anchors, there will be a large envelope to search. Moreover, the use of a pillow-shaped envelope to somewhat constrain the search could cause problems if large sections of the text have been moved around or deleted, as then the correct alignments for certain sentences may lie outside the search envelope.

Chen (1993)

Chen (1993) does sentence alignment by constructing a simple word-to-word translation model as he goes along. The best alignment is then the one that maximizes the likelihood of generating the corpus given the translation model. This best alignment is again found by using dynamic programming. Chen argues that whereas previous length-based methods lacked robustness and previous lexical methods were too slow to be practical for large tasks, his method is robust, fast enough to be practical (thanks to using a simple translation model and thresholding methods to improve the search for the best alignment), and more accurate than previous methods.

The model is essentially like that of Gale and Church (1993), except that a translation model is used to estimate the cost of a certain alignment. So, to align two texts S and T, we divide them into a sequence of sentence beads B_k, each containing zero or more sentences of each language as before, so that the sequence of beads covers the corpus:

$$B_k = (s_{a_k}, \ldots, s_{b_k}; t_{c_k}, \ldots, t_{d_k})$$

Then, assuming independence between sentence beads, the most probable alignment $A = B_1, \ldots, B_{m_A}$ of the corpus is determined by:

$$\arg\max_A P(S, T, A) = \arg\max_A P(L) \prod_{k=1}^{m_A} P(B_k)$$

The term $P(L)$ is the probability that one generates an alignment of L beads, but Chen effectively ignores this term by suggesting that this distribution is uniform up to some suitably high ℓ greater than the number of sentences in the corpus, and zero thereafter.

The task then is to determine a translation model that gives a more accurate probability estimate, and hence cost for a certain bead than a model based only on the length of the respective sentences. Chen argues that for reasons of simplicity and efficiency one should stick to a fairly simple translation model. The model used ignores issues of word order, and the possibility of a word corresponding to more than one word in WORD BEADS the translation. It makes use of word beads, and these are restricted to 1:0, 0:1, and 1:1 word beads. The essence of the model is that if a word is commonly translated by another word, then the probability of the corresponding 1:1 word bead will be high, much higher than the product of the probability of the 1:0 and 0:1 word beads using the same words. We omit the details of the translation model here, since it is a close relative of the model introduced in section 13.3. For the probability of an alignment, the program does not sum over possible word beadings derived from the sentences in the bead, but just takes the best one. Indeed, it does not even necessarily find the best one since it does a greedy search for the best word beading: the program starts with a 1:0 and 0:1 beading of the putative alignment, and greedily replaces a 1:0 and a 0:1 bead with the 1:1 bead that produces the biggest improvement in the probability of the alignment until no further improvement can be gained.

The parameters of Chen's model are estimated by a Viterbi version of the EM algorithm.[2] The model is bootstrapped from a small corpus of 100 sentence pairs that have been manually aligned. It then reestimates parameters using an incremental version of the EM algorithm on an (unannotated) chunk of 20,000 corresponding sentences from each language. The model then finally aligns the corpora using a single pass through the data. The method of finding the best total alignment uses dynamic programming as in Gale and Church (1993). However, thresholding is used for speed reasons (to give a linear search rather than the quadratic performance of dynamic programming): a beam search is used and only partial prefix alignments that are almost as good as the best partial alignment are maintained in the beam. This technique for limiting search is generally very effective, but it causes problems when there are large deletions or insertions in one text (vanilla dynamic programming should be much more robust against such events, but see Simard and Plamondon (1996)). However, Chen suggests it is easy to detect large deletions (the probability of all alignments becomes low, and so the beam becomes very wide), and a special procedure is then invoked to search for a clear alignment after the deletion, and the regular alignment process is then restarted from this point.

This method has been used for large scale alignments: several million sentences each of English and French from both Canadian Hansard and European Economic Community proceedings. Chen has estimated the error rate based on assessment of places where the proposed alignment is different from the results of Brown et al. (1991c). He estimates an error rate of 0.4% over the entire text whereas others have either reported higher error rates or similar error rates over only a subset of the text. Finally Chen suggests that most of the errors are apparently due to the not-terribly-good sentence boundary detection method used, and that further

---

2. In the standard EM algorithm, for each data item, one sums over all ways of doing something to get an expectation for a parameter. Sometimes, for computational reasons, people adopt the expedient of just using the probabilities of the best way of doing something for each data item instead. This method is referred to as a Viterbi version of the EM algorithm. It is heuristic, but can be reasonably effective.

improvements in the translation model are unlikely to improve the alignments, while tending to make the alignment process much slower. We note, however, that the presented work limits matches to 1:0, 0:1, 1:1, 2:1, and 1:2, and so it will fail to find the more exotic alignments that do sometimes occur. Extending the model to other alignment types appears straightforward, although we note that in practice Gale and Church had less success in finding unusual alignment types. Chen does not present any results broken down according to the type of alignment involved.

Haruno and Yamazaki (1996)

Haruno and Yamazaki (1996) argue that none of the above methods work effectively when trying to align short texts in structurally different languages. Their proposed method is essentially a variant of Kay and Röscheisen (1993), but nevertheless, the paper contains several interesting observations.[3] Firstly they suggest that for structurally very different languages like Japanese and English, including function words in lexical matching actually impedes alignment, and so the authors leave all function words out and do lexical matching on content words only. This is achieved by using part of speech taggers to classify words in the two languages. Secondly, if trying to align short texts, there are not enough repeated words for reliable alignment using the techniques Kay and Röscheisen (1993) describe, and so they use an online dictionary to find matching word pairs. Both these techniques mark a move from the knowledge-poor approach that characterized early Statistical NLP work to a knowledge-rich approach. For practical purposes, since knowledge sources like taggers and online dictionaries are widely available, it seems silly to avoid their use purely on ideological grounds. On the other hand, when dealing with more technical texts, Haruno and Yamazaki point out that finding word correspondences in the text is still important – using a dictionary is not a substitute for this. Thus, using a combination of methods they are able to achieve quite good results on even short texts between very different languages.

---

3. On the other hand some of the details of their method are questionable: use of mutual information to evaluate word matching (see the discussion in section 5.4 – adding use of a *t* score to filter the unreliability of mutual information when counts are low is only a partial solution) and the use of an ad hoc scoring function to combine knowledge from the dictionary with corpus statistics.

13.1.5   Summary

The upshot seems to be that if you have clean texts from a controlled translation environment, sentence alignment does not seem that difficult a problem, and there are now many methods that perform well. On the other hand, real world problems and less literal translations, or languages with few cognates and different writing systems can pose considerable problems. Methods that model relationships between lexical items in one way or another are much more general and robust in circumstances of this sort. Both signal processing techniques and whole sentence alignment techniques are crude approximations to the fine-grained structure of a match between a sentence and its translation (compare, again, the elaborate microstructure of the match shown in figure 13.2), but they have somewhat different natures. The choice of which to use should be determined by the languages of interest, the required accuracy, and the intended application of the text alignment.

13.1.6   Exercises

Exercise 13.1   [⋆]

For two languages you know, find an example where the basic assumption of the length-based approach breaks down, that is a short and a long sentence are translations of each other. It is easier to find examples if length is defined as number of words.

Exercise 13.2   [⋆]

Gale and Church (1993) argue that measuring length in number of characters is preferable because the variance in number of words is greater. Do you agree that word-based length is more variable? Why?

Exercise 13.3   [⋆]

The dotplot figure is actually incorrect: it is not symmetric with respect to the main diagonal. (Verify this!) It should be. Why?

13.2   Word Alignment

BILINGUAL
DICTIONARIES
TERMINOLOGY
DATABASES

A common use of aligned texts is the derivation of bilingual dictionaries and terminology databases. This is usually done in two steps. First the text alignment is extended to a word alignment (unless we are dealing with an approach in which word and text alignment are induced simultaneously). Then some criterion such as frequency is used to select aligned pairs for which there is enough evidence to include them in the bilingual dictionary. For example, if there is just one instance of the word alignment "*adeptes – products*" (an alignment that might be derived from figure 13.2), then we will probably not include it in a dictionary (which is the right decision here since *adeptes* means 'users' in the context, not 'products').

One approach to word alignment was briefly discussed in section 5.3.3: ASSOCIATION word alignment based on measures of association. Association measures such as the χ^2 measure used by Church and Gale (1991b) are an efficient way of computing word alignments from a bitext. In many cases, they are sufficient, especially if a high confidence threshold is used. However, association measures can be misled in situations where a word in L_1 frequently occurs with more than one word in L_2. This was the example of *house* being incorrectly translated as *communes* instead of *chambre* because, in the Hansard, *House* most often occurs with both French words in the phrase *Chambre de Communes*.

Pairs like *chambre↔house* can be identified if we take into account a source of information that is ignored by pure association measures: the fact that, on average, a given word is the translation of only one other word in the second language. Of course, this is true for only part of the words in an aligned text, but assuming one-to-one correspondence has been shown to give highly accurate results (Melamed 1997b). Most algorithms that incorporate this type of information are implementations of the EM algorithm or involve a similar back-and-forth between a hypothesized dictionary of word correspondences and an alignment of word tokens in the aligned corpus. Examples include Chen (1993) as described in the previous section, Brown et al. (1990) as described in the next section, Dagan et al. (1993), Kupiec (1993a), and Vogel et al. (1996). Most of these approaches involve several iterations of recomputing word correspondences from aligned tokens and then recomputing the alignment of tokens based on the improved word correspondences. Other authors address the additional complexity of deriving correspondences between PHRASES *phrases* since in many cases the desired output is a database of terminological expressions, many of which can be quite complex (Wu 1995; Gaussier 1998; Hull 1998). The need for several iterations makes all of these algorithms somewhat less efficient than pure association methods.

As a final remark, we note that future work is likely to make significant use of the prior knowledge present in existing bilingual dictionaries rather than attempting to derive everything from the aligned text. See

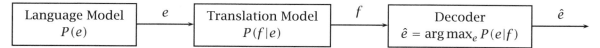

Figure 13.6 The noisy channel model in machine translation. The Language Model generates an English sentence *e*. The Translation Model transmits *e* as the French sentence *f*. The decoder finds the English sentence *ê* which is most likely to have given rise to *f*.

Klavans and Tzoukermann (1995) for one example of such an approach.

13.3   Statistical Machine Translation

NOISY CHANNEL
MODEL In section 2.2.4, we introduced the *noisy channel model*. One of its applications in NLP is machine translation as shown in figure 13.6. In order to translate from French to English, we set up a noisy channel that receives as input an English sentence *e*, transforms it into a French sentence *f*, and sends the French sentence *f* to a decoder. The decoder then determines the English sentence *ê* that *f* is most likely to have arisen from (and which is not necessarily identical to *e*).

We thus have to build three components for translation from French to English: a language model, a translation model, and a decoder. We also have to estimate the parameters of the model, the *translation probabilities*.

Language model.   The language model gives us the probability $P(e)$ of the English sentence. We already know how to build language models based on *n*-grams (chapter 6) or probabilistic grammars (chapter 11 and chapter 12), so we just assume here that we have an appropriate language model.

Translation model.   Here is a simple translation model based on word alignment:

(13.5) $$P(f|e) = \frac{1}{Z} \sum_{a_1=0}^{l} \cdots \sum_{a_m=0}^{l} \prod_{j=1}^{m} P(f_j|e_{a_j})$$

We use the notation of Brown et al. (1993): *e* is the English sentence; *l* is the length of *e* in words; *f* is the French sentence; *m* is the length of *f*;

TRANSLATION
PROBABILITY

f_j is word j in f; a_j is the position in e that f_j is aligned with; e_{a_j} is the word in e that f_j is aligned with; $P(w_f|w_e)$ is the *translation probability*, the probability that we will see w_f in the French sentence given that we see w_e in the English sentence; and Z is a normalization constant.

The basic idea of this formula is fairly straightforward. The m sums $\sum_{a_1=0}^{l} \cdots \sum_{a_m=0}^{l}$ sum over all possible alignments of French words to English words. The meaning of $a_j = 0$ for an a_j is that word j in the French sentence is aligned with the *empty cept*, that is, it has no (overt) translation. Note that an English word can be aligned with multiple French words, but that each French word is aligned with at most one English word.

EMPTY CEPT

For a particular alignment, we multiply the m translation probabilities, assuming independence of the individual translations (see below for how to estimate the translation probabilities). So for example, if we want to compute:

P(Jean aime Marie|John loves Mary)

for the alignment (*Jean, John*), (*aime, loves*), and (*Marie, Mary*), then we multiply the three corresponding translation probabilities.

$P(\textit{Jean}|\textit{John}) \times P(\textit{aime}|\textit{loves}) \times P(\textit{Marie}|\textit{Mary})$

To summarize, we compute $P(f|e)$ by summing the probabilities of all alignments. For each alignment, we make two (rather drastic) simplifying assumptions: Each French word is generated by exactly one English word (or the empty cept); and the generation of each French word is independent of the generation of all other French words in the sentence.[4]

Decoder. We saw examples of decoders in section 2.2.4 and this one does the same kind of maximization, based on the observation that we can omit $P(f)$ from the maximization since f is fixed:

(13.6) $\hat{e} = \arg\max_{e} P(e|f) = \arg\max_{e} \dfrac{P(e)P(f|e)}{P(f)} = \arg\max_{e} P(e)P(f|e)$

The problem is that the search space is infinite, so we need a heuristic search algorithm. One possibility is to use stack search (see section 12.1.10). The basic idea is that we build an English sentence incrementally. We keep a stack of partial translation hypotheses. At each

---

4. Going in the other direction, note that one English word can correspond to multiple French words.

point, we extend these hypotheses with a small number of words and alignments and then prune the stack to its previous size by discarding the least likely extended hypotheses. This algorithm is not guaranteed to find the best translation, but can be implemented efficiently.

Translation probabilities. The translation probabilities are estimated using the EM algorithm (see section 14.2.2 for a general introduction to EM). We assume that we have a corpus of aligned sentences.

As we discussed in the previous section on word alignment, one way to guess at which words correspond to each other is to compute an association measure like χ^2. But that will generate many spurious correspondences because a source word is not penalized for being associated with more than one target word (recall the example *chambre↔house*, *chambre↔chamber*).

CREDIT ASSIGNMENT   The basic idea of the EM algorithm is that it solves the *credit assignment* problem. If a word in the source is strongly aligned with a word in the target, then it is not available anymore to be aligned with other words in the target. This avoids cases of double and triple alignment on the one hand, and an excessive number of unaligned words on the other hand.

We start with a random initialization of the translation probabilities $P(w_f | w_e)$. In the E step, we compute the expected number of times we will find w_f in the French sentence given that we have w_e in the English sentence.

$$z_{w_f, w_e} = \sum_{(e,f) \text{ s.t. } w_e \in e, w_f \in f} P(w_f | w_e)$$

where the summation ranges over all pairs of aligned sentences such that the English sentence contains w_e and the French sentence contains w_f. (We have simplified slightly here since we ignore cases where words occur more than once in a sentence.)

The M step reestimates the translation probabilities from these expectations:

$$P(w_f | w_e) = \frac{z_{w_f, w_e}}{\sum_v z_{w_f, v}}$$

where the summation ranges over all English words v.

What we have described is a very simple version of the algorithms described by Brown et al. (1990) and Brown et al. (1993) (see also Kupiec (1993a) for a clear statement of EM for alignment). The main part we have simplified is that, in these models, implausible alignments are penalized. For example, if an English word at the beginning of the English sentence is aligned with a French word at the end of the French sentence, then this *distortion* in the positions of the two aligned words will decrease the probability of the alignment.

DISTORTION

FERTILITY

Similarly, a notion of *fertility* is introduced for each English word which tells us how many French words it usually generates. In the unconstrained model, we do not distinguish the case where each French word is generated by a different English word, or at least approximately so (which somehow seems the normal case) from the case where all French words are generated by a single English word. The notion of fertility allows us to capture the tendency of word alignments to be one-to-one and one-to-two in most cases (and one-to-zero is another possibility in this model). For example, the most likely fertility of *farmers* in the corpus that the models were tested on is 2 because it is most often translated as two words: *les agriculteurs*. For most English words, the most likely fertility is 1 since they tend to be translated by a single French word.

An evaluation of the model on the aligned Hansard corpus found that only about 48% of French sentences were decoded (or translated) correctly. The errors were either incorrect decodings as in (13.7) or ungrammatical decodings as in (13.8) (Brown et al. 1990: 84).

(13.7)   a. **Source sentence.** Permettez que je donne un example à la chambre.

        b. **Correct translation.** Let me give the House one example.

        c. **Incorrect decoding.** Let me give an example in the House.

(13.8)   a. **Source sentence.** Vous avez besoin de toute l'aide disponible.

        b. **Correct translation.** You need all the help you can get.

        c. **Ungrammatical decoding.** You need of the whole benefits available.

A detailed analysis in (Brown et al. 1990) and (Brown et al. 1993) reveals several problems with the model.

- **Fertility is asymmetric.** Often a single French word corresponds to several English words. For example, *to go* is translated as *aller*. There is no way to capture this generalization in the formalization proposed. The model can get individual sentences with *to go* right by translating *to* as the empty set and *go* as *aller*, but this is done in an error-prone way on a case by case basis instead of noting the general correspondence of the two expressions.

Note that there is an asymmetry here since we can formalize the fact that a single English word corresponds to several French words. This is the example of *farmers* which has fertility 2 and produces two words *les* and *agriculteurs*.

- **Independence assumptions.** As so often in Statistical NLP, many independence assumptions are made in developing the probabilistic model that don't strictly hold. As a result, the model gives an unfair advantage to short sentences because, simply put, fewer probabilities are multiplied and therefore the resulting likelihood is a larger number. One can fix this by multiplying the final likelihood with a constant c^l that increases with the length l of the sentence, but a more principled solution would be to develop a more sophisticated model in which inappropriate independence assumptions need not be made. See Brown et al. (1993: 293), and also the discussion in section 12.1.11.

- **Sensitivity to training data.** Small changes in the model and the training data (e.g., taking the training data from different parts of the Hansard) can cause large changes in the estimates of the parameters. For example, the 1990 model has a translation probability $P(le|the)$ of 0.610, the 1993 model has 0.497 instead (Brown et al. 1993: 286). It does not necessarily follow that such discrepancies would impact translation performance negatively, but they certainly raise questions about how close the training text and the text of application need to be in order to get acceptable results. See section 10.3.2 for a discussion of the effect of divergence between training and application corpora in the case of part-of-speech tagging.

- **Efficiency.** Sentences of more than 30 words had to be eliminated from the training set presumably because decoding them took too long (Brown et al. 1993: 282).

On the surface, these are problems of the model, but they are all related to the lack of linguistic knowledge in the model. For example, syntactic analysis would make it possible to relate subparts of the sentence to each other instead of simulating such relations inadequately using the notion of fertility. And a stronger model would make fewer independence assumptions, make better use of the training data (since a higher bias reduces variance in parameter estimates) and reduce the search space with potential benefits for efficiency in decoding.

Other problems found by Brown et al. (1990) and Brown et al. (1993) show directly that the lack of linguistic knowledge encoded in the system causes many translation failures.

- **No notion of phrases.** The model relates only individual words. As the examples of words with high fertility show, one should really model relationships between phrases, for example, the relationship between *to go* and *aller* and between *farmers* and *les agriculteurs*.

- **Non-local dependencies.** Non-local dependencies are hard to capture with 'local' models like *n*-gram models (see page 98 in chapter 3). So even if the translation model generates the right set of words, the language model will not assemble them correctly (or will give the re-assembled sentence a low probability) if a long-distance dependency occurs. In later work that builds on the two models we discuss here, sentences are preprocessed to reduce the number of long-distance dependencies in order to address this problem (Brown et al. 1992a). For example, *is she a mathematician* would be transformed to *she is a mathematician* in a preprocessing step.

- **Morphology.** Morphologically related words are treated as separate symbols. For example, the fact that each of the 39 forms of the French verb *diriger* can be translated as *to conduct* and *to direct* in appropriate contexts has to be learned separately for each form.

- **Sparse data problems.** Since parameters are solely estimated from the training corpus without any help from other sources of information about words, estimates for rare words are unreliable. Sentences with rare words were excluded from the evaluation in (Brown et al. 1990) because of the difficulty of deriving a good characterization of infrequent words automatically.

In summary, the main problem with the noisy channel model that we have described here is that it incorporates very little domain knowledge about natural language. This is an argument that is made in both (Brown et al. 1990) and (Brown et al. 1993). All subsequent work on statistical machine translation (starting with Brown et al. (1992a)) has therefore

focussed on building models that formalize the linguistic regularities inherent in language.

Non-linguistic models are fairly successful for word alignment as
shown by Brown et al. (1993) among others. The research results we have
discussed in this section suggest that they fail for machine translation.

Exercise 13.4   [⋆ ⋆]

The model's task is to find an English sentence given a French input sentence.
Why don't we just estimate $P(e|f)$ and do without a language model? What
would happen to ungrammatical French sentences if we relied on $P(e|f)$? What
happens with ungrammatical French sentences in the model described above
that relies on $P(f|e)$? These questions are answered by (Brown et al. 1993: 265).

Exercise 13.5   [⋆]

Translation and fertility probabilities tell us which words to generate, but not
where to put them. Why do the generated words end up in the right places in
the decoded sentence, at least most of the time?

Exercise 13.6   [⋆ ⋆]

VITERBI TRANSLATION   The *Viterbi translation* is defined as the translation resulting from the maximum
likelihood alignment. In other words, we don't sum over all possible alignments
as in the translation model in equation (13.5). Would you expect there to be
significant differences between the Viterbi translation and the best translation
according to equation (13.5)?

Exercise 13.7   [⋆ ⋆]

Construct a small training example for EM and compute at least two iterations.

Exercise 13.8   [⋆ ⋆]

For the purposes of machine translation, *n*-gram models are reasonable language
models for short sentences. However, with increasing sentence length it becomes
more likely that there are several (semantically distinct) ways of ordering the
words into a grammatical sentence. Find a set of (a) 4 English words, (b) 10
English words that can be turned into two semantically distinct and grammatical
sequences.

13.4 Further Reading

For more background on statistical methods in MT, we recommend the
overview article by Knight (1997). Readers interested in efficient decoding algorithms (in practice one of the hardest problems in statistical MT)
should consult Wu (1996), Wang and Waibel (1997), and Nießen et al.
(1998). Alshawi et al. (1997), Wang and Waibel (1998), and Wu and Wong

(1998) attempt to replace the statistical word-for-word approach with a statistical transfer approach (in the terminology of figure 13.1). An algorithm for statistical generation is proposed by Knight and Hatzivassiloglou (1995).

EXAMPLE-BASED

An 'empirical' approach to MT that is different from the noisy channel model we have covered here is *example-based* translation. In example-based translation, one translates a sentence by using the closest match in an aligned corpus as a template. If there is an exact match in the aligned corpus, one can just retrieve the previous translation and be done. Otherwise, the previous translation needs to be modified appropriately. See Nagao (1984) and Sato (1992) for descriptions of example-based MT systems.

TRANSLITERATION

One purpose of word correspondences is to use them in translating unknown words. However, even with automatic acquisition from aligned corpora, there will still be unknown words in any new text, in particular names. This is a particular problem when translating between languages with different writing systems since one cannot use the unknown string verbatim in the translation of, say, Japanese to English. Knight and Graehl (1997) show how many proper names can be handled by a *transliteration* system that infers the written form of the name in the target language directly from the written form in the source language. Since the roman alphabet is transliterated fairly systematically into character sets like Cyrillic, the original Roman form can often be completely recovered.

Finding word correspondences can be seen as a special case of the more general problem of knowledge acquisition for machine translation. See Knight et al. (1995) for a more high-level view of acquisition in the MT context that goes beyond the specific problems we have discussed here.

Using parallel texts as a knowledge source for word sense disambiguation is described in Brown et al. (1991b) and Gale et al. (1992d) (see also section 7.2.2). The example of the use of text alignment as an aid for translators revising product literature is taken from Shemtov (1993). The alignment example at the beginning of the chapter is drawn from an example text from the UBS data considered by Gale and Church (1993), although they do not discuss the word level alignment. Note that the text in both languages is actually a translation from a German original. A search interface to examples of aligned French and English Canadian Hansard sentences is available on the web; see the website.

BEAD
BITEXT
BITEXT MAP

The term *bead* was introduced by Brown et al. (1991c). The notion of a *bitext* is from (Harris 1988), and the term *bitext map* comes from

(Melamed 1997a). Further work on signal-processing-based approaches to parallel text alignment appears in (Melamed 1997a) and (Chang and Chen 1997). A recent evaluation of a number of alignment systems is available on the web (see website). Particularly interesting is the very divergent performance of the systems on different parallel corpora presenting different degrees of difficulty in alignment.

14 *Clustering*

CLUSTERING ALGORITHMS partition a set of objects into groups or *clusters*. Figure 14.1 gives an example of a clustering of 22 high-frequency words from the Brown corpus. The figure is an example of a *dendrogram*, a branching diagram where the apparent similarity between nodes at the bottom is shown by the height of the connection which joins them. Each node in the tree represents a cluster that was created by merging two child nodes. For example, *in* and *on* form a cluster and so do *with* and *for*. These two subclusters are then merged into one cluster with four objects. The "height" of the node corresponds to the decreasing similarity of the two clusters that are being merged (or, equivalently, to the order in which the merges were executed). The greatest similarity between any two clusters is the similarity between *in* and *on* – corresponding to the lowest horizontal line in the figure. The least similarity is between *be* and the cluster with the 21 other words – corresponding to the highest horizontal line in the figure.

While the objects in the clustering are all distinct as tokens, normally objects are described and clustered using a set of features and values (often known as the *data representation model*), and multiple objects may have the same representation in this model, so we will define our clustering algorithms to work over *bags* – objects like sets except that they allow multiple identical items. The goal is to place similar objects in the same group and to assign dissimilar objects to different groups.

What is the notion of 'similarity' between words being used here? First, the left and right neighbors of tokens of each word in the Brown corpus were tallied. These distributions give a fairly true implementation of Firth's idea that one can categorize a word by the words that occur around it. But now, rather than looking for distinctive collocations, as in

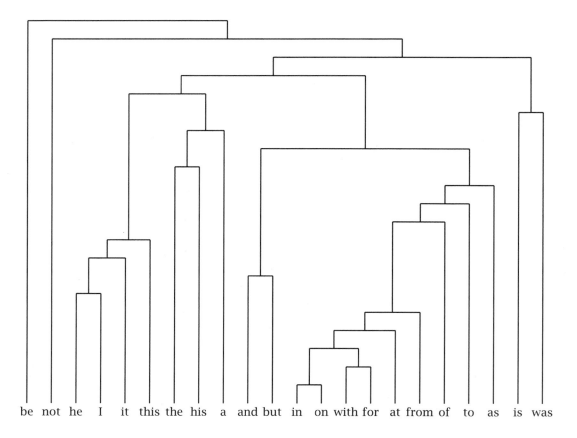

be not he   I   it this the his   a   and but in   on with for   at from of   to   as   is   was

Figure 14.1 A single-link clustering of 22 frequent English words represented as a dendrogram.

chapter 5, we are capturing and using the whole distributional pattern of the word. Word similarity was then measured as the degree of overlap in the distributions of these neighbors for the two words in question. For example, the similarity between *in* and *on* is large because both words occur with similar left and right neighbors (both are prepositions and tend to be followed by articles or other words that begin noun phrases, for instance). The similarity between *is* and *he* is small because they share fewer immediate neighbors due to their different grammatical functions. Initially, each word formed its own cluster, and then at each step in the clustering, the two clusters that are closest to each other are merged into a new cluster.

EXPLORATORY DATA ANALYSIS

There are two main uses for clustering in Statistical NLP. The figure demonstrates the use of clustering for *exploratory data analysis* (EDA). Somebody who does not know English would be able to derive a crude grouping of words into parts of speech from figure 14.1 and this insight may make subsequent analysis easier. Or we can use the figure to evaluate neighbor overlap as a measure of part-of-speech similarity, assuming we know what the correct parts of speech are. The clustering makes apparent both strengths and weaknesses of a neighbor-based representation. It works well for prepositions (which are all grouped together), but seems inappropriate for other words such as *this* and *the* which are not grouped together with grammatically similar words.

Exploratory data analysis is an important activity in any pursuit that deals with quantitative data. Whenever we are faced with a new problem and want to develop a probabilistic model or just understand the basic characteristics of the phenomenon, EDA is the first step. It is always a mistake to not first spend some time getting a feel for what the data at hand look like. Clustering is a particularly important technique for EDA in Statistical NLP because there is often no direct pictorial visualization for linguistic objects. Other fields, in particular those dealing with numerical or geographic data, often have an obvious visualization, for example, maps of the incidence of a particular disease in epidemiology. Any technique that lets one visualize the data better is likely to bring to the fore new generalizations and to stop one from making wrong assumptions about the data.

There are other well-known techniques for displaying a set of objects in a two-dimensional plane (such as pages of books); see section 14.3 for references. When used for EDA, clustering is thus only one of a number of techniques that one might employ, but it has the advantage that it can produce a richer hierarchical structure. It may also be more convenient to work with since visual displays are more complex. One has to worry about how to label objects shown on the display, and, in contrast to clustering, cannot give a comprehensive description of the object next to its visual representation.

GENERALIZATION

The other main use of clustering in NLP is for *generalization*. We referred to this as *forming bins* or *equivalence classes* in section 6.1. But there we grouped data points in certain predetermined ways, whereas here we induce the bins from data.

As an example, suppose we want to determine the correct preposition to use with the noun *Friday* for translating a text from French into English. Suppose also that we have an English training text that contains the phrases *on Sunday*, *on Monday*, and *on Thursday*, but not *on Friday*. That *on* is the correct preposition to use with *Friday* can be inferred as follows. If we cluster English nouns into groups with similar syntactic and semantic environments, then the days of the week will end up in the same cluster. This is because they share environments like "*until* day-of-the-week," "*last* day-of-the-week," and "day-of-the-week *morning*." Under the assumption that an environment that is correct for one member of the cluster is also correct for the other members of the cluster, we can infer the correctness of *on Friday* from the presence of *on Sunday*, *on Monday* and *on Thursday*. So clustering is a way of *learning*.

LEARNING

We group objects into clusters and generalize from what we know about some members of the cluster (like the appropriateness of the preposition *on*) to others.

CLASSIFICATION

Another way of partitioning objects into groups is *classification*, which is the subject of chapter 16. The difference is that classification is *supervised* and requires a set of labeled training instances for each group. Clustering does not require training data and is hence called *unsupervised* because there is no "teacher" who provides a training set with class labels. The result of clustering only depends on natural divisions in the data, for example the different neighbors of prepositions, articles and pronouns in the above dendrogram, not on any pre-existing categorization scheme. Clustering is sometimes called automatic or unsupervised classification, but we will not use these terms in order to avoid confusion.

HIERARCHICAL
FLAT
NON-HIERARCHICAL

There are many different clustering algorithms, but they can be classified into a few basic types. There are two types of structures produced by clustering algorithms, *hierarchical clusterings* and *flat* or *non-hierarchical clusterings*. Flat clusterings simply consist of a certain number of clusters and the relation between clusters is often undetermined.

ITERATIVE

Most algorithms that produce flat clusterings are *iterative*. They start with a set of initial clusters and improve them by iterating a reallocation operation that reassigns objects.

A hierarchical clustering is a hierarchy with the usual interpretation that each node stands for a subclass of its mother's node. The leaves of the tree are the single objects of the clustered set. Each node represents the cluster that contains all the objects of its descendants. Figure 14.1 is an example of a hierarchical cluster structure.

Another important distinction between clustering algorithms is whether they perform a *soft clustering* or *hard clustering*. In a hard assignment, each object is assigned to one and only one cluster. Soft assignments allow degrees of membership and membership in multiple clusters. In a probabilistic framework, an object x_i has a probability distribution $P(\cdot|x_i)$ over clusters c_j where $P(c_j|x_i)$ is the probability that x_i is a member of c_j. In a vector space model, degree of membership in multiple clusters can be formalized as the similarity of a vector to the center of each cluster. In a vector space, the center of the M points in a cluster c, otherwise known as the *centroid* or *center of gravity* is the point:

SOFT CLUSTERING
HARD CLUSTERING

CENTROID
CENTER OF GRAVITY

(14.1) $$\vec{\mu} = \frac{1}{M} \sum_{\vec{x} \in c} \vec{x}$$

In other words, each component of the centroid vector $\vec{\mu}$ is simply the average of the values for that component in the M points in c.

In hierarchical clustering, assignment is usually 'hard.' In non-hierarchical clustering, both types of assignment are common. Even most soft assignment models assume that an object is assigned to only one cluster. The difference from hard clustering is that there is uncertainty about which cluster is the correct one. There are also true multiple assignment models, so-called *disjunctive clustering* models, in which an object can truly belong to several clusters. For example, there may be a mix of syntactic and semantic categories in word clustering and *book* would fully belong to both the semantic "object" and the syntactic "noun" category. We will not cover disjunctive clustering models here. See (Saund 1994) for an example of a disjunctive clustering model.

DISJUNCTIVE
CLUSTERING

Nevertheless, it is worth mentioning at the beginning the limitations that follow from the assumptions of most clustering algorithms. A hard clustering algorithm has to choose one cluster to which to assign every item. This is rather unappealing for many problems in NLP. It is a commonplace that many words have more than one part of speech. For instance *play* can be a noun or a verb, and *fast* can be an adjective or an adverb. And many larger units also show mixed behavior. Nominalized clauses show some verb-like (clausal) behavior and some noun-like (nominalization) behavior. And we suggested in chapter 7 that several senses of a word were often simultaneously activated. Within a hard clustering framework, the best we can do in such cases is to define additional clusters corresponding to words that can be either nouns or verbs, and so on. Soft clustering is therefore somewhat more appropriate for many prob-

Hierarchical clustering:	Non-hierarchical clustering:
▪ Preferable for detailed data analysis	▪ Preferable if efficiency is a consideration or data sets are very large
▪ Provides more information than flat clustering	▪ K-means is the conceptually simplest method and should probably be used first on a new data set because its results are often sufficient
▪ No single best algorithm (each of the algorithms we describe has been found to be optimal for some application)	▪ K-means assumes a simple Euclidean representation space, and so cannot be used for many data sets, for example, nominal data like colors
▪ Less efficient than flat clustering (for n objects, one minimally has to compute an $n \times n$ matrix of similarity coefficients, and then update this matrix as one proceeds)	▪ In such cases, the EM algorithm is the method of choice. It can accommodate definition of clusters and allocation of objects based on complex probabilistic models.

Table 14.1   A summary of the attributes of different clustering algorithms.

lems in NLP, since a soft clustering algorithm can assign an ambiguous word like *play* partly to the cluster of verbs and partly to the cluster of nouns.

The remainder of the chapter looks in turn at various hierarchical and non-hierarchical clustering methods, and some of their applications in NLP. In table 14.1, we briefly characterize some of the features of clustering algorithms for the reader who is just looking for a quick solution to an immediate clustering need.

For a discussion of the pros and cons of different clustering algorithms see Kaufman and Rousseeuw (1990). The main notations that we will use in this chapter are summarized in table 14.2.

14.1   Hierarchical Clustering

The tree of a hierarchical clustering can be produced either bottom-up, by starting with the individual objects and grouping the most similar

Notation	Meaning
$X = \{x_1, \ldots, x_n\}$	the set of n objects to be clustered
$C = \{c_1, \ldots, c_j, \ldots c_k\}$	the set of clusters (or cluster hypotheses)
$\mathcal{P}(X)$	powerset (set of subsets) of X
$\text{sim}(\cdot, \cdot)$	similarity function
$S(\cdot)$	group average similarity function
m	Dimensionality of vector space $\mathbb{R}^m$
M_j	Number of points in cluster c_j
$\vec{s}(c_j)$	Vector sum of vectors in cluster c_j
N	number of word tokens in training corpus
$w_{i,\ldots,j}$	tokens i through j of the training corpus
$\pi(\cdot)$	function assigning words to clusters
$C(w^1 w^2)$	number of occurrences of string $w^1 w^2$
$C(c_1 c_2)$	number of occurrences of string $w^1 w^2$ s.t. $\pi(w^1) = c_1$, $\pi(w^2) = c_2$
$\vec{\mu}_j$	Centroid for cluster c_j
Σ_j	Covariance matrix for cluster c_j

Table 14.2 Symbols used in the clustering chapter.

ones, or top-down, whereby one starts with all the objects and divides them into groups so as to maximize within-group similarity. Figure 14.2 describes the bottom-up algorithm, also called *agglomerative clustering*. Agglomerative clustering is a greedy algorithm that starts with a separate cluster for each object (3,4). In each step, the two most similar clusters are determined (8), and merged into a new cluster (9). The algorithm terminates when one large cluster containing all objects of S has been formed, which then is the only remaining cluster in C (7).

AGGLOMERATIVE CLUSTERING

Let us flag one possibly confusing issue. We have phrased the clustering algorithm in terms of similarity between clusters, and therefore we join things with *maximum* similarity (8). Sometimes people think in terms of distances between clusters, and then you want to join things that are the *minimum* distance apart. So it is easy to get confused between whether you're taking maximums or minimums. It is straightforward to produce a similarity measure from a distance measure d, for example by $\text{sim}(x, y) = 1/(1 + d(x, y))$.

Figure 14.3 describes top-down hierarchical clustering, also called *divisive clustering* (Jain and Dubes 1988: 57). Like agglomerative clustering

DIVISIVE CLUSTERING

1 Given: a set $\mathcal{X} = \{x_1, \dots x_n\}$ of objects
2   a function sim: $\mathcal{P}(\mathcal{X}) \times \mathcal{P}(\mathcal{X}) \rightarrow \mathbb{R}$
3 **for** $i := 1$ **to** n **do**
4      $c_i := \{x_i\}$ **end**
5 $C := \{c_1, \dots, c_n\}$
6 $j := n + 1$
7 **while** $C > 1$
8          $(c_{n_1}, c_{n_2}) := \arg\max_{(c_u, c_v) \in C \times C} \text{sim}(c_u, c_v)$
9          $c_j = c_{n_1} \cup c_{n_2}$
10         $C := C \backslash \{c_{n_1}, c_{n_2}\} \cup \{c_j\}$
11         $j := j + 1$

Figure 14.2   Bottom-up hierarchical clustering.

1 Given: a set $\mathcal{X} = \{x_1, \dots x_n\}$ of objects
2   a function coh: $\mathcal{P}(\mathcal{X}) \rightarrow \mathbb{R}$
3   a function split: $\mathcal{P}(\mathcal{X}) \rightarrow \mathcal{P}(\mathcal{X}) \times \mathcal{P}(\mathcal{X})$
4 $C := \{\mathcal{X}\}$ $(= \{c_1\})$
5 $j := 1$
6 **while** $\exists c_i \in C$ s.t. $|c_i| > 1$
7          $c_u := \arg\min_{c_v \in C} \text{coh}(c_v)$
8          $(c_{j+1}, c_{j+2}) = \text{split}(c_u)$
9          $C := C \backslash \{c_u\} \cup \{c_{j+1}, c_{j+2}\}$
10         $j := j + 2$

Figure 14.3   Top-down hierarchical clustering.

it is a greedy algorithm. Starting from a cluster with all objects (4), each iteration determines which cluster is least coherent (7) and splits this cluster (8). Clusters with similar objects are more coherent than clusters with dissimilar objects. For example, a cluster with several identical members is maximally coherent.

Hierarchical clustering only makes sense if the similarity function is
MONOTONIC   *monotonic:*

(14.2)   **Monotonicity.**
$\forall c, c', c'' \subseteq S : \min(\text{sim}(c, c'), \text{sim}(c, c'')) \geq \text{sim}(c, c' \cup c'')$

In other words, the operation of merging is guaranteed to not increase similarity. A similarity function that does not obey this condition makes

Function	Definition
single link	similarity of two most similar members
complete link	similarity of two least similar members
group-average	average similarity between members

Table 14.3 Similarity functions used in clustering. Note that for group-average clustering, we average over all pairs, including pairs from the same cluster. For single-link and complete-link clustering, we quantify over the subset of pairs from different clusters.

the hierarchy uninterpretable since dissimilar clusters, which are placed far apart in the tree, can become similar in subsequent merging so that 'closeness' in the tree does not correspond to conceptual similarity anymore.

Most hierarchical clustering algorithms follow the schemes outlined in figures 14.2 and 14.3. The following sections discuss specific instances of these algorithms.

14.1.1 Single-link and complete-link clustering

Table 14.3 shows three similarity functions that are commonly used in information retrieval (van Rijsbergen 1979: 36ff). Recall that the similarity function determines which clusters are merged in each step in bottom-up clustering. In single-link clustering the similarity between two clusters is the similarity of the two closest objects in the clusters. We search over all pairs of objects that are from the two different clusters and select the pair with the greatest similarity.

LOCAL COHERENCE   Single-link clusterings have clusters with good *local coherence* since the similarity function is locally defined. However, clusters can be elongated or "straggly" as shown in figure 14.6. To see why single-link clustering produces such elongated clusters, observe first that the best moves in figure 14.4 are to merge the two top pairs of points and then the two bottom pairs of points, since the similarities a/b, c/d, e/f, and g/h are the largest for any pair of objects. This gives us the clusters in figure 14.5. The next two steps are to first merge the top two clusters, and then the bottom two clusters, since the pairs b/c and f/g are closer than all others that are not in the same cluster (e.g., closer than b/f and c/g). After doing these two merges we get figure 14.6. We end up with two clusters that

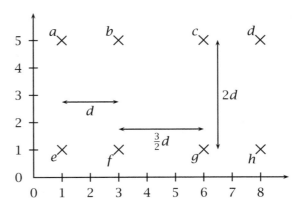

Figure 14.4   A cloud of points in a plane.

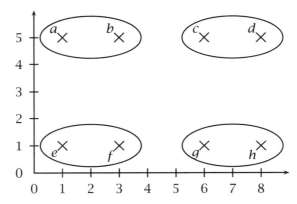

Figure 14.5   Intermediate clustering of the points in figure 14.4.

are locally coherent (meaning that close objects are in the same cluster), but which can be regarded as being of bad global quality. An example of bad global quality is that a is much closer to e than to d, yet a and d are in the same cluster whereas a and e are not.

The tendency of single-link clustering to produce this type of elongated CHAINING EFFECT   cluster is sometimes called the *chaining effect* since we follow a chain of large similarities without taking into account the global context.

MINIMUM SPANNING   Single-link clustering is closely related to the *minimum spanning tree*
TREE   (MST) of a set of points. The MST is the tree that connects all objects with edges that have the largest similarities. That is, of all trees connecting the set of objects the sum of the length of the edges of the MST is mini-

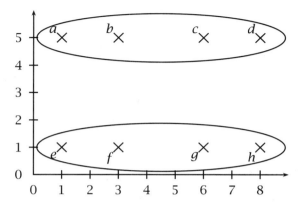

Figure 14.6 Single-link clustering of the points in figure 14.4.

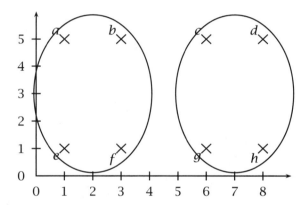

Figure 14.7 Complete-link clustering of the points in figure 14.4.

mal. A single-link hierarchy can be constructed top-down from an MST by removing the longest edge in the MST so that two unconnected components are created, corresponding to two subclusters. The same operation is then recursively applied to these two subclusters (which are also MSTs).

Complete-link clustering has a similarity function that focuses on *global* cluster quality (as opposed to *locally* coherent clusters as in the case of single-link clustering). The similarity of two clusters is the similarity of their two most dissimilar members. Complete-link clustering avoids elongated clusters. For example, in complete-link clustering the two best merges in figure 14.5 are to merge the two left clusters, and then the two right clusters, resulting in the clusters in figure 14.7. Here, the minimally similar pair for the left clusters (a/f or b/e) is "tighter" than the minimally similar pair of the two top clusters (a/d).

So far we have made the assumption that 'tight' clusters are better than 'straggly' clusters. This reflects an intuition that a cluster is a group of objects centered around a central point, and so compact clusters are to be preferred. Such an intuition corresponds to a model like the Gaussian distribution (section 2.1.9), which gives rise to sphere-like clusters. But this is only one possible underlying model of what a good cluster is. It is really a question of our prior knowledge about and model of the data which determines what a good cluster is. For example, the Hawai'ian islands were produced (and are being produced) by a volcanic process which moves along a straight line and creates new volcanoes at more or less regular intervals. Single-link is a very appropriate clustering model here since local coherence is what counts and elongated clusters are what we would expect (say, if we wanted to group several chains of volcanic islands). It is important to remember that the different clustering algorithms that we discuss will generally produce different results which incorporate the somewhat ad hoc biases of the different algorithms. Nevertheless, in most NLP applications, the sphere-shaped clusters of complete-link clustering are preferable to the elongated clusters of single-link clustering.

The disadvantage of complete-link clustering is that it has time complexity $O(n^3)$ since there are n merging steps and each step requires $O(n^2)$ comparisons to find the smallest similarity between any two objects for each cluster pair (where n is the number of objects to be clustered).[1] In contrast, single-link clustering has complexity $O(n^2)$. Once the $n \times n$ similarity matrix for all objects has been computed, it can be updated after each merge in $O(n)$: if clusters c_u and c_v are merged into $c_j = c_u \cup c_v$, then the similarity of the merge with another cluster c_k is simply the maximum of the two individual similarities:

$$\text{sim}(c_j, c_k) = \max(\text{sim}(c_u, c_k), \text{sim}(c_v, c_k))$$

Each of the $n - 1$ merges requires at most n constant-time updates. Both merging and similarity computation thus have complexity $O(n^2)$

---

1. '$O(n^3)$' is an instance of 'Big Oh' notation for algorithmic complexity. We assume that the reader is familiar with it, or else is willing to skip issues of algorithmic complexity. It is defined in most books on algorithms, including (Cormen et al. 1990). The notation describes just the basic dependence of an algorithm on certain parameters, while ignoring constant factors.

in single-link clustering, which corresponds to an overall complexity of $O(n^2)$.

Single-link and complete-link clustering can be graph-theoretically interpreted as finding a maximally connected and maximally complete graph (or clique), respectively, hence the term "complete link" for the latter. See (Jain and Dubes 1988: 64).

14.1.2   Group-average agglomerative clustering

Group-average agglomerative clustering is a compromise between single-link and complete-link clustering. Instead of the greatest similarity between elements of clusters (single-link) or the least similarity (complete link), the criterion for merges is average similarity. We will see presently that average similarity can be computed efficiently in some cases so that the complexity of the algorithm is only $O(n^2)$. The group-average strategy is thus an efficient alternative to complete-link clustering while avoiding the elongated and straggly clusters that occur in single-link clustering.

Some care has to be taken in implementing group-average agglomerative clustering. The complexity of computing average similarity directly is $O(n^2)$. So if the average similarities are computed from scratch each time a new group is formed, that is, in each of the n merging steps, then the algorithm would be $O(n^3)$. However, if the objects are represented as length-normalized vectors in an m-dimensional real-valued space and if the similarity measure is the *cosine*, defined as in (8.40), then we have:

COSINE

(14.3) $$\text{sim}(\vec{x}, \vec{y}) = \cos(\vec{x}, \vec{y}) = \frac{\vec{x} \cdot \vec{y}}{|\vec{x}||\vec{y}|} = \frac{\sum_{i=1}^{m} x_i \times y_i}{\sqrt{\sum_{i=1}^{m} x_i^2} \times \sqrt{\sum_{i=1}^{m} y_i^2}} = \vec{x} \cdot \vec{y}$$

then there exists an algorithm that computes the average similarity of a cluster in constant time from the average similarity of its two children. Given the constant-time for an individual merging operation, the overall time complexity is $O(n^2)$.

We write $\mathcal{X}$ for the set of objects to be clustered, each represented by a m-dimensional vector:

$$\mathcal{X} \subseteq \mathbb{R}^m$$

For a cluster $c_j \subseteq \mathcal{X}$, the average similarity S between vectors in c_j is defined as follows. (The factor $|c_j|(|c_j| - 1)$ calculates the number of (non-zero) similarities added up in the double summation.)

$$(14.4) \quad S(c_j) = \frac{1}{|c_j|(|c_j| - 1)} \sum_{\vec{x} \in c_j} \sum_{\vec{x} \neq \vec{y} \in c_j} \mathrm{sim}(\vec{x}, \vec{y})$$

Let C be the set of current clusters. In each iteration, we identify the two clusters c_u and c_v which maximize $S(c_u \cup c_v)$. This corresponds to step 8 in figure 14.2. A new, smaller, partition C' is then constructed by merging c_u and c_v (step 10 in figure 14.2):

$$C' = (C - \{c_u, c_v\}) \cup \{c_u \cup c_v\}$$

For cosine as the similarity measure, the inner maximization can be done in linear time (Cutting et al. 1992: 328). One can compute the average similarity between the elements of a candidate pair of clusters in constant time by precomputing for each cluster the sum of its members $\vec{s}(c_j)$.

$$\vec{s}(c_j) = \sum_{\vec{x} \in c_j} \vec{x}$$

The sum vector $\vec{s}(c_j)$ is defined in such a way that: (i) it can be easily updated after a merge (namely by simply summing the $\vec{s}$ of the clusters that are being merged), and (ii) the average similarity of a cluster can be easily computed from them. This is so because the following relationship between $\vec{s}(c_j)$ and $S(c_j)$ holds:

$$(14.5) \quad \begin{aligned} \vec{s}(c_j) \cdot \vec{s}(c_j) &= \sum_{\vec{x} \in c_j} \vec{x} \cdot \vec{s}(c_j) \\ &= \sum_{\vec{x} \in c_j} \sum_{\vec{y} \in c_j} \vec{x} \cdot \vec{y} \\ &= |c_j|(|c_j| - 1)S(c_j) + \sum_{\vec{x} \in c_j} \vec{x} \cdot \vec{x} \\ &= |c_j|(|c_j| - 1)S(c_j) + |c_j| \\ \text{Thus,} \quad S(c_j) &= \frac{\vec{s}(c_j) \cdot \vec{s}(c_j) - |c_j|}{|c_j|(|c_j| - 1)} \end{aligned}$$

Therefore, if $\vec{s}(\cdot)$ is known for two groups c_i and c_j, then the average similarity of their union can be computed in constant time as follows:

$$(14.6) \quad S(c_i \cup c_j) = \frac{(\vec{s}(c_i) + \vec{s}(c_j)) \cdot (\vec{s}(c_i) + \vec{s}(c_j)) - (|c_i| + |c_j|)}{(|c_i| + |c_j|)(|c_i| + |c_j| - 1)}$$

Given this result, this approach to group-average agglomerative clustering has complexity $O(n^2)$, reflecting the fact that initially all pairwise similarities have to be computed. The following step that performs n mergers (each in linear time) has linear complexity, so that overall complexity is quadratic.

This form of group-average agglomerative clustering is efficient enough to deal with a large number of features (corresponding to the dimensions of the vector space) and a large number of objects. Unfortunately, the constant time computation for merging two groups (by making use of the quantities $\vec{s}(c_j)$) depends on the properties of vector spaces. There is no general algorithm for group-average clustering that would be efficient independent of the representation of the objects that are to be clustered.

14.1.3   An application: Improving a language model

LANGUAGE MODEL

Now that we have introduced some of the best known hierarchical clustering algorithms, it is time to look at an example of how clustering can be used for an application. The application is building a better *language model*. Recall that language models are useful in speech recognition and machine translation for choosing among several candidate hypotheses. For example, a speech recognizer may find that *President Kennedy* and *precedent Kennedy* are equally likely to have produced the acoustic observations. However, a language model can tell us what are *a priori* likely phrases of English. Here it tell us that *President Kennedy* is much more likely than *precedent Kennedy*, and so we conclude that *President Kennedy* is probably what was actually said. This reasoning can be formalized by the equation for the noisy channel model, which we introduced in section 2.2.4. It says that we should choose the hypothesis H that maximizes the product of the probability given by the language model, $P(H)$, and the conditional probability of observing the speech signal D (or the foreign language text in machine translation) given the hypothesis, $P(D|H)$.

$$\hat{H} = \arg\max_H P(H|D) = \arg\max_H \frac{P(D|H)P(H)}{P(D)} = \arg\max_H P(D|H)P(H)$$

Clustering can play an important role in improving the language model (the computation of $P(H)$) by way of *generalization*. As we saw in chapter 6, there are many rare events for which we do not have enough training data for accurate probabilistic modeling. If we mediate probabilistic inference through clusters, for which we have more evidence in the training set, then our predictions for rare events are likely to be more accurate. This approach was taken by Brown et al. (1992c). We first describe the formalization of the language model and then the clustering algorithm.

The language model

CROSS ENTROPY

PERPLEXITY

The language model under discussion is a bigram model that makes a first order Markov assumption that a word depends only on the previous word. The criterion that we optimize is a decrease in *cross entropy* or, equivalently, *perplexity* (section 2.2.8), the amount by which the language model reduces the uncertainty about the next word. Our aim is to find a function π that assigns words to clusters which decreases perplexity compared to a simple word bigram model.

We first approximate the cross entropy of the corpus $L = w_1 \ldots w_N$ for the cluster assignment function π by making the Markov assumption that a word's occurrence only depends on its predecessor:

$$(14.7) \quad H(L, \pi) \quad = \quad -\frac{1}{N} \log P(w_{1,\ldots,N})$$

$$(14.8) \quad \approx \quad \frac{-1}{N-1} \log \prod_{i=2}^{N} P(w_i | w_{i-1})$$

$$(14.9) \quad \approx \quad \frac{-1}{N-1} \sum_{w^1 w^2} C(w^1 w^2) \log P(w^2 | w^1)$$

Now we make the basic assumption of cluster-based generalization that the occurrence of a word from cluster c_2 only depends on the cluster c_1 of the preceding word:[2]

$$(14.10) \quad H(L, \pi) \approx \frac{-1}{N-1} \sum_{w^1 w^2} C(w^1 w^2) \log P(c_2 | c_1) P(w^2 | c_2)$$

Formula (14.10) can be simplified as follows:

$$(14.11) \quad H(L, \pi) \quad \approx \quad -\left[\sum_{w^1 w^2} \frac{C(w^1 w^2)}{N-1} [\log P(w^2 | c_2) + \log P(c_2)] \right.$$

2. One can observe that this equation is very similar to the probabilistic models used in tagging, which we discuss in chapter 10, except that we induce the word classes from corpus evidence instead of taking them from our linguistic knowledge about parts of speech.

$$+ \sum_{w^1 w^2} \frac{C(w^1 w^2)}{N-1} [\log P(c_2|c_1) - \log P(c_2)] \Bigg]$$

$$(14.12) \qquad = \quad - \Bigg[\sum_{w^2} \frac{\sum_{w^1} C(w^1 w^2)}{N-1} \log P(w^2|c_2) P(c_2)$$

$$+ \sum_{c_1 c_2} \frac{C(c_1 c_2)}{N-1} \log \frac{P(c_2|c_1)}{P(c_2)} \Bigg]$$

$$(14.13) \qquad \approx \quad - \Bigg[\sum_w P(w) \log P(w) + \sum_{c_1 c_2} P(c_1 c_2) \log \frac{P(c_1 c_2)}{P(c_1) P(c_2)} \Bigg]$$

$$(14.14) \qquad = \quad H(w) - I(c_1; c_2)$$

In (14.13) we rely on the approximations $\frac{\sum_{w^1} C(w^1 w^2)}{N-1} \approx P(w^2)$ and $\frac{C(c_1 c_2)}{N-1} \approx P(c_1 c_2)$, which hold for large n. In addition, $P(w^2|c_2) P(c_2) = P(w^2 c_2) = P(w^2)$ holds since $\pi(w^2) = c_2$.

Equation (14.14) shows that we can minimize the cross entropy by choosing the cluster assignment function π such that the mutual information between adjacent clusters $I(c_1; c_2)$ is maximized. Thus we should get the optimal language model by choosing clusters that maximize this mutual information measure.

Clustering

The clustering algorithm is bottom-up with the following merge criterion which maximizes the mutual information between adjacent classes:

$$(14.15) \qquad \text{MI-loss}(c_i, c_j) = \sum_{c_k \in C \setminus \{c_i, c_j\}} I(c_k; c_i) + I(c_k; c_j) - I(c_k; c_i \cup c_j)$$

In each step, we select the two clusters whose merge causes the smallest loss in mutual information. In the description of bottom-up clustering in figure 14.2, this would correspond to the following selection criterion for the pair of clusters that is to be merged next:

$$(c_{n_1}, c_{n_2}) := \underset{(c_i, c_j) \in C \times C}{\arg\min} \; \text{MI-loss}(c_i, c_j)$$

The clustering is stopped when a pre-determined number k of clusters has been reached ($k = 1000$ in (Brown et al. 1992c)). Several shortcuts are necessary to make the computation of the MI-loss function and the clustering of a large vocabulary efficient. In addition, the greedy algorithm ("do the merge with the smallest MI-loss") does not guarantee an optimal clustering result. The clusters can be (and were) improved by moving individual words between clusters. The interested reader can look up the specifics of the algorithm in (Brown et al. 1992c).

Here are three of the 1000 clusters found by Brown et al. (1992c):

- plan, letter, request, memo, case, question, charge, statement, draft

- day, year, week, month, quarter, half

- evaluation, assessment, analysis, understanding, opinion, conversation, discussion

We observe that these clusters are characterized by both syntactic and semantic properties, for example, nouns that refer to time periods.

The perplexity for the cluster-based language model was 277 compared to a perplexity of 244 for a word-based model (Brown et al. 1992c: 476), so no direct improvement was achieved by clustering. However, a linear interpolation (see section 6.3.1) between the word-based and the cluster-based model had a perplexity of 236, which is an improvement over the word-based model (Brown et al. 1992c: 476). This example demonstrates the utility of clustering for the purpose of generalization.

We conclude our discussion by pointing out that clustering and cluster-based inference are integrated here. The criterion we optimize on in clustering, the minimization of $H(L, \pi) = H(w) - I(c_1; c_2)$, is at the same time a measure of the quality of the language model, the ultimate goal of the clustering. Other researchers first induce clusters and then use these clusters for generalization in a second, independent step. An integrated approach to clustering and cluster-based inference is preferable because it guarantees that the induced clusters are optimal for the particular type of generalization that we intend to use the clustering for.

14.1.4   Top-down clustering

Hierarchical top down clustering as described in figure 14.3 starts out with one cluster that contains all objects. The algorithm then selects the least coherent cluster in each iteration and splits it. The functions we introduced in table 14.3 for selecting the best pair of clusters to merge in bottom-up clustering can also serve as measures of cluster coherence in top-down clustering. According to the single-link measure, the coherence of a cluster is the smallest similarity in the minimum spanning tree for the cluster; according to the complete-link measure, the coherence is the smallest similarity between any two objects in the cluster; and according to the group-average measure, coherence is the average similarity between objects in the cluster. All three measures can be used to select the least coherent cluster in each iteration of top-down clustering.

Splitting a cluster is also a clustering task, the task of finding two sub-clusters of the cluster. Any clustering algorithm can be used for the splitting operation, including the bottom-up algorithms described above and non-hierarchical clustering. Perhaps because of this recursive need for a second clustering algorithm, top-down clustering is less often used than bottom-up clustering.

However, there are tasks for which top-down clustering is the more natural choice. An example is the clustering of probability distributions using the *Kullback-Leibler (KL) divergence*. Recall that KL divergence which we introduced in section 2.2.5 is defined as follows:

KULLBACK-LEIBLER
DIVERGENCE

$$(14.16) \quad D(\mathrm{p} \parallel \mathrm{q}) = \sum_{x \in X} \mathrm{p}(x) \log \frac{\mathrm{p}(x)}{\mathrm{q}(x)}$$

This "dissimilarity" measure is not defined for $\mathrm{p}(x) > 0$ and $\mathrm{q}(x) = 0$. In cases where individual objects have probability distributions with many zeros, one cannot compute the matrix of similarity coefficients for all objects that is required for bottom-up clustering.

An example of such a constellation is the approach to distributional clustering of nouns proposed by (Pereira et al. 1993). Object nouns are represented as probability distributions over verbs, where $\mathrm{q}_n(v)$ is estimated as the relative frequency that, given the object noun n, the verb v is its predicate. So for example, for the noun *apple* and the verb *eat*, we will have $\mathrm{q}_n(v) = 0.2$ if one fifth of all occurrences of *apple* as an object noun are with the verb *eat*. Any given noun only occurs with a limited number of verbs, so we have the above-mentioned problem with singularities in computing KL divergence here, which prevents us from using bottom-up clustering.

DISTRIBUTIONAL
NOUN CLUSTERING

To address this problem, *distributional noun clustering* instead performs top-down clustering. Cluster centroids are computed as (weighted and normalized) sums of the probability distributions of the member nouns. This leads to cluster centroid distributions with few zeros that have a defined KL divergence with all their members. See Pereira et al. (1993) for a complete description of the algorithm.

14.2   Non-Hierarchical Clustering

Non-hierarchical algorithms often start out with a partition based on randomly selected seeds (one seed per cluster), and then refine this initial

partition. Most non-hierarchical algorithms employ several passes of *reallocating* objects to the currently best cluster whereas hierarchical algorithms need only one pass. However, reallocation of objects from one cluster to another can improve hierarchical clusterings too. We saw an example in section 14.1.3, where after each merge objects were moved around to improve global mutual information.

If the non-hierarchical algorithm has multiple passes, then the question arises when to stop. This can be determined based on a measure of goodness or cluster quality. We have already seen candidates of such a measure, for example, group-average similarity and mutual information between adjacent clusters. Probably the most important stopping criterion is the likelihood of the data given the clustering model which we will introduce below. Whichever measure we choose, we simply continue clustering as long as the measure of goodness improves enough in each iteration. We stop when the curve of improvement flattens or when goodness starts decreasing.

The measure of goodness can address another problem: how to determine the right number of clusters. In some cases, we may have some prior knowledge about the right number of clusters (for example, the right number of parts of speech in part-of-speech clustering). If this is not the case, we can cluster the data into n clusters for different values of n. Often the goodness measure improves with n. For example, the more clusters the higher the maximum mutual information that can be attained for a given data set. However, if the data naturally fall into a certain number k of clusters, then one can often observe a substantial increase in goodness in the transition from $k - 1$ to k clusters and a small increase in the transition from k to $k + 1$. In order to automatically determine the number of clusters, we can look for a k with this property and then settle on the resulting k clusters.

A more principled approach to finding an optimal number of clusters
is the *Minimum Description Length* (MDL) approach in the *AUTOCLASS* system (Cheeseman et al. 1988). The basic idea is that the measure of goodness captures both how well the objects fit into the clusters (which is what the other measures we have seen do) and how many clusters there are. A high number of clusters will be penalized, leading to a lower good-

ness value. In the framework of MDL, both the clusters and the objects
are specified by code words whose length is measured in bits. The more
clusters there are, the fewer bits are necessary to encode the objects. In
order to encode an object, we only encode the difference between it and
the cluster it belongs to. If there are more clusters, the clusters describe
objects better, and we need fewer bits to describe the difference between
objects and clusters. However, more clusters obviously take more bits
to encode. Since the cost function captures the length of the code for
both data and clusters, minimizing this function (which maximizes the
goodness of the clustering) will determine both the number of clusters
and how to assign objects to clusters.[3]

It may appear that it is an advantage of hierarchical clustering that the
number of clusters need not be determined. But the full cluster hierarchy
of a set of objects does not define a particular clustering since the tree
can be cut in many different ways. For a usable set of clusters in hierarchical clustering one often needs to determine a desirable number of
clusters or, alternatively, a value of the similarity measure at which links
of the tree are cut. So there is not really a difference between hierarchical
and non-hierarchical clustering in this respect. For some non-hierarchical
clustering algorithms, an advantage is their speed.

We cover two non-hierarchical clustering algorithms in this section, K-
means and the EM algorithm. K-means clustering is probably the simplest
clustering algorithm and, despite its limitations, it works sufficiently well
in many applications. The EM algorithm is a general template for a family
of algorithms. We describe its incarnation as a clustering algorithm first
and then relate it to the various instantiations that have been used in
Statistical NLP, some of which like the inside-outside algorithm and the
forward-backward algorithm are more fully treated in other chapters of
this book.

14.2.1 K-means

K-MEANS   *K-means* is a hard clustering algorithm that defines clusters by the center of mass of their members. We need a set of initial cluster centers in
the beginning. Then we go through several iterations of assigning each
object to the cluster whose center is closest. After all objects have been
RECOMPUTATION   assigned, we *recompute* the center of each cluster as the centroid or *mean*

---

3. AUTOCLASS can be downloaded from the internet. See the website.

1 Given: a set $\mathcal{X} = \{\vec{x}_1, \ldots, \vec{x}_n\} \subseteq \mathbb{R}^m$
2   a distance measure $d : \mathbb{R}^m \times \mathbb{R}^m \to \mathbb{R}$
3   a function for computing the mean $\mu : \mathcal{P}(\mathbb{R}) \to \mathbb{R}^m$
4 Select k initial centers $\vec{f}_1, \ldots, \vec{f}_k$
5 **while** stopping criterion is not true **do**
6   **for** all clusters c_j **do**
7 $c_j = \{\vec{x}_i \mid \forall \vec{f}_l \; d(\vec{x}_i, \vec{f}_j) \le d(\vec{x}_i, \vec{f}_l)\}$
8   **end**
9   **for** all means $\vec{f}_j$ **do**
10 $\vec{f}_j = \mu(c_j)$
11   **end**
12 **end**

Figure 14.8   The K-means clustering algorithm.

$\vec{\mu}$ of its members (see figure 14.8), that is $\vec{\mu} = (1/|c_j|) \sum_{\vec{x} \in c_j} \vec{x}$. The distance function is Euclidean distance.

A variant of K-means is to use the L_1 norm instead (section 8.5.2):

$$L_1(\vec{x}, \vec{y}) = \sum_l |x_l - y_l|$$

This norm is less sensitive to outliers. K-means clustering in Euclidean space often creates singleton clusters for outliers. Clustering in L_1 space will pay less attention to outliers so that there is higher likelihood of getting a clustering that partitions objects into clusters of similar size. The L_1 norm is often used in conjunction with *medoids* as cluster centers. The difference between medoids and centroids is that a medoid is one of the objects in the cluster – a prototypical class member. A centroid, the average of a cluster's members, is in most cases not identical to any of the objects.

MEDOIDS

The time complexity of K-means is $O(n)$ since both steps of the iteration are $O(n)$ and only a constant number of iterations is computed.

Figure 14.9 shows an example of one iteration of the K-means algorithm. First, objects are assigned to the cluster whose mean is closest. Then the means are recomputed. In this case, any further iterations will not change the clustering since an assignment to the closest center does not change the cluster membership of any object, which in turn means that no center will be changed in the recomputation step. But this is

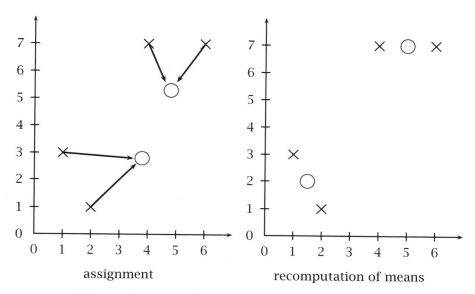

Figure 14.9 One iteration of the K-means algorithm. The first step assigns objects to the closest cluster mean. Cluster means are shown as circles. The second step recomputes cluster means as the center of mass of the set of objects that are members of the cluster.

not the case in general. Usually several iterations are required before the algorithm converges.

One implementation problem that the description in figure 14.8 does not address is how to break ties in cases where there are several centers with the same distance from an object. In such cases, one can either assign objects randomly to one of the candidate clusters (which has the disadvantage that the algorithm may not converge) or perturb objects slightly so that their new positions do not give rise to ties.

Here is an example of how to use K-means clustering. Consider these twenty words from the *New York Times* corpus in chapter 5.

> Barbara, Edward, Gov, Mary, NFL, Reds, Scott, Sox, ballot, finance, inning, payments, polls, profit, quarterback, researchers, science, score, scored, seats

Cluster	Members
1	*ballot* (0.28), *polls* (0.28), *Gov* (0.30), *seats* (0.32)
2	*profit* (0.21), *finance* (0.21), *payments* (0.22)
3	*NFL* (0.36), *Reds* (0.28), *Sox* (0.31), *inning* (0.33), *quarterback* (0.30), *scored* (0.30), *score* (0.33)
4	*researchers* (0.23), *science* (0.23)
5	*Scott* (0.28), *Mary* (0.27), *Barbara* (0.27), *Edward* (0.29)

Table 14.4 An example of K-means clustering. Twenty words represented as vectors of co-occurrence counts were clustered into 5 clusters using K-means. The distance from the cluster centroid is given after each word.

Table 14.4 shows the result of clustering these words using K-means with $k = 5$. We used the data representation from chapter 8 that is also the basis of table 8.8 on page 302. The first four clusters correspond to the topics 'government,' 'finance,' 'sports,' and 'research,' respectively. The last cluster contains names. The benefit of clustering is obvious here. The clustered display of the words makes it easier to understand what types of words occur in the sample and what their relationships are.

Initial cluster centers for K-means are usually picked at random. It depends on the structure of the set of objects to be clustered whether the choice of initial centers is important or not. Many sets are well-behaved and most initializations will result in clusterings of about the same quality.

BUCKSHOT   For ill-behaved sets, one can compute good cluster centers by first running a hierarchical clustering algorithm on a subset of the objects. This is the basic idea of the *Buckshot* algorithm. Buckshot first applies group-average agglomerative clustering (GAAC) to a random sample of the data that has size square root of the complete set. GAAC has quadratic time complexity, but since $(\sqrt{n})^2 = n$, applying GAAC to this sample results in overall linear complexity of the algorithm. The K-means reassignment step is also linear, so that the overall complexity is $O(n)$.

14.2.2   The EM algorithm

One way to introduce the EM algorithm is as a 'soft' version of K-means clustering. Figure 14.10 shows an example. As before, we start with a set of random cluster centers, c_1 and c_2. In K-means clustering we would

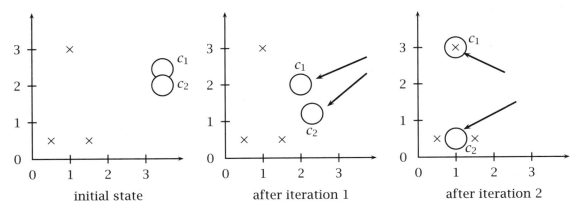

initial state   after iteration 1   after iteration 2

Figure 14.10 An example of using the EM algorithm for soft clustering.

arrive at the final centers shown on the right side in one iteration. The EM algorithm instead does a soft assignment, which, for example, makes the lower right point mostly a member of c_2, but also partly a member of c_1. As a result, both cluster centers move towards the centroid of all three objects in the first iteration. Only after the second iteration do we reach the stable final state.

An alternative way of thinking of the EM algorithm is as a way of estimating the values of the hidden parameters of a model. We have seen some data X, and can estimate $P(X|\mathrm{p}(\Theta))$, the probability of the data according to some model p with parameters Θ. But how do we find the model which maximizes the likelihood of the data? This point will be a maximum in the parameter space, and therefore we know that the probability surface will be flat there. So for each model parameter θ_i, we want to set $\frac{\partial}{\partial \theta_i} \log P(\ldots) = 0$ and solve for the θ_i. Unfortunately this (in general) gives a non-linear set of equations for which no analytical methods of solution are known. But we can hope to find the maximum using the EM algorithm.

In this section, we will first introduce the EM algorithm for the estimation of Gaussian mixtures, the soft clustering algorithm that figure 14.10 is an example of. Then we will describe the EM algorithm in its most general form and relate the general form to specific instances like the inside-outside algorithm and the forward-backward algorithm.

EM for Gaussian mixtures

In applying EM to clustering, we view clustering as estimating a mixture of probability distributions. The idea is that the observed data are generated by several underlying causes. Each cause contributes independently to the generation process, but we only see the final mixture – without information about which cause contributed what. We formalize this notion by representing the data as a pair. There is the *observable* data $X = \{\vec{x}_i\}$, where each $\vec{x}_i = (x_{i1}, \ldots, x_{im})^T$ is simply the vector that corresponds to the ith data point. And then there is the *unobservable* data $Z = \{\vec{z}_i\}$, where within each $\vec{z}_i = z_{i1}, \ldots, z_{ik}$, the component z_{ij} is 1 if object i is a member of cluster j (that is, it is assumed to be generated by that underlying cause) and 0 otherwise.

OBSERVABLE

UNOBSERVABLE

We can cluster with the EM algorithm if we know the type of distribution of the individual clusters (or causes). When estimating a Gaussian mixture, we make the assumption that each cluster is a Gaussian. The EM algorithm then determines the most likely estimates for the parameters of the distributions (in our case, the mean and variance of each Gaussian), and the prior probability (or relative prominence or weight) of the individual causes. So in sum, we are supposing that the data to be clustered consists of n m-dimensional objects $X = \{\vec{x}_1 \ldots \vec{x}_n\} \subseteq \mathbb{R}^m$ generated by k Gaussians $\mathrm{n}_1 \ldots \mathrm{n}_k$.

Once the mixture has been estimated we can view the result as a clustering by interpreting each cause as a cluster. For each object $\vec{x}_i$, we can compute the probability $P(\omega_j | \vec{x}_i)$ that cluster j generated i. An object can belong to several clusters, with varying degrees of confidence.

Multivariate normal distributions. The (multivariate) m-dimensional *Gaussian* family is parameterized by a mean or center $\vec{\mu}_j$ and an $m \times m$ invertible positive definite symmetric matrix, the *covariance matrix* Σ_j. The probability density function for a Gaussian is given by:

GAUSSIAN

COVARIANCE MATRIX

$$(14.17) \quad \mathrm{n}_j(\vec{x};\ \vec{m}_j, \Sigma_j) = \frac{1}{\sqrt{(2\pi)^m |\Sigma_j|}} \exp\left[-\frac{1}{2}(\vec{x} - \vec{\mu}_j)^T \Sigma_j^{-1}(\vec{x} - \vec{\mu}_j)\right]$$

Since we are assuming that the data is generated by k Gaussians, we wish to find the maximum likelihood model of the form:

$$(14.18) \quad \sum_{j=1}^{k} \pi_j \mathrm{n}(\vec{x};\ \vec{\mu}_j, \Sigma_j)$$

Main cluster	Word	$P(w_i\|c_j) = n_j(\vec{x}_i; \mu_j\Sigma_j)$				
		1	2	3	4	5
1	*ballot*	0.63	0.12	0.04	0.09	0.11
1	*polls*	0.58	0.11	0.06	0.10	0.14
1	*Gov*	0.58	0.12	0.03	0.10	0.17
1	*seats*	0.55	0.14	0.08	0.08	0.15
2	*profit*	0.11	0.59	0.02	0.14	0.15
2	*finance*	0.15	0.55	0.01	0.13	0.16
2	*payments*	0.12	0.66	0.01	0.09	0.11
3	*NFL*	0.13	0.05	0.58	0.09	0.16
3	*Reds*	0.05	0.01	0.86	0.02	0.06
3	*Sox*	0.05	0.01	0.86	0.02	0.06
3	*inning*	0.03	0.01	0.93	0.01	0.02
3	*quarterback*	0.06	0.02	0.82	0.03	0.07
3	*score*	0.12	0.04	0.65	0.06	0.13
3	*scored*	0.08	0.03	0.79	0.03	0.07
4	*researchers*	0.08	0.12	0.02	0.68	0.10
4	*science*	0.12	0.12	0.03	0.54	0.19
5	*Scott*	0.12	0.12	0.11	0.11	0.54
5	*Mary*	0.10	0.10	0.05	0.15	0.59
5	*Barbara*	0.15	0.11	0.04	0.12	0.57
5	*Edward*	0.16	0.18	0.02	0.12	0.51

Table 14.5 An example of a Gaussian mixture. The five cluster centroids from table 14.4 are the means $\vec{\mu}_j$ of the five clusters. A uniform diagonal covariance matrix $\Sigma = 0.05 \cdot I$ and uniform priors $\pi_j = 0.2$ were used. The posterior probabilities $P(w_i\|c_j)$ can be interpreted as cluster membership probabilities.

In this model, we need to assume a prior or weight π_j for each Gaussian, so that the integral of the combined Gaussians over the whole space is 1.

Table 14.5 gives an example of a Gaussian mixture, using the centroids from the K-means clustering in table 14.4 as cluster centroids $\vec{\mu}_j$ (this is a common way of initializing EM for Gaussian mixtures). For each word, the cluster from table 14.4 is still the dominating cluster. For example, *ballot* has a higher membership probability in cluster 1 (its cluster from the K-means clustering) than in other clusters. But each word also has some non-zero membership in all other clusters. This is useful for assessing the strength of association between a word and a topic. Comparing two

members of the 'sports' cluster, *inning* and *score*, we can see that *inning*
is strongly associated with 'sports' ($p = 0.93$) whereas *score* has some
affinity with other clusters as well (e.g., $p = 0.12$ with the 'government'
cluster). This is a good example of the utility of soft clustering.

We now develop the EM algorithm for estimating the parameters of a
Gaussian mixture. Let us write $\theta_j = (\vec{\mu}_j, \Sigma_j, \pi_j)$. Then, for the parameters
of the model, we end up with $\Theta = (\theta_1, \ldots, \theta_k)^T$. The log likelihood of the
data X given the parameters Θ is:

$$(14.19) \quad l(X|\Theta) = \log \prod_{i=1}^{n} P(\vec{x}_i) \;\; = \;\; \log \prod_{i=1}^{n} \sum_{j=1}^{k} \pi_j n_j(\vec{x}_i; \vec{\mu}_j, \Sigma_j)$$

$$= \;\; \sum_{i=1}^{n} \log \sum_{j=1}^{k} \pi_j n_j(\vec{x}_i; \vec{\mu}_j, \Sigma_j)$$

The set of parameters Θ with the maximum likelihood gives us the best
model of the data (assuming that it was generated by a mixture of k
Gaussians). So our goal is to find parameters Θ that maximize the log
likelihood given in the equation above. Here, we have to fiddle with all
the parameters so as to try to make the likelihood of each data point
a maximum, while still observing various constraints on the values of
the parameters (so that the area under the pdf remains 1, for instance).
This is a nasty problem in constrained optimization. We cannot calculate
the maximum directly since it involves the log of a sum. Instead, we
approximate the solution by iteration using the EM algorithm.

The EM algorithm is an iterative solution to the following circular statements:

Estimate: If we knew the value of Θ we could compute the expected values of the hidden structure of the model.

Maximize: If we knew the expected values of the hidden structure of the
model, then we could compute the maximum likelihood value of Θ.

EXPECTATION STEP
MAXIMIZATION STEP

We break the circularity by beginning with a guess for Θ and iterating
back and forth between an *expectation step* and a *maximization step*,
hence the name EM algorithm. In the expectation step, we compute expected values for the hidden variables z_{ij} which can be interpreted as
cluster membership probabilities. Given the current parameters, we compute how likely it is that an object belongs to any of the clusters. The
maximization step computes the most likely parameters of the model

given the cluster membership probabilities. This procedure improves our estimates of the parameters so that the parameters of a cluster better reflect the properties of objects with high probability of membership in it.

A key property of the EM algorithm is monotonicity: With each iteration of E and M steps, the likelihood of the model given the data increases. This guarantees that each iteration produces model parameters that are more likely given the data we see. However, while the algorithm will eventually move to a local maximum, it will often not find the globally best solution. This is an important difference from least-squares methods like SVD (covered in chapter 15), which are guaranteed to find the global optimum.

In what follows we describe the EM algorithm for estimating a Gaussian mixture. We follow here the discussion in (Dempster et al. 1977), (Mitchell 1997: ch. 6), and (Ghahramani 1994). See also (Duda and Hart 1973: 193).

To begin, we **initialize** all the parameters. Here, it would be appropriate to initialize the covariance matrices Σ_j of each Gaussian as an identity matrix, each of the weights π_j as $\frac{1}{k}$, and the k means $\vec{\mu}_j$ are each chosen to be a random perturbation away from a data point randomly selected from X.

The **E-step** is the computation of parameters h_{ij}. h_{ij} is the expectation of the hidden variable z_{ij} which is 1 if n_j generated $\vec{x}_i$ and 0 otherwise.

$$(14.20) \quad h_{ij} = E(z_{ij}|\vec{x}_i; \Theta) = \frac{P(\vec{x}_i|n_j; \Theta)}{\sum_{l=1}^{k} P(\vec{x}_i|n_l; \Theta)}$$

The **M-step** is to recompute the parameters Θ (mean, variance, and prior for each Gaussian) as maximum likelihood estimates given expected values h_{ij}:

$$(14.21) \quad \vec{\mu}'_j = \frac{\sum_{i=1}^{n} h_{ij} \vec{x}_i}{\sum_{i=1}^{n} h_{ij}}$$

$$(14.22) \quad \Sigma'_j = \frac{\sum_{i=1}^{n} h_{ij}(\vec{x}_i - \vec{\mu}'_j)(\vec{x}_i - \vec{\mu}'_j)^T}{\sum_{i=1}^{n} h_{ij}}$$

These are the maximum-likelihood estimates for the mean and variance of a Gaussian (Duda and Hart 1973: 23).

The weights of the Gaussians are recomputed as:

$$(14.23) \quad \pi'_j = \frac{\sum_{i=1}^{n} h_{ij}}{\sum_{j=1}^{k} \sum_{i=1}^{n} h_{ij}} = \frac{\sum_{i=1}^{n} h_{ij}}{n}$$

Once means, variances, and priors have been recomputed, we **repeat,** by performing the next iteration of the E and M steps. We keep iterating as long as the log likelihood keeps improving significantly at each step.

EM and its applications in Statistical NLP

This description of the EM algorithm has been for clustering and Gaussian mixtures, but the reader should be able to recognize other applications of EM as instantiations of the same general scheme, for example, the forward-backward algorithm and the inside-outside algorithm, which we covered in earlier chapters. Here is the most general formulation of EM (Dempster et al. 1977: 6).

Define a function Q as follows:

$$Q(\Theta|\Theta^k) = E(l(X,Z)|\Theta)|X,\Theta^k)$$

Here, the z are the hidden variables (the vectors $z_{i1}, \ldots, z_{iM}$ above), the x are the observed data (the vectors $\vec{x}_i$ above). Θ are the parameters of the model, the mean, variances and priors in the case of Gaussian mixtures. $l((x,z)|\Theta)$ is (the log of) the joint probability distribution of observable and unobservable data given the parameters Θ.

Then the E and M step take the following form:

- E-step: Compute $Q(\Theta|\Theta^k)$.

- M-step: Choose Θ^{k+1} to be a value of Θ that maximizes $Q(\Theta|\Theta^k)$.

For the Gaussian mixture case, computing Q corresponds to computing the h_{ij}, the expected values of the hidden variable z. The M step chooses the parameters Θ that maximize $Q(\Theta|\Theta^k)$.

This general formulation of EM is not literally an algorithm. We are not told how to compute the M-step in general. (There are cases where it cannot be computed.) However, for a large class of problems there exist such algorithms, for example, for all distributions of the exponential family, of which the Gaussian distribution is an example. The remainder of this section briefly discusses how certain other algorithms covered in this book are instances of the EM algorithm.

Baum-Welch reestimation.   In the Baum-Welch or forward-backward algorithm (see section 9.3.3), the E step computes (i) for each state i, the expected number of transitions from i in the observed data; (ii) for each pair (i, j) of states, the expected number of transitions from state i to state j. The unobservable data here are the unobservable state transitions. In the E step, we compute expected values for these unobservables given the current parameters of the model.

The M step computes new maximum likelihood estimates of the parameters given the expected values for the unobservables. For Baum-Welch, these parameters are the initial state probabilities π_i, the state transition probabilities a_{ij} and the symbol emission probabilities b_{ijk}.

Inside-outside algorithm. The unobservable data in this algorithm (see section 11.3.4) are whether a particular rule $N^j \rightarrow \zeta$ is used to generate a particular subsequence w_{pq} of words or not. The E step computes expectations over these data, corresponding to the expected number of times that a particular rule will be used. We use the symbols $u_i(p, q, j, r, s)$ and $v_i(p, q, j)$ for these expectations in section 11.3.4. (The difference between the u_i and the v_i is that the u_i are for rules that produce nonterminals and the v_i are for rules that produce preterminals. The subscript i refers to sentence i in the training set.)

The M step then computes maximum-likelihood estimates of the parameters based on the f_i and g_i. The parameters here are the rule probabilities and maximum-likelihood simply consists of summing and renormalizing the f_i or g_i for a particular nonterminal.

Unsupervised word sense disambiguation. The unsupervised word sense disambiguation algorithm in section 7.4 is a clustering algorithm very similar to EM estimation of Gaussian mixtures, except that the probability model is different. The E step again computes expectations of hidden binary variables z_{ij} that record cluster memberships, but the probabilities are computed based on the Bayesian independence model described in that section, not a Gaussian mixture. The probability that a cluster (or sense, which is what we interpret each cluster as) generates a particular word is then recomputed in the M step as a maximum-likelihood estimate given the expectation values.

K-means. K-means can be interpreted as a special case of estimating a Gaussian mixture with EM. To see this, assume that we only recompute the mean of each Gaussian in each iteration of the algorithm. Priors and variances are fixed. If we fix the variances to be very small, then the shape of the Gaussian will be that of a sharp peak that falls off steeply from the center. As a result, if we look at the probability $P(n_j|\vec{x}_i)$ of the 'best' cluster j and the probability $P(n_{j'}|\vec{x}_i)$ of the next best cluster j', then the first will be much larger than the second.

This means that based on the posterior probabilities computed in the E step, each object will be a member of one cluster with probability very close to 1.0. In other words, we have an assignment that is a hard assignment for the purpose of recomputing the means since the contributions of objects with a very small membership probability will have a negligible influence on the computation of the means.

So an EM estimation of a Gaussian mixture with fixed small variances is very similar to K-means. However, there is a difference for ties. Even in the case of small variances, tied objects will have equal probabilities of membership for two clusters. In contrast, K-means makes a hard choice for ties.

Summary. The EM algorithm is very useful, and is currently very popular, but it is sensible to also be aware of its deficiencies. On the down-side, the algorithm is very sensitive to the initialization of the parameters, and unless parameters are initialized well, the algorithm usually gets stuck in one of the many local maxima that exist in the space. One possibility that is sometimes used is to use the results of another clustering algorithm to initialize the parameters for the EM algorithm. For instance, the K-means algorithm is an effective way of finding initial estimates for the cluster centers for EM of Gaussian mixtures. The rate of convergence of the EM algorithm can also be very slow. While reestimation via the EM algorithm is guaranteed to improve (or at least to not have a detrimental effect on) the likelihood of the data according to the model, it is also important to remember that it isn't guaranteed to improve other things that aren't actually in the model, such as the ability of a system to assign part of speech tags according to some external set of rules. Here there is a mismatch between what the EM algorithm is maximizing and the objective function on which the performance of the system is being evaluated, and, not surprisingly, in such circumstances the EM algorithm might have deleterious effects. Finally, it is perhaps worth pointing out that the EM algorithm is only really called for when there isn't a more straightforward way of solving the constrained optimization problem at hand. In simple cases where there is an algebraic solution or the solution can be found by a simple iterative equation solver such as Newton's method, then one may as well do that.

14.3   Further Reading

General introductions to clustering are (Kaufman and Rousseeuw 1990) and (Jain and Dubes 1988). Overviews of work on clustering in information retrieval can be found in (van Rijsbergen 1979), (Rasmussen 1992) and (Willett 1988).

MINIMUM SPANNING TREE

Algorithms for constructing *minimum spanning trees* can be found in (Cormen et al. 1990: ch. 24). For the general case, these algorithms run in $O(n \log n)$ where n is the number of nodes in the graph.

To the extent that clustering is used for data analysis and comprehension, it is closely related to visualization techniques that project a high-dimensional space onto (usually) two or three dimensions. Three

PRINCIPAL COMPONENT ANALYSIS

commonly used techniques are *principal component analysis* (PCA) (see (Biber et al. 1998) for its application to corpora), Multi-Dimensional Scaling (MDS) (Kruskal 1964a,b) and Kohonen maps or Self-Organizing Maps (SOM) (Kohonen 1997). These spatial representations of a multi-dimensional space are alternatives to the dendrogram in figure 14.1.

Clustering can also be viewed as a form of category induction in cognitive modeling. Many researchers have attempted to induce syntactic categories by clustering corpus-derived word representations (Brill et al. 1990; Finch 1993). We used the clustering method proposed by Schütze (1995) for figure 14.1. Waterman (1995) attempts to find clusters of semantically related words based on syntactic evidence.

An early influential paper in which object nouns are clustered on the basis of verbs in a way similar to (Pereira et al. 1993) is (Hindle 1990). Li and Abe (1998) develop a symmetric model of verb-object pair clustering in which clusters generate both nouns and verbs. A pure verb clustering approach is adopted by Basili et al. (1996). An example of adjective clustering can be found in (Hatzivassiloglou and McKeown 1993).

The efficiency of clustering algorithms is becoming more important as text collections and NLP data sets increase in size. The Buckshot algorithm was proposed by Cutting et al. (1992). Even more efficient constant-time algorithms (based on precomputation of a cluster hierarchy) are described by Cutting et al. (1993) and Silverstein and Pedersen (1997).

14.4   Exercises

Exercise 14.1   [★★]

Retrieve the word space data from the website and do a single-link, complete-link, and group-average clustering of a subset.

Exercise 14.2   [★]

Construct an example data set for which the K-means algorithm takes more than one iteration to converge.

Exercise 14.3   [★]

Create a data set with 10 points in a plane where each point is a distance of 1 or less from the origin. Place an eleventh point (the outlier) in turn at distance (a) 2, (b) 4, (c) 8, and (d) 16 from the origin. For each of these cases run K-means clustering with two clusters (i) in Euclidean space and (ii) in L_1 space. (Pick the initial two centers from the 10 points near the origin.) Do the two distance measures give different results? What are the implications for data sets with outliers?

Exercise 14.4   [★★]

Since the EM algorithm only finds a local minimum, different starting conditions will lead to different clusterings. Run the EM algorithm 10 times with different initial seeds on the 1000 most frequent words from the website and analyze the differences. Compute the percentage of pairs of words that are in the same cluster in all 10 clusterings, in 9 clusterings, etc.

Exercise 14.5   [★]

Discuss the trade-off between time and the quality of clustering that needs to be made when choosing one of the three agglomerative algorithms or K-means.

Exercise 14.6   [★]

The model proposed by Brown et al. (1992c) is optimal in that it finds clusters that improve the evaluation measure directly. But it actually did not improve the measure in their experiment, or only after linear interpolation. What are possible reasons?

Exercise 14.7   [★]

Show that K-means converges if there are no ties. Compute as a goodness measure of the clustering the sum squared error that is incurred when each object is replaced by its cluster's center. Then show that this goodness measure decreases (or stays the same) in both the reassignment and the recomputation steps.

15 *Topics in Information Retrieval*

INFORMATION RETRIEVAL (IR) RESEARCH is concerned with developing algorithms and models for retrieving information from document repositories. IR might be regarded as a natural subfield of NLP because it deals with a particular application of natural language processing. (Traditional IR research deals with text although retrieval of speech, images and video are becoming increasingly common.) But in actuality, interactions between the fields have been limited, partly because the special demands of IR were not seen as interesting problems in NLP, partly because statistical methods, the dominant approach in IR, were out of favor in NLP.

With the resurgence of quantitative methods in NLP, the connections between the fields have increased. We have selected four examples of recent interaction between the fields: probabilistic models of term distribution in documents, a problem that has received attention in both Statistical NLP and IR; discourse segmentation, an NLP technique that has been used for more effective document retrieval; and the Vector Space Model and Latent Semantic Indexing (LSI), two IR techniques that have been used in Statistical NLP. Latent Semantic Indexing will also serve as an example of *dimensionality reduction*, an important statistical technique in itself. Our selection is quite subjective and we refer the reader to the IR literature for coverage of other topics (see section 15.6). In the following section, we give some basic background on IR, and then discuss the four topics in turn.

15.1 Some Background on Information Retrieval

The goal of IR research is to develop models and algorithms for retrieving information from document repositories, in particular, textual information. The classical problem in IR is the *ad-hoc retrieval problem*. In ad-hoc retrieval, the user enters a query describing the desired information. The system then returns a list of documents. There are two main models. *Exact match* systems return documents that precisely satisfy some structured query expression, of which the best known type is *Boolean queries*, which are still widely used in commercial information systems. But for large and heterogeneous document collections, the result sets of exact match systems usually are either empty or huge and unwieldy, and so most recent work has concentrated on systems which rank documents according to their estimated relevance to the query. It is within such an approach that probabilistic methods are useful, and so we restrict our attention to such systems henceforth.

AD-HOC RETRIEVAL PROBLEM

EXACT MATCH
BOOLEAN QUERIES

An example of ad-hoc retrieval is shown in figure 15.1. The query is '"glass pyramid" Pei Louvre,' entered on the internet search engine Alta Vista. The user is looking for web pages about I. M. Pei's glass pyramid over the Louvre entrance in Paris. The search engine returns several relevant pages, but also some non-relevant ones – a result that is typical for ad-hoc searches due to the difficulty of the problem.

Some of the aspects of ad-hoc retrieval that are addressed in IR research are how users can improve the original formulation of a query interactively, by way of *relevance feedback*; how results from several text databases can be merged into one result list (*database merging*); which models are appropriate for partially corrupted data, for example, OCRed documents; and how the special problems that languages other than English pose can be addressed in IR.

RELEVANCE FEEDBACK
DATABASE MERGING

Some subfields of information retrieval rely on a training corpus of documents that have been classified as either relevant or non-relevant to a particular query. In *text categorization*, one attempts to assign documents to two or more pre-defined categories. An example is the subject codes assigned by Reuters to its news stories (Lewis 1992). Codes like CORP-NEWS (corporate news), CRUDE (crude oil) or ACQ (acquisitions) make it easier for subscribers to find stories of interest to them. A financial analyst interested in acquisitions can request a customized newsfeed that only delivers documents tagged with ACQ.

TEXT
CATEGORIZATION

Filtering and *routing* are special cases of text categorization with only

FILTERING
ROUTING

[AltaVista] [Advanced Query] [Simple Query] [Private eXtension Products] [Help with Query]

Search the **Web Usenet**
Display results **Compact Detailed**

Tip: When in doubt use lower-case. Check out Help for better matches.

`Word count: glass pyramid:  about 200; Pei:9453; Louvre:26578`

Documents 1-10 of about 10000 matching the query, best matches first.

Paris, France
> Paris, France. Practical Info.-A Brief Overview. Layout: One of the most densely populated cities in Europe, Paris is also one of the most accessible,...
> *http://www.catatravel.com/paris.htm - size 8K - 29 Sep 95*

Culture
> Culture. French culture is an integral part of France's image, as foreign tourists are the first to acknowledge by thronging to the Louvre and the Centre..
> *http://www.france.diplomatie.fr/france/edu/culture.gb.html - size 48K - 20 Jun 96*

Travel World - Science Education Tour of Europe
> Science Education Tour of Europe. B E M I D J I S T A T E U N I V E R S I T Y Science Education Tour of EUROPE July 19-August 1, 1995...
> *http://www.omnitravel.com/007etour.html - size 16K - 21 Jul 95*
> *http://www.omnitravel.com/etour.html - size 16K - 15 May 95*

FRANCE REAL ESTATE RENTAL
> LOIRE VALLEY RENTAL. ANCIENT STONE HOME FOR RENT. Available to rent is a furnished, french country decorated, two bedroom, small stone home, built in the..
> *http://frost2.flemingc.on.ca/~pbell/france.htm size 10K - 21 Jun 96*

LINKS
> PAUL'S LINKS. Click here to view CNN interactive and WEBNEWSor CNET. Click here to make your own web site. Click here to manage your cash. Interested in...
> *http://frost2.flemingc.on.ca/~pbell/links.htm size 9K - 19 Jun 96*

Digital Design Media, Chapter 9: Lines in Space
> Construction planes... Glass-sheet models... Three-dimensional geometric transformations... Sweeping points... Space curves... Structuring wireframe...
> *http://www.gsd.harvard.edu/~malcolm/DDM/DDM09.html size 36K - 22 Jul 95*

No Title
> Boston Update 94: A VISION FOR BOSTON'S FUTURE. Ian Menzies. Senior Fellow, McCormack Institute. University of Massachusetts Boston. April 1994. Prepared..
> *http://www.cs.umb.edu/~serl/mcCormack/Menzies.html size 25K - 31 Jan 96*

Paris - Photograph
> The Arc de Triomphe du Carrousel neatly frames IM Pei's glass pyramid, Paris 1/6. © 1996 Richard Nebesky.

Figure 15.1 Results of the search ' "glass pyramid" Pei Louvre' on an internet search engine.

INFORMATION NEED   two categories: relevant and non-relevant to a particular query (or *infor-mation need*). In routing, the desired output is a ranking of documents according to estimated relevance, similar to the ranking shown in figure 15.1 for the ad-hoc problem. The difference between routing and ad-hoc is that training information in the form of relevance labels is available in routing, but not in ad-hoc retrieval. In filtering, an estimation of relevance has to be made for each document, typically in the form of a probability estimate. Filtering is harder than routing because an absolute ('Document d is relevant') rather than a relative assessment of relevance ('Document d_1 is more relevant than d_2') is required. In many practical applications, an absolute assessment of relevance for each individual document is necessary. For example, when a news group is filtered for stories about a particular company, users do not want to wait for a month, and then receive a ranked list of all stories about the company in the past month, with the most relevant shown at the top. Instead, it is desirable to deliver relevant stories as soon as they come in without knowledge about subsequent postings. As special cases of classification, filtering and routing can be accomplished using any of the classification algorithms described in chapter 16 or elsewhere in this book.

15.1.1   Common design features of IR systems

INVERTED INDEX   Most IR systems have as their primary data structure an *inverted index*. An inverted index is a data structure that lists for each word in the col-
POSTINGS   lection all documents that contain it (the *postings*) and the frequency of occurrence in each document. An inverted index makes it easy to search for 'hits' of a query word. One just goes to the part of the inverted index that corresponds to the query word and retrieves the documents listed there.

POSITION   A more sophisticated version of the inverted index also contains *posi-*
INFORMATION   *tion information*. Instead of just listing the documents that a word occurs in, the positions of all occurrences in the document are also listed. A position of occurrence can be encoded as a byte offset relative to the beginning of the document. An inverted index with position information
PHRASES   lets us search for *phrases*. For example, to search for 'car insurance,' we simultaneously work through the entries for *car* and *insurance* in the inverted index. First, we intersect the two sets so that we only have documents in which both words occur. Then we look at the position information and keep only those hits for which the position information

a	also	an	and	as	at	be	but	by
can	could	do	for	from	go			
have	he	her	here	his	how			
i	if	in	into	it	its			
my	of	on	or	our	say	she		
that	the	their	there	therefore	they			
this	these	those	through	to	until			
we	what	when	where	which	while	who	with	would
you	your							

Table 15.1 A small stop list for English. Stop words are function words that can be ignored in keyword-oriented information retrieval without a significant effect on retrieval accuracy.

indicates that *insurance* occurs immediately after *car*. This is much more efficient than having to read in and process all documents of the collection sequentially.

The notion of *phrase* used here is a fairly primitive one. We can only search for fixed phrases. For example, a search for 'car insurance rates' would not find documents talking about *rates for car insurance*. This is an area in which future Statistical NLP research can make important contributions to information retrieval. Most recent research on phrases in IR has taken the approach of designing a separate phrase identification module and then indexing documents for identified phrases as well as words. In such a system, a phrase is treated as no different from an ordinary word. The simplest approach to phrase identification, which is anathema to NLP researchers, but often performs surprisingly well, is to just select the most frequent bigrams as phrases, for example, those that occur at least 25 times.

In cases where phrase identification is a separate module, it is very similar to the problem of discovering collocations. Many of the techniques in chapter 5 for finding collocations can therefore also be applied to identifying good phrases for indexing and searching.

In some IR systems, not all words are represented in the inverted index.
STOP LIST A *stop list* of 'grammatical' or *function words* lists those words that are
FUNCTION WORDS deemed unlikely to be useful for searching. Common stop words are *the*, *from* and *could*. These words have important semantic functions in English, but they rarely contribute information if the search criterion is

a simple word-by-word match. A small stop list for English is shown in table 15.1.

A stop list has the advantage that it reduces the size of the inverted index. According to Zipf's law (see section 1.4.3), a stop list that covers a few dozen words can reduce the size of the inverted index by half. However, it is impossible to search for phrases that contain stop words once the stop list has been applied – note that some occasionally used phrases like *when and where* consist *entirely* of words in the stop list in table 15.1. For this reason, many retrieval engines do not make use of a stop list for indexing.

STEMMING

Another common feature of IR systems is *stemming*, which we briefly discussed in section 4.2.3. In IR, stemming usually refers to a simplified form of morphological analysis consisting simply of truncating a word. For example, *laughing*, *laugh*, *laughs* and *laughed* are all stemmed to *laugh-*. Common stemmers are the *Lovins* and *Porter* stemmers, which differ in the actual algorithms used for determining where to truncate words (Lovins 1968; Porter 1980). Two problems with truncation stemmers are that they conflate semantically different words (for example, *gallery* and *gall* may both be stemmed to *gall-*) and that the truncated stems can be unintelligible to users (for example, if *gallery* is presented as *gall-*). They are also much harder to make work well for morphology-rich languages.

LOVINS STEMMER
PORTER STEMMER

15.1.2 Evaluation measures

Since the quality of many retrieval systems depends on how well they manage to rank relevant documents before non-relevant ones, IR researchers have developed evaluation measures specifically designed to evaluate rankings. Most of these measures combine precision and recall in a way that takes account of the ranking. As we explained in section 8.1, precision is the percentage of relevant items in the returned set and recall is the percentage of all relevant documents in the collection that is in the returned set.

Figure 15.2 demonstrates why the ranking of documents is important. All three retrieved sets have the same number of relevant and not relevant documents. A simple measure of precision (50% correct) would not distinguish between them. But ranking 1 is clearly better than ranking 2 for a user who scans a returned list of documents from top to bottom

Evaluation	Ranking 1	Ranking 2	Ranking 3
	d1: ✓	d10: ×	d6: ×
	d2: ✓	d9: ×	d1: ✓
	d3: ✓	d8: ×	d2: ✓
	d4: ✓	d7: ×	d10: ×
	d5: ✓	d6: ×	d9: ×
	d6: ×	d1: ✓	d3: ✓
	d7: ×	d2: ✓	d5: ✓
	d8: ×	d3: ✓	d4: ✓
	d9: ×	d4: ✓	d7: ×
	d10: ×	d5: ✓	d8: ×
precision at 5	1.0	0.0	0.4
precision at 10	0.5	0.5	0.5
uninterpolated av. prec.	1.0	0.3544	0.5726
interpolated av. prec. (11-point)	1.0	0.5	0.6440

Table 15.2 An example of the evaluation of rankings. The columns show three different rankings of ten documents, where a ✓ indicates a relevant document and a × indicates a non-relevant document. The rankings are evaluated according to four measures: precision at 5 documents, precision at 10 documents, uninterpolated average precision, and interpolated average precision over 11 points.

(which is what users do in many practical situations, for example, when web searching).

CUTOFF   One measure used is precision at a particular *cutoff*, for example 5 or 10 documents (other typical cutoffs are 20 and 100). By looking at precision for several initial segments of the ranked list, one can gain a good impression of how well a method ranks relevant documents before non-relevant documents.

UNINTERPOLATED   *Uninterpolated average precision* aggregates many precision numbers AVERAGE PRECISION into one evaluation figure. Precision is computed for each point in the list where we find a relevant document and these precision numbers are then averaged. For example, for ranking 1 precision is 1.0 for d1, d2, d3, d4 and d5 since for each of these documents there are only relevant documents up to that point in the list. The uninterpolated average is therefore also 1.0. For ranking 3, we get the following precision numbers for the relevant documents: 1/2 (d1), 2/3 (d2), 3/6 (d3), 4/7 (d5), 5/8 (d4), which averages to 0.5726.

If there are other relevant documents further down the list then these also have to be taken into account in computing uninterpolated average precision. Precision at relevant documents that are not in the returned set is assumed to be zero. This shows that average precision indirectly measures *recall*, the percentage of relevant documents that were returned in the retrieved set (since omitted documents are entered as zero precision).

Interpolated average precision is more directly based on recall. Precision numbers are computed for various *levels of recall*, for example for the levels 0%, 10%, 20%, 30%, 40%, 50%, 60%, 70%, 80%, 90%, and 100% in the case of an 11-point average (the most widely used measure). At recall level α, precision β is computed at the point of the ranked list where the proportion of retrieved relevant documents reaches α. However, if precision goes up again while we are moving down the list, then we *interpolate* and take the highest value of precision anywhere beyond the point where recall level α was first reached. For example, for ranking 3 in figure 15.2 interpolated precision for recall level 60% is not 4/7, the precision at the point where 60% recall is first reached as shown in the top diagram of figure 15.2. Instead, it is 5/8 > 4/7 as shown in the bottom diagram of figure 15.2. (We are assuming that the five relevant documents shown are the only relevant documents.) The thinking here is that the user will be willing to look at more documents if the precision goes up. The two
graphs in figure 15.2 are so-called *precision-recall curves*, with interpolated and uninterpolated values for 0%, 20%, 40%, 60%, 80%, and 100% recall for ranking 3 in table 15.2.

There is an obvious trade-off between precision and recall. If the whole collection is retrieved, then recall is 100%, but precision is low. On the other hand, if only a few documents are retrieved, then the most relevant-seeming documents will be returned, resulting in high precision, but recall will be low.

Average precision is one way of computing a measure that captures
both precision and recall. Another way is the *F measure*, which we introduced in section 8.1:

(15.1) $$F = \frac{1}{\alpha \frac{1}{P} + (1 - \alpha) \frac{1}{R}}$$

where P is the precision, R is the recall and α determines the weighting of precision and recall. The F measure can be used for evaluation at fixed cutoffs if both recall and precision are important.

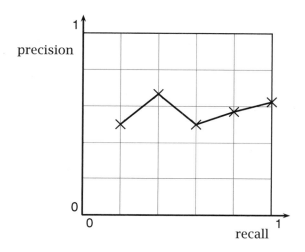

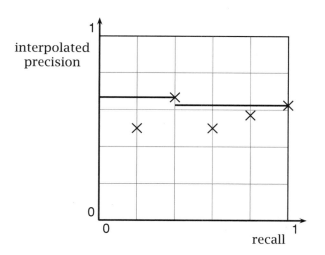

Figure 15.2 Two examples of precision-recall curves. The two curves are for ranking 3 in table 15.2: uninterpolated (above) and interpolated (below).

Any of the measures discussed above can be used to compare the performance of information retrieval systems. One common approach is to run the systems on a corpus and a set of queries and average the performance measure over queries. If the average of system 1 is better than the average of system 2, then that is evidence that system 1 is better than system 2.

Unfortunately, there are several problems with this experimental design. The difference in averages could be due to chance. Or it could be due to one query on which system 1 outperforms system 2 by a large margin with performance on all other queries being about the same. It is therefore advisable to use a statistical test like the t test for system comparison (as shown in section 6.2.3).

15.1.3   The probability ranking principle (PRP)

Ranking documents is intuitively plausible since it gives the user some control over the tradeoff between precision and recall. If recall for the first page of results is low and the desired information is not found, then the user can look at the next page, which in most cases trades higher recall for lower precision.

The following principle is a guideline which is one way to make the assumptions explicit that underlie the design of retrieval by ranking. We present it in a form simplified from (van Rijsbergen 1979: 113):

> **Probability Ranking Principle (PRP).** Ranking documents in order of decreasing probability of relevance is optimal.

The basic idea is that we view retrieval as a greedy search that aims to identify the most valuable document at any given time. The document d that is most likely to be valuable is the one with the highest estimated probability of relevance (where we consider all documents that haven't been retrieved yet), that is, with a maximum value for $P(R|d)$. After making many consecutive decisions like this, we arrive at a list of documents that is ranked in order of decreasing probability of relevance.

Many retrieval systems are based on the PRP, so it is important to be clear about the assumptions that are made when it is accepted.

One assumption of the PRP is that documents are independent. The clearest counterexamples are duplicates. If we have two duplicates d_1 and d_2, then the estimated probability of relevance of d_2 does not change after we have presented d_1 further up in the list. But d_2 does not give the user any information that is not already contained in d_1. Clearly, a better design is to show only one of the set of identical documents, but that violates the PRP.

Another simplification made by the PRP is to break up a complex information need into a number of queries which are each optimized in isolation. In practice, a document can be highly relevant to the complex information need as a whole even if it is not the optimal one for an intermediate step. An example here is an information need that the user initially expresses using ambiguous words, for example, the query *jaguar* to search for information on the animal (as opposed to the car). The optimal response to this query may be the presentation of documents that make the user aware of the ambiguity and permit disambiguation of the query. In contrast, the PRP would mandate the presentation of documents that are highly relevant to either the car or the animal.

A third important caveat is that the probability of relevance is only estimated. Given the many simplifying assumptions we make in designing probabilistic models for IR, we cannot completely trust the probability VARIANCE estimates. One aspect of this problem is that the *variance* of the estimate of probability of relevance may be an important piece of evidence in some retrieval contexts. For example, a user may prefer a document that we are certain is probably relevant (low variance of probability estimate) to one whose estimated probability of relevance is higher, but that also has a higher variance of the estimate.

15.2 The Vector Space Model

VECTOR SPACE MODEL   The *vector space model* is one of the most widely used models for ad-hoc retrieval, mainly because of its conceptual simplicity and the appeal of the underlying metaphor of using spatial proximity for semantic proximity. Documents and queries are represented in a high-dimensional space, in which each dimension of the space corresponds to a word in the document collection. The most relevant documents for a query are expected to be those represented by the vectors closest to the query, that is, documents that use similar words to the query. Rather than considering the magnitude of the vectors, closeness is often calculated by just looking at angles and choosing documents that enclose the smallest angle with the query vector.

In figure 15.3, we show a vector space with two dimensions, corre-

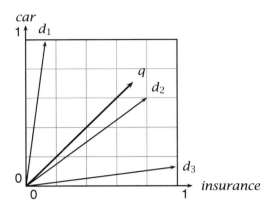

Figure 15.3   A vector space with two dimensions. The two dimensions correspond to the terms *car* and *insurance*. One query and three documents are represented in the space.

TERM WEIGHTS

sponding to the words *car* and *insurance*. The entities represented in the space are the query *q* represented by the vector $(0.71, 0.71)$, and three documents d_1, d_2, and d_3 with the following coordinates: $(0.13, 0.99)$, $(0.8, 0.6)$, and $(0.99, 0.13)$. The coordinates or *term weights* are derived from occurrence counts as we will see below. For example, *insurance* may have only a passing reference in d_1 while there are several occurrences of *car* – hence the low weight for *insurance* and the high weight for *car*. (In the context of information retrieval, the word *term* is used for both words and phrases. We say *term weights* rather than *word weights* because dimensions in the vector space model can correspond to phrases as well as words.)

In the figure, document d_2 has the smallest angle with q, so it will be the top-ranked document in response to the query *car insurance*. This is because both 'concepts' (*car* and *insurance*) are salient in d_2 and therefore have high weights. The other two documents also mention both terms, but in each case one of them is not a centrally important term in the document.

15.2.1   Vector similarity

To do retrieval in the vector space model, documents are ranked according to similarity with the query as measured by the *cosine* measure or *normalized correlation coefficient*. We introduced the cosine as a measure of vector similarity in section 8.5.1 and repeat its definition here:

(15.2) $$\cos(\vec{q},\vec{d}) = \frac{\sum_{i=1}^{n} q_i d_i}{\sqrt{\sum_{i=1}^{n} q_i^2}\sqrt{\sum_{i=1}^{n} d_i^2}}$$

where $\vec{q}$ and $\vec{d}$ are n-dimensional vectors in a real-valued space, the space of all terms in the case of the vector space model. We compute how well the occurrence of term i (measured by q_i and d_i) correlates in query and document and then divide by the Euclidean length of the two vectors to scale for the magnitude of the individual q_i and d_i.

Recall also from section 8.5.1 that cosine and Euclidean distance give rise to the same ranking for normalized vectors:

(15.3)
$$\begin{aligned}
(|\vec{x} - \vec{y}|)^2 &= \sum_{i=1}^{n} (x_i - y_i)^2 \\
&= \sum_{i=1}^{n} x_i^2 - 2\sum_{i=1}^{n} x_i y_i + \sum_{i=1}^{n} y_i^2 \\
&= 1 - 2\sum_{i=1}^{n} x_i y_i + 1 \\
&= 2\left(1 - \sum_{i=1}^{n} x_i y_i\right)
\end{aligned}$$

So for a particular query $\vec{q}$ and any two documents $\vec{d_1}$ and $\vec{d_2}$ we have:

(15.4) $$\cos(\vec{q},\vec{d_1}) > \cos(\vec{q},\vec{d_2}) \quad \Leftrightarrow \quad |\vec{q} - \vec{d_1}| < |\vec{q} - \vec{d_2}|$$

which implies that the rankings are the same. (We again assume normalized vectors here.)

If the vectors are normalized, we can compute the cosine as a simple dot product. Normalization is generally seen as a good thing – otherwise longer vectors (corresponding to longer documents) would have an unfair advantage and get ranked higher than shorter ones. (We leave it as an exercise to show that the vectors in figure 15.3 are normalized, that is, $\sqrt{\sum_i d_i^2} = 1$.)

15.2.2   Term weighting

We now turn to the question of how to weight words in the vector space model. One could just use the count of a word in a document as its term

Quantity	Symbol	Definition
term frequency	$\text{tf}_{i,j}$	number of occurrences of w_i in d_j
document frequency	df_i	number of documents in the collection that w_i occurs in
collection frequency	cf_i	total number of occurrences of w_i in the collection

Table 15.3   Three quantities that are commonly used in term weighting in information retrieval.

Word	Collection Frequency	Document Frequency
insurance	10440	3997
try	10422	8760

Table 15.4   Term and document frequencies of two words in an example corpus.

TERM FREQUENCY
DOCUMENT
FREQUENCY
COLLECTION
FREQUENCY

weight, but there are more effective methods of term weighting. The basic information used in term weighting is *term frequency, document frequency*, and sometimes *collection frequency* as defined in table 15.3. Note that $\text{df}_i \leq \text{cf}_i$ and that $\sum_j \text{tf}_{i,j} = \text{cf}_i$. It is also important to note that document frequency and collection frequency can only be used if there is a collection. This assumption is not always true, for example if collections are created dynamically by selecting several databases from a large set (as may be the case on one of the large on-line information services), and joining them into a temporary collection.

The information that is captured by term frequency is how salient a word is within a given document. The higher the term frequency (the more often the word occurs) the more likely it is that the word is a good description of the content of the document. Term frequency is usually dampened by a function like $f(\text{tf}) = \sqrt{\text{tf}}$ or $f(\text{tf}) = 1 + \log(\text{tf}), \text{tf} > 0$ because more occurrences of a word indicate higher importance, but not as much relative importance as the undampened count would suggest. For example, $\sqrt{3}$ or $1 + \log 3$ better reflect the importance of a word with three occurrences than the count 3 itself. The document is somewhat more important than a document with one occurrence, but not three times as important.

The second quantity, document frequency, can be interpreted as an indicator of informativeness. A semantically focussed word will often occur several times in a document if it occurs at all. Semantically unfocussed words are spread out homogeneously over all documents. An example from a corpus of *New York Times* articles is the words *insurance* and *try* in table 15.4. The two words have about the same collection frequency, the total number of occurrences in the document collection. But *insurance* occurs in only half as many documents as *try*. This is because the word *try* can be used when talking about almost any topic since one can *try* to do something in any context. In contrast, *insurance* refers to a narrowly defined concept that is only relevant to a small set of topics. Another property of semantically focussed words is that, if they come up once in a document, they often occur several times. *Insurance* occurs about three times per document, averaged over documents it occurs in at least once. This is simply due to the fact that most articles about health insurance, car insurance or similar topics will refer multiple times to the concept of insurance.

One way to combine a word's term frequency $\text{tf}_{i,j}$ and document frequency df_i into a single weight is as follows:

$$(15.5) \qquad \text{weight}(i,j) = \begin{cases} (1 + \log(\text{tf}_{i,j})) \log \frac{N}{\text{df}_i} & \text{if } \text{tf}_{i,j} \geq 1 \\ 0 & \text{if } \text{tf}_{i,j} = 0 \end{cases}$$

where N is the total number of documents. The first clause applies for words occurring in the document, whereas for words that do not appear ($\text{tf}_{i,j} = 0$), we set $\text{weight}(i,j) = 0$.

Document frequency is also scaled logarithmically. The formula $\log \frac{N}{\text{df}_i} = \log N - \log \text{df}_i$ gives full weight to words that occur in 1 document ($\log N - \log \text{df}_i = \log N - \log 1 = \log N$). A word that occurred in all documents would get zero weight ($\log N - \log \text{df}_i = \log N - \log N = 0$).

This form of document frequency weighting is often called *inverse document frequency* or idf weighting. More generally, the weighting scheme in (15.5) is an example of a larger family of so-called *tf.idf* weighting schemes. Each such scheme can be characterized by its term occurrence weighting, its document frequency weighting and its normalization. In one description scheme, we assign a letter code to each component of the tf.idf scheme. The scheme in (15.5) can then be described as "ltn" for logarithmic occurrence count weighting (l), logarithmic document frequency weighting (t), and no normalization (n). Other weighting possibilities are listed in table 15.5. For example, "ann" is augmented term occurrence weighting, no document frequency weighting and no normalization. We refer to vector length normalization as cosine normalization because the inner product between two length-normalized vectors (the query-document similarity measure used in the vector space model) is

INVERSE DOCUMENT
FREQUENCY
IDF
TF.IDF

Term occurrence		Document frequency		Normalization	
n (natural)	$\text{tf}_{t,d}$	n (natural)	df_t	n	(no normalization)
l (logarithm)	$1 + \log(\text{tf}_{t,d})$	t	$\log \frac{N}{\text{df}_t}$	c	(cosine)
a (augmented)	$0.5 + \frac{0.5 \times \text{tf}_{t,d}}{\max_t(\text{tf}_{t,d})}$				$\frac{1}{\sqrt{w_1^2 + w_2^2 + \ldots + w_n^2}}$

Table 15.5 Components of tf.idf weighting schemes. $\text{tf}_{t,d}$ is the frequency of term t in document d, df_t is the number of documents t occurs in, N is the total number of documents, and w_i is the weight of term i.

their cosine. Different weighting schemes can be applied to queries and documents. In the name "ltc.lnn," the halves refer to document and query weighting, respectively.

The family of weighting schemes shown in table 15.5 is sometimes criticized as 'ad-hoc' because it is not directly derived from a mathematical model of term distributions or relevancy. However, these schemes are effective in practice and work robustly in a broad range of applications. For this reason, they are often used in situations where a rough measure of similarity between vectors of counts is needed.

15.3 Term Distribution Models

An alternative to tf.idf weighting is to develop a model for the distribution of a word and to use this model to characterize its importance for retrieval. That is, we wish to estimate $P_i(k)$, the proportion of times that word w_i appears k times in a document. In the simplest case, the distribution model is used for deriving a probabilistically motivated term weighting scheme for the vector space model. But models of term distribution can also be embedded in other information retrieval frameworks.

ZIPF'S LAW   Apart from its importance for term weighting, a precise characterization of the occurrence patterns of words in text is arguably at least as important a topic in Statistical NLP as *Zipf's law*. Zipf's law describes word behavior in an *entire corpus*. In contrast, term distribution models capture regularities of word occurrence in *subunits of a corpus* (e.g., documents or chapters of a book). In addition to information retrieval, a good understanding of distribution patterns is useful wherever we want to assess the likelihood of a certain number of occurrences of a specific word in a unit of text. For example, it is also important for author identification where one compares the likelihood that different writers produced a text of unknown authorship.

Most term distribution models try to characterize how informative a word is, which is also the information that inverse document frequency is getting at. One could cast the problem as one of distinguishing content words from non-content (or function) words, but most models have a graded notion of how informative a word is. In this section, we introduce several models that formalize notions of informativeness. Three are based on the Poisson distribution, one motivates inverse document frequency as a weight optimal for Bayesian classification and the final one, *residual inverse document frequency*, can be interpreted as a combination of idf and the Poisson distribution.

15.3.1 The Poisson distribution

POISSON
DISTRIBUTION

The standard probabilistic model for the distribution of a certain type of event over units of a fixed size (such as periods of time or volumes of liquid) is the *Poisson distribution*. Classical examples of Poisson distributions are the number of items that will be returned as defects in a given period of time, the number of typing mistakes on a page, and the number of microbes that occur in a given volume of water.

The definition of the Poisson distribution is as follows.

Poisson Distribution. $\quad p(k; \lambda_i) = e^{-\lambda_i} \dfrac{\lambda_i^k}{k!} \quad$ for some $\lambda_i > 0$

In the most common model of the Poisson distribution in IR, the parameter $\lambda_i > 0$ is the average number of occurrences of w_i per document, that is, $\lambda_i = \frac{cf_i}{N}$ where cf_i is the collection frequency and N is the total number of documents in the collection. Both the mean and the variance of the Poisson distribution are equal to λ_i:

$$E(p) = \text{Var}(p) = \lambda_i$$

Figure 15.4 shows two examples of the Poisson distribution.

In our case, the event we are interested in is the occurrence of a particular word w_i and the fixed unit is the document. We can use the Poisson distribution to estimate an answer to the question: What is the probability that a word occurs a particular number of times in a document. We might say that $P_i(k) = p(k; \lambda_i)$ is the probability of a document having exactly k occurrences of w_i, where λ_i is appropriately estimated for each word.

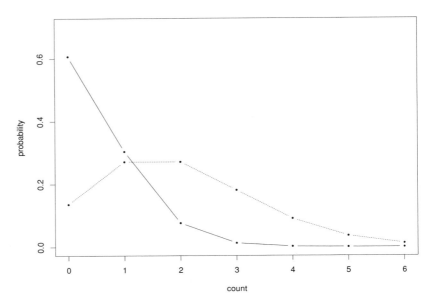

Figure 15.4 The Poisson distribution.   The graph shows p(k; 0.5) (solid line) and p(k; 2.0) (dotted line) for $0 \le k \le 6$. In the most common use of this distribution in IR, k is the number of occurrences of term i in a document, and p(k; λ_i) is the probability of a document with that many occurrences.

The Poisson distribution is a limit of the binomial distribution. For the binomial distribution b(k; n, p), if we let $n \to \infty$ and $p \to 0$ in such a way that np remains fixed at value $\lambda > 0$, then b(x; n, p) $\to$ p(k; λ). Assuming a Poisson distribution for a term is appropriate if the following conditions hold.

- The probability of one occurrence of the term in a (short) piece of text is proportional to the length of the text.

- The probability of more than one occurrence of a term in a short piece of text is negligible compared to the probability of one occurrence.

- Occurrence events in non-overlapping intervals of text are independent.

We will discuss problems with these assumptions for modeling the distribution of terms shortly. Let us first look at some examples.

Word	df_i	cf_i	λ_i	$N(1 - p(0; \lambda_i))$	Overestimation
follows	21744	23533	0.2968	20363	0.94
transformed	807	840	0.0106	835	1.03
soviet	8204	35337	0.4457	28515	3.48
students	4953	15925	0.2008	14425	2.91
james	9191	11175	0.1409	10421	1.13
freshly	395	611	0.0077	609	1.54

Table 15.6   Document frequency (df) and collection frequency (cf) for 6 words in the *New York Times* corpus. Computing $N(1 - p(0; \lambda_i))$ according to the Poisson distribution is a reasonable estimator of df for non-content words (like *follows*), but severely overestimates df for content words (like *soviet*). The parameter λ_i of the Poisson distribution is the average number of occurrences of term *i* per document. The corpus has $N = 79291$ documents.

Table 15.6 shows for six terms in the *New York Times* newswire how well the Poisson distribution predicts document frequency. For each word, we show document frequency df_i, collection frequency cf_i, the estimate of λ (collection frequency divided by total number of documents (79291)), the predicted df, and the ratio of predicted df and actual df.

Examining document frequency is the easiest way to check whether a term is Poisson distributed. The number of documents predicted to have at least one occurrence of a term can be computed as the complement of the predicted number with no occurrences. Thus, the Poisson predicts that the document frequency is $\widehat{df_i} = N(1 - P_i(0))$ where N is the number of documents in the corpus. A better way to check the fit of the Poisson is to look at the complete distribution: the number of documents with 0, 1, 2, 3, etc. occurrences. We will do this below.

In table 15.6, we can see that the Poisson estimates are good for non-content words like *follows* and *transformed*. We use the term *non-content word* loosely to refer to words that taken in isolation (which is what most IR systems do) do not give much information about the contents of the document. But the estimates for content words are much too high, by a factor of about 3 (3.48 and 2.91).

This result is not surprising since the Poisson distribution assumes independence between term occurrences. This assumption holds approximately for non-content words, but most content words are much more likely to occur again in a text once they have occurred once, a property

BURSTINESS
TERM CLUSTERING that is sometimes called *burstiness* or *term clustering*. However, there are some subtleties in the behavior of words as we can see for the last two words in the table. The distribution of *james* is surprisingly close to Poisson, probably because in many cases a person's full name is given at first mention in a newspaper article, but following mentions only use the last name or a pronoun. On the other hand, *freshly* is surprisingly non-Poisson. Here we get strong dependence because of the genre of recipes in the *New York Times* in which *freshly* frequently occurs several times. So non-Poisson-ness can also be a sign of clustered term occurrences in a particular genre like recipes.

The tendency of content word occurrences to cluster is the main problem with using the Poisson distribution for words. But there is also the opposite effect. We are taught in school to avoid repetitive writing. In many cases, the probability of reusing a word immediately after its first occurrence in a text is lower than in general. A final problem with the Poisson is that documents in many collections differ widely in size. So documents are not a uniform unit of measurement as the second is for time or the kilogram is for mass. But that is one of the assumptions of the Poisson distribution.

15.3.2   The two-Poisson model

TWO-POISSON MODEL A better fit to the frequency distribution of content words is provided by the *two-Poisson Model* (Bookstein and Swanson 1975), a mixture of two Poissons. The model assumes that there are two classes of documents associated with a term, one class with a low average number of occurrences (the non-privileged class) and one with a high average number of occurrences (the privileged class):

$$\text{tp}(k;\ \pi, \lambda_1, \lambda_2) = \pi e^{-\lambda_1} \frac{\lambda_1{}^k}{k!} + (1 - \pi)e^{-\lambda_2} \frac{\lambda_2{}^k}{k!}$$

where π is the probability of a document being in the privileged class, $(1 - \pi)$ is the probability of a document being in the non-privileged class, and λ_1 and λ_2 are the average number of occurrences of word w_i in the privileged and non-privileged classes, respectively.

The two-Poisson model postulates that a content word plays two different roles in documents. In the non-privileged class, its occurrence is accidental and it should therefore not be used as an index term, just as a non-content word. The average number of occurrences of the word in this class is low. In the privileged class, the word is a central content word. The average number of occurrences of the word in this class is high and it is a good index term.

Empirical tests of the two-Poisson model have found a spurious "dip" at frequency 2. The model incorrectly predicts that documents with 2 occurrences of a term are less likely than documents with 3 or 4 occurrences. In reality, the distribution for most terms is monotonically decreasing. If $P_i(k)$ is the proportion of times that word w_i appears k times in a document, then $P_i(0) > P_i(1) > P_i(2) > P_i(3) > P_i(4) > \ldots$. As a fix, one can NEGATIVE BINOMIAL use more than two Poisson distributions. The *negative binomial* is one such mixture of an infinite number of Poissons (Mosteller and Wallace 1984), but there are many others (Church and Gale 1995). The negative binomial fits term distributions better than one or two Poissons, but it can be hard to work with in practice because it involves the computation of large binomial coefficients.

15.3.3 The K mixture

A simpler distribution that fits empirical word distributions about as well as the negative binomial is Katz's K mixture:

$$P_i(k) = (1 - \alpha)\delta_{k,0} + \frac{\alpha}{\beta + 1}\left(\frac{\beta}{\beta + 1}\right)^k$$

where $\delta_{k,0} = 1$ iff $k = 0$ and $\delta_{k,0} = 0$ otherwise and α and β are parameters that can be fit using the observed mean λ and the observed inverse document frequency IDF as follows.

$$\lambda = \frac{\text{cf}}{N}$$

$$\text{IDF} = \log_2 \frac{N}{\text{df}}$$

$$\beta = \lambda \times 2^{\text{IDF}} - 1 = \frac{\text{cf} - \text{df}}{\text{df}}$$

$$\alpha = \frac{\lambda}{\beta}$$

The parameter β is the number of "extra terms" per document in which the term occurs (compared to the case where a term has only one occurrence per document). The decay factor $\frac{\beta}{\beta+1} = \frac{\text{cf}-\text{df}}{\text{cf}}$ (extra terms per term occurrence) determines the ratio $\frac{P_i(k)}{P_i(k-1)}$. For example, if there are $\frac{1}{10}$ as

Word							k				
		0	1	2	3	4	5	6	7	8	≥ 9
follows	act.	57552.0	20142.0	1435.0	148.0	18.0	1.0				
	est.	57552.0	20091.0	1527.3	116.1	8.8	0.7	0.1	0.0	0.0	0.0
trans-	act.	78489.0	776.0	29.0	2.0						
formed	est.	78489.0	775.3	30.5	1.2	0.0	0.0	0.0	0.0	0.0	0.0
soviet	act.	71092.0	3038.0	1277.0	784.0	544.0	400.0	356.0	302.0	255.0	1248.0
	est.	71092.0	1904.7	1462.5	1122.9	862.2	662.1	508.3	390.3	299.7	230.1
students	act.	74343.0	2523.0	761.0	413.0	265.0	178.0	143.0	112.0	96.0	462.0
	est.	74343.0	1540.5	1061.4	731.3	503.8	347.1	239.2	164.8	113.5	78.2
james	act.	70105.0	7953.0	922.0	183.0	52.0	24.0	19.0	9.0	7.0	22.0
	est.	70105.0	7559.2	1342.1	238.3	42.3	7.5	1.3	0.2	0.0	0.0
freshly	act.	78901.0	267.0	66.0	47.0	8.0	4.0	2.0	1.0		
	est.	78901.0	255.4	90.3	31.9	11.3	4.0	1.4	0.5	0.2	0.1

Table 15.7 Actual and estimated number of documents with k occurrences for six terms. For example, there were 1435 documents with 2 occurrences of *follows*. The K mixture estimate is 1527.3.

many extra terms as term occurrences, then there will be ten times as many documents with 1 occurrence as with 2 occurrences and ten times as many with 2 occurrences as with 3 occurrences. If there are no extra terms (cf = df $\Rightarrow \frac{\beta}{\beta+1} = 0$), then we predict that there are no documents with more than 1 occurrence.

The parameter α captures the absolute frequency of the term. Two terms with the same β have identical ratios of collection frequency to document frequency, but different values for α if their collection frequencies are different.

Table 15.7 shows the number of documents with k occurrences in the *New York Times* corpus for the six words that we looked at earlier. We observe that the fit is always perfect for $k = 0$. It is easy to show that this is a general property of the K mixture (see exercise 15.3).

The K mixture is a fairly good approximation of term distribution, especially for non-content words. However, it is apparent from the empirical numbers in table 15.7 that the assumption:

$$\frac{P_i(k)}{P_i(k+1)} = c, \quad k \geq 1$$

does not hold perfectly for content words. As in the case of the two-Poisson mixture we are making a distinction between low base rate of occurrence and another class of documents that have clusters of occurrences. The K mixture assumes $\frac{P_i(k)}{P_i(k+1)} = c$ for $k \geq 1$, which concedes that $k = 0$ is a special case due to a low base rate of occurrence for many words. But the ratio $\frac{P_i(k)}{P_i(k+1)}$ seems to decline for content words even for $k \geq 1$. For example, for *soviet* we have:

$$\frac{P_i(0)}{P_i(1)} = \frac{71092}{3038} \approx 23.4 \qquad \frac{P_i(1)}{P_i(2)} = \frac{3038}{1277} \approx 2.38$$

$$\frac{P_i(2)}{P_i(3)} = \frac{1277}{784} \approx 1.63 \qquad \frac{P_i(3)}{P_i(4)} = \frac{784}{544} \approx 1.44$$

$$\frac{P_i(4)}{P_i(5)} = \frac{544}{400} \approx 1.36$$

In other words, each occurrence of a content word we find in a text decreases the probability of finding an additional term, but the decreases become consecutively smaller. The reason is that occurrences of content words tend to cluster in documents whose core topic is associated with the content word. A large number of occurrences indicates that the content word describes a central concept of the document. Such a central concept is likely to be mentioned more often than a "constant decay" model would predict.

We have introduced Katz's K mixture here as an example of a term distribution model that is more accurate than the Poisson distribution and the two-Poisson model. The interested reader can find more discussion of the characteristics of content words in text and of several probabilistic models with a better fit to empirical distributions in (Katz 1996).

15.3.4   Inverse document frequency

We motivated inverse document frequency (IDF) heuristically in section 15.2.2, but we can also derive it from a term distribution model. In the derivation we present here, we only use *binary* occurrence information and do not take into account term frequency.

ODDS OF RELEVANCE

To derive IDF, we view ad-hoc retrieval as the task of ranking documents according to the *odds of relevance*:

$$O(d) = \frac{P(R|d)}{P(\neg R|d)}$$

where $P(R|d)$ is the probability of relevance of d and $P(\neg R|d)$ is the probability of non-relevance. We then take logs to compute the log odds, and apply Bayes' formula:

$$\log O(d) \;=\; \log \frac{P(R|d)}{P(\neg R|d)}$$

$$= \log \frac{\frac{P(d|R)P(R)}{P(d)}}{\frac{P(d|\neg R)P(\neg R)}{P(d)}}$$

$$= \log P(d|R) - \log P(d|\neg R) + \log P(R) - \log P(\neg R)$$

Let us assume that the query Q is the set of words $\{w_i\}$, and let the indicator random variables X_i be 1 or 0, corresponding to occurrence and non-occurrence of word w_i in d. If we then make the conditional independence assumption discussed in section 7.2.1, we can write:

$$\log O(d) = \sum_i [\log P(X_i|R) - \log P(X_i|\neg R)] + \log P(R) - \log P(\neg R)$$

Since we are only interested in ranking, we can create a new ranking function $g(d)$ which drops the constant term $\log P(R) - \log P(\neg R)$. With the abbreviations $p_i = P(X_i = 1|R)$ (word i occurring in a relevant document) and $q_i = P(X_i = 1|\neg R)$ (word i occurring in a non-relevant document), we can write $g(d)$ as follows. (In the second line, we make use of $P(X_i = 1|\_) = y = y^1(1-y)^0 = y^{X_i}(1-y)^{1-X_i}$ and $P(X_i = 0|\_) = 1 - y = y^0(1-y)^1 = y^{X_i}(1-y)^{1-X_i}$ so that we can write the equation more compactly.)

$$
\begin{aligned}
g(d) &= \sum_i [\log P(X_i|R) - \log P(X_i|\neg R)] \\
&= \sum_i [\log(p_i^{X_i}(1-p_i)^{1-X_i}) - \log(q_i^{X_i}(1-q_i)^{1-X_i})] \\
&= \sum_i X_i \log \frac{p_i(1-q_i)}{(1-p_i)q_i} + \sum_i \log \frac{1-p_i}{1-q_i} \\
&= \sum_i X_i \log \frac{p_i}{1-p_i} + \sum_i X_i \log \frac{1-q_i}{q_i} + \sum_i \log \frac{1-p_i}{1-q_i}
\end{aligned}
$$

In the last equation above, $\sum_i \log \frac{1-p_i}{1-q_i}$ is another constant term which does not affect the ranking of documents, and so we can drop it as well giving the final ranking function:

(15.6) $$g'(d) = \sum_i X_i \log \frac{p_i}{1-p_i} + \sum_i X_i \log \frac{1-q_i}{q_i}$$

If we have a set of documents that is categorized according to relevance to the query, we can estimate the p_i and q_i directly. However, in ad-hoc retrieval we do not have such relevance information. That means we have to make some simplifying assumptions in order to be able to rank documents in a meaningful way.

First, we assume that p_i is small and constant for all terms. The first term of g' then becomes $\sum_i X_i \log \frac{p_i}{1-p_i} = c \sum_i X_i$, a simple count of the number of matches between query and document, weighted by c.

The fraction in the second term can be approximated by assuming that most documents are not relevant so $q_i = P(X_i = 1|\neg R) \approx P(w_i) = \frac{df_i}{N}$, which is the maximum likelihood estimate of $P(w_i)$, the probability of occurrence of w_i not conditioned on relevance.

$$\frac{1 - q_i}{q_i} = \frac{1 - \frac{df_i}{N}}{\frac{df_i}{N}} = \frac{N - df_i}{df_i} \approx \frac{N}{df_i}$$

The last approximation, $\frac{N-df_i}{df_i} \approx \frac{N}{df_i}$, holds for most words since most words are relatively rare. After applying the logarithm, we have now arrived at the IDF weight we introduced earlier. Substituting it back into the formula for g' we get:

(15.7) $\quad g'(d) \approx c \sum_i X_i + \sum_i X_i \mathrm{idf}_i$

This derivation may not satisfy everyone since we weight the term according to the 'opposite' of the probability of non-relevance rather than directly according to the probability of relevance. But the probability of relevance is impossible to estimate in ad-hoc retrieval. As in many other cases in Statistical NLP, we take a somewhat circuitous route to get to a desired quantity from others that can be more easily estimated.

15.3.5 Residual inverse document frequency

RESIDUAL INVERSE DOCUMENT FREQUENCY RIDF

An alternative to IDF is *residual inverse document frequency* or *RIDF*. Residual IDF is defined as the difference between the logs of actual inverse document frequency and inverse document frequency predicted by Poisson:

$$\mathrm{RIDF} = \mathrm{IDF} - \log_2 \frac{1}{1 - p(0; \lambda_i)} = \mathrm{IDF} + \log_2(1 - p(0; \lambda_i))$$

where $\mathrm{IDF} = \log_2 \frac{N}{df}$, and p is the Poisson distribution with parameter $\lambda_i = \frac{cf_i}{N}$, the average number of occurrences of w_i per document. $1 - p(0; \lambda_i)$ is the Poisson probability of a document with at least one occurrence. So, for example, RIDF for *insurance* and *try* in table 15.4 would be 1.29 and 0.16, respectively (with $N = 79291$ – verify this!).

	Term 1	Term 2	Term 3	Term 4
Query	user	interface		
Document 1	user	interface	HCI	interaction
Document 2			HCI	interaction

Table 15.8 Example for exploiting co-occurrence in computing content similarity. For the query and the two documents, the terms they contain are listed in their respective rows.

As we saw above, the Poisson distribution only fits the distribution of non-content words well. Therefore, the deviation from Poisson is a good predictor of the degree to which a word is a content word.

15.3.6   Usage of term distribution models

We can exploit term distribution models in information retrieval by using the parameters of the model fit for a particular term as indicators of relevance. For example, we could use RIDF or the β in the K mixture as a replacement for IDF weights (since content words have large β and large RIDF, non-content words have smaller β and smaller RIDF).

Better models of term distribution than IDF have the potential of assessing a term's properties more accurately, leading to a better model of query-document similarity. Although there has been little work on employing term distribution models different from IDF in IR, it is to be hoped that such models will eventually lead to better measures of content similarity.

15.4   Latent Semantic Indexing

In the previous section, we looked at the occurrence patterns of individual words. A different source of information about terms that can be CO-OCCURRENCE exploited in information retrieval is *co-occurrence*: the fact that two or more terms occur in the same documents more often than chance. Consider the example in table 15.8. Document 1 is likely to be relevant to the query since it contains all the terms in the query. But document 2 is also a good candidate for retrieval. Its terms *HCI* and *interaction* co-occur with *user* and *interface*, which can be evidence for semantic relatedness. LATENT SEMANTIC   *Latent Semantic Indexing* (LSI) is a technique that projects queries and
INDEXING

$$
A = \begin{array}{c|cccccc}
 & d_1 & d_2 & d_3 & d_4 & d_5 & d_6 \\
\hline
\text{cosmonaut} & 1 & 0 & 1 & 0 & 0 & 0 \\
\text{astronaut} & 0 & 1 & 0 & 0 & 0 & 0 \\
\text{moon} & 1 & 1 & 0 & 0 & 0 & 0 \\
\text{car} & 1 & 0 & 0 & 1 & 1 & 0 \\
\text{truck} & 0 & 0 & 0 & 1 & 0 & 1
\end{array}
$$

Figure 15.5   An example of a term-by-document matrix A.

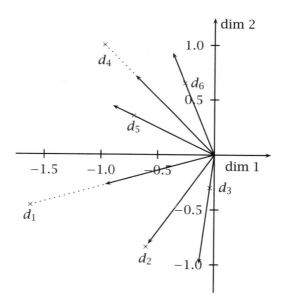

Figure 15.6 Dimensionality reduction.   The documents in matrix 15.5 are shown after the five-dimensional term space has been reduced to two dimensions. The reduced document representations are taken from figure 15.11. In addition to the document representations $d_1, \ldots, d_6$, we also show their length-normalized vectors, which show more directly the similarity measure of cosine that is used after LSI is applied.

documents into a space with "latent" semantic dimensions. Co-occurring terms are projected onto the same dimensions, non-co-occurring terms are projected onto different dimensions. In the latent semantic space, a query and a document can have high cosine similarity even if they do not share any terms – as long as their terms are semantically similar according to the co-occurrence analysis. We can look at LSI as a similarity metric that is an alternative to word overlap measures like tf.idf.

The latent semantic space that we project into has fewer dimensions than the original space (which has as many dimensions as terms). LSI is thus a method for *dimensionality reduction*. A dimensionality reduction technique takes a set of objects that exist in a high-dimensional space and represents them in a low-dimensional space, often in a two-dimensional or three-dimensional space for the purposes of visualization. The example in figure 15.5 may demonstrate the basic idea. This matrix defines a five-dimensional space (whose dimensions are the five words *astronaut, cosmonaut, moon, car* and *truck*) and six objects in the space, the documents $d_1, \ldots, d_6$. Figure 15.6 shows how the six objects can be displayed in a two-dimensional space after the application of SVD (dimension 1 and dimension 2 are taken from figure 15.11, to be explained later). The visualization shows some of the relations between the documents, in particular the similarity between d_4 and d_5 (*car/truck* documents) and d_2 and d_3 (space exploration documents). These relationships are not as clear in figure 15.5. For example, d_2 and d_3 have no terms in common.

There are many different mappings from high-dimensional spaces to low-dimensional spaces. Latent Semantic Indexing chooses the mapping that, for a given dimensionality of the reduced space, is optimal in a sense to be explained presently. This setup has the consequence that the dimensions of the reduced space correspond to the *axes of greatest variation*. Consider the case of reducing dimensionality to 1 dimension. In order to get the best possible representation in 1 dimension, we will look for the axis in the original space that captures as much of the variation in the data as possible. The second dimension corresponds to the axis that best captures the variation remaining after subtracting out what the first axis explains and so on. This reasoning shows that Latent Semantic Indexing is closely related to *Principal Component Analysis* (PCA), another technique for dimensionality reduction. One difference between the two techniques is that PCA can only be applied to a square matrix whereas LSI can be applied to any matrix.

Latent semantic indexing is the application of a particular mathemat-

DIMENSIONALITY
REDUCTION

PRINCIPAL
COMPONENT ANALYSIS

ical technique, called Singular Value Decomposition or SVD, to a word-by-document matrix. SVD (and hence LSI) is a least-squares method. The projection into the latent semantic space is chosen such that the representations in the original space are changed as little as possible when measured by the sum of the squares of the differences. We first give a simple example of a least-squares method and then introduce SVD.

15.4.1 Least-squares methods

LINEAR REGRESSION

Before defining the particular least-squares method used in LSI, it is instructive to study the most common least-squares approximation: fitting a line to a set of points in the plane by way of *linear regression*.

Consider the following problem. We have a set of n points: (x_1, y_1), (x_2, y_2), ..., (x_n, y_n). We would like to find the line:

$$f(x) = mx + b$$

with parameters m and b that fits these points best. In a least-squares approximation, the best fit is the one that minimizes the sum of the squares of the differences:

(15.8) $\quad SS(m, b) = \sum_{i=1}^{n} (y_i - f(x_i))^2 = \sum_{i=1}^{n} (y_i - mx_i - b)^2$

We compute b by solving $\frac{\partial SS(m,b)}{\partial b} = 0$, the value of b for which $SS(m, b)$ reaches its minimum:

$$\frac{\partial SS(m, b)}{\partial b} = \sum_{i=1}^{n} [2(y_i - mx_i - b)(-1)] = 0$$

$$\Leftrightarrow \quad [\sum_{i=1}^{n} y_i] - [m \sum_{i=1}^{n} x_i] - [nb] = 0$$

(15.9) $\quad \Leftrightarrow \quad b = \bar{y} - m\bar{x}$

where $\bar{y} = \frac{\sum_{i=1}^{n} y_i}{n}$ and $\bar{x} = \frac{\sum_{i=1}^{n} x_i}{n}$ are the means of the x and y coordinates, respectively.

We now substitute (15.9) for b in (15.8) and solve $\frac{\partial SS(m,b)}{\partial m} = 0$ for m:

$$\frac{\partial SS(m, b)}{\partial m} = \frac{\partial \sum_{i=1}^{n} (y_i - mx_i - \bar{y} + m\bar{x})^2}{\partial m} = 0$$

$$\Leftrightarrow \quad \sum_{i=1}^{n} 2(y_i - mx_i - \bar{y} + m\bar{x})(-x_i + \bar{x}) = 0$$

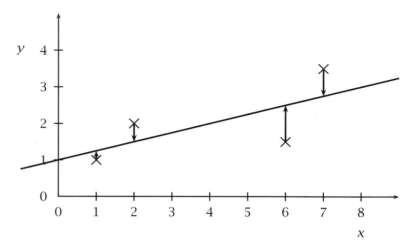

Figure 15.7 An example of linear regression.   The line $y = 0.25x + 1$ is the best least-squares fit for the four points (1,1), (2,2), (6,1.5), (7,3.5). Arrows show which points on the line the original points are projected to.

$$\Leftrightarrow \quad 0 = -\sum_{i=1}^{n} (\bar{y} - y_i)(\bar{x} - x_i) + m \sum_{i=1}^{n} (\bar{x} - x_i)^2$$

(15.10) $\Leftrightarrow \quad m = \dfrac{\sum_{i=1}^{n} (\bar{y} - y_i)(\bar{x} - x_i)}{\sum_{i=1}^{n} (\bar{x} - x_i)^2}$

Figure 15.7 shows an example of a least square fit for the four points $(1, 1), (2, 2), (6, 1.5), (7, 3.5)$. We have:

$$\bar{x} = 4, \bar{y} = 2, m = \frac{\sum_{i=1}^{n} (\bar{y} - y_i)(\bar{x} - x_i)}{\sum_{i=1}^{n} (\bar{x} - x_i)^2} = \frac{6.5}{26} = 0.25$$

and

$$b = \bar{y} - m\bar{x} = 2 - 0.25 \times 4 = 1$$

15.4.2   Singular Value Decomposition

As we have said, we can view Singular Value Decomposition or SVD as a method of word co-occurrence analysis. Instead of using a simple word overlap measure like the cosine, we instead use a more sophisticated similarity measure that makes better similarity judgements based on word co-occurrence. Equivalently, we can view SVD as a method for dimensionality reduction. The relation between these two viewpoints is that in the process of dimensionality reduction, co-occurring terms are mapped onto the same dimensions of the reduced space, thus increasing similarity in the representation of semantically similar documents.

Co-occurrence analysis and dimensionality reduction are two 'functional' ways of understanding LSI. We now look at the formal definition of LSI. LSI is the application of Singular Value Decomposition (SVD) to document-by-term matrices in information retrieval. SVD takes a matrix A and represents it as $\hat{A}$ in a lower dimensional space such that the "distance" between the two matrices as measured by the 2-norm is minimized:

(15.11) $\quad \Delta = \|A - \hat{A}\|_2$

The 2-norm for matrices is the equivalent of Euclidean distance for vectors. SVD is in fact very similar to fitting a line, a one-dimensional object, to a set of points, which exists in the two-dimensional plane. Figure 15.7 shows which point on the one-dimensional line each of the original points corresponds to (see arrows).

Just as the linear regression in figure 15.7 can be interpreted as projecting a two-dimensional space onto a one-dimensional line, so does SVD project an n-dimensional space onto a k-dimensional space where $n \gg k$. In our application (word-document matrices), n is the number of word types in the collection. Values of k that are frequently chosen are 100 and 150. The projection transforms a document's vector in n-dimensional word space into a vector in the k-dimensional reduced space.

One possible source of confusion is that equation (15.11) compares the original matrix and a lower-dimensional approximation. Shouldn't the second matrix have fewer rows and columns, which would make equation (15.11) ill-defined? The analogy with line fitting is again helpful here. The fitted line exists in two dimensions, but it is a one-dimensional object. The same is true for $\hat{A}$: it is a matrix of lower rank, that is, it could be represented in a lower-dimensional space by transforming the axes of the space. But for the particular axes chosen it has the same number of rows and columns as A.

The SVD projection is computed by decomposing the document-by-term matrix $A_{t \times d}$ into the product of three matrices, $T_{t \times n}$, $S_{n \times n}$, and $D_{d \times n}$:

(15.12) $\quad A_{t \times d} = T_{t \times n} S_{n \times n} (D_{d \times n})^{\mathrm{T}}$

$$T = \begin{pmatrix}
 & \text{Dim. 1} & \text{Dim. 2} & \text{Dim. 3} & \text{Dim. 4} & \text{Dim. 5} \\
\hline
\text{cosmonaut} & -0.44 & -0.30 & 0.57 & 0.58 & 0.25 \\
\text{astronaut} & -0.13 & -0.33 & -0.59 & 0.00 & 0.73 \\
\text{moon} & -0.48 & -0.51 & -0.37 & 0.00 & -0.61 \\
\text{car} & -0.70 & 0.35 & 0.15 & -0.58 & 0.16 \\
\text{truck} & -0.26 & 0.65 & -0.41 & 0.58 & -0.09
\end{pmatrix}$$

Figure 15.8   The matrix T of the SVD decomposition of the matrix in figure 15.5. Values are rounded.

$$S = \begin{pmatrix}
2.16 & 0.00 & 0.00 & 0.00 & 0.00 \\
0.00 & 1.59 & 0.00 & 0.00 & 0.00 \\
0.00 & 0.00 & 1.28 & 0.00 & 0.00 \\
0.00 & 0.00 & 0.00 & 1.00 & 0.00 \\
0.00 & 0.00 & 0.00 & 0.00 & 0.39
\end{pmatrix}$$

Figure 15.9   The matrix of singular values of the SVD decomposition of the matrix in figure 15.5. Values are rounded.

where $n = \min(t, d)$. We indicate dimensionality by subscripts: A has t rows and d columns, T has t rows and n columns and so on. D^T is the transpose of D, the matrix D rotated around its diagonal: $D_{ij} = (D^T)_{ji}$.

Examples of A, T, S, and D are given in figure 15.5 and figures 15.8 through 15.10. Figure 15.5 shows an example of A. A contains the document vectors with each column corresponding to one document. In other words, element a_{ij} of the matrix records how often term i occurs in document j. The counts should be appropriately weighted (as discussed in section 15.2). For simplicity of exposition, we have not applied weighting and assumed term frequencies of 1.

Figures 15.8 and 15.10 show T and D, respectively. These matrices have *orthonormal* columns. This means that the column vectors have ORTHONORMAL
unit length and are all orthogonal to each other. (If a matrix C has orthonormal columns, then $C^T C = I$, where I is the diagonal matrix with a diagonal of 1's, and zeroes elsewhere. So we have $T^T T = D^T D = I$.)

We can view SVD as a method for rotating the axes of the n-dimensional space such that the first axis runs along the direction of largest variation

$$D^T = \begin{pmatrix} & d_1 & d_2 & d_3 & d_4 & d_5 & d_6 \\ \text{Dimension 1} & -0.75 & -0.28 & -0.20 & -0.45 & -0.33 & -0.12 \\ \text{Dimension 2} & -0.29 & -0.53 & -0.19 & 0.63 & 0.22 & 0.41 \\ \text{Dimension 3} & 0.28 & -0.75 & 0.45 & -0.20 & 0.12 & -0.33 \\ \text{Dimension 4} & 0.00 & 0.00 & 0.58 & 0.00 & -0.58 & 0.58 \\ \text{Dimension 5} & -0.53 & 0.29 & 0.63 & 0.19 & 0.41 & -0.22 \end{pmatrix}$$

Figure 15.10   The matrix D^T of the SVD decomposition of the matrix in figure 15.5. Values are rounded.

among the documents, the second dimension runs along the direction with the second largest variation and so forth. The matrices T and D represent terms and documents in this new space. For example, the first column of T corresponds to the first row of A, and the first column of D corresponds to the first column of A.

The diagonal matrix S contains the singular values of A in descending order (as in figure 15.9). The ith singular value indicates the amount of variation along the ith axis. By restricting the matrices T, S, and D to their first $k < n$ columns one obtains the matrices $T_{t \times k}$, $S_{k \times k}$, and $(D_{d \times k})^{\text{T}}$. Their product $\hat{A}$ is the best least square approximation of A by a matrix of rank k in the sense defined in equation (15.11). One can also prove that SVD is unique, that is, there is only one possible decomposition of a given matrix.[1] See Golub and van Loan (1989) for an extensive treatment of SVD including a proof of the optimality property.

That SVD finds the optimal projection to a low-dimensional space is the key property for exploiting word co-occurrence patterns. SVD represents terms and documents in the lower dimensional space as well as possible. In the process, some words that have similar co-occurrence patterns are projected (or collapsed) onto the same dimension. As a consequence, the similarity metric will make topically similar documents and queries come out as similar even if different words are used for describing the topic. If we restrict the matrix in figure 15.8 to the first two dimensions, we end up with two groups of terms: space exploration terms (*cosmonaut, astronaut,* and *moon*) which have negative values on the second dimension

---

1. SVD is unique up to sign flips. If we flip all signs in the matrices D and T, we get a second solution.

	d_1	d_2	d_3	d_4	d_5	d_6
Dimension 1	−1.62	−0.60	−0.04	−0.97	−0.71	−0.26
Dimension 2	−0.46	−0.84	−0.30	1.00	0.35	0.65

Figure 15.11   The matrix $B = S_{2\times2}D_{2\times n}$ of documents after rescaling with singular values and reduction to two dimensions. Values are rounded.

	d_1	d_2	d_3	d_4	d_5	d_6
d_1	1.00					
d_2	0.78	1.00				
d_3	0.40	0.88	1.00			
d_4	0.47	−0.18	−0.62	1.00		
d_5	0.74	0.16	−0.32	0.94	1.00	
d_6	0.10	−0.54	−0.87	0.93	0.74	1.00

Table 15.9   The matrix of document correlations $B^{\mathrm{T}}B$. For example, the normalized correlation coefficient of documents d_3 and d_2 (when represented as in figure 15.11) is 0.88. Values are rounded.

and automobile terms (*car* and *truck*) which have positive values on the second dimension. The second dimension directly reflects the different co-occurrence patterns of these two groups: space exploration terms only co-occur with other space exploration terms, automobile terms only co-occur with other automobile terms (with one exception: the occurrence of *car* in d_1). In some cases, we will be misled by such co-occurrences patterns and wrongly infer semantic similarity. However, in most cases co-occurrence is a valid indicator of topical relatedness.

These term similarities have a direct impact on document similarity. Let us assume a reduction to two dimensions. After rescaling with the singular values, we get the matrix $B = S_{2\times2}D_{2\times n}$ shown in figure 15.11 where $S_{2\times2}$ is S restricted to two dimensions (with the diagonal elements 2.16, 1.59). Matrix B is a dimensionality reduction of the original matrix A and is what was shown in figure 15.6.

Table 15.9 shows the similarities between documents when they are represented in this new space. Not surprisingly, there is high similarity between d_1 and d_2 (0.78) and d_4, d_5, and d_6 (0.94, 0.93, 0.74). These document similarities are about the same in the original space (i.e. when we compute correlations for the original document vectors in figure 15.5). The key change is that d_2 and d_3, whose similarity is 0.00 in the original space, are now highly similar (0.88). Although d_2 and d_3 have no common terms, they are now recognized as being topically similar because of the co-occurrence patterns in the corpus.

Notice that we get the same similarity as in the original space (that is, zero similarity) if we compute similarity in the transformed space without any dimensionality reduction. Using the full vectors from figure 15.10 and rescaling them with the appropriate singular values we get:

$$-0.28 \times -0.20 \times 2.16^2 + -0.53 \times -0.19 \times 1.59^2 +$$

$$-0.75 \times 0.45 \times 1.28^2 + 0.00 \times 0.58 \times 1.00^2 + 0.29 \times 0.63 \times 0.39^2 \approx 0.00$$

(If you actually compute this expression, you will find that the answer is not quite zero, but this is only because of rounding errors. But this is as good a point as any to observe that many matrix computations are quite sensitive to rounding errors.)

We have computed document similarity in the reduced space using the product of D and S. The correctness of this procedure can be seen by looking at $A^T A$, which is the matrix of all document correlations for the original space:

(15.13) $\quad A^T A = (TSD^T)^T TSD^T = DS^T T^T TSD^T = (DS)(DS)^T$

Because T has orthonormal columns, we have $T^T T = I$. Furthermore, since S is diagonal, $S = S^T$. Term similarities are computed analogously since one observes that the term correlations are given by:

(15.14) $\quad AA^T = TSD^T (TSD^T)^T = TSD^T DS^T T^T = (TS)(TS)^T$

One remaining problem for a practical application is how to fold queries and new documents into the reduced space. The SVD computation only gives us reduced representations for the document vectors in matrix A. We do not want to do a completely new SVD every time a new query is launched. In addition, in order to handle large corpora efficiently we may want to do SVD for only a sample of the documents (for example a third or a fourth). The remaining documents would then be folded in.

The equation for folding documents into the space can again be derived from the basic SVD equation:

(15.15) $\qquad A = TSD^T$

$\quad \Leftrightarrow \qquad T^T A = T^T TSD^T$

$\quad \Leftrightarrow \qquad T^T A = SD^T$

So we just multiply the query or document vector with the transpose of the term matrix T (after it has been truncated to the desired dimensionality). For example, for a query vector $\vec{q}$ and a reduction to dimensionality k, the query representation in the reduced space is $T_{t \times k}{}^T \vec{q}$.

15.4.3   Latent Semantic Indexing in IR

LATENT SEMANTIC
INDEXING

The application of SVD to information retrieval was originally proposed by a group of researchers at Bellcore (Deerwester et al. 1990) and called *Latent Semantic Indexing* (LSI) in this context. LSI has been compared to standard vector space search on several document collections. It was found that LSI performs better than vector space search in many cases, especially for high-recall searches (Deerwester et al. 1990; Dumais 1995). LSI's strength in high-recall searches is not surprising since a method that takes co-occurrence into account is expected to achieve higher recall. On the other hand, due to the noise added by spurious co-occurrence data one sometimes finds a decrease in precision.

The appropriateness of LSI also depends on the document collection. Recall the example of the vocabulary problem in figure 15.8. In a heterogeneous collection, documents may use different words to refer to the same topic like *HCI* and *user interface* in the figure. Here, LSI can help identify the underlying semantic similarity between seemingly dissimilar documents. However, in a collection with homogeneous vocabulary, LSI is less likely to be useful.

The application of SVD to information retrieval is called *Latent Semantic Indexing* because the document representations in the original term space are transformed to representations in a new reduced space. The dimensions in the reduced space are linear combinations of the original dimensions (this is so since matrix multiplications as in equation (15.16) are linear operations). The assumption here (and similarly for other forms of dimensionality reduction like principal component analysis) is that these new dimensions are a better representation of documents and queries. The metaphor underlying the term "latent" is that these new dimensions are the true representation. This true representation was then obscured by a generation process that expressed a particular dimension with one set of words in some documents and a different set of words in another document. LSI analysis recovers the original semantic structure of the space and its original dimensions. The process of assigning different words to the same underlying dimension is sometimes interpreted as a form of soft term clustering since it groups terms according to the dimensions that they are represented on in the reduced space.

One could also argue that the SVD representation is not only better (since it is based on the 'true' dimensions), but also more compact. Many documents have more than 150 unique terms. So the sparse vector representation will take up more storage space than the compact SVD representation if we reduce to 150 dimensions. However, the efficiency gain due to more compact representations is often outweighed by the additional cost of having to go through a high-dimensional matrix multiplication whenever we map a query or a new document to the reduced space. Another problem is that an inverted index cannot be constructed for SVD representations. If we have to compute the similarity between the query and every single document, then an SVD-based system can be slower than a term-based system that searches an inverted index.

The actual computation of SVD is quadratic in the rank of the document by term matrix (the rank is (bounded by) the smaller of the number of documents and the number of terms) and cubic in the number of singular values that are computed (Deerwester et al. 1990: 395).[2] For very large collections subsampling of documents and selection of terms according to frequency is often employed in order to reduce the cost of computing the Singular Value Decomposition.

NORMALITY
ASSUMPTION

One objection to SVD is that, along with all other least-squares methods, it is really designed for normally-distributed data. But, as can be seen from the discussion earlier in this chapter, such a distribution is inappropriate for count data, and count data is, after all, what a term-by-document matrix consists of. The link between least squares and normal distribution can be easily seen by looking at the definition of the normal distribution (section 2.1.9):

$$n(x;\ \mu,\sigma) = \frac{1}{\sigma\sqrt{2\pi}} \exp\left[-\frac{1}{2}\left(\frac{x-\mu}{\sigma}\right)^2 \right]$$

where μ is the *mean* and σ the *covariance*. The smaller the squared deviation from the mean $(x - \mu)^2$, the higher the probability $n(x;\ \mu,\sigma)$. So the least squares solution is the maximum likelihood solution. But this is only true if the underlying data distribution is normal. Other distri-

---

2. However, others have suggested that given the particular characteristics of the matrices that SVD is applied to in information retrieval the complexity is linear in the number of documents and (approximately) quadratic in the number of singular values. See (Oard and DeClaris 1996), (Berry et al. 1995), and (Berry and Young 1995) for discussion.

butions like Poisson or negative binomial are more appropriate for term counts. One problematic feature of SVD is that, since the reconstruction $\hat{A}$ of the term-by-document matrix A is based on a normal distribution, it can have negative entries, clearly an inappropriate approximation for counts. A dimensionality reduction based on Poisson would not predict such impossible negative counts.

In defense of LSI (and the vector space model in general which can also be argued to assume a normal distribution), one can say that the matrix entries are not counts, but weights. Although this is not an issue that has been investigated systematically, the normal distribution could be appropriate for the weighted vectors even if it is not for count vectors.

From a practical point of view, LSI has been criticized for being computationally more expensive than other word co-occurrence methods while not being more effective. Another method that also uses co-occurrence
PSEUDO-FEEDBACK   is *pseudo-feedback* (also called *pseudo relevance feedback* and *two-stage retrieval*, Buckley et al. 1996; Kwok and Chan 1998). In pseudo-feedback, the top n documents (typically the top 10 or 20) returned by an ad-hoc query are assumed to be relevant and added to the query. Some of these top n documents will not actually be relevant, but a large enough proportion usually is to improve the quality of the query. Words that occur frequently with query words will be among the most frequent in the top n. So pseudo-feedback can be viewed as a cheap query-specific way of doing co-occurrence analysis and co-occurrence-based query modification.

Still, in contrast to many heuristic methods that incorporate term co-occurrence into information retrieval, LSI has a clean formal framework and a clearly defined optimization criterion (least squares) with one global optimum that can be efficiently computed. This conceptual simplicity and clarity make LSI one of the most interesting IR approaches that go beyond query-document term matching.

15.5 Discourse Segmentation

Text collections are increasingly heterogeneous. An important aspect of heterogeneity is length. On the world wide web, document sizes range from home pages with just one sentence to server logs of half a megabyte.

The weighting schemes discussed in section 15.2.2 take account of different lengths by applying cosine normalization. However, cosine normalization and other forms of normalization that discount term weights according to document length ignore the distribution of terms within a document. Suppose that you are looking for a short description of angioplasty. You would probably prefer a document in which the occurrences of angioplasty are concentrated in one or two paragraphs since such a concentration is most likely to contain a definition of what angioplasty is. On the other hand, a document of the same length in which the occurrences of angioplasty are scattered uniformly is less likely to be helpful.

We can exploit the structure of documents and search over structurally defined units like sections and paragraphs instead of full documents. However, the best subpart of a document to be returned to the user often encompasses several paragraphs. For example, in response to a query on angioplasty we may want to return the first two paragraphs of a subsection on angioplasty, which introduce the term and its definition, but not the rest of the subsection that goes into technical detail.

Some documents are not structured into paragraphs and sections. Or, in the case of documents structured by means of a markup language like HTML, it is not obvious how to break them apart into units that would be suitable for retrieval.

These considerations motivate an approach that breaks documents into topically coherent multi-paragraph subparts. In the rest of this subsection we will describe one approach to multiparagraph segmentation, TEXTTILING the *TextTiling* algorithm (Hearst and Plaunt 1993; Hearst 1994, 1997).

15.5.1 TextTiling

The basic idea of this algorithm is to search for parts of a text where the SUBTOPIC vocabulary shifts from one subtopic to another. These points are then interpreted as the boundaries of multi-paragraph units.

Sentence length can vary considerably. Therefore, the text is first di-
TOKEN SEQUENCES vided into small fixed size units, the *token sequences*. Hearst suggests a size of 20 words for token sequences. We refer to the points between GAPS token sequences as *gaps*. The TextTiling algorithm has three main components: the *cohesion scorer*, the *depth scorer* and the *boundary selector.*
COHESION SCORER The *cohesion scorer* measures the amount of 'topic continuity' or cohesion at each gap, that is, the amount of evidence that the same subtopic is prevalent on both sides of the gap. Intuitively, we want to consider gaps with low cohesion as possible segmentation points.
DEPTH SCORER The *depth scorer* assigns a depth score to each gap depending on how low its cohesion score is compared to the surrounding gaps. If cohesion

at the gap is lower than at surrounding gaps, then the depth score is high. Conversely, if cohesion is about the same at surrounding gaps, then the depth score is low. The intuition here is that cohesion is relative. One part of the text (say, the introduction) may have many successive shifts in vocabulary. Here we want to be cautious in selecting subtopic boundaries and only choose those points with the lowest cohesion scores compared to their neighbors. Another part of the text may have only slight shifts for several pages. Here it is reasonable to be more sensitive to topic changes and change points that have relatively high cohesion scores, but scores that are low compared to their neighbors.

BOUNDARY SELECTOR   The *boundary selector* is the module that looks at the depth scores and selects the gaps that are the best segmentation points.

Several methods of cohesion scoring have been proposed.

- *Vector Space Scoring.* We can form one artificial document out of the token sequences to the left of the gap (the *left block*) and another artificial document to the right of the gap (the *right block*). (Hearst suggests a length of two token sequences for each block.) These two blocks are then compared by computing the correlation coefficient of their term vectors, using the weighting schemes that were described earlier in this chapter for the vector space model. The idea is that the more terms two blocks share the higher their cohesion score and the less likely they will be classified as a segment boundary. Vector Space Scoring was used by Hearst and Plaunt (1993) and Salton and Allen (1993).

- *Block comparison.* The block comparison algorithm also computes the correlation coefficient of the gap's left block and right block, but it only uses within-block term frequency without taking into account (inverse) document frequency.

- *Vocabulary introduction.* A gap's cohesion score in this algorithm is the negative of the number of new terms that occur in left and right block, that is terms that have not occurred up to this point in the text. The idea is that subtopic changes are often signaled by the use of new vocabulary (Youmans 1991). (In order to make the score a cohesion score we multiply the count of new terms by −1 so that larger scores (fewer new terms) correspond to higher cohesion and smaller scores (more new terms) correspond to lower cohesion.)

The experimental evidence in (Hearst 1997) suggests that Block Comparison is the best performing of these three algorithms.

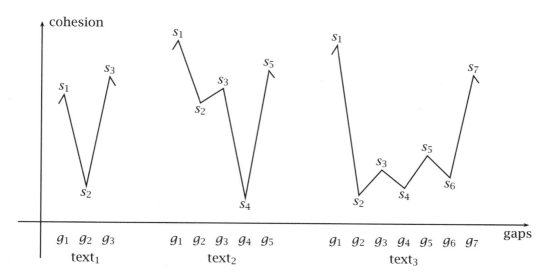

Figure 15.12 Three constellations of cohesion scores in topic boundary identification.

The second step in TextTiling is the transformation of cohesion scores into *depth scores*. We compute the depth score for a gap by summing the heights of the two sides of the valley it is located in, for example $(s_1 - s_2) + (s_3 - s_2)$ for g_2 in text 1 in figure 15.12. Note that high absolute values of the cohesion scores by themselves will not result in the creation of a segment boundary. TextTiling views subtopic changes and segmentation as relative. In a text with rapid fluctuations of topic or vocabulary from paragraph to paragraph only the most radical changes will be accorded the status of segment boundaries. In a text with only subtle subtopic changes the algorithm will be more discriminating.

For a practical implementation, several enhancements of the basic algorithm are needed. First, we need to smooth cohesion scores to address situations like the one in text 2 in figure 15.12. Intuitively, the difference $s_1 - s_2$ should contribute to the depth score of gap g_4. This is achieved by *smoothing* scores using a low pass filter. For example, the depth score s_i for g_i is replaced by $(s_{i-1} + s_i + s_{i+1})/3$. This procedure effectively takes into consideration the cohesion scores of gaps at a distance of two from the central gap. If they are as high as or higher than the two immediately surrounding gaps, they will increase the score of the central gap.

We also need to add heuristics to avoid a sequence of many small segments (this type of segmentation is rarely chosen by human judges when they segment text into coherent units). Finally, the parameters of the methods for computing cohesion and depth scores (size of token sequence, size of block, smoothing method) may have to be adjusted depending on the text sort we are working with. For example, a corpus with long sentences will require longer token sequences.

The third component of TextTiling is the boundary selector. It estimates average μ and standard deviation σ of the depth scores and selects all gaps as boundaries that have a depth score higher than $\mu - c\sigma$ for some constant c (for example, $c = 0.5$ or $c = 1.0$). We again try to avoid using absolute scores. This method selects gaps that have 'significantly' low depth scores, where significant is defined with respect to the average and the variance of scores.

In an evaluation, Hearst (1997) found good agreement between segments found by TextTiling and segments demarcated by human judges. It remains an open question to what degree segment retrieval leads to better information retrieval performance than document retrieval when evaluated on precision and recall. However, many users prefer to see a hit in the context of a natural segment which makes it easier to quickly understand the context of the hit (Egan et al. 1989).

Text segmentation could also have important applications in other areas of Natural Language Processing. For example, in word sense disambiguation segmentation could be used to find the natural units that are most informative for determining the correct sense of a usage. Given the increasing diversity of document collections, discourse segmentation is guaranteed to remain an important topic of research in Statistical NLP and IR.

15.6   Further Reading

Two major venues for publication of current research in IR are the TREC proceedings (Harman 1996, see also the links on the website), which report results of competitions sponsored by the US government, and the ACM SIGIR proceedings series. Prominent journals are *Information Processing & Management*, the *Journal of the American Society for Information Science*, and *Information Retrieval*.

The best known textbooks on information retrieval are books by van

Rijsbergen (1979), Salton and McGill (1983) and Frakes and Baeza-Yates (1992). See also (Losee 1998) and (Korfhage 1997). A collection of seminal papers was recently edited by Sparck Jones and Willett (1998). Smeaton (1992) and Lewis and Jones (1996) discuss the role of NLP in information retrieval. Evaluation of IR systems is discussed in (Cleverdon and Mills 1963), (Tague-Sutcliffe 1992), and (Hull 1996). Inverse document frequency as a term weighting method was proposed by Sparck Jones (1972). Different forms of tf.idf weighting were extensively investigated within the SMART project at Cornell University, led by Gerard Salton (Salton 1971b; Salton and McGill 1983). Two recent studies are (Singhal et al. 1996) and (Moffat and Zobel 1998).

The Poisson distribution is further discussed in most introductions to probability theory, e.g., (Mood et al. 1974: 95). See (Harter 1975) for a way of estimating the parameters π, λ_1, and λ_2 of the two-Poisson model without having to assume a set of documents labeled as to their class membership. Our derivation of IDF is based on (Croft and Harper 1979)). RIDF was introduced by Church (1995).

Apart from work on better phrase extraction, the impact of NLP on IR in recent decades has been surprisingly small, with most IR researchers focusing on shallow analysis techniques. Some exceptions are (Fagan 1987; Bonzi and Liddy 1988; Sheridan and Smeaton 1992; Strzalkowski 1995; Klavans and Kan 1998). However, recently there has been much more interest in tasks such as automatically summarizing documents rather than just returning them as is (Salton et al. 1994; Kupiec et al. 1995), and such trends may tend to increase the usefulness of NLP in IR applications.

One task that has benefited from the application of NLP techniques is *cross-language information retrieval* or *CLIR* (Hull and Grefenstette 1998; Grefenstette 1998). The idea is to help a user who has enough knowledge of a foreign language to understand texts, but not enough fluency to formulate a query. In CLIR, such a user can type in a query in her native language, the system then translates the query into the target language and retrieves documents in the target language. Recent work includes (Sheridan et al. 1997; Nie et al. 1998) and the Notes of the AAAI symposium on cross-language text and speech retrieval (Hull and Oard 1997). Littman et al. (1998b) and Littman et al. (1998a) use Latent Semantic Indexing for CLIR.

CROSS-LANGUAGE
INFORMATION
RETRIEVAL
CLIR

We have only presented a small selection of work on modeling term distributions in IR. See (van Rijsbergen 1979: ch. 6) for a more systematic introduction. (Robertson and Sparck Jones 1976) and (Bookstein and

Swanson 1975) are other important papers (the latter is a decision theoretic approach). Information theory has also been used to motivate IDF (Wong and Yao 1992). An application of residual inverse document frequency to the characterization of index terms is described by Yamamoto and Church (1998).

The example in table 15.8 is adapted from (Deerwester et al. 1990). The term-by-document matrix we used as an example for SVD is small. It can easily be decomposed using one of the standard statistical packages (we used S-plus). For a large corpus, we have to deal with several hundred thousand terms and documents. Special algorithms have been developed for this purpose. See (Berry 1992) and NetLib on the world wide web for a description and implementation of several such algorithms.

Apart from term-by-document matrices, SVD has been applied to word-by-word matrices by Schütze and Pedersen (1997) and to discourse segmentation (Kaufmann 1998). Dolin (1998) uses LSI for query categorization and distributed search, using automated classification for collection summarization.

Latent Semantic Indexing has also been proposed as a cognitive model for human memory. Landauer and Dumais (1997) argue that it can explain the rapid vocabulary growth found in school-age children.

TEXT SEGMENTATION   Text segmentation is an active area of research. Other work on the problem includes (Salton and Buckley 1991), (Beeferman et al. 1997) and (Berber Sardinha 1997). Kan et al. (1998) make an implementation of their segmentation algorithm publicly available (see website). An information source that is different from the word overlap measure used in TextTiling LEXICAL CHAINS   is so-called *lexical chains*: chains of usages of one or more semantically related words throughout a text. By observing starts, interruptions, and terminations of such chains, one can derive a different type of description of the subtopic structure of text (Morris and Hirst 1991).

Text segmentation is a rather crude treatment of the complexity of written texts and spoken dialogues which often have a hierarchical and non-linear structure. Trying to do justice to this complex structure is a much harder task than merely detecting topic changes. Finding the best approach to this problem is an active area of research in Statistical DISCOURSE ANALYSIS   NLP. The special issue of Computational Linguistics on empirical *discourse analysis*, edited by Walker and Moore (1997), is a good starting point for interested readers.

When Statistical NLP methods became popular again in the early 1990s, discourse modeling was initially an area with a low proportion of statisti-

cal work, but there has been a recent surge in the application of quantita-
tive methods. For some examples, see (Stolcke et al. 1998), (Walker et al.
DIALOG MODELING   1998) and (Samuel et al. 1998) for probabilistic approaches to *dialog mod-
eling* and (Kehler 1997) and (Ge et al. 1998) for probabilistic approaches
ANAPHORA   to *anaphora resolution.*
RESOLUTION

15.7   Exercises

Exercise 15.1   [⋆]

Try to find out the characteristics of various internet search engines. Do they
use a stop list? Try to search for stop words. Can you search for the phrase *the
the*? Do the engines use stemming? Do they normalize words to lowercase? For
example, does a search for *iNfOrMaTiOn* return anything?

Exercise 15.2   [⋆]

The simplest way to process phrases in the vector space model is to add them as
separate terms. For example, the query *car insurance rates* might be translated
into an internal representation that contains the terms *car, insurance, rates, car
insurance, insurance rates.* This means that phrases and their constituent words
are treated as independent sources of evidence. Discuss why this is problematic.

Exercise 15.3   [⋆]

Show that Katz's K mixture satisfies:

$$P_i(0) = 1 - \frac{\mathrm{df}_i}{N}.$$

That is, the fit of the estimate to the actual count is always perfect for the number of documents with zero occurrences.

Exercise 15.4   [⋆]

Compute Residual IDF for the words in table 15.7. Are content words and non-
content words well separated?

Exercise 15.5   [⋆]

Select a non-content word, a content word and a word which you are not sure
how to classify and compute the following quantities for them: (a) document
frequency and collection frequency, (b) IDF, (c) RIDF, and (d) α and β of the
K mixture. (You can use any reasonable size corpus of your choice.)

Exercise 15.6   [⋆]

Depending on λ, the Poisson distribution is either monotonically falling or has
the shape of a curve that first rises, and then falls. Find examples of each. What
is the property of λ that determines the shape of the graph?

Exercise 15.7   [★]

Compute the SVD decomposition of the term-by-document matrix in figure 15.5 using S-Plus or another software package.

Exercise 15.8   [★ ★]

In this exercise, we look at two assumptions about subtopic structure that are made in TextTiling.

First, TextTiling performs a *linear* segmentation, that is, a text is divided into a sequence of segments. No attempt is made to impose further structure. One example where the assumption of linearity is not justified is noted by Hearst: a sequence of three paragraphs that is then summarized in a fourth paragraph. Since the summary paragraph has vocabulary from paragraphs 1 and 2 that does not occur in paragraph 3 a segment boundary between 3 and 4 is inferred. Propose a modification of TextTiling that would recognize paragraphs 1–4 as a unit.

Another assumption that TextTiling relies on is that most segment boundaries are characterized by pronounced valleys like the one in text 1 in figure 15.12. But sometimes there is a longer flat region between two segments. Why is this a problem for the formulation of the algorithm described above? How could one fix it?

16 *Text Categorization*

THIS CHAPTER both introduces an important NLP problem, text categorization, and provides a more general perspective on classification, including coverage of a number of important classification techniques that are not covered elsewhere in the book. *Classification* or *categorization* is the task of assigning objects from a universe to two or more *classes* or *categories*. Some examples are shown in table 16.1. Many of the tasks that we have already studied in detail, such as tagging, word sense disambiguation, and prepositional phrase attachment are classification tasks. In tagging and disambiguation, we look at a word in context and classify it as being an instance of one of its possible part of speech tags or an instance of one of its senses. In PP attachment, the two classes are the two different attachments. Two other NLP classification tasks are author and language identification. Determining whether a newly discovered poem was written by Shakespeare or by a different author is an example of author identification. A language identifier tries to pick the language that a document of unknown origin is written in (see exercise 16.6).

In this chapter, we will concentrate on another classification problem, *text categorization*. The goal in text categorization is to classify the topic or theme of a document. A typical set of topic categories is the one used in the Reuters text collection, which we will introduce shortly. Some of its topics are "mergers and acquisitions," "wheat," "crude oil," and "earnings reports." One application of text categorization is to filter a stream of news for a particular interest group. For example, a financial journalist may only want to see documents that have been assigned the category "mergers and acquisitions."

In general, the problem of statistical classification can be characterized as follows. We have a *training set* of objects, each labeled with one or

CLASSIFICATION
CATEGORIZATION
CLASSES
CATEGORIES

TEXT
CATEGORIZATION

TRAINING SET

Problem	Object	Categories
tagging	context of a word	the word's tags
disambiguation	context of a word	the word's senses
PP attachment	sentence	parse trees
author identification	document	authors
language identification	document	languages
text categorization	document	topics

Table 16.1 Some examples of classification tasks in NLP. For each example, the table gives the type of object that is being classified and the set of possible categories.

DATA
REPRESENTATION
MODEL

more classes, which we encode via a *data representation model*. Typically each object in the training set is represented in the form $(\vec{x}, c)$, where $\vec{x} \in \mathbb{R}^n$ is a vector of measurements and c is the class label. For text categorization, the information retrieval vector space model is frequently used as the data representation. That is, each document is represented as a vector of (possibly weighted) word counts (see section 15.2). Finally,

MODEL CLASS
TRAINING PROCEDURE

we define a *model class* and a *training procedure*. The model class is a parameterized family of classifiers and the training procedure selects one classifier from this family.[1] An example of such a family for binary classification is linear classifiers which take the following form:

$$g(\vec{x}) = \vec{w} \cdot \vec{x} + w_0$$

where we choose class c_1 for $g(\vec{x}) > 0$ and class c_2 for $g(\vec{x}) \leq 0$. This family is parameterized by the vector $\vec{w}$ and the threshold w_0.

We can think of training procedures as algorithms for function fitting, which search for a good set of parameter values, where 'goodness' is determined by an optimization criterion such as misclassification rate or entropy. Some training procedures are guaranteed to find the optimal set of parameters. However, many iterative training procedures are only guaranteed to find a better set in each iteration. If they start out in the wrong part of the search space, they may get stuck in a local optimum without ever finding the global optimum. An example of such a training

GRADIENT DESCENT
HILL CLIMBING

procedure for linear classifiers is *gradient descent* or *hill climbing* which we will introduce below in the section on perceptrons.

1. Note however that some classifiers like nearest-neighbor classifiers are non-parametric and are harder to characterize in terms of a model class.

	YES is correct	NO is correct
YES was assigned	a	b
NO was assigned	c	d

Table 16.2 Contingency table for evaluating a binary classifier. For example, a is the number of objects in the category of interest that were correctly assigned to the category.

TEST SET

Once we have chosen the parameters of the classifier (or, as we usually say, *trained* the classifier), it is a good idea to see how well it is doing on a *test set*. This test set should consist of data that was not used during training. It is trivial to do well on data that the classifier was trained on. The real test is an evaluation on a representative sample of unseen data since that is the only measure that will tell us about actual performance in an application.

ACCURACY

For binary classification, classifiers are typically evaluated using a table of counts like table 16.2. An important measure is classification *accuracy* which is defined as $\frac{a+d}{a+b+c+d}$, the proportion of correctly classified objects. Other measures are precision, $\frac{a}{a+b}$, recall, $\frac{a}{a+c}$, and fallout, $\frac{b}{b+d}$. See section 8.1.

MACRO-AVERAGING
MICRO-AVERAGING

In classification tasks with more than two categories, one begins by making a 2×2 contingency table for each category c_i separately (evaluating c_i versus $\neg c_i$). There are then two ways to proceed. One can compute an evaluation measure like accuracy for each contingency table separately and then average the evaluation measure over categories to get an overall measure of performance. This process is called *macro-averaging*. Or one can do *micro-averaging*, in which one first makes a single contingency table for all the data by summing the scores in each cell for all categories. The evaluation measure is then computed for this large table. Macro-averaging gives equal weight to each category whereas micro-averaging gives equal weight to each object. The two types of averaging can give divergent results when precision is averaged over categories with different sizes. Micro-averaged precision is dominated by the large categories whereas macro-averaged precision will give a better sense of the quality of classification across all categories.

In this chapter we describe four classification techniques: decision trees, maximum entropy modeling, perceptrons, and k nearest neighbor classification. These are either important classification techniques

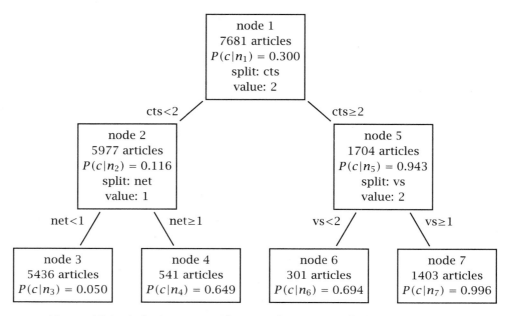

Figure 16.1 A decision tree. This tree determines whether a document is part of the topic category "earnings" or not. $P(c|n_i)$ is the probability of a document at node n_i to belong to the "earnings" category c.

in their own right, or, in the case of the perceptron, are the simplest example of an important class of techniques, neural networks. We conclude with some pointers to further reading.

16.1 Decision Trees

DECISION TREES   As the first class of classification models, we introduce *decision trees*. An example of a decision tree is shown in figure 16.1. This tree decides whether to assign documents to the Reuters category "earnings." We classify a document by starting at the top node, testing its question, branching to the appropriate node, and then repeating this process until we reach a leaf node. For example, a document with weight 1 for *cts* and weight 3 for *net* takes the left branch at the top node and then the right branch at the child node. Its probability $P(c|n_4)$ of being in the category "earnings" given that it belongs to node 4 is then estimated as 0.649. At each node, we show the number of articles in the training set that belong

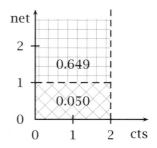

Figure 16.2 Geometric interpretation of part of the tree in figure 16.1.

to the node, the probability of a member of the node being in the category "earnings," the word (or dimension) we split on at this node, and the weight of the word we split on.

Another way to visualize the tree is shown in figure 16.2. The horizontal axis corresponds to the weight for *cts*, the vertical axis to the weight for *net*. Questions ask whether the value of some feature is less than some value or not. The top node in figure 16.1 defines a decision boundary corresponding to the vertical line "*cts* = 2" in figure 16.2. The left child node subdivides the left region into two regions above and below "*net* = 1." The upper subregion (marked with $P(c|n) = 0.649$) corresponds to node 4, the lower subregion to node 4. Note that the region to the right of the decision boundary "*cts* = 2" is not further subdivided because node 5 splits on *vs*, not on *net*. We would need a three-dimensional graph to also show the effect of node 5.

The text categorization task that we use as an example in this chapter is to build categorizers that distinguish the "earnings" category in the REUTERS *Reuters* collection. The Reuters collection is currently the most popular database for evaluating text categorization research. The version we use (based on the so-called Modified Apte Split, Apté et al. 1994) consists of 9603 training articles and 3299 test articles that were sent over the Reuters newswire in 1987. The articles are categorized with more than 100 topics such as "mergers and acquisitions" and "interest rates." An example of an article in this category is shown in figure 16.3. See the website for references to the Reuters collection.

The first task in text categorization is to find an appropriate data rep-

```
<REUTERS NEWID="11">
<DATE>26-FEB-1987 15:18:59.34</DATE>
<TOPICS><D>earn</D></TOPICS>
<TEXT>
<TITLE>COBANCO INC &lt;CBCO> YEAR NET</TITLE>
<DATELINE>    SANTA CRUZ, Calif., Feb 26 - </DATELINE>
<BODY>Shr 34 cts vs 1.19 dlrs
    Net 807,000 vs 2,858,000
    Assets 510.2 mln vs 479.7 mln
    Deposits 472.3 mln vs 440.3 mln
    Loans 299.2 mln vs 327.2 mln
    Note: 4th qtr not available. Year includes 1985
extraordinary gain from tax carry forward of 132,000 dlrs,
or five cts per shr.
 Reuter
</BODY></TEXT>
</REUTERS>
```

Figure 16.3 An example of a Reuters news story in the topic category "earnings." Parts of the original have been omitted for brevity.

resentation model. This is an art in itself, and usually depends on the particular categorization method used, but to simplify things, we will use a single data representation throughout this chapter. It is based on the 20 words whose X^2 score with the category "earnings" in the training set was highest (see section 5.3.3 for the X^2 measure). The words *loss*, *profit*, and *cts* (for "cents"), all three of which seem obvious as good indicators for an earnings report, are some of the 20 words that were selected. Each document was then represented as a vector of $K = 20$ integers, $\vec{x}_j = (s_{1j}, \ldots, s_{Kj})$, where s_{ij} was computed as the following quantity:

$$(16.1) \quad s_{ij} = \text{round}\left(10 \times \frac{1 + \log(tf_{ij})}{1 + \log(l_j)}\right)$$

Here, tf_{ij} is the number of occurrences of term i in document j and l_j is the length of document j. The score s_{ij} is set to 0 for no occurrences of the term. So for example, if *profit* occurs 6 times in a document of length 89 words, then the score for *profit* would be $s_{ij} = 10 \times \frac{1+\log(6)}{1+\log(89)} \approx 5.09$

Word w^j Term weight s_{ij} Classification

$$
\vec{x} =
\begin{pmatrix}
5 \\
5 \\
3 \\
3 \\
3 \\
4 \\
0 \\
0 \\
0 \\
4 \\
0 \\
3 \\
2 \\
0 \\
0 \\
0 \\
0 \\
3 \\
2 \\
0
\end{pmatrix}
\qquad c = 1
$$

Word w^j
vs
mln
cts
;
&
000
loss
,
"
3
profit
dlrs
1
pct
is
s
that
net
lt
at

Table 16.3 The representation of document 11, shown in figure 16.3. This illustrates the data representation model which we use for classification in this chapter.

which would be rounded to 5. This weighting scheme does log weighting similar to the schemes discussed in chapter 15, while at the same time incorporating weight normalization. We round values to make it easier to present and inspect data for pedagogical reasons.

The representation of the document in figure 16.3 is shown in table 16.3. As tends to happen when using an automatic feature selection method, some of the selected words don't seem promising as indicators of "earnings," for example, *that* and *s*. The three symbols "&", "lt", and ";" were selected because of a formatting peculiarity in the publicly available Reuters collection: a large proportion of articles in the category "earnings" have a company tag like <CBCO> in the title line whose left angle bracket was converted to an SGML character entity. We can think of this

entropy at node 1, $P(C|N) = 0.300$ 0.611
entropy at node 2, $P(C|N) = 0.116$ 0.359
entropy at node 5, $P(C|N) = 0.943$ 0.219
weighted sum of 2 and 5 $\frac{5977}{7681} \times 0.359 + \frac{1704}{7681} \times 0.219 = 0.328$
information gain $0.611 - 0.328 = 0.283$

Table 16.4 An example of information gain as a splitting criterion. The table shows the entropies for nodes 1, 2, and 5 in figure 16.1, the weighted sum of the child nodes and the information gain for splitting 1 into 2 and 5.

left angle bracket as indicating: "This document is about a particular company." We will see that this 'meta-tag' is very helpful for classification. The title line of the document in figure 16.3 has an example of the meta-tag.[2]

Now that we have a model class (decision trees) and a representation for the data (20-element vectors), we need to define the training procedure. Decision trees are usually built by first growing a large tree and then *pruning* it back to a reasonable size. The pruning step is necessary because very large trees *overfit* the training set. Overfitting occurs when classifiers make decisions based on accidental properties of the training set that will lead to errors on the test set (or any new data). For example, if there is only one document in the training set that contains both the words *dlrs* and *pct* (for "dollars" and "percent") and this document happens to be in the earnings category, then the training procedure may grow a large tree that categorizes all documents with this property as being in this category. But if there is only one such document in the training set, this is probably just a coincidence. When the tree is pruned back, then the part that makes the corresponding inference (assign to "earnings" if one finds both *dlrs* and *pct*), will be cut off, thus leading to better performance on the test set.

PRUNING
OVERFITTING

SPLITTING CRITERION
STOPPING CRITERION

For growing the tree, we need a *splitting criterion* for finding the feature and its value that we will split on and a *stopping criterion* which determines when to stop splitting. The stopping criterion can trivially be that all elements at a node have an identical representation or the same category so that splitting would not further distinguish them.

The splitting criterion which we will use here is to split the objects at a

2. The string "<" should really have been tokenized as a unit, but it can serve as an example of the low-level data problems that occur frequently in text categorization.

node into two piles in the way that gives us maximum information gain. *Information gain* (Breiman et al. 1984: 25, Quinlan 1986: section 4, Quinlan 1993) is an information-theoretic measure defined as the difference of the entropy of the mother node and the weighted sum of the entropies of the child nodes:

(16.2) $G(a, y) = H(t) - H(t|a) = H(t) - (p_L H(t_L) + p_R H(t_R))$

where a is the attribute we split on, y is the value of a we split on, t is the distribution of the node that we split, p_L and p_R are the proportion of elements that are passed on to the left and right nodes, and t_L and t_R are the distributions of the left and right nodes. As an example, we show the values of these variables and the resulting information gain in table 16.4 for the top node of the decision tree in figure 16.1.

Information gain is intuitively appealing because it can be interpreted as measuring the reduction of uncertainty. If we make the split that maximizes information gain, then we reduce the uncertainty in the resulting classification as much as possible. There are no general algorithms for finding the optimal splitting value efficiently. In practice, one uses heuristic algorithms that find a near-optimal value.[3]

LEAF NODE   A node that is not split by the algorithm because of the stopping criterion is a *leaf node*. The prediction we make at a leaf node is based on its members. We can compute maximum likelihood estimates, but smoothing is often appropriate. For example, if a leaf node has 6 members in the category "earnings" and 2 other members, then we would estimate the category membership probability of a new document d in the node as $P(\text{earnings}|d) = \frac{6+1}{2+6+1+1} = 0.7$ if we use add-one smoothing (section 6.2.2).

Once the tree has been fully grown, we prune it to avoid overfitting and to optimize performance on new data. At each step, we select the remaining leaf node that we expect by some criterion to be least helpful (or even harmful) for accurate classification. One common pruning criterion is to compute a measure of confidence that indicates how much evidence there is that the node is 'helpful' (Quinlan 1993). We repeat the pruning process until no node is left. Each step in the process (from the full tree to the empty tree) defines a classifier – the classifier that corresponds to the decision tree with the nodes remaining at this point. One way to se-

---

3. We could afford an exhaustive search for the optimal splitting value here because the s_{ij} are integers in a small interval.

lect the best of these n trees (where n is the number of internal nodes of the full tree) is by *validation* on held out data.

Validation evaluates a classifier on a held-out data set, the *validation set* to assess its accuracy. For the same reason as needing independent test data, in order to evaluate how much to prune a decision tree we need to look at a new set of data – which is what evaluation on the validation set does. (See section 6.2.3 for the same basic technique used in smoothing.)

An alternative to pruning a decision tree is to keep the whole tree, but to make the classifier probability estimates a function of internal as well as leaf nodes. This is a means of getting at the more reliable probability distributions of higher nodes without actually pruning away the nodes below them. For each leaf node, we can read out the sequence of nodes and associated probability distributions from that node to the root of the decision tree. Rather than using held out data for pruning, held out data can be used to train the parameters of a linear interpolation (section 6.3.1) of all these distributions for each leaf node, and these interpolated distributions can then be used as the final classification functions. Magerman (1994) argues that this gives superior performance to pruning, at least for the statistical parsing problem on which he was working (see section 12.2.2).

Figure 16.4 shows how performance of a decision tree depends on pruning. The x-axis corresponds to number of nodes pruned, the y-axis to classification accuracy. In order to produce the graph we grew the tree on 80% of the training set (7681 documents) and set 20% (1922 documents) aside as the validation set. The pruning of the top node is not shown in the graph.[4]

The pattern we find is standard: performance on the training set is maximum for the full tree and then falls off continuously. Since we optimize the initial construction of the full tree on the training set, larger trees will fit the properties of the training set better than pruned trees, hence the decrease in performance on the training set as we go from left to right.

Accuracy for validation and test sets peaks somewhere in the middle. When performance peaks we have reached the point where parts of the tree that fit accidental properties of the training set have been pruned

---

4. The pruning criterion was to select the leaf node with the lowest information gain on the validation set.

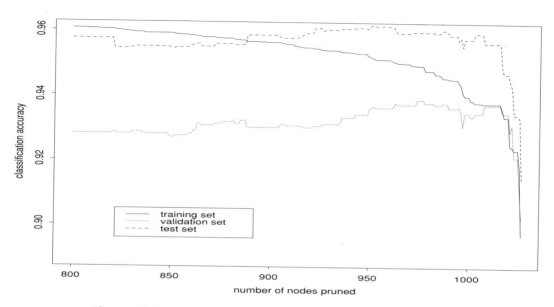

Figure 16.4   Pruning a decision tree. The graph shows how classification accuracy of a decision tree depends on pruning. Optimal performance on the test set (96.21% accuracy) is reached for 951 nodes pruned. Optimal performance on the validation set (93.91% accuracy) is reached for 974–977 nodes pruned. For these four pruned trees, performance on the test set is 96.00%, close to optimal performance. Performance on the training set is monotonically decreasing.

away. Oversimplifying a little bit, any further pruning will delete nodes that capture correct generalizations about the "earnings" category, hence the decrease in performance.

One strategy for selecting a tree is to pick the one that performs best for the validation set. As we can see in the picture it does not perfectly coincide with the peak for the test set, but it is close enough. The tree that performs best on the validation set will often be slightly overtrained or slightly undertrained, but usually it will be close to optimal performance.

Table 16.5 evaluates performance of the tree with 50 internal nodes on the test set. This is the smallest tree with the optimal performance of 93.91% accuracy on the validation set.

A problem with setting aside a validation set is that a relatively large part of the full training set is wasted. A better method is to use *n*-fold CROSS-VALIDATION   *cross-validation* (cf. section 6.2.4) to estimate a good size for the pruned

"earnings"	"earnings" correct?	
assigned?	YES	NO
YES	1024	69
NO	63	2143

Table 16.5 Contingency table for a decision tree for the Reuters category "earnings." Classification accuracy on the test set is 96.0%.

decision tree. For example, in 5-fold cross-validation we split the data into five parts. We reserve one part as a validation set, train the tree on the other four parts and then prune it back based on the held-out part. This process is repeated four times using each of the other four parts as a validation set. We then determine the average size of an optimally performing pruned tree. Finally, a new tree is grown for the *entire* training set and pruned back to what we have calculated to be the optimal size.

The interdependence of complexity of the learning device and accuracy on the training set is an important characteristic of many classification methods. If the device is too complex (or has too many parameters), then we risk overfitting and low accuracy on new data. If the device is not complex enough, it is not able to make maximum use of the training data, which again leads to lower than optimal accuracy on new data. The trick is to find just the right balance and cross-validation is one approach to doing that.

Another common property of classification methods is shown in figure 16.5, the dependence of classification accuracy on the amount of training data available. Not surprisingly, the more training data, the better – up to a point where performance improvement levels off. Sometimes one gets lucky with a small set (hence the fluctuations), but one cannot be sure that a tree trained on a small data set will perform well.

LEARNING CURVES   Computing *learning curves* like those in figure 16.5 is important to determine the size of an appropriate training set. Many training procedures are computationally expensive, so it is advantageous to avoid overly large training sets. But on the other hand, insufficient training data will result in suboptimal classification accuracy. Looking at the curve lets one decide how much data is enough for optimal performance. (Of course, there are many cases in which one has no control over the amount of training data available and has to live with a small training set even though a larger one would give much better performance.)

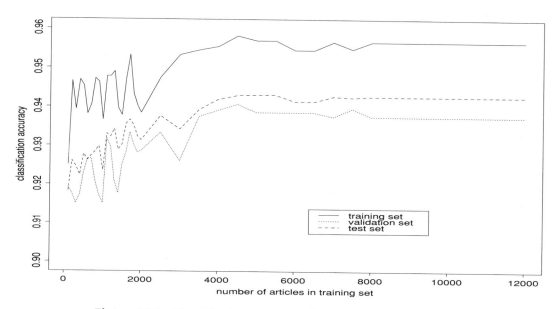

Figure 16.5 Classification accuracy depends on the amount of training data available. The *x* axis corresponds to the number of training documents the decision tree was trained on. The *y* axis corresponds to accuracy on the test set for a decision tree selected based on a constant size validation set. Classification accuracy is highly variable for small training set sizes and increases and levels off for larger sets.

When are decision trees appropriate for a classification task in NLP? Decision trees are more complex than classifiers like Naive Bayes (section 7.2.1), linear regression (section 15.4.1), and logistic regression. If the classification problem is simple (in particular, if it is *linearly separable*, see below), then these simpler methods are often preferable. Decision trees also split the training set into smaller and smaller subsets. This makes correct generalization harder, since there may not be enough data for reliable prediction, and incorrect generalization easier, since smaller sets have accidental regularities that don't generalize. Figure 16.6 gives a simple example of this problem from the domain of learning phonological rules. Pruning addresses this problem to some extent, but some learning problems are better handled by methods that look at all features simultaneously. The other three methods we introduce in this chapter all have this property.

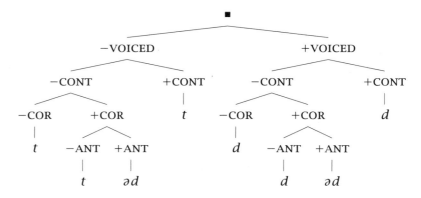

Figure 16.6 An example of how decision trees use data inefficiently from the domain of phonological rule learning. The regular rule for the English past tense is that one gets /t/ after a voiceless sound, and /d/ after a voiced sound, except after [−CONT, +COR, +ANT] sounds (i.e., /t/, /d/) where one gets /əd/. Because the voicing feature has the greatest information gain, the tree splits on that feature first, but that makes the remaining conditioning harder to learn because the relevant data has been subdivided into different bins within which learning is attempted independently.

The greatest advantage of decision trees is that they can be interpreted so easily. It is easy to trace the path from the root to a leaf node for a couple of articles and to develop an intuition as to how the decision tree works. This is not only invaluable in debugging one's own code and understanding a new problem domain, but it also allows one to explain the classifier to researchers and laymen alike, an important property in research collaboration and practical applications.

Exercise 16.1   [⋆]
What is the classification accuracy of the trivial tree with one leaf node for the "earnings" category?

Exercise 16.2   [⋆]
In section 7.1, we introduced upper and lower bounds as a way to assess how hard a particular classification problem is. What are upper and lower bounds for the 'earnings' category?

Exercise 16.3   [⋆⋆]
An important application of text categorization is the detection of spam (also known as unsolicited bulk email). Try to collect at least a hundred spam messages and non-spam messages, divide them into training and test sets and build

a decision tree that detects spam. Finding the right features is paramount for this task, so design your feature set carefully.

Exercise 16.4 [★ ★]

Another important application of text categorization is the detection of 'adult' content, that is, content that is not appropriate for children because it is sexually explicit. Collect training and test sets of adult and non-adult material from the World Wide Web and build a decision tree that can block access to adult material.

Exercise 16.5 [★ ★]

Collect a reasonable amount of text written by yourself and by a friend. You may want to break up individual texts (e.g., term papers) into smaller pieces to get a large enough set. Build a decision tree that automatically determines whether you are the author of a piece of text. Note that it is often the 'little' words that give an author away (for example, the relative frequencies of words like *because* or *though*).

Exercise 16.6 [★ ★]

Download a set of English and non-English texts from the World Wide Web or use some other multilingual source. Build a decision tree that can distinguish between English and non-English texts. (See also exercise 6.10.)

16.2 Maximum Entropy Modeling

Maximum entropy modeling is a framework for integrating information from many heterogeneous information sources for classification. The data for a classification problem is described as a (potentially large) number of features. These features can be quite complex and allow the experimenter to make use of prior knowledge about what types of information are expected to be important for classification. Each feature corresponds to a constraint on the model. We then compute the *maximum entropy model*, the model with maximum entropy of all the models that satisfy the constraints. This term may initially seem perverse, since we have spent most of the book trying to minimize the (cross) entropy of models, but the idea is that we do not want to go beyond the data. If we chose a model with less entropy, we would add 'information' constraints to the model that are not justified by the empirical evidence available to us. Choosing the maximum entropy model is motivated by the desire to preserve as much uncertainty as possible.

We have simplified matters in this chapter by neglecting the problem of feature selection (we use the same 20 features throughout). In maximum entropy modeling, feature selection and training are usually integrated.

Ideally, this enables us to specify all potentially relevant information at the beginning, and then to let the training procedure worry about how to come up with the best model for classification. We will only introduce the basic method here and refer the reader to the Further Reading for feature selection.

For a given set of features, we first compute the *expectation* of each feature based on the training set. Each feature then defines the constraint

EMPIRICAL
EXPECTATION

that this *empirical expectation* be the same as the expectation the feature has in our final maximum entropy model. Of all probability distributions

MAXIMUM ENTROPY
DISTRIBUTION

that obey these constraints, we attempt to find the *maximum entropy distribution*, the one with the highest entropy. One can show that there is a unique such maximum entropy distribution and there exists an algorithm, generalized iterative scaling, which is guaranteed to converge to it.

The features f_i are binary functions that can be used to characterize any property of a pair $(\vec{x}, c)$, where $\vec{x}$ is a vector representing an input element (in our case the 20-dimensional vector of word weights representing an article as in table 16.3), and c is the class label (1 if the article is in the "earnings" category, 0 otherwise). For text categorization, we define features as follows:

$$(16.3) \quad f_i(\vec{x}_j, c) = \begin{cases} 1 & \text{if } s_{ij} > 0 \text{ and } c = 1 \\ 0 & \text{otherwise} \end{cases}$$

Recall that s_{ij} is the term weight for word i in Reuters article j. Note that the use of binary features is different from the rest of this chapter: The other classifiers use the magnitude of the weight, not just the presence or absence of a word.[5]

The model class for the particular variety of maximum entropy model-

LOGLINEAR MODELS

ing that we introduce here is *loglinear models* of the following form:

$$(16.4) \quad p(\vec{x}, c) = \frac{1}{Z} \prod_{i=1}^{K} \alpha_i^{f_i(\vec{x}, c)}$$

where K is the number of features, α_i is the weight for feature f_i and Z is a normalizing constant, used to ensure that a probability distribution results. To use the model for text categorization, we compute $p(\vec{x}, 0)$ and

---

5. While the maximum entropy approach is not in principle limited to binary features, known reasonably efficient solution procedures such as generalized iterative scaling, which we introduce below, do only work for binary features.

$p(\vec{x}, 1)$ and, in the simplest case, choose the class label with the greater probability.

FEATURES   Note that, in this section, *features* contain information about the *class* of the object in addition to the *'measurements'* of the object we want to classify. Here, we are following most publications on maximum entropy modeling in defining feature in this sense. The more common use of the term "feature" (which we have adopted for the rest of the book) is that it only refers to some characteristic of the object, independent of the class the object is a member of.

Equation (16.4) defines a loglinear model because, if we take logs on both sides, then $\log p$ is a linear combination of the logs of the weights:

(16.5) $$\log p(\vec{x}, c) = -\log Z + \sum_{i=1}^{K} f_i(\vec{x}, c) \log \alpha_i$$

Loglinear models are an important class of models for classification. Other examples of the class are logistic regression (McCullagh and Nelder 1989) and decomposable models (Bruce and Wiebe 1999). We introduce the maximum entropy modeling approach here because maximum entropy models have been the most widely used loglinear models in Statistical NLP and because it is an application of the important maximum entropy principle.

16.2.1   Generalized iterative scaling

GENERALIZED
ITERATIVE SCALING   *Generalized iterative scaling* is a procedure for finding the maximum entropy distribution p^* of form (16.4) that obeys the following set of constraints:

(16.6) $E_{p^*} f_i = E_{\tilde{p}} f_i$

In other words, the expected value of f_i for p^* is the same as the expected value for the empirical distribution (in other words, the training set).

The algorithm requires that the sum of the features for each possible $(\vec{x}, c)$ be equal to a constant C:[6]

(16.7) $\forall \vec{x}, c \quad \sum_i f_i(\vec{x}, c) = C$

---

6. See Berger et al. (1996) for *Improved Iterative Scaling*, a variant of generalized iterative scaling that does not impose this constraint.

In order to fulfil this requirement, we define C as the greatest possible feature sum:

$$C \stackrel{\text{def}}{=} \max_{\vec{x},c} \sum_{i=1}^{K} f_i(\vec{x}, c)$$

and add a feature f_{K+1} that is defined as follows:

$$f_{K+1}(\vec{x}, c) = C - \sum_{i=1}^{K} f_i(\vec{x}, c)$$

Note that this feature is not binary, in contrast to the others.

$E_p f_i$ is defined as follows:

(16.8) $$E_p f_i = \sum_{\vec{x},c} p(\vec{x}, c) f_i(\vec{x}, c)$$

where the sum is over the event space, that is, all possible vectors $\vec{x}$ and class labels c. The empirical expectation is easy to compute:

(16.9) $$E_{\tilde{p}} f_i = \sum_{\vec{x},c} \tilde{p}(\vec{x}, c) f_i(\vec{x}, c) = \frac{1}{N} \sum_{j=1}^{N} f_i(\vec{x}_j, c)$$

where N is the number of elements in the training set and we use the fact that the empirical probability for a pair that doesn't occur in the training set is 0.

In general, the maximum entropy distribution $E_p f_i$ cannot be computed efficiently since it would involve summing over all possible combinations of $\vec{x}$ and c, a potentially infinite set. Instead, we use the following approximation (Lau 1994: 25):

(16.10) $$E_p f_i = \frac{1}{N} \sum_{j=1}^{N} \sum_{c} p(c|\vec{x}_j) f_i(\vec{x}_j, c)$$

where c ranges over all possible classes, in our case $c \in \{0, 1\}$.

Now we have all the pieces to state the generalized iterative scaling algorithm:

1. Initialize $\{\alpha_i^{(1)}\}$. Any initialization will do, but usually we choose $\alpha_i^{(1)} = 1, \forall 1 \le j \le K + 1$. Compute $E_{\tilde{p}} f_i$ as shown above. Set $n = 1$.

2. Compute $p^{(n)}(\vec{x}, c)$ for the distribution $p^{(n)}$ given by the $\{\alpha_i^{(n)}\}$ for each element $(\vec{x}, c)$ in the training set:

(16.11) $$p^{(n)}(\vec{x}, c) = \frac{1}{Z} \prod_{i=1}^{K+1} (\alpha_i^{(n)})^{f_i(x,c)}$$

$\vec{x}$ profit	c "earnings"	f_1	f_2	$\beta = f_1 \log \alpha_1 + f_2 \log \alpha_2$	2^β
(0)	0	0	1	1	2
(0)	1	0	1	1	2
(1)	0	0	1	1	2
(1)	1	1	0	2	4

Table 16.6 An example of a maximum entropy distribution in the form of equation (16.4). The vector $\vec{x}$ consists of a single element, indicating the presence or absence of the word *profit* in the article. There are two classes (member of "earnings" or not). Feature f_1 is 1 if and only if the article is in "earnings" and *profit* occurs. f_2 is the "filler" feature f_{K+1}. For one particular choice of the parameters, namely $\log \alpha_1 = 2.0$ and $\log \alpha_2 = 1.0$, we get after normalization ($Z = 2 + 2 + 2 + 4 = 10$) the following maximum entropy distribution: $p(0,0) = p(0,1) = p(1,0) = 2/Z = 0.2$ and $p(1,1) = 4/Z = 0.4$. An example of a data set with the same empirical distribution is $((0,0),(0,1),(1,0),(1,1),(1,1))$.

3. Compute $E_{p^{(n)}} f_i$ for all $1 \leq i \leq K + 1$ according to equation (16.10).

4. Update the parameters α_i:

(16.12)
$$\alpha_i^{(n+1)} = \alpha_i^{(n)} \left(\frac{E_{\tilde{p}} f_i}{E_{p^{(n)}} f_i} \right)^{\frac{1}{C}}$$

5. If the parameters of the procedure have converged, stop, otherwise increment n and go to 2.

We present the algorithm in this form for readability. In an actual implementation, it is more convenient to do the computations using logarithms.

One can show that this procedure converges to a distribution p* that obeys the constraints (16.6), and that of all such distributions it is the one that maximizes the entropy $H(p)$ and the likelihood of the data. Darroch and Ratcliff (1972) show that this distribution always exists and is unique.

A toy example of a maximum entropy distribution that generalized iterative scaling will converge to is shown in table 16.6.

Exercise 16.7 [★]

What are the classification decisions for the distribution in table 16.6? Compute $P(\text{"earnings"}|\textit{profit})$ and $P(\text{"earnings"}|\neg\textit{profit})$.

| Does *profit* | Is topic "earnings"? | |
occur?	YES	NO
YES	20	9
NO	8	13

Table 16.7 An empirical distribution whose corresponding maximum entropy distribution is the one in table 16.6.

Exercise 16.8   [⋆]

Show that the distribution in table 16.6 is a fixed point for iterative generalized scaling. That is, computing one iteration should leave the distribution unchanged.

Exercise 16.9   [⋆]

Consider the distribution in table 16.7. Show that for the features defined in table 16.6, this distribution has the same feature expectations E_p as the one in table 16.6.

Exercise 16.10   [⋆]

Compute a number of iterations of generalized iterative scaling for the data in table 16.7 (using the features defined in table 16.6). The procedure should converge towards the distribution in table 16.6.

Exercise 16.11   [⋆ ⋆]

Select one of exercises 16.3 through 16.6 and build a maximum entropy model for the corresponding text categorization task.

16.2.2   Application to text categorization

We have already suggested how to define appropriate features for text categorization in equation (16.3). For the task of identifying Reuters "earnings" articles we end up with 20 features, each corresponding to one of the selected words, and the f_{K+1} feature introduced at the start of the last subsection.

Table 16.8 shows the weights found by generalized iterative scaling after convergence (500 iterations). We trained on the 9603 articles in the training set. The features with the highest weights are *vs*, *cts*, *profit* and *lt*. If we use $P(\text{"earnings"}|\vec{x}) > P(\neg\text{"earnings"}|\vec{x})$ as our decision rule, we get the classification results in table 16.9. Classification accuracy is 88.6%.

An important question in an implementation is when to stop the iteration. One way to test for convergence is to compute the log difference

Word w^i	Feature weight $\log \alpha_i$
vs	0.613
mln	−0.110
cts	1.298
;	−0.432
&	−0.429
000	−0.413
loss	−0.332
'	−0.085
"	0.202
3	−0.463
profit	0.360
dlrs	−0.202
1	−0.211
pct	−0.260
is	−0.546
s	−0.490
that	−0.285
net	−0.300
lt	1.016
at	−0.465
f_{K+1}	0.009

Table 16.8 Feature weights in maximum entropy modeling for the category "earnings" in Reuters.

"earnings" assigned?	"earnings" correct?	
	YES	NO
YES	735	24
NO	352	2188

Table 16.9 Classification results for the distribution corresponding to table 16.8 on the test set. Classification accuracy is 88.6%.

between empirical and estimated feature expectations ($\log E_{\tilde{p}} - \log E_{p^{(n)}}$), which should approach zero. Ristad (1996) recommends to also look at the largest α when doing iterative scaling. If the largest weight becomes too large, then this indicates a problem with either the data representation or the implementation.

When is the maximum entropy framework presented in this section appropriate as a classification method? The somewhat lower performance on the "earnings" task compared to some of the other methods indicates one characteristic that is a shortcoming in some situations: the restriction to binary features seems to have led to lower performance. In text categorization, we often need a notion of "strength of evidence" which goes beyond a simple binary feature recording presence or absence of evidence. The feature-based representation we use for maximum entropy modeling is not optimal for this purpose.

Generalized iterative scaling can also be computationally expensive due to slow convergence (but see (Lau 1994) for suggestions for speeding up convergence). For binary classification, the loglinear model defines a linear separator that is in principle no more powerful than *Naive Bayes* or *linear regression*, classifiers that can be trained more efficiently. However, it is important to stress that, apart from the theoretical power of a classification method, the training procedure is crucial. Generalized iterative scaling takes dependence between features into account in contrast to Naive Bayes and other linear classifiers. If feature dependence is not expected to a be a problem, then Naive Bayes is a better choice than maximum entropy modeling.

NAIVE BAYES
LINEAR REGRESSION

Finally, the lack of smoothing can also cause problems. For example, if we have a feature that always predicts a certain class, then this feature may get an excessively high weight. One way to deal with this is to 'smooth' the empirical data by adding events that did not occur. In practice, features that occur less than five times are usually eliminated.

One of the strengths of maximum entropy modeling is that it offers a framework for specifying all possibly relevant information. The attraction of the method lies in the fact that arbitrarily complex features can be defined if the experimenter believes that these features may contribute useful information for the classification decision. For example, Berger et al. (1996: 57) define a feature for the translation of the preposition *in* from English to French that is 1 if and only if *in* is translated as *pendant* and *in* is followed by the word *weeks* within three words. There is also no need to worry about heterogeneity of features or weighting features, two problems that often cause difficulty in other classification approaches. Model selection is well-founded in the maximum entropy principle: we should not add any information over and above what we find in the empirical evidence. Maximum entropy modeling thus provides a well-motivated probabilistic framework for integrating information from heterogeneous sources.

We could only allude here to another strength of the method: an integrated framework for feature selection and classification. (The fact that we have not done maximum entropy feature selection here is perhaps the main reason for the lower classification accuracy.) Most classification methods cannot deal with a very large number of features. If there are too many features initially, an (often ad-hoc) method has to be used to winnow the feature set down to a manageable size. This is what we have done here, using the X^2 test for words. In maximum entropy modeling one can instead specify all potentially relevant features and use extensions of the basic method such as those described by Berger et al. (1996) to simultaneously select features and fit the classification model. Since the two are integrated, there is a clear probabilistic interpretation (in terms of maximum entropy and maximum likelihood) of the resulting classification model. Such an interpretation is less clear for other methods such as perceptrons and k nearest neighbors.

In this section we have only attempted to give enough information to help the reader to decide whether maximum entropy modeling is an appropriate framework for their classification task when compared to other classification methods. More detailed treatments of maximum entropy modeling are mentioned in the Further Reading.

16.3   Perceptrons

GRADIENT DESCENT
HILL CLIMBING

We present perceptrons here as a simple example of a *gradient descent* (or reversing the direction of goodness, *hill climbing*) algorithm, an important class of iterative learning algorithms. In gradient descent, we attempt to optimize a function of the data that computes a goodness criterion like squared error or likelihood. In each step, we compute the derivative of the function and change the parameters of the model in the direction of the steepest gradient (steepest ascent or descent, depending on the optimality function). This is a good idea because the direction of

```
 1  comment: Categorization Decision
 2  funct decision(x⃗, w⃗, θ)  ≡
 3     if w⃗ · x⃗ > θ then
 4                        return yes
 5              else
 6                        return no
 7     fi.
 9  comment: Initialization
10  w⃗ = 0
11  θ = 0
12  comment: Perceptron Learning Algorithm
13  while not converged yet do
14          for all elements x⃗_j in the training set  do
15              d = decision(x⃗_j, w⃗, θ)
16              if class(x⃗_j) = d then
17                                continue
18              elsif class(x⃗_j) = yes and d = no then
19                                                θ = θ - 1
20                                                w⃗ = w⃗ + x⃗_j
21              elsif class(x⃗_j) = no and d = yes then
22                                                θ = θ + 1
23                                                w⃗ = w⃗ - x⃗_j
24              fi
25          end
26  end
```

Figure 16.7 The Perceptron Learning Algorithm. The perceptron decides "yes" if the inner product of weight vector and data vector is greater than θ and "no" otherwise. The learning algorithm cycles through all examples. If the current weight vector makes the right decision for an instance, it is left unchanged. Otherwise, the data vector is added to or subtracted from the weight vector, depending on the direction of the error.

steepest gradient is the direction where we can expect the most improvement in the goodness criterion.

Without further ado, we introduce the perceptron learning algorithm in figure 16.7. As before, text documents are represented as term vectors. Our goal is to learn a weight vector $\vec{w}$ and a threshold θ, such that comparing the dot product of the weight vector and the term vector against the threshold provides the categorization decision. We decide "yes" (the article is in the "earnings" category) if the inner product of weight vector and document vector is greater than the threshold and "no" otherwise:

$$\text{Decide "yes" iff} \quad \vec{w} \cdot \vec{x} = \sum_{i=1}^{K} w_i x_{ij} > \theta$$

where K is the number of features ($K = 20$ for our example as before) and x_{ij} is component i of vector $\vec{x}_j$.

The basic idea of the perceptron learning algorithm is simple. If the weight vector makes a mistake, we move it (and θ) in the direction of greatest change for our optimality criterion $\sum_{i=1}^{K} w_i x_{ij} - \theta$. To see that the changes to $\vec{w}$ and θ in figure 16.8 are made in the direction of greatest change, we first define an optimality criterion ϕ that incorporates θ into the weight vector:

$$\phi(\vec{w}') = \phi\left(\begin{pmatrix} w_1 \\ w_2 \\ \vdots \\ w_K \\ \theta \end{pmatrix}\right) = \vec{w}' \cdot \vec{x}' = \begin{pmatrix} w_1 \\ w_2 \\ \vdots \\ w_K \\ \theta \end{pmatrix} \cdot \begin{pmatrix} x_1 \\ x_2 \\ \vdots \\ x_K \\ -1 \end{pmatrix}$$

The gradient of ϕ (which is the direction of greatest change) is the vector $\vec{x}'$:

$$\nabla \phi(\vec{w}') = \vec{x}'$$

Of all vectors of a given length that we can add to $\vec{w}'$, $\vec{x}'$ is the one that will change ϕ the most. So that is the direction we want to take for gradient descent; and it is indeed the change that is implemented in figure 16.7.

Figure 16.8 shows one error-correcting step of the algorithm for a two-dimensional problem. The figure also illustrates the class of models that can be learned by perceptrons: linear separators. Each weight vector defines an orthogonal line (or a plane or hyperplane in higher dimensions) that separates the vector space into two halves, one with positive values,

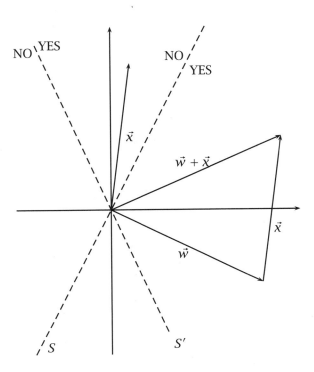

Figure 16.8 One error-correcting step of the perceptron learning algorithm. Data vector $\vec{x}$ is misclassified by the current weight vector $\vec{w}$ since it lies on the "no"-side of the decision boundary S. The correction step adds $\vec{x}$ to $\vec{w}$ and (in this case) corrects the decision since $\vec{x}$ now lies on the "yes"-side of S', the decision boundary of the new weight vector $\vec{w} + \vec{x}$.

one with negative values. In figure 16.8, the separator is S, defined by $\vec{w}$. Classification tasks in which the elements of two classes can be perfectly separated by such a hyperplane are called *linearly separable*.

LINEARLY SEPARABLE

One can show that the perceptron learning algorithm always converges towards a separating hyperplane when applied to a linearly separable problem. This is the *perceptron convergence theorem*. It might seem plausible that the perceptron learning algorithm will eventually find a solution if there is one, since it keeps adjusting the weights for misclassified elements, but since an adjustment for one element will often reverse classification decisions for others, the proof is not trivial.

PERCEPTRON
CONVERGENCE
THEOREM

Word w^i	Weight
vs	11
mln	6
cts	24
;	2
&	12
000	−4
loss	19
,	−2
"	7
3	−7
profit	31
dlrs	1
1	3
pct	−4
is	−8
s	−12
that	−1
net	8
lt	11
at	−6
θ	37

Table 16.10 Perceptron for the "earnings" category. The weight vector $\vec{w}$ and θ of a perceptron learned by the perceptron learning algorithm for the category "earnings" in Reuters.

Table 16.10 shows the weights learned by the perceptron learning algorithm for the "earnings" category after about 1000 iterations. As with the model parameters in maximum entropy modeling we get high weights for *cts*, *profit* and *lt*. Table 16.11 shows the classification results on the test set. Overall accuracy is 83%. This suggests that the problem is not linearly separable. See the exercises.

A perceptron in 20 dimensions is hard to visualize, so we reran the algorithm with just two dimensions, *mln* and *cts*. The weight vector and the linear separator defined by it are shown in figure 16.9.

The perceptron learning algorithm is guaranteed to learn a linearly sep-

"earnings"	"earnings" correct?	
assigned?	YES	NO
YES	1059	521
NO	28	1691

Table 16.11 Classification results for the perceptron in table 16.10 on the test set. Classification accuracy is 83.3%.

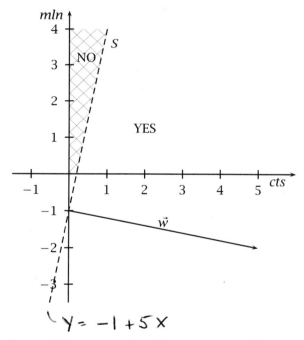

Figure 16.9 Geometric interpretation of a perceptron. The weight for *cts* is 5, the weight for *mln* is −1, and the threshold is 1. The linear separator *S* divides the upper right quadrant into a NO and a YES region. Only documents with many more occurrences of *mln* than *cts* are categorized as not belonging to "earnings."

LOCAL OPTIMUM

GLOBAL OPTIMUM

arable problem. There are similar convergence theorems for some other gradient descent algorithms, but in most cases convergence will only be to a *local optimum*, locations in the weight space that are locally optimal, but inferior to the globally optimal solution. Perceptrons converge to a *global optimum* because they select a classifier from a class of simple models, the linear separators. There are many important problems that are not linearly separable, the most famous being the XOR problem. The XOR (i.e., eXclusive OR) problem involves a classifier with two features C_1 and C_2 where the answer should be "yes" if C_1 is true and C_2 false or vice versa. A decision tree can easily learn such a problem, whereas a perceptron cannot. After some initial enthusiasm about perceptrons (Rosenblatt 1962), researchers realized these limitations. As a consequence, interest in perceptrons and related learning algorithms faded quickly and remained low for decades. The publication of (Minsky and Papert 1969) is often seen as the point at which the interest in this genre of learning algorithms started to wane. See Rumelhart and Zipser (1985) for a historical summary.

If the perceptron learning algorithm is run on a problem that is not linearly separable, the linear separator will sometimes move back and forth erratically while the algorithm tries in vain to find a perfectly separating plane. This is in fact what happened when we ran the algorithm on the "earnings" data. Classification accuracy fluctuated between 72% and 93%. We picked a state that lies in the middle of this spectrum of accuracy for tables 16.10 and 16.11. Perceptrons have not been used much in NLP because most NLP problems are not linearly separable and the perceptron learning algorithm does not find a good approximate separator in such cases. However, in cases where a problem is linearly separable, perceptrons can be an appropriate classification method due to their simplicity and ease of implementation.

A resurgence of work on gradient descent learning algorithms occurred in the eighties when several learning algorithms were proposed that overcame the limitations of perceptrons, most notably the *backpropagation* algorithm which is used to train *multi-layer perceptrons* (MLPs), otherwise known as *neural networks* or *connectionist models*. Backpropagation applied to MLPs can in principle learn any classification function including XOR. But it converges more slowly than the perceptron learning algorithm and it can get caught in *local optima*. Pointers to uses of neural networks in NLP appear in the Further Reading.

BACKPROPAGATION

NEURAL NETWORKS
CONNECTIONIST
MODELS

Exercise 16.12   [★ ★]

Build an animated visualization that shows how the perceptron's decision boundary moves during training and run it for a two-dimensional classification problem.

Exercise 16.13   [★ ★]

Select a subset of 10 "earnings" and 10 non-"earnings" documents. Select two words, one for the x axis, one for the y axis and plot the 20 documents with class labels. Is the set linearly separable?

Exercise 16.14   [★]

How can one show that a set of data points from two classes is not linearly separable?

Exercise 16.15   [★]

Show that the "earnings" data set is not linearly separable.

Exercise 16.16   [★]

Suppose a problem is linearly separable and we train a perceptron to convergence. In such a case, classification accuracy will often not be 100%. Why?

Exercise 16.17   [★ ★]

Select one of exercises 16.3 through 16.6 and build a perceptron for the corresponding text categorization task.

16.4   *k* Nearest Neighbor Classification

NEAREST NEIGHBOR
CLASSIFICATION RULE
    The rationale for the *nearest neighbor classification rule* is remarkably simple. To classify a new object, find the object in the training set that is most similar. Then assign the category of this nearest neighbor.

    The basic idea is that if there is an identical article in the training set (or at least one with the same representation), then the obvious decision is to assign the same category. If there is no identical article, then the most similar one is our best bet.

k NEAREST NEIGHBOR
    A generalization of the nearest neighbor rule is *k nearest neighbor* or *KNN* classification. Instead of using only one nearest neighbor as the basis for our decision, we consult k nearest neighbors. KNN for $k > 1$ is more robust than the '1 nearest neighbor' method.

    The complexity of KNN is in finding a good measure of similarity. As an example of what can go wrong consider the task of deciding whether there is an eagle in an image. If we have a drawing of an eagle that we want to classify and all exemplars in the database are photographs of eagles, then KNN will classify the drawing as non-eagle because according to any low-level similarity metric based on image features drawings and photographs will come out as very different no matter what their content (and how to implement high-level similarity is an unsolved problem). If one doesn't have a good similarity metric, one can't use KNN.

Fortunately, many NLP tasks have simple similarity metrics that are quite effective. For the "earnings" data, we implemented cosine similarity (see section 8.5.1), and chose $k = 1$. This '1NN algorithm' for binary categorization can be stated as follows.

- Goal: categorize $\vec{y}$ based on the training set X.

- Determine the largest similarity with any element in the training set:
  $\text{sim}_{\max}(\vec{y}) = \max_{\vec{x} \in X} \text{sim}(\vec{x}, \vec{y})$

- Collect the subset of X that has highest similarity with $\vec{y}$:

  $A = \{\vec{x} \in X | \text{sim}(\vec{x}, \vec{y}) = \text{sim}_{\max}(\vec{y})\}$

- Let n_1 and n_2 be the number of elements in A that belong to the two classes c_1 and c_2, respectively. Then we estimate the conditional probabilities of membership as follows:

(16.13) $$P(c_1|\vec{y}) = \frac{n_1}{n_1 + n_2} \qquad\qquad P(c_2|\vec{y}) = \frac{n_2}{n_1 + n_2}$$

- Decide c_1 if $P(c_1|\vec{y}) > P(c_2|\vec{y})$, c_2 otherwise.

This version deals with the case where there is a single nearest neighbor (in which case we simply adopt its category) as well as with cases of ties. For the Reuters data, 2310 of the 3299 articles in the test set have one nearest neighbor. The other 989 have 1NN neighborhoods with more than 1 element (the largest neighborhood has 247 articles with identical representation). Also, 697 articles of the 3299 have a nearest neighbor with identical representation. The reason is not that there are that many duplicates in the test set. Rather, this is a consequence of the feature representation which can give identical representations to two different documents.

It should be obvious how this algorithm generalizes for the case $k > 1$: one simply chooses the k nearest neighbors, again with suitable provisions for ties, and decides based on the majority class of these k neighbors. It is often desirable to weight neighbors according to their similarity, so that the nearest neighbor gets more weight than the farthest.

"earnings"	"earnings" correct?	
assigned?	YES	NO
YES	1022	91
NO	65	2121

Table 16.12 Classification results for an 1NN categorizer for the "earnings" category. Classification accuracy is 95.3%.

BAYES ERROR RATE

One can show that for large enough training sets, the error rate of KNN approaches twice the Bayes error rate. The *Bayes error rate* is the optimal error rate that is achieved if the true distribution of the data is known and we use the decision rule "c_1 if $P(c_1|\vec{y}) > P(c_2|\vec{y})$, otherwise c_2" (Duda and Hart 1973: 98).

The results of applying 1NN to the "earnings" category in Reuters are shown in table 16.12. Overall accuracy is 95.3%.

As alluded to above, the main difficulty with KNN is that its performance is very dependent on the right similarity metric. Much work in implementing KNN for a problem often goes into tuning the similarity metric (and to a lesser extent k, the number of nearest neighbors used). Another potential problem is efficiency. Computing similarity with all training exemplars takes more time than computing a linear classification function or determining the appropriate path of a decision tree.

However, there are ways of implementing KNN search efficiently, and often there is an obvious choice for a similarity metric (as in our case). In such cases, KNN is a robust and conceptually simple method that often performs remarkably well.

Exercise 16.18   [⋆]

Two of the classifiers we have introduced in this chapter have a linear decision boundary. Which?

Exercise 16.19   [⋆]

If a classifier's decision boundary is linear, then it cannot achieve perfect accuracy on a problem that is not linearly separable. Does this necessarily mean that it will perform worse on a classification task than a classifier with a more complex decision boundary? Why not? (See Roth (1998) for discussion.)

Exercise 16.20   [⋆ ⋆]

Select one of exercises 16.3 through 16.6 and build a nearest neighbors classifier for the corresponding text categorization task.

16.5 Further Reading

The purpose of this chapter is to give the student interested in classification for NLP some orientation points. A recent in-depth introduction to machine learning is (Mitchell 1997). Comparisons of several learning algorithms applied to text categorization can be found in (Yang 1999), (Lewis et al. 1996), and (Schütze et al. 1995).

The features and the data representation based on the features used in this chapter can be downloaded from the book's website.

Some important classification techniques which we have not covered are: logistic regression and linear discriminant analysis (Schütze et al. 1995); decision lists, where an ordered list of rules that change the classification is learned (Yarowsky 1994); winnow, a mistake-driven online linear threshold learning algorithm (Dagan et al. 1997a); and the Rocchio algorithm (Rocchio 1971; Schapire et al. 1998).

NAIVE BAYES Another important classification technique, *Naive Bayes*, was introduced in section 7.2.1. See (Domingos and Pazzani 1997) for a discussion of its properties, in particular the fact that it often does surprisingly well even when the feature independence assumed by Naive Bayes does not hold.

Other examples of the application of decision trees to NLP tasks are parsing (Magerman 1994) and tagging (Schmid 1994). The idea of using held out training data to train a linear interpolation over all the distributions between a leaf node and the root was used both by Magerman (1994) and earlier work at IBM. Rather than simply using cross-validation to determine an optimal tree size, an alternative is to grow multiple decision trees and then to average the judgements of the individual trees.

BAGGING Such techniques go under names like *bagging* and *boosting*, and have re-
BOOSTING cently been widely explored and found to be quite successful (Breiman 1994; Quinlan 1996). One of the first papers to apply decision trees to text categorization is (Lewis and Ringuette 1994).

MAXIMUM ENTROPY Jelinek (1997: ch. 13-14) provides an in-depth introduction to maxi-
MODELING mum entropy modeling. See also (Lau 1994) and (Ratnaparkhi 1997b). Darroch and Ratcliff (1972) introduced the generalized iterative scaling procedure, and showed its convergence properties. Feature selection algorithms are described by Berger et al. (1996) and Della Pietra et al. (1997).

Maximum entropy modeling has been used for tagging (Ratnaparkhi 1996), text segmentation (Reynar and Ratnaparkhi 1997), prepositional phrase attachment (Ratnaparkhi 1998), sentence boundary detection (Mikheev 1998), determining coreference (Kehler 1997), named entity recognition (Borthwick et al. 1998) and partial parsing (Skut and Brants 1998). Another important application is language modeling for speech recognition (Lau et al. 1993; Rosenfeld 1994, 1996). Iterative proportional fitting, a technique related to generalized iterative scaling, was used by Franz (1996, 1997) to fit loglinear models for tagging and prepositional phrase attachment.

NEURAL NETWORKS   Neural networks or multi-layer perceptrons were one of the statistical techniques that revived interest in Statistical NLP in the eighties based on work by Rumelhart and McClelland (1986) on learning the past tense of English verbs and Elman's (1990) paper "Finding Structure in Time," an attempt to come up with an alternative framework for the conceptualization and acquisition of hierarchical structure in language. Introductions to neural networks and backpropagation are (Rumelhart et al. 1986), (McClelland et al. 1986), and (Hertz et al. 1991). Other neural network research on NLP problems includes tagging (Benello et al. 1989; Schütze 1993), sentence boundary detection (Palmer and Hearst 1997), and parsing (Henderson and Lane 1998). Examples of neural networks used for text categorization are (Wiener et al. 1995) and (Schütze et al. 1995). Mikkulainen (1993) develops a general neural network framework for NLP.

The Perceptron Learning Algorithm in figure 16.7 is adapted from (Littlestone 1995). A proof of the perceptron convergence theorem appears in (Minsky and Papert 1988) and (Duda and Hart 1973: 142).

KNN, or *memory-based learning* as it is sometimes called, has also been applied to a wide range of different NLP problems, including pronunciation (Daelemans and van den Bosch 1996), tagging (Daelemans et al. 1996; van Halteren et al. 1998), prepositional phrase attachment (Zavrel et al. 1997), shallow parsing (Argamon et al. 1998), word sense disambiguation (Ng and Lee 1996) and smoothing of estimates (Zavrel and Daelemans 1997). For KNN-based text categorization see (Yang 1994), (Yang 1995), (Stanfill and Waltz 1986; Masand et al. 1992), and (Hull et al. 1996). Yang (1994, 1995) suggests methods for weighting neighbors according to their similarity. We used cosine as the similarity measure. Other common metrics are Euclidean distance (which is different only if vectors are not normalized, as discussed in section 8.5.1) and the Value Difference Metric (Stanfill and Waltz 1986).

Tiny Statistical Tables

THESE TINY TABLES are not a substitute for a decent statistics text-book or computer software, but they give the key values most commonly needed in Statistical NLP applications.

Standard normal distribution. Entries give the proportion of the area under a standard normal curve from $-\infty$ to z for selected values of z.

z	-3	-2	-1	0	1	2	3
Proportion	0.0013	0.023	0.159	0.5	0.841	0.977	0.9987

(Student's) t test critical values. A t distribution with d.f. degrees of freedom has percentage C of the area under the curve between $-t^*$ and t^* (two-tailed), and proportion p of the area under the curve between t^* and ∞ (one tailed). The values with infinite degrees of freedom are the same as critical values for the z test.

	p	0.05	0.025	0.01	**0.005**	0.001	0.0005
	C	90%	95%	98%	**99%**	99.8%	99.9%
d.f.	1	6.314	12.71	31.82	63.66	318.3	636.6
	10	1.812	2.228	2.764	3.169	4.144	4.587
	20	1.725	2.086	2.528	2.845	3.552	3.850
(z)	∞	1.645	1.960	2.326	**2.576**	3.091	3.291

χ^2 critical values. A table entry is the point χ^{2*} with proportion p of the area under the curve being in the right-hand tail from χ^{2*} to ∞ of a χ^2 curve with d.f. degrees of freedom. (When using an $r \times c$ table, there are $(r-1)(c-1)$ degrees of freedom.)

p	0.99	0.95	0.10	**0.05**	0.01	0.005	0.001
d.f. 1	0.00016	0.0039	2.71	**3.84**	6.63	7.88	10.83
2	0.020	0.10	4.60	5.99	9.21	10.60	13.82
3	0.115	0.35	6.25	7.81	11.34	12.84	16.27
4	0.297	0.71	7.78	9.49	13.28	14.86	18.47
100	70.06	77.93	118.5	124.3	135.8	140.2	149.4

Bibliography

The following conference abbreviations are used in this bibliography:

ACL n Proceedings of the nth Annual Meeting of the Association for Computational Linguistics

ANLP n Proceedings of the nth conference on Applied Natural Language Processing

COLING n Proceedings of the nth International Conference on Computational Linguistics (COLING-*year*)

EACL n Proceedings of the nth Conference of the European Chapter of the Association for Computational Linguistics

EMNLP n Proceedings of the nth Conference on Empirical Methods in Natural Language Processing

WVLC n Proceedings of the nth Workshop on Very Large Corpora

These conference proceedings are all available from the Association for Computational Linguistics, P.O. Box 6090, Somerset NJ 08875, USA, acl@aclweb.org, http://www.aclweb.org.

SIGIR 'y Proceedings of the $(y - 77)^{th}$ Annual International ACM/SIGIR Conference on Research and Development in Information Retrieval. Available from the Association for Computing Machinery, acmhelp@acm.org, http://www.acm.org.

Many papers are also available from the Computation and Language subject area of the Computing Research Repository e-print archive, a part of the xxx.lanl.gov e-print archive on the World Wide Web.

Abney, Steven. 1991. Parsing by chunks. In Robert C. Berwick, Steven P. Abney, and Carol Tenny (eds.), *Principle-Based Parsing*, pp. 257–278. Dordrecht: Kluwer Academic.

Abney, Steven. 1996a. Part-of-speech tagging and partial parsing. In Steve Young and Gerrit Bloothooft (eds.), *Corpus-Based Methods in Language and Speech Processing*, pp. 118–136. Dordrecht: Kluwer Academic.

Abney, Steven. 1996b. Statistical methods and linguistics. In Judith L. Klavans and Philip Resnik (eds.), *The Balancing Act: Combining Symbolic and Statistical Approaches to Language*, pp. 1–26. Cambridge, MA: MIT Press.

Abney, Steven P. 1997. Stochastic attribute-value grammars. *Computational Linguistics* 23:597–618.

Ackley, D. H., G. E. Hinton, and T. J. Sejnowski. 1985. A learning algorithm for Boltzmann machines. *Cognitive Science* 9:147–169.

Aho, Alfred V., Ravi Sethi, and Jeffrey D. Ullman. 1986. *Compilers: Principles, Techniques, and Tools.* Reading, MA: Addison-Wesley.

Allen, James. 1995. *Natural Language Understanding.* Redwood City, CA: Benjamin Cummings.

Alshawi, Hiyan, Adam L. Buchsbaum, and Fei Xia. 1997. A comparison of head transducers and transfer for a limited domain translation application. In *ACL 35/EACL 8*, pp. 360–365.

Alshawi, Hiyan, and David Carter. 1994. Training and scaling preference functions for disambiguation. *Computational Linguistics* 20:635–648.

Anderson, John R. 1983. *The architecture of cognition.* Cambridge, MA: Harvard University Press.

Anderson, John R. 1990. *The adaptive character of thought.* Hillsdale, NJ: Lawrence Erlbaum.

Aone, Chinatsu, and Douglas McKee. 1995. Acquiring predicate-argument mapping information from multilingual texts. In Branimir Boguraev and James Pustejovsky (eds.), *Corpus Processing for Lexical Acquisition*, pp. 175–190. Cambridge, MA: MIT Press.

Appelt, D. E., J. R. Hobbs, J. Bear, D. Israel, and M. Tyson. 1993. Fastus: A finite-state processor for information extraction from real-world text. In *Proc. of the 13th IJCAI*, pp. 1172–1178, Chambéry, France.

Apresjan, Jurij D. 1974. Regular polysemy. *Linguistics* 142:5–32.

Apté, Chidanand, Fred Damerau, and Sholom M. Weiss. 1994. Automated learning of decision rules for text categorization. *ACM Transactions on Information Systems* 12:233–251.

Argamon, Shlomo, Ido Dagan, and Yuval Krymolowski. 1998. A memory-based approach to learning shallow natural language patterns. In *ACL 36/COLING 17*, pp. 67–73.

Atwell, Eric. 1987. Constituent-likelihood grammar. In Roger Garside, Geoffrey Leech, and Geoffrey Sampson (eds.), *The Computational Analysis of English: A Corpus-Based Approach*. London: Longman.

Baayen, Harald, and Richard Sproat. 1996. Estimating lexical priors for low-frequency morphologically ambiguous forms. *Computational Linguistics* 22: 155-166.

Bahl, Lalit R., Frederick Jelinek, and Robert L. Mercer. 1983. A maximum likelihood approach to continuous speech recognition. *IEEE Transactions on Pattern Analysis and Machine Intelligence* PAMI-5:179-190. Reprinted in (Waibel and Lee 1990), pp. 308-319.

Bahl, Lalit R., and Robert L. Mercer. 1976. Part-of-speech assignment by a statistical decision algorithm. In *International Symposium on Information Theory*, Ronneby, Sweden.

Baker, James K. 1975. Stochastic modeling for automatic speech understanding. In D. Raj Reddy (ed.), *Speech Recognition: Invited papers presented at the 1974 IEEE symposium*, pp. 521-541. New York: Academic Press. Reprinted in (Waibel and Lee 1990), pp. 297-307.

Baker, James K. 1979. Trainable grammars for speech recognition. In D. H. Klatt and J. J. Wolf (eds.), *Speech Communication Papers for the 97th Meeting of the Acoustical Society of America*, pp. 547-550.

Baldi, Pierre, and Søren Brunak. 1998. *Bioinformatics: The Machine Learning Approach*. Cambridge, MA: MIT Press.

Barnbrook, Geoff. 1996. *Language and computers: a practical introduction to the computer analysis of language*. Edinburgh: Edinburgh University Press.

Basili, Roberto, Maria Teresa Pazienza, and Paola Velardi. 1996. Integrating general-purpose and corpus-based verb classification. *Computational Linguistics* 22:559-568.

Basili, Roberto, Gianluca De Rossi, and Maria Teresa Pazienza. 1997. Inducing terminology for lexical acquisition. In *EMNLP 2*, pp. 125-133.

Baum, L. E., T. Petrie, G. Soules, and N. Weiss. 1970. A maximization technique occurring in the statistical analysis of probabilistic functions of Markov chains. *Annals of Mathematical Statistics* 41:164-171.

Beeferman, Doug, Adam Berger, and John Lafferty. 1997. Text segmentation using exponential models. In *EMNLP 2*, pp. 35-46.

Bell, Timothy C., John G. Cleary, and Ian H. Witten. 1990. *Text Compression*. Englewood Cliffs, NJ: Prentice Hall.

Benello, Julian, Andrew W. Mackie, and James A. Anderson. 1989. Syntactic category disambiguation with neural networks. *Computer Speech and Language* 3:203-217.

Benson, Morton. 1989. The structure of the collocational dictionary. *International Journal of Lexicography* 2:1-14.

Benson, Morton, Evelyn Benson, and Robert Ilson. 1993. *The BBI combinatory dictionary of English*. Amsterdam: John Benjamins.

Berber Sardinha, A. P. 1997. *Automatic Identification of Segments in Written Texts*. PhD thesis, University of Liverpool.

Berger, Adam L., Stephen A. Della Pietra, and Vincent J. Della Pietra. 1996. A maximum entropy approach to natural language processing. *Computational Linguistics* 22:39-71.

Berry, Michael W. 1992. Large-scale sparse singular value computations. *The International Journal of Supercomputer Applications* 6:13-49.

Berry, Michael W., Susan T. Dumais, and Gavin W. O'Brien. 1995. Using linear algebra for intelligent information retrieval. *SIAM Review* 37:573-595.

Berry, Michael W., and Paul G. Young. 1995. Using latent semantic indexing for multilanguage information retrieval. *Computers and the Humanities* 29: 413-429.

Bever, Thomas G. 1970. The cognitive basis for linguistic structures. In J. R. Hayes (ed.), *Cognition and the development of language*. New York: Wiley.

Biber, Douglas. 1993. Representativeness in corpus design. *Literary and Linguistic Computing* 8:243-257.

Biber, Douglas, Susan Conrad, and Randi Reppen. 1998. *Corpus Linguistics: Investigating Language Structure and Use*. Cambridge: Cambridge University Press.

Black, Ezra. 1988. An experiment in computational discrimination of English word senses. *IBM Journal of Research and Development* 32:185-194.

Black, E., S. Abney, D. Flickinger, C. Gdaniec, R. Grishman, P. Harrison, D. Hindle, R. Ingria, F. Jelinek, J. Klavans, M. Liberman, M. Marcus, S. Roukos, B. Santorini, and T. Strzalkowski. 1991. A procedure for quantitatively comparing the syntactic coverage of English grammars. In *Proceedings, Speech and Natural Language Workshop*, pp. 306-311, Pacific Grove, CA. DARPA.

Black, Ezra, Fred Jelinek, John Lafferty, David M. Magerman, Robert Mercer, and Salim Roukos. 1993. Towards history-based grammars: Using richer models for probabilistic parsing. In *ACL 31*, pp. 31-37. Also appears in the Proceedings of the DARPA Speech and Natural Language Workshop, Feb. 1992, pp. 134-139.

Bod, Rens. 1995. *Enriching Linguistics with Statistics: Performance Models of Natural Language*. PhD thesis, University of Amsterdam.

Bod, Rens. 1996. Data-oriented language processing: An overview. Technical Report LP-96-13, Institute for Logic, Language and Computation, University of Amsterdam.

Bod, Rens. 1998. *Beyond Grammar: An experience-based theory of language.* Stanford, CA: CSLI Publications.

Bod, Rens, and Ronald Kaplan. 1998. A probabilistic corpus-driven model for lexical-functional analysis. In *ACL 36/COLING 17*, pp. 145–151.

Bod, Rens, Ron Kaplan, Remko Scha, and Khalil Sima'an. 1996. A data-oriented approach to lexical-functional grammar. In *Computational Linguistics in the Netherlands 1996*, Eindhoven, The Netherlands.

Boguraev, Bran, and Ted Briscoe. 1989. *Computational Lexicography for Natural Language Processing.* London: Longman.

Boguraev, Branimir, and James Pustejovsky. 1995. Issues in text-based lexicon acquisition. In Branimir Boguraev and James Pustejovsky (eds.), *Corpus Processing for Lexical Acquisition*, pp. 3–17. Cambridge MA: MIT Press.

Boguraev, Branimir K. 1993. The contribution of computational lexicography. In Madeleine Bates and Ralph M. Weischedel (eds.), *Challenges in natural language processing*, pp. 99–132. Cambridge: Cambridge University Press.

Bonnema, R. 1996. Data-oriented semantics. Master's thesis, Department of Computational Linguistics, University of Amsterdam.

Bonnema, Remko, Rens Bod, and Remko Scha. 1997. A DOP model for semantic interpretation. In *ACL 35/EACL 8*, pp. 159–167.

Bonzi, Susan, and Elizabeth D. Liddy. 1988. The use of anaphoric resolution for document description in information retrieval. In *SIGIR '88*, pp. 53–66.

Bookstein, Abraham, and Don R. Swanson. 1975. A decision theoretic foundation for indexing. *Journal of the American Society for Information Science* 26:45–50.

Booth, Taylor L. 1969. Probabilistic representation of formal languages. In *Tenth Annual IEEE Symposium on Switching and Automata Theory*, pp. 74–81.

Booth, Taylor L., and Richard A. Thomson. 1973. Applying probability measures to abstract languages. *IEEE Transactions on Computers* C-22:442–450.

Borthwick, Andrew, John Sterling, Eugene Agichtein, and Ralph Grishman. 1998. Exploiting diverse knowledge sources via maximum entropy in named entity recognition. In *WVLC 6*, pp. 152–160.

Bourigault, Didier. 1993. An endogeneous corpus-based method for structural noun phrase disambiguation. In *EACL 6*, pp. 81–86.

Box, George E. P., and George C. Tiao. 1973. *Bayesian Inference in Statistical Analysis.* Reading, MA: Addison-Wesley.

Brants, Thorsten. 1998. Estimating Hidden Markov Model Topologies. In Jonathan Ginzburg, Zurab Khasidashvili, Carl Vogel, Jean-Jacques Lévy, and Enric Vallduví (eds.), *The Tbilisi Symposium on Logic, Language and Computation: Selected Papers*, pp. 163–176. Stanford, CA: CSLI Publications.

Brants, Thorsten, and Wojciech Skut. 1998. Automation of treebank annotation. In *Proceedings of NeMLaP-98*, Sydney, Australia.

Breiman, Leo. 1994. Bagging predictors. Technical Report 421, Department of Statistics, University of California at Berkeley.

Breiman, L., J. H. Friedman, R. A. Olshen, and C. J. Stone. 1984. *Classification and Regression Trees*. Belmont, CA: Wadsworth International Group.

Brent, Michael R. 1993. From grammar to lexicon: Unsupervised learning of lexical syntax. *Computational Linguistics* 19:243–262.

Brew, Chris. 1995. Stochastic HPSG. In *EACL 7*, pp. 83–89.

Brill, Eric. 1993a. Automatic grammar induction and parsing free text: A transformation-based approach. In *ACL 31*, pp. 259–265.

Brill, Eric. 1993b. *A Corpus-Based Approach to Language Learning*. PhD thesis, University of Pennsylvania.

Brill, Eric. 1993c. Transformation-based error-driven parsing. In *Proceedings Third International Workshop on Parsing Technologies*, Tilburg/Durbuy, The Netherlands/Belgium.

Brill, Eric. 1995a. Transformation-based error-driven learning and natural language processing: A case study in part-of-speech tagging. *Computational Linguistics* 21:543–565.

Brill, Eric. 1995b. Unsupervised learning of disambiguation rules for part of speech tagging. In *WVLC 3*, pp. 1–13.

Brill, Eric, David Magerman, Mitch Marcus, and Beatrice Santorini. 1990. Deducing linguistic structure from the statistics of large corpora. In *Proceedings of the DARPA Speech and Natural Language Workshop*, pp. 275–282, San Mateo CA. Morgan Kaufmann.

Brill, Eric, and Philip Resnik. 1994. A transformation-based approach to prepositional phrase attachment disambiguation. In *COLING 15*, pp. 1198–1204.

Briscoe, Ted, and John Carroll. 1993. Generalized probabilistic LR parsing of natural language (corpora) with unification-based methods. *Computational Linguistics* 19:25–59.

Britton, J. L. (ed.). 1992. *Collected Works of A. M. Turing: Pure Mathematics*. Amsterdam: North-Holland.

Brown, Peter F., John Cocke, Stephen A. Della Pietra, Vincent J. Della Pietra, Fredrick Jelinek, John D. Lafferty, Robert L. Mercer, and Paul S. Roossin. 1990. A statistical approach to machine translation. *Computational Linguistics* 16: 79–85.

Brown, Peter F., Stephen A. Della Pietra, Vincent J. Della Pietra, John D. Lafferty, and Robert L. Mercer. 1992a. Analysis, statistical transfer, and synthesis in machine translation. In *Proceedings of the 4th International Conference on Theoretical and Methodological Issues in Machine Translation*, pp. 83–100.

Brown, Peter F., Stephen A. Della Pietra, Vincent J. Della Pietra, Jennifer C. Lai, and Robert L. Mercer. 1992b. An estimate of an upper bound for the entropy of English. *Computational Linguistics* 18:31–40.

Brown, Peter F., Stephen A. Della Pietra, Vincent J. Della Pietra, and Robert L. Mercer. 1991a. A statistical approach to sense disambiguation in machine translation. In *Proceedings of the DARPA Workshop on Speech and Natural Language Workshop*, pp. 146–151.

Brown, Peter F., Stephen A. Della Pietra, Vincent J. Della Pietra, and Robert L. Mercer. 1991b. Word-sense disambiguation using statistical methods. In *ACL 29*, pp. 264–270.

Brown, Peter F., Stephen A. Della Pietra, Vincent J. Della Pietra, and Robert L. Mercer. 1993. The mathematics of statistical machine translation: Parameter estimation. *Computational Linguistics* 19:263–311.

Brown, Peter F., Vincent J. Della Pietra, Peter V. deSouza, Jenifer C. Lai, and Robert L. Mercer. 1992c. Class-based *n*-gram models of natural language. *Computational Linguistics* 18:467–479.

Brown, Peter F., Jennifer C. Lai, and Robert L. Mercer. 1991c. Aligning sentences in parallel corpora. In *ACL 29*, pp. 169–176.

Bruce, Rebecca, and Janyce Wiebe. 1994. Word-sense disambiguation using decomposable models. In *ACL 32*, pp. 139–145.

Bruce, Rebecca F., and Janyce M. Wiebe. 1999. Decomposable modeling in natural language processing. *Computational Linguistics*. to appear.

Brundage, Jennifer, Maren Kresse, Ulrike Schwall, and Angelika Storrer. 1992. Multiword lexemes: A monolingual and contrastive typology for natural language processing and machine translation. Technical Report 232, Institut fuer Wissensbasierte Systeme, IBM Deutschland GmbH, Heidelberg.

Buckley, Chris, Amit Singhal, Mandar Mitra, and Gerard Salton. 1996. New retrieval approaches using SMART: TREC 4. In D. K. Harman (ed.), *The Second Text REtrieval Conference (TREC-2)*, pp. 25–48.

Buitelaar, Paul. 1998. *CoreLex: Systematic Polysemy and Underspecification*. PhD thesis, Brandeis University.

Burgess, Curt, and Kevin Lund. 1997. Modelling parsing constraints with high-dimensional context space. *Language and Cognitive Processes* 12:177–210.

Burke, Robin, Kristian Hammond, Vladimir Kulyukin, Steven Lytinen, Noriko Tomuro, and Scott Schoenberg. 1997. Question answering from frequently asked question files. *AI Magazine* 18:57–66.

Caraballo, Sharon A., and Eugene Charniak. 1998. New figures of merit for best-first probabilistic chart parsing. *Computational Linguistics* 24:275–298.

Cardie, Claire. 1997. Empirical methods in information extraction. *AI Magazine* 18:65–79.

Carletta, Jean. 1996. Assessing agreement on classification tasks: The kappa statistic. *Computational Linguistics* 22:249–254.

Carrasco, Rafael C., and Jose Oncina (eds.). 1994. *Grammatical inference and applications: second international colloquium, ICGI-94*. Berlin: Springer-Verlag.

Carroll, G., and E. Charniak. 1992. Two experiments on learning probabilistic dependency grammars from corpora. In Carl Weir, Stephen Abney, Ralph Grishman, and Ralph Weischedel (eds.), *Working Notes of the Workshop Statistically-Based NLP Techniques*, pp. 1–13. Menlo Park, CA: AAAI Press.

Carroll, John. 1994. Relating complexity to practical performance in parsing with wide-coverage unification grammars. In *ACL 32*, pp. 287–294.

Chang, Jason S., and Mathis H. Chen. 1997. An alignment method for noisy parallel corpora based on image processing techniques. In *ACL 35/EACL 8*, pp. 297–304.

Chanod, Jean-Pierre, and Pasi Tapanainen. 1995. Tagging French – comparing a statistical and a constraint-based method. In *EACL 7*, pp. 149–156.

Charniak, Eugene. 1993. *Statistical Language Learning*. Cambridge, MA: MIT Press.

Charniak, Eugene. 1996. Tree-bank grammars. In *Proceedings of the Thirteenth National Conference on Artificial Intelligence (AAAI '96)*, pp. 1031–1036.

Charniak, Eugene. 1997a. Statistical parsing with a context-free grammar and word statistics. In *Proceedings of the Fourteenth National Conference on Artificial Intelligence (AAAI '97)*, pp. 598–603.

Charniak, Eugene. 1997b. Statistical techniques for natural language parsing. *AI Magazine* pp. 33–43.

Charniak, Eugene, Curtis Hendrickson, Neil Jacobson, and Mike Perkowitz. 1993. Equations for part-of-speech tagging. In *Proceedings of the Eleventh National Conference on Artificial Intelligence*, pp. 784–789, Menlo Park, CA.

Cheeseman, Peter, James Kelly, Matthew Self, John Stutz, Will Taylor, and Don Freeman. 1988. AutoClass: A Bayesian classification system. In *Proceedings of the Fifth International Conference on Machine Learning*, pp. 54-64, San Francisco, CA. Morgan Kaufmann.

Chelba, Ciprian, and Frederick Jelinek. 1998. Exploiting syntactic structure for language modeling. In *ACL 36/COLING 17*, pp. 225-231.

Chen, Jen Nan, and Jason S. Chang. 1998. Topical clustering of MRD senses based on information retrieval techniques. *Computational Linguistics* 24:61-95.

Chen, Stanley F. 1993. Aligning sentences in bilingual corpora using lexical information. In *ACL 31*, pp. 9-16.

Chen, Stanley F. 1995. Bayesian grammar induction for language modeling. In *ACL 33*, pp. 228-235.

Chen, Stanley F., and Joshua Goodman. 1996. An empirical study of smoothing techniques for language modeling. In *ACL 34*, pp. 310-318.

Chen, Stanley F., and Joshua Goodman. 1998. An empirical study of smoothing techniques for language modeling. Technical Report TR-10-98, Center for Research in Computing Technology, Harvard University.

Chi, Zhiyi, and Stuart Geman. 1998. Estimation of probabilistic context-free grammars. *Computational linguistics* 24:299-305.

Chitrao, Mahesh V., and Ralph Grishman. 1990. Statistical parsing of messages. In *Proceedings of the DARPA Speech and Natural Language Workshop, Hidden Valley, PA*, pp. 263-266. Morgan Kaufmann.

Chomsky, Noam. 1957. *Syntactic Structures*. The Hague: Mouton.

Chomsky, Noam. 1965. *Aspects of the Theory of Syntax*. Cambridge, MA: MIT Press.

Chomsky, Noam. 1980. *Rules and Representations*. New York: Columbia University Press.

Chomsky, Noam. 1986. *Knowledge of Language: Its Nature, Origin, and Use*. New York: Prager.

Chomsky, Noam. 1995. *The Minimalist Program*. Cambridge, MA: MIT Press.

Choueka, Yaacov. 1988. Looking for needles in a haystack or locating interesting collocational expressions in large textual databases. In *Proceedings of the RIAO*, pp. 43-38.

Choueka, Yaacov, and Serge Lusignan. 1985. Disambiguation by short contexts. *Computers and the Humanities* 19:147-158.

Church, Kenneth, William Gale, Patrick Hanks, and Donald Hindle. 1991. Using statistics in lexical analysis. In Uri Zernik (ed.), *Lexical Acquisition: Exploiting On-Line Resources to Build a Lexicon*, pp. 115-164. Hillsdale, NJ: Lawrence Erlbaum.

Church, Kenneth, and Ramesh Patil. 1982. Coping with syntactic ambiguity or how to put the block in the box on the table. *Computational Linguistics* 8: 139-149.

Church, Kenneth W. 1988. A stochastic parts program and noun phrase parser for unrestricted text. In *ANLP 2*, pp. 136-143.

Church, Kenneth Ward. 1993. Char_align: A program for aligning parallel texts at the character level. In *ACL 31*, pp. 1-8.

Church, Kenneth Ward. 1995. One term or two? In *SIGIR '95*, pp. 310-318.

Church, Kenneth W., and William A. Gale. 1991a. A comparison of the enhanced Good-Turing and deleted estimation methods for estimating probabilities of English bigrams. *Computer Speech and Language* 5:19-54.

Church, Kenneth W., and William A. Gale. 1991b. Concordances for parallel text. In *Proceedings of the Seventh Annual Conference of the UW Centre for the New OED and Text Research*, pp. 40-62, Oxford.

Church, Kenneth W., and William A. Gale. 1995. Poisson mixtures. *Natural Language Engineering* 1:163-190.

Church, Kenneth Ward, and Patrick Hanks. 1989. Word association norms, mutual information and lexicography. In *ACL 27*, pp. 76-83.

Church, Kenneth Ward, and Mark Y. Liberman. 1991. A status report on the ACL/DCI. In *Proceedings of the 7th Annual Conference of the UW Centre for New OED and Text Research: Using Corpora*, pp. 84-91.

Church, Kenneth W., and Robert L. Mercer. 1993. Introduction to the special issue on computational linguistics using large corpora. *Computational Linguistics* 19:1-24.

Clark, Eve, and Herbert Clark. 1979. When nouns surface as verbs. *Language* 55: 767-811.

Cleverdon, Cyril W., and J. Mills. 1963. The testing of index language devices. *Aslib Proceedings* 15:106-130. Reprinted in (Sparck Jones and Willett 1998).

Coates-Stephens, Sam. 1993. The analysis and acquisition of proper names for the understanding of free text. *Computers and the Humanities* 26:441-456.

Collins, Michael John. 1996. A new statistical parser based on bigram lexical dependencies. In *ACL 34*, pp. 184-191.

Collins, Michael John. 1997. Three generative, lexicalised models for statistical parsing. In *ACL 35/EACL 8*, pp. 16-23.

Collins, Michael John, and James Brooks. 1995. Prepositional phrase attachment through a backed-off model. In *WVLC 3*, pp. 27-38.

Copestake, Ann, and Ted Briscoe. 1995. Semi-productive polysemy and sense extension. *Journal of Semantics* 12:15-68.

Cormen, Thomas H., Charles E. Leiserson, and Ronald L. Rivest. 1990. *Introduction to Algorithms*. Cambridge, MA: MIT Press.

Cottrell, Garrison W. 1989. *A Connectionist Approach to Word Sense Disambiguation*. London: Pitman.

Cover, Thomas M., and Joy A. Thomas. 1991. *Elements of Information Theory*. New York: John Wiley & Sons.

Cowart, Wayne. 1997. *Experimental syntax: Applying objective methods to sentence judgments*. Thousand Oaks, CA: Sage Publications.

Croft, W. B., and D. J. Harper. 1979. Using probabilistic models of document retrieval without relevance information. *Journal of Documentation* 35:285–295.

Crowley, Terry, John Lynch, Jeff Siegel, and Julie Piau. 1995. *The Design of Language: An introduction to descriptive linguistics*. Auckland: Longman Paul.

Crystal, David. 1987. *The Cambridge Encyclopedia of Language*. Cambridge, England: Cambridge University Press.

Cutting, Doug, Julian Kupiec, Jan Pedersen, and Penelope Sibun. 1991. A practical part-of-speech tagger. In *ANLP 3*, pp. 133–140.

Cutting, Douglas R., David R. Karger, and Jan O. Pedersen. 1993. Constant interaction-time scatter/gather browsing of very large document collections. In *SIGIR '93*, pp. 126–134.

Cutting, Douglas R., Jan O. Pedersen, David Karger, and John W. Tukey. 1992. Scatter/gather: A cluster-based approach to browsing large document collections. In *SIGIR '92*, pp. 318–329.

Daelemans, Walter, and Antal van den Bosch. 1996. Language-independent data-oriented grapheme-to-phoneme conversion. In J. Van Santen, R. Sproat, J. Olive, and J. Hirschberg (eds.), *Progress in Speech Synthesis*, pp. 77–90. New York: Springer Verlag.

Daelemans, Walter, Jakub Zavrel, Peter Berck, and Steven Gillis. 1996. MBT: A memory-based part of speech tagger generator. In *WVLC 4*, pp. 14–27.

Dagan, Ido, Kenneth Church, and William Gale. 1993. Robust bilingual word alignment for machine aided translation. In *WVLC 1*, pp. 1–8.

Dagan, Ido, and Alon Itai. 1994. Word sense disambiguation using a second language monolingual corpus. *Computational Linguistics* 20:563–596.

Dagan, Ido, Alon Itai, and Ulrike Schwall. 1991. Two languages are more informative than one. In *ACL 29*, pp. 130–137.

Dagan, Ido, Yael Karov, and Dan Roth. 1997a. Mistake-driven learning in text categorization. In *EMNLP 2*, pp. 55–63.

Dagan, Ido, Lillian Lee, and Fernando Pereira. 1997b. Similarity-based methods for word sense disambiguation. In *ACL 35/EACL 8*, pp. 56–63.

Dagan, Ido, Fernando Pereira, and Lillian Lee. 1994. Similarity-based estimation of word cooccurrence probabilities. In *ACL 32*, pp. 272–278.

Damerau, Fred J. 1993. Generating and evaluating domain-oriented multi-word terms from texts. *Information Processing & Management* 29:433–447.

Darroch, J. N., and D. Ratcliff. 1972. Generalized iterative scaling for log-linear models. *The Annals of Mathematical Statistics* 43:1470–1480.

de Saussure, Ferdinand. 1962. *Cours de linguistique générale*. Paris: Payot.

Deerwester, Scott, Susan T. Dumais, George W. Furnas, Thomas K. Landauer, and Richard Harshman. 1990. Indexing by latent semantic analysis. *Journal of the American Society for Information Science* 41:391–407.

DeGroot, Morris H. 1975. *Probability and Statistics*. Reading, MA: Addison-Wesley.

Della Pietra, Stephen, Vincent Della Pietra, and John Lafferty. 1997. Inducing features of random fields. *IEEE Transactions on Pattern Analysis and Machine Intelligence* 19.

Demers, A.J. 1977. Generalized left corner parsing. In *Proceedings of the Fourth Annual ACM Symposium on Principles of Programming Languages*, pp. 170–181.

Dempster, A.P., N.M. Laird, and D.B. Rubin. 1977. Maximum likelihood from incomplete data via the EM algorithm. *J. Royal Statistical Society Series B* 39: 1–38.

Dermatas, Evangelos, and George Kokkinakis. 1995. Automatic stochastic tagging of natural language texts. *Computational Linguistics* 21:137–164.

DeRose, Steven J. 1988. Grammatical category disambiguation by statistical optimization. *Computational Linguistics* 14:31–39.

Derouault, Anne-Marie, and Bernard Merialdo. 1986. Natural language modeling for phoneme-to-text transcription. *IEEE Transactions on Pattern Analysis and Machine Intelligence* 8:742–649.

Dietterich, Thomas G. 1998. Approximate statistical tests for comparing supervised classification learning algorithms. *Neural Computation* 10:1895–1924.

Dini, Luca, Vittorio Di Tomaso, and Frédérique Segond. 1998. Error-driven word sense disambiguation. In *ACL 36/COLING 17*, pp. 320–324.

Dolan, William B. 1994. Word sense ambiguation: Clustering related senses. In *COLING 15*, pp. 712–716.

Dolin, Ron. 1998. *Pharos: A Scalable Distributed Architecture for Locating Heterogeneous Information Sources*. PhD thesis, University of California at Santa Barbara.

Domingos, Pedro, and Michael Pazzani. 1997. On the optimality of the simple Bayesian classifier under zero-one loss. *Machine Learning* 29:103–130.

Doran, Christy, Dania Egedi, Beth Ann Hockey, B. Srinivas, and Martin Zaidel. 1994. XTAG system – a wide coverage grammar for English. In *COLING 15*, pp. 922–928.

Dorr, Bonnie J., and Mari Broman Olsen. 1997. Deriving verbal and compositional lexical aspect for nlp applications. In *ACL 35/EACL 8*, pp. 151–158.

Dras, Mark, and Mike Johnson. 1996. Death and lightness: Using a demographic model to find support verbs. In *Proceedings of the 5th International Conference on the Cognitive Science of Natural Language Processing*, Dublin.

Duda, Richard O., and Peter E. Hart. 1973. *Pattern classification and scene analysis*. New York: Wiley.

Dumais, Susan T. 1995. Latent semantic indexing (LSI): TREC-3 report. In *The Third Text REtrieval Conference (TREC 3)*, pp. 219–230.

Dunning, Ted. 1993. Accurate methods for the statistics of surprise and coincidence. *Computational Linguistics* 19:61–74.

Dunning, Ted. 1994. Statistical identification of language. Technical report, Computing Research Laboratory, New Mexico State University.

Durbin, Richard, Sean Eddy, Anders Krogh, and Graeme Mitchison. 1998. *Biological sequence analysis: probabilistic models of proteins and nucleic acids*. Cambridge: Cambridge University Press.

Eeg-Olofsson, Mats. 1985. A probability model for computer-aided word class determination. *Literary and Linguistic Computing* 5:25–30.

Egan, Dennis E., Joel R. Remde, Louis M. Gomez, Thomas K. Landauer, Jennifer Eberhardt, and Carol C. Lochbaum. 1989. Formative design-evaluation of superbook. *ACM Transactions on Information Systems* 7:30–57.

Eisner, Jason. 1996. Three new probabilistic models for dependency parsing: An exploration. In *COLING 16*, pp. 340–345.

Ellis, C. A. 1969. *Probabilistic Languages and Automata*. PhD thesis, University of Illinois. Report No. 355, Department of Computer Science.

Elman, Jeffrey L. 1990. Finding structure in time. *Cognitive Science* 14:179–211.

Elworthy, David. 1994. Does Baum-Welch re-estimation help taggers? In *ANLP 4*, pp. 53–58.

Estoup, J. B. 1916. *Gammes Sténographiques*, 4th edition. Paris.

Evans, David A., Kimberly Ginther-Webster, Mary Hart, Robert G. Lefferts, and Ira A. Monarch. 1991. Automatic indexing using selective NLP and first-order thesauri. In *Proceedings of the RIAO*, volume 2, pp. 624–643.

Evans, David A., and Chengxiang Zhai. 1996. Noun-phrase analysis in unrestricted text for information retrieval. In *ACL 34*, pp. 17–24.

Fagan, Joel L. 1987. Automatic phrase indexing for document retrieval: An examination of syntactic and non-syntactic methods. In *SIGIR '87*, pp. 91–101.

Fagan, Joel L. 1989. The effectiveness of a nonsyntactic approach to automatic phrase indexing for document retrieval. *Journal of the American Society for Information Science* 40:115–132.

Fano, Robert M. 1961. *Transmission of information; a statistical theory of communications.* New York: MIT Press.

Fillmore, Charles J., and B. T. S. Atkins. 1994. Starting where the dictionaries stop: The challenge of corpus lexicography. In B.T.S. Atkins and A. Zampolli (eds.), *Computational Approaches to the Lexicon*, pp. 349–393. Oxford: Oxford University Press.

Finch, Steven, and Nick Chater. 1994. Distributional bootstrapping: From word class to proto-sentence. In *Proceedings of the Sixteenth Annual Conference of the Cognitive Science Society*, pp. 301–306, Hillsdale, NJ. Lawrence Erlbaum.

Finch, Steven Paul. 1993. *Finding Structure in Language.* PhD thesis, University of Edinburgh.

Firth, J. R. 1957. A synopsis of linguistic theory 1930–1955. In *Studies in Linguistic Analysis*, pp. 1–32. Oxford: Philological Society. Reprinted in F. R. Palmer (ed), *Selected Papers of J. R. Firth 1952–1959*, London: Longman, 1968.

Fisher; R. A. 1922. On the mathematical foundations of theoretical statistics. *Philosophical Transactions of the Royal Society* 222:309–368.

Fontenelle, Thierry, Walter Brüls, Luc Thomas, Tom Vanallemeersch, and Jacques Jansen. 1994. DECIDE, MLAP-Project 93-19, deliverable D-1a: survey of collocation extraction tools. Technical report, University of Liege, Liege, Belgium.

Ford, Marilyn, Joan Bresnan, and Ronald M. Kaplan. 1982. A competence-based theory of syntactic closure. In Joan Bresnan (ed.), *The Mental Representation of Grammatical Relations*, pp. 727–796. Cambridge, MA: MIT Press.

Foster, G. F. 1991. Statistical lexical disambiguation. Master's thesis, School of Computer Science, McGill University.

Frakes, William B., and Ricardo Baeza-Yates (eds.). 1992. *Information Retrieval.* Englewood Cliffs, NJ: Prentice Hall.

Francis, W. Nelson, and Henry Kučera. 1964. *Manual of information to accompany a standard corpus of present-day edited American English, for use with digital computers.* Providence, RI: Dept of Linguistics, Brown University.

Francis, W. Nelson, and Henry Kučera. 1982. *Frequency Analysis of English Usage: Lexicon and Grammar.* Boston, MA: Houghton Mifflin.

Franz, Alexander. 1996. *Automatic Ambiguity Resolution in Natural Language Processing,* volume 1171 of *Lecture Notes in Artificial Intelligence.* Berlin: Springer Verlag.

Franz, Alexander. 1997. Independence assumptions considered harmful. In *ACL 35/EACL 8,* pp. 182–189.

Franz, Alexander Mark. 1995. *A Statistical Approach to Syntactic Ambiguity Resolution.* PhD thesis, CMU.

Frazier, Lyn. 1978. *On Comprehending Sentences: Syntactic Parsing Strategies.* PhD thesis, University of Connecticut.

Freedman, David, Robert Pisani, and Roger Purves. 1998. *Statistics.* New York: W. W. Norton. 3rd ed.

Friedl, Jeffrey E. F. 1997. *Mastering Regular Expressions.* Sebastopol, CA: O'Reilly & Associates.

Fu, King-Sun. 1974. *Syntactic Methods in Pattern Recognition.* London: Academic Press.

Fung, Pascale, and Kenneth W. Church. 1994. K-vec: A new approach for aligning parallel texts. In *COLING 15,* pp. 1096–1102.

Fung, Pascale, and Kathleen McKeown. 1994. Aligning noisy parallel corpora across language groups: Word pair feature matching by dynamic time warping. In *Proceedings of the Association for Machine Translation in the Americas (AMTA-94),* pp. 81–88.

Gale, William A., and Kenneth W. Church. 1990a. Estimation procedures for language context: Poor estimates of context are worse than none. In *Proceedings in Computational Statistics (COMPSTAT 9),* pp. 69–74.

Gale, William A., and Kenneth W. Church. 1990b. Poor estimates of context are worse than none. In *Proceedings of the June 1990 DARPA Speech and Natural Language Workshop,* pp. 283–287, Hidden Valley, PA.

Gale, William A., and Kenneth W. Church. 1991. A program for aligning sentences in bilingual corpora. In *ACL 29,* pp. 177–184.

Gale, William A., and Kenneth W. Church. 1993. A program for aligning sentences in bilingual corpora. *Computational Linguistics* 19:75–102.

Gale, William A., and Kenneth W. Church. 1994. What's wrong with adding one? In Nelleke Oostdijk and Pieter de Haan (eds.), *Corpus-Based Research into Language: in honour of Jan Aarts.* Amsterdam: Rodopi.

Gale, William A., Kenneth W. Church, and David Yarowsky. 1992a. Estimating upper and lower bounds on the performance of word-sense disambiguation programs. In *ACL 30,* pp. 249–256.

Gale, William A., Kenneth W. Church, and David Yarowsky. 1992b. A method for disambiguating word senses in a large corpus. *Computers and the Humanities* 26:415–439.

Gale, William A., Kenneth W. Church, and David Yarowsky. 1992c. A method for disambiguating word senses in a large corpus. Technical report, AT&T Bell Laboratories, Murray Hill, NJ.

Gale, William A., Kenneth W. Church, and David Yarowsky. 1992d. Using bilingual materials to develop word sense disambiguation methods. In *Proceedings of the 4th International Conference on Theoretical and Methodological Issues in Machine Translation (TMI-92)*, pp. 101–112.

Gale, William A., Kenneth W. Church, and David Yarowsky. 1992e. Work on statistical methods for word sense disambiguation. In Robert Goldman, Peter Norvig, Eugene Charniak, and Bill Gale (eds.), *Working Notes of the AAAI Fall Symposium on Probabilistic Approaches to Natural Language*, pp. 54–60, Menlo Park, CA. AAAI Press.

Gale, William A., and Geoffrey Sampson. 1995. Good-Turing frequency estimation without tears. *Journal of Quantitative Linguistics* 2:217–237.

Gallager, Robert G. 1968. *Information theory and reliable communication.* New York: Wiley.

Garside, Roger. 1995. Grammatical tagging of the spoken part of the British National Corpus: a progress report. In Geoffrey N. Leech, Greg Myers, and Jenny Thomas (eds.), *Spoken English on computer: transcription, mark-up, and application.* Harlow, Essex: Longman.

Garside, Roger, and Fanny Leech. 1987. The UCREL probabilistic parsing system. In Roger Garside, Geoffrey Leech, and Geoffrey Sampson (eds.), *The Computational Analysis of English: A Corpus-Based Approach*, pp. 66–81. London: Longman.

Garside, Roger, Geoffrey Sampson, and Geoffrey Leech (eds.). 1987. *The Computational analysis of English: a corpus-based approach.* London: Longman.

Gaussier, Éric. 1998. Flow network models for word alignment and terminology extraction from bilingual corpora. In *ACL 36/COLING 17*, pp. 444–450.

Ge, Niyu, John Hale, and Eugene Charniak. 1998. A statistical approach to anaphora resolution. In *WVLC 6*, pp. 161–170.

Ghahramani, Zoubin. 1994. Solving inverse problems using an EM approach to dnesity estimation. In Michael C. Mozer, Paul Smolensky, David S. Touretzky, and Andreas S. Weigend (eds.), *Proceedings of the 1993 Connectionist Models Summer School*, Hillsdale, NJ. Erlbaum Associates.

Gibson, Edward, and Neal J. Pearlmutter. 1994. A corpus-based analysis of psycholinguistic constraints on prepositional-phrase attachment. In Charles

Clifton, Jr., Lyn Frazier, and Keith Rayner (eds.), *Perspectives on Sentence Processing*, pp. 181–198. Hillsdale, NJ: Lawrence Erlbaum.

Gold, E. Mark. 1967. Language identification in the limit. *Information and Control* 10:447–474.

Goldszmidt, Moises, and Mehran Sahami. 1998. A probabilistic approach to full-text document clustering. Technical Report SIDL-WP-1998-0091, Stanford Digital Library Project, Stanford, CA.

Golub, Gene H., and Charles F. van Loan. 1989. *Matrix Computations*. Baltimore: The Johns Hopkins University Press.

Good, I. J. 1953. The population frequencies of species and the estimation of population parameters. *Biometrika* 40:237–264.

Good, I. J. 1979. Studies in the history of probability and statistics. XXXVII: A. M. Turing's statistical work in World War II. *Biometrika* 66:393–396.

Goodman, Joshua. 1996. Parsing algorithms and metrics. In *ACL 34*, pp. 177–183.

Greenbaum, Sidney. 1993. The tagset for the International Corpus of English. In Eric Atwell and Clive Souter (eds.), *Corpus-based Computational Linguistics*, pp. 11–24. Amsterdam: Rodopi.

Greene, Barbara B., and Gerald M. Rubin. 1971. Automatic grammatical tagging of English. Technical report, Brown University, Providence, RI.

Grefenstette, Gregory. 1992a. Finding semantic similarity in raw text: the deese antonyms. In Robert Goldman, Peter Norvig, Eugene Charniak, and Bill Gale (eds.), *Working Notes of the AAAI Fall Symposium on Probabilistic Approaches to Natural Language*, pp. 61–65, Menlo Park, CA. AAAI Press.

Grefenstette, Gregory. 1992b. Use of syntactic context to produce term association lists for text retrieval. In *SIGIR '92*, pp. 89–97.

Grefenstette, Gregory. 1994. *Explorations in Automatic Thesaurus Discovery*. Boston: Kluwer Academic Press.

Grefenstette, Gregory. 1996. Evaluation techniques for automatic semantic extraction: Comparing syntactic and window-based approaches. In Branimir Boguraev and James Pustejovsky (eds.), *Corpus Processing for Lexical Acquisition*, chapter 11, pp. 205–216. Cambridge, MA: MIT Press.

Grefenstette, Gregory (ed.). 1998. *Cross-language information retrieval*. Boston, MA: Kluwer Academic Publishers.

Grefenstette, Gregory, and Pasi Tapanainen. 1994. What is a word, what is a sentence? Problems of tokenization. In *Proceedings of the Third International Conference on Computational Lexicography (COMPLEX '94)*, pp. 79–87, Budapest. Available as Rank Xerox Research Centre technical report MLTT-004.

Grenander, Ulf. 1967. Syntax-controlled probabilities. Technical report, Division of Applied Mathematics, Brown University.

Günter, R., L. B. Levitin, B. Shapiro, and P. Wagner. 1996. Zipf's law and the effect of ranking on probability distributions. *International Journal of Theoretical Physics* 35:395–417.

Guthrie, Joe A., Louise Guthrie, Yorick Wilks, and Homa Aidinejad. 1991. Subject-dependent co-occurrence and word sense disambiguation. In *ACL 29*, pp. 146–152.

Guthrie, Louise, James Pustejovsky, Yorick Wilks, and Brian M. Slator. 1996. The role of lexicons in natural language processing. *Communications of the ACM* 39:63–72.

Halliday, M. A. K. 1966. Lexis as a linguistic level. In C. E. Bazell, J. C. Catford, M. A. K. Halliday, and R. H. Robins (eds.), *In memory of J. R. Firth*, pp. 148–162. London: Longmans.

Halliday, M. A. K. 1994. *An introduction to functional grammar*, 2nd edition. London: Edward Arnold.

Harman, D.K. (ed.). 1996. *The Third Text REtrieval Conference (TREC-4)*. Washington DC: U.S. Department of Commerce.

Harman, D. K. (ed.). 1994. *The Second Text REtrieval Conference (TREC-2)*. Washington DC: U.S. Department of Commerce. NIST Special Publication 500-215.

Harnad, Stevan (ed.). 1987. *Categorical perception: the groundwork of cognition*. Cambridge: Cambridge University Press.

Harris, B. 1988. Bi-text, a new concept in translation theory. *Language Monthly* 54.

Harris, T. E. 1963. *The Theory of Branching Processes*. Berlin: Springer.

Harris, Zellig. 1951. *Methods in Structural Linguistics*. Chicago: University of Chicago Press.

Harrison, Philip, Steven Abney, Ezra Black, Dan Flickinger, Ralph Grishman Claudia Gdaniec, Donald Hindle, Robert Ingria, Mitch Marcus, Beatrice Santorini, and Tomek Strzalkowski. 1991. Natural Language Processing Systems Evaluation Workshop, Technical Report RL-TR-91-362. In Jeannette G. Neal and Sharon M. Walter (eds.), *Evaluating Syntax Performance of Parser/Grammars of English*, Rome Laboratory, Air Force Systems Command, Griffis Air Force Base, NY 13441-5700.

Harter, Steve. 1975. A probabilistic approach to automatic keyword indexing: Part II. an algorithm for probabilistic indexing. *Journal of the American Society for Information Science* 26:280–289.

Haruno, Masahiko, and Takefumi Yamazaki. 1996. High-performance bilingual text alignment using statistical and dictionary information. In *ACL 34*, pp. 131–138.

Hatzivassiloglou, Vasileios, and Kathleen R. McKeown. 1993. Towards the automatic identification of adjectival scales: clustering adjectives according to meaning. In *ACL 31*, pp. 172–182.

Hawthorne, Mark. 1994. The computer in literary analysis: Using TACT with students. *Computers and the Humanities* 28:19–27.

Hearst, Marti, and Christian Plaunt. 1993. Subtopic structuring for full-length document access. In *SIGIR '93*, pp. 59–68.

Hearst, Marti A. 1991. Noun homograph disambiguation using local context in large text corpora. In *Seventh Annual Conference of the UW Centre for the New OED and Text Research*, pp. 1–22, Oxford.

Hearst, Marti A. 1992. Automatic acquisition of hyponyms from large text corpora. In *COLING 14*, pp. 539–545.

Hearst, Marti A. 1994. *Context and Structure in Automated Full-Text Information Access*. PhD thesis, University of California at Berkeley.

Hearst, Marti A. 1997. TextTiling: Segmenting text into multi-paragraph subtopic passages. *Computational Linguistics* 23:33–64.

Hearst, Marti A., and Hinrich Schütze. 1995. Customizing a lexicon to better suit a computational task. In Branimir Boguraev and James Pustejovsky (eds.), *Corpus Processing for Lexical Acquisition*, pp. 77–96. Cambridge, MA: MIT Press.

Henderson, James, and Peter Lane. 1998. A connectionist architecture for learning to parse. In *ACL 36/COLING 17*, pp. 531–537.

Hermjakob, Ulf, and Raymond J. Mooney. 1997. Learning parse and translation decisions from examples with rich context. In *ACL 35/EACL 8*, pp. 482–489.

Hertz, John A., Richard G. Palmer, and Anders S. Krogh. 1991. *Introduction to the theory of neural computation*. Redwood City, CA: Addison-Wesley.

Herwijnen, Eric van. 1994. *Practical SGML*, 2nd edition. Dordrecht: Kluwer Academic.

Hickey, Raymond. 1993. Lexa: Corpus processing software. Technical report, The Norwegian Computing Centre for the Humanities, Bergen.

Hindle, Donald. 1990. Noun classification from predicate argument structures. In *ACL 28*, pp. 268–275.

Hindle, Donald. 1994. A parser for text corpora. In B.T.S. Atkins and A. Zampolli (eds.), *Computational Approaches to the Lexicon*, pp. 103–151. Oxford: Oxford University Press.

Hindle, Donald, and Mats Rooth. 1993. Structural ambiguity and lexical relations. *Computational Linguistics* 19:103–120.

Hirst, Graeme. 1987. *Semantic Interpretation and the Resolution of Ambiguity.* Cambridge: Cambridge University Press.

Hodges, Julia, Shiyun Yie, Ray Reighart, and Lois Boggess. 1996. An automated system that assists in the generation of document indexes. *Natural Language Engineering* 2:137–160.

Holmes, V. M., L. Stowe, and L. Cupples. 1989. Lexical expectations in parsing complement-verb sentences. *Journal of Memory and Language* 28:668–689.

Honavar, Vasant, and Giora Slutzki (eds.). 1998. *Grammatical inference: 4th international colloquium, ICGI-98.* Berlin: Springer.

Hopcroft, John E., and Jeffrey D. Ullman. 1979. *Introduction to automata theory, languages, and computation.* Reading, MA: Addison-Wesley.

Hopper, Paul J., and Elizabeth Closs Traugott. 1993. *Grammaticalization.* Cambrige: Cambridge University Press.

Hornby, A. S. 1974. *Oxford Advanced Learner's Dictionary of Current English.* Oxford: Oxford University Press. Third Edition.

Horning, James Jay. 1969. *A study of grammatical inference.* PhD thesis, Stanford.

Huang, T., and King Sun Fu. 1971. On stochastic context-free languages. *Information Sciences* 3:201–224.

Huddleston, Rodney. 1984. *Introduction to the Grammar of English.* Cambridge: Cambridge University Press.

Hull, David. 1996. Stemming algorithms – A case study for detailed evaluation. *Journal of the American Society for Information Science* 47:70–84.

Hull, David. 1998. A practical approach to terminology alignment. In Didier Bourigault, Christian Jacquemin, and Marie-Claude L'Homme (eds.), *Proceedings of Computerm '98*, pp. 1–7, Montreal, Canada.

Hull, David, and Doug Oard (eds.). 1997. *AAAI Symposium on Cross-Language Text and Speech Retrieval.* Stanford, CA: AAAI Press.

Hull, David A., and Gregory Grefenstette. 1998. Querying across languages: A dictionary-based approach to multilingual information retrieval. In Karen Sparck Jones and Peter Willett (eds.), *Readings in Information Retrieval.* San Francisco: Morgan Kaufmann.

Hull, David A., Jan O. Pedersen, and Hinrich Schütze. 1996. Method combination for document filtering. In *SIGIR '96*, pp. 279–287.

Hutchins, S. E. 1970. *Stochastic Sources for Context-free Languages.* PhD thesis, University of California, San Diego.

Ide, Nancy, and Jean Véronis (eds.). 1995. *The Text Encoding Initiative: Background and Context*. Dordrecht: Kluwer Academic. Reprinted from *Computers and the Humanities* 29(1-3), 1995.

Ide, Nancy, and Jean Véronis. 1998. Introduction to the special issue on word sense disambiguation: The state of the art. *Computational Linguistics* 24:1-40.

Ide, Nancy, and Donald Walker. 1992. Introduction: Common methodologies in humanities computing and computational linguistics. *Computers and the Humanities* 26:327-330.

Inui, K., V. Sornlertlamvanich, H. Tanaka, and T. Tokunaga. 1997. A new formalization of probabilistic GLR parsing. In *Proceedings of the Fifth International Workshop on Parsing Technologies (IWPT-97)*, pp. 123-134, MIT.

Isabelle, Pierre. 1987. Machine translation at the TAUM group. In Margaret King (ed.), *Machine Translation Today: The State of the Art*, pp. 247-277. Edinburgh: Edinburgh University Press.

Jacquemin, Christian. 1994. FASTR: A unification-based front-end to automatic indexing. In *Proceedings of RIAO*, pp. 34-47, Rockefeller University, New York.

Jacquemin, Christian, Judith L. Klavans, and Evelyne Tzoukermann. 1997. Expansion of multi-word terms for indexing and retrieval using morphology and syntax. In *ACL 35/EACL 8*, pp. 24-31.

Jain, Anil K., and Richard C. Dubes. 1988. *Algorithms for Clustering Data*. Englewood Cliffs, NJ: Prentice Hall.

Jeffreys, Harold. 1948. *Theory of Probability*. Oxford: Clarendon Press.

Jelinek, Frederick. 1969. Fast sequential decoding algorithm using a stack. *IBM Journal of Research and Development* pp. 675-685.

Jelinek, Frederick. 1976. Continuous speech recognition by statistical methods. *IEEE* 64:532-556.

Jelinek, Frederick. 1985. Markov source modeling of text generation. In J. K. Skwirzynski (ed.), *The Impact of Processing Techniques on Communications*, volume E91 of *NATO ASI series*, pp. 569-598. Dordrecht: M. Nijhoff.

Jelinek, Fred. 1990. Self-organized language modeling for speech recognition. Printed in (Waibel and Lee 1990), pp. 450-506.

Jelinek, Frederick. 1997. *Statistical Methods for Speech Recognition*. Cambridge, MA: MIT Press.

Jelinek, Frederick, Lalit R. Bahl, and Robert L. Mercer. 1975. Design of a linguistic statistical decoder for the recognition of continuous speech. *IEEE Transactions on Information Theory* 21:250-256.

Jelinek, F., J. Lafferty, D. Magerman, R. Mercer, A. Ratnaparkhi, and S. Roukos. 1994. Decision tree parsing using a hidden derivation model. In *Proceedings of the 1994 Human Language Technology Workshop*, pp. 272-277. DARPA.

Jelinek, Fred, and John D. Lafferty. 1991. Computation of the probability of initial substring generation by stochastic context-free grammars. *Computational Linguistics* 17:315–324.

Jelinek, F., J. D. Lafferty, and R. L. Mercer. 1990. Basic methods of probabilistic context free grammars. Technical Report RC 16374 (#72684), IBM T. J. Watson Research Center.

Jelinek, F., J. D. Lafferty, and R. L. Mercer. 1992a. Basic methods of probabilistic context free grammars. In P. Laface and R. De Mori (eds.), *Speech Recognition and Understanding: Recent Advances, Trends, and Applications*, volume 75 of *Series F: Computer and Systems Sciences*. Springer Verlag.

Jelinek, Fred, and Robert Mercer. 1985. Probability distribution estimation from sparse data. *IBM Technical Disclosure Bulletin* 28:2591–2594.

Jelinek, Frederick, Robert L. Mercer, and Salim Roukos. 1992b. Principles of lexical language modeling for speech recognition. In Sadaoki Furui and M. Mohan Sondhi (eds.), *Advances in Speech Signal Processing*, pp. 651–699. New York: Marcel Dekker.

Jensen, Karen, George E. Heidorn, and Stephen D. Richardson (eds.). 1993. *Natural language processing: The PLNLP approach*. Boston: Kluwer Academic Publishers.

Johansson, Stig, G. N. Leech, and H. Goodluck. 1978. *Manual of information to accompany the Lancaster-Oslo/Bergen Corpus of British English, for use with digital computers*. Oslo: Dept of English, University of Oslo.

Johnson, Mark. 1998. The effect of alternative tree representations on tree bank grammars. In *Proceedings of Joint Conference on New Methods in Language Processing and Computational Natural Language Learning (NeMLaP3/CoNLL98)*, pp. 39–48, Macquarie University.

Johnson, W. E. 1932. Probability: deductive and inductive problems. *Mind* 41: 421–423.

Joos, Martin. 1936. Review of *The Psycho-Biology of Language*. *Language* 12: 196–210.

Jorgensen, Julia. 1990. The psychological reality of word senses. *Journal of Psycholinguistic Research* 19:167–190.

Joshi, Aravind K. 1993. Tree-adjoining grammars. In R. E. Asher (ed.), *The Encyclopedia of Language and Linguistics*. Oxford: Pergamon Press.

Justeson, John S., and Slava M. Katz. 1991. Co-occurrences of antonymous adjectives and their contexts. *Computational Linguistics* 17:1–19.

Justeson, John S., and Slava M. Katz. 1995a. Principled disambiguation: Discriminating adjective senses with modified nouns. *Computational Linguistics* 24: 1–28.

Justeson, John S., and Slava M. Katz. 1995b. Technical terminology: some linguistic properties and an algorithm for identification in text. *Natural Language Engineering* 1:9-27.

Kahneman, Daniel, Paul Slovic, and Amos Tversky (eds.). 1982. *Judgment under uncertainty: heuristics and biases.* Cambridge: Cambridge University Press.

Kan, Min-Yen, Judith L. Klavans, and Kathleen R. McKeown. 1998. Linear segmentation and segment significance. In *WVLC 6*, pp. 197-205.

Kaplan, Ronald M., and Joan Bresnan. 1982. Lexical-Functional Grammar: A formal system for grammatical representation. In Joan Bresnan (ed.), *The Mental Representation of Grammatical Relations*, pp. 173-281. Cambridge, MA: MIT Press.

Karlsson, Fred, Atro Voutilainen, Juha Heikkilä, and Arto Anttila. 1995. *Constraint Grammar: A Language-Independent System for Parsing Unrestricted Text.* Berlin: Mouton de Gruyter.

Karov, Yael, and Shimon Edelman. 1998. Similarity-based word sense disambiguation. *Computational Linguistics* 24:41-59.

Karttunen, Lauri. 1986. Radical lexicalism. Technical Report 86-68, Center for the Study of Language and Information, Stanford CA.

Katz, Slava M. 1987. Estimation of probabilities from sparse data for the language model component of a speech recognizer. *IEEE Transactions on Acoustics, Speech, and Signal Processing* ASSP-35:400-401.

Katz, Slava M. 1996. Distribution of content words and phrases in text and language modelling. *Natural Language Engineering* 2:15-59.

Kaufman, Leonard, and Peter J. Rousseeuw. 1990. *Finding groups in data.* New York: Wiley.

Kaufmann, Stefan. 1998. Second-order cohesion: Using wordspace in text segmentation. Department of Linguistics, Stanford University.

Kay, Martin, and Martin Röscheisen. 1993. Text-translation alignment. *Computational Linguistics* 19:121-142.

Kehler, Andrew. 1997. Probabilistic coreference in information extraction. In *EMNLP 2*, pp. 163-173.

Kelly, Edward, and Phillip Stone. 1975. *Computer Recognition of English Word Senses.* Amsterdam: North-Holland.

Kempe, André. 1997. Finite state transducers approximating hidden markov models. In *ACL 35/EACL 8*, pp. 460-467.

Kennedy, Graeme. 1998. *An Introduction to Corpus Linguistics.* London: Longman.

Kent, Roland G. 1930. Review of *Relative Frequency as a Determinant of Phonetic Change. Language* 6:86–88.

Kilgarriff, Adam. 1993. Dictionary word sense distinctions: An enquiry into their nature. *Computers and the Humanities* 26:365–387.

Kilgarriff, Adam. 1997. "i don't believe in word senses". *Computers and the Humanities* 31:91–113.

Kilgarriff, Adam, and Tony Rose. 1998. Metrics for corpus similarity and homogeneity. Manuscript, ITRI, University of Brighton.

Kirkpatrick, S., C. D. Gelatt, and M. P. Vecchi. 1983. Optimization by simulated annealing. *Science* 220:671–680.

Klavans, Judith, and Min-Yen Kan. 1998. Role of verbs in document analysis. In *ACL 36/COLING 17*, pp. 680–686.

Klavans, Judith L., and Evelyne Tzoukermann. 1995. Dictionaries and corpora: Combining corpus and machine-readable dictionary data for building bilingual lexicons. *Journal of Machine Translation* 10.

Klein, Sheldon, and Robert F. Simmons. 1963. A computational approach to grammatical coding of English words. *Journal of the Association for Computing Machinery* 10:334–347.

Kneser, Reinhard, and Hermann Ney. 1995. Improved backing-off for m-gram language modeling. In *Proceedings of the IEEE Conference on Acoustics, Speech and Signal Processing*, volume 1, pp. 181–184.

Knight, Kevin. 1997. Automating knowledge acquisition for machine translation. *AI Magazine* 18:81–96.

Knight, Kevin, Ishwar Chander, Matthew Haines, Vasileios Hatzivassiloglou, Eduard Hovy, Masayo Iida, Steve Luk, Richard Whitney, and Kenji Yamada. 1995. Filling knowledge gaps in a broad-coverage MT system. In *Proceedings of IJCAI-95*.

Knight, Kevin, and Jonathan Graehl. 1997. Machine transliteration. In *ACL 35/EACL 8*, pp. 128–135.

Knight, Kevin, and Vasileios Hatzivassiloglou. 1995. Two-level, many-paths generation. In *ACL 33*, pp. 252–260.

Knill, Kate M., and Steve Young. 1997. Hidden markov models in speech and language processing. In Steve Young and Gerrit Bloothooft (eds.), *Corpus-Based Methods in Language and Speech Processing*, pp. 27–68. Dordrecht: Kluwer Academic.

Kohonen, Teuvo. 1997. *Self-Organizing Maps*. Berlin, Heidelberg, New York: Springer Verlag. Second Extended Edition.

Korfhage, Robert R. 1997. *Information Storage and Retrieval*. Berlin: John Wiley.

Krenn, Brigitte, and Christer Samuelsson. 1997. The linguist's guide to statistics. manuscript, University of Saarbrucken.

Krovetz, Robert. 1991. Lexical acquisition and information retrieval. In Uri Zernik (ed.), *Lexical Acquisition: Exploiting On-Line Resources to Build a Lexicon*, pp. 45–64. Hillsdale, NJ: Lawrence Erlbaum.

Kruskal, J. B. 1964a. Multidimensional scaling by optimizing goodness of fit to a nonmetric hypothesis. *Psychometrika* 29:1–27.

Kruskal, J. B. 1964b. Nonmetric multidimensional scaling: A numerical method. *Psychometrika* 29:115–129.

Kučera, Henry, and W. Nelson Francis. 1967. *Computational Analysis of Present-Day American English.* Providence, RI: Brown University Press.

Kupiec, Julian. 1991. A trellis-based algorithm for estimating the parameters of a hidden stochastic context-free grammar. In *Proceedings of the Speech and Natural Language Workshop*, pp. 241–246. DARPA.

Kupiec, Julian. 1992a. An algorithm for estimating the parameters of unrestricted hidden stochastic context-free grammars. In *COLING 14*, pp. 387–393.

Kupiec, Julian. 1992b. Robust part-of-speech tagging using a Hidden Markov Model. *Computer Speech and Language* 6:225–242.

Kupiec, Julian. 1993a. An algorithm for finding noun phrase correspondences in bilingual corpora. In *ACL 31*, pp. 17–22.

Kupiec, Julian. 1993b. MURAX: A robust linguistic approach for question answering using an on-line encyclopedia. In *SIGIR '93*, pp. 181–190.

Kupiec, Julian, Jan Pedersen, and Francine Chen. 1995. A trainable document summarizer. In *SIGIR '95*, pp. 68–73.

Kwok, K. L., and M. Chan. 1998. Improving two-stage ad-hoc retrieval for short queries. In *SIGIR '98*, pp. 250–256.

Lafferty, John, Daniel Sleator, and Davy Temperley. 1992. Grammatical trigrams: A probabilistic model of link grammar. In *Proceedings of the 1992 AAAI Fall Symposium on Probabilistic Approaches to Natural Language.*

Lakoff, George. 1987. *Women, fire, and dangerous things.* Chicago, IL: University of Chicago Press.

Landauer, Thomas K., and Susan T. Dumais. 1997. A solution to Plato's problem: The latent semantic analysis theory of acquisition, induction and representation of knowledge. *Psychological Review* 104:211–240.

Langacker, Ronald W. 1987. *Foundations of Cognitive Grammar*, volume 1. Stanford, CA: Stanford University Press.

Langacker, Ronald W. 1991. *Foundations of Cognitive Grammar*, volume 2. Stanford, CA: Stanford University Press.

Laplace, Pierre Simon marquis de. 1814. *Essai philosophique sur les probabilites.* Paris: Mme. Ve. Courcier.

Laplace, Pierre Simon marquis de. 1995. *Philosophical Essay On Probabilities.* New York: Springer-Verlag.

Lari, K., and S. J. Young. 1990. The estimation of stochastic context-free grammars using the inside-outside algorithm. *Computer Speech and Language* 4: 35-56.

Lari, K., and S. J. Young. 1991. Application of stochastic context free grammar using the inside-outside algorithm. *Computer Speech and Language* 5:237-257.

Lau, Raymond. 1994. Adaptive statistical language modelling. Master's thesis, Massachusetts Institute of Technology.

Lau, Ray, Ronald Rosenfeld, and Salim Roukos. 1993. Adaptive language modeling using the maximum entropy principle. In *Proceedings of the Human Language Technology Workshop*, pp. 108-113. ARPA.

Lauer, Mark. 1995a. Corpus statistics meet the noun compound: Some empirical results. In *ACL 33*, pp. 47-54.

Lauer, Mark. 1995b. *Designing Statistical Language Learners: Experiments on Noun Compounds.* PhD thesis, Macquarie University, Sydney, Australia.

Leacock, Claudia, Martin Chodorow, and George A. Miller. 1998. Using corpus statistics and Wordnet relations for sense identification. *Computational Linguistics* 24:147-165.

Lesk, Michael. 1986. Automatic sense disambiguation: How to tell a pine cone from an ice cream cone. In *Proceedings of the 1986 SIGDOC Conference*, pp. 24-26, New York. Association for Computing Machinery.

Lesk, M. E. 1969. Word-word association in document retrieval systems. *American Documentation* 20:27-38.

Levin, Beth. 1993. *English Verb Classes and Alternations.* Chicago: The University of Chicago Press.

Levine, John R., Tony Mason, and Doug Brown. 1992. *Lex & Yacc*, 2nd edition. Sebastopol, CA: O'Reilly & Associates.

Levinson, S. E., L. R. Rabiner, and M. M. Sondhi. 1983. An introduction to the application of the theory of probabilistic functions of a Markov process to automatic speech recongition. *Bell System Technical Journal* 62:1035-1074.

Lewis, David D. 1992. An evaluation of phrasal and clustered representations on a text categorization task. In *SIGIR '92*, pp. 37-50.

Lewis, David D., and Karen Sparck Jones. 1996. Natural language processing for information retrieval. *Communications of the ACM* 39:92-101.

Lewis, David D., and Marc Ringuette. 1994. A comparison of two learning algorithms for text categorization. In *Proc. SDAIR 94*, pp. 81–93, Las Vegas, NV.

Lewis, David D., Robert E. Schapire, James P. Callan, and Ron Papka. 1996. Training algorithms for linear text classifiers. In *SIGIR '96*, pp. 298–306.

Li, Hang, and Naoki Abe. 1995. Generalizing case frames using a thesaurus and the mdl principle. In *Proceedings of Recent Advances in Natural Language Processing*, pp. 239–248, Tzigov Chark, Bulgaria.

Li, Hang, and Naoki Abe. 1996. Learning dependencies between case frame slots. In *COLING 16*, pp. 10–15.

Li, Hang, and Naoki Abe. 1998. Word clustering and disambiguation based on co-occurrence data. In *ACL 36/COLING 17*, pp. 749–755.

Li, Wentian. 1992. Random texts exhibit Zipf's-law-like word frequency distribution. *IEEE Transactions on Information Theory* 38:1842–1845.

Lidstone, G. J. 1920. Note on the general case of the Bayes-Laplace formula for inductive or *a priori* probabilities. *Transactions of the Faculty of Actuaries* 8: 182–192.

Light, Marc. 1996. Morphological cues for lexical semantics. In *ACL 34*, pp. 25–31.

Littlestone, Nick. 1995. Comparing several linear-threshold learning algorithms on tasks involving superfluous attributes. In A. Prieditis (ed.), *Proceedings of the 12th International Conference on Machine Learning*, pp. 353–361, San Francisco, CA. Morgan Kaufmann.

Littman, Michael L., Susan T. Dumais, and Thomas K. Landauer. 1998a. Automatic cross-language information retrieval using latent semantic indexing. In Gregory Grefenstette (ed.), *Cross Language Information Retrieval*. Kluwer.

Littman, Michael L., Fan Jiang, and Greg A. Keim. 1998b. Learning a language-independent representation for terms from a partially aligned corpus. In Jude Shavlik (ed.), *Proceedings of the Fifteenth International Conference on Machine Learning*, pp. 314–322. Morgan Kaufmann.

Losee, Robert M. (ed.). 1998. *Text Retrieval and Filtering*. Boston, MA: Kluwer Academic Publishers.

Lovins, Julie Beth. 1968. Development of a stemming algorithm. *Translation and Computational Linguistics* 11:22–31.

Luhn, H. P. 1960. Keyword-in-context index for technical literature (KWIC index). *American Documentation* 11:288–295.

Lyons, John. 1968. *Introduction to Theoretical Linguistics*. Cambridge: Cambridge University Press.

MacDonald, M. A., N. J. Pearlmutter, and M. S. Seidenberg. 1994. The lexical nature of syntactic ambiguity resolution. *Psychological Review* 101:676–703.

MacKay, David J. C., and Linda C. Peto. 1990. Speech recognition using hidden Markov models. *The Lincoln Laboratory Journal* 3:41–62.

Magerman, David M. 1994. *Natural language parsing as statistical pattern recognition*. PhD thesis, Stanford University.

Magerman, David M. 1995. Statistical decision-tree models for parsing. In *ACL 33*, pp. 276–283.

Magerman, David M., and Mitchell P. Marcus. 1991. Pearl: A probabilistic chart parser. In *EACL 4*. Also published in the Proceedings of the 2nd International Workshop for Parsing Technologies.

Magerman, David M., and Carl Weir. 1992. Efficiency, robustness, and accuracy in Picky chart parsing. In *ACL 30*, pp. 40–47.

Mandelbrot, Benoit. 1954. Structure formelle des textes et communcation. *Word* 10:1–27.

Mandelbrot, Benoit B. 1983. *The Fractal Geometry of Nature*. New York: W. H. Freeman.

Mani, Inderjeet, and T. Richard MacMillan. 1995. Identifying unknown proper names in newswire text. In Branimir Boguraev and James Pustejovsky (eds.), *Corpus Processing for Lexical Acquisition*, pp. 41–59. Cambridge, MA: MIT Press.

Manning, Christopher D. 1993. Automatic acquisition of a large subcategorization dictionary from corpora. In *ACL 31*, pp. 235–242.

Manning, Christopher D., and Bob Carpenter. 1997. Probabilistic parsing using left corner language models. In *Proceedings of the Fifth International Workshop on Parsing Technologies (IWPT-97)*, pp. 147–158, MIT.

Marchand, Hans. 1969. *Categories and types of present-day English word-formation*. München: Beck.

Marcus, Mitchell, Grace Kim, Mary Ann Marcinkiewicz, Robert MacIntyre, Ann Bies, Mark Ferguson, Karen Katz, and Britta Schasberger. 1994. The Penn Treebank: Annotating predicate argument structure. In *ARPA Human Language Technology Workshop*, pp. 110–115.

Marcus, Mitchell P., Beatrice Santorini, and Mary Ann Marcinkiewicz. 1993. Building a large annotated corpus of English: The Penn treebank. *Computational Linguistics* 19:313–330.

Markov, Andrei A. 1913. An example of statistical investigation in the text of 'Eugene Onyegin' illustrating coupling of 'tests' in chains. In *Proceedings of the Academy of Sciences, St. Petersburg*, volume 7 of *VI*, pp. 153–162.

Marr, David. 1982. *Vision: A Computational Investigation into the Human Representation and Processing of Visual Information.* New York: W. H. Freeman.

Marshall, Ian. 1987. Tag selection using probabilistic methods. In Roger Garside, Geoffrey Sampson, and Geoffrey Leech (eds.), *The Computational analysis of English: a corpus-based approach*, pp. 42–65. London: Longman.

Martin, James. 1991. Representing and acquiring metaphor-based polysemy. In Uri Zernik (ed.), *Lexical Acquisition: Exploiting On-Line Resources to Build a Lexicon*, pp. 389–415. Hillsdale, NJ: Lawrence Erlbaum.

Martin, W. A., K. W. Church, and R. S. Patil. 1987. Preliminary analysis of a breadth-first parson algorithm: Theoretical and experimental results. In Leonard Bolc (ed.), *Natural Language Parsing Systems.* Berlin: Springer Verlag. Also MIT LCS technical report TR-261.

Masand, Brij, Gordon Linoff, and David Waltz. 1992. Classifying news stories using memory based reasoning. In *SIGIR '92*, pp. 59–65.

Maxwell, III, John T. 1992. The problem with mutual information. Manuscript, Xerox Palo Alto Research Center, September 15, 1992.

McClelland, James L., David E. Rumelhart, and the PDP Research Group (eds.). 1986. *Parallel Distributed Processing. Explorations in the Microstructure of Cognition. Volume 2: Psychological and Biological Models.* Cambridge, MA: The MIT Press.

McCullagh, Peter, and John A. Nelder. 1989. *Generalized Linear Models*, 2nd edition, chapter 4, pp. 101–123. Chapman and Hall.

McDonald, David D. 1995. Internal and external evidence in the identification and semantic categorization of proper names. In Branimir Boguraev and James Pustejovsky (eds.), *Corpus Processing for Lexical Acquisition*, pp. 21–39. Cambridge MA: MIT Press.

McEnery, Tony, and Andrew Wilson. 1996. *Corpus Linguistics.* Edinburgh: Edinburgh University Press.

McGrath, Sean. 1997. *PARSEME.1ST: SGML for Software Developers.* Upper Saddle River, NJ: Prentice Hall PTR.

McMahon, John G., and Francis J. Smith. 1996. Improving statistical language model performance with automatically generated word hierarchies. *Computational Linguistics* 22:217–247.

McQueen, C.M. Sperberg, and Lou Burnard (eds.). 1994. *Guidelines for Electronic Text Encoding and Interchange (TEI P3).* Chicago, IL: ACH/ACL/ALLC (Association for Computers and the Humanities, Association for Computational Linguistics, Association for Literary and Linguistic Computing).

McRoy, Susan W. 1992. Using multiple knowledge sources for word sense disambiguation. *Computational Linguistics* 18:1–30.

Melamed, I. Dan. 1997a. A portable algorithm for mapping bitext correspondence. In *ACL 35/EACL 8*, pp. 305–312.

Melamed, I. Dan. 1997b. A word-to-word model of translational equivalence. In *ACL 35/EACL 8*, pp. 490–497.

Mel'čuk, Igor Aleksandrovich. 1988. *Dependency Syntax: theory and practice.* Albany: State University of New York.

Mercer, Robert L. 1993. Inflectional morphology needs to be authenticated by hand. In *Working Notes of the AAAI Spring Syposium on Building Lexicons for Machine Translation*, pp. 99–99, Stanford, CA. AAAI Press.

Merialdo, Bernard. 1994. Tagging English text with a probabilistic model. *Computational Linguistics* 20:155–171.

Miclet, Laurent, and Colin de la Higuera (eds.). 1996. *Grammatical inference: learning syntax from sentences: Third International Colloquium, ICGI-96.* Berlin: Springer.

Miikkulainen, Risto (ed.). 1993. *Subsymbolic Natural Language Processing.* Cambridge MA: MIT Press.

Mikheev, Andrei. 1998. Feature lattices for maximum entropy modelling. In *ACL 36*, pp. 848–854.

Miller, George A., and Walter G. Charles. 1991. Contextual correlates of semantic similarity. *Language and Cognitive Processes* 6:1–28.

Miller, Scott, David Stallard, Robert Bobrow, and Richard Schwartz. 1996. A fully statistical approach to natural language interfaces. In *ACL 34*, pp. 55–61.

Minsky, Marvin Lee, and Seymour Papert (eds.). 1969. *Perceptrons: an introduction to computational geometry.* Cambridge, MA: MIT Press. Partly reprinted in (Shavlik and Dietterich 1990).

Minsky, Marvin Lee, and Seymour Papert (eds.). 1988. *Perceptrons: an introduction to computational geometry.* Cambridge, MA: MIT Press. Expanded edition.

Mitchell, Tom M. 1980. The need for biases in learning generalizations. Technical Report Department of Computer Science. CBM-TR-117, Rutgers University. Reprinted in (Shavlik and Dietterich 1990), pp. 184–191.

Mitchell, Tom M. (ed.). 1997. *Machine Learning.* New York: McGraw-Hill.

Mitra, Mandar, Chris Buckley, Amit Singhal, and Claire Cardie. 1997. An analysis of statistical and syntactic phrases. In *Proceedings of RIAO*.

Moffat, Alistair, and Justin Zobel. 1998. Exploring the similarity space. *ACM SIGIR Forum* 32.

Mood, Alexander M., Franklin A. Graybill, and Duane C. Boes. 1974. *Introduction to the theory of statistics.* New York: McGraw-Hill. 3rd edition.

Mooney, Raymond J. 1996. Comparative experiments on disambiguating word senses: An illustration of the role of bias in machine learning. In *EMNLP 1*, pp. 82–91.

Moore, David S., and George P. McCabe. 1989. *Introduction to the practice of statistics*. New York: Freeman.

Morris, Jane, and Graeme Hirst. 1991. Lexical cohesion computed by thesaural relations as an indicator of the structure of text. *Computational Linguistics* 17: 21–48.

Mosteller, Frederick, and David L. Wallace. 1984. *Applied Bayesian and Classical Inference – The Case of The Federalist Papers*. Springer Series in Satistics. New York: Springer-Verlag.

Nagao, Makoto. 1984. A framework of a mechanical translation between Japanese and English by analogy principle. In Alick Elithorn and Ranan B. Banerji (eds.), *Artificial and Human Intelligence*, pp. 173–180. Edinburgh: North-Holland.

Neff, Mary S., Brigitte Bläser, Jean-Marc Langé, Hubert Lehmann, and Isabel Zapata Dominguez. 1993. Get it where you can: Acquiring and maintaining bilingual lexicons for machine translation. In *Working Notes of the AAAI Spring Syposium on Building Lexicons for Machine Translation*, pp. 98–98, Stanford, CA. AAAI Press.

Nevill-Manning, Craig G., Ian H. Witten, and Gordon W. Paynter. 1997. Browsing in digital libraries: a phrase-based approach. In *Proceedings of ACM Digital Libraries*, pp. 230–236, Philadelphia, PA. Association for Computing Machinery.

Newmeyer, Frederick J. 1988. *Linguistics: The Cambridge Survey*. Cambridge, England: Cambridge University Press.

Ney, Hermann, and Ute Essen. 1993. Estimating 'small' probabilities by leaving-one-out. In *Eurospeech '93*, volume 3, pp. 2239–2242. ESCA.

Ney, Hermann, Ute Essen, and Reinhard Kneser. 1994. On structuring probabilistic dependencies in stochastic language modeling. *Computer Speech and Language* 8:1–28.

Ney, Hermann, Sven Martin, and Frank Wessel. 1997. Statistical language modeling using leaving-one-out. In Steve Young and Gerrit Bloothooft (eds.), *Corpus-Based Methods in Language and Speech Processing*, pp. 174–207. Dordrecht: Kluwer Academic.

Ng, Hwee Tou, and John Zelle. 1997. Corpus-based approaches to semantic interpretation in natural language processing. *AI Magazine* 18:45–64.

Ng, Hwee Tou, and Hian Beng Lee. 1996. Integrating multiple knowledge sources to disambiguate word sense: An exemplar-based approach. In *ACL 34*, pp. 40–47.

Nie, Jian-Yun, Pierre Isabelle, Pierre Plamondon, and George Foster. 1998. Using a probablistic translation model for cross-language information retrieval. In *WVLC 6*, pp. 18-27.

Nießen, S., S. Vogel, H. Ney, and C. Tillmann. 1998. A DP based search algorithm for statistical machine translation. In *ACL 36/COLING 17*, pp. 960-967.

Nunberg, Geoffrey. 1990. *The Linguistics of Punctuation*. Stanford, CA: CSLI Publications.

Nunberg, Geoff, and Annie Zaenen. 1992. Systematic polysemy in lexicology and lexicography. In *Proceedings of Euralex II*, Tampere, Finland.

Oaksford, M., and N. Chater. 1998. *Rational Models of Cognition*. Oxford, England: Oxford University Press.

Oard, Douglas W., and Nicholas DeClaris. 1996. Cognitive models for text filtering. Manuscript, University of Maryland, College Park.

Ostler, Nicholas, and B. T. S. Atkins. 1992. Predictable meaning shift: Some linguistic properties of lexical implication rules. In James Pustejovsky and Sabine Bergler (eds.), *Lexical Semantics and Knowledge Representation: Proceedings fof the 1st SIGLEX Workshop*, pp. 76-87. Berlin: Springer Verlag.

Paik, Woojin, Elizabeth D. Liddy, Edmund Yu, and Mary McKenna. 1995. Categorizing and standardizing proper nouns for efficient information retrieval. In Branimir Boguraev and James Pustejovsky (eds.), *Corpus Processing for Lexical Acquisition*, pp. 61-73. Cambridge MA: MIT Press.

Palmer, David D., and Marti A. Hearst. 1994. Adaptive sentence boundary disambiguation. In *ANLP 4*, pp. 78-83.

Palmer, David D., and Marti A. Hearst. 1997. Adaptive multilingual sentence boundary disambiguation. *Computational Linguistics* 23:241-267.

Paul, Douglas B. 1990. Speech recognition using hidden markov models. *The Lincoln Laboratory Journal* 3:41-62.

Pearlmutter, N., and M. MacDonald. 1992. Plausibility and syntactic ambiguity resolution. In *Proceedings of the 14th Annual Conference of the Cognitive Society*.

Pedersen, Ted. 1996. Fishing for exactness. In *Proceedings of the South-Central SAS Users Group Conference*, Austin TX.

Pedersen, Ted, and Rebecca Bruce. 1997. Distinguishing word senses in untagged text. In *EMNLP 2*, pp. 197-207.

Pereira, Fernando, and Yves Schabes. 1992. Inside-outside reestimation from partially bracketed corpora. In *ACL 30*, pp. 128-135.

Pereira, Fernando, Naftali Tishby, and Lillian Lee. 1993. Distributional clustering of English words. In *ACL 31*, pp. 183-190.

Pinker, Steven. 1994. *The Language Instinct.* New York: William Morrow.

Pollard, Carl, and Ivan A. Sag. 1994. *Head-Driven Phrase Structure Grammar.* Chicago, IL: University of Chicago Press.

Pook, Stuart L., and Jason Catlett. 1988. Making sense out of searching. In *Information Online 88*, pp. 148-157, Sydney. The Information Science Section of the Library Association of Australia.

Porter, M. F. 1980. An algorithm for suffix stripping. *Program* 14:130-137.

Poznański, Victor, and Antonio Sanfilippo. 1995. Detecting dependencies between semantic verb subclasses and subcategorization frames in text corpora. In Branimir Boguraev and James Pustejovsky (eds.), *Corpus Processing for Lexical Acquisition*, pp. 175-190. Cambridge, MA: MIT Press.

Press, W. H., B. P. Flannery, S. A. Teukolsky, and W. T. Vetterling. 1988. *Numerical Recipes in C.* Cambridge: Cambridge University Press.

Procter, P. (ed.). 1978. *Longman dictionary of contemporary English.* Harlow, England: Longman Group.

Prokosch, E. 1933. Review of selected studies of the principle of relative frequency in language. *Language* 9:89-92.

Pustejovsky, James. 1991. The generative lexicon. *Computational Linguistics* 17:409-441.

Pustejovsky, James, Sabine Bergler, and Peter Anick. 1993. Lexical semantic techniques for corpus analysis. *Computational Linguistics* 19:331-358.

Qiu, Yonggang, and H.P. Frei. 1993. Concept based query expansion. In *SIGIR '93*, pp. 160-169.

Quinlan, J. R. 1986. Induction of decision trees. *Machine Learning* 1:81-106. Reprinted in (Shavlik and Dietterich 1990).

Quinlan, John Ross. 1993. *C4.5: Programs for machine learning.* San Mateo, CA: Morgan Kaufmann Publishers.

Quinlan, J. R. 1996. Bagging, boosting, and C4.5. In *Proceedings of the Thirteenth National Conference on Artificial Intelligence (AAAI '96)*, pp. 725-730.

Quirk, Randolf, Sidney Greenbaum, Geoffrey Leech, and Jan Svartvik. 1985. *A Comprehensive Grammar of the English Language.* London: Longman.

Rabiner, Lawrence, and Biing-Hwang Juang. 1993. *Fundamentals of Speech Recognition.* Englewood Cliffs, NJ: PTR Prentice-Hall.

Rabiner, Lawrence R. 1989. A tutorial on hidden markov models and selected applications in speech recognition. *Proceedings of IEEE* 77:257-286. Reprinted in (Waibel and Lee 1990), pp. 267-296.

Ramsey, Fred L., and Daniel W. Schafer. 1997. *The statistical sleuth: a course in methods of data analysis.* Belmont, CA: Duxbury Press.

Ramshaw, Lance A., and Mitchell P. Marcus. 1994. Exploring the statistical derivation of transformational rule sequences for part-of-speech tagging. In *The Balancing Act. Proceedings of the Workshop*, pp. 86–95, Morristown NJ. Association of Computational Linguistics.

Rasmussen, Edie. 1992. Clustering algorithms. In William B. Frakes and Ricardo Baeza-Yates (eds.), *Information Retrieval*, pp. 419–442. Englewood Cliffs, NJ: Prentice Hall.

Ratnaparkhi, Adwait. 1996. A maximum entropy model for part-of-speech tagging. In *EMNLP 1*, pp. 133–142.

Ratnaparkhi, Adwait. 1997a. A linear observed time statistical parser based on maximum entropy models. In *EMNLP 2*, pp. 1–10.

Ratnaparkhi, Adwait. 1997b. A simple introduction to maximum entropy models for natural language processing. Technical Report IRCS Report 97–08, Institute for Research in Cognitive Science, Philadelphia, PA.

Ratnaparkhi, Adwait. 1998. Unsupervised statistical models for prepositional phrase attachment. In *ACL 36/COLING 17*, pp. 1079–1085.

Ratnaparkhi, Adwait, Jeff Reynar, and Salim Roukos. 1994. A maximum entropy model for prepositional phrase attachment. In *Proceedings of the ARPA Workshop on Human Language Technology*, pp. 250–255, Plainsboro, NJ.

Read, Timothy R. C., and Noel A. C. Cressie. 1988. *Goodness-of-fit statistics for discrete multivariate data.* New York: Springer Verlag.

Resnik, Philip. 1992. Probabilistic tree-adjoining grammar as a framework for statistical natural language processing. In *COLING 14*, pp. 418–425.

Resnik, Philip. 1996. Selectional constraints: an information-theoretic model and its computational realization. *Cognition* 61:127–159.

Resnik, Philip, and Marti Hearst. 1993. Structural ambiguity and conceptual relations. In *WVLC 1*, pp. 58–64.

Resnik, Philip, and David Yarowsky. 1998. A perspective on word sense disambiguation methods and their evaluation. In *Proceedings of the SIGLEX workshop Tagging Text with Lexical Semantics*, pp. 79–86, Washington, DC.

Resnik, Philip Stuart. 1993. *Selection and Information: A Class-Based Approach to Lexical Relationships.* PhD thesis, University of Pennsylvania.

Reynar, Jeffrey C., and Adwait Ratnaparkhi. 1997. A maximum entropy approach to identifying sentence boundaries. In *ANLP 5*, pp. 16–19.

Riley, Michael D. 1989. Some applications of tree-based modeling to speech and language indexing. In *Proceedings of the DARPA Speech and Natural Language Workshop*, pp. 339–352. Morgan Kaufmann.

Riloff, Ellen, and Jessica Shepherd. 1997. A corpus-based approach for building semantic lexicons. In *EMNLP 2*, pp. 117–124.

Ristad, Eric Sven. 1995. A natural law of succession. Technical Report CS-TR-495-95, Princeton University.

Ristad, Eric Sven. 1996. Maximum entropy modeling toolkit. Manuscript, Princeton University.

Ristad, Eric Sven, and Robert G. Thomas. 1997. Hierarchical non-emitting Markov models. In *ACL 35/EACL 8*, pp. 381–385.

Roark, Brian, and Eugene Charniak. 1998. Noun-phrase co-occurrence statistics for semi-automatic semantic lexicon construction. In *ACL 36/COLING 17*, pp. 1110–1116.

Robertson, S.E., and K. Sparck Jones. 1976. Relevance weighting of search terms. *Journal of the American Society for Information Science* 27:129–146.

Rocchio, J. J. 1971. Relevance feedback in information retrieval. In Gerard Salton (ed.), *The Smart Retrieval System – Experiments in Automatic Document Processing*, pp. 313–323. Englewood Cliffs, NJ: Prentice-Hall.

Roche, Emmanuel, and Yves Schabes. 1995. Deterministic part-of-speech tagging with finite-state transducers. *Computational Linguistics* 21:227–253.

Roche, Emmanuel, and Yves Schabes. 1997. *Finite-State Language Processing*. Boston, MA: MIT Press.

Roget, P. M. 1946. *Roget's International Thesaurus*. New York: Thomas Y. Crowell.

Rosenblatt, Frank (ed.). 1962. *Principles of neurodynamics; perceptrons and the theory of brain mechanisms*. Washington, DC: Spartan Books.

Rosenfeld, Ronald. 1994. *Adaptive Statistical Language Modeling: A Maximum Entropy Approach*. PhD thesis, CMU. Technical report CMU-CS-94-138.

Rosenfeld, Roni. 1996. A maximum entropy approach to adaptive statistical language modelling. *Computer Speech and Language* 10:187–228.

Rosenfeld, Ronald, and Xuedong Huang. 1992. Improvements in stochastic language modeling. In *Proceedings of the DARPA Speech and Natural Language Workshop*, pp. 107–111. Morgan Kaufmann.

Rosenkrantz, Stanley J., and Philip M. Lewis, II. 1970. Deterministic left corner parser. In *IEEE Conference Record of the 11th Annual Syposium on Switching and Automata*, pp. 139–152.

Ross, Ian C., and John W. Tukey. 1975. Introduction to these volumes. In John Wilder Tukey (ed.), *Index to Statistics and Probability*, pp. iv–x. Los Altos, CA: R & D Press.

Roth, Dan. 1998. Learning to resolve natural language ambiguities: A unified approach. In *Proceedings of the Fifteenth National Conference on Artificial Intelligence*, Menlo Park CA. AAAI Press.

Rumelhart, D. E., and J. L. McClelland. 1986. On learning the past tenses of English verbs. In James L. McClelland, David E. Rumelhart, and the PDP Research Group (eds.), *Parallel Distributed Processing. Explorations in the Microstructure of Cognition. Volume 2: Psychological and Biological Models*, pp. 216–271. Cambridge, MA: The MIT Press.

Rumelhart, David E., James L. McClelland, and the PDP research group (eds.). 1986. *Parallel Distributed Processing. Explorations in the Microstructure of Cognition. Volume 1: Foundations.* Cambridge, MA: The MIT Press.

Rumelhart, David E., and David Zipser. 1985. Feature discovery by competitive learning. *Cognitive Science* 9:75–112.

Russell, Stuart J., and Peter Norvig. 1995. *Artificial Intelligence: A Modern Approach.* Englewood Cliffs, NJ: Prentice Hall.

Sakakibara, Y., M. Brown, R. Hughey, I. S. Mian, K. Sjölander, R. C. Underwood, and D. Haussler. 1994. Stochastic context-free grammars for tRNA modeling. *Nucleic Acids Research* 22:5112–5120.

Salton, Gerard. 1971a. Experiments in automatic thesaurus construction for information retrieval. In *Proceedings IFIP Congress*, pp. 43–49.

Salton, Gerard (ed.). 1971b. *The Smart Retrieval System – Experiments in Automatic Document Processing.* Englewood Cliffs, NJ: Prentice-Hall.

Salton, Gerard. 1989. *Automatic Text Processing: The Transformation, Analysis, and Retrieval of Information by Computer.* Reading, MA: Addison Wesley.

Salton, G., J. Allan, C. Buckley, and A. Singhal. 1994. Automatic analysis, theme generation and summarization of machine-readable texts. *Science* 264:1421–1426.

Salton, Gerard, and James Allen. 1993. Selective text utilization and text traversal. In *Proceedings of ACM Hypertext 93*, New York. Association for Computing Machinery.

Salton, Gerard, and Chris Buckley. 1991. Global text matching for information retrieval. *Science* 253:1012–1015.

Salton, Gerard, Edward A. Fox, and Harry Wu. 1983. Extended boolean information retrieval. *Communications of the ACM* 26:1022–1036.

Salton, Gerard, and Michael J. McGill. 1983. *Introduction to modern information retrieval.* New York: McGraw-Hill.

Salton, Gerard, and R. W. Thorpe. 1962. An approach to the segmentation problem in speech analysis and language translation. In *Proceedings of the 1961*

International Conference on Machine Translation of Languages and Applied Language Analysis, volume 2, pp. 703–724, London. Her Majesty's Stationery Office.

Sampson, Geoffrey. 1989. How fully does a machine-usable dictionary cover English text? *Literary and Linguistic Computing* 4:29–35.

Sampson, Geoffrey. 1995. *English for the Computer*. New York: Oxford University Press.

Sampson, Geoffrey. 1997. *Educating Eve*. London: Cassell.

Samuel, Ken, Sandra Carberry, and K. Vijay-Shanker. 1998. Dialogue act tagging with transformation-based learning. In *ACL 36/COLING 17*, pp. 1150–1156.

Samuelsson, Christer. 1993. Morphological tagging based entirely on bayesian inference. In *9th Nordic Conference on Computational Linguistics*, Stockholm University, Stockholm, Sweden.

Samuelsson, Christer. 1996. Handling sparse data by successive abstraction. In *COLING 16*, pp. 895–900.

Samuelsson, Christer, and Atro Voutilainen. 1997. Comparing a linguistic and a stochastic tagger. In *ACL 35/EACL 8*, pp. 246–253.

Sanderson, Mark, and C. J. van Rijsbergen. 1998. The impact on retrieval effectiveness of the skewed frequency distribution of a word's senses. *ACM Transactions on Information Systems*. To appear.

Sankoff, D. 1971. Branching processes with terminal types: applications to context-free grammars. *Journal of Applied Probability* 8:233–240.

Santorini, Beatrice. 1990. Part-of-speech tagging guidelines for the Penn treebank project. 3rd Revision, 2nd printing, Feb. 1995. University of Pennsylvania.

Sapir, Edward. 1921. *Language: an introduction to the study of speech*. New York: Harcourt Brace.

Sato, Satoshi. 1992. CTM: An example-based translation aid system. In *COLING 14*, pp. 1259–1263.

Saund, Eric. 1994. Unsupervised learning of mixtures of multiple causes in binary data. In J. Cowan, G. Tesauro, and J. Alspector (eds.), *Advances in Neural Information Processing Systems 6*. San Mateo, CA: Morgan Kaufmann Publishers.

Schabes, Yves. 1992. Stochastic lexicalized tree-adjoining grammars. In *COLING 14*, pp. 426–432.

Schabes, Yves, Anne Abeillé, and Aravind Joshi. 1988. Parsing strategies with lexicalized grammars: Tree adjoining grammars. In *COLING 12*, pp. 578–583.

Schabes, Yves, Michal Roth, and Randy Osborne. 1993. Parsing the Wall Street Journal with the Inside-Outside algorithm. In *EACL 6*, pp. 341–347.

Schapire, Robert E., Yoram Singer, and Amit Singhal. 1998. Boosting and Rocchio applied to text filtering. In *SIGIR '98*, pp. 215–223.

Schmid, Helmut. 1994. Probabilistic part-of-speech tagging using decision trees. In *International Conference on New Methods in Language Processing*, pp. 44–49, Manchester, England.

Schütze, Carson T. 1996. *The empirical base of linguistics: grammaticality judgments and linguistic methodology.* Chicago, IL: University of Chicago Press.

Schütze, Hinrich. 1992a. Context space. In Robert Goldman, Peter Norvig, Eugene Charniak, and Bill Gale (eds.), *Working Notes of the AAAI Fall Symposium on Probabilistic Approaches to Natural Language*, pp. 113–120, Menlo Park, CA. AAAI Press.

Schütze, Hinrich. 1992b. Dimensions of meaning. In *Proceedings of Supercomputing '92*, pp. 787–796, Los Alamitos, CA. IEEE Computer Society Press.

Schütze, Hinrich. 1993. Part-of-speech induction from scratch. In *ACL 31*, pp. 251–258.

Schütze, Hinrich. 1995. Distributional part-of-speech tagging. In *EACL 7*, pp. 141–148.

Schütze, Hinrich. 1997. *Ambiguity Resolution in Language Learning.* Stanford, CA: CSLI Publications.

Schütze, Hinrich. 1998. Automatic word sense discrimination. *Computational Linguistics* 24:97–124.

Schütze, Hinrich, David A. Hull, and Jan O. Pedersen. 1995. A comparison of classifiers and document representations for the routing problem. In *SIGIR '95*, pp. 229–237.

Schütze, Hinrich, and Jan O. Pedersen. 1995. Information retrieval based on word senses. In *Fourth Annual Symposium on Document Analysis and Information Retrieval*, pp. 161–175, Las Vegas, NV.

Schütze, Hinrich, and Jan O. Pedersen. 1997. A cooccurrence-based thesaurus and two applications to information retrieval. *Information Processing & Management* 33:307–318.

Schütze, Hinrich, and Yoram Singer. 1994. Part-of-speech tagging using a variable memory Markov model. In *ACL 32*, pp. 181–187.

Shannon, Claude E. 1948. A mathematical theory of communication. *Bell System Technical Journal* 27:379–423, 623–656.

Shannon, Claude E. 1951. Prediction and entropy of printed English. *Bell System Technical Journal* 30:50–64.

Shavlik, Jude W., and Thomas G. Dietterich (eds.). 1990. *Readings in Machine Learning.* San Mateo, CA: Morgan Kaufmann.

Shemtov, Hadar. 1993. Text alignment in a tool for translating revised documents. In *EACL 6*, pp. 449-453.

Sheridan, Paraic, and Alan F. Smeaton. 1992. The application of morphosyntactic language processing to effective phrase matching. *Information Processing & Management* 28:349-370.

Sheridan, Paraic, Martin Wechsler, and Peter Schäuble. 1997. Cross language speech retrieval: Establishing a baseline performance. In *SIGIR '97*, pp. 99-108.

Shimohata, Sayori, Toshiyuko Sugio, and Junji Nagata. 1997. Retrieving collocations by co-occurrences and word order constraints. In *ACL 35/EACL 8*, pp. 476-481.

Siegel, Sidney, and N. John Castellan, Jr. 1988. *Nonparametric Statistics for the Behavioral Sciences*, 2nd edition. New York: McGraw Hill.

Silverstein, Craig, and Jan O. Pedersen. 1997. Almost-constant-time clustering of arbitrary corpus subsets. In *SIGIR '97*, pp. 60-66.

Sima'an, Khalil. 1996. Computational complexity of probabilistic disambiguation by means of tree-grammars. In *COLING 16*, pp. 1175-1180.

Sima'an, Khalil, Rens Bod, S. Krauwer, and Remko Scha. 1994. Efficient disambiguation by means of stochastic tree substitution grammars. In *Proceedings International Conference on New Methods in Language Processing*.

Simard, Michel, G. F. Foster, and P. Isabelle. 1992. Using cognates to align sentences in bilingual corpora. In *Proceedings of the Fourth International Conference on Theoretical and Methodological Issues in Machine Translation (TMI-92)*, pp. 67-81.

Simard, Michel, and Pierre Plamondon. 1996. Bilingual sentence alignment: Balancing robustness and accuracy. In *Proceedings of the First Conference of the Association for Machine Translation in the Americas (AMTA-96)*, pp. 135-144.

Sinclair, John (ed.). 1995. *Collins COBUILD English dictionary*. London: Harper Collins. New edition, completely revised.

Singhal, Amit, Gerard Salton, and Chris Buckley. 1996. Length normalization in degraded text collections. In *Fifth Annual Symposium on Document Analysis and Information Retrieval*, pp. 149-162, Las Vegas, NV.

Sipser, Michael. 1996. *Introduction to the theory of computation*. Boston, MA: PWS Publishing Company.

Siskind, Jeffrey Mark. 1996. A computational study of cross-situational techniques for learning word-to-meaning mappings. *Cognition* 61:39-91.

Skut, Wojciech, and Thorsten Brants. 1998. A maximum-entropy partial parser for unrestricted text. In *WVLC 6*, pp. 143-151.

Smadja, Frank. 1993. Retrieving collocations from text: Xtract. *Computational Linguistics* 19:143–177.

Smadja, Frank, Kathleen R. McKeown, and Vasileios Hatzivassiloglou. 1996. Translating collocations for bilingual lexicons: A statistical approach. *Computational Linguistics* 22:1–38.

Smadja, Frank A., and Kathleen R. McKeown. 1990. Automatically extracting and representing collocations for language generation. In *ACL 28*, pp. 252–259.

Smeaton, Alan F. 1992. Progress in the application of natural language processing to information retrieval tasks. *The Computer Journal* 35:268–278.

Smith, Tony C., and John G. Cleary. 1997. Probabilistic unification grammars. In *1997 Australasian Natural Language Processing Summer Workshop*, pp. 25–32, Macquarie University.

Snedecor, George Waddel, and William G. Cochran. 1989. *Statistical methods*. Ames: Iowa State University Press. 8th edition.

Sparck Jones, Karen. 1972. A statistical interpretation of term specificity and its application in retrieval. *Journal of Documentation* 28:11–21.

Sparck Jones, Karen, and Peter Willett (eds.). 1998. *Readings in Information Retrieval*. San Francisco: Morgan Kaufmann.

Sproat, Richard William. 1992. *Morphology and computation*. Cambridge, MA: MIT Press.

Sproat, Richard W., Chilin Shih, William Gale, and Nancy Chang. 1996. A stochastic finite-state word-segmentation algorithm for Chinese. *Computational Linguistics* 22:377–404.

St. Laurent, Simon. 1998. *XML: A Primer*. Foster City, CA: MIS Press/IDG Books.

Stanfill, Craig, and David Waltz. 1986. Toward memory-based reasoning. *Communications of the ACM* 29:1213–1228.

Steier, Amy M., and Richard K. Belew. 1993. Exporting phrases: A statistical analysis of topical language. In R. Casey and B. Croft (eds.), *Second Annual Symposium on Document Analysis and Information Retrieval*, pp. 179–190, Las Vegas, NV.

Stolcke, Andreas. 1995. An efficient probabilistic context-free parsing algorithm that computes prefix probabilities. *Computational Linguistics* 21:165–202.

Stolcke, Andreas, and Stephen M. Omohundro. 1993. Hidden Markov model induction by Bayesian model merging. In S. J. Hanson, J. D. Cowan, and C. Lee Giles (eds.), *Advances in Neural Information Processing Systems 5*, pp. 11–18, San Mateo, CA. Morgan Kaufmann.

Stolcke, Andreas, and Stephen M. Omohundro. 1994a. Best-first model merging for hidden Markov model induction. Technical Report TR-94-003, International Computer Science Institute, University of California at Berkeley.

Stolcke, Andreas, and Stephen M. Omohundro. 1994b. Inducing probabilistic grammars by Bayesian model merging. In *Grammatical Inference and Applications: Proceedings of the Second International Colloquium on Grammatical Inference*. Springer Verlag.

Stolcke, A., E. Shriberg, R. Bates, N. Coccaro, D. Jurafsky, R. Martin, M. Meteer, K. Ries, P. Taylor, and C. Van Ess-Dykema. 1998. Dialog act modeling for conversational speech. In *Applying Machine Learning to Discourse Processing*, pp. 98–105, Menlo Park, CA. AAAI Press.

Stolz, Walter S., Percy H. Tannenbaum, and Frederick V. Carstensen. 1965. A stochastic approach to the grammatical coding of English. *Communications of the ACM* 8:399–405.

Strang, Gilbert. 1988. *Linear algebra and its applications*, 3rd edition. San Diego: Harcourt, Brace, Jovanovich.

Strzalkowski, Tomek. 1995. Natural language information retrieval. *Information Processing & Management* 31:397–417.

Stubbs, Michael. 1996. *Text and corpus analysis: computer-assisted studies of language and culture*. Oxford: Blackwell.

Suppes, Patrick. 1970. Probabilistic grammars for natural languages. *Synthese* 22:95–116.

Suppes, Patrick. 1984. *Probabilistic Metaphysics*. Oxford: Blackwell.

Suppes, Patrick, Michael Böttner, and Lin Liang. 1996. Machine learning comprehension grammars for ten languages. *Computational Linguistics* 22:329–350.

Tabor, Whitney. 1994. *Syntactic Innovation: A Connectionist Model*. PhD thesis, Stanford.

Tague-Sutcliffe, Jean. 1992. The pragmatics of information retrieval experimentation, revisited. *Information Processing & Management* 28:467–490. Reprinted in (Sparck Jones and Willett 1998).

Talmy, Leonard. 1985. Lexicalization patterns: Semantic structure in lexical form. In Timothy Shopen (ed.), *Language Typology and Syntactic Description III: Grammatical Categories and the Lexicon*, pp. 57–149. Cambridge, MA: Cambridge University Press.

Tanenhaus, M. K., and J. C. Trueswell. 1995. Sentence comprehension. In J. Miller and P. Eimas (eds.), *Handbook of Perception and Cognition*, volume 11, pp. 217–262. San Diego: Academic Press.

Tesnière, Lucien. 1959. *Éléments de Syntaxe Structurale*. Paris: Librairie C. Klincksieck.

Tomita, Masaru (ed.). 1991. *Generalized LR parsing*. Boston: Kluwer Academic.

Towell, Geoffrey, and Ellen M. Voorhees. 1998. Disambiguating highly ambiguous words. *Computational Linguistics* 24:125–146.

Trask, Robert Lawrence. 1993. *A dictionary of grammatical terms in linguistics.* London: Routledge.

van Halteren, Hans, Jakub Zavrel, and Walter Daelemans. 1998. Improving data driven wordclass tagging by system combination. In *ACL 36/COLING 17*, pp. 491–497.

van Riemsdijk, Henk, and Edwin Williams. 1986. *Introduction to the Theory of Grammar.* Cambridge, MA: MIT Press.

van Rijsbergen, C. J. 1979. *Information Retrieval.* London: Butterworths. Second Edition.

Velardi, Paola, and Maria Teresa Pazienza. 1989. Computer aided interpretation of lexical cooccurrences. In *ACL 27*, pp. 185–192.

Viegas, Evelyne, Boyan Onyshkevych, Victor Raskin, and Sergei Nirenburg. 1996. From submit to submitted via submission: On lexical rules in large-scale lexicon acquisition. In *ACL 34*, pp. 32–39.

Viterbi, A. J. 1967. Error bounds for convolutional codes and an asymptotically optimum decoding algorithm. *IEEE Transactions on Information Theory* IT-13: 1260–269.

Vogel, Stephan, Hermann Ney, and Christoph Tillmann. 1996. HMM-based word alignment in statistical translation. In *COLING 16*, pp. 836–841.

Voutilainen, A. 1995. A syntax-based part of speech analyser. In *EACL 7*, pp. 157–164.

Waibel, Alex, and Kai-Fu Lee (eds.). 1990. *Readings in Speech Recognition.* San mateo, CA: Morgan Kaufmann.

Walker, Donald E. 1987. Knowledge resource tools for accessing large text files. In Sergei Nirenburg (ed.), *Machine Translation: Theoretical and methodological issues*, pp. 247–261. Cambridge: Cambridge University Press.

Walker, Donald E., and Robert A. Amsler. 1986. The use of machine-readable dictionaries in sublanguage analysis. In Ralph Grishman and Richard Kittredge (eds.), *Analyzing language in restricted domains: sublanguage description and processing*, pp. 69–84. Hillsdale, NJ: Lawrence Erlbaum.

Walker, Marilyn A., Jeanne C. Fromer, and Shrikanth Narayanan. 1998. Learning optimal dialogue strategies: A case study of a spoken dialogue agent for email. In *ACL 36/COLING 17*, pp. 1345–1351.

Walker, Marilyn A., and Johanna D. Moore. 1997. Empirical studies in discourse. *Computational Linguistics* 23:1–12.

Wang, Ye-Yi, and Alex Waibel. 1997. Decoding algorithm in statistical machine translation. In *ACL 35/EACL 8*, pp. 366–372.

Wang, Ye-Yi, and Alex Waibel. 1998. Modeling with structures in statistical machine translation. In *ACL 36/COLING 17*, pp. 1357–1363.

Waterman, Scott A. 1995. Distinguished usage. In Branimir Boguraev and James Pustejovsky (eds.), *Corpus Processing for Lexical Acquisition*, pp. 143–172. Cambridge, MA: MIT Press.

Weaver, Warren. 1955. Translation. In William N. Locke and A. Donald Booth (eds.), *Machine Translation of Languages: Fourteen Essays*, pp. 15–23. New York: John Wiley & Sons.

Webster, Mort, and Mitch Marcus. 1989. Automatic acquisition of the lexical semantics of verbs from sentence frames. In *ACL 27*, pp. 177–184.

Weinberg, Sharon L., and Kenneth P. Goldberg. 1990. *Statistics for the behavioral sciences*. Cambridge: Cambridge University Press.

Weischedel, Ralph, Marie Meteer, Richard Schwartz, Lance Ramshaw, and Jeff Palmucci. 1993. Coping with ambiguity and unknown words through probabilistic models. *Computational Linguistics* 19:359–382.

Wiener, Erich, Jan Pedersen, and Andreas Weigend. 1995. A neural network approach to topic spotting. In *Proc. SDAIR 95*, pp. 317–332, Las Vegas, NV.

Wilks, Yorick, and Mark Stevenson. 1998. Word sense disambiguation using optimized combination of knowledge sources. In *ACL 36/COLING 17*, pp. 1398–1402.

Willett, Peter. 1988. Recent trends in hierarchic document clustering: A critical review. *Information Processing & Management* 24:577–597.

Willett, P., and V. Winterman. 1986. A comparison of some measures for the determination of inter-molecular structural similarity. *Quantitative Structure-Activity Relationships* 5:18–25.

Witten, Ian H., and Timothy C. Bell. 1991. The zero-frequency problem: Estimating the probabilities of novel events in adaptive text compression. *IEEE Transactions on Information Theory* 37:1085–1094.

Wittgenstein, Ludwig. 1968. *Philosophical Investigations [Philosophische Untersuchungen]*, 3rd edition. Oxford: Basil Blackwell. Translated by G. E. M. Anscombe.

Wong, S. K. M., and Y. Y. Yao. 1992. An information-theoretic measure of term specificity. *Journal of the American Society for Information Science* 43:54–61.

Wood, Mary McGee. 1993. *Categorial Grammars*. London: Routledge.

Woolf, Henry Bosley (ed.). 1973. *Webster's new collegiate dictionary*. Springfield, MA: G. & C. Merriam Co.

Wu, Dekai. 1994. Aligning a parallel English-Chinese corpus statistically with lexical criteria. In *ACL 32*, pp. 80–87.

Wu, Dekai. 1995. Grammarless extraction of phrasal examples from parallel texts. In *Sixth International Conference on Theoretical and Methodological Issues in Machine Translation*.

Wu, Dekai. 1996. A polynomial-time algorithm for statistical machine translation. In *ACL 34*, pp. 152–158.

Wu, Dekai, and Hongsing Wong. 1998. Machine translation with a stochastic grammatical channel. In *ACL 36/COLING 17*, pp. 1408–1415.

Yamamoto, Mikio, and Kenneth W. Church. 1998. Using suffix arrays to compute term frequency and document frequency for all substrings in a corpus. In *WVLC 6*, pp. 28–37.

Yang, Yiming. 1994. Expert network: Effective and efficient learning from human decisions in text categorization and retrieval. In *SIGIR '94*, pp. 13–22.

Yang, Yiming. 1995. Noise reduction in a statistical approach to text categorization. In *SIGIR '95*, pp. 256–263.

Yang, Yiming. 1999. An evaluation of statistical approaches to text categorization. *Information Retrieval* 1:69–90.

Yarowsky, David. 1992. Word-sense disambiguation using statistical models of Roget's categories trained on large corpora. In *COLING 14*, pp. 454–460.

Yarowsky, David. 1994. Decision lists for lexical ambiguity resolution: Application to accent restoration in Spanish and French. In *ACL 32*, pp. 88–95.

Yarowsky, David. 1995. Unsupervised word sense disambiguation rivaling supervised methods. In *ACL 33*, pp. 189–196.

Youmans, Gilbert. 1991. A new tool for discourse analysis: The vocabulary-management profile. *Language* 67:763–789.

Younger, D. H. 1967. Recognition and parsing of context free languages in time n^3. *Information and Control* 10:198–208.

Zavrel, Jakub, and Walter Daelemans. 1997. Memory-based learning: Using similarity for smoothing. In *ACL 35/EACL 8*, pp. 436–443.

Zavrel, Jakub, Walter Daelemans, and Jorn Veenstra. 1997. Resolving PP attachment ambiguities with memory-based learning. In *Proceedings of the Workshop on Computational Natural Language Learning*, pp. 136–144, Somerset, NJ. Association for Computational Linguistics.

Zernik, Uri. 1991a. Introduction. In *Lexical Acquisition: Exploiting On-Line Resources to Build a Lexicon*, pp. 1–26. Hillsdale, NJ: Lawrence Erlbaum.

Zernik, Uri. 1991b. Train1 vs. train2: Tagging word sense in corpus. In Uri Zernik (ed.), *Lexical Acquisition: Exploiting On-Line Resources to Build a Lexicon*, pp. 91–112. Hillsdale, NJ: Lawrence Erlbaum.

Zipf, George Kingsley. 1929. Relative frequency as a determinant of phonetic change. *Harvard Studies in Classical Philology* 40:1–95.

Zipf, George Kingsley. 1935. *The Psycho-Biology of Language*. Boston, MA: Houghton Mifflin.

Zipf, George Kingsley. 1949. *Human Behavior and the Principle of Least Effort*. Cambridge, MA: Addison-Wesley.

Index